The Great Society and the High Tide of Liberalism

A Volume in the Series

Political Development of the American Nation:
Studies in Politics and History

Edited by Sidney M. Milkis and
Jerome M. Mileur

The Great Society and the High Tide of Liberalism

Edited by
Sidney M. Milkis
and
Jerome M. Mileur

University of Massachusetts Press
Amherst and Boston

Copyright © 2005 by University of Massachusetts Press
All rights reserved
Printed in the United States of America
LC 2005011750
ISBN 1-55849-494-4 (library cloth ed.); 493-6 (paper)
Set in Galliard and Univers
Printed and bound by The Maple-Vail Book Manufacturing Group, Inc.

Library of Congress Cataloging-in-Publication Data

The Great Society and the high tide of liberalism / edited by Sidney M. Milkis and Jerome M. Mileur.
    p. cm. — (Political development of the American nation)
    Includes bibliographical references and index.
    ISBN 1-55849-493-6 (pbk. : alk. paper) — ISBN 1-55849-494-4 (library cloth : alk. paper)
    1. Johnson, Lyndon B. (Lyndon Baines), 1908–1973. 2. Liberalism—United States. 3. United States—Social policy. 4. United States—Economic policy. 5. United States—Politics and government—20th century. I. Milkis, Sidney M. II. Mileur, Jerome M. III. Series.
    HN65.G743 2005
    973.923—dc22
                                                                              2005011750

British Library Cataloguing in Publication data are available.

*We dedicate this volume to the memory of
Richard Cloward, Hugh Davis Graham, and Wilson Carey McWilliams—
generous colleagues, superb scholars, and committed citizens.*

Contents

Preface   xi

Lyndon Johnson, the Great Society, and the
"Twilight" of the Modern Presidency   1
     Sidney M. Milkis

Part I
Rethinking the Great Society   51
Ideology, Institutions, and Social Movements

Sixties Civics   53
     Hugh Heclo

Pluralism, Postwar Intellectuals, and the Demise
of the Union Idea   83
     Nelson Lichtenstein

Contested Rights   115
The Great Society between Home and Work
     Eileen Boris

Making Pluralism "Great"   145
Beyond a Re*cycled* History of the Great Society
     Brian Balogh

Part II
Lyndon Johnson and the American Presidency — 183

Lyndon Johnson in the Shadow of Franklin Roosevelt — 185
William E. Leuchtenburg

Great Societies and Great Empires — 214
Lyndon Johnson and Vietnam
Wilson Carey McWilliams

Lyndon Johnson — 233
Means and Ends, and What His Presidency Means in the End
David M. Shribman

Part III
The Great Society in Action — 251

The Politics of the Great Society — 253
Frances Fox Piven and Richard A. Cloward

The New Politics of Participatory Democracy Viewed through a Feminist Lens — 270
Rosalyn Baxandall

Freedom from Ignorance? — 289
The Great Society and the Evolution of the Elementary and Secondary Education Act of 1965
Patrick McGuinn and Frederick Hess

Medicare — 320
The Great Society's Enduring National Health Insurance Program
Edward Berkowitz

Justices and Justice — 351
Reflections on the Warren Court's Legacy
Henry J. Abraham

Part IV
Legacies 363

The Great Society's Civil Rights Legacy 365
Continuity 1, Discontinuity 3
    Hugh Davis Graham

From Tax and Spend to Mandate and Sue 387
Liberalism after the Great Society
    R. Shep Melnick

The Great Society and the Demise of New Deal Liberalism 411
    Jerome M. Mileur

Contributors 457
Index 461

Preface

This volume marks the third we have edited on political reform in the twentieth century. In important respects, these three volumes—on the Progressive Era, the New Deal, and the Great Society—tell the story of a long secular development. Twentieth-century America was a country in transition from a localist and provincial regime to a more national and socially advanced state, but one that strove mightily to keep faith with its past—with the principles and purposes implicit in its founding. The twentieth century witnessed reform in the reconstitution of America's governance and politics at home as well as in its role in the world at large. Domestic and foreign affairs intersected in terms of both policy and politics with dramatic and unanticipated consequences. The nation's understanding of itself underwent a transformation, as did the social and geographic construction of the nation.

The result was a century of dramatic reversals: the rejection of the laissez-faire philosophy, limited government, and localist politics of the nineteenth century; its replacement through the Progressive, New Deal, and Great Society eras with a more centralized, activist, and bureaucratic state; and the end-of-the-century political reaction against the expanded national government these liberal reform eras had produced. Decried as "big government," the reformed American state was cast by conservatives as a threat to traditional American values—to moral individualism, freedom with responsibility, family and neighborhood, schools and religion—and to the entrepreneurial spirit that, in their view, had built the nation and made it great. This was not a new appeal for conservatives, but their call for a return to first principles—a more decentralized, privatized, and individualistic America—was more populist in tone and resonated in new ways with the American public after the 1960s.

The long era of liberal reform that began in the first decade of the twentieth century and continued through six more was largely the work of "advanced" social thinkers, influenced by European models of the modern social-service state, though some conservatives, especially those with strong civil libertarian and internationalist sentiments, joined for parts of the ride.[1] Centered in the Democratic Party and in the energetic presidencies of Woodrow Wilson, Franklin Roosevelt, Harry Truman, and Lyndon Johnson, it ended in war abroad and riots at home. The reaction, centered in the Republican Party, was driven primarily by a new breed of "principled" conservatives who sprang from the Southwest and the West and were joined by a collection of libertarians, Christian fundamentalists, and neoconservatives, as well as more-traditional GOP conservatives, to mount a successful challenge to the "liberalism" of the Democrats.

Authors of the essays in this volume explore how the Great Society both extended and marked an important departure from the Progressive Era and the New Deal. The ideology of liberal reform in twentieth-century America evolved from Progressivism through the New Deal and cold war to form the political and intellectual backdrop for the Great Society. The reformist call had been for a more activist national state with a greatly enlarged role for the president as leader of public opinion and for an executive branch that was the repository of expertise in policy and administration. Reform was an organic doctrine that grew in different ways as conditions of life changed for Americans across the century, adding layers of thought that modified and adjusted liberalism without altering its statist impulse. The Great Society was no exception to this pattern, except that elements of its liberal idea worked in practice to erode the powers of the president and to contribute to a growing popular suspicion of government and politics in the nation, especially at the national level.

The New Deal had transformed Progressivism into a yet more executive-centered liberal state grounded in the notion of an economic bill of rights that vastly expanded the positive role of government in attending to the material needs of the nation at home. The cold war adjusted the domestic economic liberalism of FDR to the new international realities after World War II, retaining a commitment to the unfinished agenda but adding a foreign policy that embraced a determined anticommunism and also evincing a more technocratic style of politics and governance. John F. Kennedy was the model cold war liberal. Concerned more with foreign affairs than domestic, he saw the great challenge to America as the survival of its constitutional system of individual liberties and freedom.

Kennedy was a generation apart from Franklin Roosevelt, and while he supported the domestic agenda left from the 1930s, its realization was not the passion that drove his presidency. It was different with his successor Lyndon Johnson, who was at once both a New Deal and a cold war liberal but whose passion lay in the former. For Johnson, FDR was the model president, whose domestic program LBJ intended not only to complete but also to exceed. In his essay for this volume, William Leuchtenburg notes that as president, Johnson wanted to be "the greatest of them all, the whole bunch of them"—an ambition that drove him to achieve an unprecedented outpouring of legislation in the pursuit of a "great society" at home, but one that also tormented him in foreign policy with a war he inherited which he could not win and would not lose.

Johnson was a presidentialist, whose conception of the office was similar to that of FDR and who was comfortable with the style of politics practiced by Roosevelt. Johnson believed that strong presidential leadership was required to produce change in the American system, and like Roosevelt he wanted to strengthen the managerial tools of the modern presidency. Indeed, most of the federal programs that came from the Johnson years were executive centered and bureaucratic, much like those of the New Deal. But the 1960s were not the 1930s. Unlike the latter, the sixties was an era of prosperity in which economic security and material well-being, although still important, were not the paramount issues they had been thirty years earlier. There were those, such as the activist Michael Harrington, who found desperate poverty in a society of plenty, but the overriding social problem, as detailed by the sociologist David Riesman and others, was the alienation felt by modern men and women living in a mass society—their "loneliness" in the crowd, the anomie and estrangement. The social issue was thus *qualitative*, not quantitative, and the question was how to deal with the sense of powerlessness that resulted.[2]

Lyndon Johnson embraced this new understanding of the social issue for his May 1964 speech at the University of Michigan in which he set forth his vision for the Great Society. To be sure, Johnson's liberalism demanded an end to poverty and racial injustice, but he went on to describe the good society as one in which "the city of man serves not only the needs of the body and the demands of commerce but the desire for beauty and hunger for community."[3] Elaborating later, he told the nation that the Great Society required three things: economic growth, racial justice, and the "fulfillment of our lives." "A great people," he intoned, "flower not from wealth and power, but from a society which spurs them to the fullness of their genius. That alone is the Great Society." Prosperity alone was not enough, because, LBJ continued, "in the midst of abundance modern man walks oppressed by forces which menace and confine the quality of his life, and which individual abundance alone will not overcome." From this came a rush of noneconomic goals intended to create "a flourishing community where our people can come to live the good life."[4]

As the essay by Sidney Milkis shows, Lyndon Johnson had doubts that the Great Society could be built with national administrative power as the agent of change; many reformers in the sixties rejected this approach. Indeed, they saw the modern presidency and a powerful national administrative state as impediments to the realization of an authentic democracy. They sought instead to recast administrative power through a "participatory democracy" that would confront government power with popular power. The reformers who embraced participatory democracy believed that the interventionist and activist state of the New Deal tied liberalism too closely to a bureaucratic system of top-down power that left scant space for localized activism, and they urged a return to a politics that engaged the largest possible number of people in decisions that affected them directly.

The idea of participatory democracy found clear expression in the Port Huron statement issued by the Students for a Democratic Society (SDS). Drawing on the arguments of John Dewey that "democracy" was a means of realizing the full potential of human beings, SDS called for a political system in which citizens were actively engaged as participants in the decisions that affected them. Democracy was central to the SDS vision of the "good society." But an authentic democracy required more than economic security and social equality; it required a politics of maximum citizen participation so that individuals might realize their full potential. It was this call for participatory democracy that separated the New Left from the Old Left.[5] Like the New Dealers, the Great Society reformers embraced an expansive notion of rights, but as Nelson Lichtenstein argues in his essay for this volume, the rights-conscious liberalism that sought to protect individual men and women from racism, sexism, and bureaucratic indifference was complaisant about, if not avowedly hostile to, the rights of workers.

The idea of participatory democracy did not play a large part in LBJ's Great Society programs, but it found its way into some of them, such as the community action programs, where it served as an important prelude to the emergence of participatory democracy as a leading principle of reformers in the late 1960s and 1970s. It was a central principle guiding the Democratic Party reforms after 1968, which sought to open the party's presidential nominating process to greater involvement by rank-and-file party members and to make the party's national convention more visibly representative of the groups, especially minorities and women, who made up the party coalition.[6] The idea of participatory democracy was embodied in the student, antiwar, and other social movements of the sixties, which moved liberalism away from its economic and quantitative moorings in the New Deal toward a revised liberalism that was more social in focus, emphasizing quality-of-life issues.

The reform politics of the sixties also animated the organization of consumers, environmentalists, and others into additional movements that, in turn, inspired the self-styled "public interest" advocates of the seventies, for whom the presidency and the executive branch were targets for reform. Ironically, the Great Society helped bring to power issue-oriented independents, representing broad causes and movements, who resisted presidential management and who were less willing to delegate policy responsibility to administrative agencies. As Hugh Heclo points out in his essay for this volume, the recasting of liberalism in the 1960s resulted in an "odd amalgam of aspiration and alienation in public affairs."

The essays that follow explore both the policy changes that were part of the liberal reforms of the Great Society as well as the underlying ideological and political changes in liberalism itself. Many of the essayists argue, some with regret, that politically, the Great Society was the "last hurrah" for the liberalism of Roosevelt and the New Deal, and this third great reform era of the twentieth century, which included the activist Warren Court and extended into the mid-1970s, provided the primary targets for the new conservatism, which emerged nationally in the mid-1960s and came to power in the 1980s. Just as Republicans had been slow in the 1930s to recognize that the election and administration of FDR had ushered in a new ideological and partisan era in American politics, Democrats in the 1970s were slow to recognize that a new ideological and partisan era was at hand. As conservatives in the 1930s believed that most Americans shared their values and vision for the nation and would return to their senses once "that man" was gone from the White House, so too liberals in the 1970s believed that most Americans remained faithful to their statist approach to the nation's governance and that all would be well once the agony of Vietnam was behind them.[7] And as Republican Party divisions between a moderately conservative, eastern, internationalist, Wall Street, establishment wing and an old-time conservative, midwestern, small-town, isolationist, Main Street wing became increasingly apparent after the 1930s, Democratic Party divisions between a traditional urban, working-class wing grounded in economics and a suburban, college-educated, moderate wing centered on social and cultural issues became more and more evident in the 1970s.

Teaching Americans both to expect more from government and to trust it less, the Great Society was the fulcrum on which the decline of liberalism and the rise of conservatism tilted. The authors who have contributed to this volume depict its successes and disappointments with both theoretical insight and careful attention to detail. The Great Society made good in many ways on the unfinished agenda of New Deal liberalism—housing, education, health care—and it moved liberalism philosophically into even greater association with an expanding realm of *positive* rights (or entitlements) and with state regulation that extended this doctrine in new and different ways, some of which contributed to its demise. For Democrats (and for liberals especially), the decade of the 1960s was a roller coaster ride, begun with the promise of Camelot, shattered by assassination, renewed by the dreams of a Great Society, only to be crushed again by the continuing misadventures in Vietnam. It was a decade in which the methods of politics changed as social movements championing civil rights, peace, women, welfare rights, consumerism, and the environment rose to compete with political parties for the loyalties of American voters—and one in which the parties themselves changed, owing in part to Democratic Party reforms and in part to the new technologies and styles of campaigning. It was also a decade tossed and tormented at home by violence in the nation's cities, by continuing protests, and by a new counterculture that seemed to present outrageous challenges to all things conventional. By 1968, with the murders of Martin Luther King and Robert Kennedy, a Democratic Party convention scarred by violence in the streets and on the floor, continuing turmoil in the inner cities and on college campuses, and a seemingly endless war in Southeast Asia that pitted hawk against dove at home, it seemed to many as if the very social fabric of the nation was being torn beyond repair. The final blow for liberals in that fateful year came with the election of their political nemesis of two decades, Richard Nixon, to the White House.

Nonetheless, as R. Shep Melnick argues in his essay, the Great Society years did not end with Lyndon Johnson's departure from the White House. It not only continued but surged into the 1970s, even as general public distrust in government was growing. The 1970s brought ambitious new regulations to deal with environmental challenges, consumer protection, workplace safety, gender discrimination, rights of the disabled, and political campaigning. Hugh Davis Graham's essay shows that it was in the 1970s rather than the 1960s that affirmative action and many other civil rights measures became a real presence in American society.

Moreover, as Heclo points out, the Great Society changed not only the Left but the Right as well. In the wake of the Great Society's sweeping new commitments to activist national government—to innovative programs and insurgent politics that dramatically eroded the separation of the public and private spheres—self-styled conservatives were no longer content with a politics of forbearance. No less than liberals, conservatives practiced an activist politics that expected government to solve national problems. Ronald Reagan, the apostle of contemporary conservatism, promised to "get government off the backs of the American people," but his administration became committed to expanding the national government's role in containing communism, protecting the domestic economy, and preserving "family values."[8] George W. Bush, a self-professed Reagan disciple, seeks solutions to society's ills in government-supported, "faith-based" groups (a conservative version of community action) and educational reforms which ensure that "no child is left behind."

By the end of the 1960s, Democrats and Republicans, conservatives and liberals, had all become, as Heclo puts it, "policy minded," thus they have remained committed to finding public solutions to economic and social problems. Moreover, this commitment to government activism has been allied to a distrust of centralized power that has encouraged aggressive oversight of executive administration and insurgent assaults on the "Washington establishment." Rather than pursuing solutions to the nation's problems with New Deal–style executive-centered and pragmatic policy measures, contemporary political activists engage in ideological and institutional confrontation that defies consensus and diminishes public trust in government.

Although it was greeted with scorn and derision when delivered, Jimmy Carter's "malaise" speech of July 15, 1979, captured the essence of the Great Society's legacy for American politics and society. In fact, Carter never used the word "malaise"; the press, taking its cues from the White House pollster Patrick Caddell, dubbed it so. Still, the meaning was there. "This is not a message of happiness or reassurance," Carter announced gravely, "but it is the truth. And it is a warning." Carter's unhappy truth told of a "crisis of confidence":

> We have always believed in something called progress. We have always had a faith that the days of our children would be better than our own. Our people are losing that faith. Not only in government itself, but in their ability to serve as the ultimate rulers and shapers of our democracy. . . . In a nation that was proud of hard work, strong families, close-knit communities and our faith in God, too many of us now tend to worship self-indulgence and consumption. Human identity is no longer defined by what one does but by what one owns. But we have discovered that owning things and consuming things does not satisfy our longing for meaning.

Like Lyndon Johnson's sermons a decade earlier, Carter sought to summon the American people to a higher calling. But his speech lacked the hopefulness that animated the Great Society; in contrast to LBJ's celebration of government reform, Carter's words bespoke a profound distrust, indeed a "growing disrespect," for government and its leaders. "Looking for a way out of this crisis, our people have turned to the Federal Government and found it isolated from the mainstream of the nation's life," he lamented.[9]

By speaking truth to the fractious politics and public estrangement of America, Carter hoped that he could rally its people to the moral equivalent of a war against economic problems, such as the energy crisis, and societal infirmities, such as greediness and alienation. But the president's words seemed only to reinforce the country's growing doubts about the liberal order. Carter's "crisis of confidence" anticipated the Reagan "revolution" that would force Carter from office. More penetratingly, however, Carter's tortured moralism sheds light on the love-hate relationship that Americans had formed with the state—the defining characteristic of the Great Society's legacy for political life in the United States.

The essays in this volume reveal the profound drawbacks of this Ibsen-esque love-hate relationship between government and the people in the United States. At the same time, they suggest that the Great Society represents a critical chapter in the timeless story of the American republic, of its exalted wayward attempt to make practical self-rule on a grand scale. From the very beginning, as the historian Barry Karl has pointed out, Americans have been fearful that the national government would not meet its fundamental responsibility to protect our rights. Nevertheless, we have found it necessary to look to it for redress when the industrialization of the nation and its emergence as an international power required us to think and act as a nation. To the extent that it has weakened our ties with the more familiar state and local governments, the development of a more-active and better-equipped national state has "threatened our sense of ourselves as citizens." The Great Society marked a noble if flawed effort to rediscover a sense of citizenship and community amid the recognition that the expansion of national administrative power was inevitable. It left us accepting the national state forged on the crucible of twentieth-century reform, but uneasily. That the Great Society taught us both to embrace and to distrust this "uneasy state" may be diagnosed as an unhealthy political schizophrenia. But perhaps we should credit the reformers of the 1960s for recognizing that the uneasy state born of the 1960s—and the conflict it engendered between our need for government and our deep suspicion of it—had its source in our oldest and most profound need: our need to govern ourselves.[10]

The authors who contributed to this volume share an understanding that the Great Society marked a transformation of political life no less important than the Progressive Era and the New Deal. The examination of the Great Society that follows encompasses a number of different perspectives. But the rich variety of analysis and evaluation included seems appropriate, given the complex way in which our political system has been changing since the sixties. Even if this book does not make complete order out of chaos, it suggests, we believe, that a common set of principles and an enduring pattern of institutional arrangements have emerged since the 1960s that define a system of governance, albeit one characterized by a disconcerting tendency toward uncertain political attachments and intractable group demands. More generally, the Great Society entailed the culmination of a century's struggle to reconcile "big government" and the dignity of the democratic individual. Recent developments—the unspeakable horror of September 11, 2001, and the War on Terrorism that followed—confirm dramatically that this struggle has continued into the twenty-first century.

We dedicate this book to the memory of three of our authors, Hugh Davis Graham, Richard Cloward, and Wilson Carey McWilliams, who died after writing their essays for this volume. They will be sorely missed by their friends, their colleagues, and their fellow citizens. Hugh, Richard, and Carey were very different people and very different scholars. But all shared a passion for scholarship that mattered—they sought to understand and meet the imposing challenges of sustaining the vitality of self-government in a complex bureaucratic society. Each also, in his own way, was a political activist who was willing to challenge established power in the service of free inquiry and democratic accountability. They understood the deeper meaning of the popular sixties phrase, "the personal is the political." In their scholarship and political activism, they recognized that political justice is rooted in private morality; and they championed political participation as an activity that taught a rights-conscious people about their responsibility to one another.

Sidney M. Milkis
Jerome M. Mileur

Notes

1. See James T. Kloppenberg, *Uncertain Victory: Social Democracy and Progressivism in European and American Thought, 1879–1920* (New York: Oxford University Press, 1986).

2. See Michael Harrington, *The Other America: Poverty in the United States* (New York: Macmillan, 1963); see also David Riesman, *The Lonely Crowd* (New Haven: Yale University Press, 1961).

3. *Public Papers of the Presidents of the United States: Lyndon Baines Johnson,* 1963–64, 2 vols. (Washington, D.C.: Government Printing Office, 1965),

1:704. On the origins and significance of the Great Society speech, see Richard Goodwin, *Remembering America: A Voice from the Sixties* (Boston: Little, Brown, 1988), 274, 276.

4. *Public Papers of the Presidents of the United States: Lyndon Baines Johnson, 1966*, 2 vols. (Washington, D.C.: Government Printing Office, 1967), 1:3–7.

5. See Kevin Mattson, *Intellectuals in Action* (University Park: Pennsylvania State University Press, 2002), esp. chap. 5.

6. See William Crotty, *Decision for the Democrats: Reforming the Party Structure* (Baltimore: Johns Hopkins University Press, 1978), and Byron E. Shafer, *Quiet Revolution: The Struggle for the Democratic Party and the Shaping of Post-Reform Politics* (New York: Russell Sage Foundation, 1983).

7. On Republicans in the 1930s, see Clyde P. Weed, *The Nemesis of Reform: The Republican Party during the New Deal* (New York: Columbia University Press, 1994).

8. Commission on Presidential Debates, transcript of the Carter-Reagan presidential debate, October 28, 1980, www.debates.org.

9. Transcript of President Carter's "Address to the Country on Energy Problems," *New York Times*, July 16, 1979.

10. Barry D. Karl, *The Uneasy State: The United States from 1915–1945* (Chicago: University of Chicago Press, 1983), 238–39.

Lyndon Johnson, the Great Society, and the "Twilight" of the Modern Presidency

Sidney M. Milkis

The place in history of Lyndon B. Johnson and the Great Society is a difficult matter to assess. As the essays in this volume reveal, the Great Society marks both an extension of and a critical departure from the New Deal. In this essay I seek to make sense of the continuities and discontinuities between the 1930s and 1960s by exploring Lyndon Johnson's complicated relationship to Franklin Roosevelt and the New Deal. More than John F. Kennedy, LBJ committed his administration to expanding the New Deal political order. JFK considered the Roosevelt legacy the stuff of the past, from which he and the Democratic Party needed to be liberated. Johnson, in contrast, both reverentially and competitively drew inspiration from Roosevelt, whom he resembled as a political leader far more than Kennedy ever did.

Whereas Kennedy seemed intent on providing leadership for a generation far removed from the political struggles of the 1930s, LBJ's political career was launched by the heated battles that stirred a constitutional crisis during Roosevelt's second term. Johnson came to Congress in a special House election, held in 1937, in which he gained the favor of the Roosevelt administration and managed to distinguish himself from a field of eight other, better-known candidates, by running as the most devoted follower of the New Deal. Championing controversial initiatives that FDR proposed so as to expand national administrative power, such as the "Court-packing" plan and the Executive Reorganization Act,

Johnson gave a series of addresses during the House campaign that revealed his understanding of the deeper dynamics of the New Deal and strikingly foretold the task that would dominate his presidency. As he remarked in a radio address of March 1937: "If the administration program were a temporary thing the situation would be different. But it is not for a day or for a year, but for an age. It must be worked out through time, and long after Roosevelt leaves the White House, it will still be developing, expanding. . . . The man who goes to Congress this year, or next year, must be prepared to meet this condition. He must be capable of growing and progressing with it."[1]

Johnson's hope to participate actively in the development of New Deal liberalism was frustrated by the political pressures of representing a conservative state in the House and later the Senate. But as president, he hoped to resurrect the reformist zeal of the New Deal, long stalled by the conservative coalition in Congress. As one columnist wrote in 1965, the Johnson administration's initiatives in health care, education, and civil rights did much to "codify the New Deal vision of the good society."[2]

Nevertheless, Johnson is not easily characterized as a loyal son of the New Deal.[3] As William Leuchtenburg points out in this volume, Johnson was not content to complete the New Deal political order. He was not satisfied to go down in the history books as a successful president in the Roosevelt tradition. Johnson's feelings for FDR were as competitive as they were pious. His consuming dream was to be the greatest reform president in American history—to exercise leadership in the service of a reform program that would surpass FDR's New Deal.

Johnson's landslide victory over conservative Republican Barry Goldwater in the 1964 election surpassed FDR's triumph in 1936 as the largest popular vote margin in the history of presidential elections. It also swelled the Democratic margins in Congress and led Johnson to believe that he had a popular mandate to out-Roosevelt Roosevelt. The victory, he believed, bestowed authority on him not only to expand but also to redefine the reform aspirations of the 1930s—to build a "great society." From the beginning of his presidency, Johnson pursued an ambitious program that both advanced the New Deal goal of economic security and enhanced the "quality of American life." Johnson's leadership in the service of this program played a major part in formulating a new version of liberalism, a new philosophy of government that would remake American politics during the late 1960s and 1970s.

Scholars tend to agree that the reforms of the 1960s and 1970s marked a transformation of political life no less important than the Progressive Era and the New Deal.[4] Unlike these earlier reform periods, however, the Great Society and its aftermath did not embrace national administrative power as an instrument of social and economic justice.[5] Indeed, Johnson's reform ambitions led him to deliberately initiate and help legitimize an assault on New Deal institutional forms. Like FDR, Johnson was a presidentialist: the thrust of his institutional approach was to strengthen the managerial tools of the presidency with a view to enhancing the programmatic vision and energy in the executive branch. But the vision of the Great Society suggested the limits of "enlightened administration." LBJ summoned the American people to "a Great Society of the highest order," a calling that ultimately aroused a new generation of reformers who posed hard challenges to the executive-centered administrative state forged on the anvil of the New Deal.[6] Implicit in this philosophy of liberalism that emerged during the 1960s was the view that the problems afflicting the well-to-do and the poor could not be solved by centralized administration and federal largesse alone but required a more creative intervention of the state that would address the underlying causes of social and political discontent: alienation, powerlessness, and the decline of community. The emergence of a new version of liberalism during the Johnson presidency, trumpeted by LBJ himself, was a leading, if not the first, cause of a fundamental change in the principles and institutional arrangements of American government.

Johnson's commitment to ameliorating centralized administration was not merely rhetorical flourish. It followed from programmatic ambition and practical experience. He made his political mark first as the Texas director of the National Youth Administration (NYA), the New Deal agency that Roosevelt created in 1935 to rescue young people from ignorance, unemployment, and enduring hardship. The NYA, headed by the militant southern liberal Aubrey Williams, was both more idealistic and less bureaucratic than most other New Deal agencies. Its programs were administered from state offices and under state relief administrators, who were encouraged to develop innovative grassroots reforms that would provide meaningful work for young people and help keep them in school long enough to become self-sufficient.[7]

Johnson, just twenty-seven years old, the youngest of state directors, found the NYA to be a perfect outlet for his enormous ambition and boundless energy. Under his relentless leadership, the Texas NYA gained national recognition for innovations such as youth unemployment programs that created roadside parks and freshman college centers that offered credit courses, usually in high schools, for young people who could not enroll in college. Johnson soon gained the reputation of "youthful bureaucratic genius, as the ablest NYA director in the country."[8] The Roosevelt administration took appreciative note of how Johnson and the Texas NYA gained the support of and developed close ties to local communities, thus giving the New Deal a tangible presence in one of the largest and most politically important states in the country.

Johnson recognized that the problem of poverty in the 1960s was not the same as that of the Depression, but he considered the NYA experiences relevant to his presidential aspirations. As he wrote in his memoirs, "Those NYA experiences were valuable to me, suggesting some of the solutions we were searching for in the present."[9] Indeed, the social movements that emerged in the 1960s suggested that ideas and administrative practices which were marginal during the New Deal might become the foundation of a new reform program. As Johnson aide Richard Goodwin has pointed out, "The Civil Rights revolution demonstrated not only the power and possibility of organized protests, but the unsuspected fragility of resistance to liberating changes." The civil rights movement established the model for other social movements that grew out of the 1960s—feminism, consumerism, environmentalism, and others. Another social movement for which civil rights politics was paradigmatic, the antiwar movement, would play a major role in driving LBJ from office. But in the relatively halcyon early days of LBJ's leadership, Goodwin, and the president himself, envisioned social forces as potential agents of a new generation of reform. "Johnson intended to align himself with the cause of blacks and women and consumers," Goodwin claims. "And I saw [their causes] as evidence that the country was ready for leadership committed to social change."[10]

The civil rights movement, cresting in the August 1963 March on Washington, highlighted the unrest of a disenchanted minority most affected by poverty. The Johnson administration was eager to launch a national program to give the movement direction and purpose. Influenced by intellectuals such as Michael Harrington and John Kenneth Galbraith, the White House considered the problem of poverty as more than material deprivation; it was a symptom of deep-rooted social and political problems. As Harrington wrote in *The Other America*, the poor in post–World War II America were both estranged and invisible: "They think and feel differently; they look upon a different America than the middle class looks upon."[11] The core of the administration's War on Poverty, the community action program, which became the signature innovation of the Great Society, was designed to treat the deeper maladies that afflicted impoverished Americans. Its objective, War on Poverty director Sargent Shriver told Congress, was "to get action initiated against poverty at the point closest to where the people live by encouraging and inspiring local governmental units, and local private voluntary agencies, to initiate programs at the local level." Its deeper purpose, Shriver acknowledged, was "to change institutions as well as people," to challenge "hostile or uncaring or exploitive institutions" in an attempt to make them responsive to the peculiar needs of the "whole community."[12]

Viewed as a "profound and innovative concept of basic social participation," the concept of community action was written into the 1964 act that launched the War on Poverty.[13] The law required community action agencies to be "developed, conducted, and administered with the maximum feasible participation of residents of the areas and groups involved." As Frances Fox Piven and Richard Cloward show in their essay in this volume, the idealistic thrust of community action quickly gave way to the more practical objective of enabling poor people to obtain welfare benefits. But the Community Action Program was an important and revealing prelude to the emergence of "participatory democracy" as a leading principle of the reformers of the late 1960s and 1970s who gained influence as Johnson's support in the country declined and the White House became the target, rather than the catalyst, of social activism.

Johnson's reform commitments appeared to call in artillery on his own encampment. At the center of the administrative state stood the modern presidency—the most important institutional legacy of the New Deal. Institutional and programmatic reform of the New Deal made the modern executive, born of the Progressive Era, an enduring part of American political life; it consolidated developments in which the president, rather than Congress or localized parties, became the main instrument of popular rule in the United States. With FDR's long reign, a politics of administration emerged—centered in the White House Office and the Executive Office of the President—that depended primarily on a presidency-generated administrative state for coherence and energy.[14]

LBJ would extend this institutional legacy. As David Broder wrote in October 1966, more than those of any predecessor, including Kennedy, Lyndon Johnson's program depended "for its success largely on the skill, negotiating ability, and maneuvering of the president."[15] But no sooner had presidential government been proclaimed, than its very legitimacy came into question. By the end of Johnson's presidency, George Reedy, one of LBJ's aides, saw the "first lengthening shadows that will become the twilight of the [modern] presidency."[16] The startling, unhappy denouement of LBJ's presidency—his withdrawal from the 1968 election amid the collapse of the liberal political order—appeared to confirm Reedy's observation. Much was still demanded of presidents. They remained at the center of citizens' ever-expanding expectations of government. Yet Johnson's domestic and foreign policy failures fostered public cynicism about the merits of presidential policies, opposition to unilateral use of presidential power, and a greater inclination in the news media to challenge the wisdom and veracity of presidential statements and proposals.

Jerome Mileur's essay in this volume suggests how the Great Society contributed to the rise of its own antithetical force—a conservative movement that would achieve considerable influence by the end of the 1970s and seize power with the elevation of Ronald Reagan to the White House in 1980. But the rise of conservative insurgency was part of an unruly development, a change that was less a transformation than a fracturing of order—or in Brian Balogh's more optimistic view, a flowering of a "great (more diverse) pluralism." Moreover, Johnson was not merely the victim of a conservative "backlash." Ironically, by contributing so much to this development, LBJ helped to construct the platform that eventually enabled insurgents to challenge his presidency; more enduringly, the Great Society loosed political forces that challenged the modern presidency and remade the institutions of the administrative state.

Trumpeting the Great Society

Lyndon Johnson was caught between two worlds—a product of the New Deal, his ambition drove him to transcend it—to empower a new generation of reformers who created a political order in which he did not fit. White House special counsel Harry McPherson described LBJ's tragic fall from political grace as resulting from a generation the president expected to lead: "Johnson was a manipulator of men when there was a rejection of power politics; he was a believer in institutions at a time when spontaneity was being celebrated; he was a paternalist when paternal authority was rejected; and he came to political maturity during the 1930s, when democracy was threatened by fascism and communism, making him an unbending anticommunist."[17]

Johnson was a ruthless, sometimes crude manipulator of power, but he was not consumed by power for its own sake. From the beginning of his presidency, he pursued an ambitious reform program that would leave its (and his) mark on history.[18] He gave the signature speech of his administration on May 22, 1964, in a commencement address at the University of Michigan. To the surprise, and for the most part delight, of militant liberal reformers, Johnson did not merely call for an extension of FDR's economic constitutional order, which emphasized programs that would protect individual men and women from the uncertainties of the marketplace. He ignored the advice of several aides, such as Reedy, White House press secretary; Jack Valenti, a key member of Johnson's White House staff; and Wilbur Cohen, the assistant secretary of health, education, and welfare, that the speech should call for the intrepid forward march of New Deal programs. Johnson allied himself with White House aides, such as Bill Moyers and Richard Goodwin, who encouraged him to pronounce, instead, a bold new course of reform. Rejecting a toned-down version of the speech advocated by Reedy and Valenti, LBJ chose to deliver a provocative message that Goodwin had drafted. As Moyers wrote in fending off the cautionary importuning of other White House staffers, "This is a political year, but the President is not just thinking of the next election—*he is thinking of the next generation.* . . . He believes there is a danger that the *primacy of politics* this year will prevent the Nation from looking at the longer pull—hence *his deliberate decision to cast the spotlight on certain issues which ought to be imbedded in the Nation's consciousness.*"[19]

"The Great Society," Johnson told the graduating seniors and their families, "demand[ed] an end to poverty and racial injustice," but this was "just the beginning." Challenging the students and their parents to embrace more ambitious goals for America, LBJ described his vision of a "great society" as a place "where every child can find knowledge to enrich his mind and to enlarge his talents. It is a place where leisure is a welcome chance to build and reflect, not a feared cause of boredom and restlessness. It is a place where the city of man serves not only the needs of the body and the demands of commerce but the desire for beauty and the hunger for community."[20]

Johnson remained strongly committed to this more ambitious form of liberalism, even as he took America into a war in Southeast Asia. In his 1966 State of the Union address he declared that "we will not permit those who fire on us in Vietnam to win the victory over the desires and intentions of the American people."[21] Valenti had urged Johnson to emphasize foreign policy rather than domestic reform in the State of the Union message. He gave LBJ a draft speech, written by John Kenneth Galbraith, that offered a sweeping, idealistic defense of the administration's foreign policy and its intervention in Vietnam.[22] But once again LBJ allied himself with the voices of a new liberalism; he adopted a draft written by Goodwin that insisted, "This nation is mighty enough—its society healthy enough—its people strong enough—to pursue our goals in every corner of the earth and to continue to build a Great Society at home."[23] Highlighting his administration's record of the previous two years, Johnson declared that the Great Society led the nation along three roads—economic growth, "justice" for all races, and finally "liberation," which would use the economic success of the nation, so robust at this stage of the country's history, for the "fulfillment of our lives": "A great people flower not from wealth and power, but from a society which spurs them to the fullness of their genius. That alone is the Great Society. . . . [S]lowly, painfully, on the edge of victory, has come the knowledge that shared prosperity is not enough. In the midst of abundance modern man walks oppressed by forces which menace and confine the quality of his life, and which individual abundance alone will not overcome."[24]

There followed a list of noneconomic policy goals: an expansion of health and education programs; the rebuilding of entire sections of neighborhoods in urban areas to establish "a flourishing community where our people come to live the good life"; a stronger effort to put an end to the "continued poisoning of our rivers and air"; a highway safety act to seek an end to "the destruction of life and property on our highways"; and action to prevent the exploitation of the American consumer by deceptive business practices.[25]

This shift from concern with the "quantity" to the "quality" of life in America was the vehicle by which Johnson hoped to become "a national interest leader," as his aide Horace Busby put it, to surpass FDR's rights-based, interest group politics.[26] Some of Johnson's aides, if not the president himself, viewed the Great Society as an effort to marry New Deal liberalism with some of the ideas of the New Left that gained currency among the social activists of the 1960s. In discussing the preparation of Johnson's Great Society speech, Goodwin credits the Port Huron statement, a New Left tract, published in 1962 by the Students for a Democratic Society (SDS), at the same site Johnson chose, not coincidentally, for his landmark address—the University of Michigan. One aspect of that manifesto, in particular, impressed the presidential aide as expressing a yearning that went well beyond the utopian vision of radical fringe groups and was shared by a great many Americans. As the statement read:

> Some would have us believe that Americans feel contentment amidst prosperity—but might it not better be called a glaze above deeply felt anxieties about their role in the new world? And if those anxieties produce a developed indifference to human affairs, do they not as well produce a yearning to believe there is an alternative to the present, that something can be done to change circumstances in the schools, the workplaces, the bureaucracies, the government? It is to this latter yearning, at once the spark and agent of change, that we direct our present appeal. The search for truly democratic alternatives to the present, and the commitment to social experimentation with them, is a worthy and fulfilling enterprise, one which moves us and, we hope, others today.[27]

Hard as it is to imagine Lyndon Johnson embracing such New Left doctrine, he was not merely a cipher—a mouthpiece for speechwriters such as Goodwin. Johnson's ambition and background inclined him to embrace Goodwin's phrasing and to reject the more conventional ideas of Cohen, Valenti, and Reedy. The ideas that informed the Great Society were not so far afield from certain aspects of the New Deal, to more communal reform ideas and practices that Johnson understood well as a result of his experiences as the Texas director of the National Youth Administration. The 1943 report of the National Resources Planning Board (NRPB), a planning agency created in 1939 as part of the newly formed Executive Office of the President, singled out the NYA for avoiding bureaucratic inertia; it was one of the few New Deal agencies, the NRPB found, that did not "divorce the average citizen from participation in the problems involved in public-aid policy and administration."[28]

The praise New Deal planners bestowed on the NYA revealed the influence that such progressives as John Dewey had on the New Deal mind. Dewey defended an alternative vision of liberalism, one that went beyond the rights-based "economic constitutional order" that had given shape to the New Deal. "No economic state of affairs is merely economic," he argued. "Any liberalism that does not make full cultural freedom supreme and that does not see the relations between it and genuine industrial freedom as a way of life is a degenerate and delusive freedom."[29] Dewey's fingerprints could be found in the NRPB report, which gave the first detailed account of the economic bill of rights, dubbed the "Second Bill of Rights"—the centerpiece of FDR's 1944 State of the Union address. To the more conventional economic rights, such as the right to a job and the right to health care, the NRPB added one more expansive right that foretold importantly of developments during the 1960s: it called for "the right to rest, recreation, and adventure, the opportunity to enjoy life and take part in an advancing civilization."[30] FDR, believing such a "right" was extravagant in an era of depression and war, would transform this entitlement to cultural enrichment into a more conventional idea, the "right to recreation"—to the understandable proposition that modern American workers and their families had the right to take a vacation.

The prosperity and restlessness of the 1960s nurtured a more extravagant political aspiration: the desire to ally the welfare state to cultural resources of civilization, presupposing a shift in emphasis from the "quantity" to the "quality" of life in America, became the centerpiece of the Great Society.[31] Even the Johnson administration's War on Poverty was informed by the need to address the quality of American life. In fact, Vice President Hubert Humphrey had suggested at the program's inception that the administration coin "a better phrase than the 'War on Poverty,'" proposing alternative phrases such as "an adventure in opportunity" and "an opportunity crusade."[32]

Johnson was less exuberant than his vice president in his characterization of the poverty program. Indeed, he sometimes took the position that the 1964 Economic Opportunity Act was properly understood as an extension of the New Deal.[33] Speaking in Franklin D. Roosevelt Square in Gainesville, Georgia, where thirty years before FDR had urged attention to the "one-third of our people" who were "ill clad, ill fed, and ill housed," Johnson praised New Deal programs, which he credited for "moving that thirty percent down to twenty percent." Recalling the New Deal quest to provide "freedom from want," LBJ pledged his administration "to keep on and keep on and keep on, in our war on poverty, until we drive poverty into the face of the earth and it no longer exists in our beloved America."[34]

Nonetheless, Johnson insisted, an "unconditional war on poverty" could not be won by distributing checks or providing jobs alone. Gareth Davies notes that Johnson instructed a young economic adviser, Lester Thurow, to remove from the text of the bill any portion that could be viewed as a cash support program—the emphasis was to be on *opportunity*, not *entitlement*. As the opening "Declaration of Purpose" announced, the War on Poverty aimed "to eliminate the paradox of poverty in the midst of plenty" by "opening to everyone the opportunity for education and training, the opportunity to work, and the opportunity to live in decency and dignity." The commitment to eliminate poverty, Davies observes, "was dramatic and new, but the rights of the poor were opportunities, not outcomes."[35]

But the right of the poor to these opportunities did not invoke nineteenth-century individualism. Instead, the Great Society idea of opportunity was informed by the fundamental cultural changes of the 1960s that challenged the traditional liberal commitment, honored by New Deal liberalism, to the pursuit of material self-interest. These changes demanded not just security but also, as Johnson put it, "the chance for fulfillment and prosperity and hope." By the same token, the 1960s posed new leadership challenges. As Johnson told a 1964 Convention of the Communications Workers, "In Franklin Roosevelt's time there was a sense of crisis, of desperate danger, of threatening disaster. The need for action was plain." In contrast, LBJ warned, the Great Society summoned the country to address problems that were virtually invisible—"like some giant iceberg." The government's most important task in the 1960s was not to ameliorate the contest between the rich and the poor. The greatest challenge was to alert an "indifferent" nation, which ignored subterranean but potentially fatal social ills tied to excessive individualism, to "the need to solve problems." The contest today, LBJ preached, was not "so much between the oppressed and the privileged, as between the farsighted and those without any vision."[36]

The commitment to treat the deeper causes of the country's maladies contributed to the Johnson administration's decision to make community action an integral part of the War on Poverty. The federal Office of Economic Opportunity (OEO), the new White House agency charged with leading the War on Poverty, would award "special consideration to programs which give promise of effecting a permanent increase in the capacity of individuals, groups, and communities to deal with their problems without further assistance." This task would be abetted by delegating administrative authority to community action agencies (CAPs), a policy design that resembled, as Davies observes, the traditional American commitment to local self-government—to prescribing "local solutions to local problems."[37] But Johnson and the architects of the War on Poverty had no affinity for local self-government as it had traditionally worked in the United States. Instead, federal guidelines concerning CAPs, requiring "maximum feasible participation of residents of the areas of the groups served," entailed a commitment to "participatory democracy" that would operate independently of existing local and state governments.[38] The ideals of local community and political participation had to be redefined to address the underlying problems of America's poor. As the OEO's administrative history of the War on Poverty put it, "CAP gave a vocabulary, and then a language, and then a voice to the poor. They did not, any longer, have to be silent."[39]

As later events would reveal, Johnson did not fully grasp the disruptive potential of the community action agencies. Community action was based partly on the premise that the principal hope for the poor was for them "to develop sufficient strength and skill to maneuver themselves, largely by their own efforts, out of where they are and into something better." But an important corollary to this notion was the "belief that if any reforms are feasible in the existing social system they will have to be accomplished through vesting poor people with the political and administrative power necessary to force the changes *they* consider important upon the power structure."[40]

Johnson did not share the hope of OEO director Sargent Shriver and other militant reformers that community action programs might become agents of disruptive political change. Viewing the War on Poverty as an expanded version of the NYA, Johnson was primarily interested in launching jobs programs that would have close ties to local communities. Indeed, when a dispute broke out in Congress over the role of religious organizations in community action programs, a frustrated Johnson considered eliminating the community action provisions from the legislation and investing poverty funds in federal job programs such as the Job Corps camps.[41] Gently encouraged by aides such as Moyers and

Shriver, LBJ eventually accepted community action as the core of the Economic Opportunity Act. He took great pleasure from the establishment of one of the first community programs in San Marcos, the site of his alma mater, Southwest Texas State College. In a November 1964 visit to San Marcos, he acknowledged that the War on Poverty and the pursuit of a Great Society were closely linked—and that the goals they embodied meant that American men and women had to "participate in the affairs of your community and your State and your Nation." The success of his presidency and his program, Johnson insisted, could not be attained at the hand of "beneficent government" but instead required a new political activism: "A President can lead and teach, and explore, and set goals. He can have his eyes on the stars, with a vision that will flow therefrom, and he can have his feet on the ground, with a solid foundation that we need. . . . But no leader can make a people more than they are, or make them more than they really want to be. . . . These goals are going to demand your effort and your work and your sacrifice, and the best from every American."[42]

The Modern Presidency Meets the "New" Politics

In the end, Johnson would become the target, rather than the leader, of those who practiced the new politics of the 1960s. White House aide Hayes Redmon saw the handwriting on the wall as early as the summer of 1966, when LBJ's support began to unravel. In a June 9 memorandum to his boss, Bill Moyers, Redmon conveyed the troubling accusations of Fred Dutton, a former White House assistant to John Kennedy, who later would serve as the principal assistant in Robert Kennedy's presidential campaign. "Dutton accused us of being old fashioned and somewhat out of step with the temper of the time," Redmon reported ruefully. There was no easy solution for this infirmity; Redmon and other White House aides were not optimistic about the prospects of making over LBJ's image. Dutton agreed, Redmon's memo concluded, "that it would be 'phony' to attempt to move Lyndon Johnson into the era of the 'politics of existentialism.'"[43]

LBJ's image as an old-fashioned politician was not necessarily an indictment of his leadership. It bespoke a lack of charisma and an unwillingness to appeal directly to public opinion, to become the type of popular leader who might weaken governing institutions.[44] Unlike Dwight

Eisenhower, LBJ was not a constitutional conservative. He wanted to excite the nation, to accomplish more than any president had ever achieved. Johnson felt best able to do so with his laws and policies, but he was to learn that he was unable to cultivate a stable basis of popular support for his domestic and foreign policies. As he told Walter Cronkite regretfully in 1969, during the first of a series of television interviews, his disadvantage as a leader could be succinctly described as "a general inability to stimulate, inspire, and unite all the people of the country, which I think is an essential function of the Presidency."[45]

LBJ's failures as a popular leader were not merely a matter of personal deficiencies, however; they also followed from the inherent tension between executive power and the Great Society. Johnson's bold leadership was tempered by reticence. Firmly rooted in FDR's tradition, Johnson would seek to uphold, even expand on, the modern presidency—to embellish, rather than curtail, the New Deal's abiding commitment to, as Roosevelt called it, "enlightened administration."[46] In fact, the early years of the Johnson administration marked the historical high point of "presidential government": major domestic policy departures that formed the heart of the Great Society, such as War on Poverty and Model Cities, were conceived in the White House, hastened through Congress by the extraordinary legislative skill of the president and his sophisticated legislative liaison team, and administered by new or refurbished executive agencies that had been designed to respond to the president's directives. Moreover, Johnson attempted to establish a personal governing coalition that reached beyond and lessened the importance of the Democratic Party.[47]

The separation of presidential politics and the party would eventually isolate Johnson, depriving his administration of a stable basis of popular support. Indeed, the 1966 off-year election proved disastrous for LBJ and the Democrats, in no small part because the president had neglected the regular party apparatus. But from a broader historical perspective, Johnson's reliance on presidential politics was a logical response to the New Deal and its consolidation of the modern presidency. Although FDR's leadership had been the principal ingredient in a full-scale Democratic realignment, it had aimed to establish the president rather than the party as the steward of public welfare. Like the New Deal, the Great Society was less a partisan program than an exercise in expanding the president's power and nonpartisan administration of the affairs of state.

What Johnson, for all his savvy, failed to appreciate adequately was the profound differences between the 1930s and the 1960s—differences that his own celebration of a Great Society accentuated. The Roosevelt revolution dedicated itself to tangible government entitlements, thereby forging a coalition of African Americans, liberal intellectuals and professionals, labor union members, and white ethnic groups who looked to the modern presidency and the "liberal establishment" for leadership and programmatic benefits. The Great Society helped to bring to power issue-oriented independents, representing broad causes and movements, who resisted "presidential management"—and were less willing to delegate policy responsibility to administrative agencies.[48] The movements and groups that all previous presidents had kept at a distance—those representing minorities, women, environmentalists, and consumers—Johnson hoped to incorporate into the Great Society coalition. He was surprised and hurt that his efforts, from the start of his presidency, to invite civil rights leaders into the White House to listen to their concerns and to express support for their causes were not appreciated by some of the more militant voices in the African American community.[49] In resenting this unrequited commitment to diversity, Johnson showed that he badly misjudged the difficulty of expanding the liberal coalition to movements that, as Bruce Miroff observes, were in "the process of exploding the usual categories of American group politics." The more moderate—"responsible"—civil rights leadership was losing its influence on the movement, and the rising younger militants particularly mistrusted established leaders whom the White House appeared to have co-opted.[50]

Johnson's tempestuous years in the White House revealed that modern presidents, despite significant prerogative power and freed from the constraints of partisan responsibility, could not escape the need to achieve consensus and popular support for their programs. Johnson knew that even presidents with large reform ambition had to keep some distance from social movements and causes so as to avoid alienating other supporters. The Johnson White House attempted to advance progressive reform, to serve the same ideas represented by the social movements of the 1960s: racial justice, equal treatment of women, consumer protection, and a healthy environment. At the same time, its cooperation with social movements coexisted uneasily with the need to cultivate a nonpartisan consensus for the Great Society program. Johnson was to find that it was impossible to maintain a "balance point," as Miroff puts it, between national consensus and idealistic zeal.[51]

Johnson and the Civil Rights Movement

Johnson's uneasy relationship with the civil rights movement provides perhaps the best example of the strengths and weaknesses of the Great Society—and of the importance and limitations of the modern presidency's relationship to social movements. In a 1987 interview, Horace Busby said that the Johnson White House viewed coming to terms with the race issue as the major challenge in completing the work left undone by Roosevelt: "It's just not true that FDR was a friend of blacks. . . . In 1936, FDR participated in a ceremony unveiling the Robert E. Lee statue in Dallas, Texas. He said that he welcomed the chance to do this and that Lee was a great Christian gentleman. No president could get away with such a thing today. Johnson acted to fill the gap in the New Deal left as a result of the inattention to racial problems."[52]

When Johnson assumed the presidency, he had substantial reasons for taking a strong civil rights stand. By this time, the Solid South was no more, as Eisenhower and Nixon had won substantial support below the Mason-Dixon Line. The best hope for shoring up the national Democratic Party lay in expanding the black vote. Black voters were suspicious of a southern president, as were many northern liberals who had become strongly committed to the civil rights cause after the demonstrations in Birmingham, Alabama, and the March on Washington in 1963. Johnson felt the need to prove himself to the growing civil rights movement by carrying out—indeed surpassing—the civil rights program of the Kennedy administration.[53]

Even more, Johnson wanted to make his own historic mark on the presidency; he viewed civil rights reform and an alliance with the leaders of the civil rights movement as critical to the success of the Great Society. If he and the architects of the Great Society were New Dealers, they wedded themselves to that side of the New Deal which demanded a relentless pursuit of reform. As vice president, Johnson had urged JFK to go after Jim Crow aggressively, telling Kennedy aide Theodore Sorenson that "the Negroes are tired of this patient stuff and tired of this piecemeal stuff and what they want more than anything else is not an executive order or legislation, they want a moral commitment that he's [Kennedy's] behind them." Johnson recalled that FDR had attempted a failed "purge" campaign in the 1938 primary campaigns, trying to replace conservative southern and border state Democrats with 100 percent New Dealers who were committed to economic reform. The president's moral commitment to civil rights, LBJ believed, should not be expressed in an effort to purge southern Democrats but in an appeal to their consciences: "I think the President could do this in North Carolina or some place. I'd invite the congressmen and senators to be on the platform. . . . I'd have him talk about the contributions that they had made and then I'd say, 'Now, we have a problem here. No Nation—a hundred years ago in the Lincoln-Douglas debate, Lincoln said, "No Nation can long endure half slave and half free." Now no world can long endure half slave and half free and we've got to do something about it in our own country.'"[54]

To a remarkable degree during the early days of his presidency, Johnson was able to practice what he preached. In May 1964 he gave two courageous speeches in Georgia, one before the state legislature where he declared unequivocally that the time had come for "justice among the races." "Heed not," the president urged the southern lawmakers at a breakfast meeting in Atlanta, "those who seek to stir old hostilities and kindle old hatreds, who preach battle between neighbors and bitterness between States." Johnson insisted that he would never feel that he had done justice to his "high office"—the national constitutional office—so long as those old hatreds continued to rend the country. He would not have fulfilled his responsibility as president "until every section of the country is linked, in single purpose and joined devotion, to bring an end to injustice, to bring an end to poverty, and to bring an end to the threat of conflict among nations."[55] Johnson did not scold or preach; his tone was one of gentle persuasion rather than threat or coercion. The president sought to stir the conscience of his southern audience—to moderate their racial prejudice with an appeal to their bias for law and the Constitution: "In your search for justice, the Constitution of the United States must be your guide. Georgians helped write the Constitution. Georgians have fought and Georgians have died to protect that Constitution. . . . Because the Constitution requires it, because justice demands it, we must protect the constitutional rights of all of our citizens, regardless of race, religion, or the color of their skin."[56]

Johnson's campaign to take his civil rights fight into the deep South was a great triumph, one that reverberated far beyond Georgia's borders.

In going before the legislature of a southern state to make an unflinching statement on civil rights, he gained the hard-won respect of northern liberals. It was "becoming of the President of the United States," a *Washington Post* editorial declared, that he should make such a "forthright statement" below the Mason-Dixon Line. Johnson's words were not novel; he and other presidents had said as much before. "But said in this setting," the *Post* recognized, "the words have special impact, special meaning. They throw down the gauntlet of a challenge: they say to the South—in part because they are spoken by a President of the United States who is himself a Southerner—'Remember that you are Americans; remember that you belong to a Union, not a confederacy.'"[57]

The reaction to Johnson's moral appeal was hardly less impressive in the South than it was in the North. He did not overcome all resistance. At the breakfast meeting in Atlanta, which also included Governor Carl E. Sanders and Senator Herman Talmadge, the audience applauded the president on several occasions, but not when he spoke of equal rights.[58] Similarly, when he thumped the podium at his second stop in Georgia, the town of Gainesville, and shouted that "the Constitution of the United States applies to every American of every race, of every religion, of every region in this beloved country," there was no applause from the large and otherwise enthusiastic audience. Nonetheless, as the *Richmond Times Dispatch* admitted, "despite his uncompromising civil rights stand, the President's public appeal made its impact." No major Georgia official, save the unreconstructed states' rights senator Richard Russell, boycotted LBJ's visit. Moreover, although there were notes of disagreement among the huge crowds that greeted the president in Atlanta and Gainesville—white workers wearing coveralls held up a sign along the Atlanta motorcade that read "Kill the Bill"—the overwhelming response to Johnson's visit was remarkably positive, an indication, LBJ insisted, that a "new South" was ready to turn the page of racial intolerance.[59] As an editorial in the *Atlanta Constitution* put it, "It was typical of the President's directness that he came South to state the case for racial justice, to say that 'no one is fully free until all of us are fully free.' . . . But it was also very much in his style that he said the words not as a hickory-stick teacher but rather as a compassionate friend. . . . It was as though he were placing a fatherly hand on the shoulders of the South and saying: 'Look, I am of your same soil. I understand. But it is time to put aside this stultifying issue of race and get on with the business of the nation.'"

Reminding its readership that Franklin Roosevelt had once visited Gainesville in the cause of economic justice, the editorial concluded: "Georgia and the nation responded with deep enthusiasm for FDR. And if the surging crowds in Atlanta and Gainesville . . . were any measure, they are doing the same for LBJ."[60]

Johnson's remarkable and widely praised trip to Georgia strengthened his resolve to achieve major civil rights reform. Much is made, and rightfully so, of Johnson's skill in moving legislation through a recalcitrant Congress. The 1964 Civil Rights Act and the 1965 Voting Rights Act represented LBJ's largest and most enduring achievement—the virtual elimination of legal barriers to black equality; the end of Jim Crow in the South; and the enfranchisement of millions of Americans. What is often overlooked is how the fight for civil rights reform saw Johnson's mastery of the legislative process joined to moral leadership—how LBJ used the presidency to pique the conscience of the nation. LBJ's greatest strength as majority leader of the Senate had been personal persuasion, a talent he now used to convince the Senate Republican leader, Everett Dirksen, to endorse the bill and enlist moderate Republicans in the cause. Johnson's success with Dirksen, however, was greatly aided by the senator's perception that public support for civil rights was building in the country. Investing the prestige of his office in a cause and a movement, Johnson persuaded Dirksen and most members of Congress that civil rights reform could no longer be resisted. As Dirksen put it, paraphrasing Victor Hugo's diary: "No army is stronger than an idea whose time has come."[61] Dirksen's support sounded the death knell for the conservative coalition of southern Democrats and Republicans against civil rights. Congress passed the bill, and Johnson signed it on July 2, 1964.

Johnson also joined forces with civil rights activists in the dramatic prelude to the enactment of the 1965 voting rights legislation. Amid a crisis in Selma, Alabama, which saw civil rights marchers confront an oppressive barrier of state troopers, Johnson spoke with unusual feeling to a joint session of Congress in March 1965 about the Voting Rights Act. His speech warned that the enactment of the voting rights bill would not end the battle for civil rights; rather, it was but one front in a large war: "What happened in Selma is part of a far larger movement which reaches into every section and State of America. It is the effort of American Negroes to secure for themselves the full blessings of American life. Their cause must be our cause too. Because it is not just Negroes, but really it is all of us, who must overcome the crippling legacy of bigotry and injustice. And we shall overcome."[62]

Johnson thus adopted as his own rallying cry a line from an old hymn that had become the slogan of the civil rights movement. "Much of his audience," Paul Conkin has written in his biography of Johnson, "was in tears, for he had succeeded in doing what he had asked Kennedy to do in 1963—use the presidency as a moral platform."[63] LBJ had not won over southern congressmen, most of whom slumped in their seats, as the joint session erupted in applause. Nonetheless, he had triumphed where FDR failed: without embroiling himself in an enervating purge campaign, he had discredited southern resistance to liberal reform.

Johnson's alliance with the civil rights movement was fraught with political risks. The Democrats had depended on their southern base to win national elections. "He knew very well what the impact would be of an all-out civil rights program," White House aide McPherson related many years later. "He would be considered a traitor."[64] Johnson's triumphant visit to Georgia gave him hope that he would be forgiven by poor white southerners; this was the very purpose of his appeal to conscience. "I can't make people integrate," he told Goodwin, "but maybe we can make them feel guilty if they don't."[65] The elections of November 1966, however, revealed that the South was not in a forgiving mood. Three segregationist Democrats—Lester Maddox in Georgia, James Johnson in Arkansas, and George P. Mahoney in Maryland, won their party's gubernatorial nomination. In Alabama, moreover, voters ratified a caretaker administration for Lurleen Wallace, since her husband, George, was not permitted to succeed himself. George Wallace, dubbed the "prime minister" of Alabama, had by 1966 emerged as a serious threat to consummate the North-South split in the Democratic Party, either by entering the 1968 presidential primaries or running as a third-party candidate. What happened in the 1966 gubernatorial race in California, where former movie star Ronald Reagan handily defeated the Democratic incumbent Edmund G. Brown, revealed that this conservative insurgency was not limited to southern Democrats.

The prospect of losing the White House in 1968 made certain members of the administration nervous, if not completely repentant, about Johnson having alienated southern Democrats. A few days after the midterm election, one aide, Ervin Duggan, urged immediate attention to the problem: "Bill Moyers once [said] that Lyndon Johnson's mission might be to 'free the white South from itself.' If President Johnson is to accomplish that, he'd better get busy. Bitterness and resentment and outright hatred for the President in the South are bad—and getting worse. If they are to be moderated, if Wallace is to be stopped and the South saved for the President's party, we should start developing a Southern strategy now."[66]

The fear of "white backlash"—the new phrase for white resentment of black gains through political action—did not shake Johnson's determination to obtain civil rights progress through legislation and executive action. Johnson had no stomach for a "southern strategy" that retreated from civil rights. The defense of this cause above all was how he intended to make his mark on history, and Johnson's place in history meant more to him than serving another term as president or the standing of the Democratic Party. Moreover, the civil rights movement had been far too powerful and the issues it raised too riveting for a return to relatively "safe" New Deal issues such as economic security and educational opportunity. Johnson believed that as long as the economy remained strong, the Democrats "could still squeeze through." "But whatever the consequences," McPherson has insisted, LBJ "was determined to make major advances in the area of civil rights."[67]

To Johnson's deep disappointment, however, the growing militancy of the civil rights movement gave further impetus to "white backlash" and also created a rift between the White House and the social movements that Johnson hoped to enlist in the Great Society. LBJ had dedicated his presidency to a more activist and experimental form of progressive politics. By 1967, however, radical insurgency represented the greatest threat to his presidency.

Toward the end of 1965, the energy and resources committed to the Great Society began to suffer, threatened more and more by Johnson's preoccupation with the Vietnam War. African Americans were among the first to sense this change, and civil rights leaders, such as Martin Luther King Jr., became visible participants in the antiwar movement. In late November, Hayes Redmon lamented these efforts of civil rights activists. "I am increasingly concerned over the involvement of civil rights groups with anti-war demonstrators," he wrote in a memo to Moyers. "The anti-Vietnam types are driving the middle class to the right. This is the key group that is slowly being won over to the civil rights cause. Negro leadership involvement with anti-Vietnam groups will set their programs back substantially."[68]

Johnson had tried to renew ties with King earlier in the year. In August, soon after race riots broke out in Watts, he called the civil rights leader to express his continued, indeed strengthened support for civil rights and to question him about rumors that he was opposed to the administration's actions in Vietnam.[69] Johnson feared that the Watts riot was but the most dramatic episode in what was becoming a routine conflagration, a pattern of lawlessness that would defy his hope to exert leadership in the cause of an enduring civil rights program.[70] He urged King to take seriously and help publicize a recent commencement address the president had given at Howard University, in which Johnson had raised the stakes of civil rights reform. That speech, LBJ told King, which proclaimed that "freedom was not enough" and that the time had come to "seek . . . not just equality as a right and a theory but equality as a fact and as a result," demonstrated his administration's commitment to deal with the deep-rooted symptoms of racial inequality.[71] He also urged the civil rights leader to support the administration on Vietnam, telling King: "I want peace as much as you do if not more so," because "I'm the fellow who had to wake up to 50 marines killed."[72]

King acknowledged that Johnson's Howard University speech was "the best statement and analysis of the problem" he had seen and that "no president ever said it like that before."[73] Nonetheless, King saw himself, and not the president, as the leader of the civil rights movement. Moreover, he feared that tying himself too closely to Johnson, in an atmosphere of mounting racial tension, would weaken his standing in the civil rights community. As David Carter has written, "In this period of growing polarization it had become increasingly clear to civil rights leaders, and ultimately even to the President and his staff, that a White House blessing of a leader was tantamount to a curse."[74]

Indeed, King was the least of the administration's problems. Much more troublesome was the emergence of a new generation of black leaders dedicated to "Black Power," a militant, more threatening type of activism. People like Stokely Carmichael, newly elected head of the Student Nonviolent Coordinating Committee (SNCC), and other angry young civil rights leaders such as Floyd McKissick of the Committee of Racial Equality (CORE) were not only dissatisfied with the achievements of the Johnson administration's civil rights program but also contemptuous of its objective of racial integration. The growing militancy of black America erupted during the summer of 1966 as urban riots swept across the nation. In the wake of these developments, the moderately conservative middle class, as Redmon feared, grew impatient with reform. The administration's string of brilliant triumphs in civil rights was snapped. Its 1966 civil rights bill, an open-housing proposal, fell victim to a Senate filibuster. Johnson's leadership of the civil rights movement was a great asset to him in 1964; it had become something of a liability by the summer of 1966.

Since the emergence of the modern presidency in the Progressive Era, presidents had considered the White House to be a superior vantage point for guiding economic and social reform. Johnson had effectively intervened in civil rights matters during the summer of 1964, the first of the long hot summers. Riots erupted in July of that year, soon after the Republican national convention nominated conservative Arizona senator Barry Goldwater for president. Although proclaiming himself an opponent of discrimination, Goldwater had voted against the recently enacted Civil Rights Act; his acceptance speech denounced it as unconstitutional and prescribed a reliance on the states for the advancement of constitutional protections owed blacks. As the rioting spread and civil rights demonstrations continued in 1964 after the passage of the Civil Rights Act, the administration feared that racial unrest would turn white voters against a president identified with the cause of African Americans. In July, at LBJ's request, leaders of major civil rights organizations, including King, held a meeting in New York, where they called for a moratorium on black unrest.[75]

Johnson also actively intervened a month later in the struggle over the seating of the Mississippi delegation at the 1964 Democratic Convention. The Mississippi Freedom Democratic Party (MFDP) challenged the "regular" delegation, on grounds that the Democratic Party in the state excluded blacks from membership. The conflict confronted Johnson and the Democratic Party leaders with a dilemma, since they risked antagonizing the civil rights forces if they banned the Freedom Party delegation, and much or all of the South if they seated it. To avoid these unpalatable prospects, Johnson, with considerable help from Minnesota senator Hubert Humphrey and the leader of the United Automobile Workers, Walter Reuther, worked assiduously behind the scenes to achieve a compromise. The compromise plan included the seating of the regular Mississippi delegation, provided its members signed a loyalty oath that pledged them to support the presidential ticket; the symbolic gesture of making MFDP delegates honored guests at the convention, with two of its members seated as special delegates at large; and a prohibition of racial discrimination in delegate selection at the 1968 convention, to be enforced by a special committee to assist state parties in complying with this expectation.

Johnson's intervention in these two episodes was resented by more-militant civil rights leaders. John Lewis of SNCC and James Farmer of CORE dissented from the moratorium on demonstrations, signaling their commitment to "direct action" as a critical method of civil rights progress. Moreover, SNCC and CORE rejected the White House–negotiated compromise at the 1964 Democratic Convention and bitterly criticized Johnson for his willingness to sacrifice their moral cause on the altar of expediency. But the MFDP, through its lawyer, Joseph Rauh, accepted the compromise, which was adopted by the convention without notable objection.[76] And most civil rights activists, including King, accepted the White House's leadership on these two occasions. King joined Whitney Young, the executive director of the National Urban League; Roy Wilkins, executive secretary of the National Association for the Advancement of Colored People; and A. Philip Randolph, chairman of the Negro American Labor Council, in signing the moratorium statement. Johnson's heroic support for the Civil Rights Act and Goldwater's opposition to it, they believed, put a special premium not only on the election but also on the need to cultivate a climate in which racial progress could continue. As the declaration read, "Our own estimate of the present situation is that it presents such a serious threat to the implementation of the Civil Rights Act and to subsequent expansion of civil rights gains that we recommend a voluntary, temporary alteration in strategy and procedure."[77]

Similar considerations persuaded most civil rights leaders to swallow the MFDP compromise, albeit not without creating a great "sense of distress" in King and other moderate activists.[78] Not only were southern states threatening to walk out of the convention if the regular Mississippi delegation was purged, but Johnson and Democratic leaders also warned civil rights leaders that an unruly convention would cost the party the support of several border states and deprive Democrats of a chance to win by a historic landslide—and a mandate for further reform.[79] Just as important, LBJ helped to diffuse the Mississippi controversy by championing a fundamental reform of convention rules that would have enormous long-term consequences for the Democratic Party. Previously, state parties had sole authority to establish delegate selection procedures. Johnson's proposed solution to the MFDP compromise established the centralizing principle that henceforth the national party agencies not only would decide how many votes each state delegation got at the national convention but also enforce uniform rules on what kinds of persons could be selected. As the president told Reuther, "We don't want to cut off our nose to spite our face. If they [MFDP protesters] give us four years, I'll guarantee the Freedom delegation somebody representing views like [theirs] will be seated four years from now."[80] Contrary to conventional wisdom, LBJ made it clear to all parties—civil rights reformers and regular southern delegates alike—that he did not propose this compromise merely as a short-term, stopgap measure to ensure peace at the 1964 convention. Rather, he viewed the new nondiscrimination rule as a justified extension of the national party's power over state delegations that carried on discriminatory practices. As Humphrey confirmed with Johnson in a telephone conversation soon after the compromise plan was accepted, the MFDP representatives should "be heralded not as delegates from the state of Mississippi" but "as an expression of the conscience of the Democratic Party, as to the importance of the right to vote, political participation by all peoples in this country, and that we, in this historic period when we passed a civil rights act, which establishes a whole new pattern of social conduct in the country, that we're prepared to make official recognition of the all-important right to vote and of active participation in political affairs."[81]

Two years later, Harry McPherson, who played an important role as a White House liaison with the civil rights community, urged Johnson to intervene once again in the civil rights crisis of 1966.[82] He suggested that the president call an immediate meeting of civil rights leaders to address the black community's demand for further advances. Once eager to take steps that would solidify his personal ties with the civil rights movement, Johnson hesitated this time. He referred McPherson's recommendations to Attorney General Nicholas Katzenbach. Katzenbach agreed with McPherson that the racial situation had taken a disturbing turn, but in a memorandum to the White House aide he opposed an immediate meeting between the president and civil rights leaders. Underlying Katzenbach's objection was his disagreement with McPherson's characterization of Johnson as a "civil rights leader." Johnson was and would continue to be a leader toward racial progress. But to consider Johnson a civil rights leader was to assume falsely that the civil rights movement was constrained by its association with the White House—that it was a loyal part of a presidential coalition. In fact, Katzenbach observed, "one of the principal difficulties of established Negro leadership has been and will continue to be taking positions that are at the same time responsible, practical—and clearly independent of the Administration."[83]

In the end, Johnson did not meet with civil rights leaders. Instead, he followed Katzenbach's advice to send a number of his younger aides to various cities to meet with young black leaders. The attorney general's suggestion was the origin of ghetto visits that White House aides made throughout 1967; a dozen or so visited troubled black areas in more than twenty cities, including Chicago, Philadelphia, New York, Detroit, Washington, D.C., Los Angeles, and Oakland. The ghetto visits reveal the extent to which the modern presidency had assumed so many of the more important tasks once carried out by parties. Instead of relying on local party leaders for information about their communities, Johnson asked his aides to live in various ghettos for a time and then report directly to him about the state of black America. Local public officials and party leaders, even Chicago's powerful boss Richard Daley, were not told of the ghetto visits, lest they take umbrage at someone from the White House rooting about their home territories.[84] At the same time, these visits marked the declining significance of the modern presidency as the leading agent of liberal reform—a symptom of its "extraordinary isolation."[85] The awkward presence of these Johnson aides—mostly white, mostly from small towns and cities in the Midwest and the Southwest—spending a week, sometimes a weekend, in volatile ghetto environments such as Harlem and Watts was, as a leading participant put it, a "unique attempt by the President to discover what was happening in urban ghettos and why."[86] Aides were not sent to organize or manipulate or steer but solely to gain a sense of the ideas, frustrations, and attitudes at the basis of the riots.[87]

Overwhelmingly, the lengthy reports that White House aides prepared for the president indicated that volatile conditions in the ghetto did not stem from material deprivation alone. The most serious and common problem was that "the ghetto Negro lives in a world which is severed from ours." As Sherwin Markman, who organized the White House ghetto visits, wrote in his summary report, the first essential key to understanding urban America was "alienation—of the ghetto Negro from the mainstream of American life, and of white America from the ghetto Negro." Although housing, education, and employment varied from city to city, the "disconnection" blacks felt from the rest of America was "not limited to one city or region, but [was] nation-wide in its pattern, and growing." Markman related that as he left the comfortable parts of downtown and suburban U.S. cities, he had the "same feeling in the ghetto as I did when I visited the poverty stricken areas of South America a year ago. It was almost like visiting a foreign country—and the ghetto Negro tends to look on us and our government as foreign."[88]

Markman sought to persuade LBJ that the severe alienation that afflicted urban America both explained and perhaps justified the Black Power movement. The "dramatic growth" of Black Power had become the "rallying cry in the ghetto," he reported after a return visit to Chicago in February 1968. "Power" should not be confused with violence, Markman insisted, even though "some advocates of the philosophy preach violence." After talking with such intellectuals as Charles Hamilton, who had just written a book with Stokely Carmichael on Black Power, as well as militant black nationalists who championed the idea from the pulpits and in the streets, Markman concluded that this vague concept most essentially meant "an increase in race consciousness and pride." In their early visits to urban areas, White House aides had discovered, as one report put it, that "perhaps the most significant symbol of the ghetto is the *absence of proud men*." Black Power, Markman told LBJ, would bring "positive results" in filling that terrible void: "It is my judgment that the increased pride in race must inevitably lead to strong racial motivation for better social organization, better education, and better jobs. This motivation can, at least, serve the same purpose for Negroes as ethnic history has served for other minorities which have successfully made it in our society."[89]

By all accounts, Johnson was deeply moved by these reports. The president carried one of Markman's reports on the Chicago ghetto around with him and read it to members of the cabinet, Congress, and the press, with the hope that it would persuade them to accept the White House's position on civil disorders.[90] LBJ condemned the riots, declaring in a nationwide address of July 1967, "There is no American right to loot stores, or to burn buildings, or to fire rifles from the rooftops. That is a crime—and crime must be dealt with forcefully, and swiftly, and certainly—under law." At the same time, he insisted, "this is not a time for angry reaction. It is a time for action: starting with legislative action to improve the life in our cities. The strength and promise of the law are the surest remedies for tragedy in the streets."[91]

The ghetto reports apparently were pivotal in persuading Johnson to respond to the riots by redoubling his efforts to expand civil rights and the War on Poverty programs. The administration continued to push for an open-housing bill, and in the aftermath of King's assassination, one was passed in 1968. That year, LBJ also submitted and Congress passed the most extensive and most expensive public housing legislation in American history. Finally, Johnson continued to support the War on Poverty's Office of Economic Opportunity, even though its sponsorship of the Community Action Program was reportedly having a disruptive influence in many cities and was the target of bitter complaints from local party leaders.[92] The president seethed privately about the "revolutionary" activity that some CAPs were fomenting. Nonetheless, encouraged by the ghetto reports of their valuable work in ameliorating the alienation of urban dwellers from American society and government, he never repudiated them and continued to support federal funds for neighborhood organizations. The appropriate response to the riots, Johnson and his aides concluded, did not call for a return to steak-and-potato issues of the New Deal; rather, the estrangement of ghetto life required a reaffirmation of the core principles of the Great Society. As Markman concluded dramatically after a visit to the California East Bay communities of Oakland, Berkeley, and Richmond: "The only way the Negro can identify with the [War on Poverty] is by being an integral part of it. The War on Poverty is the great bulwark against the total disaffection of the ghetto Negro, which in the long run can lead only to guerilla warfare. The Poverty program succeeds by involving the Negro totally in the dreams and destiny of this Nation."[93]

The Modern Presidency and Community Action

Johnson's ambivalent relationship with the War on Poverty helps explain how he both extended the reach of the modern presidency and built the skids for its diminishing influence. In part, delegation of administrative responsibility by the Johnson White House to these local citizen groups was intended to be an extension of the modern presidency. LBJ and his aides viewed state and local governments, and the party organizations that governed them, as obstacles to good government, to the "enlightened" management of social policy. They conceived of CAPs as a local arm of the Office of Economic Opportunity, thus enabling the Johnson administration to bypass local governments and the entrenched, usually Democratic political machines.[94] Federal guidelines, in fact, stipulated that the community action program had to be conducted by a public or private nonprofit agency (or some combination thereof) other than a political party.[95]

From this perspective, the CAP was evidence of a further displacement of localized party politics by executive administration. As Samuel Beer has pointed out, "the antipoverty program was not shaped by the demands of pressure groups and the poor—there were none—but by deliberations of [White House] task forces" based on theories of social action and social psychology that had been germinating in some universities for several decades.[96] At least in part, then, the communal concerns of the Johnson presidency were closely connected to administrative invention; the CAP was a bold new initiative that embodied, in Nathan Glazer's words, "the professionalization of reform in modern society."[97] Moreover, in the hands of the Johnson administration, which relied to an unprecedented extent on presidential politics and governance, this invention never fulfilled its stated objective of popular participation. Under the banner of community control, Daniel Patrick Moynihan observed, "the essential decisions about local affairs came increasingly to be made in Washington via the direct CAP-OEO line of communication and funding."[98] Especially after 1967, following the recommendations of the Heineman Task Force on Government Organization, Johnson tried to tighten White House management over the CAPs.[99] The following year, George Nicolau, stepping down after eighteen months of running the Harlem Community Action Agency (HARYOU-ACT), the largest in the nation, declared himself "a victim of that process which in the space of three short years created and has almost been overwhelmed by its own complexities and its own bureaucracy."[100]

Nevertheless, although administrative centralization enervated the participatory aspirations of the War on Poverty, "participatory democracy" would became the clarion call of reformers who gained influence with the demise of Johnson's political fortunes. The Johnson administration's expressed concern for "community" involvement revealed how "qualitative" liberalism was potentially in tension with the centralization of authority required by an extensive welfare state. Furthermore, the administrative innovation that gave rise to the War on Poverty was an attempt to respond to real problems that could not be readily addressed by executive administration. Moynihan argued that the Johnson administration blundered into the community action program and that the mandate phrased "maximum feasible participation" was a shallow rhetorical bow to the Jeffersonian tradition of local self-government. Yet, as James Morone points out, Johnson and his aides were not so simple-minded; rather, they were attempting to identify a controversial program with a deeply rooted tradition in the United States—"by invoking the powerful myths of the American democratic wish."[101] As Johnson wrote in his memoirs with respect to his attraction to the idea of community action: "This plan had the sound of something brand new and even faintly radical. Actually, it was based on one of the oldest ideas of our democracy, as old as the New England town meeting—self-determination at the local level."[102]

In an admittedly halting, often awkward way, Johnson was seeking to reconcile the New Deal state with the historical antipathy in the United States to bureaucracy. His experiences as director of the Texas National Youth Administration, no doubt, gave him a practical sense of the difficulty of accomplishing this objective. Especially when the NYA was created, the 1943 NRPB report claimed, it was an outstanding example of a federal organization that was highly decentralized, with a considerable amount of discretion being left to state administrators. Even as the agency matured, although there was some increase in centralized administration, it retained a significant commitment to local determination. This character of the NYA was its greatest strength, but also the source of some concern among New Deal planners:

> The present arrangement has made for adaptability of the program to local conditions and community needs and has permitted experimentation in methods and techniques. . . . On the other hand, it has resulted in a marked lack of uniformity in program and methods and techniques and a wide diversity of achievement. The situation would appear to be particularly serious in view of the national significance of the problems of unem-

ployed youth, and the fact that so large a proportion of the young unemployed population is concentrated in areas where both social and economic conditions are likely to inhibit the development of appropriate projects if reliance is so largely placed upon local initiative.[103]

The cultural changes and social circumstances of the 1960s greatly aggravated the tension between enlightened administration and community control. After reading his White House aides' accounts of ghetto conditions, Johnson developed a deeper appreciation of the limits of executive administration in fighting a war against racial discrimination and economic deprivation. More important, the riots and the White House aides' reports of them confirmed the Johnson administration's view that "community action" was a critical element of their program to establish a post–New Deal version of the welfare state. The architects of the Great Society were well aware of the political risks involved in delegating administrative responsibility to community action agencies; however, these risks were taken in the hope of revitalizing, and indeed surpassing, the militant side of New Deal liberalism. Interestingly, the evaluations of the task forces charged by the Johnson White House with investigating the administrative problems of the War on Poverty are strikingly reminiscent of the NRPB's critique of the NYA. The "Task Force Report on Intergovernmental Program Coordination" noted in a typical analysis that the decentralized management of the Office of Economic Opportunity, while creating problems of administrative fragmentation and uneven performance standards, should not be condemned out of hand: "Administrative tidiness is not the only test of effective government. In truth, some Federal programs operating from new and revolutionary postulates (e.g., the Community Action Program) may have to measure their success, in part, in terms of what they temporarily disrupt. Furthermore, total program coordination can be bought at too high a price: the imposition of 'commissar' sanctions by one agency or one level of government over other agencies, levels, and jurisdictions, and a deadening multiplication of paper work and inter-agency clearance."[104]

Johnson's surprising patience with community action programs, his continuing, albeit certainly not unqualified, support of the War on Poverty, in the face of blistering criticism from Congress and local government officials, suggests that he did not disagree with this assessment.[105] He did not fully appreciate the tension between executive management and local self-determination. Nor did he sufficiently appreciate that the civil rights movement was a catalyst for a "new" politics that was inherently suspicious of presidential leadership. As one policy analyst has written, "It was precisely because the civil rights movement had already built organizations and mobilized community resources that 'maximum feasible participation' was translated so quickly from abstraction to reality."[106] The community action agencies took on the energy and aspirations of the civil rights movement and refocused it, thus giving a new generation of black leaders entrée into local and administrative politics. As a 1967 Senate investigation of the War on Poverty put it: "The Office of Opportunity policies and programs have produced a cadre of citizen leadership, heretofore neither seen nor heard in the community arena." They have brought "to the fore a sizeable cadre, for the first time in the Negro community, especially, of young energetic and striving leadership."[107] That cadre of striving leaders, instrumental in both the increasing election of black mayors in American cities and the growing influence of civil rights groups on social policy during the late 1960s and 1970s, developed political bases that were not tied directly to the Democratic Party or the White House. Nonetheless, having invested his immense ambition in the Great Society, having staked his political fortunes in the social movements that it empowered, Johnson had little choice but to support the Office of Economic Opportunity and the community organizations it spawned, even as he grew increasingly aware that it aroused leadership and social forces that he could not control.

Lyndon Johnson's Complex Legacy

Since Franklin Roosevelt died, the Democratic Party had been confronted with the reality that the New Deal realignment had failed in itself to protect the administrative and policy changes associated with his years. In a partisan sense, the New Deal realignment had always been fragile, subordinate to the task of refurbishing the presidency and executive agencies. New Deal liberalism, which for more than a quarter of a century had been tied to the modern executive, seemed in jeopardy when Lyndon Johnson, catching nearly every one of his aides off-guard, concluded his prepared speech on the evening of March 31, 1968, with the announcement that he would neither seek nor accept the nomination of his party for another term as president. As Herbert Parmet has written, "It does not take much exaggeration to consider [that night] as a landmark for the post–New Deal Democratic Party, as a moment when the old coalition finally yielded to a new fragmentation, when the old politics gave way to the new."[108]

The "new" politics represented an odd meld of the New Deal and the New Left. It did not oppose the programmatic and legal achievements of the New Deal but sought to extend and redirect them. "This new liberalism," Jack Newfield, an assistant editor of the *Village Voice*, wrote in late 1967, was "more urban, more activist, and more experimental than the old. Decentralist rather than bureaucratic. . . . More geared to the non-working poor than the fat, belching unions. More interested in sympathizing with the unborn revolutions in the Third World, than in containment or NATO."[109]

As such, Johnson's abdication marked a failure of his ambition, first announced at the University of Michigan in 1964, to align himself and the powers of the modern executive with the carriers of the new politics—civil rights activists, consumer and environmental advocates, and those fighting for women's rights. Johnson had in rhetoric and program sought to "manage" these political forces. But he was too much of a New Dealer, too dedicated to the presidency, to accept the consequences of "movement politics." By 1968, he had become the hated symbol of the status quo, forced into retirement lest he contribute further to the destruction of the liberal consensus. As he told Hubert Humphrey in their meeting of April 5, 1968: "I could not be the rallying force to unite the country and meet the problems confronted by the nation abroad and at home in the face of a contentious campaign and the negative attitudes towards [me] of the youth, Negroes, and academics."[110]

As Wilson Carey McWilliams makes clear in his essay for this volume, the Vietnam War contributed to this estrangement between LBJ and his former liberal allies. But the movement that emerged to protest the war was a sign of more than a foreign policy controversy; the estrangement between Johnson and the new liberal activists he once sponsored was a signal of new political and social forces that called the modern presidency to account. The two most significant facts of the reforms of the Great Society were the aggrandizement of executive power and, in seeming contrast to that, a deep suspicion of centralized administration. The reach of "enlightened administration"—the authority invested in the presidency and administrative agencies—became a great deal more intrusive in the

1960s. "Almost any legislation, even welfare measures," Conkin has written, "involved new rules, new guidelines, that circumscribed the behavior of some Americans, at times even those who collected subsidies."[111] Nonetheless, the Great Society's celebration of a "desire for beauty," "hunger for community," and "maximum feasible participation" called for efforts to limit the discretionary power of New Deal institutions. The Community Action Program, resulting from an attempt to reconcile administrative invention and the rejection of centralized administration, perfectly captured the paradox of Lyndon Johnson's Great Society.

As R. Shep Melnick shows in his essay in this volume, this intriguing and disconcerting paradox—the love-hate relationship with administrative power—would intensify during the 1970s. In the end it left liberalism in a funk, a "malaise," as Jimmy Carter would later characterize it: liberal reformers would continue to look to the national government to solve the problems of an industrial, and postindustrial, order; but, unlike New Dealers, they denigrated presidential leadership and administrative agencies, without which expansive government responsibility would become a chimera.

The reformers who took control of the Democratic Party after the Chicago convention followed the progressive tradition of scorning partisanship—of desiring a direct relationship between presidential candidates and the people. In this respect, the expansion of presidential primaries and other changes in nomination politics initiated by the McGovern-Fraser Commission were the logical extension of the modern presidency. But these reformers, champions of the "new politics," rejected the concept of popular presidential leadership that prevailed during the Progressive and New Deal eras. "New politics" liberals viewed the president as an *instrument* rather than the *steward* of the public welfare. Failing to address the question of the type of leadership or the type of executive that was desired, party reformers of the 1970s took for granted the general ideas current in the late 1960s and 1970s that presidential politics should be directed by social movements.[112]

Still, the institutional reforms of the 1960s and 1970s are miscast as an antinomian attack on government authority. There was a large element of hostility to centralized administrative power evident in the politics of New Left reformers who played an important part in the civil rights and antiwar movements of the 1960s. Moreover, the reform politics of these movements, celebrating community action and grassroots participation, inspired the self-styled "public interest advocates" of the 1970s who advanced policies that increased the national government's responsibilities to ameliorate racial and sexual discrimination and to enhance consumer and environmental protection. Notwithstanding their antiestablishment rhetoric and profound suspicion of centralized power, however, reform activists of the 1970s were intrepid liberals who sought to remake rather than dismantle government institutions. As Jeffrey Berry has written, "Leaders of the new [public interest groups] wanted to transcend 'movement politics' with organizations that could survive beyond periods of intense emotion."[113] The public interest movement, Berry shows, harnessed the revolutionary fervor of the civil rights and antiwar movements as an agent of change within the system.

Hoping to reconcile national authority with the New Left's dedication to participatory democracy, public interest reformers rejected the New Deal practice of delegating power to the executive branch. They championed statutes and court rulings that would reduce the discretionary authority of presidents and administrative agencies. Just as significant, reform activists played a principal part in revamping administrative law during the 1970s, so that liberal provisions were established for public participation. Taking account of these changes, Samuel Beer noted at the end of that decade "it would be difficult today to find a program involving regulation or delivery of services in such fields as education, welfare, and the environment that does not provide for 'community input.'"[114]

In part, the effort of reformers to circumscribe executive administration followed from the emergence of "divided government" as a regular feature of political life in the United States. Richard Nixon's election in 1968 marked the beginning of an increased tendency for voters to place the presidency in Republican hands and Congress under the control of Democrats; this pattern of ticket splitting would endure for the better part of two decades. Progressive and New Deal reforms were conceived with the view that the modern presidency would be an ally of programmatic reform; in contrast, public interest activism was born of institutional confrontation between a conservative Republican president and a reform-minded Democratic Congress. Greatly suspicious, if not avowedly hostile to, presidential power, reformers of the 1970s and their allies on the Hill were determined to protect liberal programs from unfriendly executive administration.

The battles waged by Democrats and Republicans for control of departments and agencies transcended narrow partisanship, however. As the unhappy term of Jimmy Carter revealed, one-party control of the White House and Congress did not assure institutional harmony. In fact, the restraints imposed on presidential power during the late 1960s and 1970s reflected an effort to ameliorate what Alexis de Tocqueville called the "puerilities of administrative tyranny."[115] There is a real sense in which the reforms of the 1970s attempted to make national administrative power legitimate by appealing to the antistatism that was so deeply rooted in the principles and historical traditions of the United States.

Significantly, with the maturing of the new politics, reformers' dedication to participatory democracy evolved into a commitment to new rights: the right to be free of discrimination; the so-called collective rights associated with consumer and environmental protection; and the right of those affected by government programs (and those representing the "public") to participate in the administration of those programs. As public participation evolved into new programmatic and procedural rights during the late 1960s and 1970s, the courts became vigilant in making sure that federal agencies adhered to the newly recognized entitlements.[116]

The institutionalization of Great Society liberalism and the emergence of the courts as the guardian of the "the rights revolution" of the late 1960s and 1970s followed in large part from the landmark laws that were Lyndon Johnson's greatest accomplishment. White House aide Harry McPherson foresaw this possibility in the midst of the civil rights crisis in Selma, Alabama. In seeking civil rights reform, McPherson urged the president, it was important "to describe both the possibilities and limitations of Federal action":

> Some sense of the *power* of the law—of the Constitution and the civil rights acts—is vital. The Selma Negroes and their supporters . . . think Federal law is an ineffective abstraction. You cannot change that feeling overnight. But you can assure the country that the power is there to back up the decrees of the courts. . . . [Y]ou are not after vengeance on the perpetrators of the outrage in Selma. . . . Your vision of America—expressed in the poverty program [and] the education program—includes them, as well as the men and women they have wronged. In an educated America, in an America of opportunity and hope, they will have a part. Then they can cast aside the truncheon and the whip. . . . Then the differences between men can be settled where they should be—in the courts.[117]

Yet three years later, at the twilight of the Johnson presidency, as well as the twilight of the modern presidency, McPherson expressed the concern that this expansion of legal rights had left the country without a national purpose; the Great Society, he lamented, had helped to bring to power issue-oriented independents who failed to acknowledge a transcendent public interest. "Does this lack of a central core," a fellow White House assistant asked McPherson, "explain the emptiness we all sense . . . as Peer Gynt discovered when he peeled the onion?"[118]

Just as Ibsen's Peer Gynt discovered the limits of his search for the "true self," so the architects of the Great Society discovered the limits of reform in American politics. At the same time, as Brian Balogh argues in his essay in this volume, it is hard to deny that the battles they waged to advance civil rights and to enhance the quality of American life left the country better than it had been in the 1950s. Lyndon Johnson's Great Society may have failed to call the nation to a higher purpose, but in this failure they responded to the American people's concern to regain control and play a real part in the development of their communities and the nation. The tragedy of Lyndon Johnson reveals the extraordinary possibilities and profound weaknesses of modern executive power. In his boundless ambition and desire for fame, LBJ reminds us that responsible political leadership presupposes an active and competent citizenry. And this assumption imposes on presidents above all an obligation to recognize the limits and appropriate uses of administrative power.

Notes

I thank Donald Zinman for research help in preparing this chapter.

1. Lyndon Johnson, "Eight in the Dark," radio address over KNOW, March 18, 1937, Lyndon Baines Johnson Library, Austin, Texas (hereafter Johnson Library).

2. Richard A. Rovere, "A Man for This Age Too," *New York Times Magazine*, April 11, 1965, 118.

3. LBJ's role as a "faithful son" of FDR and the New Deal is explored by Stephen Skowronek in his seminal work on presidential leadership and American political development *The Politics Presidents Make: Leadership from John Adams to Bill Clinton* (Cambridge: Harvard University Press, 1997). Johnson's presidency, Skowronek argues, displayed the "politics of articulation"—he was constrained by the New Deal regime, the product of Roosevelt's "reconstructive politics," and could not become a regime builder in his own right. Still, Skowronek acknowledges that the emergence of the "modern" presidency, es-

tablishing the president as the principal agent of American politics, tempts all contemporary presidents, especially those with immense ambition, to engage in reconstructive politics, to disrupt, not sustain, the prevailing regime. Johnson's enormous ambition, Skowronek speculates, given considerable play by the power of the modern presidency, may have "gut[ted] the whole idea of a faithful son in the American Presidency" (330).

4. For example, see Anthony King, ed., *The New American Political System* (Washington, D.C.: American Enterprise Institute, 1978), and Richard A. Harris and Sidney M. Milkis, eds., *Remaking American Politics* (Boulder, Colo.: Westview, 1989).

5. Hugh Heclo, "The Sixties' False Dawn: Awakenings, Movements, and Postmodern Policy-Making," *Journal of Policy History* 8, no. 1 (1996): 41.

6. Remarks of the President and Mrs. Johnson to Fund-Raising Dinner of the Democratic Club of Cook County, Chicago, Illinois, April 23, 1964, White House Central Files, SP (SP 3-20), Johnson Library. Johnson's remarks at this dinner marked his first use of the term "Great Society." Encouraged by the enthusiastic response to his declaration of a new reform era, the president made the obligation to build a great society the central theme of his signature speech, a commencement address a month later at the University of Michigan. I discuss this speech at length in the next section.

7. On Johnson and the National Youth Administration, see Paul Conkin, *Big Daddy from the Pedernales: Lyndon B. Johnson* (Boston: Twayne, 1986), 74–79; Robert Dallek, *Lone Star Rising: Lyndon Johnson and His Times, 1908–1960* (New York: Oxford University Press, 1991), 123–44; and Robert A. Caro, *The Years of Lyndon Johnson*, vol. 1, *The Path to Power* (New York: Vintage Books, 1983), chap. 19.

8. Conkin, *Big Daddy from the Pedernales*, 76.

9. Lyndon Baines Johnson, *The Vantage Point: Perspectives on the Presidency, 1963–1969* (New York: Holt, Rinehart and Winston, 1971), 73.

10. Richard Goodwin, *Remembering America: A Voice from the Sixties* (Boston: Little, Brown, 1988), 275.

11. Harrington, cited in Office of Economic Opportunity (OEO), "The Office of Economic Opportunity during the Administration of President Lyndon B. Johnson: November 1963–January 1969," 1:5, Special Files: Administrative History, OEO, Johnson Library.

12. Ibid., 40, 55.

13. Ibid., 55.

14. I develop this point more fully in *The President and the Parties: The Transformation of the American Party System since the New Deal* (New York: Oxford University Press, 1993).

15. David Broder, "Consensus Politics: End of an Experiment," *Atlantic Monthly*, October 1966, 62.

16. George Reedy, *The Twilight of the Presidency* (New York: New American Library, 1970), xv.

17. Harry McPherson, interview with the author, Washington, D.C., July 30, 1985.

18. LBJ's complexity is somehow ignored in Robert Caro's epic biography. In the most recent volume, Johnson, like the Senate itself, is depicted as a ruthless power seeker without any purpose other than his own ambition, as someone who would do the right thing only if it cost him nothing and was sure to advance his interests (*Master of the Senate* [New York: Knopf, 2002]). As Ronald Steel points out in a penetrating review, "Lyndon Johnson was a man of operatic dimensions. Robert Caro sees the action but does not hear the music" ("Fatal Attraction," *Atlantic* Monthly, July/August 2002). Johnson was enthralled by a characterization that Walker Stone, editor in chief of Scripps-Howard newspapers, gave of his leadership. He heard of Stone's evaluation from Frank Dobie, a renowned folklorist and University of Texas faculty member. Dobie's letter to LBJ, written in December 1963, quoted Stone's assessment of the transition between Kennedy and Johnson: "The White House never had, nor is it likely to have again, more graceful and gallant occupants than the Kennedys. They radiate youth and wit and charm and warmth. But his [Kennedy's] administration, in balance, in my opinion, was a weak one. You and I know better than most the weaknesses and shortcomings of Johnson. But it is my belief that his will be a stronger and more productive administration. Lyndon has a surer instinct for power, and more knowledge of and ruthless skill in its uses. The times call for his talents." Johnson's secretary, Juanita Roberts, wrote eight days later in her filing instructions for the letter, "This is priceless. The President carried it around in his pocket until today when he told me to file it." Juanita Roberts to Dorothy Territo, January 14, 1964, Diary Backup, Johnson Library; Frank Dobie to LBJ, December 29, 1963, ibid. Johnson called Walker Stone on January 6 to thank him for his support; see Johnson Tapes, Johnson Library (hereafter Johnson Tapes). I thank Kent Germany, University of Virginia, for bringing this material to my attention.

19. Memorandum, Bill Moyers to George Reedy, May 21, 1964, White House Central Files, SP, Johnson Library (emphasis in original). Moyers had presented his case for a bold speech to Johnson a few days earlier. Urging the president to resuscitate the original draft of the speech, written by Richard Goodwin, which Valenti had watered down, Moyers and Goodwin appealed to LBJ's ambition and his desire to be taken as seriously as was John Kennedy—to be anointed a man of ideas. The bold version of the speech, Moyers and Goodwin wrote, is "designed to make people like Reston and Lippmann, Pusey and Goheen, sit up and say: 'This President is *really* thinking about the *future problems of America*.'" Memorandum for the President, May 18, 1964, ibid. Reedy noted in his recollections of the White House scuffle over the address that "the phrase [Great Society] bothered me because it seemed pompous and had many overtones of Marxist-style planning." He lamented that his efforts to get LBJ to "soft-pedal" the idea failed. Memorandum, Reedy to Juanita Roberts, September 13, 1968, ibid.

20. *Public Papers of the Presidents of the United States: Lyndon Baines Johnson,* 1963–64, 2 vols. (Washington, D.C.: Government Printing Office, 1965), 1:704.

21. *Public Papers of the Presidents of the United States: Lyndon Baines Johnson,* 1966, 2 vols. (Washington, D.C.: Government Printing Office, 1967), 1:3.

22. Memorandum, Jack Valenti to LBJ, and attached draft speech by John Kenneth Galbraith, December 9, 1965, Statements, Johnson Library.

23. Richard Goodwin, Draft Speech, January 12, 1966, ibid. The words of the final speech were very close to Goodwin's draft: "This Nation is mighty enough, its society is healthy enough, its people are strong enough, to pursue our goals in the rest of the world while still building a Great Society at home." *Public Papers of the Presidents of the United States: Lyndon B. Johnson,* 1966, 1:3.

24. *Public Papers of the Presidents of the United States: Lyndon B. Johnson,* 1966, 1:5–6.

25. Ibid., 6–7.

26. Horace Busby to LBJ, July 13, 1964, and attached memorandum, "The Democratic Party and the Presidency in the Twentieth Century, 1900–1960," Office Files of Horace Busby, Johnson Library.

27. Students for a Democratic Society, "Port Huron Statement," printed in *The New Left: A Documentary History,* ed. Missimo Teodori (Indianapolis: Bobbs-Merrill, 1969), 165.

28. *National Resources Development Report for 1943,* pt. 2, "Security, Work, and Relief Policies" (Washington, D.C.: Government Printing Office, 1943), 486.

29. John Dewey, "The Future of Liberalism," *Journal of Philosophy* 32, no. 9 (1935): 230.

30. *National Resources Development Report for 1943,* pt. 1, "Post-War Plan and Program," 3.

31. The idea of redefining liberalism for a new age had been in the air for some time. In 1956, Arthur Schlesinger Jr. published an essay in *The Reporter* titled "The Future of Liberalism," which anticipated the Great Society: "Liberalism in an age of abundance must begin shifting its emphasis. Instead of the quantitative liberalism of the 1930s, rightly dedicated to the struggle to secure the economic basis of life, we need now a 'qualitative liberalism' dedicated to bettering the quality of people's lives and opportunities. Instead of talking as if the necessities of living—a job, a square meal, a suit of clothes, and a roof—were still at stake, we should be able to count that fight won and move on to the more subtle and complicated problem of fighting for individual dignity, identity, and fulfillment in a mass society." Schlesinger sent a copy of this article to Richard Goodwin in March 1965, attaching a note, "I'm glad you fellows are catching up." Schlesinger to Goodwin, March 2, 1965, and attached article from *The Reporter* (May 3, 1956), Office Files of Richard Goodwin, Johnson Library. Schlesinger, of course, worked in the Kennedy White House, where some notions of a "qualitative liberalism" informed JFK's New Frontier. But Kennedy's rhetoric and policies were never as bold as Johnson's on this score.

32. Memorandum, the Vice President to Marvin Watson, White House Central Files, Aides, Watson, Johnson Library.

33. Occasionally, when seeking the support of southerners and conservatives for his poverty program, Johnson would express its purpose using rough language and racial stereotypes. He told Walker Stone, the conservative editor in chief of Scripps-Howard newspapers, an Oklahoma native, in a telephone conversation of January 6, 1964, "I'm going to try to teach these nigras that don't know anything how to work for themselves, instead of just breeding. I'm going to teach these Mexicans [that] can't talk English to learn it, so they can work for themselves. I'm going to try to build a road in eastern Kentucky and northern West Virginia and a few of these places so they can get down and go to school, and get off our taxpayers' back, and so forth. And that I'm going to call poverty." Johnson Tapes.

34. "Remarks in Franklin D. Roosevelt Square, Gainesville, Georgia," May 8, 1964, *Public Papers of the Presidents of the United States: Lyndon B. Johnson*, 1963–64, 1:653.

35. Gareth Davies, *From Opportunity to Entitlement: The Transformation and Decline of Great Society Liberalism* (Lawrence: University Press of Kansas, 1996), 34.

36. "Remarks in Cleveland at the Convention of the Communications Workers in America," June 17, 1964, *Public Papers of the Presidents of the United States: Lyndon B. Johnson*, 1963–64, 1:778–79. Johnson's understanding of his leadership challenge may have been influenced by an article that appeared in the British press. Carl T. Rowan, director of the United States Information Agency, brought the piece to the president's attention a month before the Cleveland address. This "highly laudatory" article predicted "greatness" for Johnson, but only if he could "persuade an affluent but conservative giant to pursue and expand a number of liberal policies . . . which are physically possible but are also, on the full scale required, 'unthinkable.' " Memorandum, Rowan to the President, May 16, 1964, and attached article, "Mr. Johnson's Chance of Greatness," by a Special Correspondent, *London Times,* May 11, 1964, White House Central Files, FG1, Johnson Library.

37. Davies, *From Opportunity to Entitlement*, 35.

38. OEO, "Office of Economic Opportunity during the Administration of President Lyndon B. Johnson," 1:157.

39. Ibid., 165.

40. Ibid., 9 (emphasis in the original).

41. On the legislative struggle over the relationship of the War on Poverty to religious organizations, see Guian McKee, "Prelude to Faith-Based Initiatives?" *Miller Center Report*, Winter 2003, 21–27.

42. Lyndon Johnson, "Remarks at Southwest Texas State College, San Marcos, Texas," November 20, 1964, *Public Papers of the Presidents of the United States: Lyndon B. Johnson*, 1963–64, 1:168–69.

43. Memorandum, Hayes Redmon to Bill Moyers, June 9, 1966, Office Files of Bill Moyers, Johnson Library. Fred Dutton's view of LBJ reflected the deep

antipathy between Johnson and Robert Kennedy. But that antipathy reflected deeper tension between the modern presidency and the social movements of the 1960s.

44. On the tendency of twentieth-century presidents to seek the support of public opinion so as to circumvent or impose popular pressure on Congress, see Jeffrey Tulis, *The Rhetorical Presidency* (Princeton: Princeton University Press, 1987).

45. "Why I Chose Not to Run," transcript of CBS Cronkite interview with Lyndon Johnson, tape 1, December 27, 1969, p. 5, Johnson Library.

46. As Roosevelt put it in his very important Commonwealth Club address, delivered during the 1932 campaign, "The day of enlightened administration has come." Franklin D. Roosevelt, *Public Papers and Addresses,* ed. Samuel I. Rosenman, 13 vols. (New York: Random House, 1938–50), 1:752.

47. For a detailed discussion of Johnson's influence on the institution of the presidency, see Milkis, *The President and the Parties,* chap. 8.

48. On the Johnson administration's efforts to manage the civil rights movement, see Bruce Miroff, "Presidential Leverage over Social Movements: The Johnson White House and Civil Rights," *Journal of Politics* 43 (February 1981): 1–23.

49. Johnson's problems in forming an alliance with the civil rights movement were evident from his first days in the White House. He took umbrage at criticism in the black press, especially a piece written by Simeon Booker, Washington bureau chief for the black magazine *Jet.* In the December 3, 1963, edition of the magazine, Booker wrote that when "Johnson was sworn in a wave of pessimism and dejection began to build across Negro Americans." He claimed that as vice president, "Johnson didn't get involved" in the struggle for the civil rights bill. Once president, Booker wrote, Johnson kept civil rights leaders at a distance and refused to have his picture taken with those he deigned to meet with in the White House. After reading the article, Johnson complained to Andy Hatcher, a Kennedy holdover, the first African American to work in the White House Press Office, that he did have his picture taken with all the civil rights leaders who came to the White House. This was his reward, the president complained, for "being the first president who just went out of my way to have every one of them come in and have a picture made, have coffee, and sit down and talk to them, and then go to bat for them." Reminding Hatcher of other efforts to make African Americans an important presence in his administration, LBJ added that he also intended to get "a Mexican and bring him in here, and put him on the staff here in the White House," and that the first White House aide he hired was Jack Valenti, "a good Italian." Telephone conversation between LBJ and Andy Hatcher, December 23, 1963, Recordings of Telephone Conversations, JFK Series, Recordings and Transcripts of Conversations and Meetings, Johnson Library. Johnson's traditional view of interest group politics at a time when the interest group universe was undergoing a radical transformation foreshadowed serious problems that would plague him throughout his presidency.

50. Miroff, "Presidential Leverage over Social Movements," 11.

51. Ibid., 14.

52. Horace Busby, interview with the author, June 25, 1987. Busby's memory of this event was accurate. FDR dedicated the Robert E. Lee Memorial Statue in Dallas, Texas, on June 12, 1936, offering the following words to the occasion: "We recognize Robert E. Lee as one of our greatest American Christians and one of our greatest gentlemen." Roosevelt, *Public Papers and Addresses,* 5:214.

53. Louis Martin, editor and publisher of the black newspaper *Michigan Chronicle* and an important official of the Democratic National Committee during the Johnson years, where he served as an effective liaison between the White House and the African American community, saw LBJ's southern background as the key to understanding the president's strong civil rights record: "Now my feeling about Johnson . . . is that since [he] was a southerner, he would normally, being a good politician, lean over backwards to prove that he was not a racist. Further, there's something in the folklore of Negro life that a reconstructed southerner is really far more liberal than a liberal Yankee. . . . Johnson did many things that Kennedy would never have done." Oral History of Louis Martin, May 14, 1969, transcript of interview by David G. McComb, tape 1, p. 22, Johnson Library. Pointing to the fragile yet indispensable link between civil rights reformers and the Johnson White House, Martin admitted that he "exploited this part of folklore," just as LBJ exploited his African American advisers and civil rights leaders to make his distinctive mark on American history.

54. Transcript of telephone conversation between Lyndon Johnson and Ted Sorenson, June 3, 1963, pp. 6, 10, George Reedy Office Files, box 1, Johnson Library.

55. Lyndon B. Johnson, "Remarks at a Breakfast of the Georgia Legislature," May 8, 1964, *Public Papers of the Presidents of the United States: Lyndon B. Johnson, 1963–64,* 1:648.

56. Ibid., 649.

57. "LBJ's Challenge," editorial, *Washington Post,* May 9, 1964, A8.

58. *Washington Post,* May 9, 1964, A1.

59. *Richmond Times Dispatch,* May 9, 1964, 1, 11.

60. "With South in His Tongue and Heart, LBJ Sounds Call for Justice for All," editorial, *Atlanta Constitution,* May 9, 1964, 4.

61. Dirksen cited in Byron Hulsey, *Everett Dirksen and His Presidents: How a Senate Giant Shaped American Politics* (Lawrence: University Press of Kansas, 2000), 196.

62. Lyndon B. Johnson, "Special Message to Congress: The American Promise," March 15, 1965, *Public Papers of the Presidents of the United States: Lyndon B. Johnson,* 1965 (Washington, D.C.: Government Printing Office, 1966), 1:284.

63. Conkin, *Big Daddy from the Pedernales,* 334.

64. McPherson interview.

65. Goodwin, *Remembering America,* 316. Johnson was very disappointed that he lost Georgia to Barry Goldwater in the 1964 election. After learning that

he had lost Georgia and four other deep southern states, LBJ told two White House aides, "I'm sorry about Georgia. I don't care about the other southern states. Louisiana is a bunch of crooks. And Mississippi's too ignorant to know any better. And Alabama's the same way. But Georgia knows better." Johnson did not abandon his view that Georgia might become a beachhead of racial moderation below the Mason-Dixon Line. He believed that conflict between Carl E. Sanders, the young moderate governor, and Richard Russell, the unreconstructed segregationist senator, and not civil rights, had led to defeat there. Telephone conversation between Lyndon Johnson, Bill Moyers, and McGeorge Bundy, November 3, 1964, Johnson Tapes.

66. Memorandum, Ervin Duggan to Douglas Cater, November 9, 1966, Henry Wilson Papers, Johnson Library.

67. McPherson interview.

68. Memoranda, Hayes Redmon to Bill Moyers, November 27, 1965, and November 30, 1965, Office Files of Bill Moyers.

69. Johnson telephone conversation with Martin Luther King, August 20, 1965, Johnson Tapes.

70. Oral History of Lee White, transcript of taped interview by Joe B. Frantz, March 2, 1971, p. 20, Johnson Library.

71. Johnson telephone conversation with King; Lyndon Johnson, "Commencement Address at Howard University: 'To Fulfill These Rights,'" June 4, 1965, *Public Papers of the Presidents of the United States: Lyndon B. Johnson, 1965*, 2:636. Johnson complained to King that civil rights leaders had largely ignored his Howard University speech.

72. Johnson telephone conversation with King.

73. Ibid.

74. David Charles Carter, "Two Nations: Social Insurgency and National Civil Rights Policymaking in the Johnson Administration, 1965–1968" (Ph.D. diss., Duke University, 2001), 320.

75. Because LBJ's efforts were sub rosa, direct evidence of his efforts to influence the civil rights leadership is lacking, but leaders of the major organizations convened on July 29 and issued statements that conformed to LBJ's immediate political objectives. See *New York Times*, July 30, 1964, 12, and Miroff, "Presidential Leverage over Social Movements," 10–11. Martin Luther King implied that the civil rights leadership was doing the White House bidding in asking for Johnson's cooperation in resolving the Mississippi Freedom Democratic Party controversy that threatened to disrupt the national Democratic convention, which was held a month later in Atlantic City, New Jersey. As White House aide Lee White wrote in a memorandum to LBJ, "[King] expressed the thought that those leaders who had signed the moratorium were in a difficult situation. They needed to be supported." Memorandum, Lee C. White to the President, August 13, 1964, White House Central Files, Ex & Gen PL, Johnson Library.

76. E-mail to author from Sherwin J. Markman, a Johnson White House aide, who was heavily involved in the resolving the MFDP controversy, January 13, 2004.

77. "Text of Statement by Negro Leaders," printed in the *New York Times*, July 30, 1964, 12.

78. White to Johnson memorandum, August 13, 1964.

79. Johnson also was concerned, even at this early stage of his presidency, that an unruly convention might open the door to a Robert Kennedy candidacy. Markman written communication.

80. Johnson telephone conversation with Walter Reuther, August 9, 1964, Johnson Tapes.

81. Johnson telephone conversation with Hubert Humphrey and Walter Reuther, August 25, 1964, Johnson Tapes. On the Mississippi seating controversy, see Mark Stern, "Lyndon Johnson and the Democratization of the Democratic National Delegate Selection Process" (paper delivered at the 1990 annual meeting of the American Political Science Association, San Francisco, California, August 29–September 1, 1990). Johnson kept apprised of the Democratic National Committee's implementation of the 1964 convention's call for greater participation; given the tight reins the White House kept on the committee, these activities certainly would not have gone on without the president's approval. See Memorandum, Marvin Watson to LBJ, April 19, 1967, Marvin Watson Files, Johnson Library. As became clear at the 1968 convention, the rule was no paper tiger. Having found no evidence that the Mississippi Democratic Party had "complied with either the spirit or the letter" of the convention call prohibiting racial discrimination, the Credentials Committee voted overwhelmingly to bar the Mississippi regular delegation from its seats. A biracial delegation, including many members of the 1964 Mississippi Freedom Party, was seated in its place. See Milkis, *The President and the Parties*, 210–16.

82. Memorandum, Harry McPherson to Lyndon Johnson, September 12, 1966, Office Files of Harry McPherson, Johnson Library.

83. Memorandum, Nicholas de B. Katzenbach to Harry McPherson, September 17, 1966, ibid.

84. The fact that Johnson did not consult Daley about these visits is striking testimony to how he de-emphasized party politics in favor of a presidential coalition—and an alliance with social movements. Daley was one of the few urban party leaders regarded highly by Johnson; moreover, his Cook County Democratic organization was widely recognized as one of the few effective local machines still in existence. For example, see James R. Jones to Marvin Watson, September 15, 1967, Marvin Watson Files, Johnson Library. But Johnson's aspiration to be a civil rights leader somewhat compromised his relationship with the Chicago mayor. As White House intern Bill Graham (who shared a name with the famous evangelical minister) noted in his report on a visit to the Chicago ghetto, "Mayor Daley has remarkable support from the business community, the universities—and the white majority, as is evident from his last election. *When Daley is criticized, it is on the civil rights issue.*" Memorandum, Bill Graham to the President, May 18, 1967, White House Central Files, We9, Johnson Library (emphasis in original).

85. The term *extraordinary isolation* is Woodrow Wilson's. See Wilson, *Con-*

stitutional Government in the United States (New York: Columbia University Press, 1908), 69.

86. Markman written communication.

87. For a primary account of the ghetto visits, see the Oral History of Sherwin J. Markman, transcript of interview by Dorothy Pierce McSweeney, May 21, 1969, tape 1, pp. 24–36, Johnson Library. Markman, the most enthusiastic and influential of the White House aides who participated in the ghetto visits, notes that one of the biggest tactical problems the Johnson aides faced is how they would "go about living in the ghetto without getting [their heads] cut off." The solution was that every white, middle-class Johnson man had to find a black official in the administration who could serve as his guide and protector during visits to the ghetto (25). The most detailed account of the ghetto visits is Carter, "Two Nations," chap. 5.

88. Sherwin J. Markman, "American Ghettos: Our Challenge and Response," April 5, 1967, and Memorandum, Markman to the President, February 1, 1967, both in White House Central Files, We9, Johnson Library.

89. Memorandum, Markman to the President, February 17, 1968, ibid.; White House fellow Thomas E. Cronin, who visited Baltimore, spoke of the "*absence of proud men.*" See Memorandum, Cronin to LBJ, May 11, 1967, ibid. (emphasis in original).

90. See Oral History of Sherwin J. Markman, 28; Notes of a Meeting with Peter Lisigor, of the *Chicago Daily News*, August 4, 1967, Tom Johnson's Notes of Meetings, box 1, folder: July 1967—May 1968, Meetings with Correspondents, Johnson Library; and Memorandum, Tom Johnson to the President, August 10, 1967, with attached notes of meeting with labor leaders, folder: August 9, 1967, ibid. Although Johnson did not refer directly to the ghetto reports in a meeting with labor leaders, his discussion of the riots was certainly informed by them. As he told the union heads, "In Detroit, four out of five people arrested had jobs with salaries of $120 per week. So you see it is not just a matter of jobs. A lot of it is also a matter of rats and poor housing. And we are concerned about it. Pending before Congress are a half a dozen bills which would alleviate these problems. We have worked on them for weeks and months and years." Johnson also told the labor leaders, "Some people tell me that some of the unions you represent discriminate. I hope you will put an end to this. It's just not American."

91. *Public Papers of the Presidents of the United States: Lyndon B. Johnson, 1967*, 2 vols. (Washington, D.C.: Government Printing Office, 1968), 1:721, 723.

92. In June 1965, James Rowe, who ran Johnson's 1964 campaign, informed the president that the Office of Economic Opportunity was "giving instructions and grants to local private groups for the purpose of training the Negro poor on how to conduct sit-ins and protest meetings against government agencies, federal, state and local. . . . When neighborhood workers are organizing groups in the poorest neighborhoods to 'protest' and take 'direct action' which is not in behalf of any program or anything constructive, I am sure the tax payer and voter will not be happy!" Johnson passed this memo on to Bill Moyers, with a pointed note: "For God's sake get on top of this and stop it at once." Memorandum,

James Rowe to the President, June 29, 1965, White House Central Files, Aides, Moyers, Johnson Library. Shriver "started a damn revolution," LBJ complained to Richard Daley a few months later. Telephone conversation with Richard Daley, December 24, 1965, Johnson Tapes.

93. Memorandum, Sherwin Markman to the President, March 14, 1967, White House Central Files, We9, Johnson Library.

94. The OEO was conceived as the president's managerial arm that could "cut across departmental lines to facilitate coordination." As its director, Sargent Shriver testified before a House committee, the placement of the OEO in the White House bestowed "an authority which the President wants because he wants to be at the focal point with respect to this aspect of our domestic effort." This line of reasoning invoked the administrative science of the Brownlow Committee report, the blueprint for the creation of the Executive Office of the President during Franklin Roosevelt's second term. Shriver is quoted in OEO, "Office of Economic Opportunity during the Administration of President Lyndon B. Johnson," 1:35–36. On the Brownlow Committee report and the role it played during the Roosevelt years, see Milkis, *The President and the Parties*, chaps. 5–6.

95. *Economic Opportunity Act of 1964*, title 2, pt. A, sec. 202 (a), in *U.S. Statutes at Large* (Washington, D.C.: Government Printing Office, 1965), 78:508–16.

96. Samuel Beer, "In Search of a New Public Philosophy," in King, *New American Political System*, 16. Beer notes that the research-based theories of two Columbia University sociologists, Richard Cloward and Lloyd Ohlin, had an especially important influence on the presidential task forces that shaped the antipoverty program. For Cloward's thoughts on the origins and development of the Community Action Program during the Great Society, see the essay by Frances Fox Piven and Richard A. Cloward in this volume. See also OEO, "Office of Economic Opportunity during the Administration of President Lyndon B. Johnson," vol. 1, chap. 1.

97. Glazer cited in OEO, "Office of Economic Opportunity during the Administration of President Lyndon B. Johnson," 1:18.

98. Daniel Patrick Moynihan, *Maximum Feasible Misunderstanding: Community Action in the War on Poverty* (New York: Free Press, 1970), 139.

99. The Task Force on Government Organization, chaired by Ben Heineman, was the second group to report on government organization during the Johnson presidency; the first, chaired by Don K. Price, issued its study in 1964. The Johnson administration's embarrassment at the criticism of the Office of Economic Opportunity placed the management of the War on Poverty program at the top of the Heineman task force's agenda. Its recommendations appear in two lengthy memoranda: Task Force on Government Organization, Memorandum to the President, December 15, 1966, White House Central Files, and "A Final Report by the President's Task Force on Government Organization," June 15, 1967, 18–20, Outside Task Forces, both in Johnson Library.

100. Nicolau cited in Moynihan, *Maximum Feasible Misunderstanding*, 139.

101. James Morone, *The Democratic Wish: Popular Participation and the Limits of American Government*, rev. ed. (New Haven: Yale University Press, 1998), 226.

102. Johnson, *Vantage Point*, 74.

103. *National Resources Development Report for 1943*, 394–95.

104. "Task Force Report on Intergovernmental Program Coordination," December 22, 1965, i, Outside Task Forces, Johnson Library.

105. Johnson voiced such a view in his memoirs. "I heard bitter complaints from the mayors of several cities," he wrote. "Some funds were used to finance questionable activities. Some were badly mismanaged. That was all part of the risk. We created new bureaus and consolidated old ones. We altered priorities. We learned from mistakes. But as I used to tell our critics, 'We have to pull the drowning man out of the water and talk about it later' " (*Vantage Point*, 81). David Welborn and Jesse Burkhead show that even though he feared it was unduly influenced by "Kooks and Sociologists," Johnson stuck with the War on Poverty and was deeply involved in the fight for its authorization in 1967. See their *Intergovernmental Relations in the Administrative State* (Austin: University of Texas Press, 1989), 56–76. To win the approval of Congress, the administration gave tacit approval to an amendment added to the reauthorization act, sponsored by Congresswoman Edith Green (D-Ore.), that allowed local elected officials to take control of privately run community action programs. Although this amendment was denounced publicly as a betrayal of the War on Poverty's participatory ethos, the White House came to the conclusion that reauthorization would be impossible without the support of conservative Democrats, who demanded that local officials be granted more control over poverty programs. See Davies, *From Opportunity to Entitlement*, 194–97. By 1967, however, the concept of community action had become so firmly established throughout the nation that it was impossible for local government officials to absorb community action programs. As the administrative history of the OEO reported in 1968, "it was clear that the concept of community action, as it was formalized and implemented through OEO, had a profound, and continuing effect on community structure in American society" (OEO, "Office of Economic Opportunity during the Administration of President Lyndon B. Johnson, 1:190).

106. Lillian B. Rubin, "Maximum Feasible Participation: The Origins, Implications, and Present Status," *Annals* 385 (September 1969): 17.

107. *Examination of the War on Poverty*, prepared for the Subcommittee on Employment, Manpower and Poverty of the Committee on Labor and Public Welfare, United States Senate (Washington, D.C.: Government Printing Office, 1967), 5:1238, 1241–42. For this quote and many of the ideas expressed in the discussion of the Community Action Program, I am indebted to Morone, *Democratic Wish*, chap. 6; the quotation is on p. 247.

108. Herbert S. Parmet, *The Democrats: The Years after FDR* (New York: Macmillan, 1976), 248.

109. Jack Newfield, "A Man for This Season," *Commonweal*, December 29, 1967, 400–401.

110. W. W. Rostow, Memorandum of Conversation, Participants: The President; the Vice President; Charles Murphy; W. W. Rostow, April 5, 1968, White House Famous Names, box 6, folder: Robert F. Kennedy, 1968 Campaign, Johnson Library.

111. Conkin, *Big Daddy from the Pedernales,* 239.

112. James Ceaser, *Presidential Selection: Theory and Development* (Princeton: Princeton University Press, 1979), 283.

113. Jeffrey Berry, *The Interest Group Society* (Boston: Little, Brown, 1984), 28.

114. Samuel Beer, "In Search of a New Public Philosophy," 27–28. For a more complete account of the reform of national administration during the 1970s, see Sidney M. Milkis, "Remaking Government Institutions in the 1970s: Participatory Democracy and the Triumph of Administrative Politics," *Journal of Policy History* 10, no. 1 (1998): 51–74.

115. Alexis de Tocqueville, *Democracy in America* (Garden City, N.Y.: Doubleday, 1969), 263.

116. As Frances Fox Piven and Richard Cloward point out in their essay for this volume, the community action programs helped poor people gain access to welfare—and to strengthen welfare rights: "The federal Great Society programs, together with the urban protests that helped shape them, brought something like the rule of law to welfare administration."

117. Memorandum, Harry McPherson to the President, March 12, 1965, White House Diary Backup, Johnson Library.

118. Memorandum, Fred Panzer to Harry McPherson, February 21, 1968, White House Central Files, EX-SP, Johnson Library.

Part I

Rethinking the Great Society
Ideology, Institutions, and Social Movements

Sixties Civics

Hugh Heclo

In a time when "teach-ins" became a campus fashion, the sixties as a whole constituted the biggest teach-in of all. The period became a school of sorts for teaching Americans how to think about public affairs. Its curriculum developed in thousands of campus debates, TV exposés, street demonstrations, and newspaper and magazine stories. Less dramatically, the teaching also occurred through official government pronouncements and denials, social science reports, professors' books, and pundits' commentaries. New policy undertakings—projects that put the "programmatic" into the Great Society's programmatic liberalism—were shaped by this schooling, and in turn, the various government programs added further applications to its lessons. Overall, Americans living through this period participated in a kind of informal, ongoing civics tutorial. The impact down to the present day has been profound.

As in any school, the civics lessons of the Great Society era were often confusing and difficult to understand. Americans were taught, for example, that this was a time for promoting more participatory democracy, yet they were also taught that unelected judges in the national courts were now to be a powerful force in directing the course of public affairs. They were taught that sex education should be a public responsibility in the schools but that religion should now be regarded as a private concern walled off from public endorsement in the schools. Indeed, the new teaching was that what earlier generations had assumed to be intimate, "private" issues about sex and reproduction should be topics for open discussion in the public square, which the entertainment industry and mass media appeared bent on turning into a pubic square. Older Americans were taught that young people, once applauded for being seen but not heard, should be now be recognized as the voices of political conscience, even if their "lifestyles" (a nonjudgmental term becoming popular at the time) seemed a threat to all traditional morality. In this new television age, Americans could live out the oxymoron of passive participation; for the first time, citizens were spectators watching their national life unfold in live pictures projected into the intimacy of their living rooms and bedrooms. They learned that Washington politics and the media now weighted race relations, previously assumed a local matter, with huge national significance. So, too, they learned that anyone who could not see that women's personal struggles were also national political issues was simply "out of it." And not least of all, Americans learned they could expect that their presidents would knowingly lie to them.

Was there any underlying lesson that tied these and many other teachings together? There was indeed one such central theme. Americans were taught that so far as the governing system is concerned, one should both expect more and trust less than ever before. That sounds simple enough, but the paradox of greater entrusting and greater distrusting was a powerful generator of new patterns in public life. From it came a distinctive syndrome of civic behavior—a sixties civics.[1] Like one of today's "oldies" radio stations that keeps recycling the rock classics, the public square in twenty-first-century America continues to echo the melody and tones of this sixties civics. On the one hand, the new civics taught Americans to look to government for solving problems on a vast new scale. Public authority became the default setting of expectations, the presumptive agent to which one should turn for securing the most vital purposes of personal and national life. Eventually, the name for this expanding domain of demands and hopes was simply "public policy." On the other hand, all motives in the public square should be considered suspect. Disinterestedness was a fiction—not a constructive myth but a hypocritical ploy in a world where any realistic understanding required a strict focus on questions of power. The various names for the domain of suspicion and mistrust were the establishment, the status quo, or, simply, "the system."

Whatever the terms employed from one issue to the next, the central thrust of this sixties' mentality was both to entrust and to distrust, to be pro-policy and antigovernment. It would be easy to misunderstand and see nothing exceptional in this lesson. It might appear as a familiar "blind date" story—expectations are built up but disappointed, and then faith is lost in the date's matchmaker. However, sixties civics is not a sequencing of two different viewpoints, first one thing producing another. It expresses a single, twofold certitude. To repeat the basic point: this affirmation and negation are not two opposing judgments but two elements within the same judgment. From political decision making, one should simultaneously expect much and trust little. The Great Society did not launch a disappointing blind date but an Ibsen-esque love-hate relationship.

There is no simple way to explain how this happened. Sixties civics was embedded into the political culture not by design but as a way of thinking that emerged while people went about the political business of the day. Like all enduring lessons, the new civics was caught more than taught. It was promulgated not only by what was said but even more by what came to be assumed in the speaking. To appreciate the workings of the great sixties teach-in, we would do well to follow the advice of Alfred North Whitehead: "When considering the philosophy of an epoch, do not chiefly direct your attention to those intellectual positions which its exponents feel it necessary explicitly to defend. There will be some fundamental assumptions which adherents of all the variant systems within the epoch unconsciously presuppose. Such assumptions appear so obvious that people do not know what they are assuming because no other way of putting things has ever occurred to them."[2]

For twenty-first-century Americans, one of these largely unconscious presuppositions is the sixties' twofold viewpoint of high expectations and low trust. Without intending to either condemn or endorse it, I explore that odd amalgam of aspiration and alienation in public affairs I call "sixties civics." Some may wonder if, in this sense, the events of September 11, 2001, finally brought "the sixties" to an end. After foreign terrorists' greatest success against the United States, opinion polls and everyday evidence showed a revival of trust in government and a general prevalence of political goodwill. This sense of patriotic unity was especially evident among younger Americans.

Two points need to be kept in mind, however. First, political reactions to the attacks of September 11 continued the trend of ramping up expectations on government and public policy. In this case the policy aim was not only to provide fail-safe security for Americans' normal lifestyle in the homeland but also, as the nation's political leaders put it, to "preserve Western civilization" and eliminate such "evil" everywhere in the world—no small mission. Appropriately enough, one early version of the administration's antiterrorist campaign was dubbed Operation Infinite Justice. Second, as Whitehead might caution, presuppositions are not displaced by mood swings. Through many large and small acts of instruction, stretching over many years, public thinking acquires not only structures but also roots. When America graduated from the Great Society and that broader period of tumult known as the sixties, something deeply, culturally important had happened in the American democratic mind. It is not something that will be readily subject to remedial education by foreign terrorists and a surge of rally-round-the-flag sentiments. By the time the last of the debris from the World Trade Center was being hauled off, loads of new public grievances were being hauled into view—political finger-pointing about officials' financial misdeeds and even their advance knowledge of the September 11 attacks, a season of Enron and WorldCom, Martha Stewart and Arthur Anderson, pedophile priests and sleazeball sports millionaires. By the summer of 2002, ten months after the terrorist attacks, polls showed that Americans' dissatisfaction with and distrust in government and American institutions more generally were back to their pre–September 11 levels.[3] A majority of federal employees even reported a sense of decreased trust in their organizations and in the federal government generally since September 11. Sixties civics is not the whole story of today's public thinking, but it is certainly much more than a historical curiosity. In some very important respects, "then" is still now.

Onloading Policy Expectations

Writing at the close of the 1950s, Walter Lippmann described a public outlook that would soon undergo a massive transformation. In that gentle spring of 1960, the nation's premier political commentator declared that "the public mood of the country is defensive, to hold on and to conserve, not to push forward and to create. We talk about ourselves these days as if we were a completed society, one which has achieved its purposes, and has no further great business to transact."[4]

In addition to supplying a subtle endorsement of Senator John F. Kennedy's run for the presidency ("to get the country moving again," as the candidate usually put it), Lippmann's influential voice expressed a widely recognized sense of the times. Complacency ruled, but uneasy lay the crown upon the king's head. Complacency was anxious about itself. That summer, *Life* magazine sought to address the national languor by launching a five-part series devoted to articulating "the national purpose." Readers were offered the well-modulated views of eight eminent Americans.[5] It is not surprising that these pronouncements had little to say about most of the causes that would shake America during the sixties. The agenda for the nation would not be written by a Waspish elite of white males but by all sorts of activists, mostly people who were young and prone to take to the streets. The latter were not people who, in Adlai Stevenson's phrase, showed "a slackness about public problems."

However, there was at least one common element between the gently imploring voices of *Life* and the raucous demands of the coming sixties activists (whom the magazine's editor, Henry Luce, would soon despise). Both were continuing a project traceable to the New Deal of the 1930s. In both cases, the point was to direct public thinking toward activist national government to address an underdeveloped sense of national problems. In Samuel Beer's words, the people had to be taught "to turn to Washington as the center of power on which to exert their pressures and project their expectations." Beer, who was one of FDR's bright young men and later chairman of Americans for Democratic Action (ADA) and a distinguished Harvard professor, has described the deliberate and uphill struggle during the 1930s in trying to teach Americans to look to national government and national politics for answers. "During 1935–1936 I worked in the Resettlement Administration, my job being to draft articles that appeared under the name of Rexford G. Tugwell, a leading New Dealer. Frequently I also helped Thomas G. Corcoran, then a rising brain-truster, with speeches for President Roosevelt. I vividly recall our preoccupation with persuading people to look to Washington for the solution of problems and our sense of what a great change in public attitudes this involved."[6] By the beginning of the 1960s, it took less effort than it had in the New Deal years to teach Americans to focus on Washington for societal problem solving. By the time the sixties era ended, most people seemed able to look nowhere else.

There is probably a general impression among Americans that

government got bigger in the Great Society era. This is certainly true with respect to the number of federal programs and regulations; somewhat true of Washington's domestic spending (which actually increased more under Nixon in the early 1970s); but hardly true at all when it comes to numbers of federal bureaucrats (which has increased only very modestly throughout the entire period after the Second World War). What really got "big" about big government was the scope and ambitiousness of its missions. Other essays in this volume chronicle the Great Society program commitments in areas such as education, medical care, civil rights, environmental protection, and other spheres. Moreover, as R. Shep Melnick shows, these policy commitments endured and, if anything, deepened their hold on people's expectations regarding government.

If one takes the term "Great Society" to signify sweeping new commitments to activist national government, it is clear that the Great Society years did not end with Lyndon Johnson's departure from the White House but surged into the 1970s even as general public distrust in government was growing. In these later years, the national government began telling Americans what they could and could not do with regard to abortions, capital punishment, and bilingual education. The 1970s also brought new and more-sweeping national regulations to deal with environmental challenges, consumer protection, workplace safety, gender discrimination, the rights of those with disabilities, and political campaigning. It was in the 1970s rather than the 1960s that affirmative action and many other civil rights measures became a real presence in American society.

To be sure, as the 1970s drew to a close, overt political opposition to big government gathered force. Tax revolts, the Reagan revolution, New Democrats, the 1994 Contract with America—all have come, chipped away, and gone. But the overall edifice of programmatic liberalism has remained standing tall. A 1975 policy wonk transported twenty-five years forward in time would feel quite at home in today's policy environment. By contrast, if sent twenty-five years backward to the early 1950s, he would probably feel disoriented and estranged. This is because in going backward from 1975, the time traveler would recross what James Q. Wilson has called "the legitimacy barrier."[7] In one policy field after another, the age-old question of whether the federal government had authority to act became a nonissue. The claim of states' rights against national authority yielded to an unprecedented, deliberately pursued enlargement of national power at the expense of state and local governments.[8] If anything, the claim that powers not granted to the federal government were reserved to the people now became even more passé than the idea of powers reserved to the states. In other words, the idea of the Constitution as a design for limited national government—and there being any serious meaning attached to the Constitution's Tenth Amendment—receded into history as a premodern curiosity. The lesson of sixties civics was that virtually any domain of human life could be a legitimate topic on the national policy agenda.

To speak of crossing the "legitimacy barrier" can make the development sound unduly legalistic, an invitation to memorize the appropriate Supreme Court cases. However, that is not good enough if we aim to steer by Whitehead's previously noted insight, namely, to pay less attention to the intellectual positions that exponents explicitly argue and more attention to the generally prevailing presuppositions behind those arguments. In that light, court cases are merely signs of something more fundamental. Likewise, the stories one can tell by tallying up the list of new Great Society programs or federal budget expenditures are not the *real* story. The nub of the matter lies deeper.

To get to that deeper level, we might consider an illustration used by James Q. Wilson.[9] In 1956, federal legislation authorized the nation's first interstate highway system and the taxes to pay for it. In a bare twenty-eight pages, the Federal Highway Act set the massive continental building program in motion through Washington's Bureau of Public Roads and did so with a handful of stipulated constraints (there would have to be public hearings, consultation with state highway departments, and building contracts paying the prevailing wages). Fast-forward thirty-five years. The program was reauthorized in 1991 with a law (the Intermodal Surface Transportation Efficiency Act) of over 280 pages that bristled with constraints and requirements. The head of the federal Department of Transportation (itself a new creation in 1966) was directed not only to relieve congestion but also to reduce drunk driving, improve air quality, preserve historic sites, enforce metropolitan transportation planning, encourage use of seat belts, control erosion and outdoor advertising, and produce a stream of environmental impact statements. The agency was to earmark 10 percent of construction funds for disadvantaged small business owners, restrict iron and steel purchases to U.S. firms, give preferential treatment to Native Americans on road projects near reservations, and the list went on. It is no accident that these provisions were in the 1991 law but not the 1956 act. Every one of these directives (as well as many more that could be mentioned) expressed a particular policy issue that somebody somewhere cared about very much.

Highway building is just one example of a pervasive phenomenon. Sixties civics taught the essential lesson that the one thing of any real public consequence is policy. This point may seem too obvious for a contemporary reader even to notice. In and of itself, policy is certainly nothing new in politics. A policy is simply a course of action (or inaction) deliberately pursued under the coercive power of government aiming to deal with some perceived public problem. Clashes over policy have always been an important part of American political history. Contemporary students find it utterly mysterious to read about the partisan lightning and thunder that could be unleashed when nineteenth-century politicians addressed such matters as the national bank, the tariff issue, internal improvements, temperance, the single tax, or a free-silver monetary policy. What was new about sixties civics was not policy but *policy mindedness.* To be policy minded is to think that everything in public life besides policy is secondary. It is an outlook that elevates and cleaves to one essential insight: when governing is happening or when partisan politics is churning, when all the affairs of public affairs are coming and going, the one thing that is *really* happening is this or that choice. In the language of the time, policy choice is the "happening" thing. Understanding that, one can be relevant, tuned in to the issues, "with it." Not understanding that, one is "out of it," and the great sixties teach-in is lost on you.

This lesson was not lost on either political activists or ordinary American citizens. It was inculcated and absorbed so deeply that over time it became difficult to think in any other way. To appreciate just how deeply, we might consider the paradox of a phrase popularized in the 1960s by the women's movement: "the personal is the political." The trials women faced in their personal lives were denominated into a new awareness of public measures that were needed to liberate women from their oppressive situation. What had once been accepted as a condition was now perceived as a problem, one that had to be addressed through collective action. The personal was the political because it was a question of policy. We now fast-forward a generation. The president of the United States is exposed not only for engaging in sexual encounters in the Oval Office with a young lady his daughter's age but also for lying about it publicly and under legal oath. Despite the best, and ultimately self-defeating, efforts of his political opponents, impeachment could not dislodge public support for the president. He was considered to be doing a good job, and his personal peccadilloes were regarded by feminists and many other Americans as irrelevant to his performance. In other words, in judging Clinton, the personal was not the political because what really mattered in judging a political leader's performance were his or her policies. Policy mindedness had become the universal solvent for making and not making the personal into the political.

Policy mindedness was at the core of sixties civics on many fronts. It was a period when academics began devoting new attention to the terms "decision making" and "policymaking," even though decision-making theory seemed "not about making decisions but about getting ready to make decisions."[10] Businesses and foundations ramped up investments in a flock of new so-called think tanks, where the thing for scholars to think about was how to be "policy relevant." More dramatically, claims about the decisions to be made were put forward by a growing multitude of political activists, people whose involvement had far more to do with policy agendas than with any traditional party chores as Democrats or Republicans. New public interest groups were created and grew. They, as well as older interest groups, converged on Washington and planted permanent offices there. For even the most venal of lobbying organizations, the tax law made it advantageous to spin off new so-called policy research and public education units, whose financing was tax deductible.

Policy mindedness did not follow any one straight line but grew out of a nonstop flow of contesting claims about public problems, from economic to cultural. In the mainstream of this flow were more or less standard liberal efforts to deal with postwar social and economic issues that FDR's New Deal had neglected, for one reason or another. Particularly after the 1958 midterm elections, reformers in Congress (including the now extinct species, liberal Republican) laid some of the groundwork for important federal initiatives in health care, aid to education, civil rights, unemployment, and regional economic development.[11] It is revealing that in proposing a modest civil rights bill, President John F. Kennedy used the novel term "constitutional policy" to refer to his initiative. Further to the left, ferment was growing over structural inequalities in society, environmental degradation, and participatory democracy. Soon the traditional economic critique offered by America's version of a social democratic Left was being trumped by a self-conscious New Left championing a "countercultural" agenda. Here the search was on for new types of community empowerment and new personal identities "on the far side of power politics, the bourgeois home, and the Protestant work ethic."[12]

We would be missing half the picture, however, if we traced policy mindedness only to the advocates of activist government and the political Left. Although it may be harder to perceive, their opponents, too, were policy promoters. In the previous generation, "Mr. Republican," Senator Robert A. Taft, had called himself a liberal to the end of his days (harkening back to the nineteenth-century use of that term). In the 1960s, Barry Goldwater became the first major American politician to embrace the conservative label. In doing so, Goldwater represented an array of policy aspirations from the political Right, beginning in the 1950s with anticommunism and white resentment of civil rights agitation. As time passed, some of the new conservative movement's greatest hostility turned against the ambitions for social change that had charged beyond the New Deal's basic agenda of economic security. If the counterculture had an agenda, right-thinking Americans could have a counter-countercultural agenda. In that sense, many activists on the right were New Deal conservatives, and with Goldwater marginalized after his 1964 loss to LBJ, Ronald Reagan became their new champion and, in 1966, California's governor. The foot soldiers in this conservative movement were not downtrodden rural reactionaries but educated, suburban, middle- and upper-middle-class individuals who claimed to understand the issues.[13] Their activism gained momentum in backyard barbeques, coffee klatches, study groups, and school board battles. Adding social science brainpower to their cause were "neoconservative" intellectuals, mostly former Democrats who produced powerful critiques showing the counterproductive results of ill-conceived social programs. When conservative Republicans finally won control of Congress in 1994, their Contract with America served to highlight the larger point: conservatives were also people with policy ideas.

Sixties civics was about the triumph not of policies—many of which were failures and ruthlessly criticized—but of policy itself. It was not big government that people came to believe in but big policy. Those who liked activist, positive government might invoke such terms as "quality-of-life issues." Those who did not like it advocated new measures to counter the liberals' "social engineering." Policy could mean "tax and spend," but it could also mean "deregulate and cut." The approach Melnick calls "mandate and sue" was policy, as was "decentralize and contract out." To give government aid was policy, and to refuse to give aid was policy. Before the triumph of sixties civics—when someone like Taft used "liberal" in its nineteenth-century sense—one might reject public action in the name of constitutionalism, self-sufficiency, or personal independence. Or even more likely, the idea of appealing for public policy action would not have arisen in the first place. In the new mind-set, however, not to believe in policy answers was an admission of irrelevance. By the end of the sixties teach-in, Democrats and Republicans, liberals and conservatives, had all become the party of Policy. And so they have remained.

All of this can seem quite curious. But before pursuing the puzzle of policy mindedness any further, we would do well to follow along the second major theme of the sixties' curriculum.

Offloading Trust and Doubt

As with policy, an element of distrust is nothing new to the American political scene. It lay at the Whiggish core of republican thought and the Founders' experiment in self-government.[14] Eighteenth-century distrust split government power into three branches, split the predominant branch into two houses, and then gave each piece of the machinery a part of the other's business. It required that national government powers be enumerated, and then still not satisfied, it insisted on a Bill of Rights.

As with policy mindedness, however, the kind of distrust that Americans learned in the 1960s was distinctive. Sixties civics posited bad faith throughout public affairs, which *was* something new. Of course, not everyone thought the same way on every issue, but here I am concentrating on central tendencies of the time. A distrust deeper and more pervasive than traditional American dubiousness about power was precisely such a central tendency.

The point becomes clearer when we recognize that the opposite of trust is not doubt but affirmation—the affirmation that what one is encountering is untrustworthy. Traditional American distrust is more like doubt. To question things from a position of doubt leaves the issue of trustworthiness open to being decided one way or another. Traditional distrust-as-doubt remains unconvinced about good intentions and thus watchful. It can believe enough to trust, but what it believes in most is a show-me attitude. Doubt is skeptical, with the doors to both trust and distrust left half ajar. Not everyone is a friend but maybe not an enemy either, and so, as the old American saying has it, you "keep your powder dry."

The overall thrust of sixties civics was to teach a purer form of distrust, one going beyond doubt. The emphasis shifted from the traditional suspicion of power to a postmodern distrust of motive. Intentions of those in authority were never to be trusted, precisely because they were in authority. Opposition to one's cause came from hostile rather than merely benighted forces. In facing either authority or opposition, doors that doubt tended to leave ajar were now slammed shut. The working assumption in public affairs favored cynicism rather than skepticism. Indeed, the 1960s ushered in a withdrawal not simply of trust but of doubt as well, privileging a stance of pervasive mistrust of the public motives and actions of any opponents.

So enveloping has been the distrust taught by the sixties that it takes a special effort to perceive its influence. One way to throw its presence into relief is by imagining a public world where doubt rather than distrust predominated. As we are walking into the public square, we see that an important problem has come into debate. Public controversy is erupting. There is disagreement, uncertainty, information and misinformation, intelligent and stupid things being said. There is nothing to suggest that all is sweetness and light, but remember, we are going about public business in an atmosphere of doubt rather than distrust. Amid their contentions, the participants are also able to acknowledge that some things are possibly being spoken and done in good faith. The possibility remains open for giving each other the aptly named "benefit of the doubt." At least some of the people some of the time find it plausible to think that certain participants might have better information or sounder judgments that are worth listening to. Even one's opponents might have some truth on their side, since a dubious person is able to doubt his or her own doubts. In this public square of doubt rather than distrust, there is the possibility of both asserting and deferring, of making a claim and of acknowledging some merits in another's claim against it.

Engaging in such a mental experiment, one may sense a kind of freshness in the public conversation—a healthiness in the air that today's citizen might not even notice is missing. Coming out of the mental experiment, a person may also sense something of the airless, enervating feeling imparted by sixties civics. It vaunts an openness that really is not open to the possibility of good faith, deference, or disinterestedness in public debate. It is assured of its own good intentions but no one else's. No opponent is given what is quite literally the benefit of the doubt. Sixties civics celebrates voicing but not listening. It carries a righteous insistence on opening the public square for all of the previously excluded to be heard, without a serious effort to really hear and weigh other views. By its nature, it is an inclusiveness that divides. It assumes unity is additive, a function of putting more seats at the table. It dismisses as oppressive the older assimilationist idea that unity is singular, a function of having the common denominator of one table and one meal at which the seats are placed. Some of the linear descendants of this sixties outlook are today's ideologically segmented radio talk shows, multiculturalism, "gotcha" journalism, and verbal wrestling matches by TV pundits.

By now, the growth of distrust in the sixties has attracted a good deal of scholarly attention. Public opinion polling has documented some of these changing attitudes.[15] While the statistical data do not go back much earlier, it seems clear that a general decline in the public's trust in government began in the 1960s, even as government was being enlisted to undertake more activities. After 1965, a more or less steadily growing proportion of Americans said they felt that government could not be trusted to do the right thing at least most of the time. Likewise, a growing portion of the population thought that government is run by people and groups simply looking out for themselves. Changes in party control of the White House seemed merely to provide the opportunity for a new section of the population to feel aggrieved. Between 1965 and 1972, with the fall of Johnson's presidency and the rise of Richard Nixon, the sharpest drop in trust in government occurred among self-described liberals and Democrats. As ideological polarization between the two parties grew, voters in the middle became one of the most distrustful segments of the population.[16]

Polls can only hint at the changing political atmosphere and presuppositions during and surrounding the Great Society years. Those on the leading edge of popular culture, for example, embraced a new kind of political commentary. Humorists in the tradition of a Mr. Dooley, Mark Twain, Will Rodgers, and Bob Hope had poked fun at the human foibles that politics invariably puts on display. Now in the sixties, such figures as Mort Sahl, Lenny Bruce, George Carlin, and their many successors found an enthusiastic response not only to irony but to sarcasm in its most literal sense. Their messages aimed less at poking fun and more at cutting with ridicule and tearing away pretenses. Whether expressing an embittered, resigned, or lighthearted sense of "being had" by the system, the important thing was to be in the know, hip, not taken in. Coolness became a social norm, respected and envied even among those who were not part of the disaffected minority. And to be cool was to be distrustful. Eventually, the result was a comic nihilism that masses of post-sixties Americans have found enormously attractive.[17]

What satirists did in 1960s popular culture, influential intellectuals had already been doing years before at elite levels. The match between comedians and professors was not perfect, but it was close enough to contribute to the same climate of distrust. Mid-twentieth-century liberalism was a chastened way of thinking about public affairs. The upbeat liberalism of the earlier Progressive Era had been abandoned in favor of a tough-minded liberal realism. To see how this set the stage for a compounding of distrust in the body politic, we might return to Walter Lippmann.

Over thirty years before his 1960 contribution to *Life* magazine, Lippmann had analyzed the distrust that had already become a feature of modern life in the 1920s. As he saw it, modern man found the old religious faiths simply unbelievable. Traditional authority and the morality derived from it were no longer considered authentic for the way millions of Americans were living in the "Great Society."[18] But Lippmann was no modern liberal, much less a child of the sixties. For him, what modernity now required was diffusion to the general population of the wisdom that "high religion" had historically imparted to an educated few. The essence of that wisdom was "disinterestedness." By this, Lippmann meant a mature, self-controlled outlook that submitted to the discipline of objective information in an adult world, a clear-headed stoicism that follows "what the heart desires without transgressing what is right."[19] In saying this, Lippmann was simply expressing an intellectualized, natural law formulation of the worldview that had been associated with Progressivism for decades, even though most reformers in the early twentieth century endorsed a more straightforward Protestant Christianity. In either case, for the public-spirited Progressives of this earlier generation, disinterestedness was a compelling answer.[20] For sixties satirists, disinterestedness was a joke. For the generation of midcentury liberal intellectuals, it was a naïve illusion, and therein lay the next turn in the story of distrust.

By the middle of the twentieth century, liberals had seen enough of modern war and mass cruelty to lose any Progressive-style faith in progress or the triumph of virtue. In his influential 1949 volume *The Vital Center*, Arthur M. Schlesinger Jr. summarized the new realistic and hard-edged cast of liberalism and, according to one reviewer, "announced the spirit of an age to itself."[21] Humans had to be taken as they were—flawed and corruptible. Human rationality and virtue were problematic at best (although liberals assumed a certain righteousness associated with their own hard-edged intelligence). Against the reality of people's short-sighted, self-seeking impulses, Lippmann's disinterestedness was illusory. Worse, it was a dangerous sentimentality to hope for a society or world rationally harmonized beyond conflicts of interest. Nevertheless, humans could not escape moral responsibility for acting against suffering and evil in the world. Power had to be met with power, not sentimental calls for disinterestedness. A realistic, responsible liberalism would accept the compromises and moral ambiguities required by political action. Without denying the importance of moral convictions, midcentury liberalism eagerly accepted the tragedy of political engagement. As Richard N. Goodwin, one of the youngest Kennedy and Johnson advisers, put it, "Goethe said to act is to sin, and so you have to be willing to sin a little."[22]

In saying all this, the new liberalism had absorbed a great deal of Reinhold Niebuhr's critique of the early Progressives' faith in human innocence and progress—in fact everything about Niebuhr's "Christian realism" except its Christianity.[23] As Schlesinger saw in retrospect, this chastened liberalism was an outlook combining "a certain operational optimism with a certain historical pessimism." It offered a positive view of government's ability to produce needed change (thus liberal and hopeful) and a negative view of people's behavior in the world as it is (thus realistic and unsentimental). In the American context, government planning had been an ideal expressing the high-minded, disinterested presuppositions of the old Progressivism. Policy, with its shrewd, utilitarian acceptance of selfish interests, gave focus to the new realism. With policy came programs that could be designed to use those competing interests for public ends. Thus the philosophy of liberal realism shaded into programmatic liberalism and the burst of government initiatives in the Great Society era. Taking leave from his chair in history at Harvard, Schlesinger would go on in 1960 to become the leading public thinker in Kennedy's White House and one of the tough-minded, liberal "action intellectuals" who were influential in Washington throughout the sixties.[24]

This, of course, was not the end of the story. The realist outlook in turn opened up liberalism to charges from youthful radicals in the sixties that it was more concerned with power than ideals. Its methods were seen as manipulative and its promises hypocritical, offering yet more evidence of a morally bankrupt status quo. Against this corrupt power of the establishment, activists sought to mobilize social movements from below. The unfolding disaster in Vietnam helped greatly in making these charges stick to both hawkish cold war liberals and the action intellectuals from elite universities and foundations. By reaping distrust while attempting to sow realism, programmatic liberalism of the mid-twentieth century took its place in what Niebuhr had called the "irony of American history."

Political leaders and events of the time were effective if unwitting teachers in the sixties school of distrust. Distrust was the only sane response in the face of revelations about covert FBI operations against Dr. Martin Luther King, CIA-sponsored assassinations and coups in other countries, recurrent scandals in Congress, and ongoing deceptions perpetrated by Presidents Johnson and Nixon, not to mention outright criminal conduct in high places.

Yet, even if such official misdeeds had never occurred, the social movements of the sixties were propitiously aligned for turning doubt into distrust. It was a time of mobilizing behind social causes, and whether of the Left or the Right, red or green, movements tend to prod activists into an ideological hardness toward nonbelievers. As one peace activist has observed: "Ideology, not compassion, tends to become the driving force of much activism. Compassion, however much the word may be used, rarely thrives within the climate of movements and causes, except a very narrow compassion focused like a spotlight on a victim group whose needs legitimate the cause.... One feels compassion for the baby seal being slaughtered for its fur but not for the man whose family may presently depend upon the fur trade."[25] With ideological movements comes anger at others for opposing or not caring enough to join the cause, as well as guilt toward oneself for never being able to do all that the cause deserves.

Selective compassion, smoldering guilt, diffuse anger—these came trailing in the wake of one good cause after another in the sixties. The civil rights movement brought an overwhelming indictment against the disparity between American ideals and the evasions and deceptions of the white power structure. The women's movement extended this case against an oppressive male power structure. Lame apologists for irresponsible business practices were easy targets for environmental and consumer movements. Ongoing contests among mainstream culture, the counterculture, and the counter-counterculture reinforced the general proposition that everybody was part of some status quo that somebody else found objectionable and dangerous. In sum, the social movements of the sixties were in the business of making claims for bold new government policy commitments while advancing a wholly negative view of anything that might be identified with the status quo. Charity toward one's opponents and assumptions of good intentions were the first things to make shipwreck in this political whirlpool. Meanwhile, casting about amid the politics of resentment, voters in the middle had every reason to become the most distrustful segment of the population.

Distrust taught in the school of the sixties went to something deeper than just particular political misdeeds, social movements, and policy disputes of the time. The decline in public trust began before Vietnam and Watergate, and it was directed against not just government but all institutions. It occurred in other developed countries besides the United States. Perhaps easiest to overlook is that the distrust of the sixties was not solely an eruption from below. There were abundant signs that many occupying the commanding heights of the status quo distrusted themselves and the legitimacy of their own authority. That became evident as significant numbers of university leaders surrendered traditional standards to student protestors. Self-doubt appeared in a healthier form as many in America's white establishment came to accept demands for racial justice under the Constitution and, in effect, became willing collaborators in the de-WASPing of America's power elite.[26] Some business leaders saw that a degraded environment and unsafe products really were not worth defending. Ordinary Americans did not have to become hippies to realize that postwar materialism threatened authentic living. Even some men could see that their sexist claims on women's lives were, to put it politely, less than equitable. In thousands of different ways, the forces of the status quo displayed their loss of confidence, which is to say, their self-distrust.

From the perspective of the early twenty-first century, the distrust embedded in sixties civics can appear quite unremarkable, regardless of how positively or negatively one evaluates its effects. Today there seems nothing at all strange about finding people routinely cynical about public figures and political affairs. Yet, this distrust represents the collapse of an entire region in the American public mind. It is the region that once had really believed disinterestedness, goodwill, and public spiritedness were workable ideals rather than hypocritical ploys, sentimentalism, or jokes. Not surprisingly, it was generally in the 1960s that people's attachment to political and other public heroes more or less disappeared from American culture.[27]

As with policy mindedness, we have now traced along the stream of distrust to a point that runs beyond particular events and personalities of the sixties. The eventual destination where distrust merges with policy expectations sends us venturing into deeper waters. To be sure, we have seen that midcentury liberals had joined policy advocacy with a kind of distrustful pessimism, but this was only a prelude. It was a viewpoint of intellectuals whose books and ideas were almost entirely unknown to the mass of citizens. The general ascendancy of sixties civics forces us to confront more powerful forces, a juncture of historical currents oceanic in scale.

The Journey to Uncivil Civics

So far, we have followed one theme of policy mindedness and a second of distrust, but we have not yet come to their essential union. It is a truly curious combination. In the latter years of Ronald Reagan's presidency, negotiations with the Soviet Union popularized the motto "trust but verify." Sixties civics represented the mirror image of that idea: distrust but demand. On reflection, the former appears a hopeful view, the latter a rather resigned morbidity.

One might think there is nothing remarkable in the conjoining of these two themes. With more expectations placed on government, there is more for people to disagree about. But that would imply only more argument and contentiousness in the public square, not necessarily more distrust and cynicism. Or, again, one might think that with more policies there are more chances for things to go wrong and for the unintentional production of negative consequences. As critics of the Great Society pointed out at length, that certainly did happen. Yet there could also be more chances for things to go right, and on the face of it, there is no necessary reason to think that unintended consequences must always be perverse rather than positive.[28] All this misses the essential point with which we began, namely, that policy mindedness and public distrust were simultaneous developments, not a story of high aspirations followed by dashed hopes and disappointment. Sixties civics is a design for aspirations and alienation, entrusting and distrusting all wrapped up together. It pictures loading a vehicle with ever more weight while letting ever more air out of the tires. In this sense, the common formulation that the American public is ideologically conservative but operationally liberal gets it exactly backward.[29] Sixties civics is ideologically radical but operationally conservative, hoping for great policy projects but withholding the commitments of faith to accomplish them.

If it really is a matter of both entrusting and distrusting, then the lesson of the sixties is not about splitting the difference between the two poles but about combining ferocious opposites and keeping each ferocious. Some overbelief, almost a theology, must be present to make this paradox not only possible but sustainable and thriving. There was and is such an overbelief. It is a vision of the people redeeming a flawed society or, if you will, democracy in a modern passion play. Policy mindedness was the expression of the democratic element of this vision, and distrust the expression of its modern face. In this redeeming work, policy and distrust were commensal with rather than contradictory to each other.

We noted earlier that the growth in policy expectations was not the obvious result of any great political debate about the role of government. In fact, if we think about the intellectual environment, the thrust of the most advanced thinking leading up to these times was largely in the other direction. It is difficult to convey today how hopeful planning advocates had been in the 1940s and how thoroughly they were routed, first politically by Congress as early as 1943 and then intellectually during subsequent years. Midcentury liberalism embraced "realism" precisely because it was under heavy attack. By the onset of the sixties, the offensive against central government planning had become intellectually and politically triumphant in America. However, in a manner of speaking, this merely destroyed general headquarters. In the larger picture, sketched earlier and discussed at length elsewhere in this volume, policy surged across the legitimacy barrier on a host of fronts, flooding the political landscape with what I have called policy mindedness. Opponents of planning defined a "plan" as "a feasible and rational course of action that someone believes will achieve a set of ends."[30] This was, of course, exactly what became the political preoccupation on one issue after another in the sixties. Having reached central headquarters, the enemies of planning looked around and found that on all sides, planning had become policymaking. Planners disappeared in the 1960s but so too did antiplanners. Everyone, including conservatives, had become would-be policymakers responding to the people's concerns.

That the people's ostensible concerns could now be probed through scientific opinion polls, displayed through mass electronic communications, massaged by the new craft of public relations, dramatized by staged media events, marketed on a continental scale—all this mattered greatly in a way it never had before. America was now experiencing a fulfillment of democratic tendency that had been a long time in the making. In short, policy mindedness is the outworking of a mass democratic mentality.

Although they did not have a word for it, policy mindedness is what perceptive observers such as Alexis de Tocqueville and the German historian Jacob Burckhardt saw as they looked ahead from the democratizing tendencies of the nineteenth century. For the French aristocrat writing in the 1830s, the bright side of this democratic vision was a society of ordinary people taking enlightened self-interest in their common business. It was local road building and temperance movements. On a darker side, democracy's triumph could be a "new physiognomy of servitude": "an innumerable multitude of men, all equal and alike, incessantly endeavoring to procure the petty and paltry pleases with which they glut their lives. . . . Above this race of men stands an immense and tutelary power, which takes upon itself alone to secure their gratification and to watch over their fate. . . . For their happiness such a government willingly labors."[31]

For Burckhardt lecturing in the 1860s, to become more open to public scrutiny and more accepting of various forms of citizen participation, to adopt an ever more expansive concept of who this common man or woman might be—in other words, to become more democratic—was to become committed to a never-ending agenda of social problem solving: "The State is thus, on the one hand, the realization and expression of the cultural ideas of every party; on the other, merely the visible vestures of civic life and only *ad hoc* almighty. It should be able to do everything, yet allowed to do nothing. . . . Everything that people know or feel Society will not undertake is simply heaped on to the daily growing burden of the State."[32]

If all this sounds too negative, recall that it is the same democratic tendency to which the economist Amartya Sen pointed in our own time to explain why food shortages no longer become famines in India or, for that matter, in any other poor countries where democratic forces can make themselves felt.[33] Democracy sets the people on the throne (at Whitehead's presuppositional level if not always in empirical reality). Policy mindedness constitutes one long complaint that government should do something about the way things are because of what other people are doing. The essence of complaining is putting oneself at the center of things. Once people have come to believe that they alone have the right to rule, it is only a short step (short logically, though not necessarily short in historical time, as I have noted) to believing that social conditions should accommodate them. When the world does not cooperate in making this accommodation, it is an even shorter step to demanding that something should be done about it, done by those whom the people have empowered. This is what we have called "public policy."

Obviously, democratic aspirations mattered greatly in the sixties, but it is democracy plus modernity that matters most for our discussion. Political prophets like Tocqueville and Burckhardt were able to have a much clearer view of the former than of the latter. Though stalled and seemingly defeated at times, democratization was what one could see happening everywhere in the nineteenth century. Moreover, there were also rich historical precedents to use in thinking about the subject. Eruptions of popular demands and grievances under "government by the many" were nothing new. Stories about Athenian democracy and Roman republicanism were the common property of any educated nineteenth-century person. With modernity it was different. Living in an era before electricity, graduate schools, psychiatrists, traffic jams, manufactured toilet paper or the term "nihilist" existed, no observer could anticipate the character of democracy under the conditions of a modern society. The thing that made modernity modern was that there had never been anything like it before.

Among many other things, to be modern meant to become more dependent on professionally trained experts. It meant to grow more involved in impersonal, bureaucratically organized forms of social interaction. As the twentieth century progressed, this modernizing character was becoming very deeply imprinted on American public affairs. One could see it in civic life, in which voluntary associations became more bureaucratized and professional engagements with public concerns became more narrowly compartmentalized.[34] The same tendency could be found in the partisan political arena. Politics grew professionalized not only with professional politicians but also with new cadres of political professions that sold special skills to manage what were becoming permanent political campaigns.[35] In and around government it simply became a fact of life that the complexities of public policy in modern society demanded the skills of experts, some of whom were subject-matter specialists, some experts in techniques of political activism, and some experts in both.

Modernization enhanced policy mindedness, but only on its own terms—by seeing social conditions as therapeutic challenges. Favored by the new social science professions and burgeoning research universities of the modern era, the therapeutic point of view taught the idea of a sick society in need of treatment. In the early stages of industrialization, socialists had thought the great change in political society would come from collectivizing the means of production. What turned out to be the leverage point was collectivizing fault. The source of disorders troubling the people was not any class, section, or individual ethical failings but society itself. Policy became modern democracy's answer to socialism, communism, and every other ism claiming a master plan for society's future. As the premise of a sick but treatable society was accepted, democratic government (not necessarily the same thing as centralized government planning) became the only plausible place to look. Advised by the proper experts, it was the only physician with the reach to deal with such a patient.

Thus while the fulfillment of democratic tendencies promoted policy mindedness, modernization transformed politics and policy into something *done to* ordinary, ambivalent citizens with everyday concerns, rather than something *done by* them.[36] Herein lay grounds for alienation, distrust, and cynicism. That is precisely why sixties civics was what it was and not some updated version of New Deal politics or midcentury liberalism. As Samuel Beer reminds us, Franklin Roosevelt not only said the federal government would take the lead but he also urged the people to demand and shape that lead. Government in Washington "consisted simply of the people themselves acting in their national capacity."[37] Ever after, advocates of positive national government tried mightily to sustain this idea. In one way or another, liberals commonly invoked a formula borrowed from Herbert Croly's 1909 book *The Promise of American Life*. The claim was that national reformers were using Hamiltonian means to achieve Jeffersonian ends, national power to perfect the democratic ideal of the common man. However, once policies became facts rather than rhetorical formulas, the notion that federal policy was "the people" acting in their national capacity simply could not be sustained. Federal policy was bureaucrats, program offices, regulators, professional specialists, interest group insiders, policy activists, political consultants, and (in George Wallace's excellent phrase) "pointy-headed intellectuals." By the Great Society era, Washington policies were no more the people acting in their national capacity than sprawling public school bureaucracies were the people acting in their local capacity. And ordinary people knew it.

Watching the expanding policy demands and deflating public trust of the sixties, radicals of the Left saw new grounds for hope. They and others judged that modern democratic capitalism must be approaching a massive legitimacy crisis.[38] In retrospect we now realize that if sixties civics implied delegitimization of the regime, it was an oddly weak form of delegitimation. It had to be weak because there was no positive alternative anyone could trust enough to endorse. At the beginning of the century, Lippmann, Graham Wallas, and others had followed Nietzsche in observing that it was not only the authority of traditional institutions that was losing its grip on people. The very idea of any ultimate, authoritative truth was yielding to the demand for self-liberation and self-realization, first at the elite and then the mass levels. With this shift in outlook, the cultural power of anything like orthodox religion was dissolving in the so-called acids of modernity. For some observers, modernity's golden rule that there is no golden rule was its most portentous feature. It seems at least plausible to think that after the "great time-out" for the Depression and World War II, the "great disruption" of the sixties drew out the implications of these deeper currents.[39] Sixties civics carried forward what G. K. Chesterton sixty years earlier had called "modern man in revolt": "The Jacobin could tell you not only the system he would rebel against, but (what was more important) the system he would *not* rebel against, the system he would trust. But the new rebel is a skeptic, and will not entirely trust anything. He has no loyalty; therefore he can never be really a revolutionist. . . . In his book on politics he attacks men for tramping on morality; in his book on ethics he attacks morality for trampling on men."[40]

On a more extended popular level than Chesterton could have imagined, this situation was roughly that which characterized the sixties turmoil. Delegitimization was self-limiting. When protesters denounced "the system," it was an artistic free-form exercise that also rejected any firm authority for justifying the denunciations. As in the earlier twentieth century, youth seemed to assume an immense authority, often aided by the shame and envy of their elders.[41] A popular song of the time celebrated the San Francisco scene, claiming "there's a whole generation / with a new explanation."[42] But youth had no new explanation. They had critiques of hypocrisy and the morality of unmasking pretensions of conventional morality. But they had little positive to put in its place.[43] In fact, the triumphant nonjudgmentalism was ruthless in judging any claim of ultimate, binding standards. To say, as many did, that one was advancing the cause of individual choice ducked the issue of what is right and good and slipped silently through the back door of indifference, redefined as tolerance. To say, as many did, that you were championing liberty and freedom gave no grounds for justifying the limits required if freedom and liberty were to have any real meaning. It was playing tennis with the net down and the foul lines erased. Slogans for freedom, personal choice and tolerance really declared the goodness of not deciding what is good. All this was perhaps best foreshadowed in Nicholas Ray's 1955 film *Rebel without a Cause*. On the issue of what to rebel against, the answer was, "What have you got?" On what to really believe in, with full, committed faith, the hero must stay cool. Of course, there would be plenty of causes in the Great Society era. Shorn of vague references to "the people," it was the idea of genuine authority that went missing.

Thus, the school of the sixties was uncivil but not uncivic. There was a busy, indeed hyperactive, concern with the public business. Yet it was a concern inherently negative in spirit. For over two centuries, America had gone through certain periods of intense cultural confusion, attended by zealous efforts at personal purification and institutional reform. Some scholars later called these "awakenings." If the sixties was one of these awakenings, it was the first such struggle for revitalization that was not grounded in religious revival of a culturally dominant Christianity.[44] Sixties civics offered ever closer attention to what things are wrong, together with an ever more ambivalent view of what things are right. Like the new breed of satirists filling the comedy clubs, reformers were the black knights of the implied positive. Their relentless critiques implied a yearning for a vague perfection that would yet somehow be personally unconstricting or, as Mort Sahl, the patriarch of the new comedians, could best define the goal, "something good to replace the bad."[45] The therapeutic mind-set could offer no solace because there was no agreement on what constituted normal health. By definition, any standard of what was good would be too confining. Americans were taught to be critical but nonjudgmental.

Looking at the whole package—a darkly critical view of traditional authority, scripts concentrating on victimization and revenge, a preoccupation with detecting societal evils, punishing wrongs, and constructing institutions of policy correction—one is tempted to call the sixties' curriculum Gothic. To say that, however, does injustice to the Gothic mind, since the cathedral builders always drew their inspiration from something higher that ultimately produced redemption and regeneration. Sixties civics had none of that. In military language, by the 1960s, religion, social criticism, and public political authority had mutually exceeded each other's "supporting distance," which is to say, the gap beyond which one unit cannot come to the aid of another before it is defeated.

Just as no two faces are the same and yet all faces are alike, sixties civics put different faces on public affairs, but it had a single visage. We can perceive the variations only because it *is* one thing, whether coming from a comedy club satirist, liberal professor, investigative journalist, or disgruntled voter. This is the singularity I have tried to examine in these pages. We should remember that sixties civics was not the whole story of Americans' civic outlook, even in the Great Society era. Mort Sahl's first four record albums sold 125,000 copies, but the gentle domestic humor of Shelley Berman sold one million;[46] religious thinkers were writing modestly successful books about the "death of god," but Billy Graham crusades were filling arenas; protesters were in the streets, but Ronald Reagan was twice elected California's governor preaching the old-time political religion of Americanism.

Sixties civics was certainly not the whole story of the sixties. Neither is it the only teaching at work in our politics today. Unlike the minority of political activists, ordinary citizens typically pay little regard to the combative outlook I have been describing. Most Americans seem to glance at the public contests of advocates and adversaries and give an uncitizenly shrug at "them" and the political games they play. One assumes this is just the way things are. The public square is not an enlivening civic meeting place but a dreary, distasteful presence one has to endure in the news.

That assumption, however, is precisely the point. Sixties civics is associated with features of American political life that each succeeding generation now takes for granted. All of us, political activists and nonactivists alike, expect that institutions are little more than stages for public performances. We assume the political parties will be ideologically at each other's throats. We assume that "spin"—or what was traditionally known as sophistry and a deception objectionable to all right-thinking persons— is what everybody in the public square is doing. We expect every group to refuse to give an inch to another group because there is no goodwill that would prevent an inch on the slippery slope from turning into a mile. We expect that the public conversation is always about talking to win rather than to discover the truth of things. We expect a public realm that is tolerant in not judging anyone's values but committed to distrusting everyone's motives. And in the end, the more we resist claims of authority, the more we expect respect.

That we can walk through the public square and not even notice such things as strange demonstrates the enduring legacy of sixties civics.

Notes

1. The problem with decade labeling is that history does not occur in ten-year chunks ending in zero. In discussing the cultural revolution in four countries, Arthur Marwick dates the "sixties" as roughly 1958 through 1974. It is a reasonable approximation of the unruly, nondecadal decade that I am discussing in this essay and avoids the fruitless argument about whether the sixties or the seventies contained the "real" radical shift. Cf. Arthur Marwick, *The Sixties: Cul-*

tural Revolution in Britain, France, Italy, and the United States, c. 1958–c. 1974 (New York: Oxford University Press, 1998), and David Frum, *How We Got Here: America since the Seventies—for Better and Worse* (New York: Basic Books, 1999).

2. Alfred North Whitehead, *Science and the Modern World* (1925; reprint, New York: Mentor Edition, 1952), 49–50.

3. David S. Broder, "Time to Face Fiscal Reality," *Washington Post*, July 24, 2002, A19; *A Workforce at Risk: The Troubled State of the Federal Public Service*, Brookings Briefing (Washington, D.C.: Brookings Institution Press, 2002).

4. Quoted in *Life*, May 23, 1960, 24.

5. Adlai Stevenson (two-time Democratic candidate for president), Archibald MacLeish, Billy Graham, David Sarnoff (chairman of RCA), John Gardner (president of the Carnegie Corporation), Albert Wohlstetter (defense specialist for the Rand Corporation), Clinton Rossiter (Cornell University professor of government), and Lippmann.

6. Samuel H. Beer, "In Search of a New Public Philosophy," in *The New American Political System*, ed. Anthony King (Washington, D.C.: American Enterprise Institute, 1978), 8 n. 5.

7. James Q. Wilson, "New Politics, New Elites, Old Publics," in *The New Politics of Public Policy*, ed. Marc C. Landy and Martin A. Levin, 249–67 (Baltimore: Johns Hopkins University Press, 1995).

8. See Martha Derthick, "Crossing Thresholds: Federalism in the 1960s," in her collection of essays *Keeping the Compound Republic: Essays on American Federalism* (Washington: Brookings Institution Press, 2001), esp. 147, 152.

9. James Q. Wilson, "Reinventing Public Administration," *PS: Political Science and Politics*, December 1994, 673.

10. Joseph M. Bessette, *Toward a More Perfect Union: Writings of Herbert J. Storing* (Washington, D.C.: American Enterprise Institute Press, 1995), 427.

11. James L. Sundquist, *Politics and Policy: The Eisenhower, Kennedy, and Johnson Years* (Washington, D.C.: Brookings Institution, 1968)

12. Theodore Roszak, "Youth and the Great Refusal," *The Nation*, March 25, 1968.

13. The contrast is evident in more-recent books such as Catherine McNicol Stock, *Rural Radicals* (Ithaca: Cornell University Press, 1996); Lisa McGirr, *Suburban Warriors: The Origins of the New American Right* (Princeton: Princeton University Press, 2001); and Rick Perlstein, *Before the Storm: Barry Goldwater and the Unmaking of the American Consensus* (New York: Hill and Wang, 2001).

14. Bernard Bailyn, *The Ideological Origins of the American Revolution* (Harvard University Press, 1973); Gordon Wood, *The Creation of the American Republic* (Chapel Hill: University of North Carolina Press, 1969).

15. Much of this information is collected and analyzed in Joseph Nye, Philip D. Zelikow, and David C. King, *Why People Don't Trust Government* (Cambridge: Harvard University Press, 1997); William G. Mayer, *The Changing*

American Mind (Ann Arbor: University of Michigan Press, 1993); and Seymour Martin Lipset and William Schneider, *The Confidence Gap* (Baltimore: Johns Hopkins University Press, 1987).

16. Lipset and Schneider, *Confidence Gap*, 333; David C. King, "The Polarization of American Parties and Mistrust of Government," in Nye, Zelikow, and King, *Why People Don't Trust Government*, 155–78.

17. Thomas S. Hibbs, *Shows about Nothing* (Dallas: Spence Publishing, 1999).

18. Lippmann had imported the term "Great Society" from his British intellectual colleague Graham Wallas. In the book he was working on at his death (*Social Judgement* [New York: Harcourt, Brace, 1935]), Wallas also sought to describe a working secular philosophy that was emerging in modern society and could grow. Like Lippmann's, it was a public-spirited, humanistic outlook uniting emotional empathy and rational knowledge.

19. Walter Lippmann, *A Preface to Morals* (New York: Macmillan, 1929), 327. On other points mentioned, see esp. 228–30 and 320–30. This perspective and its subsequent loss among contemporary elites is discussed in John Judis, *The Paradox of American Democracy* (New York: Pantheon, 2000).

20. Thus in early 1930, before the Depression had taken hold or the New Deal had come to Washington, Harvard Law professor Felix Frankfurter lectured on "the paradox of both distrusting and burdening government." FDR's future Supreme Court justice saw this as revealing the lack of "a conscious philosophy of politics" and went on to argue that such an outdated view had to be replaced with disinterested thinking, expert administration, and enlightened public judgment to meet the ever-growing demands on government. Felix Frankfurter, *The Public and Its Government* (New Haven: Yale University Press, 1930), 4, 6, and chaps. 3, 4.

21. Schlesinger discusses *The Vital Center: The Politics of Freedom* (Boston: Houghton Mifflin, 1949) in his memoir, *A Life in the Twentieth Century: Innocent Beginnings, 1917–1950* (Boston: Houghton Mifflin, 2001). An insightful review is offered by James Nuechterlein, "The Last Liberal," *First Things*, August/September 2001, 39.

22. *Life*, June 9, 1967, 57.

23. Never a realist who believed that a good cause would hallow any weapon, Niebuhr's subtleties of thought were overlooked by secularists like Schlesinger and are now largely forgotten; however, they still repay close attention. Standard references include Reinhold Niebuhr's *Moral Man and Immoral Society: A Study in Ethics and Politics* (New York: Charles Scribner's Sons, 1932); *The Children of Light and the Children of Darkness* (New York: Scribners, 1944); and *The Irony of American History* (New York: Scribner, 1952).

24. Theodore H. White wrote a series of profiles and articles titled "The Action Intellectuals," which were published in *Life* magazine on June 9, 16, and 23, 1967. They gained almost no attention because of the concurrent outbreak and conclusion of Israel's Six Days' War. Schlesinger's characterization of operational optimism and historical pessimism is quoted in Nuechterlein, "Last Liberal," 40.

25. Jim Forest, "Mrs. Jellyby and St. John of the Cross," *Touchstone,* October 2001, 19.

26. Robert C. Christopher, *Crashing the Gates* (New York: Simon and Schuster, 1989).

27. Peter H. Gibbon, *A Call to Heroism* (New York: Atlantic Monthly Press, 2002)

28. Albert O. Hirschman, *The Rhetoric of Reaction* (Cambridge: Harvard University Press, Belknap Press, 1991), esp. chap. 2.

29. Lloyd Free and Hadley Cantril, *The Political Beliefs of Americans* (New Brunswick, N.J.: Rutgers University Press, 1967).

30. James Q. Wilson, "A Connecticut Yankee in King Arthur's Court: A Biography," in *Edward C. Banfield: An Appreciation,* Henry Salvatori Center Monograph, new ser., no. 3, April 2002, 52.

31. Alexis de Tocqueville, *Democracy in America* (New York: Anchor Books, 1969), 2:336.

32. Jacob Burckhardt, *Force and Freedom: Reflections on History* (New York: Pantheon Books, 1943), 227–28.

33. Amartya Sen, *Development as Freedom* (New York: Oxford University Press, 1999).

34. See especially part 2 in Theda Skocpol and Morris P. Fiorina, eds., *Civic Engagement in American Democracy* (Washington: Brookings Institution Press, 1999).

35. Norman Ornstein and Thomas Mann, eds., *The Permanent Campaign and Its Future* (Washington, D.C.: American Enterprise Institute, 2000).

36. This theme is developed in any number of quite different studies. See, for example, James L. Nolan, *The Therapeutic State: Justifying Government at Century's End* (New York: New York University Press, 1998); Robert H. Wiebe, *Self-Rule: A Cultural History of American Democracy* (Chicago: University of Chicago Press, 1995); and Christopher Lasch, *The Revolt of the Elites and the Betrayal of Democracy* (New York: Norton, 1995).

37. Beer, "In Search of a New Public Philosophy," 8.

38. Jurgen Habermas, *Legitimation Crisis* (Boston: Beacon, 1975).

39. The terms derive from Francis Fukuyama's *The Great Disruption: Human Nature and the Reconstitution of Social Order* (New York: Free Press, 1999), and James Q. Wilson's review of that book in *Public Interest,* Fall 1999.

40. G. K. Chesterton, *Orthodoxy,* in *The Collected Works of G. K. Chesterton* (San Francisco: Ignatius Press, 1986), 1:244–45.

41. As early as 1921, André Gide captured the spirit precisely: "I believe the truth lies in youth; I believe it is always right against us. I believe that, far from trying to teach it, it is in youth that we, the elders, must seek our lessons.... I believe that each new generation arrives bearing a message it must deliver; our role is to help that delivery. I believe that what is called 'experience' is often but an unavowed fatigue, resignation, blighted hope" (*The Journals of André Gide,* trans. Justin O'Brien [New York: Vintage, 1956], entry of December 26, 1921, 1:312).

42. The song is "San Francisco," chords and lyrics by John Phillips.

43. One is speaking here of anything on a scale compared with the religious-cultural traditions being dismissed. Of course some did try, as mentioned in note 12 above. See, for example, documents attempting to develop a political creed in Mitchell Cohen and Dennis Hale, eds., *The New Student Left: An Anthology* (Boston: Beacon, 1967) or, in a more economic vein, Michael Harrington, *The Twilight of Capitalism* (New York: Simon and Schuster, 1976).

44. Hugh Heclo, "The Sixties' False Dawn: Awakenings, Movements, and Postmodern Policy-Making," in *Integrating the Sixties*, ed. Brian Balogh (University Park: Pennsylvania State University Press, 1996), 34–63.

45. Quoted in a special cover story on the new brand of comedians in *Time*, August 15, 1960, 48.

46. Ibid.

Pluralism, Postwar Intellectuals, and the Demise of the Union Idea

Nelson Lichtenstein

Trade union movements in the industrialized West normally stand on the left side of a nation's political culture, and they usually reap benefits of great organizational and political value when left-wing ideas circulate freely and when social democratic regimes come to power. This is true in most of Western Europe, Canada, and even Poland, Spain, South Africa, and South Korea, where the rights-conscious values and radical impulses characteristic of "the sixties," even when delayed for a decade or more, dramatically increased trade union numbers, prestige, and power.

But little of this happened in the United States. Trade union membership did grow modestly, largely as a result of a successful organizing breakthrough in public employment, but union density continued a slow decline, and the political influence of organized labor, even under two activist Democratic presidents, seemed muted at best. Indeed, the reputation of American unions and of the entire New Deal bargaining system began a precipitous decline in the 1960s. During the very same years in which the social imagination of American reformers took wing, labor's historic agenda—for a democratic workplace, an organizational breakthrough into the new white-collar occupations, and a progressive reform of the labor law—sank from sight in all but the most radical circles. At the very moment in which a rights-conscious revolution began to transform American political culture, the model of collective action, of democratic empowerment embodied in the Wagner Act, was reaching something close to an ideological dead end.

The Devaluation of "Big Labor"

There are many explanations for this extraordinary state of affairs. One is the very real success of the American economy and the union role in capturing a share of that bounty for the working class. Real wages doubled between 1947 and 1973. The old "labor question," which had animated politics during the Progressive Era and the New Deal, seemed to evaporate under the prosperous postwar sky. Organized labor's success robbed the unions of their social movement character, a state of affairs made depressingly evident during the sensational McClellan Committee hearings of 1957 and 1958, when Teamster union arrogance and corruption were displayed before a television audience of millions. The standoffishness of the AFL-CIO toward the civil rights movement, combined with its steadfast support for the Vietnam War policy, seemed to confirm labor's conservative parochialism, at least for the sixties' Left. Finally, the trade unions never really became corporatist partners within American politics or economic life. There was no stable, consensual "labor-management" accord even during those midcentury decades when unionism was politically and economically most potent. From the late 1950s the unions faced a business community that had begun to mobilize against union bargaining clout and a resurgent right wing whose standard bearers denounced "monopoly unionism" and attacked labor's capacity to use its collective resources in electoral politics.[1]

This analysis of labor's postwar decline has become a cottage industry. But the most consequential sources of unionism's ideological and cultural devaluation during this era lie in the ideas, ideologies, and values that made the long decade of the 1960s such a watershed. No single great economic, technological, or political change can account for the devaluation of the union idea during the 1950s and 1960s. Rather, the midcentury transformation in the labor question was a product of many of the same ideological transmutations that made the sixties such a effervescent moment. Even as unions reached their twentieth-century apogee as economic institutions and mass membership organizations, trade unionism and the old "labor question" practically vanished from popular political and cultural discourse.

As early as 1960, a generation of intellectuals, jurists, journalists, academics, and politicians had come to see the unions as little more than a self-aggrandizing interest group, no longer a lever for progressive change. This was a project not so much of the political Right, which had long polemicized against big labor, but of radical intellectuals and centrist liberals, whose critique of postwar trade unionism proved far more demoralizing and, in the long run, more ideologically and jurisprudentially debilitating. The radical sociologist C. Wright Mills looked well beyond "the labor metaphysic" to find efficacious sources of social change, while liberal economists such as Clark Kerr argued that writers and intellectuals had been profoundly mistaken to see the labor movement as some kind of "institutionalized messiah."[2] This critique soon became the new orthodoxy, especially within the main, innovative body of American liberalism. But this new skepticism would also have a vast influence in the academy, among "new social movement" activists of the 1960s and 1970s, as well as on the judiciary, where a discourse of rights soon came to have a powerfully corrosive effect on the legitimacy and integrity of the union idea itself.

This devaluation of organized labor was not just an ideological and cultural phenomenon, for it was advanced by a highly visible transformation of the trade unions themselves. They were now "Big Labor": in the 1950s and 1960s it seemed to many former allies that caution, bureaucracy, and self-interest had replaced the visionary quest for solidarity and social transformation that had been a hallmark of the Depression decade. Collective bargaining had become a self-contained system, and the unions, so it was thought, had "matured," even become part of the "establishment."[3] This indictment rested upon much social myth, but an institutional reality was there as well. Compared with those in Europe and Canada and with much of the New Deal world of American labor, individual trade unions were now internal oligarchies, administratively top-heavy with technicians and officials, and increasingly parochial in their bargaining strategy and political outlook.

The stolid quality of postwar U.S. unionism reflected the institutional constraints and legal structures under which the unions were forced to function. The firm-centered system of U.S. bargaining generated a positively baroque industrial relations regime. By the 1980s, when labor claimed only about 16 percent of the wage and salary workers as members, there were nevertheless 175,000 collective bargaining agreements in force. American workers were represented by 70,000 local unions, roughly 275 state and regional organizations, and 174 national unions, of which only 108 were affiliated with the AFL-CIO.[4] All this activity sustained the largest and best-paid stratum of full-time salaried officers in the labor movement world. Of every three hundred unionists in 1960, one was a paid functionary. The United States had sixty thousand full-time union officers then, compared with just four thousand in Great Britain.[5] Not unexpectedly, these top-heavy, well-paid bureaucracies proved highly resistant to rotation in office, just as much in the United Automobile Workers (UAW), where the leadership advertised the union's adherence to democratic procedure in an extravagant fashion, as in the Teamsters or the building trades, where little pretense was made of following such democratic norms.[6]

In politics as well as collective bargaining, the fragmentation of the unions sharply limited their influence. What had changed between the 1930s and the 1950s was not some abstract measure of political consciousness but the range of opportunities for social action and organizational mobilization that confronted workers and their institutions. In the quarter century that followed the end of World War II, a solid majority of all unionists remained faithful Democrats, especially when voting for president or their representative in Congress. When the sociologist Arthur Kornhauser surveyed the political attitudes of Detroit autoworkers in 1952, he found that they "are not going 'middle class,'" a view sustained by the incisive reportage of journalist Samuel Lubell, who found that "this same kind of class voting can be seen in every American city."[7] But labor's electoral mobilizations never bore the fruit expected of them. Although unions in meatpacking, steel, automobiles, and electrical products sought to link their bargaining posture to a larger social democratic project, the concentration of their membership and economic clout to a northeastern/midwestern industrial heartland limited their political leverage. Meanwhile, the Teamsters and the construction trades often allied themselves with conservative municipal machines, some Republican in party affiliation, and in the South the vacuum created by the absence of a union presence in textiles, food processing, and light manufacturing meant that the national Democratic Party contained a militant southern wing hostile to unionism or to a significant rise in the social wage. "He who would understand politics in the large may ponder the status of labor," wrote political scientist V. O. Key in 1953, the year in which labor's membership stood at its numerical apogee, "a numerically great force in a society adhering to the doctrine of the rule of numbers, yet without proportionate durable political power as a class."[8]

Pluralism: Industrial and Otherwise

Given these difficulties, one of the most remarkable features of the early postwar landscape is the extent to which mainstream intellectuals, legal experts, and labor economists celebrated what we can now so clearly see as the gross deformities inherent in this laborite world. At midcentury, most American liberals thought the doctrine of "industrial pluralism" constituted the twentieth-century solution to the labor question. From the Progressive Era forward, such policymaking intellectuals as John R. Commons, William Leiserson, Harry Millis, and Edwin Witte saw the unfolding of a state-sponsored collective bargaining regime as the sure path to social peace, class equilibrium, and industrial democracy. But the meaning of such pluralistic bargaining had a very different resonance in the years before and after 1940.

During the Progressive Era and the New Deal, collective bargaining was inextricably linked to the republican ideal of "industrial democracy." Louis Brandeis made this clear in 1915 when he told a Faneuil Hall audience that the task of the hour was the translation, under twentieth-century social and economic conditions, of those eighteenth-century "rights which our Constitution guarantees." All Americans, argued Brandeis in a formulation typical of his generation of reformers, must have "a reasonable income," decent "working conditions," and "some system of social insurance." However, the "essentials of American citizenship" were not simply material. There could be no more "political democracy" in contemporary America, Brandeis told the U.S. Industrial Commission that same year, without an "industrial democracy" that gave workers actual participation in the governance of the firms for which they worked.[9]

This was the spirit that gave such luminosity to the 1935 Wagner Act. Arguing for the labor law that would bear his name, New York senator Robert Wagner asserted that "industrial tyranny is incompatible with a Republican form of government." Collective bargaining was the mechanism, not unlike that of a two-party parliamentary body, that would bring to the shop floor those procedures and standards that had long been venerated in civil society. Industrial democrats envisioned an "industrial jurisprudence" that would generate a constitutionalized factory regime. Although hardly a radical, Yale Law School professor Harry Shulman, one of the founders of labor arbitration, endorsed the Brandeis-Wagner vision, seeing collective bargaining as "the essential condition of political democracy, the means of providing for the workers' lives in industry the sense of worth, of freedom, and of participation that democratic government promises them as citizens."[10] For millions of workers, a majority immigrants, the offspring of immigrants, or migrants from the American South, trade unionism and collective bargaining proved a highway to civil rights, civil liberties, and real citizenship.

By the 1950s, however, industrial pluralism had acquired a far more constrained and a much more depoliticized character. The cold war made suspect the whole discourse of "industrial democracy," celebrating instead an ideology of "free collective bargaining" that made a virtue out of the depoliticized insularity that increasingly characterized the collective bargaining regime. Even as American trade unions enrolled more than a third of all nonfarm workers, industrial relations scholars and practitioners took this political-organizational retreat and recast it as a triumphal solution to issues of class conflict and social inequality, in the process turning the idea of industrial pluralism into something very close to a celebration of the status quo.

"Collective bargaining is the great social invention that has institutionalized industrial conflict," wrote the sociologist Robert Dublin in 1954. "In much the same way that the electoral process and majority rule have institutionalized political conflict in a democracy, collective bargaining has created a stable means for resolving industrial conflict." To drive the ideological point home, economist Arthur Ross offered an elbow to those whose politics had once been more expansive. "One of the great virtues of collective bargaining . . . is that it permits the formulation of limited issues which are amenable to resolution and blurs over large differences of principle. . . . This, of course, is revolting to those who will settle for nothing less than 'basic solutions.'"[11]

Such sentiments clearly misjudged the long-term industrial dynamic at work in postwar America. The collective bargaining system was hardly stable and universal; indeed, management was becoming increasingly hostile to unionism of any sort. Why, then, did so many American academics and intellectuals engage in such wishful social thinking? Why did industrial pluralism become so ideologically well rooted, despite its manifest illusions?

For those who presumed to analyze midcentury industrial life, the history of contemporary capitalism was a nightmare from which they were trying to escape. American liberals, indeed many radicals, were in full flight from the class politics of the European socialist tradition and the ambitious social engineering that had been part of both Progressive Era reform and New Deal state building. All the most influential intellectuals and academics of this era had been adults in the 1930s or early 1940s, and a considerable number had stood on the left, including Seymour Martin Lipset, Daniel Bell, Reinhold Niebuhr, John Kenneth Galbraith, Will Herberg, Clark Kerr, Robert Dahl, and James Burnham. But these were the "twice born," to use Daniel Bell's phrase, men and women who had rejected the socialism of their youth for a more sober and limited creed.[12] To them, feckless majorities in a mass, industrialized society generated a runaway democracy that might well subvert liberal values and democratic processes. The political ambitions projected by the fascist and Stalinist regimes of Europe made a decentralized, non-ideological, interest-group theory of politics on this side of the Atlantic seem desperately attractive, even more so when "populist" demagogues, from Huey Long to Joseph McCarthy, threatened civil liberties and democratic comity. Classes, capitalists, and collective struggle might yet exist, but these social theorists sought and found an Americanized ideal that repudiated the ideological polarization of prewar Europe. To the influential sociologist Seymour Martin Lipset, the American class struggle would always be "a fight without ideologies, without red flags, without May Day parades."[13]

A wishful but potent illusion underlay this optimistic conservatism. Postwar students of industrial society were not pro-capitalist ideologues. Many remained critics of the corporation and disdainful of business leadership. But that was just the problem: they devalued capitalism as a system of power and in its place saw profits and production within a bureaucratically structured matrix. Thus Peter Drucker, the Austrian émigré who became the nation's most important management theorist since Frederick Taylor, considered the modern U.S. corporation the paradigmatic institution of the contemporary world, "the representative social actuality." But if Drucker was a herald of corporate America, he was equally determined to divorce such views from any taint of the old, free-wheeling laissez-faire. To Drucker and to a generation of societal savants who would follow, the corporation was essentially a political planning mechanism, a Weberian rationalization of industrial society. The "rights of capital" had been replaced by the "responsibilities of management." As a result, in his pioneering study of General Motors, published just after World War II, Drucker eschewed the usual categories of business analysis—profits, prices, labor costs, and the like—and emphasized "the traditional questions of politics and political analysis" as applied to the internal life of the large corporation.[14]

This perspective was given a metahistorical coherence by the nation's most influential theorists of the postwar industrial relations system. In 1951, when Clark Kerr, John Dunlop, Frederick Harbison, and Charles A. Myers proposed that the new and immensely rich Ford Foundation fund a worldwide study of "labor relations and democratic policy," echoes of the Depression era's Whiggish, radical pluralism could still be found beneath the cold war overlay that justified their ambitious research design. These Depression-bred social scientists argued that the "condition, character, and beliefs of the working classes will be among the decisive influences upon the political structure of modern nations." Ford turned aside this suggested probe into the worldwide "labor question" but soon funded a revised, and very different, application titled "Utilization of Human Resources: A Comparative Analysis," which eliminated all mention of the phrase "working class" and instead advanced more explicitly the emerging discourse of modernization, industrialization, and human resources.[15]

By the time Clark Kerr, John Dunlop, and their associates published *Industrialism and Industrial Man* in 1960, they had reached the conclusion that the process of "industrialization" had replaced the dialectics of capitalism as a worldwide principle framing the evolution of society. As Kerr put it with characteristic bravado, "In our times it is no longer the specter of Communism which is haunting Europe, but rather emerging industrialization in many forms that is confronting the whole world. The giant of industrialization is stalking the earth, transforming almost all features of older and traditional societies." Classes would still exist in such a society, and unions remained important institutions that represented the interests of lower-skilled manual workers. But, Kerr concluded, "conflict will take place in a system of pluralistic industrialism . . . tak[ing] less the form of the open strife or the revolt and more the form of the bureaucratic contest. Persuasion, pressure, and manipulation will take the place of the face-to-face combat of an earlier age." Whatever the nature of the conflict, the stakes would be far lower than those once imagined by industrial democrats. Regardless of the form of industrialization—Soviet, Western, or in the underdeveloped world—a universal "web of rules" was intrinsic to industrialism's Weberian universe. These technocratic and rationalist constraints devalued collective action, marginalized the role of government, and heightened the centrality of the managerial elite as the "initiators" and "manipulators" of the industrial system.[16]

All this made the appeal of pluralist theory and the political culture that enfolded it well nigh irresistible. If capitalism had begun to morph into a politically more malleable system, if classes did not really clash in the United States, and if a technocratic web of rules structured the realm of production, then a theory of society that put interest group parochialism at its center might well flourish. Thus did postwar American intellectuals begin their love affair with what Amherst College political scientist Earl Latham called "the group basis of politics." To Columbia's David Truman, "this pluralistic structure is a central fact of the distribution of power in the society."[17] Stable, nonideological conflict was the natural product of the peaceful clash of interest groups. "Mature capitalism does not lead to more class consciousness, but to a multitude of views," wrote Kerr in 1961. "Pluralism rather than class solidarity characterizes the new industrial society."[18]

"In a pressure group society, labor has a legitimate political role," wrote Daniel Bell, in 1952 the labor editor of *Fortune* magazine. From this influential post he offered the kind of analytic cynicism that made labor relations palatable to a skeptical business readership. Bell thus labeled modern trade unionism "the capitalism of the proletariat," positing an inevitable conflict in which the unions as a market-shaping interest group won out against organized labor considered as an "ideological conception."[19] Likewise, Reinhold Niebuhr, who had denounced Henry Ford from a Detroit pulpit in the 1920s, summed up much conventional wisdom at the end of the 1950s. "Collective bargaining has come to be regarded as almost as basic as the right to vote," he told the labor liberals who read the staunchly anticommunist *New Leader*, adding that "the equilibrium of power achieved between management and labor . . . is one of the instruments used by a highly technical society, with ever larger aggregates of power, to achieve that tolerable justice which has rendered Western Civilization immune to the Communist virus."[20]

If political pluralism and its industrial variant, collective bargaining, were to function effectively, then the interest groups involved required the kind of internal discipline necessary to sustain a coherent leadership and a de facto oligarchy. Robert Dahl actually defined twentieth-century democracy as a "polyarchy," in which real pluralism flourishes, but only as competing elites bargain, compromise, and govern.[21] When it came to labor and management, therefore, the old dream of an industrial democracy animated by a mass of alert citizen-workers seemed suddenly antique. Just as management represented an enlightened bureaucracy, so too did the unions best advance the interests of their members when they were led by officers of expertise and long tenure. "Union memberships are traditionally apathetic except in some crisis, and very little can be done about it," observed Kerr in 1958. "Compulsory strike votes proved a farce in World War II," he added. "And most bargaining issues cannot properly be put to membership vote."[22] Lipset would give Kerr's Weberian observations a categorical élan. The oligarchic governance of American trade unions was a good thing because too much democracy led to internal division, ideological politics, and weakness in the face of the corporate enemy. "Unions, like all other large-scale organizations, are constrained to develop bureaucratic structures," wrote Lipset in his 1960 masterwork *Political Man: The Social Basis of Politics*. To Lipset, these private oligarchies provide "a secure base for factionalism and real vested interests at the same time that they limit individual freedom within the organization and allow a degree of autonomy of action for both the leaders and the organization."[23]

This perspective was hardly confined to the academy. The wildcat strikes that proliferated during World War II and Korea made managers more appreciative of a "responsible" union leadership. Thus the Taft-Hartley Act made the international union legally responsible for actions by subordinate locals and minor officials. And when Dwight D. Eisenhower spoke at the AFL's 1952 convention, the GOP presidential nominee asserted that "unions have a secure place in our industrial life. . . . [H]ealthy collective bargaining requires responsible unions and responsible employers. Weak unions cannot be responsible."[24]

Six years later, Arthur Goldberg, the influential counsel for the United Steel Workers (USW), made the same point, albeit with some left-wing flavoring. Justifying the high-handed methods used by USW officials to defeat their internal union opponents, Goldberg argued that trade unions were in a state of chronic warfare with a set of corporate adversaries who took every opportunity to exploit divisions within the workforce to subvert them. "Even where the existence and status of a union is unquestioned—as, for example, in the basic steel industry—it is unlike political government in that it cannot legislate by itself on the matters of primary concern to it—wages, hours and working conditions. . . . If there is analogy to political government, the analogy is to a political government [during] a revolution, and which is periodically at war."[25]

The labor law sustained this pluralist perspective. Liberals such as Supreme Court justice William O. Douglas and Harvard Law professor Archibald Cox were determined to shape the law to strengthen the union capacity to uphold its side of the collective bargaining relationship. "The collective bargaining agreement," argued Douglas, "calls into being a new common law—the common law of a particular industry or of a particular plant . . . a system of industrial self-government."[26] Thus despite the spread of right-to-work legislation in the South and Mountain West, the Court generally sustained the capacity of unions to discipline scabs during strikes and penalize those who refused to pay their dues.[27] In a series of "duty of fair representation" cases during the 1940s and 1950s, the courts intervened to make sure that racial minorities were given equal treatment. But most jurists, the liberals especially, refrained from second-guessing internal union decisions as to most other complaints, including administration of the grievance procedure.[28]

Radical Disillusionment

Not everyone was a pluralist. America's left-wing intellectuals were not numerous in the 1950s and early 1960s, but their influence on liberal thought, academic scholarship, and judicial opinion was soon to become quite potent. During the two decades after World War II, they remained largely immune to the lures of industrial pluralism, developing instead a critique of the unions and of the entire industrial relations regime that put a large minus sign next to the collaboration, the incrementalism, and the hostility to left-wing ideology that was celebrated by Lipset, Kerr, Bell, and Drucker. Radical voices were lonely protests in the 1950s, but within a decade they became something far more influential, when pluralist ideology, in almost all its forms, began to decompose. Then, their disillusionment would become the common coin of American liberalism.

In the United States, as in Europe, the Left had long maintained a heavy ideological investment in the trade union movement, even when the actual leadership and program of organized labor proved hostile to the radical vision of a transformed society. C. Wright Mills captured this sensibility at the end of World War II. His *New Men of Power: America's Labor Leaders* (1948) was written during that creative, pre–cold war moment, before the postwar industrial relations regime had been put into place. Organized labor still had the will and power to wage strike battles that reflected the moral dichotomies of the Depression decade. To Mills, trade union leaders were a "strategic elite," the unions the "only organization capable of stopping the main drift towards war and slump." He saw union leaders as thoroughly political animals, "managers of discontent," who were nevertheless in a constant state of "conflict with the powers of property." Mills was not a pluralist, industrial or otherwise. Trade union leaders might quest for power, but they were not proponents of a pluralistic equilibrium. "Modern rebels," wrote Mills, "need not be romantic figures."[29]

The demise of this perspective came quickly. Even as *The New Men of Power* appeared, Mills was turning his back on the labor movement. By the time he published *White Collar* in 1951, he had lost any hope in a labor-based "strategic elite." Unions were at best liberal "pressure groups" that served simultaneously as agents of repression. "Trade unions," wrote Mills, "are the most reliable instruments to date for taming and channeling lower-class aspirations, for lining up the workers without internal violence during time of war, and for controlling their insurgency during times of peace and depression." And the new class of semiproletarian white-collar workers would hardly provide the social ingredients from which might spring a new round of union growth. Instead, Mills saw white-collar workers as the raw material needed by a mass coercive society, flavored perhaps by the scent of fascism. Indeed, the entire labor metaphysic had come under a cloud, if not a sustained attack.[30] To Mills and the generation of New Leftists who would follow him, the functional pluralism celebrated by Kerr, Lipset, and Dahl seemed enormously repressive, ethically and morally claustrophobic. The "iron cage" of Max Weber and Robert Michels had replaced the liberating visions of Marx and Trotsky as the most reliable guide to the inner structures of American society.

Three important developments in the late 1950s contributed to this ideological sea change in the way liberals and the Left viewed unions and their relationship to management. First, it became clear that the economy was entering a new period of structural change and dislocation. Pluralism has always been an ideology of relative social and economic stasis. Its claims have been most persuasive during those eras when classes and interests seemed stable, if not stolid. But American society was entering a new era of flux, and the recession of 1957–59, the deepest in two decades, demonstrated that postwar capitalism was hardly on automatic pilot. A self-governing equilibrium between capital and labor was hardly sufficient to make the economy function with fairness or efficiency. The recession, moreover, hit hardest in the highly unionized industrial belt that stretched from Boston to Minneapolis. In Detroit, Pittsburgh, and Chicago, where pluralist bargaining arrangements were most highly developed, they generated no solution to the wave of plant closings that swept the heartland.

The second development was the emergence of the civil rights movement, which set a new and higher standard for those who claimed to speak for the underdog. Pluralism, industrial or otherwise, celebrated interest group aggrandizement and modulated bargaining. But "the movement," as its partisans fondly called it, spotlighted those aspects of the racial, economic order that were decidedly resistant to pluralist bargaining pressures. For the post-Depression liberals, incremental social change had been the best that could be expected. In contrast, the civil rights movement of the late 1950s and first half of the 1960s stirred the social imagination, evoking a transcendent universalism that would animate a new epoch in the American democratic pageant.

Finally, there were the McClellan Committee hearings of 1957 and 1958, which had a devastating impact on the moral standing of the entire trade union world. These celebrated corruption hearings exposed the dark underside of those trade unions that conformed most closely to key elements of the pluralist ideal. The unions which had rejected ideological influences and which adhered most self-consciously to an interest group model of political and economic action were those that seemed most tainted by illegal and undemocratic self-aggrandizement on the part of their officials.

The hearings chaired by Senator John McClellan opened the door to both liberal defection and right-wing attack. They marked a true shift in the public perception of American trade unionism and the collective bargaining system within which it was embedded. Most of the distinctions between mob-connected criminality, autocratic leadership, hard bargaining, and industry-wide negotiating strength were purposefully lost on those who saw the labor corruption scandals of the 1950s as an opportunity to discredit the labor movement. The atmosphere in which the McClellan Committee was created in 1957 was alive with denunciations of big labor's overweening power. Echoing the attack on industry-wide bargaining long offered by the National Association of Manufacturers, a 1956 editorial in the *Wall Street Journal* found the "connection between crime and the wide-ranging power of unions" hardly coincidental and concluded that "when one man can determine whether a million or more men all over the country are to eat or starve, there has been set up a situation ripe for every kind of corruption all down the line."[31]

Spurred on by Chief Counsel Robert Kennedy, whose initial ignorance about all things working-class was increasingly characteristic of liberalism in this period, the committee cast Teamster president Jimmy Hoffa in the image of a larger-than-life icon whose combative persona soon made him the nation's most famous union leader. Institutionally, the International Brotherhood of Teamsters was precisely the kind of union the proponents of Taft-Hartley had hoped to encourage: decentralized, insular, and self-interested. Politically, Hoffa stood in near-perfect agreement with his conservative GOP interrogators; he would have no truck with liberal social movement unionism. But as a symbolic target the combative Teamster "boss" proved a perfect foil for a new effort to discredit union power.[32] Indeed, the McClellan Committee deliberations proved a turning point in the moral history of American unionism. In a Gallup poll, pro-union sentiment had reached 76 percent, an all-time high, in February 1957, just before the hearings began. Thereafter, it dropped steadily, reaching 50 percent in the mid-1960s and dropping even lower in subsequent decades.[33]

From this point onward it would no longer be possible for a new generation of radicals—Harvey Swados, Michael Harrington, and Tom Hayden among them—to put the trade unions at the center of their moral, democratic imagination. Although Harvey Swados had been schooled in the politics of the anti-Stalinist Left, his work prefigured New Left themes when, in 1957, he published *On the Line,* a bleak series of interconnected short stories that recounted the despair and dehumanization he encountered during a year of night-shift work in a Ford assembly plant.[34] Swados was not interested in measuring either workers or their unions by the yardstick of Bell or Mills. It was not their relationship to socialism that provoked Swados, the collaboration of the trade unions in the cold war, or even the persistence of economic inequality. Rather, Swados took the dignity and meaning of work as his touchstone, and with it the continuing reality of class in American life. Swados decried "the myth of the happy worker," arguing that "the plain truth is that factory work is degrading" and that "it is about time we faced the fact."[35]

Michael Harrington always defined himself as a pro-labor socialist, but *The Other America,* his influential 1962 rediscovery of the nation's poor, avoided any mention of socialism and kept the author's Marxism well hidden. Instead, Harrington advertised his youthful links to the Catholic Worker movement in order to appeal to the guilt of middle-class liberals and their Kennedyesque leaders. Although he praised the labor movement, unionization was not a solution, nor did pluralist democracy offer much of a way out. "The dispossessed at the bottom of society are unable to speak for themselves," wrote Harrington. "The people of the other America do not, by far and large, belong to unions, to fraternal organizations, or to political parties. They are without lobbies of their own; they put forward no legislative program." Since they had no voice or interest representation, the government could not be a passive referee but would have to step forward itself.[36]

Here was a new way—or rather a renewed way—of thinking about the old labor question. Swados and Harrington were framing the moral dichotomies that so powerfully shaped the discourse of the sixties. In the 1962 Port Huron Statement, Tom Hayden, who had grown up in a working-class suburb of Detroit, also indicted the unions, but not for a failure to build socialism. Instead, the problem was their incapacity to confront the problems of automation, joblessness, world peace, and the "Negro revolution." Hayden was actually far more hopeful about the unions than was Mills, Harrington, or Swados. At the very least, a "revitalization of the labor movement" was in his indictment, in the Port Huron Statement, of a "labor bureaucracy . . . cynical . . . and afraid of rank-and-file involvement in the work of the union."[37]

Thus, by 1963, when Swados published his famous essay "The

UAW—Over the Top or Over the Hill?," the critique of the nation's most progressive and powerful union had turned acerbic. The alienation, humiliation, and speedup experienced by automobile workers were seen less as the product of industrial life itself than of the UAW's failure to fulfill the aspirations of its founding generation. In a critique of the Reuther circle that the next generation of New Leftists would extend to other labor liberals, Swados declared that manipulation had replaced mobilization of the membership: bureaucracy had triumphed over locally initiated activism. "One cannot complain, as one might with almost any other union, of an absence of intellect," wrote Swados in *Dissent*. "What one can say, I think with justification, is that the UAW leadership no longer takes its own demands seriously."[38]

This left-wing disillusionment with the unions and with the whole structure of collective bargaining became pervasive throughout liberal political culture in the years after 1958. Pluralism's ideological architecture, in social thought, judicial opinion, and popular sentiment, became increasingly attenuated. Many liberals adopted views once held by those on the left, while the hard, antiunion Right, making good use of this critique, became increasingly vocal and aggressive. Of course, some industrial pluralists still advanced the old faith, but their audience was largely confined to the band of technocratic scholars and practitioners huddling within the embattled domain called "industrial relations." Mainstream political scientists such as E. E. Schattschneider, Theodore Lowi, and even Robert Dahl effectively deconstructed pluralism's democratic presumption. As Schattschneider put it as early as 1960, "The flaw in the pluralist heaven is that the heavenly chorus sings with a strong upper-class accent."[39]

The Demise of Industrial Pluralism

Such a critique, along with the sordid atmospherics generated by the union corruption hearings, were soon reflected throughout mainstream journalism and scholarship. There was initially a great sense of disappointment and disillusionment. Sumner Slichter, who a decade before had declared the United States a "laboristic society," in 1958 wrote that "in spite of their brilliant success, trade unions are suffering a great loss of prestige and moral influence."[40] Paul Jacobs, who had once helped purge the unions of their communist element, now won a hearing in

Commentary for a critique that bemoaned, rather than celebrated, the "inevitable current moving the trade unions toward bureaucratization and oligarchy." The culprit was the governmental effort "to maintain the kind of stable, responsible labor leadership which promotes harmony in labor-management relations."[41] When asked five years later to write an assessment of unionism for the Center for the Study of Democratic Institutions, Jacobs dolefully titled it "Old before Its Time: Collective Bargaining at Twenty-Eight."[42]

In one article after another, A. H. Raskin of the *New York Times* turned this critique into the common wisdom. Their titles tell the tale: "The Moral Issue That Confronts Labor," "New Issue: Labor as Big Business," and "Labor's Time of Troubles: The Failure of Bread-and-Butter Unionism." In "The Obsolescent Unions," published in 1963, he declared that automation, government incomes policy, and a transformation in the class structure made for an "inevitable withering of union strength." Forces beyond its control hurled labor "inexorably into obsolescence."[43] A similarly despondent cry came from Herbert Harris, who wrote in *Harper's Weekly* that labor had "lost the intellectuals" because "the American labor movement is sleepwalking along the corridors of history."[44]

Meanwhile, the idea of an industrial pluralism came under direct ideological assault, even from those who had been its most influential proponents. In 1956, Daniel Bell had denounced C. Wright Mills's *The Power Elite*, which was a radical assault on the democratic presumption inherent in pluralist polyarchial theory. But just a few years later, Bell's labor journalism began to echo themes first put forward by Mills himself. The giant 1959 steel strike was fought over the kind of job control issues that had motivated steelworkers since the 1890s, but Bell saw it as little more than a sham battle, useful so that the steel industry could "administer" a higher price schedule. "The desiccated language of collective bargaining is a trap," wrote Bell, "its syntax too constricting, its images too mechanical." It was no longer "an instrumentality for economic and social justice." Instead, collective bargaining had been subverted by both the corporation and the union, whose "interest in getting higher wages makes it become a partner in a collusive enterprise which strong-arms the rest of the community."[45]

John Kenneth Galbraith, whose influence among American liberals was then reaching its apogee, advanced much of the same cynicism in the

1960s. When Galbraith published *American Capitalism: The Theory of Countervailing Power* in 1952, his views lay entirely within a pluralist framework. He then argued that "the operation of countervailing power is to be seen with the greatest clarity in the labor market where it is also most fully developed." Fifteen years later, however, when *The New Industrial State* appeared, Galbraith had shifted toward the neo-Weberianism of Daniel Bell and Clark Kerr, if not that of C. Wright Mills. "The union belongs to a particular stage in the development of the industrial system," wrote Galbraith in his most ideologically ambitious book. "When that stage passes so does the union in anything like its original position of power." Obviously, argued Galbraith, that time had come, because in the modern "industrial system" (a term he now preferred to "capitalism"), the labor movement had lost many of its most important functions. Indeed, it now served the "technostructure" largely as a price-setting and industry-wide planning mechanism. The interests of unions and corporations were concordant. "Since World War II," Galbraith continued, "the acceptance of the union by the industrial firm and the emergence thereafter of an era of comparatively peaceful industrial relations have been hailed as the final triumph of trade unionism. On closer examination it is seen to reveal many of the features of Jonah's triumph over the whale."[46]

Soon those coming of age during the Vietnam era made their own powerful contribution to the devaluation of the trade union idea, even as the New Left made a "turn to the working class" after 1969.[47] Yet another new generation of critical intellectuals linked a systemic, neo-Weberian critique, similar to that of Mills, with the kind of rank-and-file issues that Swados and other critics of working-class alienation had moved into the spotlight. But New Leftists infused their critique of corporate power, routinized work, union bureaucracy, and the racism and sexism endemic to working-class culture, with a sense of the agency and insurgency they had earlier glimpsed in the civil rights and antiwar movements. There was plenty of cooperation between the New Left and such unions as Hospital Workers Local 1199, the American Federation of State, County, and Municipal Employees, the United Electrical Workers, and the United Farm Workers.[48]

But this process of generational interpenetration—as great as any since the Great Depression—did little to temper the critique offered by the young intellectuals and academics whose New Left voices were becoming so influential. Stanley Aronowitz, for example, argued that the modern labor agreement is the essence of "class collaboration" dismissing the union as "chiefly a force for integrating the workers into the corporate capitalist system."[49] Likewise, Alice and Staughton Lynd thought contemporary trade unions "have become a new kind of company union, financially independent of the rank and file because the company deducts union dues from the worker's pay check, and politically all-powerful because the contract takes away from rank and filers the right to strike."[50]

In *Strike!*, a book that emerged from the Students for a Democratic Society rediscovery of the class struggle, Jeremy Brecher celebrated a labor history in which "the main actors in the story are ordinary working people," whose battles against capital and the state were stymied by "unions and labor leaders [that] have most often striven to prevent or contain them."[51] Finally, Mike Davis circled back to a position not entirely different from that of Daniel Bell. By the late 1970s and early 1980s, his essays in the *New Left Review*, which would find their way into *Prisoners of the American Dream*, had abandoned even a workerist perspective on American labor, largely because of what he saw as the Reaganite success in institutionalizing a set of debilitating racial polarities within the working class. "The unions," he wrote, "have closed in around the laager of the seniority system, abandoning the unemployed, betraying the trust of working-class communities, and treating young workers as expendable pawns." Unions in the United States, concluded Davis, were "abandoning the majority of the American working class."[52]

Rights Consciousness

The rise of a dynamic, morally incisive civil rights movement ratified this shift in consciousness among both liberals and those who stood to their left. The summer of 1963 may have been the moment in the twentieth-century history of American reform when the discourse of liberalism shifted decisively out of the New Deal–labor orbit and into a world in which the racial divide colored all politics. In the great political opening that followed the Birmingham demonstrations, a legal-administrative template derived from the World War II–era Fair Employment Practices Committee was rolled into the 1964 civil rights law as Title VII. The

AFL-CIO supported the then-radical inclusion, but this injection of a racial (and later a gender-based) egalitarianism into the world of work was modeled not on the struggles of the labor movement—and certainly not on any pluralist quest for equilibrium—but on the strategic vision and legal innovations of the movement for African American civil rights. From this point onward, the most legitimate, though not necessarily the most potent, defense of American job rights would be found not through collective initiative, as codified in the Wagner Act and advanced by the unions, but through an individual's claim to his or her civil rights based on race, gender, age, or other attribute. If a new set of work rights was to be won, the decisive battles would take place not in the union hall or across the bargaining table but in courts and legislatures.

Until the mid-1960s, it had seemed as if the unions, the civil rights forces, and most judicial liberals were marching in tandem. A. Philip Randolph's plan for the 1963 March on Washington included a dramatic, pro-union reform of the labor law and a doubling of the minimum wage. A popular placard at the August 1963 march pithily asserted "Civil Rights + Full Employment = Freedom."[53] Indeed, the 1964 civil rights law was an authentically radical piece of social legislation, fully comparable to the Wagner Act in its intrusive, democratizing impact. Like the Wagner Act, it brought the power of the central government to bear on recalcitrant employers, as well as other managers of property, in order to make real the citizenship rights of those heretofore excluded and subordinate.

The law had a huge impact in the South, where patterns of Jim Crow segregation and discrimination had structured the world of African American labor for more than three generations. In southern textiles, still the manufacturing industry that employed the most workers, black employment jumped from about 6 percent to more than 25 percent in little more than a decade. In South Carolina, the black proportion of all millworkers soared from one in twenty to one in three. Segregated water fountains, time clocks, bathrooms, and dining tables were abolished. African Americans won new and better jobs throughout much of the factory hierarchy, and they called their supervisors by their first names, just like their white coworkers. Historian Gavin Wright declared the impact of Title VII a "genuine revolution" within this mainstay of the southern economy.[54]

Like the Wagner Act, Title VII generated a wave of working-class empowerment and self-organization. Before passage of the law, "we had no leg to stand on," reported a black worker. "It was difficult to do anything . . . you were scared to talk." But as workers became alive to the impact of the law, they clamored for redress. The National Association for the Advancement of Colored People (NAACP) filed numerous class action lawsuits, demanding nondiscriminatory hiring, promotion into heretofore "white" jobs, and equal and better pay. These suits generated a tangible social/political fission, not all that different from a CIO unionizing campaign in Depression-era America. As in the 1930s, once-deferential workers organized to bring their grievances and complaints to the attention of those whose knowledge of law, politics, and corporate personnel policy was essential to make effective use of the new legislation. In the late 1930s, these had been radical CIO organizers; in the late 1960s, they were often movement-oriented lawyers.[55]

This sense of rights consciousness generated a powerful impulse for the union struggle in the South. In the 1940s when southern bourbons wanted to discredit the labor movement in their region, they denounced it as a racially, politically subversive institution that strayed well beyond its role as a collective bargaining organization. Southern unions, especially African American unions, were illegitimate not because they sought collective bargaining but because they sought to transform the social structure of the South.[56] But twenty years later, the rights revolution had thoroughly transformed the ideological landscape. In Memphis, Charlestown, Danville, and Durham, union organizers cast their struggle almost entirely in terms of the civil rights movement of that era. In Charlestown, for example, Hospital Workers Local 1199B gave de facto leadership of a 1969 struggle to Andrew Young and other Southern Christian Leadership Council leaders, who put the tactics, values, and language of the civil rights movement on full and disruptive display. Conversely, South Carolina's conservative elite insisted that the conflict in the Charlestown hospitals was a question of old-fashioned trade unionism, not civil rights. State officials did not resort to the brutal tactics Sheriff Bull Connor deployed half a decade earlier in Birmingham, nor did South Carolina conservatives red-bait or race-bait the civil rights activists. Instead, they insisted that the absence of a state collective bargaining law made the effort to unionize illegal and futile. Thus, the

South Carolina governing class capitalized on the eclipse into which the union idea had fallen, while paying a backhanded tribute to the power of a rights-conscious social movement.

Indeed, rights consciousness transcended most of the usual demographic and occupational barriers. It spread to almost every segment of society, to nearly every stratum and faction. Between 1967 and 1973, workplace turmoil—black and white, public employee or private— reached levels not seen since the mid-1940s. "All authority in our society is being challenged," announced the 1973 Department of Health, Education, and Welfare report *Work in America*. "Professional athletes challenge owners, journalists challenge editors, consumers challenge manufacturers . . . and young blue-collar workers, who have grown up in an environment in which equality is called for in all institutions, are demanding the same rights and expressing the same values as university students."[57]

The legislative promulgation or judicial affirmation of workplace rights encompassing the gender, sexual orientation, age, disability, and parenthood of employees soon put a new and expanded conception of social citizenship on the employment agenda. Title VII of the 1964 Civil Rights Act therefore stands with the Wagner Act as a pillar on which the world of work has been reshaped in the twentieth century. Within just a few years, the Equal Employment Opportunity Commission (EEOC) became an even more high-profile agency than the National Labor Relations Board, and the judicial interpretation of Title VII became every bit as important and controversial as any Supreme Court labor law ruling. Unlike the Wagner Act, whose legitimacy and scope had quickly come under employer attack and judicial constraint, Title VII opened the floodgates to a series of new laws, labeled "civil rights," though actually central to the expansion of work rights within the realm of factory, office, mine, and salesroom.

The list of such legislation is quite remarkable. In 1968 came the Age Discrimination in Employment Act, in 1969 the Mine Safety Act, in 1970 the Occupational Safety and Health Act, in 1973 the Rehabilitation Act, in 1974 the Employee Retirement Income Security Act, and in 1978 the Pregnancy Discrimination Act. After a hiatus during the Reagan years, more "labor legislation" appeared: the Americans with Disabilities Act in 1990 and the Family and Medical Leave Act of 1993. Meanwhile, the EEOC expanded its authority and jurisdiction even during the period in which Republican presidents held the White House. Although highly contested, issues that encompassed the hiring, pay, promotion, and layoff of employees became subject to governmental review and private litigation to an extent the union movement could not match even in the heyday of the Wagner Act. The unfolding of a feminist consciousness within the workplace generated laws covering areas of interpersonal relations and employer-employee contact once considered exclusively private.[58]

Organized labor stood on the winning side when this social legislation made it into the statute books, but in the 1960s and afterward, American unions were unable to make the rights revolution work for them. In health care employment, in the teaching professions, and in some service trades, the civil rights impulse did merge with and advance the union cause. But for most of U.S. labor, especially that centered in the private sector, rights consciousness, which has revolutionized race and gender relations, has had little organizational payoff. Indeed, if one looks at the timing and the numbers, an inverse relationship may well link the decline of unionism and the rise of 1960s–70s rights consciousness.

The declining reputation of the unions, the decay of industrial pluralism, and the rise of a new discourse of rights eroded the legal status and devalued the meaning of the trade union idea. Labor's reliance on procedural mechanisms designed to generate a pluralistic industrial democracy came to seem far less potent and universal than the rights discourse generated by the state's conception of substantive justice and equal protection under the law. Rights are universal and individual, which means that employers and individual members of management enjoy them as much as workers do. Under a regime of rights, it becomes very difficult to privilege a trade union as an institution that stands apart from its membership.

In American law and political culture a discourse of rights has subverted the very idea, and the institutional expression, of union solidarity. Solidarity is not just a song or a sentiment but requires a measure of coercion that can enforce the social bond when not all members of the organization are in full agreement. In recent decades, employer antiunionism has become increasingly oriented toward the ostensible protection of the individual rights of workers as against undemocratic unions and restrictive contracts that hamper the free choice of employees. This began in the aftermath of the McClellan Committee hearings when a coalition of antiunion forces from the Democratic South and the Republican North inserted a rank-and-file "bill of rights" into the 1959 Landrum-Griffin Law. At the same time, the National Right-to-Work Committee, initially funded by southern textile interests, became adept at making use of the new rights language, civil libertarian if not actually that of the civil rights movement, to perforate union solidarity and discredit the union idea. The Right-to-Work Committee declared that the NAACP "prostituted" itself when the organization allied itself with the AFL-CIO legislative agenda. Because of its "marriage of convenience to monopolistic labor unions," asserted a committee official, the NAACP's "first priority goes not to restricting union racial discrimination, but to striking down all state laws against compulsory unionism."[59]

A further counterposition between the "rights" of workers and the potency of the union idea has arisen from a series of judicial decisions that privilege an extremely individualistic conception of worker rights, which differentiates between the economic and political rights of an individual worker. As early as 1961, Hugo Black, one of the Supreme Court's most aggressive civil libertarians, argued that any attempt to make a dissenting unionist contribute to the political funds of his organization was "extortion" that government had "no . . . power to enforce." Right-wing, antiunion forces soon took this species of rights liberalism and threw it back at labor in an effort to strip unions of any right to use employee dues money to endorse political candidates, mobilize their membership for a particular cause, or lobby Congress or the state legislatures.[60]

Given the evolution of the rights discourse in the United States, it is not surprising that courts have questioned the meaning of industrial solidarity itself, even in crucial strike situations. In its 1972 *Granite State* decision, for example, the Supreme Court held that workers have the right to resign their membership in the midst of a strike and then scab on their workmates free from the disciplinary penalties sought by their former union associates. "When there is a lawful dissolution of a union-member relation," the Court said, "the union has no more control over the former member than it has over the man in the street." On legal historian David Abraham's reading of this "right to resign" doctrine, the Court, once again led by its most liberal members, subverted the legal and ethical basis of collective solidarity in favor of an "abstract and atomistic conception of our society." Liberal jurists have been sensitive to the rights of dissident workers because of the often well-grounded assumption that unions are less than democratic. But liberal sensitivity on this score transformed the meaning of solidarity into a coercive set of legal/administrative pressures that merely trampled on the work rights of the individual former unionist, which was not far distant from the views promulgated by the antiunion Right.[61]

This rights-based undermining of the solidarity principle was accompanied by a perverse calcification of the industrial pluralist idea that drastically narrowed the power of unions to strike. In the 1960s, the Supreme Court severely restricted the right of a union and its workers to take part in unofficial job actions or in wildcat strikes. Indeed, the courts ruled "self-help" illegal when undertaken outside the scope of the union's grievance procedure or its system of industrial arbitration. A series of decisions, almost all written by the most liberal Supreme Court justices, institutionalized collective bargaining, but only under conditions that narrowly channeled and utterly bureaucratized the functions trade unions could perform for their members. In the 1960 *Lucas Flower* case, for example, the Supreme Court insisted that the mere presence of an arbitration clause in a collective bargaining contract meant that the union had waived its otherwise statutorily protected right to strike over grievances. In the *Boys Market* decision of 1970, the high court made virtually all work stoppages illegal during the term of a contract and in the process legitimized the usage of labor injunctions like those that had crippled the union movement during the nineteenth century.[62]

Restrictive reinterpretations of the scope of collective bargaining further undercut the potency and appeal of American trade unionism. During the very same season in which Congress passed the 1964 Civil Rights Act, the Supreme Court questioned, in its ostensibly pro-union *Fibreboard* decision, whether trade unions had the right to bargain over such issues as production planning, price schedules, and investment decisions, which lie "at the core of entrepreneurial control." By 1980, in *First National Maintenance Corporation*, the Supreme Court had made up its mind, ruling that companies have no obligation to bargain over—or even to provide advance notice of—the closure of part of their operations. The Court's position was that "the harm likely to be done to an employer's need to operate freely in deciding whether to shut down part of his business for purely economic reasons outweighs the incremental benefit that might be gained through the union's participation in making the decision."[63]

By the end of the twentieth century, the same species of rights-conscious liberalism that had abolished racial segregation, ended McCarthyism, and legalized women's rights had also undermined the ideological and legal bases of American trade unionism. This devaluation of the union idea has had two devastating aspects. To the extent that the courts continue to honor an outmoded set of pluralist assumptions governing the presumptively equal, insulated bargaining power of unions and their corporate adversaries, they generated a false equality between labor and capital. Because of corporate mobility, as well as the insulation of so many management prerogatives from the union's bargaining reach, this equation is inherently biased against the unions. The liberal effort to shoehorn labor's interests into this untenable legal system put the union impulse in an increasingly unworkable structure, while offering capital new weapons with which to marginalize its adversaries. Indeed, the failure of pluralist ideology within the realm of capital-labor conflict, which is where it first staked its most crucial claims, has discredited the idea that pluralism is much of a guide to an understanding of the dynamics of the rest of American society, during the 1960s or afterward. Although these stale pluralist constructs still find some proponents on the academic center-right, they have lost political and ideological traction everywhere else. Thus, as both the courts and popular opinion have privileged a rights-based model of industrial justice, the unions have lost their capacity to command the loyalty of their memberships, on which their strength depends. Individualistic, rights-based assumptions replaced group pluralist ones and turned solidarity into a quaint and antique notion. American labor not only missed the 1960s but also found its birthright subverted by the ideological politics of that tumultuous era.[64]

Notes

1. Bruce Nissen, "A Post–World War II 'Social Accord'?" in *U.S. Labor Relations, 1945–1989: Accommodation and Conflict,* ed. Bruce Nissen (New York: Garland Publishing, 1990), 174–79; Kim Moody, *An Injury to All: The Decline of American Unionism* (London: Verso, 1988), 24–40; Joel Rogers, "In the Shadow of the Law: Institutional Aspects of Postwar U.S. Union Decline," in *Labor Law in America,* ed. Christopher Tomlins and Andrew King, 283–302

(Baltimore: Johns Hopkins University Press, 1992); Kevin Boyle, *The UAW and the Heyday of American Liberalism, 1945–68* (Ithaca: Cornell University Press, 1995); and see also Nelson Lichtenstein, *State of the Union: A Century of American Labor* (Princeton: Princeton University Press, 2002), 98–140.

2. C. Wright Mills, *The Marxists* (New York: Delta Books, 1963), 128; Clark Kerr and Abraham Siegel, "The Structuring of the Labor Force in Industrial Society: New Dimensions and New Questions," *Industrial and Labor Relations Review* 8 (January 1955): 115.

3. Paul Jacobs, "Old before Its Time: Collective Bargaining at Twenty-Eight," in *The State of the Unions* (New York: Atheneum, 1963), 257–93; Richard Lester, *As Unions Mature: An Analysis of the Evolution of American Unionism* (Princeton: Princeton University Press, 1958).

4. Joel Rogers, "Divide and Conquer: Further 'Reflections on the Distinctive Character of American Labor Laws,'" *Wisconsin Law Review* 1 (1990): 57–59.

5. Seymour Martin Lipset, *The First New Nation: The United States in Historical and Comparative Perspective* (New York: W. W. Norton, 1979), 191–96.

6. Moody, *An Injury to All*, 41–69, 147–64; John Hutchinson, *The Imperfect Union: A History of Corruption in American Trade Unions* (New York: Dutton, 1970).

7. Arthur Kornhauser, *When Labor Votes: A Study of the Auto Workers* (New York: University Books, 1956), 19; Samuel Lubell, *The Future of American Politics* (Garden City, N.Y.: Doubleday, 1956), 229.

8. V. O. Key quoted in Rogers, "Divide and Conquer," 60.

9. Brandeis quoted in William Forbath, "Caste, Class, and Equal Citizenship," *Michigan Law Review* 98 (October 1999): 57. For an elaboration or some of these themes, see Gary Gerstle, "Ideas of the American Labor Movement, 1880–1950," in *Ideas, Ideologies, and Social Movements: The U.S. Experience since 1800*, ed. Stuart Bruchey and Peter Cocanis (Columbia: University of South Carolina Press, 1998).

10. Wagner quoted in Forbath, "Caste, Class, and Equal Citizenship," 11, 58; Harry Shulman, "Reason, Contract, and Law in Labor Relations," *Harvard Law Review* 68 (1955): 1002.

11. Robert Dublin, "Constructive Aspects of Industrial Conflict," 44, and Arthur Ross, "Conclusion," 532, both in *Industrial Conflict*, ed. Arthur Kornhauser, Robert Dublin, and Arthur Ross (New York: McGraw-Hill, 1954).

12. Daniel Bell, *The End of Ideology: On the Exhaustion of Political Ideas in the Fifties* (New York: Free Press, 1960), 300; Robert Dahl, "Workers' Control of Industry and the British Labor Party," *American Political Science Review* 41 (October 1947): 875–900.

13. Robert Booth Fowler, *Believing Skeptics: American Political Intellectuals, 1945–1964* (Westport: Greenwood Press, 1978), 176–86; Lipset quoted in Richard Pells, *The Liberal Mind in a Conservative Age: American Intellectuals in the 1940s and 1950s* (New York: Harper and Row, 1985), 141.

14. Peter Drucker, *The Practice of Management* (New York: Harper and Brothers, 1954), 3, 381–82; all Drucker quotations taken from Peter Drucker,

The Concept of the Corporation (1946; reprint, New York: John Day, 1972), 8, 12; Stephen Waring, *Taylorism Transformed: Scientific Management Theory since 1945* (Chapel Hill: University of North Carolina Press, 1991), 79–88. Of course, the executives and spokesmen for big business did not share Drucker's sanguine narrative. Alfred Sloan and other GM executives repudiated Drucker's study as "hostile" and "anti-business." See Drucker's epilogue in the 1972 reprint of *The Concept of the Corporation*, 291–310.

15. James Cochrane, *Industrialism and Industrial Man in Retrospect: A Critical Review of the Ford Foundation's Support for the Inter-University Study of Labor* (New York: Ford Foundation, 1979), 61–80.

16. Ibid., 80–95, 118–19; Clark Kerr, John T. Dunlop, Frederick Harbison, and Charles A. Myers, *Industrialism and Industrial Man* (Cambridge: Harvard University Press, 1960), 12, and see in particular chap. 3, "The Industrializing Elites and Their Strategies," 47–76, and chap. 9, "The Rule Makers and the Rules," 234–63, from which all Kerr quotations are taken. John Dunlop is generally recognized as the author of the concept of a "web of rules." See his highly influential *Industrial Relations Systems* (Cambridge: Harvard University Press, 1958). Some twelve books and twenty articles were published during the 1950s alone under the auspices of the Kerr-Dunlop Inter-University Study. Bruce E. Kaufman, *The Origins and Evolution of the Field of Industrial Relations in the United States* (Ithaca: ILR Press, 1993), 94–95.

17. Earl Latham, "The Group Basis of Politics: Notes for a Theory," *American Political Science Review* 46 (June 1952): 376–97; David Truman, "The American System in Crisis," *Political Science Quarterly* 74 (December 1959): 488.

18. As quoted in Reuel Schiller, "From Group Rights to Individual Liberties: Post-war Labor Law, Liberalism, and the Waning of Union Strength," *Berkeley Journal of Employment and Labor Law* 20 (1999): 11. These immediate postwar years were also the moment at which the cult of Alexis de Tocqueville first arose. His *Democracy in America*, which celebrated a diverse world of voluntary associations, was republished at the end of World War II. See Pells, *Liberal Mind in a Conservative Age*, 149.

19. Daniel Bell, "Taft-Hartley, Five Years Later," *Fortune*, July 1952, 69. See also Bell, *End of Ideology*, 208, 213.

20. Reinhold Niebuhr, "'End of an Era' for Organized Labor," *New Leader*, January 4, 1960, 18.

21. Dahl quoted in Fowler, *Believing Skeptics*, 178.

22. Kerr, "Unions and Union Leaders of Their Own Choosing" (1958), reprinted in Kerr, *Labor and Management in Industrial Society* (Garden City: N.Y.: Doubleday, 1964), 34. In 1955, Will Herberg would publish the pluralist classic *Protestant, Catholic, Jew*, in which he devalued the theological and cultural divide between the major denominations.

23. Seymour Martin Lipset, *Political Man: The Social Basis of Politics* (Garden City, N.Y.: Doubleday, 1960), 389, 431, 433.

24. Osar Ornati, "Union Discipline, Minority Rights, and Public Policy,"

Labor Law Journal 5 (July 1954): 473–77; "The Text of General Eisenhower's Speech at A.F.L. Convention," *New York Times*, September 18, 1952, 12.

25. As quoted in David Stebenne, *Arthur Goldberg: New Deal Liberal* (New York: Oxford University Press, 1996), 169.

26. As quoted in Melvyn Dubofsky, *The State and Labor in Modern America* (Urbana: University of Illinois Press, 1994), 213. This was the famous Steelworkers Trilogy ruling of 1960. The liberal commitment to grievance arbitration as a key element in this system of industrial self-governance therefore put them at odds both with those who advocated judicial review or new government supervision, on the one hand, and with wildcat strikers and other advocates of workplace "self-help," on the other. Staughton Lynd, "Government without Rights: The Labor Law Vision of Archibald Cox," *Industrial Relations Law Journal* 4 (1979): 483–95; Ronald Schatz, "From Commons to Dunlop: Rethinking the Field and Theory of Industrial Relations," in *Industrial Democracy in America*, ed. Nelson Lichtenstein and Howell Harris, 87–112 (New York: Cambridge University Press, 1993).

27. David J. Sousa, "'No Balance in the Equities': Union Power in the Making and Unmaking of the Campaign Finance Regime," *Studies in American Political Development* 13 (Fall 1999): 374–401.

28. Schiller, "From Group Rights to Individual Liberties," 18–29. See also Clyde Summers, "Individual Rights in Collective Agreements—a Preliminary Analysis," in *New York University Twelfth Annual Conference on Labor* (New York: New York University Press, 1959).

29. C. Wright Mills, *The New Men of Power: America's Labor Leaders* (New York: Harcourt, Brace, 1948; Urbana: University of Illinois Press, 2001), 6–7; citations are to the 1948 publication.

30. C. Wright Mills, *White Collar: The American Middle Classes* (New York: Oxford University Press, 1951), 318, 350–54.

31. As quoted in Thaddeus Russell, "Cleaning the House of Labor: The McClellan Committee and the AFL-CIO, 1956–1959" (master's thesis, Columbia University, 1992), 17.

32. I discuss this political and ideological shift in Nelson Lichtenstein, *Walter Reuther: The Most Dangerous Man in Detroit* (Urbana: University of Illinois Press, 1997), 346–50. See also David Reinhard, *The Republican Right since 1945* (Lexington: University Press of Kentucky, 1983), 138–45, and Mike Davis, *Prisoners of the American Dream* (London: Verso, 1986), 166–70.

33. Russell, "Cleaning the House of Labor," 4. Generally, see also Jean-Claude Andre, "Congress, Business, and the Postwar Decline of Labor: Rethinking the McClellan Committee, Its Origins, and Its Consequences," (master's thesis, University of Virginia, 2000), and Anthony Baltakis, "Agendas of Investigation: The McClellan Committee, 1957–1958" (Ph.D. diss., University of Akron, 1997).

34. Harvey Swados, "The Myth of the Happy Worker," reprinted in Swados, *On the Line* (Urbana: University of Illinois Press, 1990), 241–42.

35. Ibid., 243.

36. Michael Harrington, *The Other America: Poverty in the United States* (New York: Macmillan, 1962), 6; Maurice Isserman, *The Other American: The Life of Michael Harrington* (New York: Public Affairs Press, 2000), 195–98.

37. B. J. Widick, *Labor Today: The Triumphs and Failures of Unionism in the United States* (Boston: Houghton Mifflin, 1964); Port Huron Statement, quoted in James Miller, *"Democracy Is in the Streets": From Port Huron to the Siege of Chicago* (New York: Simon and Schuster, 1987), 370.

38. Harvey Swados, "The UAW—Over the Top or Over the Hill?" *Dissent*, Fall 1963, 321–43.

39. E. E. Schattschneider, *The Semisovereign People: A Realist's View of Democracy in America* (New York: Holt Rinehart, 1960), 35; Theodore Lowi, "The Public Philosophy: Interest-Group Liberalism," *American Political Science Review* 61 (March 1967): 5–24; Schatz, "From Commons to Dunlop," 105–12; Kaufman, *Origins and Evolution of the Field of Industrial Relations* (Ithaca: ILR Press, 1993), 103–55.

40. Sumner Slichter, "Are We Becoming a 'Laboristic' State?" *New York Times Magazine*, May 16, 1948, 11, 61–66; Slichter, "New Goals for the Unions," *Atlantic Monthly*, December 1958, 54.

41. Paul Jacobs, "Union Democracy and the Public Good," *Commentary*, January 1958, 74.

42. Jacobs, "Old before Its Time."

43. A. H. Raskin, "The Moral Issue That Confronts Labor," *New York Times Magazine*, March 31, 1957, 17–23; Raskin, "New Issue: Labor as Big Business," *New York Times Magazine*, February 22, 1959, 9, 69–72; Raskin, "Labor's Time of Troubles: The Failure of Bread-and-Butter Unionism," *Commentary*, August 1959, 93–99; Raskin, "The Obsolescent Unions," *Commentary*, July 1963, 18.

44. Herbert Harris, "Why Labor Lost the Intellectuals," *Harper's Weekly*, June 1964, 79.

45. Daniel Bell, "The Subversion of Collective Bargaining," *Commentary*, March 1960, 185, 195.

46. John Kenneth Galbraith, *American Capitalism: The Theory of Countervailing Power* (Boston: Houghton Mifflin, 1952), 114; Galbraith, *The New Industrial State* (Boston: Houghton Mifflin, 1967), 263–64, 274, 280–81.

47. Peter Levy, *The New Left and Labor in the 1960s* (Urbana: University of Illinois Press, 1994), 108–21. Mills was by now uncompromising in his rejection of the "labor metaphysic." In *The Marxists*, his last book, Mills declared, "Wage workers in advanced capitalism have rarely become a 'proletariat vanguard,' they have not become the agency of any revolutionary change of epoch" (*The Marxists* [New York: Delta Books, 1963], 128).

48. Levy, *The New Left and Labor*, 147–66.

49. Stanley Aronowitz "Trade Unionism in America," *Liberation*, December 1971, 27.

50. Alice Lynd and Staughton Lynd, *Rank and File: Personal Histories by Working-Class Organizers* (Boston: Beacon, 1973), 3–4.

51. Jeremy Brecher, *Strike!* (New York: Fawcett, 1972), 10. Even Burton

Hall, the veteran union democracy watchdog, who should have understood something of the dialectical relationship between union organization and rank-and-file insurgency, edited a 1972 collection titled *Autocracy and Insurgency in Organized Labor*. His main theme was that which Sylvia Kopaid first described in 1924 as "this amazing separation that exists between union leaders and union rank and file," an actual "class struggle" between leaders and those they presume to lead. See Burton Hall, ed., *Autocracy and Insurgency in Organized Labor* (New York: New Politics, 1972); Kopaid is quoted on page 2.

52. Davis, *Prisoners of the American Dream*, 153.

53. As quoted in William E. Forbath, "Why Is This Rights Talk Different from All Other Rights Talk? Demoting the Court and Reimagining the Constitution," *Stanford Law Review* 46 (July 1994): 1804.

54. Timothy Minchin, *Hiring the Black Worker: Racial Integration of the Southern Textile Industry, 1960–1980* (Chapel Hill: University of North Carolina Press, 1999), 3.

55. Ibid., 57.

56. Michael Honey, *Black Workers Remember: An Oral History of Segregation, Unionism, and the Freedom Struggle* (Berkeley: University of California Press, 1999), 213–36.

57. Department of Health, Education, and Welfare, *Work in America* (Cambridge: MIT Press, 1973), 49; see also Robert Ellis Smith, *Workrights* (New York: E. P. Dutton, 1983).

58. Sally Kenney, *For Whose Protection? Reproductive Hazards and Exclusionary Policies in the United States and Britain* (Ann Arbor: University of Michigan Press, 1992), 139–84; Vicki Schultz, "Reconceptualizing Sexual Harassment," *Yale Law Journal* 107 (1998): 1683–1805; and Gwendolyn Mink, *Hostile Environment: The Political Betrayal of Sexually Harassed Women* (Ithaca: Cornell University Press, 2000).

59. Dubofsky, *The State and Labor in Modern America*, 220–21; Right-to-Work Committee quoted in Reed Larson, "Is Monopoly in the American Tradition?" *Vital Speeches of the Day* 39 (June 15, 1973): 527–28.

60. Reuel Schiller, "Policy Ideals and Judicial Action: Expertise, Group Pluralism, and Participatory Democracy in Intellectual Thought and Legal Decision-Making, 1932–1970" (Ph.D. diss., University of Virginia, 1997), 328.

61. David Abraham, "Individual Autonomy and Collective Empowerment in Labor Law: Union Membership Resignations and Strikebreaking in the New Economy," *New York University Law Review* 63 (December 1988): 1281, 1314–23.

62. Katherine Van Wezel Stone, "The Post-war Paradigm in American Labor Law," *Yale Law Journal* 90 (June 1981): 1533–34; Christopher Tomlins, *The State and the Unions: Labor Relations, Law, and the Organized Labor Movement in America, 1880–1960* (New York: Cambridge University Press, 1985), 314–28; Staughton Lynd, "The Right to Engage in Concerted Activity after Union Recognition: A Study of Legislative History," *Indiana Law Journal* 50 (1974–75): 720–56.

63. James Atleson, *Values and Assumptions in American Labor Law* (Amherst: University of Massachusetts Press, 1983), 124–30, 130–32; Paul C. Weiler, *Governing the Workplace: The Future of Labor and Employment Law* (Cambridge: Harvard University Press, 1990), 1–48.

64. Schiller, "Policy Ideals and Judicial Action," 179.

Contested Rights

The Great Society between Home and Work

Eileen Boris

The proper relation between wage earning and family labor has stood at the center of a century-long debate over public assistance for those in need. A set of binaries has framed this discussion. Do public or private efforts sap initiative or alleviate suffering? Will marriage or economic independence relieve the poverty of single mothers and their children? Must mothers of preschool children be forced into the labor market, or can they stay home? Should charity or welfare be available only to worthy widows or women with incapacitated husbands and withheld from those without "suitable homes" or with out-of-wedlock pregnancies?

The Great Society of the 1960s faced these questions in the midst of changing expectations about women, work, and motherhood that were racialized as well as a product of both labor market demands and the aspirations of women. In grappling with the persistence of poverty amid affluence, it embodied prior policy assumptions about good homes and families, even as it reinforced emerging understandings of employment as the norm for full citizenship for women as well as men, for mothers of small children as well as other women. It looked backward to the New Deal but extended ideals of male breadwinners and female homemakers to black as well as white family life. Yet in apparent contradiction, the Great Society also embraced the movement of women of all groups into the labor force, punishing poor and black women who desired to remain at home because they could not afford to do so on their own. Initiatives grouped under the War on Poverty, initially run by the innovative Office of Economic Opportunity (OEO), crossed the boundaries between home and work, family and market, carework and waged labor. They sought to remake families through employment, provide relief through "manpower" training, and push wage labor through welfare requirements. Rather than existing in separate spheres, employment or "manpower" policy and welfare policy were interconnected. As political scientist Margaret Weir has argued, employment policy sought "to alter the supply of labor by modifying workers' characteristics rather than seeking to change the demand for labor."[1] Welfare policy, in turn, sought to fashion self-sufficiency through the labor market, not relief checks.

For those building the Great Society, economic opportunity was never dependent on the workplace alone. It would be fought through remaking the home as well. President Lyndon Baines Johnson himself recognized that the War on Poverty "must be won in . . . every private home." Launching his assault in January 1964, he claimed that "our chief weapons in a more pinpointed attack will be better schools, and better health, and better homes, and better training, and better job opportunities."[2] Failed homes, labeled as sites of broken and abnormal families and places of deprivation and blight, impeded attainment of an equal place at the starting line when it came to the competition for opportunity. So Johnson, following aide Daniel Patrick Moynihan, suggested in his 1965 Howard University commencement address, "To Fulfill These Rights": "The family [understood as the heterosexual nuclear family] is the cornerstone of our society. More than any other force it shapes the attitude, the hopes, the ambitions, and the values of the child."[3] The War on Poverty would rehabilitate families and rebuild communities in the process of providing education, training, and jobs. It promised to transform "the culture of poverty" into a culture of aspiration, if not achievement, "to fashion a world in which 'the meaning of man's life matches the marvels of man's labors,'" as OEO director Sargent Shriver reiterated Johnson's vision in the agency's first annual report in 1965.[4]

After consideration of the New Deal legacy and the overall War on Poverty, I analyze the Job Corps, a major "manpower" program, in terms of its assumptions and impact on home, family, and gender. I then turn to the better-known story of Aid to Families with Dependent Children (AFDC) or "welfare," which investment in "manpower" was to supplant, to suggest that reforms in that arena were as much about wage labor as about family. Indeed, the two realms, work and family, were—and remain—interdependent in social policy and American politics.

The New Deal Legacy: An American Welfare State

The white male breadwinner has existed at both the symbolic and policy center of America's public/private welfare regime. His labor brought social rights to the family, including pensions, health insurance, and other forms of income maintenance. The 1935 Social Security Act provided for old-age insurance, or social security; unemployment insurance; and "welfare," or Aid to Dependent Children (ADC), renamed Aid to Families with Dependent Children in 1962. It solidified this model of the citizen-worker by creating an unequal system that linked the most generous benefits to employment, but excluded agricultural and service occupations dominated by white women and men and women of color. Survivor's insurance, which came in 1939, separated single mothers into the deserving, widows whose men had contributed to the system, and the undeserving, the never-married and widows of noncontributing men, who could obtain only the less generous ADC (which was initially without a caregiver's allowance). Moreover, the benefits gained by men were federally determined and guaranteed, whereas those available to individuals outside of the primary labor market were more arbitrary as a result of their being state- and local-controlled.[5]

Labor standards—the minimum wage, maximum hour, and child labor restrictions embodied in the 1938 Fair Labor Standards Act—were similarly restricted in their reach. After 1945, some white male workers made even further gains as corporations, under pressure from strong trade unions and encouraged by favorable tax measures, offered their own systems of social insurance. Women received benefits more often through their family connection to a man, for being a wife or daughter, than for their own wage record. Like "minority" men, who disproportionately suffered from under- and unemployment, they went in and out of the labor market, worked part-time, and concentrated in workplaces uncovered by either law or union contract.[6]

Such a system doubly disadvantaged the vast majority of African American, Latina, and immigrant women who could rely on neither their men's access nor their own labor histories and thus found themselves relegated to low-waged jobs without either pensions or unemployment insurance or to stigmatized public assistance. Those without citizenship rarely gained aid; migrants from Asia, subject to immigration restriction, were prohibited from becoming citizens and were, as a result, particularly lacking any public safety net. Welfare rarely came without arbitrariness or discrimination, as "employable mother," "suitable homes," and "man in the house" rules restricted the eligibility of poor solo mothers.[7] Not until the 1960s would welfare become more of an entitlement, thanks to poverty lawyers funded by one Great Society program, Legal Services, and the protest of poor mothers themselves.[8]

Therefore, we might argue that liberalism has depended on gender division and tolerates racial distinctions. Its upholding of the private in opposition to the public reinforced the ideological basis for the separation of work from home, workers from mothers.[9] White men, through the Democratic Party and trade unions, sought to maintain the white male breadwinner as ideal worker and hence welfare state citizen. Thus this liberal state also depended on a racialized, gendered order that degendered racial minority men and women. Resulting social policy has devalued the carework or motherwork of racial minority women and denied breadwinner status to minority men, often forcing the former into the low-wage labor force and the latter out of the labor force altogether.[10]

The War on Poverty

The War on Poverty moved from a battle cry to a set of programs when Congress authorized the OEO in August 1964. As historian Gareth Davies explains, Johnson sought to enhance individual "initiative." The goal was to increase opportunity through education and training, jobs, "and the opportunity to live in decency and dignity."[11] This was no public works or relief program. Johnson assumed that Congress would refuse to allocate cash assistance to those who might support themselves but would fund programs to achieve economic self-sufficiency. Stressing "opportunity," he disassociated his war from "welfare," which by the early 1960s had become stigmatized in the public mind because of increased numbers, a shift in recipient population from white widows to African Americans and those who had never married, and reports of fraud. In urban areas, welfare had taken on a black or brown face.[12] Given this context, OEO would assist "taxeaters" to become "taxpayers."[13]

An "environmental" concept of poverty informed the new "manpower" policies. As one former administration official recalled, "If poverty could be substantially eliminated by education and training, by removing discrimination, and by a strong economy, then poverty arose from causes largely external to the poor."[14] This concern with the nation's human resources was a by-product of the cold war. Formed during the Korean conflict, the nongovernmental National Manpower Council—which included representatives from education, business, and labor—advocated long-term planning and skill development, especially in science and the professions. It worked closely with the Department of Labor (DOL), which established the Office of Manpower Administration in 1954. By the end of the decade, the DOL had begun to focus on improving apprenticeship programs and, through retraining packages, to confront unemployment that was thought to be caused by automation, especially in "depressed areas."[15] Congressional hearings on "manpower" found that "a high rate of unemployment in an otherwise relatively prosperous economy" was the "obvious symptom" of the "manpower revolution" into which the War on Poverty was born.[16]

But this structural understanding, derived from labor market analysis of geographic and technological pockets of unemployment, stood in tension with a growing body of social science that lamented the culture of poverty. The culture of poverty posited the existence of lower-class pathologies, especially among African Americans, that blocked economic and social success. These included impulsive behavior, the inability to delay gratification, and "present-time orientation." Poverty became associated with "a way of life" transmitted from one generation to the next through inadequate parenting by domineering mothers and weak, often absent fathers, who failed to earn a "family" wage large enough to support a wife and children. Over time, conservatives would embrace such descriptions of what by the 1980s was commonly called "the underclass," but twenty years earlier, liberals had considered these characteristics to be traits that their social programs could alter. Both structuralists and culturalists, however, agreed that state action could end poverty by increasing income: the former by job training and the latter by additional acculturation into white, middle-class, Protestant norms, including the work ethic, male breadwinning, and sexual restraint.[17]

The Economic Opportunity Act of 1964 created the Neighborhood Youth Corps (run by the DOL) and the Job Corps, programs to enhance the employability of teenage dropouts and potential delinquents. It authorized funds for college students under work-study programs and established Volunteers in Service to America (VISTA) as a "domestic" Peace Corps. Title II authorized the Community Action Program "to provide stimulation and incentive for urban and rural communities to mobilize their resources . . . to combat poverty," as well as the Adult Education Program to combat the illiteracy thought to lead to unemployment and dependency. Other sections focused on rural development, provided loans to small businesses, aided migrant farm labor, and formed a Work Experience Program for those on AFDC.[18]

The act also mandated the development of OEO to coordinate these programs. This was an attempt to bypass entrenched bureaucracies in the DOL and in Health, Education, and Welfare (HEW), as well as to circumvent hostile local officials. Labor secretary Willard Wirtz, for one, held that "the single immediate change which the poverty program could bring about in the lives of most of the poor would be to provide the family head with a regular, decently paid job."[19] He had wanted to incorporate any new job training into his department, where Job Corps later was relocated under Richard Nixon. Such a move may have maintained an emphasis on labor market structure over service to the needy, but it risked neglecting the special problems of the young by folding their training into the overall manpower effort. Job Corps and related programs, after all, had derived from the Kennedy administration's fight against juvenile delinquency, which sought to transform the opportunity structure open to youths for the good of society as a whole. Labor obtained the Neighborhood Youth Corps as a token, but the Job Corps went to OEO.

The Council of Economic Advisors had preferred indirect means to combat unemployment. It pushed successfully for a tax cut as a more effective device to create jobs and improve incomes, ensuring that the War on Poverty would be done on the cheap even before Vietnam drained the treasury.[20] Thus, historian Michael B. Katz explains, "by default, the War on Poverty adopted the culture of poverty."[21] That is, it sought to change workers rather than the structure of the labor market because it lacked resources for the latter. Against civil rights struggles for fair employment, equal pay, and access to jobs, it initially "ignored barriers impeding the *right* to work, emphasizing instead barriers impeding the *ability* to work," as sociologist Jill Quadagno has aptly concluded.[22]

The War on Poverty became as much a welfare scheme, providing moneys to disadvantaged households with young men, as it was a manpower or job training program. Political scientist Michael Brown has shown that it brought income into impoverished communities not only directly through stipends to participants and their families but also indirectly through the purchase of goods and services in the locales of projects.[23] Though promoted as a "machine for transforming people," it also hoped to reconfigure the black family into a male breadwinner and female homemaker by raising male wages and resocializing women away from independent wage earning and family headship.[24] To increase black male employment and earnings was certainly the goal expressed by the 1965 Moynihan Report, which recommended government-guaranteed full employment for black men, "even if this meant that some jobs had to be redesigned to enable men to fulfill them."[25]

Most civil rights leaders also emphasized jobs for black men, though without condemning the black family or black woman.[26] Others were not as generous. Rising rates of female labor force participation were used to attack poor at-home women both as lazy and as inadequate mothers by those who opposed the War on Poverty, civil rights, and women's rights. Indeed, the new feminism inadvertently provided ideological cover in its emphasis on equality in the paid labor force.[27] The extension of workfare to mothers with preschool children in the late 1960s must thus be seen as an attempt to discipline such solo mothers. The liberal goal of rehabilitating the poor morphed into a conservative dismissal of the poor as unworthy of public largesse.[28]

Saving Homes: The Job Corps Story

The "centerpiece" of the Economic Opportunity Act, recalled poverty crusader Adam Yarmolinsky, on loan from the Department of Defense at the time, "was the Job Corps." Secretary of Defense Robert S. McNamara had argued for the corps as "a social engineering solution that's got to work."[29] The corps would remove the poorest youth, aged sixteen to twenty-one, from their home environments, "ghetto tenements and rural shacks," and send them to "a clean, healthful . . . center where massive injections of remedial education and job training would turn them into law-abiding, tax-paying good neighbors," wrote Shriver's former special assistant Christopher Weeks in his defense of the program in

1967, seemingly unconscious of the assumptions about proper homes and good citizens embodied in such descriptions.[30]

Origins of the Job Corps lay in a 1958 plan of Minnesota senator Hubert H. Humphrey to establish a residential youth conservation corps, itself an echo of the New Deal's Civilian Conservation Corps (CCC). But whereas the CCC provided support through public works to a general, albeit mostly white, population during a period of economic crisis, the Job Corps during a period of "affluence" targeted one group—dropouts and "failures," that is, "youth who had benefited least from society's educational and training institutions and who might expect lives of menial work, frequent unemployment, crime, deprivation, and hopelessness," as liberal evaluators described them a decade later.[31] Senators referred to these young people as "disadvantaged" and "deprived." As survey researcher Louis Harris put it, "Most of them are black or Spanish speaking. They have had pitifully poor education, and they are young. And if they are women, they are women to boot." Thus, not only the individuals but also the program faced "tremendous handicaps."[32]

Despite the shift in population and goals from the CCC, the politics of passage required that 40 percent of the slots be allocated to rural conservation centers. This amendment included a stipulation that those most in need of remedial education would take classes and not merely clear forests and engage in other CCC-like projects. Urban centers would offer vocational training to those with at least a sixth grade education. Though envisioned as a program for men, Congress added women, with an understanding that one-third of the openings would be for them. By 1966, there existed six large (1,000 to 3,000 per unit) urban centers for men, at least eighty conservation centers for men (100 to 250 per unit), and seventeen for women (300 to 1,000 per unit). All offered health care and counseling as well as education and training.[33] Like Head Start, another War on Poverty innovation, the idea was to offer a full range of services, in this case out of the belief that job preparation required improving the entire person.

Of those remaining in the corps six months, nearly two-thirds were African American, while just over a quarter were white. After a year, blacks dropped to 57 percent of the participants, while whites rose to 30 percent. This was true among women as well as men.[34] The predominance of African Americans during a period of racial tension was not what planners had envisioned; they hoped to forge a universal program that would escape the entanglement of racial politics. "By '65, '66," Yarmolinsky remembered, "OEO was if not a black, a very dark gray agency, and when we were putting it together it hadn't the faintest gray tinge to it. If anything, color it Appalachian."[35] By 1969, African Americans had embraced the corps as their own. Irene Smith, president of the New Jersey National Association for the Advancement of Colored People (NAACP), for example, chastised those who would cut the number of centers by recalling the War on Poverty promise of "human development." "I am very concerned that this Nation put so much priority on making war and making money and putting so little value on raising citizens," she testified at a congressional hearing. "Promises unfulfilled," she argued, led to urban unrest. Those who would diminish the opportunity of the corps for African Americans, she claimed, heightened disillusionment that was fueling violence among such youth.[36]

Some centers were organized in a paramilitary fashion, and some suffered from disorganization and disciplinary chaos; others provided greater freedom to mix with the local community. Initial plans to have the Department of Defense run the centers floundered under congressional opposition, though the Department of the Interior and National Parks Service oversaw most of the conservation programs. While a few universities and state education departments ran residential centers, most contracts went to private firms, such as the Radio Corporation of America (RCA), with expertise in systems management. The political need to organize this huge undertaking quickly—to show results from the War on Poverty—encouraged a turn to corporate management. But promised efficiencies never developed; within a few years, the men's centers under private firms cost more per slot than did the others under government or universities. Dropout rates were high because of the location of centers away from families, because of the disorganization that came from rapid buildup, and because of unrealistic expectations on the part of recruits who were oversold anticipated benefits.[37]

During the Job Corps' first years, negative publicity called into question OEO director Shriver's claim that the corps housed "the kind of American who would be welcome anywhere in the United States," "carefully screened to make certain that he was of good moral character and sincerely desired a chance to prepare himself for the responsibilities of citizenship." This claim sought to calm local fears by ignoring the original emphasis on "those whose background, health, and education make them least fit for useful work," as President Johnson explained. When asked the benefits of participation during congressional hearings on closing centers in 1969, a graduate countered, "I got a skill. Now I can go out and get a job . . . [and] I learned to live with people."[38] They learned, Harris declared, "how to respect their own persons, how to control their own persons and control themselves and their own destinies"—that is, "how to stay out of trouble more."[39] But riots in and out of centers fed a portrait of the corps, based on stereotypes of the black male, as "an expensive boondoggle which ships juvenile delinquents and hoodlums across the country by jet, mollycoddles them in camps which are shot through with gang fights, looses them each weekend on defenseless communities to riot and vandalize private property, and shows no notable success in turning them into better, more productive citizens."[40]

In contrast, the first annual report of the OEO, "A Nation Aroused," interpreted the War on Poverty for the public with a can-do enthusiasm associated with its director, a Kennedy by marriage who previously had organized the popular Peace Corps. In its descriptions, the home represented "the ugly scar of poverty." The Job Corps thus justified its mission through the inadequate environments from which enrollees came, with their "substandard and overcrowded housing," families on public assistance, homes with unemployed "primary"—that is, male—wage earners and undereducated parents. These were families without adequate nurture, or so the story of one rural recruit dramatized: "He carried a small, battered suitcase and a cheap coat over his arm. His cat followed him and . . . he turned and went back, and as I watched he kissed the cat goodbye. No one came to the door, no one at all was there to send their love to him, no one to wish him well, no one to remember— only his cat." But in the next paragraph we read that "his mother gave him [a jacket] for Christmas and how he was taking it in his suitcase because he didn't want anything to happen to it," which presents a more positive representation of poor women's care of children than implied by the previous bleak image of the absence of emotion.[41]

Similarly, Head Start, with its comprehensive care of children from medical examinations and nutrition to cognitive development, promised improved chances at "future employability." Here, too, the failure of the home, where "adults . . . were too preoccupied with the daily grind of existence to offer much cheer or encouragement," had an adverse impact on the promise of opportunity. The Foster Grandparents Program also proposed to substitute for "over-worked custodians." Such custodians, by OEO definition, "have little time to cuddle them [children], to sing the lullabies or offer the reassurances that make a child feel loved and secure in an alien world."[42]

But what about the actual impact of such programs on home and family? Rather than taking the rhetoric of the Job Corps at face value, we need to entertain whether this program functioned more as a conduit to supplement the earnings of the poor—that is, as an arm of public assistance, as Michael Brown has argued—or as a facilitator of employment. By having participants allot twenty-five dollars a month to dependents (which apparently included parents) and matching these funds with an equal amount from the federal government, the Job Corps funneled money to the families from which its predominantly young, minority male members came. During the first year, this amounted to $7 million. Those who remained at least six months earned "a readjustment allowance" of fifty dollars each month, but home support funds began immediately. The OEO publicized success stories, such as that of the McNeese brothers of Centerville, Arkansas, whose combined fifty-dollar-per-month allotment allowed the family to purchase a plot of land. Other training programs, like Neighborhood Youth Corps, also channeled income to the families of participants.[43]

The Job Corps was not gender neutral, as sociologists Jill Quadagno and Catherine Fobes have shown.[44] Like other white liberals, planners crafted a race-neutral program for political reasons, as well as to fulfill their own notions of equality.[45] Sex distinction in the mid-1960s remained acceptable among liberals, however, in ways that race distinction rarely was: race difference represented pathology; gender difference, biology. The male breadwinner remained the norm, OEO director Shriver replied to Representative Edith Green (D-Ore.), who insisted on adding women to the Job Corps. He claimed that "the principal purpose of these centers was to give young men, who we hope will be heads of families and wage earners, an opportunity . . . to learn the necessary skills . . . for employment during the rest of their lives."[46]

Gender differences distinguished the development as well as the running of separate but not equal facilities. New Jersey representative Peter Frelinghuysen had insisted before the Senate Select Committee on Poverty drafting the legislation in 1964 that as "a guardian of the public morals we should put in a provision that they [men and women] should be housed separately."[47] The U.S. Employment Service recruited only for the men's centers. National women's councils (of Catholic, Jewish, and "Negro" women), along with United Church Women, formed Women in Community Service (WICS), which won a contract to recruit and screen women applicants. Men would be housed in larger units out of the mistaken belief that women could not handle such settings (subsequent events proved that neither could men). Corporations were reluctant to bid for establishing the women's centers because center size precluded economies of scale (and greater profits); developing their curriculum on "home and family life" seemed an unpromising detour toward capturing the growing market in manpower training modules.[48] Training re-inscribed occupational segregation by sex (and by race among the sexes). Women received "intensive training in home and family life and the development of values, attitudes, and skills that (would) contribute to stable family relationships and a good child-rearing environment," the Job Corps announced. But men did not. Acceptance criteria for women included lack of "opportunity for marriage to men capable of providing more than a poverty-level income." They "would not be doing conservation work on public lands, building roads, felling trees, building viaducts, and so on," Shriver had reassured Congress from the start.[49]

Successful outcomes also varied by gender. Other than employment, survey researchers classified former "corpsmen" as having achieved positive outcomes if they had "been admitted in the Armed Forces or school" or were "waiting to go or in the case of women those who have been married in the interim or have assumed an equivalent position in terms of running a household." A hostile senator recognized the fallacy in this reasoning when he asked, "How can you consider marriage a positive placement unless the Job Corps arranged it?" He answered himself by pointing out that however positive marriage might be, "it does not reduce unemployment or show that Job Corps has trained her to get or retain a job."[50] (Technically, it would reduce unemployment if the newly married woman stopped looking for employment.) Former corpswomen, especially African Americans, reportedly "felt better prepared for marriage and raising children." They also learned to make family budgets, to stretch the food dollar by shopping for bargains, and to sew "attractive clothes" for themselves. When it came to better-paying jobs, however, women benefited less than men, obtaining a lower initial increase in their hourly earnings. Among eighteen-year-olds, men received thirty-nine cents more to women's twenty-one-cent increase. "Maybe that is because being a woman is another part of being disadvantaged," surveyor Harris concluded.[51]

The Keystone Job Corps Center for Women, run by RCA in upstate Pennsylvania, typified the gendered assumptions behind job training that equated women with a family role. Its director proudly admitted, "Although we realize the economic justification for the Center . . . is to provide our people with salable business skills, while the girls are here, we want to expose them to a new set of values and way of living." Not only did the emphasis on family and home dominate discussions about women enrollees, but the focus on individual change also took a particularly gendered turn. The "most popular activity" outside of vocational and academic classes became a "modeling and charm course conducted by an attractive woman whose fashion experience includes working with larger department stores." Not only did the young women learn "grooming," "but we also try to teach the girls poise, good manners and how to handle themselves during a job interview." The director renamed the program "an 'attitudinal corps.'" Reminiscent of job preparation training later attached to workfare, such confidence building stood as the working-class version of the development of self-esteem that educators by the 1970s would advocate for girls in general.[52]

Actual training led women into what the OEO called service occupations. Similarly, "work experience" programs (noncompulsory for welfare recipients) funded by HEW placed women as health aides, orderlies, attendants, and laboratory helpers for hospitals and nursing homes; commercial and dietary kitchen workers; homemaker aides; child day-care center aides; and teacher aides. That is, skill building and work experience often directed women to the devalued and low-paid equivalents of care tasks performed for love or out of duty when for the family, which was quite in keeping with the Job Corps instruction on household and marital matters. Even small business loans rewarded the domestic, with women founding maid and dressmaking services. (However, success for "a Harlem mother of six" became leaving "the relief rolls" and being able to "afford to hire someone to care for her children of pre-school age.") Even when women gained clerical skills, their potential earnings remained far below that of the skilled trades open to men through "manpower" programs. Such earnings did not bode well for women's economic independence. "The programs sought to eliminate the 'culture of poverty' by encouraging the formation of male breadwinner/female caregiver households," concluded Quadagno and Fobes.[53]

Pregnancy and responsibility for children complicated women's involvement in the Job Corps and the Job Corps' ability to fill slots allocated to women. Before 1971, those who became pregnant while in the corps were forced out "for medical reasons," much as pregnant workers were terminated from employment in the larger economy and as women in the military had been dismissed.[54] They left with "appropriate referrals to counseling and health agencies in their home areas," but not with the resources necessary to improve the lives of the next generation, although a prime reason for including women in the poverty programs in the first place had been to discourage the carryover of poverty to their children that social scientists claimed distinguished "the culture of poverty." After a successful pilot project that showed caring for pregnancy among enrollees would not attract the already pregnant, prove disruptive, or generate adverse community responses, the corps allowed those who became pregnant to remain until their seventh month. Accompanying sex education programs actually decreased the number of corpwomen who became pregnant.[55]

The lack of childcare proved a more difficult barrier to female participation and successful completion of training courses. From the beginning, mothers with children over six weeks old could apply but had to show that "the child will be receiving adequate care and protection during the period the applicant is enrolled in the Job Corps." These young women, however, were prominent among corps dropouts and tended to make less progress in their education and training when they remained. In response, in 1971 the corps finally established an "experimental" child development center in Atlanta. This proved costly, about $3,280 per child per year, but effective. Mothers with access to this childcare remained in the program 205 days compared with 123 days for those without any care and 127 days for those without children. Into the late 1980s, lack of childcare continued to impede the participation of women, by then mandated to reach half of all slots. Job Corps remained "a full-service program" that provided all essential services but "childcare" and thus failed to reach large numbers of potential recruits.[56]

Rewarding "Work" by Changing Welfare

In 1987, when Congress addressed the dearth of childcare for mothers in the Job Corps, it justified increasing expenditures for this service by contrasting the program with welfare. Job Corps, Steny H. Hoyer (D-Md.) argued, "can end generations of welfare dependency."[57] Investment in Job Corps, an Urban Institute researcher concluded, generated savings from not spending money on "crime, welfare benefits and unemployment insurance."[58] For Yarmolinksy, evaluating the War on Poverty as early as 1973, welfare represented "the biggest single obstacle to making training programs of any kind . . . work."[59] This dichotomy—work and welfare—associated work with labor market participation and welfare with "tax receivers," as opposed to "taxpayers and participators."[60] It reflected core beliefs of the American liberal state.

Political philosopher Judith Shklar has named *earning* "a social right" of "American citizenship." "The opportunity to work and to be paid an earned reward for one's labor," she has argued, brought "public respect" or the standing crucial for citizenship, separating the "American" from both the nonwork of the European aristocrat and the forced labor of the slave.[61] Legal theorist William E. Forbath similarly placed the right to earn at the center of a social citizenship tradition that offered "opportunities for self-improvement and a measure of material independence and security for all." As Franklin D. Roosevelt proclaimed in 1932, "Government formal and informal, political and economic, owes to everyone an avenue to possess himself of a portion of . . . plenty sufficient for his needs, through his own work."[62] Yet in this paradigm, welfare reflected the illiberal assumption that male household heads represented their dependents in the body politic, whereas female ones were likely to become "wards" of the state. In 1972, influenced by the new feminism, welfare rights activist Johnnie Tillmon interpreted AFDC as "a supersexist marriage. You trade in *a* man for *the* man."[63]

In the midst of the Great Depression, crafters of Aid to Dependent Children initially assumed traditional gender norms, in which mothers could be allowed to stay home to care for children. At a time when the white woman was the norm, mothers were considered not to be workers. Into the 1960s, policymakers still claimed that mother care of children took precedence over a full-time job, even as they sought to devise programs to encourage "independence" from welfare through wage earning.[64]

But the relationship between mothers and employment was changing, at first for mothers from less privileged groups and later for all mothers. Amendments to Social Security in 1939 differentiated between the widowed, who were judged deserving because their deceased husband could have qualified for social insurance, and the divorced or never-married, who were considered undeserving because no man mediated their relation to the state. The former received survivor's insurance, whereas the latter were left to the more arbitrary and state-run welfare programs. Beginning with Louisiana in 1943, states adopted "employable mother" rules that "forced" would-be recipients into the labor market if any form of employment was available.[65] The declaration of Georgia representative Philip Landrum at 1969 House hearings reflected attitudes that had shaped eligibility for public assistance over the preceding decades. "I find many people can't get domestic help. Couldn't domestics be taken off welfare?" he suggested.[66] When labor shortages developed in low-waged sectors, states reduced their welfare caseloads.[67]

As historian Jennifer Mittelstadt has shown, the 1956 amendments to Social Security began the transformation of welfare from assistance to workfare, a movement away from a right to mother to a requirement to earn. This increased funding and coverage, but more significant, it redefined ADC as a program "to assist clients in maintaining and strengthening family life and encouraging 'self-care and self-support' among clients."[68] Washington administrators encouraged the states by funding services as well as assistance. Responding to changes in the recipient population—a shift away from white widows to the never-married, the divorced, and minorities—social welfare advocates began arguing for "rehabilitation," a notion that training, education, and other social services allowed families on welfare headed by women to become self-supporting through maternal employment.[69] Women would increase their self-worth, it was claimed, and families would become stronger. These advocates used a casework approach that focused on individual rather than structural barriers, as seemed appropriate during a period of rising affluence. Behind their talk about the psychological impact of work and the benefits of independence, however, lay a conviction, as the American Public Welfare Association found, that welfare checks "were not adequate to provide a minimum standard of living." Wage work promised a higher standard of living.[70]

But former Social Security commissioner Arthur Altemeyer in 1957 worried about the implications of such liberal welfare reform as devised by his former protégé Wilbur Cohen. "I am afraid that in the name of rehabilitation, increased self-help, and provision of constructive social services we will depreciate the need for effective income maintenance programs and weaken such principles as . . . the right of needy persons to assistance." Moreover, in arguing against the direction of reform, Altemeyer asserted that a "mother had a right to assistance even if she refused to go to work."[71]

The 1961 extension of ADC to families with unemployed parents, that is, men without employment (called ADC-UF, Aid to Dependent Families-Unemployed Father, later AFDC-UP), and the 1962 name change to AFDC further linked welfare to wage earning.[72] "An unemployed individual," the new requirements read, "whose family is receiving aid under this program should accept any reasonable offer of employment." Administrators of ADC/AFDC and the public employment service became linked. Finally, ADC-UF mandated that states establish work relief.[73] According to Special Assistant Weeks, "Through welfare, jobs had been organized for more than one thousand fathers who would otherwise have been unemployed, and whose families would otherwise have been ineligible for welfare unless the father deserted. On these jobs, the fathers worked for the equivalent of their welfare payments, in the process of which they developed some skills, retained some work habits, and helped their own community in some small way."[74] Weeks pictured this father as a displaced Appalachian miner, the target of much early planning by the poverty warriors, as we have seen. This change then appeared as the entering wedge to requiring all recipients of welfare to work off their checks. The newly established Community Work and Training programs under ADC-UF supposedly addressed the unemployment of "'employable' fathers," as Mittelstadt has contended, but they actually turned ADC into "a combination welfare-work program," challenging "the 'non-employable' status of mothers" in the process.[75]

Though women were not yet forced to participate in such work schemes, they were encouraged to obtain jobs or training. The public welfare amendments of 1962, which first made women eligible for

Community Work and Training, included funds for childcare. Cohen admitted that "the bill seems . . . designed to encourage mothers to work," which he judged a positive step. For the first time, recipients no longer would have their assistance diminished by each dollar they earned; this was the beginning of significant income incentives.[76] Historian Sonya Michel has noted the paradox of these funds: "Instead of opening the way to universal childcare, the 1962 amendment put federal welfare policy on the slippery slope toward workfare." Congress certainly drew on the language of dependency and self-sufficiency in justifying the 1962 amendments, as it would with subsequent changes in the late 1960s and early 1970s that stressed "work."[77]

Title V of the Economic Opportunity Act of 1964 incorporated Community Work and Training, renaming it Work Experience and redirecting it to single mothers but without adequate funding. It targeted "parents who are eligible for aid because of their unemployment" (with parent coded male) and those with "incapacities" that permitted "some kinds of employment." Most significant, work programs embraced "women caring for children who are old enough that, with proper safeguards for their care, they can safely be left while their mother learns and works so that she may eventually become employable." Increasing the skills of such mothers, Secretary of Health, Education, and Welfare Anthony J. Celebrezze argued in 1964, would not only make them better workers but also "strengthen family life."[78]

Rather than celebrating the maternal responsibility to remain home for carework, politicians by the mid-1960s had joined social workers in advocating employment. Thus, in 1967, Senator Wayne Morse (R-Ore.) protested to the states a proposed freeze on AFDC caseloads not merely in terms of "social justice" but also in terms of "better opportunities for children in American homes whose parents need just economic assistance from their Government in order that they may better provide for their children through taking advantage of job training programs and other economic opportunities for self-improvement."[79] The 1967 amendments established the Work Incentive Program (WIN) that pushed employment through an income disregard—the "thirty plus one-third" rule that would allow recipients to earn more without losing benefits—and funds for childcare. But states could end assistance to parents and children over sixteen if they refused participation in training or "work" programs. Amendments of 1971 mandated the employment of mothers with children older than six, encouraging states to establish their own programs.[80] For example, Work Rules, the resulting New York program, compelled "employables" "to make a 'diligent' search for day care for their young children, to follow up on each and every job 'referral' . . . and . . . accept any job offer" as a condition to receiving welfare.[81] The actual numbers forced to work or be cut off welfare remained small, however, because childcare funds proved inadequate and most states defined the majority of mothers as having a good cause for staying home.

Resistance on the part of poor solo mothers proved significant. Their rights talk challenged this growing expectation that even mothers of young children should join the labor force. Claiming to be working already for their own families, organized welfare recipients presented an alternative understanding of citizenship that broke the link between market labor and social benefits. They rejected the opportunity to work if that employment fell short of providing adequate income and dignity. Lawyers on whom welfare activists depended also refused to equate citizenship with employment. Their radical constitutional theory posited public assistance as a new form of property that enabled "individual well-being and dignity."[82]

The call for income, not jobs, contrasted with aspirations of the middle-class, predominantly white, women's movement to be included in "the right to earn." Ending workplace discrimination—marriage bars, unequal pay, firing upon becoming pregnant, as well as refusal to hire or promote—was central to the revival of feminism.[83] But policies aimed at increasing women's participation in the labor force also derived from the same cold war search for manpower, in this case labeled "womanpower."[84] Demands by organized women further suggested that they could function like men as unencumbered individuals, free from carework. Liberal feminists, as they came to be known, sought caretaker replacements, paid laborers—usually other women who were often from a lower class and from another race or culture. But their promotion of wage labor as a women's, even a mother's, right undermined the choice to stay at home for those women dependent on public assistance. As feminist author Barbara Ehrenreich has argued, it was easier to siphon off household and other domestic duties, including carework, to another woman than to convince men to do their share or rearrange the workplace to balance family and work, as the common parlance defines the social need to engage in reproductive as well as income-generating labor.[85]

An exchange during 1969 hearings between Michigan representative Martha Griffiths (Dem.), a white woman, and National Welfare Rights Organization (NWRO) leaders George Wiley and Beulah Sanders, both African Americans, most graphically expressed the tension between equal rights feminism and welfare rights. Griffiths played a major role in adding "sex" to the Civil Rights Act of 1964, in which she evoked the specter of white women being at the back of the job queue after African Americans had gained access to fair employment.[86] Her emphasis on women's self-reliance through wage labor contrasted with Wiley's call for adequate income through public assistance to poor single mothers. He, in turn, rejected her class- and race-biased perspective. Though his organization was "deeply concerned about the problems and the discrimination against women in the society and the special problem that women have in the society," Wiley named dealing with such discrimination "criminal" if it meant "penalizing all people who are poor by giving them inadequate income."[87]

Griffiths insisted that "too much emphasis is placed on what should be paid in welfare rights and too little emphasis is placed on every person has a right to a job and that is true whether it is a man or a woman and they should be given that training." Young solo mothers "should be given training, then a chance to work," she argued and claimed that Wiley disagreed with her "because you are a man." When NWRO legal counsel Carl Rachlin, a white man, pointed out how New York State would pay for a recipient to become a nurse's aide but not a nurse, since "the idea of a welfare woman becoming a professional worker . . . was just beyond them," and how stenographers earned more than women on AFDC, Griffiths interrupted with the liberal feminist mantra, "don't offer women secretarial positions only," have them become "chairman of the board."[88] Wiley countered by asking her to be "realistic," to "put your money where your mouth is." He framed his argument in terms of a consumption politics that equated dignity with the material goods of affluence available to other Americans:

> You say you want to have training. You say you want to have people out of poverty. Fine. Pay people the basic income they need to live today and then provide the training program and the other opportunities so that if those opportunities fail we will at least have the money so that the next generation of boys and girls are not going to be mentally impaired from inade-

quate diets, are not going to have dropped out of school because they didn't have the decent clothing to wear and are not going to be degraded and have the problem of having the inadequate housing and inadequate furniture and basic things that they need to live.[89]

Sanders had no problem with promoting women's self-sufficiency, but instead of forcing mothers on welfare into low-paid jobs, she called for choices: to earn wages, gain higher education, or remain at home. Despite the feminist mantra of "choice,"[90] Sanders felt that poor women lacked choice; she dismissed current training programs as wasteful and "unsuccessful." Hers was a devastating critique from the bottom up. "Even the manpower program, the people that got training under that to become lab technicians, came to our organization and said to us, 'We got our training from manpower. We can't find a job. Everywhere we go and knock on the door, it is slammed in our faces.'" Instead, speaking at the beginning of the Nixon years, she echoed the War on Poverty's call for maximum feasible participation: "Go out in the community and knock on doors and find out what the people want," she recommended.[91] This former worker on the poverty program charged, much as journalist Nicholas Lemann would argue in his history of urban poverty and civil rights, that "the money has gone into the pockets of the middle class people and made their pockets that much fatter and we are still poor."[92] Senator James Eastland (D-Miss.) obtained farm subsidies, but government refused to provide enough for the needy to survive in New York City, Sanders contended. "They spend more for dog food, the blind peoples' dogs, than they spend for human beings." But "everybody in this country has a right to share this wealth."[93]

By the late 1960s, expanding notions of a decent standard of living, added to increased costs and inadequate male wages, were turning the dual-income family into the new norm. Some wage-earning women begrudged their poorer counterparts for being paid to stay home. This politics of resentment derived not only from a taxpayer's revolt against having to pay for "laziness" but also from the time bind of the double day that led one California woman to object before the same congressional committee in 1969: "I'm getting fed up with having to work, taking my child to a baby-sitter's so some other mother can sit home and not do a blankety blank thing!"[94] Such women bought into notions held by such proponents of workfare as Louisiana's Senator Russell Long that "welfare mothers," whom he insulted as "female broodmares and 'riff-raff,'" were not "doing something constructive sitting around those homes."[95] The bottom line for Long and his ilk was that women on welfare were unworthy.

In the 1980s, Reaganite conservative Charles Murray most infamously charged that the transformation of welfare into an entitlement during the era of the Great Society destroyed the family.[96] But rules punishing conjugal relationships and the involvement of fathers, as well as pushing mothers out to work, had existed since the 1940s.[97] In contrast, during and after the Great Society, the Supreme Court provided some basic procedural safeguards to those qualifying for public assistance. *King v. Smith* struck down "man in the house" laws that interfered with the federal requirement that states provide AFDC to all who were eligible.[98] *Goldberg v. Kelly* found in the equal protection clause a right to a fair hearing.[99] The Supreme Court refused to find a substantive right to welfare in the Constitution, but it did reinforce the criteria of need, uphold the mobility of recipients, and sustain the privacy of poor women.[100]

The Great Society emphasized "a hand-up, not a hand-out," with opportunity the key discourse, yet one of its consequences was to provide an opening for political activists to challenge structures of inequality through the language of rights. NWRO activists were one group who took advantage of that political opening. Their organization emerged from the civil rights movement in 1966 to mobilize poor people to gain an adequate guaranteed income for all. NWRO organized recipients to overload the public welfare system in order to transform it. It challenged the implementation of welfare "on the ground" by demanding that caseworkers provide recipients the clothing, furniture, money, and dignity required by law and regulation and that they respect the personal autonomy and bodily integrity that are as much a product of the American creed of individualism as the work ethic. It offered an alternative to definitions of work as paid labor and public assistance as charity, reconceiving welfare as a right of citizenship. Welfare rights became a movement of poor, unmarried, mostly African American mothers, who took control of NWRO in 1972.[101]

Mandatory work requirements represented an attempt to discipline such challenges. As Senator Long exclaimed in 1967, during the first serious attempt to enact such rules, "they ought to be able to find something to do if they can find time to go demonstrate or wrap a chain around a city hall or come in here and demonstrate in the streets and impede the work of the Congress. Those people ought to be offered the opportunity to work and if they don't want to do something constructive then we just shouldn't pay them, period."[102] The African American women at the center of the NWRO rejected such a notion of opportunity that would provide Mr. and Mrs. Long with someone to do their housework. Their conception of "constructive" dismissed forced labor at low wages for choices on how to manage family and market labor that other citizens understood as their right.[103]

During the 1992 presidential campaign, Democrat Bill Clinton pledged "to end welfare as we know it." Though he planned "to make work pay" through increased funds for childcare and training, electoral weakness and divisions within his own coalition meant that Clinton could not fully control the political agenda. Only an expanded Earned Income Tax Credit (EITC) and a slight increase in the minimum wage alleviated the continued poverty that awaited those who would be forced into the low-wage labor market through welfare reform. Clinton's rhetoric that appropriated Republican themes encouraged opponents who would punish the autonomy of women under the guise of "family values" and who never accepted aid to poor solo mothers in the first place.[104]

The resulting 1996 Personal Responsibility and Work Opportunity Act replaced AFDC with Temporary Assistance for Needy Families (TANF), ending any federal entitlement to welfare. Among its provisions were work rules and time limits, as well as devolution of responsibility to the states, which received block grants to devise their own programs to move recipients from welfare to "work." As a condition of receiving benefits, solo caregivers had to obtain work outside the home within two months of going on the program. Some states have insisted that recipients take any job rather than stay in school to train for employment that might bring self-sufficiency. "Work" consisted of a range of activities, from unsubsidized and subsidized private sector employment to subsidized public sector jobs, community service programs, childcare services, some education and vocational training, job search and readiness programs, and on-the-job training.[105]

Sociologist Ann Shola Orloff has argued that this shift in public policy flowed logically from a welfare regime that privileges the market "in the provision of income and care." Maternalism, or programs that favor motherhood and women's domestic responsibilities, she has contended, always reinforces gender inequality.[106] But maternalism may have been more a discourse than a practice. To the extent that programs under its name would protect the care of children by their mother, they rarely extended to all mothers. The racialization of welfare, its association with women who were defined as laborers and whose carework remained unvalued, proved crucial in turning welfare into a work program. The War on Poverty was a war for work, that is, for waged labor, but one that hoped to reconstitute homes and families in the process. Substituting employment or training for welfare intensified during the 1960s, leaving manpower programs to undertake the maternalist project by instructing recipients how to establish proper homes, better families, and improved selves.

The current triumph of work as the basis for citizenship rights, compatible with what Orloff and others label an "equality" or "sameness" model for men and women,[107] is not new, nor does it have the same consequences for all women. In the first decade of the twenty-first century, this equality model continues to be precarious as women still earn less than men and continue to be responsible for carework and other domestic labor without adequate public, or even family, support. Home and work, family and labor, remain interdependent in law and social policy, while the dream of a Great Society remains elusive.

Notes

I thank the Institute for Social, Behavioral, and Economic Research and the Academic Senate at the University of California, Santa Barbara, for grants to support this research. I also thank Danielle Swiontek for research assistance.

1. Margaret Weir, *Politics and Jobs: The Boundaries of Employment Policy in the United States* (Princeton: Princeton University Press, 1992), 64.

2. Lyndon B. Johnson, "Annual Message to the Congress on the State of the Union, January 8, 1964," www.lbjlib.utexas.edu/johnson/archives.hom/speeches.hom/640108.

3. Lyndon B. Johnson, "Commencement Address at Howard University: 'To Fulfill These Rights,' June 4, 1965," reprinted in *Poverty and Public Policy in Modern America,* ed. Donald T. Critchlow and Ellis W. Hawley (Chicago: Dorsey Press, 1989), 250.

4. "A Nation Aroused," First Annual Report, Office of Economic Opportunity, 1965, n.p., in *The War on Poverty, 1964–1968,* part 1, White House Central Files, microfilm ed. (Bethesda, Md.: University Publications of America, 1986), reel 9.

5. I have crafted this interpretation from my reading of Linda Gordon, *Pitied but Not Entitled: Single Mothers and the History of Welfare* (New York: Free Press, 1994); Gwendolyn Mink, *The Wages of Motherhood: Inequality in the Welfare State, 1917–1942* (Ithaca: Cornell University Press, 1995); Suzanne Mettler, *Dividing Citizens: Gender and Federalism in New Deal Public Policy* (Ithaca: Cornell University Press, 1998); Robert C. Lieberman, *Shifting the Color Line: Race and the American Welfare State* (Cambridge: Harvard University Press, 1998); Alice Kessler-Harris, "In the Nation's Image: The Gendered Limits of Social Citizenship in the Depression Era," *Journal of American History* 86 (December 1999): 1251–79.

6. For elaboration, see Eileen Boris and Sonya Michel, "Social Citizenship and Women's Right to Work in Postwar America," in *Women's Rights and Human Rights: International Historical Perspectives,* ed. Patricia Grimshaw, Katie Holmes, and Marilyn Lake (New York: Palgrave, 2001), 199–219.

7. Joanne Goodwin, "'Employable Mothers' and 'Suitable Work': A Reevaluation of Welfare and Wage Earning for Women in the Twentieth-Century United States," *Journal of Social History* 29 (1995): 253–74.

8. Martha Davis, *Brutal Need: Lawyers and the Welfare Rights Movement, 1960–1973* (New Haven: Yale University Press, 1993).

9. Carole Pateman, "The Patriarchal Welfare State," in *The Disorder of Women: Democracy, Feminism, and Political Theory* (Stanford: Stanford University Press, 1989), 179–209.

10. Dorothy E. Roberts, "Welfare and the Problem of Black Citizenship," *Yale Law Journal* 105 (April 1996): 1563–1602.

11. Gareth Davies, *From Opportunity to Entitlement: The Transformation and Decline of Great Society Liberalism* (Lawrence: University Press of Kansas, 1996), 34.

12. Lisa Levenstein, "From Innocent Children to Unwanted Migrants and Unwed Moms: Two Chapters in the Public Discourse on Welfare in the United States, 1960–1961," *Journal of Women's History* 11 (Winter 200): 10–33.

13. Christopher Weeks, *Job Corps: Dollars and Dropouts* (Boston: Little, Brown, 1967), 130–31.

14. Henry J. Aaron, "Six Welfare Questions," in *The Great Society and Its Legacy: Twenty Years of U.S. Social Policy,* ed. Marshall Kaplan and Peggy Cuciti (Durham: Duke University Press, 1986), 106.

15. Weir, *Politics and Jobs,* 64–67.

16. Garth L. Mangum, introduction to *The Manpower Revolution: Its Policy Consequences; Excerpts from Senate Hearings before the Clark Subcommittee,* ed. Garth L. Mangum (Garden City, N.Y.: Doubleday, 1965), xiii. Senator Joseph S. Clark saw his hearings on manpower as contributing to building the Great Society. See Joseph S. Clark, forward to ibid., v–viii.

17. Michael B. Katz, *The Undeserving Poor: From the War on Poverty to the War on Welfare* (New York: Pantheon, 1989), 9–123; Alice O'Connor, *Poverty Knowledge: Social Science, Social Policy, and the Poor in Twentieth-Century U.S. History* (Princeton: Princeton University Press, 2001), 99–123, 196–210.

18. Davies, *From Opportunity to Entitlement*, 34–35; James T. Patterson, *Grand Expectations: The United States, 1945–1974* (New York: Oxford University Press, 1996), 538–42.

19. Cited in Katz, *Undeserving Poor*, 93.

20. Michael K. Brown, *Race, Money, and the American Welfare State* (Ithaca: Cornell University Press, 1999).

21. Katz, *Undeserving Poor*, 94. For how this happens, see Weir, *Politics and Jobs*, 69–83. See also Nicholas Lemann, *The Promised Land: The Great Migration and How It Changed America* (New York: Alfred Knopf, 1991).

22. Jill Quadagno, *The Color of Welfare: How Racism Undermined the War on Poverty* (New York: Oxford University Press, 1994), 67.

23. Brown, *Race, Money, and the American Welfare State*.

24. Sar A. Levitan and Benjamin H. Johnston, *The Job Corps: A Social Experiment That Works* (Baltimore: Johns Hopkins University Press, 1975), 30.

25. Daniel Patrick Moynihan, *The Negro Family: The Case for National Action* (Washington, D.C.: U.S. Department of Labor, Office of Policy Planning and Research, 1965), 29.

26. Dona Cooper Hamilton and Charles V. Hamilton, *The Dual Agenda: The African-American Struggle for Civil and Economic Equality* (New York: Columbia University Press, 1997).

27. Sheila Tobias, *Faces of Feminism: An Activist's Reflections on the Women's Movement* (Boulder, Colo.: Westview, 1997).

28. For this important distinction, see Jennifer L. Mittelstadt, "The Dilemmas of the Liberal Welfare State, 1945–1964: Gender, Race, and Aid to Dependent Children" (Ph.D. diss., University of Michigan, 2000).

29. Adam Yarmolinsky comment and quoting of Robert S. McNamara, "Poverty and Urban Policy," 241, unpublished conference transcript of 1973 Group Discussion of the Kennedy Administration Urban Poverty Programs and Policies, Florence Heller School for Advanced Studies in Social Welfare, Brandeis University, June 16–17, 1973, John F. Kennedy Library, Boston.

30. Weeks, *Job Corps*, 5.

31. Levitan and Johnston, *The Job Corps*, 1.

32. See Senator Gaylord Nelson (D-Wis.) at "Closing of Job Corps Centers," *Hearings before the Subcommittee on Employment, Manpower, and Poverty of the Committee on Labor and Public Welfare*, U.S. Senate, 91st Cong., 1st sess., April 18, 25, and May 2, 1969, 11; testimony of Louis Harris, ibid., 130.

33. For the politics, see Weeks, *Job Corps*, passim; on numbers formed, Levitan and Johnston, *The Job Corps*, 5.

34. "A Survey of Ex-Job Corpsmen Conducted by Louis Harris and Associates, April 1969," included in "Closing of Job Corps Centers," table: "Ethnic Groups," 28.

35. Yarmolinsky, "Poverty and Urban Policy," 162–63.

36. Testimony of Irene Smith, "Closing of Job Corps Centers," 338.

37. Weeks, *Job Corps*, 78–79, 95–102; Levitan and Johnston, *The Job Corps*, 24–30. See also "Closing of Job Corps Centers," esp. the testimony of Louis Harris, 22–145.

38. Shriver and the president quoted in Weeks, *Job Corps,* 178; testimony of Kathy Ashworth, Richmond, Va., "Closing of Job Corps Centers," 329.
39. Testimony of Harris, "Closing of Job Corps Centers," 139, 141.
40. Weeks, *Job Corps,* 231.
41. "A Nation Aroused," n.p.
42. Ibid.
43. Ibid., n.p. See also Levitan and Johnston, *The Job Corps,* 27.
44. Jill Quadagno and Catherine Fobes, "The Welfare State and the Cultural Reproduction of Gender: Making Good Girls and Boys in the Job Corps," *Social Problems* 42 (May 1965): 171–90.
45. Brown, *Race, Money, and the American Welfare State,* 215–18; Davies, *From Opportunity to Entitlement.*
46. Quadagno and Fobes, "The Welfare State and the Cultural Reproduction of Gender," 178. On Shriver's testimony, see also Patricia G. Zelman, *Women, Work, and National Policy: The Kennedy-Johnson Years* (Ann Arbor: UMI Research Press, 1982), 80–82.
47. Frelinghuysen testimony, *Economic Opportunity Act of 1964,* S 2642, *Hearings before the Select Committee on Poverty of the Committee on Labor and Public Welfare,* U.S. Senate, 88th Cong., 2d sess., June 17, 18, 23, and 25, 1964, 190.
48. Weeks, *Job Corps,* 182–83, 155–57.
49. Quadagno and Fobes, "The Welfare State and the Cultural Reproduction of Gender," 176; Shriver testimony in *Economic Opportunity Act of 1964,* 148.
50. Dialogue between Senator Winston L. Prouty (R-Vt.) and Louis Harris, "Closing of Job Corps Centers," 113.
51. Testimony of Harris, "Closing of Job Corps Centers," 138–39, 119.
52. Pat Rooney, "The Corps Does a Job," reprint, 1967, box 130, 1967–1969, reel 10, War on Poverty, microfilm edition, part 1, reel 10.
53. "A Nation Aroused," n.p.; Quadagno and Fobes, "The Welfare State and the Cultural Reproduction of Gender," 184, 186.
54. Sheila B. Kamerman, Alfred J. Kahn, and Paul Kingston, *Maternity Policies and Working Women* (New York: Columbia University Press, 1983), 35–56, 58; on the military, see Leisa D. Meyer, *Creating G.I. Jane: Sexuality and Power in the Women's Army Corps during World War II* (New York: Columbia University Press, 1996), 109–16.
55. Levitan and Johnston, *The Job Corps,* 35–36.
56. Ibid., 36–38; "Child Care Services for Job Corps," *Hearing before the Subcommittee on Employment Opportunities of the Committee on Education and Labor,* House of Representatives, 100th Cong., 1st sess., July 23, 1987, 1–8.
57. Statement of Steny H. Hoyer, "Child Care Services for Job Corps," 3.
58. Lawrence D. Maloney, "Welfare in America: Is It a Flop?" *U.S. News and World Report,* December 24, 1984, reprinted in *The Welfare Debate,* ed. Robert Emmet Long (New York: H. W. Wilson, 1989), 11.
59. Yarmolinsky, "Poverty and Urban Policy," 331.
60. Hoyer statement, in "Child Care Services for Job Corps," 5.
61. Judith N. Shklar, *American Citizenship: The Quest for Inclusion* (Cambridge: Harvard University Press, 1991), 1–2, 99.

62. William E. Forbath, "Constitutional Welfare Rights: A History, Critique and Reconstruction," *Fordham Law Review* 69 (April 2001): 1827; Roosevelt speaking in 1932 quoted at 1832.

63. Johnnie Tillmon, "Welfare Is a Women's Issue," *Liberation News Service*, no. 415, February 26, 1972, reprinted in *America's Working Women: A Documentary History, 1600 to the Present*, ed. Rosalyn Baxandall and Linda Gordon (New York: Norton, 1995), 315.

64. Mittelstadt, "Dilemmas of the Liberal Welfare State," 143.

65. For this section I rely on my essay "When Work Is Slavery," in *Whose Welfare?*, ed. Gwendolyn Mink (Ithaca: Cornell University Press, 1999), 37–38, as well as Nancy Rose, *Workfare or Fair Work: Women, Welfare, and Government Work Programs* (New Brunswick: Rutgers University Press, 1995), 73–75.

66. Representative Landrum quoted in Memorandum from Clint Fair to Andy Biemiller on Social Insurance and Welfare Hearings, October 9, 1969, collection 1, box 54, folder 62, AFL-CIO Papers, George Meany Library and Archives, Silver Spring, Maryland.

67. Southern states had engaged in such practices for all kinds of relief during the Great Depression. See Jacqueline Jones, *Labor of Love, Labor of Sorrow: Black Women, Work, and the Family* (New York: Basic Books, 1985). Ellen Reese has connected employable mother rules to structural economic factors, including the presence of agricultural labor. See "The Politics of Motherhood: The Restriction of Poor Mothers' Welfare Rights in the United States, 1949–1960," *Social Politics: International Studies in Gender, State, and Society* 8 (Spring 2001): 65–112.

68. Mittelstadt, "Dilemmas of the Liberal Welfare State," 93.

69. Robert A. Moffitt and Michele Ver Ploeg, eds., *Evaluating Welfare Reform in an Era of Transition* (Washington, D.C.: National Academy Press, 2001), 16–17, esp. figs. 1-1, 1-2.

70. For the importance of "rehabilitation," see Mittelstadt, "Dilemmas of the Liberal Welfare State," and on the American Public Welfare Association, see ibid., 140. See also Blanche D. Coll, *Safety Net: Welfare and Social Security, 1929–1979* (New Brunswick: Rutgers University Press, 1995), 164–238.

71. Altemeyer quoted in Edward D. Berkowitz, *Mr. Social Security: The Life of Wilbur J. Cohen* (Lawrence: University Press of Kansas, 1995), 106–7. I thank Jennifer Mittelstadt for calling my attention to this quotation.

72. The program changed to AFDC-UP (unemployed parent) to become gender neutral in 1979. For this history, see Gertrude Schaffner Goldberg and Sheila D. Collins, *Washington's New Poor Law: Welfare "Reform" and the Roads Not Taken, 1935 to the Present* (New York: Apex Press, 2001), 78, and Gwendolyn Mink, *Welfare's End* (Ithaca: Cornell University Press, 1998), 149 n.15.

73. Mittelstadt, "Dilemmas of the Liberal Welfare State," 220, summarizes these provisions.

74. Weeks, *Job Corps*, 57–58.

75. Mittelstadt, "Dilemmas of the Liberal Welfare State," 223.

76. Ibid., 232, 235.

77. Sonya Michel, "Childcare and Welfare (In)Justice," *Feminist Studies* 24 (Spring 1998): 45–46, 53 n. 5. Michel further notes that little of the authorized funding for childcare was actually appropriated under this amendment.

78. Mittelstadt, "Dilemmas of the Liberal Welfare State," 276–77; on Title V, see the testimony of Anthony J. Celebrezze, *Economic Opportunity Act of 1964*, 217–18.

79. "Social Security Amendments of 1967," *Hearings before the Committee on Finance*, U.S. Senate, 90th Cong., 1st sess., HR 12080, pt. 3, September 20, 21, 22, and 26, 1967, 1791.

80. James T. Patterson, *America's Struggle against Poverty, 1900–1994* (Cambridge: Harvard University, 1994), 174–77.

81. *New York State Department of Social Services v. Dublino*, 413 U.S. 405 (1972), attached *Amicus Brief of NWRO*, 11.

82. Forbath, "Constitutional Welfare Rights," 1863–67, esp. 1865. See also Felicia Kornbluh, "The Rise and Fall of Welfare Rights: Gender, Law, and Poverty in Postwar America," manuscript draft in author's possession, and Premilla Nadasen, "Expanding the Boundaries of the Women's Movement: Black Feminism and the Struggle for Welfare Rights," *Feminist Studies* 28 (Summer 2002): 271–303.

83. Tobias, *Faces of Feminism*, 93–133; Dorothy Sue Cobble, *The Other Women's Movement: Workplace Justice and Social Rights in Modern America* (Princeton: Princeton University Press, 2004).

84. Susan M. Hartmann, "Women's Employment and the Domestic Ideal in the Early Cold War Years," in *Not June Cleaver: Women and Gender in Postwar America, 1945–1960*, ed. Joanne Meyerowitz (Philadelphia: Temple University Press, 1994), 84–100.

85. Barbara Ehrenreich, "Maid to Order," *Harper's Magazine*, April 2000, 59–70.

86. *Congressional Record*, 88th Cong., 2d sess., February 8, 1964, vol. 110, pt. 2, 2578. See also Alice Kessler-Harris, "Gender Identity: Rights to Work and the Idea of Economic Citizenship," *Schweizerische Zeitschrift für Geschichte* 46 (1996): 421–25.

87. "Social Security and Welfare Proposals," *Hearings before the Committee on Ways and Means, House of Representatives*, 91st Cong., 1st. sess., pt. 1, October 15 and 16, 1969, 1027.

88. Ibid., 1030–31.

89. Ibid., 1032.

90. Rickie Solinger, *Beggars and Choosers: How the Politics of Choice Shapes Adoption, Abortion, and Welfare in the United States* (New York: Henry Holt, 2001).

91. "Social Security and Welfare Proposals," 1032.

92. Lemann, *Promised Land*; "Social Security and Welfare Proposals," 1033.

93. "Social Security and Welfare Proposals," 1032–33.

94. Ibid., 1042.

95. "Social Security Amendments of 1967," 1555–57.

96. Charles Murray, *Losing Ground: American Social Policy, 1950–1980* (New York: Basic Books, 1984).

97. Goodwin, "'Employable Mothers' and 'Suitable Work'"; Levenstein, "From Innocent Children to Unwanted Migrants and Unwed Moms."

98. *King v. Smith*, 292 U.S. 309 (1968).

99. *Goldberg v. Kelly*, 394 U.S. 254 (1970).

100. Elizabeth Bussiere, *(Dis)Entitling the Poor: The Warren Court, Welfare Rights, and the American Political Tradition* (University Park: Pennsylvania State University Press, 1997), 98–151. See also R. Shep Melnick, *Between the Lines: Interpreting Welfare Rights* (Washington, D.C.: Brookings Institution, 1994).

101. Guida West, *The National Welfare Rights Movement: The Social Protest of Poor Women* (New York: Praeger, 1981). See also Felicia Kornbluh, "To Fulfill Their 'Rightly Needs': Consumerism and the National Welfare Rights Movement," *Radical History Review*, no.69 (1997): 76–111.

102. "Social Security Amendments of 1967," 1556.

103. I elaborate on these points in "When Work Is Slavery."

104. R. Kent Weaver, "Ending Welfare As We Know It: Policymaking for Low-Income Families in the Clinton/Gingrich Era," in *The Social Divide: Political Parties and the Future of Activist Government*, ed. Margaret Weir (Washington, D.C.: Brookings Institution, 1998), 361–416.

105. Mink, *Welfare's End*; see also the essays in Mink, *Whose Welfare?*

106. Ann Shola Orloff, "Farewell to Maternalism: Welfare Reform, Ending Entitlement for Poor Single Mothers, and Expanding the Claims of Poor Employed Parents" (paper presented at the annual meeting of the American Political Science Association, San Francisco, August 30, 2001).

107. See also Alice Kessler-Harris, *In Pursuit of Equity: Women, Men, and the Quest for Economic Citizenship in Twentieth-Century America* (New York: Oxford University Press, 2001).

Making Pluralism "Great"

Beyond a Re*cycled* History of the Great Society

Brian Balogh

Explicit in the title of this essay and lurking throughout the volume is a seemingly innocuous term: "pluralism." Both Nelson Lichtenstein and Hugh Heclo argue that the Great Society killed pluralism. Lichtenstein engages pluralism in order to castigate it as a Trojan horse (designed by liberal intellectuals, no less!) that first co-opted social democracy and later succumbed to self-absorbed rights consciousness. For Heclo, the self-contradictory demands made of pluralism in the sixties—asking government to do more yet trusting government less—overwhelmed a system built on compromise. "Combining ferocious opposites and keeping each ferocious," not the compromise and bargaining essential to pluralism, animated sixties civics, as Heclo sees it. Lichtenstein's attitude toward pluralism can be characterized as "good riddance." Heclo's? "What are we to do now?"

In this essay I weigh the historical evolution of pluralism and conclude that it survived the Great Society. No doubt, the social tumult, radical demands for democratic access, and the dramatic increase in the venues for policymaking stimulated by the sixties have altered pluralism significantly. Nevertheless, the Great Society democratized politics without destroying the basic pluralist fabric which bound Americans to the public sphere in the twentieth century and which endures today.

The "Challenge Constantly Renewed"

The authors in this volume understand the Great Society to encompass several dimensions. Public policy is a central concern for the contributors, but so, too, is the growth of the presidency, the impact of war on social reform, and political ideology.

Nelson Lichtenstein frames his account of labor in a broader context of intellectual trends that overwhelmed social democracy and celebrated cold war pluralism. Like Lichtenstein, most contributors to this volume concentrate on the ideological battle for the hearts and minds of liberals. Jerome Mileur reminds us, however, that this important internecine struggle should not eclipse an even more fundamental ideological shift from liberalism to conservatism. Viewed from the perspective of the last forty years, the Great Society served as the fulcrum, possibly even a catalyst, in this evolution.[1]

Lyndon Johnson, of course, looms large in any account of the Great Society. As David Shribman and William Leuchtenburg illustrate, Johnson was larger than life, and his personal motivation, experience, strengths, and shortcomings were integrally connected to the fate of the Great Society. Sidney Milkis places Johnson's personal qualities in the context of an administrative presidency which stretches back to Franklin D. Roosevelt and which tested its limits amid the flux of Great Society demands and promises.

Vietnam also shaped the course of the Great Society. Although Johnson could do little about his personality and even less about the trajectory of the office he assumed, he did enjoy a great deal of discretion when it came to waging war or preserving peace. Johnson might have benefited from the lessons of history when American presidents often had to choose between war and reform. The Great Society seems to confirm this pattern. Yet, the same arrogance of power that drove Johnson deeper into Vietnam, Wilson Carey McWilliams argues, was crucial to the vaulting confidence necessary to imagine a "great society."

The authors in this volume analyze the way that ideas, the diffusion of those ideas, social movements, interest groups, presidential initiative, foreign policy considerations, political culture, and the venues used to convert political preferences into action produced a distinct set of public policies. Several essays examine how these policies fared as they were implemented and challenged after the 1970s through the present. The authors also comment on many aspects of the policymaking system that evolved during the heyday of the Great Society and endured despite a sharp shift to the right ideologically, and leadership styles far different from LBJ's.[2]

The relationship between politics, public policy, and society shifted during the "long" sixties. Hugh Heclo distills this change in the phrase "policy mindedness." What was new about the sixties, Hugh Heclo insists, was not policy but "policy mindedness," which was "an outlook that elevates and cleaves to one essential insight—when governing is happening or when partisan politics is churning, when all the affairs of public affairs are coming and going, the one thing that is *really* happening are choices about policy." That liberal Democrats might envision the world in these terms should come as no surprise. That the New Right ultimately embraced this perspective, as Heclo, R. Shep Melnick, and Patrick McGuinn and Frederick Hess demonstrate, suggests a more fundamental shift in social and intellectual perspective.

The breadth and complexity of the "Great Society" as a concept found no better expression than Lyndon Johnson's words at the University of Michigan commencement in May 1964. "Most of all," Johnson cautioned, "the Great Society is not a safe harbor, a resting place, a final objective, a finished work." Rather, it is a "challenge constantly renewed."[3] That its ambitions were boundless, its commitment sincere, and elements of its initial agenda long overdue meant that Great Society policymakers sometimes identified new problems and shifted their angle of attack as initial challenges proved to be more intractable than anticipated. The Great Society was a work in progress. Its progress elicited demands for more work.

Johnson's words triggered an ambitious agenda. LBJ challenged the Michigan students to "enrich and elevate our national life, and to advance the quality of our American civilization." With imagination, initiative, and indignation, they could move "not only toward the rich society and the powerful society, but upward to the Great Society." Such a society would fulfill one's desire for beauty and "hunger for community." It would be a place where one could "renew contact with nature." The Great Society would even address loneliness, boredom, and indifference. Schools would prepare students to "enjoy their hours of leisure as well as their hours of labor."[4]

The means to these sweeping ends, however, were unclear. Employing more experts was one solution that Johnson offered to a nation locked into a space race and supposedly on the verge of producing electrical power "too cheap to meter."[5] Expertise was tapped in the social and human sciences, not just in physics and engineering. Johnson told the Michigan students: "We are going to assemble the best thought and the broadest knowledge from all over the world to find . . . answers for America." But the president also cautioned against the very kind of statist intervention that many progressives sought. As LBJ told the audience, "The solution to these problems does not rest on a massive program in Washington, nor can it rely solely on the strained resources of local authority."[6] Rather than specifying the means, Johnson instead retreated to the far more politically cautious mechanism of "creative federalism." Of all the idealistic assumptions built into the early conception of a "great society," the belief that bold ends could be achieved without redistributing income and power nationally was certainly the most optimistic.[7]

Within months of the Michigan speech, Johnson created the first of what ultimately swelled to over one hundred task forces that would bring the power of expert problem solving to bear on the nation's social problems. LBJ understood the importance of timing. Departing from the inaugural ball that crowned his landslide election over Barry Goldwater, the president put his aides on notice: "Don't stay up late. There's work to be done. We're on our way to the Great Society."[8]

If legislation could make society great, the Johnson team was the one on which to bet. In the first half of 1965, the president sent sixty-five messages to Congress. James Patterson has labeled the most significant achievements in this unprecedented legislative onslaught as the "Big Four": aid to elementary and secondary education; Medicare and Medicaid; immigration reform; and the Voting Rights Act.[9] Even before the Big Four, Johnson had declared war on poverty, adopting a set of community-based experiments funded by the Ford Foundation as the centerpiece of his Office of Economic Opportunity.[10] By 1966, Johnson had delivered on his promise to address Americans' quality of life. He passed legislation concerning clean air and wilderness areas. Congress also created the National Endowment for the Arts and the National Endowment for the Humanities and expanded aid to college students.[11]

At its outset, the Great Society was a dynamic, though scattershot, effort to bring the good life to all Americans. But to do so meant addressing the problem of inequality. Those Americans who had been left behind owing to poverty or racism had to be brought into the middle class. The Great Society sought to extend to all Americans the kinds of New Deal programs that had helped to broaden the middle class in the 1940s and 1950s. It started by completing the missing link—federally subsidized health care for elderly Americans with steady work histories. As Edward Berkowitz details in this volume, it was compulsory, and it was financed by payroll taxes.

Although Social Security benefits came to be viewed as an entitlement for those who had steady employment in the core sectors of the economy, the program was built originally on the cultural bedrock of "equal opportunity." By providing for the security of hardworking Americans after retirement, during times of high unemployment, and when faced by medical problems as they aged, the Social Security Act and its extensions rewarded the work ethic. Over the years, the types of work covered slowly expanded outward from the industrial core to include agricultural and other workers who initially had been excluded from benefits. As Berkowitz notes, Social Security administrators celebrated the date (1951) that the work-related social insurance coverage finally outstripped the hated means-tested old-age assistance.

Yet for millions of Americans, opportunity remained "blocked." The Great Society addressed this neglected constituency, seeking to remove barriers to political and economic opportunity. The most straightforward, and perhaps most successful, legislation was the Voting Rights Act, which brought unprecedented federal enforcement to bear on what traditionally had been localized responsibilities—registration, redistricting, and municipal expansion. Under the banner of community action, the federal government helped to organize poor and dispossessed citizens, urging them to challenge such local and state bureaucracies as welfare departments and school boards. As Eileen Boris points out, Johnson framed his claims for aid to the poor in the rhetoric of self-sufficiency. This was not welfare. "The Goal was to increase opportunity through education and training, jobs, 'and the opportunity to live in decency and dignity.'"

Historically, education had been the great avenue of opportunity in America. But it had failed to achieve this end, particularly in urban areas. Loath to redistribute income directly or to guarantee jobs for poor people, Great Society planners viewed the Elementary and Secondary Education Act (ESEA) as the most promising engine for equalizing opportunity. As McGuinn and Hess note, a powerful equity rationale—the removal of barriers to equal opportunity—lay behind the ESEA. It was the federal government's responsibility to promote social and economic opportunity through education.

Equal access to a good education also raised the federal government's stake in desegregation. With the emergence of Black Power, frustration with the pace of progress, and a wave of riots that swept the nation's cities, programmatic liberals shifted from emphasizing opportunity to insisting on results. But the initial ESEA legislation provided little federal control as it funneled additional resources to disadvantaged students through state and local school systems. As funding directed toward traditional ends and middle-class constituents increased, the federal government intervened. McGuinn and Hess note that "federal legislative enactments, bureaucratic regulations, and court mandates in education became increasingly numerous and prescriptive, and federal influence over schools grew significantly. As a result, the political debate shifted from whether the federal government had an obligation to promote educational opportunity, to the effectiveness of these efforts."

During the sixties, the federal courts and the Office of Education leapfrogged each other in a race toward southern compliance with school desegregation. Faced with losing what, by the end of the decade, was a major source of revenue, southern systems complied with federal mandates and in many instances achieved levels of integration that far exceeded those in the North.[12]

While the Great Society was built on an important historical foundation of programs dedicated to the ideal of equal opportunity, the Johnson administration's vision was results oriented from the start when it came to serving those who already enjoyed "equal opportunity." For middle-class Americans who had long benefited from hefty government subsidies ranging from Social Security to veterans benefits to the home mortgage deduction, the Great Society promised results where it most mattered: quality of life. In February 1965, the president urged Congress to adopt environmental policies that considered "not just man's welfare, but the dignity of man's spirit."[13] Some of the most assertive new extensions of federal authority occurred in policy areas such as the arts or the environment, in programs that historically had been run by state and local authorities if they existed at all, and in policies that disproportionately advantaged middle-class and wealthy patrons.

By the end of the Johnson years, nine separate task forces had explored a range of policy issues that resulted in hundreds of conservation and beautification measures costing $12 billion.[14] Congress weighed in, passing such legislation as the 1965 Water Quality Act, even though public opinion polls at the time showed that only 17 percent of the American people considered air and water pollution a problem worthy of government attention.[15]

For the poorest quarter of Americans, the Great Society authorized the War on Poverty in order to remove barriers that denied equal opportunity whether the problem was racial discrimination, access to the political system, or unequal education. When these barriers proved to be more intractable than anticipated, those who had already embraced federal public policy as the solution to social and economic problems demanded results, not just "opportunity." Understood as a challenge constantly renewed, the Great Society did not insist on equalizing Americans' income or quality of life but instead sought to improve every American's quality of life.

Cyclical, Linear, and Proximate Historical Influences

Cycles of Reform

The interpretations of the Great Society in this volume often draw on the "cycles of reform" framework. Calling it the "last hurrah" for liberalism, Mileur labels the Great Society the "third great reform era of the twentieth century." Comparing the accomplishments of the Great Society with those of the New Deal was not merely an intellectual abstraction for LBJ. Leuchtenburg argues that it was a motivating force behind Johnson's commitment to the Great Society. Only a set of legislative accomplishments greater than FDR's would suffice. Roosevelt may have "saved" liberal democracy, McWilliams notes, but "LBJ would make it victorious."

Johnson did not always compete with the New Deal: he learned from it as well, as Shribman notes. Johnson's conviction that presidential administrations had little time to make a difference is one of these lessons. Roosevelt's "Court-packing" debacle was another lesson LBJ imbibed during the New Deal. One bad decision, Johnson concluded, could squander a huge mandate. "Franklin Roosevelt came back here in 1937 after the biggest popular landslide in history," Johnson told Turner

Catledge of the *New York Times* in December 1964. "But by April he couldn't get Congress to pass the time of day."[16]

The most significant legacy of the New Deal remained ideological. Boris notes that the New Deal's structure of social benefits was constructed around the white male breadwinner. His labor—at least in core sectors of the economy—brought with it a package of social rights that included his entire family. The Social Security Act of 1935, which translated this powerful set of ideas into a federal commitment, and the incremental extension of these benefits to cover the disabled and those working in marginal sectors of the economy, shaped Great Society planners' conception of the relationship between work, welfare, and social citizenship.[17] Thus Lyndon Johnson stressed "opportunity" and economic self-sufficiency as he promoted his War on Poverty. As Boris illustrates, the Job Corps and the Great Society's training programs continued to privilege the male breadwinner at the same time as they began to impose work requirements on women.

New Deal reforms were supported politically by a coalition that retained the Democratic Party's base of support in the Solid South but captured millions of new adherents among northern African Americans, working-class ethnics, and union members. Frayed from the start at the local level, this coalition proved to be a powerful force at the national level during the Great Society. It even drew millions of newly suburbanized voters into its ranks. The New Deal coalition was able to maintain this balancing act by deferring regularly to local administrative preferences. From welfare to public housing policy, from road building to public power, national enabling legislation was implemented through a variety of brokers who adapted New Deal programs to local preferences.

But as the Great Society nationalized public policy, some of these local arrangements fractured. As African American constituents embraced Black Power, long-standing fissures between this key northern constituency and the Democratic Party's southern base tore the party apart.[18] Nor were the cleavages purely regional. If Frances Fox Piven and Richard Cloward are correct in their thesis, programs such as the Equal Opportunity Act of 1964 were designed to take political advantage of millions of African Americans who had moved north, but these programs also fueled fires already smoldering at the local level. Figurative fires were soon replaced by real ones, as race riots swept through virtually every major American city by the end of the 1960s, illuminating even more starkly the firewall that now stood between segments of the New Deal coalition.

The Great Society's ambitious program ended in the Vietnam War. As McWilliams observes, "foreign policy is to a Great Society like a third party on a romantic date, a disruption of the mood, prose muddling poetry." While a number of scholars have demonstrated that war has often contributed to significant social reform—the emergence of the modern civil rights movement and the capacious package of veterans benefits after World War II being just two examples—there is little doubt that some of the principals, especially Lyndon Johnson himself, worried that war would kill the Great Society.[19]

Enduring Legacies

But most of the connections between the Great Society and the past are not contained within the "cycles of reform" framework. Indeed, there was a powerful strain within the Great Society that resonated deeply with some of America's longest-standing legacies. The quest for growth and mastery was one. While America's intervention in Vietnam came to symbolize the apotheosis of military, technological, and ideological optimism (if not hubris), it was just one of many examples, such as the space program, that sought to conquer the boundaries of time, place, and material restraints. Johnson was a nationalist and, like all American presidents who came before him, was committed to the goal of "mastery, abundance and command over nature."[20] Like most Americans in the mid-1960s, Johnson believed that America could not fail—in Vietnam or in its quest to build a great society.[21] While it is easy to criticize this arrogance of power in the wake of the Vietnam disaster, the noble dream embodied in the Great Society would not have been possible without that kind of chutzpah.[22] Nor was it uncharacteristic for Americans to believe that the remaining barriers to social and economic obstacles could be overcome, given the exceptional advantages in political system, resources, and technical ingenuity America enjoyed.

Regrettably, the history of exclusion of and bias toward women and minorities is another legacy that stretches far back in American history and is inextricably linked to the quest for growth and mastery. Moreover, the role of the state in enforcing these racist and sexist norms has been even more prominent than its support for expansion and technical mastery.[23] A committed handful of racial activists and a far larger number of anonymous citizens battled racial discrimination throughout the century. It was courageous work among "local people" that set the stage for legal breakthroughs in the 1960s. Liberal leaders, however, had not been as willing to take political risks at the grass roots as were their supporters. Stepping out of the shadows of the New Deal, the Great Society explicitly acknowledged America's racist history, addressing the problem directly in the Civil Rights Act of 1964, the Voting Rights Act of 1965, and the aggressive interpretation and enforcement of both.[24]

When "equal opportunity" alone failed to erase hundreds of years of racial discrimination, Great Society programs did not shy away from emphasizing results in their administrative interpretation of legislative mandates, despite the long-standing history of liberal emphasis on equal individual rights. Doing so required that certain groups be designated as "official minorities." But as Hugh Davis Graham relates in his essay, "a major barrier to designating official minorities in post–World War II America was the liberal political tradition itself, which emphasized equal individual rights, not group rights, and protected them through the negative action of antidiscrimination." Thus advocates of results-based Great Society programs had to reconstruct liberalism before they could mobilize it effectively to end racial discrimination.[25]

The Great Society had less to say about the long-standing tradition of sexism. As Boris documents, sex distinctions remained acceptable among liberals in the mid-1960s. Nevertheless, Great Society programs did begin to incorporate a subtle shift in attitude toward women and work that had been reflected in training programs as early as the mid-1950s. These programs stressed the role that training and education might play in preparing women on welfare for the workforce. By 1962, federal welfare directed toward women had begun to build work-related income incentives into the program, and in 1967, the Work Incentive Program was initiated, allowing states to end assistance to parents (of older children) if the adults refused to work or accept training. This transition paved the way for treating women and men alike—at least when it came to the relationship between work and welfare.[26] Given the system's expectation that women would continue to care for children while they worked, the biting criticism of welfare rights activist Johnnie Tillmon hit home. She compared welfare to a "supersexist marriage. You trade in *a* man for *the* man."[27]

The Great Society was part of another linear trend in the twentieth century: the growth of the administrative presidency, which, as Sidney Milkis points out, accelerated rapidly during the Johnson presidency. This trend, which dates back to the Progressive Era and gained momentum during the New Deal, divorced the presidency more and more from party and congressional control. Like many of his predecessors, Johnson sought alternative bases of support. As Milkis and as Piven and Cloward argue, Johnson established one such beachhead in the Community Action Program, which enabled the president to reach grassroots constituents by going around ossified local institutions and more traditional levers of power. Indeed, the Great Society pushed the administrative presidency to the breaking point. When push came to shove—whether in the form of urban riots, increasingly radical demands from newly empowered constituents, or opposition to the Vietnam War—Johnson's extension of the administrative presidency left him insulated, if not isolated, from his party and large segments of Congress.[28] For the previous thirty-five years, strengthening the presidency had reinforced its stature. For the first time since Roosevelt's ill-advised Court-packing scheme, a majority of Americans began to question the legitimacy of the administrative presidency.

The Cold War Influence on the Great Society

Both the ubiquitous cyclical interpretations of reform and those grounded in such persistent patterns as the quest for mastery or racism have crowded out a more proximate and the most significant historical influence on the Great Society: the cold war. The post–World War II growth of the administrative presidency, for instance, had been nurtured and in large part underwritten by the cold war, which encouraged Americans to defer to insulated, distant institutions, especially the federal government. Experts had been glamorized by their crucial role in developing the atomic bomb, radar, and other scientific triumphs that helped win World War II, and they enjoyed unprecedented authority and status by the early 1960s. Some of the luster of the physical sciences had even rubbed off on the social sciences. Many of the programs that emerged as part of the Great Society were the product of ideas supplied by well-meaning professionals, not responses to popular demand.

This merger of professional and administrative capacity, which I have elsewhere labeled the "proministrative state," reached the height of its influence during the early years of the Great Society. Ironically, at the very time when Americans were looking more and more to government and to experts to solve an ever-growing list of problems, they also began to question the ability of those experts to deliver public policy that worked. By the end of the decade, and in part as a result of failed policies in Vietnam, the American faith in even science and technology had been shaken.[29]

Yet for fifteen years, from roughly 1950 through 1965, Americans granted experts unprecedented discretion, especially in the area of national security. Few questioned the safety or economic viability of the government's role in subsidizing a nuclear power industry that promised cheap electricity at the same time as it strengthened the nation's defense. Environmental considerations, civilian health and safety, and local zoning traditions were trampled to accommodate the needs of the nation's university-military-industrial complex.[30]

The "proministrative state," responding to the pressures of the cold war, led the national government in the 1950s to undertake major new initiatives, such as the interstate highway system and the St. Lawrence Seaway. The cold war, as Mary Dudziak has argued, added a new rationale for improving race relations, as racial oppression in the United States was a heavy burden in the nation's competition with the Soviet Union for the hearts and minds of the so-called third world. It also provided a new rationale for deficit spending, as the National Security Council called for permanent mobilization to counter the Soviet threat even though it would create a deficit situation. It was the National Defense Education Act of 1958, passed in the wake of Sputnik to provide federal assistance to states to improve science, math, and language instruction, that laid the groundwork for the explosion of categorical grant programs for domestic social programs that comprised so much of the Great Society and ushered in a new era of federalism. This path of social reform was far from cyclical, nor did it owe its legacy to the New Deal, as the Johnson White House relied on critical resources and precedents created during the height of the cold war—the most significant being deficit spending—oftentimes simply taking them for granted.[31]

The cold war also had a dramatic impact on liberalism. For all of Johnson's self-reflective comparisons to Franklin Roosevelt's administration, it was cold war liberalism that informed his thinking as he sought to sustain both guns and butter. The gritty insider politics of the Truman and Eisenhower presidencies and Johnson's tenure as Senate majority leader were more proximate influences on Johnson's career as president. It was cold war liberalism that dominated ideological debate on both sides of the partisan aisle in the early 1960s.[32]

In his essay Heclo addresses the contours of cold war liberalism on the eve of the Great Society. The liberalism that built the New Deal, he argues, was constructed on a foundation of disinterestedness. Embodied in Walter Lippmann's 1929 call for an educated public that could employ a mature and self-controlled outlook to process objective information, disinterestedness lay at the heart of public-spirited Progressivism.[33] Heclo contrasts this ideal to the new realism embedded in the outlook of cold war liberals such as Arthur Schlesinger Jr. "Coolness," the characteristic most associated with John F. Kennedy's attitude toward public policy, was now the norm. This tough-minded realism, according to Schlesinger, continued to offer a positive view of the federal government's ability to carry out reform.[34] But in the wake of Nazi Germany, World War II, and the use of atomic weapons, humankind had to be regarded as flawed and corruptible. The positive attitude toward government was thus combined in cold war liberalism with a negative view of human behavior. This incubator for "big policy" grew out of cold war, not New Deal, liberalism and provided the impetus for a "new liberalism" that emerged during the Great Society.

What Was Distinctive about the Great Society?

Sensitivity to the historical context from which the Great Society grew should not obscure the social and political transformation that occurred between 1964 and the end of the decade. We cannot understand this transformation, however, if our analysis is confined to the White House or even the formal political and policymaking arenas. Instead, we need to consider profound changes in American political culture and social relations in the mid-1960s. Politicians and policymakers adapted to and, in some instances, guided this rapidly changing environment.

Social Movements

Social movements transformed liberal ideology and the cold war pluralist system. The civil rights movement fashioned a template for mobilizing hundreds of thousands of committed citizens around a concrete set of programmatic objectives and publicizing this agenda to millions of sympathetic supporters. This model was soon adopted by students protesting restrictions on free speech and, eventually, by millions more who challenged the administration's policies in Vietnam. Public interest groups, epitomized by Ralph Nader's crusade on behalf of consumers, proliferated during the second half of the decade, carrying finely tuned policy pronouncements deep into the inner sanctums of all three branches of government.

Social movements, as well as the networks of issue-related public interest groups they spawned, cared not only about the substance of policy problems but also, and sometimes more intensely, about the process by which citizens engaged public policy in a modern democratic republic. Although the solution crafted by New Left theoreticians—participatory democracy—failed in practice, the overwhelming demand for transparency left its mark on the process of governance. An acute sense of "rights consciousness" powered many of the demands advanced by social movements, issue networks, and plaintiffs who filed class action suits. From initial demands targeted at destroying the Jim Crow regime in the South to the right to a minimum income, clean air and water, or special education, the language of entitlement expanded as the decade progressed.

The civil rights movement led the way in this regard. It not only demonstrated the transformative power of organized protest, as Milkis points out, but also exposed the relatively fragile condition of political institutions that had for so long upheld the prerogatives of Jim Crow segregation. The New Left, another seminal social movement that animated student protest against the war during the 1960s, was deeply influenced by the triumphs of the Civil Rights movement. A sense of hope and possibility—even a utopian spirit at times—pervaded the New Left in its early years. The civil rights movement also provided the "how-to" guide for would-be organizers, as activists from civil rights moved on to the New Left, feminist, and even the environmental movements.[35] The lessons went well beyond personal experience. In a society that increasingly tuned to the electronic media for its news—first television, then the World Wide Web—the power of the video image was a lesson that activists soon mastered.[36] Nonviolent resistance, marches on Washington, confrontations with reactionary opponents—these tactics were adopted from the civil rights movement and used again and again by other groups demanding a hearing for their issues.

A radical reconceptualization of the boundary between public and private linked these movements. Again, the civil rights movement led the way. It trained its tactical guns on activities previously considered "private": lunch counters, transportation, employment, recreation, and even religious observance. It exposed the public power behind the seemingly private sets of decisions that excluded citizens based on race. The landmark civil rights legislation of 1964 and 1965 was "radical," to use Hugh Graham's adjective, because it embraced "the permanently expanded federal authority with effective enforcement power over vast areas of behavior previously free of national coercion, including private as well as public employment; customer choice in stores, hotels, restaurants, and places of amusement; and voting procedures." It mobilized a political, rather than a personal, response to these affronts to African American rights and dignity, and it demanded public solutions. Armed with the mantra that "the personal is the political," students at elite college campuses began to see connections between the courses they were required to take and the federally subsidized military-industrial-university complex; women noticed the discrepancy between male and female wages; and environmentalists glimpsed the relationship between personal health and protective regulation. Once engaged, issues previously considered inappropriate for public action emerged as a crucial source of new policy agendas.

Social pressure from the grass roots was instrumental in breaking the legislative logjam. The 1964 Civil Rights Act and the 1965 Voting Rights Act created templates that ultimately served the needs of many other groups. Famously, Title VII of the Civil Rights Act, originally drafted with racial discrimination in mind, was redirected toward sexual discrimination in the workplace.[37] The Voting Rights Act was expanded to cover a broad range of minorities.[38]

Indeed, the relationship between the Great Society and the emergence of feminism illustrates the enduring relationship between social movements and the policy legacy of the civil rights movement. As Boris documents, women's issues were ignored by most Great Society planners. Despite the valuable work of the network of professional women who eventually formed the National Organization of Women, the organization they created focused on relatively narrow issues of employment discrimination and electing women to office. As late as the mid-1960s, the lives of most women were circumscribed both within the family and in the workplace. It took grassroots activism and mass mobilization of women to bring changes in society that led to greater equality for women.

Only after the emergence of feminism, with the broad-based pressure it was able to exert on the political system and in the private sector, were women able to use legislation and administrative procedures initially crafted to secure the rights of African Americans to protect the rights of their sisters. The breakthrough for women required redrawing the boundary between public and private to place issues previously considered personal or private on the state's agenda and to pursue "liberation" in places previously considered "private." "The vast majority of the newly minted feminists across the country," Linda Gordon has observed, "did not belong to any organization. Participation in the movement was as much private and domestic as public, it was a new way of challenging the boss, a new way of understanding daily interactions. You were in women's liberation if you thought you were."[39] Women, just as millions of African Americans had when they embraced Black Power, addressed the political culture. The movement radically reoriented women's views about power. By embracing identities as African Americans, women, or both, activists exposed sources of repression, whether private or public, and sought to redress the balance of power in all their relationships. They demonstrated that so-called private matters, whether in the home or at work, were in fact public concerns and that public consciousness could reshape "private" relationships.

Big Policy, Little Trust

Cumulatively, these powerful thrusts from the grass roots upward democratized the political culture of the mid-1960s. As Heclo put it, the "overbelief," virtually a theology, of the sixties was "a vision of the people redeeming a flawed society, if you will, democracy in a modern passion play." Distrust of government and faith in public policy were not sequential. Rather, there was a "singularity" to this symbiotic relationship. Thus, public trust in government plummeted between 1965 and 1975. Clearly, Vietnam and Watergate were contributing factors, but mistrust of government went well beyond these seminal events. It became embedded in the very relations between students and teachers, doctors and patients, elected officials and constituents. Significantly, as Melnick notes, trust in government declined at a faster pace among liberals than conservatives. By the 1970s, nothing seemed to alarm liberal consumer advocate Ralph Nader more than the prospect of actually sharing power with the "establishment."[40]

At the same time, liberals embraced "big policy," for which they turned to the federal government. The explosion of new policy demands from democratically inspired social movements called for more government, not less. Liberation, whether black, Hispanic, women's, or gay, invariably required an active state. Milkis argues that even Lyndon Johnson was caught up in the rhetoric of liberation that permeated the political culture. It resonated with his populist roots. Johnson's Great Society speech at the University of Michigan echoed language of the Port Huron Statement drafted not far from there in 1962. As late as 1966, Johnson's State of the Union address called for "liberation" that would use the nation's economic success for the "fulfillment" of people's lives.[41] Still, liberals retained a suspicion of government authority. Even the new administrative structures created by social pressure—the Equal Employment Opportunity Commission, the Office of Economic Opportunity (OEO), and the Environmental Protection Agency (EPA)—were themselves objects of suspicion and constant vigilance by the grass roots.

Ambivalent activists, as Melnick has characterized them, quickly embraced a discourse that had become more pervasive in post–World War II liberalism—the language of individual rights. While the roots of nineteenth-century liberalism lay in protecting the integrity and rights of the individual, the "rights revolution" or "rights talk" that exploded by the end of the 1960s differed from classical liberalism in its demand that the public sector, especially the national government, actively enforce a broad range of rights and fund a generous array of direct government services to uphold these rights.[42] The New Deal laid the groundwork for this, but the range of rights pursued before the Great Society was limited.

Advocates of the vastly expanded rights agenda also stressed procedural rights, which reflected their ambivalent attitude toward a government that was asked to do more yet was not fully trusted by the very interests demanding its expansion. Policy got "bigger," while the bureaucratic discretion required to implement expanded policy was circumscribed to ensure the right of equal access to all. Robert Kagan has labeled the juxtaposition of demands that an activist government protect individuals from serious harm, injustice, and environmental dangers, on the one hand, with the heightened fear of concentrated power and demands for access, on the other, "adversarial legalism."[43]

Rights-based liberalism ultimately overwhelmed and constrained the administrative structure, especially the capacious conception of the presidency, founded during the New Deal. It opened the New Deal's entrenched administrative structures to attack from both the left and the right, according to Milkis. In education, for instance, the theme of "equal opportunity" was superceded in the 1970s by a rationale that emphasized entitlements and protecting rights.[44] Along the fractious boundary between work and welfare, the National Welfare Rights Organization broke with the Great Society's early emphasis on equal opportunity, demanding a guaranteed income as one of the rights of citizenship.[45] It was Richard Nixon, not Lyndon Johnson, who translated these demands into public policy, proposing legislation that would have ensured just such an entitlement. The quest for Civil Rights evolved from an equal opportunity rationale to one that featured "hard" affirmative action and equal results. Once again, it was Richard Nixon, through the Philadelphia Plan, who enshrined this rights-driven program.

Lowering the Legitimacy Barrier

Great Society programs lowered the "legitimacy barrier." A conception developed by the political scientist James Q. Wilson, the legitimacy barrier operated to constrain the scope of public policy, identifying certain options—such as state-owned businesses, for instance—as illegitimate, except, perhaps, during times of crisis. In many instances, the legitimacy barrier was breached when the national government moved into policy areas traditionally handled at the state and local level—such as civil rights enforcement and voter registration. Once lowered, Wilson argues, "no program is any longer 'new'—it is seen, rather, as an extension, a modification, or an enlargement of something the government is already doing."[46] The new wave of social regulation introduced in the 1970s is another important example of the legitimacy barrier breached. "In the past going back ten or fifteen years," Bernard Falk of the National Electrical Manufacturers Association complained, "you didn't have a consumer movement. The manufacturer controlled the make-up of his own product, and Washington could be ignored. Now we all have a new partner, the federal government."[47]

Starting with Johnson's expansive goals, which ranged from combating boredom to the search for beauty, Great Society policies propelled the national government into a variety of new policy areas. Each new breach in the legitimacy barrier was significant in its own right. But the most important consequence, one that Melnick has called the "most profound legacy of the Great Society," was cumulative. During the 1970s, the federal government's expansion was routinized. It no longer took a presidential assassination or powerful social movements to recalibrate the legitimacy barrier.

As Melnick illustrates in impressive detail, the Great Society gave birth to a new set of institutional patterns that privileged big policy and garnered support from conservatives as well as liberals. The implications of this shift are evident today. As President Bush sought to fulfill traditional conservative pledges to reign in "big government" by reducing domestic spending and federal regulation, he faced opposition from some of his supporters, concerned that programs which their states had come to rely on would be targeted. As the *Washington Post* reported on January 26, 2003, "two of the Senate's most conservative Republicans, Sens. John E. Sununu and Judd Gregg of New Hampshire, supported an amendment aimed at having the federal government play a more active role in protecting New England from Midwest air pollution."[48] Conservatives could play the "big policy" game too.

The Therapeutic Ethos

Where did such demands come from in the first place? Perhaps the most distinctive source of new demands during the Great Society grew out of a phenomenon broadly referred to as the "therapeutic ethos." At the core of this worldview lay the notion that virtually any problem could be solved, even problems previously defined as "personal" or "emotional." If the personal really was the political, then public policy might well hold the key to satisfaction and fulfillment. The ever-expanding list of problems, concerns, and rights to be protected by government was easier to sustain during a time of economic prosperity and rising federal revenues, which made it appear that the government could afford to meet these demands without redistributing income or power. The range of remedies for society's problems offered in the name of therapeutic progress—and the broad public acceptance of this legitimacy—helps explain why public obligations ballooned during the Great Society, ranging from the expansion of mental health and education programs to "identity-based" programs such as affirmative action.[49]

Piven and Cloward dismiss the therapeutic ethos as a trivial factor in the development of social policy in the 1960s. Heclo, however, takes this phenomenon more seriously, identifying it as a source of "big policy." In a modern society, he argues, social distress is seen as therapeutic challenge. Society is seen as a sick patient in need of therapy that public policy experts can supply. Contrasting therapeutic and socialist perspectives, Heclo writes that "socialists had thought the great change in political society would come from collectivizing the means of production. What actually turned out to be the leverage point was collectivizing fault. The source of disorders troubling the people was not any class, section, or individual ethical failings but society itself. Policy became modern democracy's answer to socialism, communism, and every other ism claiming a master plan for society's future."

In "Shrinking the Group," Peter Sheehy elucidates the key to understanding why the New Left embraced the therapeutic ethos, breaking with the Old Left's disdain for such considerations. The origins of the therapeutic ethos were individualistic and hierarchical—drawn directly from Freud's conception of the doctor-patient relationship. Sheehy, however, historicizes the rise of the therapeutic, documenting the growing emphasis among social scientists on environmental influences on the individual and the power of the group to incorporate individuals into society. The therapeutic ethos served as a catalyst for collective action. Self-realization, in a collective setting, proved to be a fruitful catalyst for exploring the possibility that the personal and the political were integrally connected.[50]

The therapeutic ethos influenced the way that Americans conceived of politics. The "environmental turn" in the therapeutic ethos shifted the emphasis in therapy away from its exclusive focus on the individual and turned it instead on the relationship of the individual to his or her environment. It also relied on group relations—not just the hierarchical analyst-patient relationship—to empower individuals. The changing nature of therapeutic theory and practice explains why techniques like "consciousness-raising" proved to be effective politically. The women's liberation movement placed private life at the center of its concerns, recognizing that subordination in the private realm could not be separated from subordination in the public realm. A hybrid of some of the organizing techniques that grew out of the civil rights movement and group therapy, consciousness-raising was particularly effective at excavating discontents that previously had been submerged and at framing these discontents in a broader political context. Just as the evolution of therapeutic practice had broken down the older Freudian hierarchy between analyst and patient, consciousness-raising abolished the distinction between political organizer and foot soldiers, reinforcing the democratic nature of this movement and connecting it to the New Left through its embrace of participatory democracy.[51] Linking the personal and the political corroded the "legitimacy barrier," generating many of the demands that fueled "big policy" in the last third of the twentieth century. Public policy was now the key not only to protecting individual life and property but also to an individual's well-being.

New Venues

Policy advocates turned to new venues in order to press their claims. Again, the quest for civil rights led the way. Hugh Graham summed up the explosive potential of the Civil Rights Act of 1964 and the Voting Rights Act of 1965: "The radicalism of these measures lay not in their command against harmful discrimination. . . . Such nondiscrimination policy had characterized liberal reform proposals and measures since the Reconstruction era." Rather, new laws were radical because they extended federal authority into venues previously untouched by the national government. Local and state prerogatives were the most significant among these.

Facing restraints and the outright opposition of Richard Nixon in his second term, liberal policy advocates replaced the New Deal–inspired tax-and-spend formula with a more intricate, but equally effective, "mandate-and-sue" strategy. Building on a power base that now lay in congressional subcommittees, the lower federal courts, and a cadre of permanent federal civil servants, liberal reformers expanded policy from bases that lay outside the White House. There were fewer "big bang" legislative initiatives but far more incremental growth through new interpretations of existing laws. There were fewer novel constitutional arguments in the Supreme Court and more "creative" statutory interpretations at the district court level.[52] Advocates of big policy worked across all three branches of government. A federal district court judge, for instance, ordered the Environmental Protection Agency to implement a rural air quality program. The court's decision rested on a few fragments of legislative history, but this was sufficient to trigger an elaborate regulatory program. Once ordered by the court, Congress expanded the program still further.

As Gary Orfield's classic study of southern school desegregation recounts, this administrative-judicial pattern of leapfrogging was established even while a liberal Democrat was president. Here, a landmark legislative act—the ESEA—got the ball rolling. But progress on desegregation followed only after civil rights advocates in the Justice Department used a combination of district court decisions and threats to cut off funding under Title VII of the Civil Rights Act to pressure both the Federal Office of Education and local school districts to desegregate.[53]

By the late 1960s, the strategy of mandate-and-sue featured three venues that emerged as crucial forums for crafting public policy: intergovernmental relations, congressional oversight, and the federal judiciary. Martha Derthick has chronicled the radical shift in the nature of federalism during the sixties.[54] The scale and scope of federal grants-in-aid increased significantly. Initially, many of these grants were administered in the age-old tradition of local discretion. But as federal funding increased and the demand for results intensified, federal administrative agencies grew more assertive. McGuinn and Hess document the case in education. The federal Office of Education had a long history of supporting states through statistics and advisory notices. As funding through the ESEA's categorical grants grew, the Office of Education moved from a supporting role to far more active supervision and oversight. But at least these mandates *were* funded. This was not the case with special education, another program overseen by the Office of Education. Established by an amendment to the ESEA in 1966, special education grew by leaps and bounds, as did the number of children served under it. Although total public school enrollment had declined between 1968 and 1986, the number of children served by special education almost doubled.

Improving environmental quality proved to be another classic case of unfunded federal mandates. Established in 1970, the Environmental Protection Agency was originally envisioned as an agency that would work in concert with the states. Indeed, pollution control had been a traditional responsibility of state and local government. But seven days after taking office, William Ruckelshaus, EPA's administrator, announced that Atlanta, Cleveland, and Detroit would have just 180 days to comply with water pollution laws.[55] Matters only grew more heated in the early 1970s when the EPA sought to enforce the Clean Air and Clean Water Acts. "This oversight," Ruckelshaus later reflected, "created a very, very difficult period between the EPA and the states. The states thought we dictated too much, were too intrusive."[56]

Eager to press ahead with big policy, yet wary of granting the administrative discretion required to fulfill demanding policy promises, Congress micromanaged programs through detailed statutory provisions and intensive oversight. In an era of divided government, if such detailed provisions could not compel executive compliance they at least could be used to pillory executive incompetence should administrative agencies fall short of these demanding mandates. Congressional hearings became an important venue for articulating still new demands and exposing executive or local foot-dragging. Increasingly shut out of the executive branch, liberal policy advocates often sought to expand public policy by exposing government failures.[57]

Perhaps the most distinctive new arena for making public policy was the federal judiciary. The Warren Court produced a series of landmark cases that invited or mandated assertive new public policies. Some, like *Reynolds v. Syms*, which proclaimed the "one person, one vote" principle, or *Harper v. Virginia Board of Education*, which eliminated the poll tax, imposed federal standards on long-standing local prerogatives. Others, such as *Green v. New Kent County*, which ordered busing to desegregate schools, and *Goldberg v. Kelly*, which ensured the right of welfare clients to a "fair hearing," propelled the Court into arenas that would soon require elaborate policy decisions on its part. Decisions that required complex policy solutions were often made with the assistance of Court-appointed masters.[58]

While federalism, fine-grained congressional management, and an activist judiciary served as beachheads for expanding the range of public policy, they would not have been effective without the dense networks of activists that circulated through them and that connected bureaucrats to social movements and judges to grassroots citizens groups. The judiciary loomed as a formidable policy player in part owing to the revolution in standing for plaintiffs that swept the courts by the 1970s. As Melnick notes, the Great Society created new centers of policy advocacy both inside and outside the government. Thus civil rights agencies, from the Equal Employment Opportunity Commission to the civil rights division of the Justice Department, worked hand in hand with such advocacy groups as the Legal Defense Fund of the National Association for the Advancement of Colored People or the National Organization for Women. It was through these more staid, buttoned-down iterations of the civil rights movement that the courage and energy that inspired a mass movement continued to shape public policy.

As already noted, advocates of big policy during this era were wary of empowering the instruments needed to carry out big policy. The most important mechanism for ensuring democratic accountability was the "citizen suit," which one environmentalist described as "a means of access for ordinary citizens to the process of governmental decisionmaking" and "a repudiation of our traditional reliance upon professional bureaucrats."[59] While these suits sometimes allowed individuals to enter the policymaking arena, the increased use of the citizen suit more often provided entrée to organized advocacy groups, such as the Natural Resources Defense League, in the case of the environment.

As the number of venues available for making public policy multiplied in the sixties, the opportunity for state-created advocacy groups multiplied as well. Hybrid creations of the new era in intergovernmental relations, such as the Community Action Program or the Model Cities Program, as Melnick states, actively recruited advocates for the poor and helped organize pressure groups to represent them. The voluntary sector also played a crucial role in shaping advocacy groups. The Ford Foundation sponsored initiatives that led to the creation of Mobilization for Youth, the Mexican American Legal Defense and Education Fund, and the National Resources Defense Council.[60]

With the explosion of policy demands, techniques long used by the federal government in defense policy, arguably the training grounds for "big policy" during the cold war, were applied to new fields. Boris, for instance, notes that after plans to have the Department of Defense run job-training centers fell through, the OEO turned to a practice that was actually more familiar to those in the Pentagon: contracted services. The provider in this instance was RCA, which had vast experience in the defense field and was hired for its expertise in systems management. Programs that addressed environmental quality also adopted systems analysis, a technique originally engineered by the military. Under the guidance of political scientist Arthur "Muddy Waters" Maass, the Harvard Water Program developed "multi-objective planning." As Paul Milazzo reveals in "Legislating the Solution to Pollution," such techniques reoriented the practices of even such inveterate dam builders as the Army Corp of Engineers. By the mid-1960s, the corps had began to develop alternative water-use policies that factored in water quality—not because this bureaucracy had turned "green" but because water quality was essential to water supply for economic development in the drought-stricken East.[61]

Thus, the Great Society reforms extended public policy into venues previously considered "private" or voluntary, linking interests to policymaking in new ways and expanding the methods of administration. Areas previously free of federal authority succumbed to federal "coercion" during the Great Society, as Graham notes, but that was only part of the story. The list included private as well as public agencies and encompassed stores, hotels, restaurants, and places of amusement. In education, the key to passing the ESEA was a compromise device that targeted federal aid at students—rather than schools—thus broaching the divide between public, parochial, and private schools.[62]

Making Pluralism "Great"

Business and professional groups forged the parameters of twentieth-century interest group pluralism.[63] When the economic crisis of the 1930s offered the possibility of social democratic alternatives to the prevailing political structure, labor also came to embrace pluralism. With its acceptance of the Wagner Act's collective bargaining provisions in 1935, labor pushed pluralism toward a far more capacious framework than the one dominated primarily by well-organized businesses, trade associations, and the professions. As Lichtenstein describes it, "For millions of workers, a majority immigrants, the offspring of immigrants, or migrants from the American South, trade unionism and collective bargaining proved a highway to civil rights, civil liberties, and real citizenship." While Boris is correct to point out just how many workers were shut out of trade union pluralism, interest group bargaining during the New Deal and the following decades secured a broad range of benefits for those workers who *were* represented by powerful unions. No wonder economists and political scientists by the 1950s treated organized labor as an interest group: not only was labor a powerful interest deeply invested in maintaining the pluralist system, but its inclusion in pluralism was also the definitive development in the policymaking system after the mid-1930s.⁶⁴

Cold War Pluralism

The cold war constrained pluralism as it hardened the boundaries between those insiders safely welded to iron triangles and constituencies excluded from these policymaking communities. It is no accident that terms such as "iron triangles" gained popularity in describing the reinforced, insulated subsystems that parceled out power and guarded access to crucial public policy decisions. Established interest groups coveted their access to congressional subcommittees and administrative bureaus. Public officials returned the favor, carefully nurturing well-organized interests. The resulting policymaking structure was indeed insular; it was best suited to deal with limited issues. It was designed to preserve stability.⁶⁵ Once inside, bargaining and negotiation were the qualities that participants valued most. New recruits, like labor, had to be reminded of this at times, but as long as the economy and tax revenues grew, negotiation yielded outcomes acceptable to everybody included in the game. During the cold war era, pluralism hunkered down, seeking to win the twilight struggle with formidable foes, emerging as a "fighting faith," in order to vanquish totalitarian alternatives.⁶⁶

By distributing decision making to dozens of iron triangles, the national policymaking structure was geared to contain conflict over issues as divergent as race relations and tax reform. "Protected by their pressure group, served by their governmental agency, assuaged by their friendly congressmen," Louis Galambos writes, interest groups "were satisfied with triocracy. They were not going to be foot soldiers in a battle to eliminate privilege for others—and certainly not for themselves."⁶⁷

The "civics lesson" that Heclo explores for the sixties examines interest group pluralism's evolution. The roots of "big policy" were firmly grounded in the cold war system of pluralism, which, "with its shrewd, utilitarian acceptance of selfish interests, gave focus to the new realism," Heclo writes. "With policy came programs that could be designed to use those competing interests for public ends. Thus the philosophy of liberal realism shaded into programmatic liberalism and the burst of government initiatives in the Great Society era." If the New Deal cast a shadow on Johnson's Great Society, cold war liberalism illuminated many of the paths that the Great Society would forge.

Key policymakers during the Great Society era, from Lyndon Johnson to Earl Warren, rose to power by mastering the cold war pluralist system. No wonder LBJ was appalled by the unwieldy politics of "the street," despite his intense desire to make society great for all Americans. As McWilliams notes, Johnson, who was "overwhelmingly persuasive" in small groups and one-to-one encounters, never mastered mass politics. The cloakroom, the subcommittee, and, when pressed, the Senate floor were the forums in which Johnson rose to power. In his preference for insulated politics, Johnson was very much a product of his political culture, a practitioner of the "suprapartisan politics," as Byron Hulsey has called it, that was practiced by the Washington establishment during the cold war in a fashion that "celebrated pragmatic compromise and ridiculed ideological obstinacy."[68]

Democratic Pluralism: Lift Every Voice

Yet this cold war system proved vulnerable on the very front that its advocates claimed to revere: democratic participation. As E. E. Schattschneider noted almost half a century ago, "The flaw in the pluralist heaven is that the heavenly chorus sings with a strong upper-class accent."[69] For such influential scholars from the mid-1960s as Theodore Lowi, interest groups were, at best, necessary evils, and the notion that the problems pluralism might encounter were self-correcting, a joke. Among political scientists, pluralism bashing became a growth industry.[70]

The treatment of African Americans was the most visible reminder of pluralism's elitist repertoire. Beginning with their efforts to convert the courage and energy of grassroots activists into social reform, Great Society programs revolutionized access to the policymaking system.[71] The Great Society reached out to some of pluralism's most severe critics: African Americans abused by what for them was only the latest system of oppression as well as to a broad range of Americans who insisted that "beauty and health" were legitimate objects of national public policy.[72] These Americans took matters into their own hands, massing in unruly and sometimes fractious movements that ebbed and flowed with the latest insult to their members' status as full participants in the exclusive pluralist chorus. The Great Society took these demands seriously, converted some into effective policies, and raised the hopes of millions that other objectives might soon be realized—that they might encompass the hopes of *all* Americans, not just a privileged few.

Lyndon Johnson embraced reforms that democratized cold war pluralism and made the public policy process accessible to millions of citizens for the first time. Whether the Supreme Court's willingness to grant class action status, the Community Action Program's "maximum feasible participation," or the Medicaid program that opened a world of federally funded benefits to those without steady work records, public policies that shaped the Great Society expanded the scope of debate.[73]

Momentarily lost in the shuffle, however, was the bitterness expressed by more-conservative business and even some cold war liberal interest groups, forced to share the pluralist stage with insurgents and activists who would have been considered intruders just a few years ago. At the same time, critics on the left scorned the now-enlarged pluralist system for its tendency to retreat from or, more often, fail to identify the moral high ground. No sooner had some interests, excluded for centuries, stepped through the conference room door than they were charged with selling or "copping" out.[74]

Even as pluralism expanded access to groups previously excluded from the political system, proministrators retained a partial grasp on their privileged perch. They played a particularly crucial role in narrowing broad-gauged demands for reform into policy packages that might fit the pluralist mold. Hugh Graham's essay illuminates an important instance—the origins of official minority status. While high-profile advisory bodies such as President Truman's Committee on Civil Rights put the issue of racial discrimination on the policymaking agenda, it was obscure government officials who first asked employers to report the number of "negro" and "other minority" employees.

This development was noted by other racial and ethnic groups, who lobbied members of Congress to pressure responsible administrators for them to be included by name. Responding to the League of United Latin American Citizens and the Mexican-American Political Action Committee, Henry Gonzales (D-Tex.) succeeded in 1962 in having "Spanish-Americans" included as a specific category on Standard Form 40. In turn, the Japanese American Citizens League, with the support of Senator Hiram L. Fong and Representative Daniel K. Inouye of Hawaii, won the addition of "Orientals" as a required category on Form 40. It was thus through the system of iron triangles that epitomized the way cold war pluralism worked that agreements were hammered out behind the scenes with little public debate and even less publicity.[75]

The number of "insiders," along with the style that they brought to pluralism, was changing as was intended in landmark legislation vesting new groups with a stake in the system. The Civil Rights Act of 1964 was one of the pillars of Johnson's Great Society. It established the Equal Employment Opportunity Commission (EEOC), which, among other responsibilities, was charged with contract compliance. This was a high-profile and highly publicized body that by 1965 operated at the epicenter of one of the most highly contested issues in post–World War II history. Martin Luther King, Malcolm X, and the Student Nonviolent Coordinating Committee (SNCC), representing three strains of a powerful social movement, were at the height of their influence. Yet, as Graham notes, the decision about which groups to include on the EEO-1 form that replaced Standard Form 40 for contract compliance purposes suffered from bureaucratic inertia: the groups that employers now had to count were Negroes, Spanish-Americans, Orientals, American Indians, and Whites.

When the Philadelphia Plan propelled the government into "hard" affirmative action a few years later, administrators had at their disposal a list of four official minorities. Yet, as Graham notes, "there is no record of civil rights leaders addressing the issue of which groups to include on the EEO-1 form, no hearings or record of discussion by the president's contract compliance committees or by the EEOC." Instead, the initiative "came from appointed federal officials and served their immediate political needs." Even at the height of the Great Society's quest for participatory politics, in a highly contested policy area thrust upon the nation's agenda by the century's most powerful social movement, crucial decisions were still hammered out in a manner that military contractors, dam builders, or the United Automobile Workers and their congressional and proministrative partners would be quite comfortable with.

The Great Society was an era of big policy: it both identified new problems and insisted that there were policy solutions to these problems. Before society could be "great," however, it had to be more egalitarian. Racial inequality was the most glaring discrepancy, and in the eyes of most Great Society advocates, little could be accomplished until this problem was addressed. As the highly visible racial divide was narrowed, it revealed another gaping discrepancy—income.

Expanding equality, or at least access to public resources in the pursuit of equality, changed the very nature of the "society" slated for greatness.

It was now far more diverse, but there was little consensus about public policy. The diversity and range of perspectives that penetrated America's policymaking system was the direct result of hard-won victories by the civil rights movement and, to a lesser extent, the New Left. By the end of the decade, feminism accounted for additional victories in the quest to democratize mainstream politics. The Great Society imbibed the rhetoric of "community" and the commitment to participation expressed by these social movements. The Great Society even subsidized, within limits, challenges to older, less representative and far less participatory state and local bureaucracies.

There was a price, however. New entrants into the policy sweepstakes had to play by pluralist rules. Efforts to reconcile a system predicated on Madisonian self-interest with the surge in morally based "public interest" politics that grew out of the social movements of the 1960s fell short of their goal. In racial politics this produced what Peter Skerry calls a "hybrid" organization: the Mexican American Legal Defense and Education Fund (MALDEF). "The organization's lawyers have played the inside game of clientelist politics," Skerry writes, excelling at the "backroom maneuvering and inside politicking needed to negotiate the maze of today's administrative state. But MALDEF has also played an aggressive outside game of high-visibility, media-oriented entrepreneurial politics."[76]

As one effervescent movement after another stepped into the policymaking arena, the shape of pluralism itself changed.[77] The size of the chorus expanded, the backgrounds of its singers diversified, and rehearsals grew more raucous. Democratizing pluralism opened the door to a host of new participants. For the first time since pluralism adapted to the demands of working-class Americans during the New Deal, the pluralist chorus really did sing with different accents and swayed to a variety of beats.

Nor was the chorus intimidated by its director. Pluralism grew unwieldy. It expanded the venues in which the chorus performed. It invited audience participation in its highly publicized performances, some of which seemed like they would never end as court-composed codas and regulatory encores kept the music going long into the night. Although liberals and conservatives both complained bitterly about the outcomes, African Americans, women, those with disabilities, those who sought to infuse public policy with moral and religious values, and a host of other

Americans had far greater access to the system than they did in 1963. Access and inclusion, along with the claims on full citizenship that went with them, made pluralism—despite all its problems—"great" in the 1960s. The decade democratized pluralism.

Some, such as Lichtenstein and Heclo, have discovered the death of pluralism in this raucous cacophony.[78] Of the current condition of labor, Lichtenstein concludes that "individualistic, rights-based assumptions replaced group pluralist ones and turned solidarity into a quaint and antique notion." For Heclo, the demise of pluralism is also an important turning point. That collapse was engineered by the demise of trust and goodwill and the belief in disinterestedness, qualities Heclo believes to be essential to any pluralist system.

I disagree. Pluralism not only survived the Great Society but remains the central feature of the American policymaking system today. It was democratic pluralism that neoconservatives and the New Right mastered as they sought to turn public policy to their own ends, and it is democratic pluralism that, for better or for worse, characterizes the way public policy is made today. What ultimately distinguished the Great Society from more radical approaches or, for that matter, conservative critiques that saw little role for the federal government at all, was the determination to break down broad social demands—the kind of objectives that would have been considered unrealistic just a decade or two earlier—into digestible bites. These could then be converted into public policies. The central mechanism used to achieve this—just as it was during the New Deal—was interest group pluralism, albeit a more vocal and energetic form of pluralism.

Pluralism remained a powerful framework, although it now reached out to a vast array of groups, many of which claimed to speak for the "public interest." Whether working in the governmental nodes of the issue networks that pushed this pluralist infrastructure to the breaking point, or on the public advocacy end of the spectrum, policy promoters embraced far more ambitious and demanding ends.

To some, the results were cacophonous; for others, polyphonic. As conservatives soon discovered, however, the restructured pluralism that emerged from the Great Society could serve the purposes of more than one ideological program. Far steadier than "cycles of reform," pluralism toughened by the cold war and democratized by the Great Society offered a mechanism for expanding the size and diversity of the chorus while ensuring that its music was still acceptable to the congregation and to church elders alike.

Notes

I thank Ed Ayers, Catherine Gavin Loss, Chris Loss, Chi Lam, Mike Lynch, Paul Milazzo, Sid Milkis, and Ed Sermier for their assistance with this essay. Unless otherwise noted, all quotations or information attributed to Rosalyn Baxandall, Edward Berkowitz, Eileen Boris, Frances Fox Piven and Richard Cloward, Hugh Davis Graham, Hugh Heclo, William Leuchtenburg, Nelson Lichtenstein, Patrick McGuinn and Frederick Hess, Wilson Carey McWilliams, R. Shep Melnick, Jerome Mileur, Sidney Milkis, and David Shribman] are from the particular author's essay in this volume.

1. See Thomas Byrne Edsall and Mary D. Edsall, *Chain Reaction: The Impact of Race, Rights, and Taxes on American Politics* (New York: W. W. Norton, 1991). Compare this with *The Origins of the Urban Crisis: Race and Inequality in Postwar Detroit* (Princeton: Princeton University Press, 1996), by Thomas J. Sugrue, who places the shift—at least at the local level—far earlier.

2. Collectively, these essays do not offer a commentary on who won and who lost or on which specific policies survived and which fell by the wayside. For examples of the former, see John E. Schwartz, *America's Hidden Success: A Reassessment of Twenty Years of Public Policy* (New York: W. W. Norton, 1983), and Charles Murray, *Losing Ground: American Social Policy, 1950–1980* (New York: Basic Books, 1984).

3. Lyndon B. Johnson, "Remarks at the University of Michigan, May 22, 1964," in *Public Papers of the Presidents of the United States: Lyndon Johnson, 1963-1964*, 2 vols. (Washington, D.C.: Government Printing Office, 1965), 1:704.

4. Ibid., 704, 706.

5. The quotation is from Lewis Strauss. For background on Strauss and the context for his statement, see Brian Balogh, *Chain Reaction: Expert Debate and Public Participation in American Commercial Nuclear Power, 1945–1975* (New York: Cambridge University Press, 1991), 113.

6. Johnson, "Remarks at the University of Michigan, May 22, 1964," 706.

7. On the assumption that the Great Society would not require a redistribution of income and power, see Allen J. Matusow, *The Unraveling of America: A History of Liberalism in the 1960s* (New York: Harper and Row, 1984).

8. James T. Patterson, *Grand Expectations: The United States, 1945–1974* (New York: Oxford University Press, 1996), 562.

9. Ibid., 563, 569.

10. Ibid., 536, 563, 569; Peter Marris and Martin Rein, *Dilemmas of Social Reform: Poverty and Community Action in the United States* (Chicago: University of Chicago Press, 1982), 24–25.

11. Patterson, *Grand Expectations,* 569.

12. See Gary Orfield, *The Reconstruction of Southern Education: The Schools and the 1964 Civil Rights Act* (New York: Wiley, 1969). See also Gary Orfield, *Must We Bus? Segregated Schools and National Policy* (Washington, D.C.: Brookings Institution, 1978), for statistics on southern desegregation. That the shift from opportunity to achievement endured long beyond the Great Society is illustrated by the willingness of both liberals and conservatives to support federal expansion. The "No Child Left Behind Act," passed in 2002, and supported by both George Bush and Ted Kennedy, significantly increased the federal government's presence in secondary and elementary education.

13. "Special Message to Congress on Natural Beauty," February 8, 1965, *Public Papers of the Presidents of the United States: Lyndon Baines Johnson, 1965*, vol. 1 (Washington, D.C.: Government Printing Office, 1966), 155–65, cited in Paul Milazzo, "Legislating the Solution to Pollution: Congress and the Development of Water Pollution Control Policy, 1945–1972" (University of Virginia, 2001), chap. 3.

14. Milazzo, "Solution to Pollution," chap. 3.

15. Milazzo, "Congress and the Environment," in *The American Congress: The Building of Democracy*, ed. Julian E. Zelizer (Boston: Houghton Mifflin, 2004).

16. "Confidential Memo on Turner Catledge's Conversation with President Johnson," box 30, Arthur Krock MSS, Princeton University, Princeton, N.J., quoted by Leuchtenburg in his essay.

17. See Edward D. Berkowitz, *Mr. Social Security: The Life of Wilbur J. Cohen* (Lawrence: University Press of Kansas, 1995).

18. Edsall and Edsall, *Chain Reaction*.

19. H. W. Brands, *The Strange Death of American Liberalism* (New Haven: Yale University Press, 2001); Robert Higgs, *Crisis and Leviathan: Critical Episodes in the Growth of American Government* (New York: Oxford University Press, 1987); Mary L. Dudziak, *Cold War Civil Rights: Race and the Image of American Democracy* (Princeton: Princeton University Press, 2000).

20. From the essay by McWilliams; on some of the unfortunate consequences of this mind-set, see Patricia N. Limerick, *Legacies of Conquest: The Unbroken Past of the American West* (New York: Norton, 1987).

21. See the essay by McWilliams.

22. Ibid., although McWilliams certainly does not use the word "chutzpah."

23. Rogers M. Smith, *Civic Ideals: Conflicting Visions of Citizenship in U.S. History* (New Haven: Yale University Press, 1997).

24. John Dittmer, *Local People: The Struggle for Civil Rights in Mississippi* (Urbana: University of Illinois Press, 1994).

25. This is not to suggest that they had to start from scratch. Roosevelt had laid the foundation for rights-based liberalism in his Commonwealth Club address of September 1932. See Sidney M. Milkis, *The President and the Parties: The Transformation of the American Party System since the New Deal* (New York: Oxford University Press, 1993), 38–51.

26. See the essay by Boris.

27. Johnnie Tillmon, "Welfare Is a Women's Issue," *Liberation News Service,* no. 415, February 26, 1972, reprinted in *America's Working Women: A Documentary History, 1600 to the Present,* ed. Rosalyn Baxandall and Linda Gordon (New York: Norton, 1995), 31, quoted in ibid.

28. See the essay in this volume by Shribman.

29. For the term "proministrative state" and faith in experts, see Balogh, *Chain Reaction.*

30. J. Edgar Hoover, "The Twin Enemies of Freedom: Crime and Communism," address before the 28th Annual Convention of the National Council of Catholic Women, Chicago, Illinois, November 9, 1956, cited in Elaine Tyler May, *Homeward Bound: American Families in the Cold War Era* (New York: Basic Books, 1988), 137.

31. Dudziak, *Cold War Civil Rights,* 13–14. See also Robert M. Collins, *The Business Response to Keynes, 1929–1964* (New York: Columbia University Press, 1981), and *More: The Politics of Economic Growth in Postwar America* (New York: Oxford University Press, 2000), 24–25, on the impact of NSC 68 on growthmanship.

32. Godfrey Hodgson, *America in Our Time* (Garden City, N.Y.: Doubleday, 1976); Richard H. Pells, *The Liberal Mind in a Conservative Age: American Intellectuals in the 1940s and 1950s* (New York: Harper and Row, 1985).

33. In his essay in this volume, Heclo cites Walter Lippmann's *Preface to Morals* (New York: Macmillan, 1929).

34. For Arthur M. Schlesinger Jr., see Heclo's essay in this volume.

35. On the succession of activist movements, Sara Evans, *Personal Politics* (New York: Knopf, 1979), is a classic. See also Terry Anderson, *The Movement and the Sixties: Protest in America from Greensboro to Wounded Knee* (New York: Oxford University Press, 1995).

36. On the electronic media, see David Garrow, *Protest at Selma: Martin Luther King, Jr., and the Voting Rights Act of 1965* (New Haven: Yale University Press, 1978), and Todd Gitlin, *The Whole World Is Watching: Mass Media in the Making and Unmaking of the New Left* (Berkeley: University of California Press, 1980).

37. Hugh Davis Graham, *The Civil Rights Era: Origins and Development of National Policy, 1960–1972* (New York: Oxford University Press, 1990); Abigail Thernstrom, *Whose Votes Count? Affirmative Action and Minority Voting Rights* (Cambridge: Harvard University Press, 1987).

38. Thernstrom, *Whose Votes Count?*

39. Linda Gordon, "Social Movements, Leadership, and Democracy: Towards Utopian Mistakes," *Journal of Women's History* 14, no. 2 (2002): 112, quoted in Baxandall, in this volume.

40. Hugh Heclo, "The Sixties' False Dawn: Awakenings, Movements, and Postmodern Policy-Making," in *Integrating the Sixties,* ed. Brian Balogh (University Park: Pennsylvania State University Press, 1996), 50–52, cited by Melnick in his essay in this volume.

41. See the essay in this volume by Milkis.

42. See the essay in the volume by Melnick. On rights talk see Mary Ann Glendon, *Rights Talk: The Impoverishment of Political Discourse* (New York: Free Press, 1991).

43. Robert Kagan, *Adversarial Legalism: The American Way of Law* (Cambridge: Harvard University Press, 2001), cited by Melnick in his essay in this volume.

44. See the essay in this volume by McGuinn and Hess. The *No Child Left Behind Act,* passed in January 2002, confirmed the national government's central role in elementary and secondary education. Richard Elmore has called it "the single largest expansion of federal power over the nation's education system in history." See Richard Elmore, "Unwarranted Intrusion," *Education Next* 2, no. 1 (2002): 31–33, cited in McGuinn and Hess.

45. See the essay by Boris.

46. James Q. Wilson, "American Politics: Then and Now," *Commentary,* February 1979, cited in Melnick. There is strong consensus among authors in this volume that the Great Society vastly expanded the range of public policies that the national government engaged in. In systematically expanding this range, the Great Society resembled the New Deal, which was decidedly "illegitimate" in the eyes of its opponents. As many of the essays emphasize, however, the very legitimacy barriers lowered by the Great Society were those established by the New Deal and its offspring.

47. Bernard Falk, quoted in Milkis, *The President and the Parties,* 245 n. 79.

48. Dan Morgan, "Senators Tried to Balance Deluge of Needs, Ceiling on Spending," *Washington Post,* January 26, 2003.

49. On social services, see Martha Derthick, *Uncontrollable Spending for Social Service Grants* (Washington: Brookings Institution, 1975); on services and mental health, see Andy Morris, "Therapy and Poverty: Private Social Service in the Area of Public Welfare" (Ph.D. diss., University of Virginia, 2003). On mental health see Peter Sheehy, "The Triumph of Group Therapeutics: Therapy, the Social Self, and Liberalism in America, 1910–1960" (Ph.D. diss., University of Virginia, 2002); on the therapeutic in education, see Catherine Gavin Loss, "Public Schools, Private Lives: American Education and Psychological Expertise, 1945–1975" (Ph.D. diss., Curry School of Education, University of Virginia, forthcoming).

50. Sheehy, "Triumph of Group Therapeutics."

51. See the essay in this volume by Baxandall.

52. See the essay in this volume by Melnick.

53. Orfield, *Reconstruction of Southern Education.*

54. See Martha Derthick, "Crossing Thresholds: Federalism in the 1960s," in Balogh, *Integrating the Sixties;* Martha Derthick, *Keeping the Compound Republic* (Washington: Brookings Institution, 2001); and the essay in this volume by McGuinn and Hess.

55. Brian Balogh, Joanna Grisinger, and Philip Zelikow, "Making Democracy

Work: A Brief History of Twentieth-Century Federal Executive Reorganization," Miller Center of Public Affairs Working Paper, Charlottesville, July 2002, p. 67.

56. Quoted in ibid.
57. See the essay in this volume by Melnick.
58. Ibid.
59. Quoted in ibid.
60. Ibid.
61. Milazzo, "Solution to Pollution," and "U.S. Water Pollution," in *Water and the Environment since 1945: Global Perspectives,* ed. Char Miller et al., 257–63 (Detroit: St. James Press/Gale Publications, 2001).
62. See the essay in this volume by McGuinn and Hess.
63. Brian Balogh, "'Mirrors of Desires': Interest Groups, Elections and the Targeted Style in Twentieth-Century America," in *The Democratic Experiment,* ed. Meg Jacobs, William Novak, and Julian Zelizer (Princeton: Princeton University Press, 2003). Pluralism has undergone significant change during the twentieth century. From the late nineteenth century forward, it has adapted to the styles of its participants. Four distinct phases of pluralism dominated twentieth-century American political culture: business/professional pluralism; labor pluralism; cold war pluralism; and democratic pluralism. Each phase added a new layer of complexity to the existing structure but hardly displaced those interests that had previously staked a claim.

See also John Mark Hansen, *Gaining Access: Congress and the Farm Lobby, 1919–1981* (Chicago: University of Chicago Press, 1991), and Lorraine Gates Schulyer, "The Weight of Their Votes: Southern Women and Politics in the 1920s" (Ph.D. diss., University of Virginia, 2001). In a brilliant history of pluralist adaptation, Elisabeth Clemens underscores the ways in which the political history of each nascent interest group shaped its strategy, modifying the nature of pluralism as new groups joined the "club." Women and farmers ultimately moved away from failed populist and social democratic efforts. But they behaved differently from such long-standing pluralist stalwarts as business interests. Women and farmers were far more likely to call for state intervention in public policy. Nevertheless, both groups narrowed the scope of their agendas and created permanent homes in Washington, D.C., for the American Farm Bureau Federation (AFBF) and the League of Women Voters (LWV). In the 1920s, such organizations as the AFBF and the LWV walked, talked, and lobbied more like interest groups than populist movements. Elisabeth S. Clemens, *The People's Lobby: Organizational Innovation and the Rise of Interest Group Politics in the United States, 1890–1925* (Chicago: University of Chicago Press, 1997).

64. See the essay in this volume by Lichtenstein. On labor commitment to interest group bargaining, see Jacob Hacker, *The Divided Welfare State: The Battle over Public and Private Social Benefits in the United States* (New York: Cambridge University Press, 2002).
65. These are the adjectives used by Lichtenstein.

66. For "fighting faith," see Arthur M. Schlesinger Jr., *The Vital Center: The Politics of Freedom* (Cambridge, Mass.: Riverside Press, 1949).

67. Louis Galambos, *America at Middle Age: A New History of the United States in the Twentieth Century* (New York: New Press, 1983), 67.

68. Byron C. Hulsey, *Everett Dirksen and His Presidents: How a Senate Giant Shaped American Politics* (Lawrence: University Press of Kansas, 2000). Lichtenstein provides a good description of this system in his essay. Pluralism provides a mechanism for formulation of limited issues, where the parties still disagree on principles.

69. E. E. Schattschneider, *The Semisovereign People: A Realist's View of Democracy in America* (1960; reprint, Hinsdale, Ill.: Dreyden Press, 1975), 34–35.

70. For an extended discussion of cold war liberalism and the attack on it, see Balogh, introduction to *Integrating the Sixties*, 13–17.

71. Dittmer, *Local People*.

72. Samuel Hays, *Beauty, Health, and Permanence: Environmental Politics in the United Staes, 1955–1985* (Cambridge: Cambridge University Press, 1987).

73. On the concept of scope of debate, see Schattschneider, *Semisovereign People*.

74. The Port Huron Statement is a good example of this. See http://coursesa.matrix.msu.edu/~hst306/documents/huron.html.

75. See the essay in this volume by Graham.

76. Peter Skerry, "We're All Moralists Now: Racial Politics in the American Administrative State," paper presented at "The Great Society: Then and Now" conference, November 17–18, 2000, University of Virginia, Charlottesville, p. 7.

77. Clemens, *People's Lobby*.

78. It is ironic that the rise of "identity" politics would mean the demise of pluralism because in the United States, ethnic politics long served as one of the foundations of pluralism.

Part II

Lyndon Johnson and the American Presidency

Lyndon Johnson in the Shadow of Franklin Roosevelt

William E. Leuchtenburg

For reasons only those captivated by psychohistory will care to explore, Lyndon Johnson went through life with a series of "daddies"—older men he revered and counted on to advance his career—and of all the daddies, by far the most important for him was Franklin Delano Roosevelt. Toward the end of his life, Johnson told Walter Cronkite: "Franklin D. Roosevelt, he was my hero, he was like a father to me. I think he saved our system, I think he saved our country, I think he saved me."[1]

So keen was Johnson to establish his credentials as an FDR legatee that he recounted episodes that almost certainly never happened. In his interview with Cronkite, Johnson recalled: "We were all hungry, we were homeless, we would have been thrown out on the streets except for the Homeowners Loan. My Daddy got an eighteen hundred dollar loan on a Homeowners Loan under President Roosevelt." There is no evidence that his family was ever "hungry" or "homeless," but Johnson felt so beholden to FDR that he may well have believed that tale. During the 1964 campaign, he divulged to Georgia legislators at a breakfast in Atlanta that "Franklin D. Roosevelt sent me to the South in 1936 to survey conditions in our Southern States," though FDR had more sense than to rely on a greenhorn for a mission requiring an old hand. In that same campaign, he told a Los Angeles rally, "Jimmy Roosevelt brought me to Washington," a statement so far from the truth that it must have confounded FDR's son. Nor is it possible to document his claim to a close association with Eleanor Roosevelt: "I remember following her on the dusty roads of Texas, in the slums of our cities."[2]

Though Johnson stood on much firmer ground in saying that he was "a Roosevelt man, lock, stock and barrel," his relationship to FDR was more complicated than that simple assertion suggests. One of FDR's assistants called him "a perfect Roosevelt man," and John Kenneth Galbraith has observed, "As with many of our generation when young, Johnson knew his political position only when the President had stated it." Johnson, however, also found his devotion to FDR, which sometimes verged on obsequiousness, a heavy burden to carry. When he became president, he continued to pay homage to Roosevelt, but he was determined to step out from under his shadow. That breakaway had portentous consequences for the country and for Johnson's place in history.[3]

As a Texas teenager, Lyndon Johnson got his first glimpse of Roosevelt at the 1928 Democratic national convention in Houston. Watching the New Yorker, who had been partly paralyzed by polio, gamely make his way across the spotlighted platform to nominate Al Smith, he developed an admiration for him that soon approached idolatry. Though Johnson, who preceded FDR to Washington as secretary to a Texas congressman, shared with other Texans hopes for the presidential aspirations in 1932 of their native son, John Nance Garner, he rejoiced when Roosevelt, after capturing the nomination, won the election.

FDR's inaugural address made an indelible impression on him. In 1964 Johnson remembered being at the Capitol on March 4, 1933, when a dispirited people saw "that great man march up and hold on to that podium and say, 'The only thing we have to fear is fear itself.'" It is hard to know what to make of Johnson's use of the word "march" for a man who was disabled, but there is no reason to doubt his conclusion: "It gave me an inspiration that has carried me all through the years since." After maneuvering to get himself picked Speaker of the "Little Congress" of congressional aides, Johnson mimicked FDR in an unintentionally comical way by promising a "New Deal" for the "forgotten man" on Capitol Hill. He even managed to persuade his archconservative, but often clueless and disengaged, boss to vote for New Deal measures the wealthy Texas congressman despised. Recalling the critical formative years of his political education, Johnson later said: "I saw all the great reform legislation born. In the angry bitterness of the depression, we forged the vision for America."[4]

By 1935, Johnson, who must have acquired a bent toward politicking in the cradle, had developed so many contacts with movers and shakers in Washington that, altogether improbably, he secured a choice position as director for the state of Texas of the newly created National Youth Administration (NYA). Though Roosevelt was reluctant to name a twenty-seven-year-old to so important an administrative post, an appointment that would make LBJ the youngest state director in the land and in geographically the largest state, the clamor from Johnson's influential backers was so relentless that the president gave in. When all the state NYA directors assembled in Washington that summer, Roosevelt sought out this phenom and asked him to hang around after the others departed. The president "kinda petted me," Johnson said. In the ensuing months, Johnson's demonically energetic performance of his assignment spread his name still further in New Deal circles. On one occasion at Hyde Park in 1936, Johnson, like a bright pupil in grade school, was summoned to sit by FDR and Eleanor Roosevelt and recite how he had put his NYA corps to work creating roadside parks. The NYA venture, Johnson remarked later, was "the most satisfying job I ever did have in my life."[5]

Johnson had still higher goals in mind. Early in 1937 he announced his candidacy in the Democratic primary for a vacant seat in Congress in a Texas district. It was a harebrained idea. Only twenty-eight, he was far less well known than some of the other candidates in the field of nine. But Johnson had one thing going for him: his link to FDR at a particular historical moment. In February the president had shocked the country by announcing a plan to add as many as six justices to the Supreme Court in order to overcome its hostility to the New Deal. His message provoked howls of indignation, but Roosevelt was confident that Congress would enact his controversial proposal if he could hold on to the usually reliable Solid South.[6]

Texas was an important battleground. Ardently behind FDR in his first term, it was mutinying against him on "Court-packing." Almost every Democrat in the Texas Senate voted to instruct the state's congressional delegation to reject his scheme, a defection from the president's party matched nowhere else in the country, and Senator Tom Connally of Texas was one of the most vocal critics.[7] FDR's opponents claimed that they reflected the views of an outraged public, but Roosevelt countered that, despite the drumbeat of newspapers and bar associations against him, the people were with him. In an age when polling was often primitive (the prestigious *Literary Digest* survey had forecast a Landon victory in 1936), no one could say confidently which side was correct in its estimate of public opinion. Hence, at a time when Court-packing was the hottest issue of the day, the eyes of the nation focused on the April Texas primary, the first significant test of popular sentiment since FDR's message.

Johnson's promoters had no doubt about where he should position himself. His principal adviser told LBJ that he had to be "a total Roosevelt man. . . . Of course, there will be those who will be bitter at you, but the hell with them. They're in the minority. The people like Roosevelt." Another friend lectured him, "Lyndon, look, the important thing about this race is FDR . . . and he's in hot water over that Court-packing thing. He needs our help and we are going to come out loud and clear for him. . . . There's not going to be any halfway stuff."[8]

Johnson, already so well disposed toward the president, had no trouble accepting this counsel. Though he was not the only candidate in the Texas primary to back Roosevelt on Court-packing, Johnson sought frenetically to create the impression that he was the one true-blue FDR man. "I'm for the President," he declared. "When he calls on me to help, I'll be where I can give him a quick lift, not out in the woodshed practicing a quick way to duck." "FRANKLIN D. AND LYNDON B.," his campaign materials announced, or "A VOTE FOR JOHNSON IS A VOTE FOR ROOSEVELT'S PROGRAM." The president's enemies, Johnson claimed, knew that of all the would-be congressmen there was "only one who will fight them until the last dog is dead. . . . They know I am that man." In his "National Whirligig" column, Ray Tucker wrote: "Major plebiscite on the supreme court will take place in Texas April 10. . . . Young Lyndon Johnson, former national youth administrator, carries FDR's judicial colors. . . . Several senators now lukewarm toward the White House scheme may suddenly shift if Mr. Roosevelt wins out there by proxy."[9]

The president and the national Democratic organization refused to endorse Johnson directly in a race where the young man's chances were so slim, but Johnson got the next best thing. In Austin, Democratic national chairman Jim Farley said that it would be inappropriate for him to intervene in "a local matter," but he added, in a muted signal, that the congressional district ought to send "a young, industrious and one-hundred percent Roosevelt man up there in this crucial hour." FDR's son Elliott was more forthright. He wired Johnson his hopes for "a glorious victory. . . . I feel sure that when you get to Congress the Administration will have a young, vigorous and ardent supporter." Little wonder that columnist Drew Pearson informed his readers, "On the surface the Administration is keeping hands off the contest, but under cover is quietly boosting Johnson."[10]

When in April Johnson surprised prognosticators by coming out first in the crowded field, the national press, which ordinarily would have paid scant attention to a Texas by-election, made the story a front-page feature across America. The people, it appeared, did indeed approve of Court-packing. "Youthful Lyndon B. Johnson, who shouted his advocacy of President Roosevelt's court reorganization all over the Tenth Texas District, was elected today," the Associated Press ticker chattered, and a headline in a Texas paper read: "Johnson Elected to Congress by Big Vote. FDR'S Court Proposal Okayed by 10th District." Johnson gave his triumph the same spin; it proved, he said, the people were "as strong as horse radish for Roosevelt." Delighted by this unexpected piece of good fortune at a time when the tide had begun to run against him, the president, on a fishing cruise in the Gulf of Mexico, got word to the governor of Texas that he wanted to meet the precocious victor as soon as he came ashore.[11]

On May 10 Johnson rode from Houston to Galveston with Elliott Roosevelt in an open touring car, and on the following day when FDR came down the gangway, there was LBJ, alongside Governor James Allred. Photographers recorded the congressman-elect shaking hands with the president, providing Johnson with an invaluable graphic memento for future use. Subsequently, Johnson joined the presidential party on a train journey, and along the way Roosevelt told him that he could use "somebody from Texas that would vote for a strong Navy." As the train pulled into the Fort Worth depot, the president wrote down a phone number and advised Johnson to call that number as soon as he reached Washington, adding that he should ask for Tom. "I've just met the most remarkable young man," Roosevelt later told Tommy Corcoran. "Now I like this boy, and you're going to help him with anything you can."[12]

Johnson could not have come to Washington in more propitious circumstances. When he took the oath of office in the well of the House of

Representatives, the fiery New Deal congressman Maury Maverick announced to the members: "Mr. Speaker, the gentleman just sworn in, Mr. Lyndon Johnson, supported the President's judiciary plan and was overwhelmingly elected," a statement that drew a round of applause from FDR's followers in the House. Instead of being lost in a swarm of 435, Johnson arrived with fanfare. "Here's one of us," Corcoran told Alben Barkley.[13]

Roosevelt ordered Corcoran to "take care of the boy," an admonition that his aide understood to have two meanings. Corcoran not only called around town to get the young Texan the place he coveted on the Naval Affairs Committee but also saw to it that LBJ's financial backer, Brown and Root, made a successful bid for the construction of a Corpus Christi naval base. The president did not leave Johnson's prospects to Corcoran alone. A powerful House Democrat wondered all through dinner at the White House what Roosevelt wanted from him until he heard, "Fred, there's a fine young man just come to the House. Fred, you know that young fellow, Lyndon Johnson? I think he would be a great help on Naval Affairs." With such sponsorship, Johnson got the committee assignment he sought.[14]

The new Texas congressman rapidly got taken up by the Roosevelt circle. Corcoran, who remembered how the New Dealers created an "atmosphere, a consensus about the new boy and his immediate future in the House," has etched him: "Tall as a plow horse and slim as a lodgepole, he boasted a slick of black curly hair and a smile as wide as the Pedernales—a very attractive guy so cocksure of himself that he never stopped talking." Johnson, always a man on the make, saw the opportunity to seize his chance. One of FDR's White House assistants, Jim Rowe, who began a close friendship with Johnson that would last a lifetime, later said: "He was one of the few young Congressmen that got to know all the young New Dealers. . . . He cultivated them. He quite early seemed to know where the buttons for power were." New Dealers learned to expect the arrival each year of a huge turkey from the Lone Star State. Thanks to the smiles of Fortune and his own determined efforts, Johnson made a special place for himself. Pa Watson, the gatekeeper to the Oval Office, told Rowe, "Your friend, Lyndon Johnson, he's always 100 percent. He can get in."[15]

The president, who appears to have had a genuine liking for the larger-than-life Texan, took him under his wing. "Roosevelt was quite fond of

Johnson," Rowe remembered. "Roosevelt was impressed by the fact that Johnson had taken on his Court plan and won." In later years, this relationship became the pith of legend. A Mississippi congressman, noting that Johnson won on a platform of "100 percent support of President Roosevelt" in 1937, recalled that "the President invited him down to the White House, and he became known overnight." In truth, it took longer than "overnight" for Johnson to develop a special connection to Roosevelt. Yet Washington did have reason to conclude that he was an FDR favorite. He persuaded the president to pour millions into the construction of Texas dams, and in 1939 Roosevelt asked him to become administrator of the Rural Electrification Administration. Johnson preferred to hold on to his seat in the House, but the offer suggests the president's high regard. Roosevelt, John Connally later wrote, "put out the word to his people. Work with that young congressman from Texas, Lyndon Johnson—he's a comer."[16]

Johnson, in turn, out of both gratitude and conviction, became a stalwart member of the Roosevelt bloc in the House. He was one of only twenty-two southerners to support FDR on a key roll call on the wages and hours bill, and when 108 Democrats broke with the president on his attempt to reorganize the executive branch, White House strategists noted that Johnson was in the cadre that could be counted on. Hence, it is not surprising that in 1940, in communicating with Roosevelt, Corcoran used the phrase "your man, Lyndon Johnson." A generation later, Johnson informed Cronkite: "I went all the way with him. He befriended me, went far beyond what any president would ordinarily do for a young Congressman."[17]

By the unusual respect he accorded Johnson, Roosevelt steadily elevated his stature in party councils. When a feud among Texas Democrats was resolved, New Dealers, with FDR's blessing, insisted that a telegram announcing the settlement be signed not only by Sam Rayburn but also by Lyndon Johnson, placing "the kid Congressman" on a par with the veteran House majority leader who would soon be Speaker. By 1940, Johnson's standing in Washington had risen so high that Roosevelt named him campaign manager to reelect Democratic members of the House. Around midnight on election night, the president phoned him to find out how many seats the party had lost. We're not going to lose," Johnson told him. "We're going to gain." A Washington column syndicated to newspapers throughout the country reported: "To the boys on the Democratic side of the House of Representatives, many of them still nervously mopping their brows over narrow escapes, the hero of the hair-raising campaign was no big shot party figure.... In the House all the praise is for the youngster whose name was scarcely mentioned.... The Democrats' unknown hero was Representative Lyndon Baines Johnson, a rangy, 32-year-old ... who ... has political magic at his finger tips." Jim Rowe later recalled, "It impressed the hell out of Roosevelt."[18]

In a lengthy communication to Senator Connally on April 21, 1941, a Texan concisely encapsulated LBJ's status:

> Johnson ... became the President's "fair-haired boy" and when he went up to Washington was immediately embraced and advanced far beyond either his calendar years or his experience in public affairs. The nation was made to know this. Then, when the national election came on, with the aid of the administration he was put in strategic campaign work and did yeoman service, thereby adding to his own ability as a useful adherent, and quite probably also in his own self-esteem.... Johnson has no machine of his own, of course, as he has never run for a state office, has really scarcely been heard of in most parts of the big State of Texas, and can lay claim only to the Roosevelt machine in a sort of preferred-right fashion.[19]

On the very next day, after meeting with Roosevelt, Johnson announced from the White House steps that he was entering the race for U.S. senator from Texas. Roosevelt was known to be wary of squandering his influence by backing losers, and a poll gave LBJ only 5 percent of the vote. But at a press conference the president, following the usual disavowal, "I can't take part in a Texas primary," added, "If you ask me about Lyndon himself, ... I can only say what is perfectly true—you all know he is a very old and close friend of mine. Now that's about all. Now don't try to tie those things together!" The reporters roared with laughter, and Roosevelt joined in. The press corps understood perfectly well that FDR was endorsing his "old friend," whom he had met only four years before. One Texas headline read: "F.D. TOSSES LYNDON'S HAT FOR SENATE."[20]

At every opportunity, Johnson emphasized that he was running as a Roosevelt man. His rallies featured an enormous picture of him shaking hands with FDR, the photo taken at their first meeting in Galveston in 1937, but now with Governor Allred airbrushed out. Beneath the photograph on a canvas backdrop ran the legend: "ROOSEVELT AND UNITY—ELECT LYNDON JOHNSON UNITED STATES SENATOR." Irving Caesar, a well-known composer, put together a forgettable ballad to the tune of "Tea for Two" that ended: "MISTER ROOSEVELT DOES AGREE—THAT UN-I-TY AND LYNDON B. WOULD HELP DEFENSE AND HELP DEMOCRACY!"[21]

Uncharacteristically, Roosevelt went all out for Johnson. "Roosevelt did everything he could to help," Rowe recalled. "Practically gave him the Treasury." The president mobilized cabinet members and other federal officials on his behalf; he even tried to recruit Houston's crusty Jesse Jones. LBJ's campaign, noted one journalist, "was cluttered with New Dealers." In mid-June, Roosevelt told the head of the Social Security League of Texas, "I do not mind reiterating to you that Congressman Lyndon Johnson is an old and trusted friend of mine," and while continuing to feign neutrality he added, "I do not think my Texas friends will misunderstand my position in the Senatorial race." A Dallas paper referred to Johnson as "FDR's Anointed." When the election returns showed Johnson trailing narrowly, the Roosevelt administration sent FBI agents into the state to cow county judges into reporting accurate figures. In the end, all the president's prestige failed to get his candidate the last few votes needed, but Johnson assured Roosevelt, "You certainly gave me support nonpareil."[22]

Johnson's loss in the 1941 Senate race might have ended his political prospects, but Roosevelt approved a plan to have the Texan invited to speak at the next national convention of the Young Democrats, giving him prominence by placing him on the same stage as the president, and Roosevelt continued to value his counsel. William S. White of the *New York Times*, the national correspondent who was closest to Johnson, said of LBJ that "as a very junior Congressman he became somewhat senior rather quick." White added:

> Before Pearl Harbor . . . Mr. Roosevelt had a very serious problem about whether the military draft would be renewed. . . . Mr. Roosevelt at that time was making a great deal of sort of private use of Lyndon Johnson. . . . Johnson, of course, was not then in the leadership of the House. Nevertheless, Mr. Roosevelt often leaned on him, particularly for inside information about the estimates of what the House would really do. . . . He called Lyndon Johnson to the White House—a very young Congressman he was too, of course—and asked his advice about how he, Mr. Roosevelt, would best move in order to have the draft continued.[23]

That close association endured to the end. The Texan even backed the president in opposing an increase in oil prices, a position certain to be unpopular in his home state. In 1944 Roosevelt showed his respect for Johnson's judgment in seeking his counsel on how to heal divisions in the Democratic Party in Texas. His loyalty to FDR paid dividends. Asked how she had first become acquainted with Johnson, Helen Gahagan Douglas, who entered Congress in 1945, replied, "Lyndon and I became friends in the Congress, as other supporters of Roosevelt became friends. . . . Our political background was similar: Roosevelt. He was the man in politics that we admired the most—President Roosevelt."[24]

The shocking news of FDR's death on April 12, 1945, shattered Johnson. Trembling, teary-eyed, he told William S. White: "He was like a daddy to me always. . . . I don't know that I'd ever have come to Congress if it hadn't been for him." Johnson's "grief was just unreal," a secretary recalled. "He just . . . literally shut himself up. His grief was vast and deep and he was crying tears. Manly tears, but he actually felt . . . that it was just like losing his father." Johnson later remembered how he had first heard of Roosevelt's death: "I was just looking up at a cartoon on the wall—a cartoon showing the President with that cigarette holder and his jaw stuck out like it always was. He had his head cocked back, you know." And when White went to LBJ's office to get his response to the awful tidings, he came upon Johnson with a cigarette holder at an angle, his jaw outthrust.[25]

Robert Caro has set down the experience of Horace Busby, who arrived in Washington in 1948 to be LBJ's speechwriter:

> Busby idolized Franklin Roosevelt, and Johnson had been told that, and when the young man was shown into Johnson's office to meet him, there, sitting behind the desk, was Franklin Roosevelt, complete to pince-nez glasses, long cigarette holder, and uptilted, outthrust jaw. "Come in, young man, come in," the figure behind the desk said, in a perfect imitation of Roosevelt's patrician voice, and, wheeling his big swivel chair around the desk since of course he was paralyzed and couldn't walk, he took the astonished young man's hand and said graciously, "Sit down, sit down." Then, with obvious difficulty, he wheeled himself slowly and painfully back behind the desk, and looked Busby directly in the eye. The big jaw thrust even farther out and up. "We have nothing to fear but fear itself," Franklin Roosevelt said. There followed one of Roosevelt's fireside chats—"about ten minutes of it," in Busby's recollection; "I looked it up later, and it was practically word for word."[26]

On entering the U.S. Senate in 1949, Johnson continued to think of himself as a Roosevelt man, but because he tailored his behavior to the conservatism of his Texas constituents, longtime New Dealers disowned him. When he waged a vicious campaign to deny Leland Olds, a revered figure in liberal circles, reappointment to the Federal Power Commission, the *New Republic* commented: "Against Olds is a onetime liberal Senator, Lyndon Johnson, born into the family of a poor farmer, brought forward by the New Deal, and carried into office by liberal and labor support. Johnson, who saw his first backer, Aubrey Williams, hounded out of government on charges of Communism, now is hounding Olds out on the same charges—Johnson, who boasted that 'Roosevelt was a daddy to me.' How Roosevelt would have scorned such backsliding." In 1952 Jim Rowe instructed Johnson's secretary, "Tell him it ain't true that 'all the Liberals' don't love him anymore, although it must be admitted that most of them don't."[27]

Johnson knew that his best, indeed his only, defense against these attacks was to call to mind FDR's faith in him. He could mimic FDR so well, one senator said, that when he did, "you *saw* Roosevelt," and in a feature article a Washington correspondent noted that "when he talks he tilts his head back in a manner reminiscent of Franklin Roosevelt (whom he reveres)." William S. White, though, reported, "He is excessively sensitive to criticism—or rather to criticism from certain sources, and especially from those liberal Democrats whose *beau ideal* is still Franklin D. Roosevelt." Johnson told a columnist, "You say I am not a liberal. Let me tell you I am more liberal than Eleanor Roosevelt and I will prove it to you. Franklin D. Roosevelt was my hero. He gave me my start."[28]

Invoking memories of FDR proved especially effective with the most prominent of the Senate liberals. To ingratiate himself with Hubert Humphrey, who started out with strong reservations about LBJ, Johnson regaled him again and again with accounts of conversations he had carried on with FDR over meals and about his friendships with New Dealers. "Johnson was a Roosevelt man," Humphrey later said. "That was his greatest joy. To remind people that Roosevelt looked upon him as his protégé. A hundred times I heard him mention that, you know. That was his great moment. . . . This made him in a sense, in his contacts with many people like myself, a sort of New Dealer." That claim to be a keeper of the flame went a long way with Humphrey. "I found him fascinating right from the beginning," he recalled. "He had been close to Roosevelt, who was my political hero." Humphrey found Johnson convincing: "Johnson, you have to keep in mind in order to understand him . . . always considered himself a New Dealer. In the real sense of the Roosevelt tradition—Social Security, yes, education, yes—he was a Rooseveltian Democrat."[29]

When Johnson was elected Senate majority leader, he instinctively turned to former New Dealers—Jim Rowe, Tommy Corcoran, Abe Fortas—and he struck precisely the right chord when, on Rowe's recommendation, he named to his staff FDR's former personal secretary. Grace Tully had no sooner arrived at the LBJ Ranch than she obligingly told a reporter how much Johnson resembled Roosevelt in his avid interest in conservation. The *San Antonio Express* headlined the story: "JOHNSON AIDE SAYS TEXAN IS LIKE FDR." George Reedy later said of this symbolic appointment:

> That was Johnson strengthening his position with the New Deal liberals. That was part of it, and part of it I think was a genuine—you know, Johnson could get very warm about some things, and Grace had been very, very useful to him when he was a young congressman. . . . He told me that he would quite often pick up Grace and take her down to the White House on his way down to work in the morning. If he had a little memorandum or something like that that he wanted Roosevelt to see, he'd slip it to Grace, and Grace would see to it that Roosevelt got it. . . . There was always a mixture of motives with Johnson. . . . Naming Tully gave him quite a bit of yardage with the New Dealers and it paid off some old debts, and at the same time he kind of liked Grace. You couldn't help but like Grace, she was one of the most likeable women I've ever known.[30]

Such bits of political theater might suffice to placate some liberals, but not Eleanor Roosevelt. After Johnson had shepherded through the Senate a badly gutted civil rights bill in 1957, she lashed out at him in a My Day column and wrote him icily, "You must realize that I understand very well your extremely clever strategy. . . . It would be fooling the people to have them think that this was a real vital step towards giving all our people the right to vote or any other civil rights."[31]

Touched to the quick by these assaults, Johnson, who knew how devilishly difficult it had been to fashion a compromise that made possible the first civil rights law of the twentieth century, responded to the former First Lady:

> I was very much disappointed by your column last Saturday. I had always thought of you as a fair-minded person who would always insist on knowing all the facts before coming to a conclusion on the motives of men.
> If I am "trying to fool the people," I have a large company with me.

Take, for example, Ben Cohen, who worked day and night to try to produce a jury trial amendment. . . . Other men who worked on the Bill—for no other reason than their devotion to the cause of Civil Rights—include Dean Acheson, Jim Rowe, and Joe O'Mahoney. It is a heavy blow to all of us to have you dismiss our work as mere fakery.[32]

Not even a ceremonial visit to Hyde Park, where Johnson paid tribute to FDR on a sultry late-spring afternoon, served to win her over. To be sure, she wrote him cordially, "On all sides I was told that this was the most successful Memorial Day Service that had ever been held," and she later complimented his parliamentary skill in getting a civil rights bill to the floor. But when he delivered his eloquent address, she brutally snubbed him by not appearing at the event. After he left Hyde Park, she said mockingly, in a sing-song cadence, "Lyndon came a-courtin'," then added, "He wants to be president, but try as I did, I couldn't learn about a single program he had formulated. . . . Franklin was *willing* to become president because only as president could he introduce legislation that he felt was essential to end the Depression!"[33]

Echoes of the 1930s continued to resound in the 1960s. Oscar Chapman, who headed the National Committee of Citizens for Johnson in 1960, told a press conference that liberals from the Roosevelt era were rallying to LBJ as their presidential candidate because he had been "one of the leading men in Congress" in putting through FDR's New Deal. "That's why I'm for him," Chapman explained. In fact, Johnson did not enter Congress until after most of Roosevelt's program had been enacted, but he did have a strong New Deal following, though that was not enough to get him the Democratic presidential nomination. When he was offered second place on the Kennedy ticket, Sam Rayburn initially wanted him to turn it down. "I saw Jack Garner agree to run twice with Roosevelt, of whose political philosophy he disapproved intensely, and go back to Texas a bitter man for life," the Speaker said. After the Kennedy-Johnson ticket prevailed in November, memory of Garner led Johnson to keep a low profile. "Your daddy," he told Franklin D. Roosevelt Jr., "never let his Vice-Presidents put their heads above water."[34]

Vice President Johnson's credentials from the FDR era helped him especially in overcoming the suspicions African Americans harbored toward a man from a former Confederate state. Louis Martin, who was named by Johnson to chair the advisory group to the Committee on Equal Employment, stated: "One of the reasons I think I was sold on him, he talked so much like Roosevelt about the problems of poverty . . . that my view was that whether he liked you as a black or not was secondary to the greatest interest he seemed to have in . . . poverty and those other things which were my overriding concern. . . . So I think it never occurred to me to doubt him because he was so convincing on these things, and his record and his admiration for the Roosevelt point of view, really, sold me almost immediately."[35]

The tragic manner in which Johnson became president in November 1963 made him more dependent than ever on veterans of the New Deal wars for emotional sustenance and for wisdom. Some three days after he entered the White House, he called in Jim Rowe to mend a rupture between them. Rowe recalled: "He apologized. I said I apologized, and he said, by God, I wouldn't apologize, I was the first fellow this president had apologized to, and he didn't want me getting into the act; it was his apology." Rowe reflected: "What I think he was doing, and it is curious, . . . was touching all his old bases as soon as he became president. I don't quite understand the psychological reason for this, but he was doing it. He was seeing all his old friends that he had known from the beginning of the New Deal. Not so much because he wanted their help, which he did want, but it's almost like a superstition, coming back and touching all these things. I remember I think the day after he saw me he saw two people, old New Dealers, who were dying. I . . . doubt he had seen them for some time. He went to call on them."[36]

From the outset Johnson let it be known that, as president, he was modeling himself on Franklin Roosevelt. He placed a bust of FDR in the Oval Office and hung in a prominent place a photograph of himself and Roosevelt under which he wrote, "I listen." At a ceremony in January 1964 commemorating the birth of Roosevelt, the new president said, "In both pride and humility, I readily admit that my own course in life has been influenced by none so much as by this great man." When seeking to categorize Johnson, the White House press corps habitually dwelt on this identification. In a 1965 broadcast, at a time when LBJ was at the apex of his power and prestige, a seasoned Washington correspondent said of him: "He was taken up by Franklin Roosevelt at a very tender age—tender for a politician—his early thirties, I believe, and perhaps without Roosevelt's patronage he would be still a Congressman. I think Roosevelt gave him most of what he has in the way of an ideology, and a good deal of what he has in the way of method."[37]

More than one commentator has traced the antecedents of the Great Society to the New Deal. "Johnson never really liked the term 'Great Society,'" Bill Moyers has said. "He didn't like it as much as he liked the New Deal. That's really what he saw himself doing." Repeatedly, he said to Moyers, "I'm going to be president for nine years and so many days, almost as long as FDR." That gave him the opportunity to complete FDR's program. Similarly, Robert Dallek has written, "His idea of the presidency was picking up where FDR's New Deal left off." Not long after Johnson took office, he invited his chums of Roosevelt days to dinner to plan a new program, and his first idea of how to begin a war on poverty was to draw on the legacy of the NYA.[38]

As Johnson framed the scaffolding of his poverty program, allusions to the age of Roosevelt came naturally to him. When he interviewed Dick Goodwin about a post on his White House staff, he told him, "You're going to be my voice, my alter ego, like Harry Hopkins." (In his memoir, Goodwin notes that each of at least five other staff members had been told that he was to be Harry Hopkins.) Borrowing from Roosevelt's rhetoric, Johnson instructed the director of the Office of Economic Opportunity (OEO), Sargent Shriver, that he wanted the poverty program to help "the ill-housed, ill-clad, ill-nourished," the very words of FDR's second inaugural address. In rejecting Robert Kennedy's notion that the OEO should be under a cabinet instrumentality, Johnson resolved that it should instead have the independence of the NYA or the Civilian Conservation Corps. "FDR," he pointed out, "always put new ideas into new hands, . . . to give them freedom, running room, a chance to be creative."[39]

When Johnson sought another term in the White House, he contrasted his enthusiasm for FDR's programs with Barry Goldwater's desire to do away with them. At twenty-nine, Goldwater had already appeared in print in a newspaper column attacking Roosevelt, whereas Johnson presented himself as FDR's heir. "As always, the LBJ eye was fixed on FDR," Eric Goldman recalled in discussing the demands Johnson placed on him for memoranda on past Democratic conventions. "Typically, the memo on acceptance speeches came back with a notation instructing, 'Give me more on R in '32.'" In May, Johnson made a pilgrimage to Franklin D. Roosevelt Square in Gainesville, Georgia, where FDR had delivered a notable address in 1938. "Today, with Franklin Roosevelt's young son, Franklin Roosevelt, Jr., by my side," Johnson said, "I have come back to Gainesville to say that his work and ours is not finished; his dreams and ours are not yet realized; his hopes and ours are not yet fulfilled." Johnson declared: "As President Franklin Roosevelt did in March 1938, I ask you today to give me your hand and to give me your heart, to work for the good of the whole people and the whole Nation." Johnson's landslide victory in November derived in no small part from popular apprehension that Goldwater, if elected, might do away with enormously popular Roosevelt programs, which Johnson would safeguard. When Goldwater campaigned against Johnson in Tennessee, an airplane soaring above his Knoxville rally towed the message, "Vote LBJ Keep TVA."[40]

As it became inescapably apparent in the closing weeks of the 1964 campaign that Lyndon Johnson was going to become, for the first time, president of the United States in his own right, the opportunity opened up for him to fulfill his dream of completing Franklin Roosevelt's program, but though he did intend to do that, he also had something considerably more daring in mind. "Lyndon Johnson," Marshall Frady has written, "wanted much—in sum, to be the greatest President in the history of the republic." And to be "the greatest of them all, the whole bunch of them," he had to roll up a record so impressive that it would exceed even the achievements of FDR. With such an ambition, he might well have pitted himself against Washington or Lincoln, but it was Roosevelt at whom he took aim.[41]

Almost everyone who came in contact with Johnson, or has written about him, grasped that he was engaged in a fierce, undeclared war with the memory of FDR. In his first interview with Johnson at the White House, Richard Goodwin has recalled, "I sensed the enormity of the man's will, the intensity of his intent . . . to leave a mark on the country that would equal, even excel, that of his youthful hero, Franklin Roosevelt. He wanted to out-Roosevelt Roosevelt." Robert Dallek, Lyndon Johnson's most astute and most judicious biographer, has observed: "He saw Franklin Roosevelt as the President to measure himself against. FDR, the winner of a historic landslide election in 1936 and the most successful reform leader and greatest war President of the century, was Johnson's model and target to surpass. This was not some casual game Johnson played with himself. His competitiveness and need to be top dog were at the core of his being. It translated into wanting unsurpassed reform accomplishments." Similarly, in his chronicle of the northward migration of southern blacks and of the War on Poverty, Nicholas Lemann has written that "there can be no doubt but that Johnson's consuming dream was to be a great—the greatest—liberal president. . . . Johnson may have made the requisite remarks about living up to the standard set by John F. Kennedy, but his real mark was Franklin Roosevelt. . . . Roosevelt's achievements, and not Kennedy's, were of Johnsonian scale."[42]

Johnson's desire to get the better of Roosevelt derived in part from resentments that had been simmering for some time. In 1964 he blurted out to members of his staff, "Hell, I was the only one to run for Congress on court-packing and he didn't even endorse me." He especially disliked being regarded as FDR's errand boy. At one Texas Democratic convention, his opponents had shouted, "Throw Roosevelt's pin-up boy out," and in his failed race for the Senate in 1941 he was derided as a "watercarrier." He revealed how defensive he was about such taunts when, at the very moment he was pouring out his sorrow at Roosevelt's death, he said, "Some of us they called 'yes men.' Sure, I yesed him plenty of times." But, he insisted, "I voted against him plenty of times." After his defeat in 1941, he wrote the president fawningly that he was "glad to be called a watercarrier" for him. "I would be glad to carry a bucket of water to the Commander-in-Chief any time his thirsty throat or his thirsty soul needed support." Johnson may have had such words in mind when, safely in the White House, he said, "I've been kissing asses all my life and I don't have to kiss them anymore."[43]

As if being in FDR's shadow were not enough, Johnson had to endure the exasperating spectacle of his wife being in Eleanor Roosevelt's shadow. A Washington correspondent, writing on Lady Bird Johnson, said that Eleanor Roosevelt was "the only other First Lady with whom she can reasonably be compared," and in drafting one of Lady Bird's addresses, Katie Louchheim was instructed to make it "up to the standards of her Eleanor Roosevelt speech." During her well-publicized whistle-stop campaign through the South in 1964 to win votes for her husband, Lady Bird found that the Eleanor Roosevelt yardstick was regularly trotted out. A *Washington Post* correspondent reported from Columbia, South Carolina: "A determined Lady Bird Johnson valiantly held her own against youthful Goldwater hecklers here today in the face of the most publicly abusive and insulting treatment any First Lady of the United States has encountered since the era of Eleanor Roosevelt."[44]

Lady Bird Johnson was in many ways an admirable figure and had her champions, but they presented her not as a pathbreaker in the style of Eleanor Roosevelt but as a "stand by your man" throwback. Though Lady Bird Johnson "admired Mrs. Roosevelt greatly, she was very different," her press secretary, Liz Carpenter, said. "Mrs. Roosevelt was an instigator, an innovator, willing to air a cause without her husband's endorsement. Mrs. Johnson was an implementer and translator of her husband and his purposes . . . a WIFE in capital letters." Early in 1966 a *New York Times* correspondent wrote of Lady Bird Johnson:

> She is the most political First Lady since Eleanor Roosevelt, but unlike Mrs. Roosevelt, who said she wanted to be "as inconspicuous as possible" during President Franklin D. Roosevelt's campaigns, Mrs. Johnson has taken to the stump with vigor every time her husband has run for office.
>
> Mrs. Roosevelt had her own causes to push. Mrs. Johnson has worked politically only for her husband and other Democrats who needed support in her 29 years in public life. . . .
>
> In her first six months in the White House she traveled many a mile for him.[45]

Johnson believed that one way he could outshine Roosevelt was by being more prudent than his predecessor, for FDR's presidency served Johnson not simply as a guidepost but also as a flashing warning light. In his memoirs, Johnson claimed that he took pains to see that certain members of Congress got advance notice of legislation he was about to propose, a practice he said derived from his experience as a young congressman. He wrote:

> I was standing in the back of the House behind the rail as Speaker Sam Rayburn listened to the House clerk read an important new administration message President Roosevelt had just sent to the Hill. Several dozen Democrats were gathered around him. As he finished, a unanimous chorus of complaints rushed forth: "Why, that message is terrible, Mr. Sam—we can't pass that." . . . "That last suggestion is awful." . . . "Why in the world did you let the President send one up like that?" . . . "Why didn't you warn us?"
>
> Speaker Rayburn listened to all the criticisms and then responded softly: "We'll just have to look at it more carefully. That's all I can say now,

fellows. We'll have to look at it more carefully." The crowd scattered. Mr. Sam and I were left alone in the back. I could see that something was wrong. "If only," he said, "the President would let me know ahead of time when these controversial messages are coming up. I could pave the way for him. I could create a base of support. I could be better prepared for criticism. I could get much better acceptance in the long run. But I never know when the damned messages are coming. This last one surprised me as much as it did all of them." He shook his head sadly and walked slowly away.

I could see that his pride was hurt. So was the President's prestige and the administration's program. I never forgot that lesson.[46]

Roosevelt's reign offered one especially salient cautionary tale. No recollection was more vivid to Johnson than his impression of the Washington scene when he was sworn into Congress in April 1937. Roosevelt had won a resounding affirmation in the 1936 election only six months before. Yet just three months after Johnson settled into his apartment in the capital and observed events from the floor of the House, FDR had sustained the worst defeat he had ever experienced when Congress entombed his Court-packing bill. That taught Johnson how quickly one wrong decision can turn the tide of popular sentiment.[47]

Johnson's aspiration to outdistance FDR became nakedly apparent on election night. As the television screens showed him sweeping all the Northeast, all the Midwest, all the upper South, all the Great Plains, and all the Pacific Coast, Johnson had every reason to be jubilant. Instead, he was short-tempered. He knew he was overwhelming Goldwater, but he was not running against Goldwater. He was running against Roosevelt. He was in a foul mood because he feared his percentage of the popular vote might fall short of FDR's in 1936. In a phone conversation after all the returns were in, Johnson boasted, "Even Roosevelt in '36 never captured the number of people and never had them jumping in the air and yelling and giving the loyalty that we did."[48]

On an early December evening in 1964, a month after his great triumph over Goldwater, Johnson revealed his plans for the next session of Congress to Turner Catledge of the *New York Times*. Above all, he declared, he would avoid a major confrontation on the Hill of the sort that had undone FDR. He explained: "Franklin Roosevelt came back here in 1937 after the biggest popular landslide in history. An electoral college landslide second only to George Washington and James Monroe. But by

April he couldn't get Congress to pass the time of day." FDR had broken his leg on the Court-packing scheme, he recounted. "You're not going to catch me getting into a mess like that."[49]

Determined to "avoid another 1937," Johnson approached the opening of the Eighty-ninth Congress in 1965 as though entered in a race with FDR. "Let's get as much as we can as fast as we can," he told his White House staff. "I know all about these mandates. Roosevelt had one in 1936, and then he came up with that foolish court-packing plan." Johnson's "grandiose" conception of a "great society," Tom Wicker has written, "was not, as the civil rights victory had been, a response to significant public demand. The Great Society was, instead, the product of the president's own vision, dreams, and political ambition to surpass or equal his model, Franklin Roosevelt, in improving the lives of the American people." Johnson cracked the whip in order to push through so many bills before the hundredth day of the session that he could boast that his Congress had achieved more than Roosevelt's in the spring of 1933. A week before the hundredth day came, he told the press: "The Senate has already passed fifteen substantial measures. . . . I think you will find that they have passed more measures already than were passed the first one hundred days of the Roosevelt administration, about which you have been writing for thirty-odd years."[50]

Johnson believed that in less than two years after he had taken office (in contrast to FDR's more than three terms), he had already overshadowed Roosevelt, and early that fall I had an opportunity to observe this attitude. In September 1965 I received a phone call from the White House inviting me to come to Washington to write about Johnson and the Eighty-ninth Congress. For two days I lived a Walter Mitty existence in which a black limousine rolled me through the White House gates up to Capitol Hill to talk to Senate and House leaders and back to the White House to quiz presidential aides and, as the climax of my visit, the president. During an exceptionally lengthy interview, Johnson made clear to me exactly how he measured himself against his illustrious predecessor. Johnson said of Roosevelt: "He did get things done. There was regulation of business, but that was unimportant. Social Security and the Wagner Act were all that really amounted to much. And none of it compares to my Education Act."[51]

Brashly, Johnson continued to maintain that more significant legislation had been enacted under his leadership than FDR had been able to achieve. In the fall of 1965, he offered the Eighty-ninth Congress his assessment of the first session: "I know the great record of the 73rd Congress under Franklin Roosevelt. That record included the Emergency Relief Act, the Securities Act, the CCC Act, the Home Owner's Loan Corporation, the TVA, the Economy Act, the Agricultural Adjustment Act, the NRA and FDIC. You have done more." Toward the end of 1966 he added: "FDR passed five major bills the first one hundred days. We passed 200 in the last two years. . . . We must dramatize that."[52]

A few commentators agreed that Johnson had trumped Roosevelt. The columnist Drew Pearson said of Johnson, "He was a disciple of Franklin Roosevelt, a great admirer of Franklin Roosevelt, but he had greater drive, greater imagination in many respects." More persuasively, one of his African American aides later reflected: "I would say that the President had a very real and deep concern for this whole matter of civil rights, and that he felt it perhaps more personally and more fervently than any man that I have ever known who was in the White House. I knew President Roosevelt and President Truman and President Kennedy. . . . I knew them all pretty well. . . . Certainly none of these other men had it down in their stomachs in the same way. . . . Lyndon Johnson actually felt ashamed for some of the things he had to do on the way up." "Johnson has outstripped Roosevelt, no doubt about that," the Senate majority leader, Mike Mansfield of Montana, told me in the fall of 1965. "He has done more than FDR ever did, or ever thought of doing."[53]

Mansfield's was decidedly a minority view. In the emergence of the welfare state, most writers concluded, Johnson was a latecomer, Roosevelt the innovator. They also maintained that Johnson's performance fell short of FDR's in other respects. When Johnson became president, noted one observer, "it became his obligation to offer moral leadership, for this, as his mentor, Franklin Roosevelt, commented, is what is expected and required of the American President," but LBJ was too "crude" to be "an inspirational figure." Lyndon Johnson, said a Virginia governor, could not project himself in public, whereas "Franklin Roosevelt would just exude." Even when observers praised Johnson they did not think he matched FDR. "Lyndon Johnson," Clark Clifford declared, "understood political power in Washington better than any President in my lifetime, with the exception of Franklin Roosevelt."[54]

Johnson's desire to "out-Roosevelt Roosevelt" not only did not succeed; it also led to his downfall. Johnson sought to climb past Roosevelt in the ratings of presidents by winning a major victory in Southeast Asia that would drastically change the balance of power in the perilous cold war at the same time as he was carrying out a program of domestic reform considerably more ambitious than the New Deal. In truth, he conflated the two. When he went on a mission to Saigon in 1961, he said that Premier Ky "sounded like Rex Tugwell," and he compared Ngo Dinh Diem to FDR. Five years later, with the Tennessee Valley Authority in mind, he declared, "We're going to turn the Mekong into a Tennessee valley."[55] It would be too much to say that Johnson's acceleration of the war in Vietnam resulted solely, or perhaps even primarily, from a passion to eclipse Roosevelt. He inherited from Kennedy a predicament that he did not know how to escape; he shared the verities of the cold war culture; and he brought to the Oval Office legends of the Alamo that challenged him to prove that he was not a quitter. Nonetheless, his competition with FDR contributed significantly to his overreaching in Southeast Asia.

Johnson's excess is best explained by his megapersonality, but his knowledge of the presidency of Franklin Roosevelt also swelled his self-conception. Well before Johnson reached Washington, a story circulated that there was concern about God's mental health: "He thinks that He is Lyndon Johnson." Not without reason, though, did Johnson remember the FDR presidency as jumbo-sized. He could not forget that he had come to Congress at the very moment that Roosevelt was flouting tradition by assaulting the Supreme Court. Johnson got his first national campaign experience in the year that FDR was breaking another taboo—against a third term. Roosevelt, Johnson well knew, never surrendered the enormous power of his office voluntarily. Only death cut short his unprecedentedly long tenure.

Johnson, however, misread FDR. True, Roosevelt both challenged the shibboleths of laissez-faire and fought a global war, flouted convention, and sometimes told downright lies, albeit in the national interest. But for the most part he did not overreach. He took care, even when he knew full well what terrible danger Hitler constituted, not to get too far ahead of the country. Roosevelt understood that, in a democracy, a president must inspire public trust and establish a bond with the people if he was to earn their affection. Though he greatly amplified the power of the chief executive, he did not confuse personal aggrandizement with statecraft, and his style was civil. He was incapable of saying, as Johnson did, that he wanted someone to kiss his ass in Macy's window and tell him how sweet it smelled. A patrician comfortable with himself, Roosevelt saw no need to engage in combat with the ghosts of those who had gone before him.

Lyndon Johnson never did understand why Roosevelt was ranked as the greatest president of the century, whereas he was regarded as a pariah. In the first spring after he retired, Lady Bird, worried sick about her husband's deep depression, tried to cheer him by reminding him of all he had accomplished as president, but he paid no heed. A visitor found that he only wanted to ruminate about "the early days—about the WPA" and the Lower Colorado River Authority. "He wouldn't speak about anything in between; he just had it completely blotted out of his mind."[56] He knew that whatever he had achieved, he had not put FDR in his shadow. In the final year of his life he learned that Roosevelt's picture hung in a place of honor at the 1972 Democratic national convention, while his was nowhere to be seen. In his own party, he was a nonperson.

His puzzlement and gloom had been painfully evident in his last year in the White House. Johnson thought he had followed FDR's model faithfully—reform and war. If he had blundered in Vietnam, if he had failed to "avoid another 1937," he was being punished as Roosevelt had not been. Far more members of the armed forces had died in World War II, after Roosevelt had pledged not to send American boys overseas, than in Southeast Asia, but FDR had never been asked how many kids he had killed that day. Roosevelt had been reelected in the midst of the fighting, whereas Johnson had been driven from office. Johnson did, though, have time to perform one more act. On January 27, 1969, his final day in office, he signed a series of proclamations. The very last edict to which he put his name created Franklin Delano Roosevelt Memorial Park.

Notes

1. Transcript of interview of Lyndon B. Johnson by Walter Cronkite, December 1, 1971, box 21, roll 3, p. 20, Burton Benjamin MSS, State Historical Society of Wisconsin, Madison. For the "daddy" phenomenon, see William E. Leuchtenburg, *In the Shadow of FDR: From Harry Truman to George W. Bush* (Ithaca: Cornell University Press, 2001). Inevitably, I have drawn on the long chapter on Lyndon Johnson in my book in writing this essay, but most of the material comes from research I have done since the book was first published—with

the subtitle *From Harry Truman to Ronald Reagan*—in 1983. Though the book has gone through several editions, the chapter on LBJ has not been revised. Since 1983, I have worked in additional archives, and I have benefited from the writings of a number of historians. I am especially indebted to the fine scholarship of Robert Dallek.

2. Johnson interview; *Public Papers of the Presidents of the United States: Lyndon Baines Johnson*, 1963–64, 2 vols. (Washington, D.C.: Government Printing Office, 1965), 1:647, 1495, 335–36. The *Public Papers* series is published at regular intervals by the Government Printing Office.

3. Alistair Cooke, *Talk about America* (New York: Knopf, 1968), 83; Ronnie Dugger, *The Politician: The Life and Times of Lyndon Johnson; The Drive for Power, from the Frontier to Master of the Senate* (New York: Norton, 1982), 254–55; John Kenneth Galbraith, *A Life in Our Times: Memoirs* (Boston: Houghton Mifflin, 1981), 446.

4. Robert Dallek, *Lone Star Rising: Lyndon Johnson and His Times, 1908–1960* (New York: Oxford University Press, 1991), 107–8.

5. Ibid., 129; John H. Binns to LBJ, February 3, 1964, Gen FG2/FDR, box 48, LBJ MSS, Lyndon B. Johnson Library, Austin, Tex. (henceforth Johnson Library); Cooke, *Talk about America*, 83. Johnson was never shy about boasting of his intimacy with Roosevelt. He told a Texas friend that the president had explored with him the post of director of the ill-fated Passamaquoddy Project to harness tides in Maine. Welly K. Hopkins Oral History, 3:19, Johnson Library. Perhaps the tale is true, but it seems improbable.

6. William E. Leuchtenburg, *The Supreme Court Reborn: The Constitutional Revolution in the Age of Roosevelt* (New York: Oxford University Press, 1995), 134–37.

7. Lindley Beckworth Oral History, p. 20, Johnson Library; George Sutherland to Tom Connally, June 5, 1937, box 6, Sutherland MSS, Library of Congress (henceforth LC); Harold Ickes, *The Secret Diary of Harold L. Ickes*, 3 vols. (New York: Simon and Schuster, 1953–54), 2:75–81; clipping from *Austin American*, February 20, 1937, in box 477, Ickes MSS, LC; clipping from *New York Sun*, March 6, 1937, in box 16, James A. Farley MSS, LC; John Henry Kirby to R. B. Dresser, February 12, 1937, ser. 7, box 1, Grenville Clark MSS, Dartmouth College, Hanover, N.H.; clipping from *New York American*, February 10, 1937, in *New York Journal-American* files, University of Texas, Austin; L. L. James to Louis D. Brandeis, April 2, 1937, G 14, folder 1, Brandeis MSS, University of Louisville Law Library, Louisville, Ky.

8. Dallek, *Lone Star Rising*, 147.

9. Ibid., 149; Alfred Steinberg, *Sam Johnson's Boy: A Close-Up of the President from Texas* (New York: Macmillan, 1968), 110; Mrs. W. S. Birdwell Scrapbook, box 193, LBJ MSS, Johnson Library. Johnson leafleted the district with the Tucker column.

10. Dallek, *Lone Star Rising*, 150; Elliott Roosevelt to James A. Farley, April 5, 1937, box 5, Farley MSS; Steinberg, *Sam Johnson's Boy*, 11.

11. *New York Times*, April 11, 1937; *San Marcos Record*, April 16, 1937, and

clipping from Wichita Falls newspaper, April 11, 1937, House of Representatives, scrapbook 1, LBJ MSS; Memorandum for the Trip Files, April 20, 1937, box 7, White House Famous Names, LBJ MSS.

12. Dallek, *Lone Star Rising*, 160–61; Bascom Timmons Oral History, pp. 6–7, Johnson Library; Steinberg, *Sam Johnson's Boy*, 118–20.

13. Dallek, *Lone Star Rising*, 161–62.

14. Thomas G. Corcoran, "Rendezvous with Democracy: The Memoirs of 'Tommy the Cork,'" box 586A, Corcoran MSS, LC; Dallek, *Lone Star Rising*, 164.

15. Dallek, *Lone Star Rising*, 162; Corcoran, "Rendezvous with Democracy"; James H. Rowe Jr. Oral History, 1:7, Johnson Library; Elizabeth Rowe Oral History, 1:11, Johnson Library; James Rowe, Eleanor Roosevelt Oral History Project, p. 20, Franklin D. Roosevelt Library, Hyde Park, N.Y. (henceforth FDRL).

16. James H. Rowe Oral History, 1:11; William Colmer Oral History, p. 68, University of Southern Mississippi, Hattiesburg; John Connally with Mickey Herskowitz, *In History's Shadow: An American Odyssey* (New York: Hyperion, 1993), 53; Clarke Newlon, *L. B. J.: The Man from Johnson City* (New York: Dodd Mead, 1970), 72–73; Arthur E. Goldschmidt and Elizabeth Wickenden Oral History, p. 11, Johnson Library; Grace Tully Oral History, 1:2, Johnson Library; Oscar L. Chapman Oral History, 2:12, 1:37, Johnson Library. See also Robert A. Caro, *The Years of Lyndon Johnson: Means of Ascent* (New York: Knopf, 1990), 9.

17. Dallek, *Lone Star Rising*, 199; Johnson interview, p. 20.

18. Dallek, *Lone Star Rising*, 196, 199–205.

19. R. H. Moodie to Tom Connally, April 21, 1941, box 97, Connally MSS, LC.

20. Press conference transcript, box 7, White House Famous Names, LBJ MSS; Dallek, *Lone Star Rising*, 209.

21. Dallek, *Lone Star Rising*, 217–19; Elster M. Haile to Stephen Early, June 25, 1941, Official File 300, box 33, FDRL.

22. James H. Rowe Jr. Oral History, 1:12; Daniel Quill Oral History, p. 13, Johnson Library; Jack Guinn, "Screwball Election in Texas," *American Mercury* 53 (September 1941): 275; FDR to D. C. McCord, June 21, 1941; telephone message from Tom Corcoran, May 24, 1941; FDR to LBJ, May 26, 1941; LBJ to FDR, May 31, 1941; James Rowe Jr., Memorandum for the President: Lyndon Johnson, June 3, 1941; FDR to LBJ, June 4, 1941, all in box 7, White House Famous Names, LBJ MSS; Dallek, *Lone Star Rising*, 214, 223, 226. To some extent, Roosevelt's intervention backfired. A Dallas man wrote Senator Tom Connally that he resented the "'Washington Crowd' . . . trying to elect a Senator from our state." He added, "It did not do the President any good when he trotted out a candidate." R. E. Abernathy to Connally, July 10, 1941, box 97, Connally MSS.

23. William S. White Oral History, 1:5–6, Johnson Library.

24. Helen Gahagan Douglas Oral History, p. 11, Johnson Library. For one of

numerous examples of Johnson's closeness to the White House, see Jonathan Daniels MS. Diary, October 11–15, 1942, Daniels MSS, Southern Historical Collection, University of North Carolina, Chapel Hill. Johnson's enemies sought to offset this advantage. When he ran for reelection in 1944, his opponent circulated a photograph of Mrs. Roosevelt shaking hands with an African American and linked LBJ to this breach of racial mores. Paul Bolton Oral History, 1:13, Johnson Library.

25. *New York Times*, April 13, 1945; Dorothy Palmie Alford to Max Starcke, with Mrs. Max Starcke and Dorothy Palmie Alford Oral History, p. 11, Johnson Library; Dallek, *Lone Star Rising*, 266; Caro, *Years of Lyndon Johnson: Means of Ascent*, 121.

26. Robert Caro, *The Years of Lyndon Johnson: Master of the Senate* (New York: Knopf, 2002), 125.

27. Ibid., 286–87; James H. Rowe Jr. to Mary Rather, June 4, 1952, box 99, Rowe MSS, FDRL. "There was a great deal of criticism among the New Dealers to which he was incredibly sensitive," Rowe remembered. James H. Rowe Jr. Oral History, 1:25.

28. Caro, *Years of Lyndon Johnson: Master of the Senate*, xvii; Cabell Phillips, "The Way Lyndon Does It," *New York Times Magazine*, July 26, 1959, 58; William S. White, "Who Is Lyndon Johnson?" *Harper's*, March 1958, 58; clipping from Robert Spivack, "The New President," *New York Herald Tribune*, December 1, 1963, in box 100, James H. Rowe Jr. MSS. The link to Roosevelt had also helped him win his very narrow victory in the 1948 Senate race. A future congressman who was one of Johnson's campaign workers in 1948, in explaining the strategy for wooing African American voters, reported, "We worked the FDR connection because all blacks supported FDR." Patrick Cox, "'Nearly a Statesman': LBJ and Texas Blacks in the 1948 Election," *Social Science Quarterly* 74 (1993): 254.

29. Caro, *Years of Lyndon Johnson: Master of the Senate*, 457, 451; Hubert Humphrey Oral History, 1:6, 3:11, 2:5, Johnson Library.

30. Caro, *Years of Lyndon Johnson: Master of the Senate*, 635–36; George Reedy Oral History, pp. 10–11, Johnson Library.

31. Leonard C. Schlup and Donald W. Whisenhunt, eds., *It Seems to Me: Selected Letters of Eleanor Roosevelt* (Lexington: University of Kentucky Press, 2001), 227.

32. LBJ to Eleanor Roosevelt, August 12, 1957, box 99, Rowe MSS.

33. Lyndon B. Johnson, *A Time for Action: A Selection from the Speeches and Writings of Lyndon B. Johnson, 1953–64* (New York: Atheneum, 1964), 66–73; Schlup and Whisenhunt, *It Seems to Me*, 238; Joseph P. Lash, *Eleanor: The Years Alone* (New York: Norton, 1972), 284; William Turner Levy and Cynthia Eagle Russett, *The Extraordinary Mrs. R: A Friend Remembers Eleanor Roosevelt* (New York: John Wiley and Sons, 1999), 205.

34. Clipping from *Dallas Morning News*, June 11, 1960, in box NA 51, John G. Tower MSS, Southwestern University, Georgetown, Texas; "Private Memorandum," box 30, Arthur Krock MSS, Princeton University, Princeton, N.J.

35. Louis Martin Oral History, 1:15, Johnson Library. See also Alex Poinsett, *Walking with Presidents: Louis Martin and the Rise of Black Political Power* (Lanham, Md.: Madison Books, 1997), 140.

36. James H. Rowe Jr. Oral History, 2:29–30.

37. Jack Bell, *The Johnson Treatment: How Lyndon B. Johnson Took Over the Presidency and Made It His Own* (New York: Harper and Row, 1965), 283; Lady Bird Johnson, *A White House Diary* (New York: Holt, Rinehart and Winston, 1970), 485; Michael Knox Beran, *The Last Patrician: Bobby Kennedy and the End of American Aristocracy* (New York: St. Martin's Press, 1998), 98; Republican National Committee, "Johnson Log," box 67, William E. Miller MSS, Cornell University Collection of Regional History, Ithaca, N.Y.; *Public Papers of the Presidents of the United States: Lyndon Baines Johnson,* 1963–64, 1:250; Frank Cormier, *LBJ: The Way He Was* (Garden City, N.Y.: Doubleday, 1977), 14, 46; Elizabeth Wickenden Goldschmidt Oral History, 1:3, Johnson Library; "Portraits of Our Time," transcript, box 5, Richard Rovere MSS, State Historical Society of Wisconsin, Madison.

38. Robert Dallek, *Flawed Giant: Lyndon Johnson and His Times, 1961–1973* (New York: Oxford University Press, 1998), 83, 60–61; Richard Goodwin, interview with the author, Middletown, Conn., December 13, 1965.

39. Richard Goodwin, *Remembering America: A Voice from the Sixties* (Boston: Little, Brown, 1988), 257; Dallek, *Flawed Giant,* 77, 75. Goodwin first made a favorable impression on the Johnson circle when he drafted a speech to be delivered by the president that received a highly favorable response. "LBJ's way of speaking," Jack Valenti told him, "is a lot closer to Roosevelt than to Kennedy." Goodwin, *Remembering America,* 253.

40. Barry Goldwater, "A Fireside Chat with Mr. Roosevelt," *Phoenix Evening Gazette,* June 23, 1938, in James M. Perry, *Barry Goldwater: A New Look at a Presidential Candidate* (Silver Spring, Md.: National Observer, 1964), 51, box 2, Dean Burch MSS, Arizona Historical Society, Tucson, Ariz.; *Public Papers of the Presidents of the United States: Lyndon Baines Johnson,* 1963–64, 1:652–53; Richard L. Strout, *TRB: Views and Perspectives on the Presidency* (New York: Macmillan, 1979), 272.

41. Marshall Frady, "Cooling Off with LBJ," *Harper's,* June 1969, 66; Eric F. Goldman, *The Tragedy of Lyndon Johnson* (New York: Dell, 1969), 21; Richard Harwood and Haynes Johnson, *Lyndon* (New York: Praeger, 1973), 177.

42. Goodwin, *Remembering America,* 259; Dallek, *Flawed Giant,* 278; Nicholas Lemann, *The Promised Land: The Great Migration and How It Changed America* (New York: Knopf, 1991), 182–83.

43. Goodwin, *Remembering America,* 317; George Tindall, *The Emergence of the New South, 1913–1945* (Baton Rouge: Louisiana State University Press, 1967), 728; Harwood and Johnson, *Lyndon,* 36; *New York Times,* April 13, 1945; George Reedy, *Lyndon B. Johnson: A Memoir* (New York: Andrews and McMeel, 1982), 138.

44. Clipping from *Washington Star,* January 12, 1969, in box 20, Katie Louchheim MSS, LC; Katie Louchheim Journals, August 11, 1964, box 79,

Louchheim MSS; Jan Jarboe Russell, *Lady Bird: A Biography of Mrs. Johnson* (New York: Scribners, 1999), 255; clipping from *Washington Post*, October 8, 1964, in box 21, Louchheim MSS.

45. Elizabeth Carpenter, *Ruffles and Flourishes* (New York: Doubleday, 1970), 74; clipping from the *New York Times*, March 6, 1966, in box 125, Bess Furman MSS, LC.

46. Telephone conversation between LBJ and Theodore Sorensen, June 3, 1963, box 1, George Reedy Office Files, Johnson Library; Bill Moyers, interview with the author, White House, November 18, 1965; "Norris Cotton Reports to You from the United States Senate, January 28, 1965," Cotton MSS, University of New Hampshire, Durham; Lyndon Baines Johnson, *The Vantage Point: Perspectives of the Presidency, 1963–1969* (New York: Holt, Rinehart and Winston, 1971), 447–48. Franklin Roosevelt's biographer Geoffrey Ward has given a different spin to the relationship in saying that "many of the charges Roosevelt's contemporaries leveled against him during the pre-presidential years were eerily reminiscent of those Caro has compiled for his indictment of LBJ." Ward contends that like Johnson, Roosevelt was judged by his contemporaries before he became president to be "slippery, self-obsessed, unreliable," a braggart, and a self-promoter. Geoffrey C. Ward, "A One-Sided Johnson," *American Heritage*, July/August 1990, 12.

47. Leuchtenburg, *Supreme Court Reborn*, 152–54.

48. Goldman, *Tragedy*, 301; Eric F. Goldman to Bill Moyers, November 3, 1964, ser. 1, box 63, Goldman MSS, LC; Michael R. Beschloss, ed., *Reaching for Glory: Lyndon Johnson's Secret White House Tapes, 1964–1965* (New York: Simon and Schuster, 2001), 120–21. After delivering his State of the Union address in 1964, Johnson, characteristically, ordered a study of whether at any time in the past a president had been interrupted so often by applause. The answer: Yes, in 1933. Lemann, *Promised Land*, 144–45.

49. "Confidential Memo on Turner Catledge's Conversation with President Johnson," box 30, Krock MSS.

50. Goldman, *Tragedy*, 307–8; *New York Times*, December 16, 1964; Philip Geyelin, *Lyndon B. Johnson and the World* (New York: Praeger, 1966), 146; Goodwin, *Remembering America*, 317; Rowland Evans and Robert Novak, *Lyndon B. Johnson: The Exercise of Power* (New York: Signet, 1968), 517; *Public Papers of the Presidents of the United States: Lyndon Baines Johnson*, 1965 (Washington, D.C.: Government Printing Office, 1966), 369; Tom Wicker, "Lyndon Johnson and the Roots of Contemporary Conservatism," in *Long Time Gone: Sixties America Then and Now*, ed. Alexander Bloom (New York: Oxford University Press, 2001), 102; "Conversation with Mac Bundy," December 15, 1967, box 32, Theodore White MSS, John F. Kennedy Library, Boston, Mass.

51. Lyndon B. Johnson, interview with the author, White House, September 22, 1965; William E. Leuchtenburg, "A Visit with LBJ," *American Heritage*, May/June 1990, 47–64.

52. Office of the White House Press Secretary, Bethesda Naval Hospital, "Prepared but Undelivered Remarks of the President," October 11, 1965,

Brooks Hays MSS, Southern Baptist Historical Collection, Wake Forest University, Winston-Salem, N.C.; Dallek, *Flawed Giant*, 339.

53. Drew Pearson Oral History, 25, Johnson Library; Hobert Taylor Jr. Oral History, 2:5, Johnson Library; Mike Mansfield, interview with the author, U.S. Senate, September 22, 1965. See also Charles Halleck Oral History, p. 28, John F. Kennedy Library, Boston, Mass.

54. James Deakin, "The Dark Side of L.B.J.," *Esquire*, August 1967, 136; J. Lindsay Almond Jr. Oral History, p. 29, Johnson Library; Clark Clifford, with Richard Holbrooke, *Counsel to the President: A Memoir* (New York: Random House, 1991), 386. Noting that even in 1964, when he would win overwhelmingly, Johnson foresaw the possibility of defeat, one commentator has remarked that "Lyndon Johnson was not Franklin D. Roosevelt, . . . a supremely confident politician." Jon Margolis, *The Last Innocent Year: America in 1964, the Beginning of the "Sixties"* (New York: Morrow, 1999), 295. See also Claude Pepper MS. Diary, March 25, 1968, Pepper MSS, Florida State University, Tallahassee.

55. Hugh Sidey, *A Very Personal Presidency: Lyndon Johnson in the White House* (New York: Atheneum, 1968), 71–87; Henry F. Graff, *The Tuesday Cabinet: Deliberation and Decision on Peace and War under Lyndon B. Johnson* (Englewood Cliffs, N.J.: Prentice-Hall, 1970), 105; Frances FitzGerald, *Fire in the Lake: The Vietnamese and the Americans in Vietnam* (Boston: Little, Brown, 1972), 234; Doris Kearns, *Lyndon Johnson and the American Dream* (New York: Harper and Row, 1976), 282–83, 286, 329, 374.

56. Dallek, *Flawed Giant*, 605.

Great Societies and Great Empires

Lyndon Johnson and Vietnam

Wilson Carey McWilliams

Always a bit larger than life, Lyndon Johnson seems even more titanic when compared with his successors. During the lackluster campaign of 2000, James MacGregor Burns, longing for a president uniting "transformational" vision and "transactional" political craft, thought immediately of "a 21st century LBJ."[1] Even among Johnson's erstwhile critics, memories are growing fonder: George McGovern recently wrote that he now rates LBJ—with the exception of Wilson, FDR, and perhaps Theodore Roosevelt—as "the greatest president since Abraham Lincoln."[2]

Johnson's contemporary admirers, however, are apt to draw a sharp distinction between the Great Society and the war in Vietnam, treating Vietnam as a virtual lapse of judgment, an intrusion on Johnson's domestic agenda.[3] LBJ himself sometimes encouraged this view. "We're doing just fine," he told Richard Russell in June 1964, "except for this damn Vietnam thing."[4] And by 1965, he was worrying, to Adlai Stevenson, that Vietnam would dwarf his domestic achievements.[5] To a point, it is a position that makes sense, since Vietnam was undeniably a political tragedy, for Johnson and for America. Yet while there was no *necessary* connection between the Great Society and the American intervention in Vietnam, there were strong, even organic links between the two.

Anyone who hopes for a Great Society is bound to be ambivalent about foreign policy. A regime, after all, is constrained to some extent by what stands outside it: the law is a text limited by context (including, if it needs saying, the limits imposed by the most inclusive contexts, nature and the divine).[6] Grander ambitions for greater societies reach for what is excellent and rare, something probably intricate and certainly vulnerable. In that sense, foreign policy is to a Great Society as a third party is to a romantic date: a disruption of the mood, prose muddling poetry.[7]

Accordingly, ideal states and societies have classically been utopias—regimes that have no place and hence no context other than one created by the theorist's imagination. Efforts to approximate the ideal in practice, especially the *democratic* ideal, have tried to maximize isolation, freedom from foreign influences, and the greatest autonomy for domestic life and politics, on the model of Plato's *Laws*.

Lyndon Johnson appreciated the moral case for democratic isolation.[8] He argued pretty forcefully against overseas involvements in the years before World War II, enough to sound like an isolationist to an alarmed Alvin Wirtz, a devoted New Dealer as well as a Johnson confidant, and since there was no serious pacifist pressure from his district, that stance has to be understood as reflecting Johnson's own convictions.[9]

But Johnson also recognized the *fact* of interdependence, the dynamics of economics, technology, and power that, overriding boundaries, drew nations willy-nilly into international life. Nor was Johnson's internationalism simply a matter of necessity. He was not attracted by Sparta, austere, cherishing her virtues and fearful of the foreign: like most advocates of a Great Society, he was inclined to side with Glaucon, the advocate of a luxurious city in Plato's *Republic*.[10]

The external world offers opportunities and resources as well as restraints and perils. Beyond goods and services, it affords occasions for glory and honor, including both the chance to "do good," the beneficence that indicates one has much where others have little, and the opportunity to advance one's beliefs or way.[11] Being admired is no small attraction, and even envy, admiration's underside, testifies to the greatness of a regime. The glory of one's country offers some solace for mortality and for the marginal dignity of individuals in a mass regime. And all those goods beckoned Lyndon Johnson.

Valuing small communities, Johnson was fundamentally a nationalist, devoted to the Framers' great republic and with it to the modern goal of mastery, abundance, and command over nature.[12] America, in fact and in Johnson's vision, is a regime that dwarfs even Athenian restlessness and drive for "growth," its dynamism a constant intrusion on the life and culture of others (and an easy target for the ambivalence of those others toward change and the disordering of traditional ways).[13]

In general, the logic of the effort to create and secure a Great Society points toward imperium. At a minimum, it prompts a quest to control whatever might threaten the project of social greatness, and it inches toward the attempt to dominate nature, an endeavor associated with, but not confined to, modernity.[14] David, we are told, building Jerusalem and loving beauty, would not let the lame and the blind, who were "hated of David's soul," enter the gates of Zion.[15]

The "arrogance of power," so often criticized in American policy toward Vietnam, is pretty much inseparable from the vaulting confidence necessary to attempt a Great Society.[16] The sense of power makes the goal seem *possible*, and any failure to achieve it, *inexcusable*.

Certainly, that is how LBJ saw it. When, in 1964, he set out his vision of a Great Society, he spoke repeatedly of "man's first chance to create a Great Society," an unparalleled opportunity and duty to build a regime in which "material progress" would be "only the foundation" for a "richer life of mind and spirit."[17] In that high ambition, moreover, it is hard not to hear a response to the challenge of Marxism.[18]

Marx had argued that, hitherto, society was shaped by the dynamics of production, so that "the social relationships of production," reflecting an earlier stage, came to "fetter" the modes of production but were eventually broken by those modes. The "bourgeois social formation" is the "closing chapter of the Prehistoric stage of human society" because, strictly speaking, *society* has had no history: human history thus far is simply the history of production and hence of class struggle. Under socialism, with the problem of production fundamentally solved, it is possible for the first time to construct a society on truly *social* terms.[19]

Johnson's rhetoric suggests that he aimed, in the Great Society, to achieve the socialist *goal* through liberal *institutions*. FDR had "saved" liberal democracy; LBJ would make it victorious, playing Caesar to Roosevelt's Marius, establishing himself as "the greatest of them all," just as he always hoped.[20] Johnson believed that American power was so monumental that it was equal to the building of a Great Society and to the demands of foreign policy, great enough that the United States simply could not fail in Vietnam even if it proved unable to prevail.[21]

In this, he reflected a general American confidence, in Washington and in the country at large. The eventual failure in Vietnam, so startling to Americans, helped set off the wave of opinion that, increasingly, has come to regard government as inept or malign or both. Like Mike Mansfield, George Ball suspected this at the time: even withdrawing from Vietnam, he argued in 1965, would damage American credibility less than proving "unable to defeat a handful of guerrillas."[22] But the domestic result was worse than anything Ball—or LBJ—feared: Vietnam did not greatly damage American credibility abroad, but it wreaked havoc at home. It shattered not only the Great Society but also our capacity for common dreams, activating both extremes, the Right and the Left, and escalating the distrust of public authority toward a kind of madness.[23]

This, too, is excess and full of dangers. Writing Gobineau in 1853, Alexis de Tocqueville set down a political lesson applicable to our times: "After having believed ourselves capable of transforming ourselves, we believe ourselves incapable of reforming ourselves; after having had an excessive pride, we have fallen into a humility that is no less excessive. We believed ourselves capable of everything, and today we believe ourselves capable of nothing."[24] Tocqueville thought it imperative to revive the sense of political possibility or, at any rate, to avoid making things worse. So it is for us and, with it, a special reason to get straight in our memory the connections between the Great Society and Vietnam.

Lyndon Johnson's defenders, especially those who are partisans of the Great Society, are apt to blame his advisers for his troubles in Vietnam. According to this version of the story, Johnson was primarily focused on his domestic agenda and an amateur in foreign policy, too easily impressed by the expertise and the aura of the staff he inherited from JFK, too inclined to defer to those advisers' confidence in their ability to manage and control events.[25]

It is true that LBJ was badly served in many ways. Kennedy's appointees, invested in the commitments they had made in and to Vietnam, were unwilling to admit to any error. (Notably, George Ball, that loyal dissenter, was not involved in Vietnam policy during the Kennedy years.)[26] Dean Rusk, scarred by the McCarthy years, leaned toward superhawkishness; McNamara, at critical points, upheld a rather extreme view of the domino theory.[27] Similarly, the Joint Chiefs spoke, in 1964, of the "overriding importance" of South Vietnam (and, after the Tet offensive, presented an exaggeratedly dark picture of the military situation, hoping to provoke full mobilization but actually dealing a fatal wound to intervention).[28] And when Johnson turned to a panel of elder statesmen in search of alternatives, these quasi-official wise men endorsed ongoing policy, including troop commitments, in an almost cavalier way.[29]

Nevertheless, Johnson had reasonable credentials in foreign policy. He ran for the Senate in 1941 as a champion of Rooseveltian internationalism, advocating the "defense of Democracy against aggression," and he was enlisted by FDR in a variety of roles involving foreign affairs.[30] Johnson's view of international politics was evidently shaped by the failure of appeasement, so that while he was at least mildly conciliatory toward the Soviet Union at the beginning of the postwar era, he moved quickly to a relatively hard-line anticommunism.[31] In 1953, he argued that the Korean truce had been obtained at the price of too many concessions; in the late 1950s, he worried publicly about the supposed "missile gap" between the United States and the Soviet Union; and during the primary season in 1960, he criticized Kennedy for JFK's willingness to apologize to the USSR for the U-2 incident.[32] Yet most appositely, Johnson argued for limiting American commitments in Asia during the Eisenhower and Kennedy years, seeing disorder and a lack of clear goals in American policy in Indochina and even, just before the fall of Dien Bien Phu, urging the Eisenhower administration to turn its eyes "homeward."[33]

Johnson was quite capable of asserting himself against the most formidable of experts. In the Senate hearings after Truman's dismissal of General Douglas MacArthur, for example, Johnson not only challenged the general but rather artfully exposed the fact that MacArthur had not thought through the global implications of his own policy.[34] That experience helped make LBJ confidently derisive with generals who assured him that China would not intervene in response to escalation in Vietnam: "MacArthur didn't think they would come in either."[35]

While as a rule Johnson probably did defer to his advisers, he was quite adroit, when so inclined, at getting the kind of advice he wanted. In May 1964, for instance, he insisted on delaying escalation in order to consult Adlai Stevenson, knowing that Stevenson's counsel would be relatively dovish and something of a check on Rusk.[36]

Moreover, Johnson clearly had reservations about the strength of America's interest in Vietnam. It helped that Richard Russell, so revered by LBJ, advised him that Vietnam "isn't important a damn bit," or that other people, such as J. William Fulbright, who counted as political friends, were even more doubtful.[37] In any event, in May 1964, Johnson told McNamara that while he did not think the United States could "get out" of Vietnam, he also did not think the place was "worth fighting for."[38]

Johnson was not much more enthusiastic about the claim that the United States was assisting the South Vietnamese to defend their freedom. Up to a point, he agreed: he was confident that, in the long term, the South Vietnamese regime would prove more hospitable to human flourishing and more popular than its rivals. But in the immediate situation, Johnson had few illusions about the quality of the South Vietnamese government, and even fewer about the strength of its legitimacy. Emphatic about the need for economic and political change, he was skeptical about the extent of America's ability to reform South Vietnam, especially given its internal divisions and its lack of stable institutions.[39] Accordingly, he had been critical of Kennedy's decision to displace Diem, shrewdly suspecting that it would only open the door to South Vietnamese factionalism.[40]

When that disarray materialized and escalated, South Vietnam's political disorder might have furnished an occasion for minimizing American involvement or even for withdrawal.[41] LBJ, after all, was hardly enchanted by the counterargument that increased American military intervention would strengthen morale in South Vietnam and buy time for political stabilization.[42] In fact, through 1964, he continued to treat the commitment of American troops as *undesirable* as well as unnecessary, arguing, as Maxwell Taylor did at the time, that U.S. military intervention would be likely to foster dependence in South Vietnam and would surely lead to resentment, making a bad political situation even worse.[43] Moreover, Johnson retained these doubts even when Taylor reversed himself in June 1965. Nor was Johnson ever sanguine about the prospects of a purely military victory.[44]

Almost desperately, Johnson sought for alternatives, room for the sort of maneuvering that was the mark of his political craft.[45] There were limits, of course: he recognized, many liberal critics to the contrary, that any effort to "neutralize" South Vietnam would be certain to fail without parallel restraints in the North, which North Vietnam was unwilling to concede.[46] But he did raise the question of whether it might not be better to withdraw, "let the dominoes fall," and "make a stand" somewhere else in Asia, on more favorable ground, and he showed serious interest in George Ball's plan for a negotiated settlement including the Vietcong.[47]

Johnson even listened to Richard Russell's hyper-Machiavellian plan for engineering a coup by a South Vietnamese nationalist who would then *ask* the United States to withdraw, allowing America to get out with dignity. Significantly, Johnson argued against this scheme in strictly *practical* terms: American involvement in such a coup could not be concealed and, once known, would cause much greater damage to our national dignity.[48] But Johnson offered no *moral* objection to the plan. In fact, he suggested a version of it in July 1965, proposing that the United States issue an ultimatum to the then prime minister Nguyen Cao Ky, demanding reforms and aiming to withdraw when turned down, only to be dissuaded by McNamara's invocation of an extreme version of the domino theory.[49]

Beyond all these schemes, Johnson allowed himself to consider Walter Lippmann's formula: negotiating a settlement that allowed North Vietnam to win through *diplomacy*, avoiding a *military* defeat.[50] Nixon was to adopt a version of this design; Johnson ultimately rejected it. He insisted on keeping the war limited and pursuing goals short of victory, but he regarded defeat as unacceptable, and at the moment of decision, he always came down against "pulling out."[51]

Yet, that stubborn determination, with all its dark consequences for American politics, did not derive from any American interest in South Vietnam or from any ideological affinity with South Vietnam's successive governments. It was linked to Johnson's view of the duty and dignity of American public life, abroad and at home, and hence to the very foundations of the Great Society.

On the evidence, one is bound to conclude that Johnson's policy in Vietnam, with its ever-increasing costs, was powerfully, perhaps decisively influenced by considerations of honor, Johnson's own as well as the country's. At the most rational level, honor involved the need to make good the word of his predecessors, who had pledged the United States to Vietnam. In that sense, at the level of high policy, the issue was never Vietnam but rather American "credibility," the need to demonstrate America's will to avoid giving any reward to aggression, any rebirth of the impulse toward appeasement. The peculiar securities of the "balance of terror" required an America willing to keep its promises and to draw lines, even at considerable cost, and such calculations took on heightened significance in late 1964, given the new uncertainties introduced by the fall of Khrushchev and the fear of a China armed with nuclear weapons.[52] But where LBJ's advisers preferred to speak of prestige and credibility as utilitarian counters in an international game of push-pin, Johnson gave them a distinctively moral shading.

Vietnam, he told Walter Lippmann, was "a commitment I inherited."[53] Johnson assigned the primary responsibility for getting us into Vietnam to Eisenhower, and LBJ remembered himself as having opposed that intervention.[54] But of course, Kennedy had moved America "from advice to partnership" in South Vietnam and, especially, into a deep entanglement with South Vietnamese politics.[55] In Johnson's judgment, it would do "irreparable" damage to break "the word of three presidents."[56]

It is hard not to hear the personal tone in such comments. Driven to be the best and to outdo his rivals, LBJ was utterly unwilling to be the first U.S. president to lose a war (a fear his advisers often played on) or to appear unmanly or dishonorable.[57] This attitude extended to Johnson's political doctrine. "When a democracy lays [*sic*] down before any ideology," he once remarked, "there is no more democracy."[58] In a sense, this looks like a non sequitur: a democracy that lies down before another regime is, on the face of it, still a democracy; it is merely a *defeated* democracy. But LBJ was speaking about the inner aspect of public life, a republican spirit underlying democratic forms: he meant that democracy presumes civic pride, a willingness to do and risk everything for self-government.

Behind LBJ's own manly willingness to do battle was a softer motive, a patriot's love of country and identification with its glory, just as his zeal to be the best reflected a desire—like Callicles with Demos—to establish a claim *on* the love of the thing he loved.[59] After all, LBJ repeatedly demonstrated his willingness to compromise purely *personal* honor in order to get some desired public result. "I've been kissing asses all my life," he said once (even as he raised the hope that he would not have to do so any more).[60] His career was built on multiple dishonors, including saying what he evidently did not mean, and even despised, about racial politics, to say nothing of the other necessities of public life in the Texas of his time. But a lover must uphold the beloved's honor with all his or her strength: so it was with Johnson and American democracy.

Dealing with disturbances in Panama in 1964, for example, Johnson proclaimed himself willing to do a "good many chicken things," but not when Panamanians were "shooting at my soldiers." Similarly, Johnson moved decisively toward escalation after the attack on the U.S. advisers at Pleiku in Vietnam in February 1965: you "can't take this kind of thing," LBJ remarked, when enemies are "killing our boys in their sleep."[61] In such comments, one is bound to hear the paternal—even erotic—dimension of LBJ's toughness. Achilles-like, Johnson was moved by warm anger, a rage against those who had injured Americans he saw as his own, reflecting an essentially Periclean eros, a need to avenge any injury to the city and the public that one loves.

By 1966, Richard J. Daley—an admirer and an ally, but already disenchanted with the war—had told LBJ that a wise man folds a losing hand. "But what about American prestige?" Johnson asked. To which Daley responded, "You put your prestige in your back pocket and walk away." But when Chicago's honor and prestige came under fire at the 1968 Democratic Convention, Daley did not heed his own advice, even though he half agreed with the demonstrators.[62] Pragmatism, as we all know, gets trumped by love.

Johnson's passionate devotion to the glory of his country and to its citizens, so much a foundation of the Great Society, helped draw him deeper into war, each new death an affront to be avenged, each new loss a reason for rejecting failure.[63] Walter Lippmann had foreseen situations like Vietnam in which America's choices would come down to a stark antithesis: whatever the advantages of our withdrawal from Vietnam, it was undeniably dishonorable.[64] And Lyndon Johnson was not the man to make such a choice.

Johnson's policy in Vietnam was thus entwined with, though possibly subordinate to, his plans for a Great Society at home. This was especially true because Johnson, with some reason, felt himself to be the only leader able to build support across racial, sectional, and class lines for his domestic program, and because—familiar with the rhythms of democratic politics—he knew he had only a short time in which to accomplish his goals.[65] Indeed, if Vietnam indicated a presidency that had become dangerously "imperial" in foreign affairs, it hinted at a presidency not imperial enough in domestic politics.[66]

The Great Society strongly influenced Johnson's decision to refrain from any full-scale mobilization for the Vietnam conflict.[67] Persuaded that Vietnam was not worth more than a limited war, he was even more convinced, from his reading of history and from personal experience, that putting the country on a "war footing," in addition to soaking up resources, would engender a patriotic militancy fatal to the impulse toward domestic reform.[68]

Guilty memories may have underlined these calculations. During the Korean War, Johnson had urged a full, quasi-permanent mobilization, with a curtailment of domestic spending.[69] Similarly, during the Second World War, he criticized labor unions that disrupted war production, arguing that justice at home must take second place to victory in war.[70]

At the same time, he worried that too much forbearance, let alone withdrawal, would allow the Right to use anticommunism to subvert domestic change, on the model of the notorious "loss" of China that had devastated liberalism.[71] Accordingly, he sought to forestall or take the steam out of such attacks: Johnson swallowed the first attack on U.S. forces in the Gulf of Tonkin, perhaps because he was aware of the moral ambiguity of the American position; part of his decision to retaliate for the second attack involved a felt need to respond to Barry Goldwater's demand for sterner measures.[72]

By contrast, at the time when critical decisions were being made, Johnson does not appear to have been overly impressed by Hubert Humphrey's warning that Johnson should fear the Right less than his left-liberal critics.[73] Liberals in Texas, recognizing their own weakness, had generally tended to put up with LBJ's bows to the Right.[74] Moreover, through the postwar decades, the peace-oriented Left, demoralized by its perceived errors in relation to Nazi and Soviet totalitarianism, had spoken in a chastened voice, pursuing a relatively responsible internationalism and contenting itself, if restively, with the leadership of cold war liberals such as Hubert Humphrey.[75] Indeed, at the beginning of the war in Vietnam, most activists were at least moderately hawkish.[76] In debates over foreign policy, the Left, for the most part, was silent, while the Right thundered. Johnson, hoping to hold the center and to minimize any threat to the Great Society, tipped in the direction of that skewed balance.[77]

The upshot was the administration's effort to pursue the war while limiting any demands on the American public, a stance that led Johnson and his advisers to minimize the costs of the war, to conceal their early escalations and to obscure their early, brief gestures toward peace.[78] Evidently, LBJ wishfully underrated the burden of the war, hoping for a quick, half-covert settlement on the model of American interventions in Latin America and relying on a misguided view of North Vietnamese "rationality" that discounted patriotism.[79] As Johnson himself sometimes suspected, our opponents' passion for Vietnam proved a more-than-adequate balance for America's relatively indifferent power.[80]

A great many people who had LBJ's ear—Mike Mansfield, for example, or Hubert Humphrey—soon came to urge, as McNamara had earlier in mid-1964, a full and open national debate aimed at winning public support for the American commitment to Vietnam.[81] American opinion was obviously the key to the war. In material terms, Hanoi could not win and knew it; the measure of its hope was set by the uncertainty of the American popular will to persist.[82] Yet on this point, Lyndon Johnson, imperial in so many ways, felt fundamentally constrained: he was convinced that it was not possible to persuade Americans to make major sacrifices for a war with *limited* ends, while full-scale war would doom the Great Society.[83] Consequently, he was forced to rely on the hope that Americans would stay the course if not asked for very much. His policy made it impossible to transform Vietnam into an all-out war; it also locked us into a limited war we were likely to lose in the end.[84]

LBJ presumed a public that could be stirred or inflamed, but one broadly uneducable, at least in the near term. He may have underrated his talents: Johnson had taught debate; he was adroit at argument; by all accounts, he had been a great teacher. Still, in Johnson's defense, it must be noted that the task of winning popular support for foreign policy—and especially for a costly but limited war—is more difficult in modern America than it was for ancient architects of great societies.

Pericles, for example, could appeal to the interest of his public more easily than could Johnson. Ancient empires financed much of their great societies directly, paying for public works and public welfare out of spoils and tribute.[85] Athenian leaders, Socrates observed, "stuffed the city with harbors and arsenals and walls and tribute," and if philosophy was disdainful, citizenries were apt to be appreciative.[86] In liberal societies, by contrast, the benefits of imperium are more likely to be indirect or limited to safety, only problematically related to the goal of a Great Society.[87]

Ancient republics, moreover, were less apt to hold themselves to moral or ideological universals. Pericles may not have been as candid as

Thucydides makes him, but he could credibly be made to say that Athens' empire was a tyranny: Athenian ends may have been noble, Clifford Orwin writes, but they were "those of the Athenians, and no one else's."[88] Greeks and Romans were rather cavalier in their treatment of barbarians and even of near kin. The only universal acknowledged at Melos and Mytilene was the good of dominion, and to be effective, any appeal to Athenian sympathy had to be cast (or so we are told) in the language of interest.[89]

But in our times, universals—such as doctrines of human rights—have become habitual in political discourse. This is a gain in many ways, setting at least some limit to indifference and cruelty, but it also involves its own moral ambiguities: while universals *inhibit* government, on the one hand, they also push it toward *total* engagement, on the other. LBJ, obviously, confronted both tendencies, his left-liberal opponents concerned to humanize and democratize policy, his conservative critics invoking ideological combat. The language of modern politics, in other words, places special constraints on foreign policymakers, especially those, like Lyndon Johnson, who speak of high duties.

Above all, the United States is a republic on the grand scale, itself an empire by ancient standards, its public a fragmented multitude, ordinarily content with comfortable decency and only rarely moved to great projects and callings.[90] Easy and overwhelmingly persuasive in small groups and one-to-one exchanges, Johnson knew that such face-to-face eloquence, which can recognize and enhance the dignity of the individual addressed, cannot be transferred to the anonymity and indignity of mass politics.[91]

He did not expect the "mediating strata" to do more than moderate those defects of national politics. Local and state governments seemed increasingly passé; he despised the media; associations he regarded as largely the voice of faction; and his belief in the virtue of political parties, while significant, was decidedly limited, especially where Republicans were concerned.[92] Following an essentially Madisonian teaching, LBJ was inclined to regard public deliberation as almost inherently the domain of unreason.[93] He preferred a "two-tier" politics in which leaders, selected by the people, work out the details of policy in private.[94]

It is not hard to make a case for Johnson's view. Nevertheless, the effort to insulate leaders from the public often results in concealing failures of leadership—not simply miscalculations of technique but also confusion about ends, both of which were evident in Vietnam.[95] It provides justification to paranoid fantasies, and risks sheltering the *public* from an acknowledgment of its share of the dangers, burdens, and obligations of political life. The most proficient leaders, after all, can encourage people to feel entitled to good outcomes and, consequently, to see themselves as ill-used by any costs or setbacks. Pericles, Socrates said, taught Athenians to "kick, butt or bite him," and in many ways, LBJ's very competence did the same.[96] Democratic greatness presumes public commitment and hence public argument. Since international forces increasingly touch the intimate details of domestic life, a democratic politics—let alone a Great Society—requires public debate about international affairs.

Since LBJ left office, despite some signal triumphs, we have endured three decades of political disappointment; confidence in our institutions is low, our sense of self-government in retreat. In 2000, the presidential election became an unfunny comedy in which the joke was on us. Tocqueville was right to argue that in such circumstances, politics needs a new measure of pride. But the patriotic ferment that followed September 11, 2001, is souring from the effect of half-truths and deceptions. We should also learn a crucial lesson from the Johnson years: that a democratic Great Society not only demands but is also *defined* by a Great People. Its test and measure is civic education, including parties and communities, churches, and, yes, bowling leagues, the whole academy of democratic politics.[97] Johnson was right to think that, among the Titans, democracy sometimes needs Atlas to hold up the heavens; even more, however, it relies on Prometheus to bring it light.

Notes

1. James MacGregor Burns, "It's the Vision Thing, Again," *Washington Post National Weekly*, May 22, 2000, 22.

2. George McGovern, "Discovering Greatness in Lyndon Johnson," *New York Times*, December 5, 1999, WK17. Similarly, Marc Landy and Sidney Milkis rate Johnson as the closest contender for greatness since FDR. See Landy and Milkis, *Presidential Greatness* (Lawrence: University Press of Kansas, 2000), 205.

3. McGovern makes essentially this argument; for an even more striking example, see John A. Andrew III, *Lyndon Johnson and the Great Society* (Chicago: Ivan Dee, 1998). Landy and Milkis are an exception to this rule (*Presidential Greatness*, 218).

4. Michael R. Beschloss, ed., *Taking Charge: The Johnson White House Tapes*,

1963–1964 (New York: Simon and Schuster, 1997), 402. Johnson made similar comments to Humphrey on election night in 1964; see Rick Perlstein, *Before the Storm: Barry Goldwater and the Unmaking of the American Consensus* (New York: Hill and Wang, 2001), 512.

5. Philip Geyelin, *Lyndon B. Johnson and the World* (New York: Praeger, 1966), 232.

6. The problem of "foreign powers" is a constant theme in Machiavelli's writing, as Harvey Mansfield indicates (*Machiavelli's New Modes and Orders* [Ithaca: Cornell University Press, 1979]).

7. In a more positive sense, an international context can set limits to national baseness, as in Herbert Marcuse's observation that the Soviet Union of the 1960s could not revert to Stalinism, given the nature of international competition (*One Dimensional Man* [Boston: Beacon, 1968], 44–45).

8. Probably best stated, in the prewar years, by Charles Beard; see, for example, *The Open Door at Home* (New York: Macmillan, 1934). For another discussion, see my "Democracy, Protest and Publics: The Problem of Foreign Policy," *Journal of International Affairs* 28 (1969): 193–94.

9. Robert Dallek, *Lone Star Rising: Lyndon Johnson and His Times, 1908–1960* (New York: Oxford University Press, 1991), 198–99.

10. On Sparta, see Clifford Orwin, *The Humanity of Thucydides* (Princeton: Princeton University Press, 1994), 75–76.

11. For Lyndon Johnson, the desire to do good was virtually tyrannical, as Doris Kearns suggests (*Lyndon Johnson and the American Dream* [New York: Harper and Row, 1976], 53–54, 65–67). In his teaching days, Dallek comments, Johnson showed "almost a desperate urgency in his desire to give . . . good things" to his pupils (*Long Star Rising*, 78).

12. Dallek, *Lone Star Rising*, 72, 167, 242; Lyndon Baines Johnson, *The Vantage Point: Perspectives of the Presidency, 1963–1969* (New York: Holt, Rinehart and Winston, 1971), 29, 72, 79, 343–44; Kearns, *Lyndon Johnson and the American Dream*, 34, 36, 64, 97, 113.

13. On Athens, see Orwin, *Humanity of Thucydides*, 44. On the relation between economic dynamism and empire, see John Gallagher and Ronald Robinson, "The Imperialism of Free Trade," *Economic History Review*, 2d ser., 6, no. 1 (1953): 1–25.

14. Richard Koebner, *Empire* (New York: Grosset and Dunlap, 1961), 1–17; Robert Wesson, *The Imperial Order* (Berkeley: University of California Press, 1967).

15. 2 Samuel 5:6, 8 (Revised Standard Version).

16. Brian Van De Mark, for example, refers to an "arrogant and stubborn faith in America's power." See his *Into the Quagmire: Lyndon Johnson and the Escalation of the Vietnam War* (New York: Oxford University Press, 1991), xiv, 219–20. See also H. W. Brands, *The Wages of Globalism: Lyndon Johnson and the Limits of American Power* (New York: Oxford University Press, 1995).

17. Andrew, *Lyndon Johnson and the Great Society*, 14; Beschloss, *Taking Charge*, 404 n. 1, 326 n. 4.

18. Jon Margolis, *The Last Innocent Year: America in 1964: The Beginning of the "Sixties"* (New York: Morrow, 1999), 215–18. Johnson claimed that the Ann Arbor speech (May 22, 1964) derived from his reading of Barbara Ward (*The Rich Nations and the Poor Nations* [New York: Norton, 1962]). Hugh Sidey thought, however, that this remark was part of a "game" designed to downplay the contributions of Richard Goodwin (*A Very Personal Presidency: Lyndon Johnson in the White House* [New York: Atheneum, 1968], 156–58).

19. Karl Marx, *A Contribution to the Critique of Political Economy*, trans. S. W. Ryazanskaya (Moscow: Progress, 1977), 21–22.

20. William Leuchtenburg, *In the Shadow of FDR: Harry Truman to Ronald Reagan* (Ithaca: Cornell University Press, 1983), 142; see also 123, 128. It is worth noting that international politics played a key role in the failure of the high aspirations of both Soviet communism and Lyndon Johnson. Marx had assumed an internationalism created by bourgeois economics and socialist politics: "*l'Internationale sera le genre humain.*" Socialism's empire would be universal, its Great Society unconstrained by foreign policy. In fact, the Soviet Union was not so fortunate; neither was LBJ.

21. Leslie Gelb and Richard Betts, *The Irony of Vietnam* (Washington: Brookings Institution, 1979).

22. George Ball, *The Past Has Another Pattern: Memoirs* (New York: Norton, 1982), 399–402; Van De Mark, *Into the Quagmire*, 104, 189.

23. Michael P. Rogin, "JFK: The Movie," *American Historical Review* 97 (1992): 502–5.

24. To Arthur de Gobineau, December 20, 1853, in Alexis de Tocqueville, *Selected Letters on Politics and Society*, ed. Roger Boesche (Berkeley: University of California Press, 1985), 303.

25. Van De Mark, *Into the Quagmire*, 219.

26. Ibid., 85–90.

27. Ibid., 11, 42, 196. It did not help that Richard Russell worried about Rusk's "softness," since that view encouraged LBJ to treat Rusk's sometimes hysterical anticommunism as relatively moderate (Beschloss, *Taking Charge*, 174–75); compare Rusk's views on the possibility of public debate about Vietnam policy (Van De Mark, *Into the Quagmire*, 160–61).

28. Beschloss, *Taking Charge*, 266; Herbert Y. Schandler, *The Unmaking of a President: Lyndon Johnson and Vietnam* (Princeton: Princeton University Press, 1977), 66–67, 79, 82, 99–101,110–11, 115–16, 183–84, 199–202, 210–11, 327–28.

29. Walter Isaacson and Evan Thomas, *The Wise Men: Six Men and the World They Made* (New York: Simon and Schuster, 1986), 650–52.

30. Dallek, *Long Star Rising*, 226–27. Ironically, the argument that LBJ, while a "whiz" at domestic politics, should—as a novice—listen to old hands at foreign policy was first made by Alvin Wirtz as part of a critique of Johnson's early doubts about entanglement in European affairs (ibid., 198–99).

31. Ibid., 275, 292, 396–97.

32. Ibid., 435, 531, 569.

33. Ibid., 444, 479–80; Van De Mark, *Into the Quagmire*, 9, 10.
34. Dallek, *Lone Star Rising*, 398, 400.
35. Van De Mark, *Into the Quagmire*, 197, 200.
36. Beschloss, *Taking Charge*, 362–63.
37. Ibid., 364, 297, 403.
38. Ibid., 370.
39. Van De Mark, *Into the Quagmire*, 35–37, 106.
40. Beschloss, *Taking Charge*, 73, 366; Van De Mark, *Into the Quagmire*, 15.
41. Van De Mark, *Into the Quagmire*, 42–46, 217–18.
42. Ibid., 53–54; Beschloss, *Taking Charge*, 263.
43. See, for example, Johnson's speeches to the American Bar Association, August 12, 1964, and at the University of Akron, October 21, 1964, in *The Public Papers of the Presidents of the United States: Lyndon B. Johnson*, 1963–64, 2 vols. (Washington, D.C.: Government Printing Office, 1965), 2:952–55, 1387–93. On Taylor's view, see Van De Mark, *Into the Quagmire*, 51, 92, 99. Obviously, these expectations were correct (Beschloss, *Taking Charge*, 359).
44. Beschloss, *Taking Charge*, 214; Johnson, inclined to discount the claims made on behalf of airpower, recognized that any U.S. military intervention would be likely to lead to the use of ground troops, a result he feared for many reasons. Van De Mark, *Into the Quagmire*, 50, 160–61; Beschloss, *Taking Charge*, 263.
45. Van De Mark, *Into the Quagmire*, 160–61, 187.
46. Beschloss, *Taking Charge*, 210, 213–14, 226–27, 367.
47. Ibid., 264, 401; Van De Mark, *Into the Quagmire*, 129, 155.
48. Beschloss, *Taking Charge*, 369–70, 411.
49. Van De Mark, *Into the Quagmire*, 196.
50. Beschloss, *Taking Charge*, 372–73, 375 n. 1.
51. Van De Mark, *Into the Quagmire*, 187, 208; *Public Papers*, 2:1122–28.
52. Kearns, *Lyndon Johnson and the American Dream*, 252; Van De Mark, *Into the Quagmire*, 215–16. In November 1964, 59 percent of respondents in a Gallup poll named China as the greatest nuclear threat; only 20 percent named the USSR (Van De Mark, *Into the Quagmire*, 242 n. 3).
53. Ronald Steel, *Walter Lippmann and the American Century* (New York: Random House, 1981), 556.
54. Beschloss, *Taking Charge*, 213, 271. Johnson had been very reticent about any involvement in Indochina, but he stopped short of outright opposition (Dallek, *Lone Star Rising*, 444).
55. Neil Sheehan et al., *The Pentagon Papers* (Boston: Beacon, 1971), 2:87–98, 652–54; Van De Mark, *Into the Quagmire*, 8.
56. Van De Mark, *Into the Quagmire*, 189. In 1965, Mike Mansfield conceded that the United States was "in too deep before you assumed office" (ibid., 104).
57. Beschloss, *Taking Charge*, 228, 410–11. Johnson was notoriously sensitive to any slights or criticism (for example, see ibid., 529–32); his father's shame and rage at any sign that his son might be thought "sissified" or cowardly had

understandable effects on LBJ's personality (Dallek, *Lone Star Rising*, 39). His competitiveness sometimes obscured his interests. He feared his longtime nemesis Bobby Kennedy as a potential (and eventual) critic of Vietnam policy, especially because Kennedy, that old McCarthyite, could go right or left as the occasion might dictate. (As one might suspect, Johnson most dreaded a hard-line critique.) Consequently, when Kennedy offered to replace Henry Cabot Lodge as ambassador to South Vietnam, Johnson might have seen it as a grand political opportunity, allowing him to link Kennedy to administration policy or leave him with a good deal of the blame for any failure. But Johnson turned him down, giving as his reason his fears for Kennedy's safety. These worries were probably sincere, but one suspects that LBJ, far from seeking to minimize his responsibility, was unwilling to give RFK so much of the limelight and the credit for possible success. See Beschloss, *Taking Charge*, 406; on the rivalry between Johnson and Kennedy, see Dallek, *Lone Star Rising*, 490, and Beschloss, *Taking Charge*, 157 n. 4; on Kennedy's McCarthyism and his possibilities as a hawkish critic, see Kearns, *Lyndon Johnson and the American Dream*, 253, and Beschloss, *Taking Charge*, 489, 519.

58. Dallek, *Lone Star Rising*, 292.

59. Plato, *Gorgias*, 481D–E, 513A–B, in Lysis, Symposium, *and* Gorgias, trans. W. R. M. Lamb (Cambridge: Harvard University Press, 1975).

60. George Reedy, *Lyndon B. Johnson: A Memoir* (New York: Andrews and McMeel, 1982), 138; Kearns, *Lyndon Johnson and the American Dream*, 76, 91, 103, 105, 113, 173; Ronnie Dugger, *The Politician: The Life and Times of Lyndon Johnson; The Drive for Power, from the Frontier to Master of the Senate* (New York: Norton, 1982), 112, 200, 204, 264, 276, 346.

61. Beschloss, *Taking Charge*, 174–75, 360; Van De Mark, *Into the Quagmire*, 64–65.

62. Adam Cohen and Elizabeth Taylor, *American Pharaoh: Richard J. Daley; His Battle for Chicago and the Nation* (Boston: Little, Brown, 2000), 445–46.

63. Van De Mark, *Into the Quagmire*, 218.

64. See Lippmann's prophetic observation in *The Cold War* (New York: Harper, 1949), 23.

65. Kearns, *Lyndon Johnson and the American Dream*, 156–57; Dallek, *Lone Star Rising*, 546.

66. See Aaron B. Wildavsky's argument in "The Two Presidencies," *Transaction* 4 (1966): 7–14.

67. Landy and Milkis, *Presidential Greatness*, 218; Kearns, *Lyndon Johnson and the American Dream*, 282–83.

68. Kearns, *Lyndon Johnson and the American Dream*, 142, 252–53, 282, 338; Sidey, *A Very Personal Presidency*, 234; Henry F. Graff, *The Tuesday Cabinet: Deliberation and Discussion on War and Peace under Lyndon B. Johnson* (Englewood Cliffs, N.J.: Prentice-Hall, 1970), 53–55; David Halberstam, *The Best and the Brightest* (New York: Random House, 1972), 424, 507, 530. It helped that, in 1965, the public was probably more hawkish than Johnson (Van De Mark, *Into the Quagmire*, 76). LBJ told Helen Gahagan Douglas that he hoped

to pay for the Great Society out of military reductions; in the end, the war made it impossible to fund the Great Society adequately (Beschloss, *Taking Charge*, 137).

69. Dallek, *Lone Star Rising*, 383–84, 389.

70. Ibid., 254–56. None of these hesitations, however, kept LBJ from appealing to patriotism when he thought it could serve his purposes: he used the Tonkin Gulf crisis to rally support for his antipoverty program (Beschloss, *Taking Charge*, 503).

71. Eric F. Goldman, *The Tragedy of Lyndon Johnson* (New York: Knopf, 1969), 484; Beschloss, *Taking Charge*, 114, 213, 261, 365–66, 369. Privately, Johnson sometimes ridiculed conservative critics: in April 1964, he referred to Nixon's demand for escalation as a policy of "unleashing" South Vietnam, mocking the Right's old enthusiasm for Chiang Kai-shek; he never discounted the public appeal of conservative policies (Beschloss, *Taking Charge*, 319).

72. Van De Mark, *Into the Quagmire*, 18.

73. Hubert H. Humphrey, *The Education of a Public Man: My Life and Politics*, ed. Norman Sherman (Garden City, N.Y.: Doubleday, 1976), 320–24.

74. Dallek, *Lone Star Rising*, 365.

75. McWilliams, "Democracy, Protest and Publics," 189–209.

76. Sidney Verba and Richard Brody, "Participation, Policy Preferences and the War in Vietnam," *Public Opinion Quarterly* 34 (1970): 325–32.

77. Dean Rusk, interestingly, did fear the Left, arguing against any full public debate on the war lest "commies" use their "apparatus" to stir up trouble (Van De Mark, *Into the Quagmire*, 160–61).

78. Ibid., 39, 54, 112, 136, 217; Larry Berman, *Planning a Tragedy* (New York: Norton, 1982); Wilson Carey McWilliams, "Lyndon B. Johnson: The Last of the Great Presidents," in *Modern Politics and the Presidency*, ed. Marc Landy (Lexington, Mass.: D. C. Heath, 1985), 175.

79. Van De Mark, *Into the Quagmire*, 102, 115; Kearns, *Lyndon Johnson and the American Dream*, 268.

80. Stanley Karnow, *Vietnam: A History* (New York: Viking, 1983), 419.

81. Van De Mark, *Into the Quagmire*, 41; Beschloss, *Taking Charge*, 397–98. By 1965, Humphrey found the public "weary and confused" (*The Education of a Public Man*, 320–24).

82. Herbert Y. Schandler, *The Unmaking of a President*, 52–53, 56; Leslie Gelb, "The Essential Domino: American Opinion and Vietnam," *Foreign Affairs* 50 (1972): 459–75.

83. Beschloss, *Taking Charge*, 372; Col. Harry Summers, *On Strategy: The Vietnam War in Context* (Carlisle, Pa.: U.S. Army War College, 1981), 8. From the beginning, popular support for the war was low and ambivalent (Beschloss, *Taking Charge*, 501; John E. Mueller, "Trends in Popular Support for the Wars in Korea and Vietnam," *American Political Science Review* 65 [1971]: 363). As LBJ recognized, however, this did not suggest a willingness to accept defeat (for example, see Joseph Alsop, "Accepting Defeat," *Washington Post*, December 23, 1964, A21).

84. At that, Johnson came close to success: it is increasingly clear how desperate Hanoi and the Vietcong were at the time of the Tet offensive (Summers, *On Strategy;* Schandler, *The Unmaking of a President,* 66–67, 79, 82, 99–101, 110–11, 115–16, 183–84, 199–202, 210–11, 327–28).

85. Michael Doyle, *Empires* (Ithaca: Cornell University Press, 1986), 63, 86–87, 92; Friedrich Engels, *Anti-Dühring* (New York: International Publishers, 1939), 199–202; William Harris, *War and Imperialism in Republican Rome* (Oxford: Clarendon Press, 1979).

86. Plato, *Gorgias* 519A.

87. Efforts to develop a "social" or "people's" imperialism have, on the whole, been political failures. See Bernard Semmel, *Imperialism and Social Reform* (London: Allen and Unwin, 1968).

88. Thucydides, *The Landmark Thucydides: A Comprehensive Guide to the Peloponnesian War,* ed. Robert Strassler (New York: Free Press, 1996), bk. 2, 63–64, 126–27; Orwin, *Humanity of Thucydides,* 18.

89. Orwin, *Humanity of Thucydides,* 99, 146–63.

90. *The Federalist,* ed. Jacob E. Cooke (Middletown, Conn.: Wesleyan University Press, 1961), #49 and, of course, #10.

91. Harry McPherson, *A Political Education* (Boston: Little, Brown, 1972), 172; Kearns, *Lyndon Johnson and the American Dream,* 122, 127, 225.

92. Johnson, *The Vantage Point,* 343–44; Kearns, *Lyndon Johnson and the American Dream,* 34, 36, 64; Reedy, *Lyndon B. Johnson,* 59–69. On Johnson's view of political parties, see Beschloss, *Taking Charge,* 534.

93. Johnson, *The Vantage Point,* 29, 72, 79, 158, 451; Kearns, *Lyndon Johnson and the American Dream,* 92, 97, 109, 113, 128, 142, 154, 244. Johnson's position parallels Madison's argument regarding deliberative bodies; see Cooke, *The Federalist,* #55. Johnson's belief was reinforced by the fact that his political maturity coincided, among intellectuals, with the perception of an affectively unreliable public, prone to the demand for simplification, if not to paranoia. See Michael Paul Rogin, *The Intellectuals vs. McCarthy: The Radical Specter* (Cambridge: Massachusetts Institute of Technology Press, 1967); McWilliams, "Democracy, Protest and Publics," 198–99.

94. Kearns, *Lyndon Johnson and the American Dream,* 112; Reedy, *Lyndon B. Johnson,* 6, 7, 12, 81; McPherson, *Political Education,* 263–64. This attitude is also Madisonian: see *The Federalist* #63. See also my essay "Two-Tier Politics and the Problem of Public Policy," in *The New Politics of Public Policy,* ed. Marc Landy and Martin Levin (Baltimore: Johns Hopkins University Press, 1995), 268–76.

95. Kenneth Waltz, *Foreign Policy and Democratic Politics* (Boston: Little, Brown, 1967), 270, 274–86.

96. Plato, *Gorgias,* 515E–516B.

97. Robert Putnam, *Bowling Alone: The Collapse and Revival of American Community* (New York: Simon and Schuster, 2000); see also Walter Berns, *Making Patriots* (Chicago: University of Chicago Press, 2001).

Lyndon Johnson

Means and Ends, and What His Presidency Means in the End

David M. Shribman

From this vantage point, where the writing of journalism ends and the crafting of history begins, the fog has lifted, the physical characteristics of the landscape of the 1960s now are clear. A third of a century later, the view is far different. At the time—when the passions were strong, the wounds raw, the heartache real—the principal figures of the age seemed to be John F. Kennedy and Richard M. Nixon. In popular portrayal, they were the martyred prince and the prince of darkness, polar opposites whose struggle for the presidency opened the decade and whose shadows dominated it. Lyndon B. Johnson was but the figure in the middle, the consequence of the death of one, the cause of the ascendancy of the other. Indeed, his triumphs (particularly the Voting Rights Act of 1965) and failures (especially Vietnam) were regarded alike as legacies of Kennedy and, because of the peculiar effect of the racial politics of the time and the toxic effect of Vietnam, principal explanations for the election of Nixon. In this view, which places LBJ as the bridge between the other two men, Johnson mixed the heroism of his predecessor and the brooding mendacity of his successor. He was the man in the middle, history's accident, a comic-book figure of exaggerated aspirations and appetites, a portrait in tragedy.

Though journalism seldom was gentle to Johnson, history may yet be. The most prominent political victim of Vietnam, the target of protesters' chants, the symbol of big-spending liberalism, the last apostle of

Washington social engineering, Johnson was for many years the subject of contempt and ridicule, particularly from fellow Democrats. But now that he has been out of office for a third of a century, a new Johnson is emerging from the historical mists and myths. The new Johnson is visionary. Sympathetic. Avuncular. Wise. Effective. A lot smarter than the smart people of the time once thought. And, as Shakespeare said of King Lear, he ended his career "a poor, infirm, weak and despis'd old man" who was "more sinn'd gainst than sinning." Lyndon B. Johnson is plausibly the dominating politician of the 1960s—and the most colorful, original, human figure of the period.

The Johnson revisionism is coming only partially from the academy. It is also coming from the arena, where in the 2000 presidential election Vice President Al Gore put Johnson on the list of presidents he most admired. The economist John Kenneth Galbraith, a onetime Johnson intimate who broke with the president over Vietnam and helped lead an insurrection designed to dump him from the 1968 Democratic ticket, has described Johnson as "the most effective political activist of our time."[1] Former senator George S. McGovern of South Dakota, as LBJ apostate and antiwar Democratic presidential nominee in 1972, argued that, aside from Woodrow Wilson, Franklin Roosevelt, and Theodore Roosevelt, "Lyndon Johnson was the greatest president since Abraham Lincoln."[2]

But the current Johnson revival also reveals as much about America at the beginning of the twenty-first century as it does about the America that, in the tumultuous Johnson years, had reached the two-thirds mark of the twentieth century. It tells us there is a yearning again, in the Democratic Party and perhaps in the nation at large, for a president with big dreams, big plans, and—this is recognized in Johnson's case more in hindsight than at the time—a big sense of self-confidence.

Long before this latest burst of revisionism, there were many Lyndon Johnsons: the striving capital schemer who ingratiated himself with Franklin D. Roosevelt and became the biggest New Dealer of them all, eventually dreaming of a New Deal for South Vietnam's Mekong Delta. The son of Depression-poor Texas who dreamed of bigger horizons for the poor, the black, and the Hispanic. The gifted Senate majority leader who felt stifled as John F. Kennedy's understudy and then, in the most tragic transition of the twentieth century, became Kennedy's successor. The shrewd Washington hand who slammed his social-activist program through Congress with deftness, only to be bogged down in a civil war in Vietnam. Now the emphasis is more on Johnson as a political magician than as a cold war tactician, with more public fascination with Johnson's role as dreamer in chief than on his failures as commander in chief.

Johnson entered office in the most strained of circumstances, taking the oath in Air Force One while the blood-stained widow of his predecessor looked on and as the shocked world trembled. Within hours, his advisers, a mix of Johnson loyalists and Kennedy holdovers, told him that Kennedy's commitment to civil rights legislation was a threat to his presidency, then regarded as fragile and temporary. They counseled him that as a southern president who had not been elected, he had every excuse to put the legislation aside for a year, or forever. He asked what the presidency was for if not for urgent national priorities such as civil rights.

That was the approach that Johnson took when proposing the Great Society, including Medicare and the Voting Rights Bill, which Johnson correctly recognized was good for America and bad for the Democratic Party (delivering the Solid South, the backbone of Democratic coalitions, to the GOP). The stain of Vietnam has not receded, and Johnson's onetime critics have not sought to erase the stain. But Galbraith said he regretted "the way in which we allowed the Vietnam War to become the totally defining effort of those years, and likewise of history," and McGovern added that it would be "a historic tragedy" if Johnson's "outstanding domestic record remained forever obscured by his involvement in a war he did not begin and did not know how to stop."[3] Vindication, after three decades, may finally be his.

Lyndon Johnson left office a broken man, in poor spirits, in poor health, and in poor odor with the American people. His valedictory year was one of the most disquieting in American history—an annus horribilis filled with a disastrous Vietcong offensive; the assassinations of two of the most intoxicating figures on the American scene, the Reverend Martin Luther King and Senator Robert F. Kennedy; a bloody political convention in Chicago; and a convulsive presidential election. He was a reviled man who had lost the support of major elements of his own party. He was a beaten man who had lost the support of a nation that was in grief at the beginning of his presidency and in shock at the end.

The prevailing view of Johnson at the end was expressed crisply by Eric F. Goldman, the Princeton historian who worked for Johnson in the White House and who came away disappointed and disillusioned. In his memorable final paragraph of a 1969 book titled, tellingly, *The Tragedy of Lyndon Johnson*, Goldman wrote: "Lyndon Johnson could win votes, enact laws, maneuver mountains. He could not acquire that something beyond, which cannot be won, enacted, or maneuvered but must be freely given. He could not command that respect, affection and rapport which alone permit an American President to lead. In his periods of triumph and of downsweep, in peace as in war, he stood the tragic figure of an extraordinarily gifted President who was the wrong man from the wrong place at the wrong time under the wrong circumstances."[4]

For years that notion persisted, with Johnson being regarded as a rogue president trapped by his own blindness in a war he could not win and ambushed by his own dishonesty at a place called Credibility Gap, the phrase that grew to describe the yawning distance between what Lyndon Johnson and his administration said and the truth. But as the century neared its end—and even before the conclusion of the Republican ascendancy in the White House, which lasted from 1969 to 1993, with the exception of the Jimmy Carter interregnum between 1977 and 1981—perceptions of Lyndon Johnson have been changing. The Vietnam War, to be sure, is still regarded as a failure of policy and vision (from the viewpoint of the Left) and of will (from the viewpoint of the Right). The war claimed fifty-five thousand lives and a sense of American innocence and inevitability, but it no longer claims Lyndon Johnson's legacy and his place in history.

Two recent publications demonstrate that. In his 1997 narrative history of the United States, *The Unfinished Nation*, the historian Alan Brinkley concludes that Johnson "proved, in the end, more effective than his predecessor in translating his goals into reality."[5] In a 1999 revision of *Witness to America*, a book first produced by Henry Steele Commanger and Allan Nevins in 1939 and updated regularly thereafter, Stephen Ambrose and Douglas Brinkley include only one entry from the Johnson presidency, the text of his Great Society speech in 1964, and do not mention Johnson's connection with Vietnam at all. The preface to the Great Society entry notes that "few people expected much more than" a continuation of Kennedy's policies from Johnson and goes on to say: "Yet in a speech at the University of Michigan in May of 1964, Johnson rebuilt a handful of Kennedy-era bills into a monument he called the 'Great Society.'" The authors continue: "Infused with idealism, the speech revealed another side of Johnson: a man with even greater ties to his hero Franklin Roosevelt than to Jack Kennedy. Where FDR's complex of New

Deal programs had sought to save the nation a crippling depression, LBJ's Great Society was offered to save the nation from a prosperity that was proving to be equally unjust."[6]

The other item pertaining to Johnson in *Witness to America* is the Ralph Ellison essay "The Myth of the Flawed White Southerner," in which Ellison describes Johnson as "far ahead of most of the intellectuals who were critical of him," places him ahead of Lincoln and Roosevelt as a liberator of American black people, and concludes: "When all of the returns are in, perhaps President Johnson will have to settle for being recognized as the greatest American President for the poor and for the Negroes, but this, as I see it, is a very great honor indeed."[7]

This transformation in the view of Johnson may be recognizable only now, in the first breath of the twenty-first century, but it was beginning to form in the Reagan years, and not only at the hands of Johnson loyalists, of whom there were remarkably few. As early as 1983, Vaughn Davis Bornet spoke of "some catastrophic policies abroad and erroneous policies at home" but also of "the many worthwhile changes [the Johnson administration] embedded deeply in legislation, in the lives of millions and in American society." Bornet writes: "During the years 1963 to 1969 the executive branch of the United States government developed, in the hands of this leader and his associates, into a dynamic administrative unit never likely to be equaled. It prodded history into new directions."[8]

Six years later, in his history of the United States in the twentieth century, James Patterson acknowledged liberals' distrust of Johnson and noted his image as something of a riverboat gambler but argued, "These unflattering portrayals overlooked other sides of Johnson." Patterson showed an appreciation for the demands placed on Senator Johnson by his white constituents in Texas who did not endorse an aggressive federal role in racial questions, noted his achievements as Senate majority leader between 1954 and 1960, and praised his gradual embrace of progressive ideas, including the 1957 Civil Rights Bill, in the passage of which Johnson played a major role. "Johnson's detractors also tended to ignore traits that made him one of the most dynamic chief executives in American history."[9]

By the 1990s, the historians' revision had begun to take root. Philip Jenkins, in a history of the United States that emphasized outsiders and the "marginal" among us, credited Johnson for large increases in social-welfare spending and for aggressive social policies that contributed to substantial declines in the number of Americans who lived below the poverty level. "There were successes to be claimed," he wrote.[10] Similarly, Norman L. Rosenberg and Emily S. Rosenberg, in a history of America since World War II, credited Johnson with "the first significant contribution to federal spending for domestic purposes since the 1930s," arguing: "As a result, by the early 1970s, many low-income people could hope to receive services, including medical care and legal advice, that more affluent Americans took for granted. Although the Great Society never fulfilled Johnson's grandiose goals, it inaugurated more than a decade of increased social spending that improved the lives of millions of Americans." To Johnson's critics on the left, the two scholars argue that Johnson did not promise a broad redistribution of wealth or power, only to use government to soften the harder edges of life. "Johnson," they write, "never intended a radical assault on postwar institutions."[11] Indeed, LBJ believed in governmental institutions and sought to use them for broad social purposes, not to destroy them.

Even so, the period 1963–69 remains deeply controversial. Though historians and political scientists examine the past with new lenses and from ever-changing perspectives, the controversy of the period has not been washed away. In a massive narrative history of the United States published in 1999, George Brown Tindall and David Emory Shi credit Johnson with "a record in the passage of landmark legislation unequalled since the time of the New Deal," but still portray him as "a compulsive worker and achiever, animated by greed, ambition, and an all-consuming lust for power, an overbearing man capable of ruthlessness and deceit."[12] The title of a 1997 book on Vietnam by H. R. McMaster, who was born a year before Johnson became president, speaks for itself: *Dereliction of Duty: Lyndon Johnson, Robert McNamara, the Joint Chiefs of Staff, and the Lies That Led to Vietnam.* And Robert A. Caro's popular volumes portray Johnson as a relentless schemer, liar, adulterer, embezzler, skimmer, and trimmer who stole an election and maneuvered himself to power both as a young man and as an adult. In some ways, the Caro volumes, immensely readable and prodigiously researched, have had the unintended consequence of contributing to a fascination with Johnson, as have the tape recordings of the president's conversations, which show the unvarnished Johnson at work.[13]

Public views of American presidents often differ substantially from those of historians; the stubborn presence of John F. Kennedy in public polls of the greatest American presidents is at variance with the judgment of historians, many of whom believe that Kennedy served too short a period to rank among the greatest presidents, who usually include such figures as George Washington, Abraham Lincoln, and Franklin Delano Roosevelt. Members of the public—and, it must be added, public officials, such as presidents and presidential candidates—generally take a less critical view of the part, often regarding history as more of a parade than as a series of episodes. This parade tends to take on a sense of inevitability, as if no other outcomes were possible, and as such the excesses of political figures tend to be blunted, apologized for, and even celebrated. The "Johnson Treatment," as his means of persuasion came to be known, is a signal example; Benjamin C. Bradlee, the *Washington Post* executive editor, once compared Johnson to a St. Bernard who "licked your face for an hour [and] pawed you all over."[14] The Johnson Treatment, sometimes reviled as a vulgar expression of domination and power, is now viewed instead as a colorful but harmless eccentricity.

In like manner, the entire sweep of the Johnson years now has a homespun aura, and though the images of the carnage of Vietnam, the anger of blacks, the rebellion of young people, the resentment of working people, the bewilderment of parents and other authority figures, and the politicization of music, theater, and the Hollywood screen remain important parts of American historical memory, they have acquired a nostalgic tint: the way we were. So, too, with the president himself. His experience with Vietnam is especially vulnerable to this process; in today's rearview mirror, it was a war Johnson did not start, did not want, and did not deserve. It helps Johnson's image substantially that, as we will see below, the president expressed grave doubts about the American course in Southeast Asia as early as his second day in office.

Instead, Johnson is remembered for an astonishing flurry of activity and achievement. The Great Society comprised some 435 bills, one for each member of the House. It included Medicare, the Appalachian Regional Development Act, the Housing and Urban Development Act, an immigration bill, landmark civil rights legislation, the Highway and Traffic Safety Act, substantial increases in funding for elementary, secondary, and higher education, and the creation of a new cabinet department, Housing and Urban Development. Much of this would fall short of its goal, some of the spending was wasted, some of the social engineering was in direct contradiction to human nature and experience. Much would be grist for the Nixon presidential campaign in 1968.

So potent was the legacy of Lyndon Johnson that it helped fuel a presidential campaign a dozen years later by former governor Ronald W. Reagan of California. Indeed, one of the principal goals of the Reagan administration was to dismantle the Great Society and to chip away at what conservatives considered the bureaucratic kudzu that had grown around government; in his 1990 autobiography, Reagan wrote that by 1960 he had come to believe that "the real enemy wasn't Big Business, it was Big Government," a perception that the Great Society only buttressed.[15] One of Reagan's most irresistible gags was to delight audiences by pretending to be a government official and say, "I'm from Washington, and I've come here to help you." The line always brought a laugh, and everyone in the crowd knew that the bureaucrat was hired by a Great Society program.

By the end of the twentieth century, the resentment toward government was largely spent. Bill Clinton's largest legacy may have been the restoration of Washington as the center of power, authority, and expertise in the nation—a repudiation of the Reagan revolution and a restoration of the Great Society ethos despite his avowal that, as he put it in his 1996 State of the Union address, "the era of big government is over." This trend was only magnified by the terrorist attacks against the United States on September 11, 2001, which gave Washington (and, ironically, a Republican president from Johnson's home state) new moral authority and new public support. Soon after the attacks on the World Trade Center and the Pentagon, public support for government had returned to levels last seen in the Johnson years.[16]

The new Johnson appeal does not grow out of a conclusion that the president was heroic, visionary, or even effective in Vietnam; his failures in Southeast Asia (and in handling the domestic reaction) remain part of the consensus. Nor do the new Johnson admirers seek to play down the importance of a war that alienated substantial portions of the population, killed tens of thousands of Americans and Asians, and warped the perspective and purpose of the nation. The current Johnson appeal comes, instead, from a new appreciation of the burden he inherited and of the accomplishments he achieved even as the conflict wore on.

Much of the new Johnson appeal comes from a reexamination of the way the president took office and consolidated power and from an appreciation of Johnson's style, determination, and courage. Some of it, moreover, grows from the contrast between Johnson, who has not been one of history's favored children, and Kennedy, whose luster remains alluring but who himself has been the subject of revisionism that centers on the unfinished business of his administration and on the personal comportment of the president himself.

As a new president, Johnson lacked the polish of Kennedy and, worse yet, knew it and felt it. Years later, Joseph A. Califano Jr., who served as Johnson's secretary of health, education, and welfare, would say that Johnson's "envy for the glamour that surrounded the Kennedys in life and the adulation that attended them in death was Shakespearean."[17] Kennedy possessed the outer moral bearing of an Ivy League president, able to talk fluently about values and Voltaire. Johnson had that of a rural southern courthouse pol, able to understand how to abuse and use worried men.

But where there was surface elegance to Kennedy, there was inner depth to Johnson. He knew politics from its grittiest, gravelly roots; he knew how to motivate men and scare them into action. He knew Washington, not so much its shiny monuments but the hidden, darker corners. He knew the secrets the most powerful chairmen harbored on Capitol Hill, he knew the secret levers of power that existed beyond the Constitution—indeed that sometimes existed beyond the conscience of most of the respectables in the capital. Kennedy and Johnson both served in the House and Senate, but Johnson's relationships on Capitol Hill were far deeper than Kennedy's. Lawmakers such as Richard Russell of Georgia and Harry Byrd of Virginia, both of whom had opposed the Civil Rights Bill of 1957, had little in common with Kennedy but had an affinity and a sense of understanding with Johnson, who could fairly be described as one of their cronies. Of both men, Johnson would ask more than Kennedy could, and would get more.

Kennedy seemed a romantic figure, but in truth Johnson was the most romantic of the romantics. He had a romance with Washington, with power, with the idea that it was possible to harness the tax revenues and regulatory power of the federal government and use them to transform the nation, whether by diverting rivers or diverting human purposes. For him, the New Deal did not end with the Roosevelt years. For Johnson, the New Deal was a process, not a program. It was an idea, and the idea was as alive in Lyndon Johnson on the Friday that John Kennedy was killed as it had been in the years when Johnson ran the National Youth Administration.

In the next hours, days, and weeks, Lyndon Johnson would take power by intuition. He knew, though no one needed to tell him, that a gentle hand was necessary. But he also knew, from his youth in Johnson City, his college days at San Marcos, and his early days in the House, that a gentle hand could be a strong one, and in this case it had to be strong, very strong. In his first day as president, in the very first memo he received from a terrified staff ("To: The President," it said, and even now the difficulty of thinking of Johnson as president is apparent on the page), the people around Johnson made it clear that he would symbolize change even as he sought to show continuity. "I don't know how many deals have been made up at the Capitol," Orville Freeman, the secretary of agriculture, told Walter Jenkins the day after the assassination, a message that Jenkins dutifully passed on to Johnson, "but I am sure that President Johnson is not bound by any of them."[18]

President Johnson was, to be sure, a different sort of president than his predecessor. He understood the complexities, totems, and taboos of Congress far better than had Kennedy. He knew where the power came from, where the hidden weaknesses were in men and institutions. He lacked the easy lyricism of Kennedy, but he had an earthy sense of reality, and he understood, intuitively, struggle—and though Kennedy spoke of long twilight struggles, Johnson had lived struggle.

The nation in 1963 was peculiarly vulnerable to Johnson's strengths—and to his weaknesses. Though the term did not yet exist, there did exist an American "underclass," and Johnson understood the heartbreak of the striving. Though the term was not yet widely employed, there did exist a "minority consciousness," and Johnson knew the agony of the life of the black and the brown. He wanted to ease their way, to open windows and doors, to think big the way Roosevelt had.

The need remained so great—no longer was a third of a nation ill-housed or ill-fed, but giant chunks were still living in poverty, still prevented from seeing the big horizon, still fettered by lack of opportunity. The civil rights movement of bus strikes and lunch counter sit-ins had, by 1963, matured, its various elements more united, more willing to move from demonstration to confrontation. These confrontations began in the fateful year of 1963, particularly in Birmingham, and they spread, through word of mouth, the pulpit, television, and the power of conscience. Johnson understood that this movement had moral authority even if local authorities did not, and he thought government should be its ally.

Then there were the weaknesses. They grew from his sense of insularity. He did not know the world, and he knew that was a weakness in a job where it was important to know de Gaulle and Adenauer and to understand the impulses of Ho Chi Minh and Castro and Mao. The realities and rhetoric of realpolitik were foreign to him, and while he relied on his instincts in domestic affairs, he did not dare to do so abroad. Vietnam was a faraway country of which he knew almost nothing, and everything he did know was processed and distilled into an American model. Hence the notion, not entirely fanciful, of a New Deal for the Mekong Delta. He would show his strength in Vietnam—his fortitude, his toughness—but in determining to show his strength, he would underline his weakness. He would not be defeated in Vietnam; he feared Republicans, impeachment, the verdict of history. He would press on, farther and farther into the swamp, though his instincts—and this is evident from his first day in office—were skeptical to the core.

From the very start, Johnson was an old man in a hurry. Later, his aides would develop what they called "the LBJ trot," a way of walking through the White House with an air of intensity and urgency, a metaphor for the intensity and urgency Johnson brought to his job and for the intensity and urgency with which he infected his aides.[19] But in the early days he knew intuitively that the nation's wound was the nation's opening, believing that if he could only move deftly and quickly enough, he might move the country. Time and again he would admonish his staff: We have a very limited window in which to make a difference. "He knew," Luci Johnson told me in an interview, "the beginning was when he had the best chance."[20]

The great turning point in Johnson's life coincided with the great turning point in postwar America: the assassination of Kennedy. The period between the assassination and Johnson's State of the Union message, in which, in a reference to Kennedy's admonition to "let us begin," Johnson told the nation, "Let us continue," stands for the great transformation of Johnson himself, the presidency, and the nation. It is not too much to say that the story of how Lyndon Johnson was thrust by another man's assassination into the most difficult and demanding job in the world, how he responded to the challenge, how he organized himself and motivated the nation resonates anew with Americans, for there is renewed respect for how Johnson consolidated power, how he decided to use it, and what he decided to use it for.

This is a story worth rethinking—or, for a new generation of readers, thinking about for the very first time. It is worth rethinking from a new perspective, not only because our knowledge of what followed—Vietnam and race tensions, plus the social upheaval and moral rootlessness that seemed to stem directly from November 1963—was unavailable to those who wrote the first draft of the story, including writers such as William Manchester, whose *Death of a President* provided many details of the most memorable weekend of the postwar period. Our image of the time was also fixed by *Life* magazine and by Theodore H. White's "Camelot" interview with Jacqueline Kennedy (which provided the soundtrack for our memories and for the mythology). Almost all our memories put John Kennedy at the center of the period. Now our perceptions put Lyndon Johnson at the center.

In this period, reports of conspiracy were in the air even as the former president's men and the new president's men were mounting palace conspiracies of their own. In this period, the course of the war in Vietnam was set for five years, a turning point that would have grave implications for American life. In this period, an accidental southern president made the most fateful decision of postwar domestic politics, risking (and losing) his party's critical southern base in a headlong attack on segregation, a turning point that would, in November 1968, deliver the South to the Republican Party and pave the way to power for Republican Speaker Newt Gingrich of the once devoutly Democratic state of Georgia and Republican Senate majority leader Trent Lott of the once-bedrock Democratic state of Mississippi.

Yet, in this period Johnson showed real heroism in his embrace of civil rights. Though told that as a southern president he could be forgiven for abandoning the administration position on civil rights, he plowed forward anyhow. Right after the assassination he called Martin Luther King. He appointed a black secretary of his staff (the first ever) and put her on the television show *What's My Line*. He later took her to the University of Texas Faculty Club on New Year's Eve, thereby instantly desegregating the club.

He set in motion not only huge growth in the federal bureaucracy but also broadened governmental responsibility for the poor. Indeed, social spending for the poor grew from 11.7 percent of gross national product in 1965 to 20 percent by 1975—an increase prompted by Johnson programs and the Johnson ethos. It is fashionable today to argue that the Great Society failed, and by some measures it did. But between 1965 and 1974 the number of Americans living below the poverty line fell by 42 percent.[21]

It is no exaggeration to say that the rest of the 1960s was set in motion by the way Johnson took power. Vietnam, civil rights, and the Great Society—all were adumbrated by this period. In remarkable off-the-record comments to many of the nation's governors, assembled in the Executive Office Building at 8:30 the morning before Kennedy's funeral, Johnson begins all this, saying that the nation had to pass the Civil Rights Bill "so that we can say to the Mexican in California or the Negro in Mississippi or the Oriental on the West Coast or the Johnsons in Johnson City that we are going to treat you all equally and fairly, and you are going to be judged on merit and not ancestry, not on how you spell your name." In that same meeting, he sketched the barest outlines of the Great Society, saying, "We will show the country that we not only deserve to be the leader of the world because we believe in mankind and in humankind; and we have done something about it, and we can set an example that they can follow."[22]

Kennedy talked big but asked for little. Johnson said little but was going to ask for a lot. Johnson married his knowledge of the country and the Congress, weighed what was necessary and what was possible, and, unlike Kennedy, argued that they both could be done. He would fight poverty, racism, and ignorance. He would harness the potential of Congress for a frontal assault on America's social needs. He would do it to prove that America was up to the task, but most of all he would do it to prove that he, Lyndon Johnson, was up to the task.

Proving the one would prove the other. This simple notion governed every step he took during the first sixty days. His days were full, and the challenge was great. The demand on him was enormous: balance leading a mourning nation, being presidential, finding his own style of executive leadership after a lifetime as a legislator, paying homage to his predecessor, succeeding a celebrity. This required great grace—but also grit. The Johnson White House, for example, rejected John Kenneth Galbraith's first draft of the new president's speech to a joint session of Congress as too much a memorial to Kennedy. "The President," Carl Kaysen wrote in a private memo to Ted Sorenson, "must be his own man"[23] He had to do all those things—plus keep the country running.

He did it with a combination of urgency and activity. The transition to power occurred with a jolt, but it unfolded in a methodical manner. "I need you now more than ever," he told Dwight Eisenhower in a telephone call from his vice presidential office in the Executive Office Building.[24] He thought about delivering a message to a joint session of Congress—"with dignity and reserve and without being down on my knees," he told Arthur Goldberg, an associate justice of the Supreme Court, "but at the same time letting them know of my respect and confidence."[25] And in a display that indicated he was conscious that the presidential election was but eleven months away, he called Richard Maguire, Kennedy's chief fund-raiser and treasurer of the Democratic National Committee, and reminded him, pointedly, "I've been on your team ever since I got here."[26]

On his first day in the White House, Johnson was a whirlwind, doing himself what the White House staff had been accustomed to doing for the president. He called 214-CA4-2294 to speak with the widow of J. D. Tippitt, the Dallas police officer killed by Lee Harvey Oswald after the assassination. He made sure a general was dispatched to greet former president Harry Truman on his arrival in Washington. He contacted John Ochs at the *New York Times* to talk about the paper's editorial stance toward the new administration. He asked Secretary of State Dean Rusk and Defense Secretary Robert S. McNamara to stay on, telling McNamara, "We must have both strength and the appearance of strength. There must be no move that would ever remotely lead others to think that our policies of strength are changing."[27] He sent the Kennedy children separate handwritten notes, thinking first—as no political figure would today—of Kennedy's young son and only later of his older daughter. He opened his first cabinet meeting by saying, "The president is dead. The president must keep the business of this government moving."[28]

Johnson's Saturday schedule alone is daunting and a measure of how furiously and thoroughly he worked to consolidate his hold on the office and to begin his own administration. At 7:00 A.M., he called Richard Thornberry and asked him to come to the White House. At 10:00, he met with McGeorge Bundy, Jack Valenti, Robert Kennedy, John Mc-

Cone, Pierre Salinger, and J. Edgar Hoover. Shortly thereafter, Bundy, former dean of arts and sciences at Harvard University, gave Johnson a brief review of the operation of the White House Situation Room, and McCone gave him an intelligence briefing. The president, at Arthur Goldberg's request, called labor leader George Meany to say that he knew he could count on the support of organized labor. After public services at St. John's Church, he met with Dwight Eisenhower for twenty minutes and then had a spate of telephone conversations—with Hubert H. Humphrey of Minnesota, a leader of the liberal wing of the Democratic Party; with Carl B. Albert, Everett Dirksen, and Speaker John McCormack, congressional leaders, asking them whether he ought to address a joint session of Congress the day after the funeral; with Fred Kappell of AT&T, asking for the support of the business community; with Senator Ralph Yarborough of Texas, who offered to "close ranks"; and with Senator George Smathers of Florida, whom Johnson quizzed about the status of the Kennedy tax bill. Many national leaders called him—Senator Warren Magnuson of Washington with words of encouragement, Governor George Romney of Michigan with prayers.

In the afternoon, Johnson met with Harry Truman. In the evening, he called Nellie Connolly, whose husband, the governor of Texas, had been injured in the gunfire that killed Kennedy. On the way home to Spring Valley, he stopped at the Mayflower Hotel to pick up a newspaper, but he was not finished yet. At 9:40 P.M., he telephoned Bundy just to be sure telegrams on the continuity of American foreign policy had been sent out. He had dinner with Nancy and Wyatt Dickerson, Mrs. Johnson, Marie Fehner, and others. Horace Busby, a longtime LBJ loyalist, joined the group, and forty minutes later, at 11:00 P.M., the two men went upstairs alone to talk. Before the day was out, he wrote Mrs. Tippitt, concluding, "If there is any solace in a dark hour like this, let it be the fact that your husband's bravery and his dedication to his country and his President will be an inspiration to law enforcement officers everywhere." He sent the letter airmail special delivery.[29]

On his second day as president, Johnson signed a National Security Action Memorandum stating that "it remains the central objective of the United States in Vietnam to assist the people and Government of that country to win their contest against the externally directed and supported Communist conspiracy." He said that he wanted particular emphasis on the Mekong Delta—military, social, political, economic, and educational. "We should seek to turn the tide not only of battle but of belief, and we should seek to increase not only the control of hamlets but the productivity of this area." Notes of a meeting of foreign policy specialists on Johnson's second day as president show the new chief executive expressing misgivings about Vietnam, suggesting that he was not sure the United States was right in upending Diem earlier that month. But it was the Johnson Vietnam memorandum that would shape his entire presidency, with repercussions from it felt unto this day.

That was just the start. There was the Panama Canal incident, upheaval in the Dominican Republic, the seizure of the *Pueblo* off Korea, the continuation of the space race, the hot summer of riots in the cities, and the emergence of Black Power, feminism, and a counterculture that would rock the performing arts, be blared on transistor radios, and fill the screens of motion picture theaters. Protest would become an American art form, with its own conventions (chants, signs, arrests). Authority would be challenged, in Washington, in the state houses, in the universities, in the schoolyard, and in homes from coast to coast and from border to border. Television would become the medium of politics, with President Johnson using it for prime-time news conferences, addresses, and, fatefully, for his March 31, 1968, announcement that he would neither seek nor accept the nomination of his party for another term as president.

In all of this, the president would be buffeted, badgered, and, sometimes, bewildered. He had lusted after the presidency once but had come to terms with his limits. Once he had the presidency, he was determined to do something with it. It was as if all his talk of "opportunity," addressed to others—to blacks, Hispanics, and the poor—were suddenly focused on him. He had the burdens of the presidency, to be sure, and they were great—a war with poorly defined aims and a social architecture with poorly designed pillars, along with the day-to-day challenges that come with being the center of political action in a multicultural society and a superpower in the nuclear age. But he had the opportunity of the presidency as well, and that was where Lyndon Johnson thought he could make a difference.

He had not sought it, but he could not shirk from it, and so he took it on. The presidency took his flaws and magnified them. It took his insecurities and diminished him. It took his moral failings and made him a figure of ridicule, even hatred. Yet so much of that seems so long ago. Now we think of the flaws and failures, but we appreciate the intelligence, intensity, and instincts of the man and, of course, the intentions of Lyndon B. Johnson. He had a tin ear for means, but he knew the importance of ends.

We know now what we could not have known then: Lyndon Johnson was the last of his kind. In a Neil Simon comedy, *Forty-five Seconds from Broadway*, the playwright says of the Café Edison where the action unfolds, "When it goes, there will be nothing left like it." The same was true of the thirty-sixth president of the United States. When he went, there was nothing left like him.

Notes

1. Galbraith quoted in R. W. Apple Jr., "Critic of War in Vietnam Is Now Praising Johnson," *New York Times,* November 27, 1999, A11.
2. George McGovern, "Discovering Greatness in Lyndon Johnson," *New York Times,* December 5, 1999, sec. 4, 17.
3. Galbraith quoted in Apple, "Critic of War"; McGovern, "Discovering Greatness."
4. Eric F. Goldman, *The Tragedy of Lyndon Johnson* (New York: Alfred Knopf, 1969), 531.
5. Alan Brinkley, *The Unfinished Nation* (New York: Alfred Knopf, 1999), 833.
6. Stephen Ambrose and Douglas Brinkley, eds., *Witness to America: An Illustrated Documentary History of the United States from the Revolution to Today* (New York: HarperCollins, 1999), 469.
7. Ibid., 475.
8. Vaughn Davis Bornet, *The Presidency of Lyndon B. Johnson* (Lawrence: University Press of Kansas, 1983), 351.
9. James T. Patterson, *America in the Twentieth Century* (San Diego: Harcourt Brace Jovanovich, 1989), 351.
10. Philip Jenkins, *A History of the United States* (New York: St. Martin's Press, 1997), 264.
11. Norman L. Rosenberg and Emily S. Rosenberg, *In Our Times: America since World War II* (New York: W. W. Norton, 1999), 125.
12. George Brown Tindall and David Emory Shi, *America: A Narrative History* (New York: W. W. Norton, 1999), 1523.
13. Robert A. Caro, *The Years of Lyndon Johnson: The Path to Power* (New York: Alfred Knopf, 1982).
14. Quoted in Irwin Unger and Debi Unger, *LBJ: A Life* (New York: John Wiley, 1999), 187.
15. Quoted in Paul Johnson, *A History of the American People* (New York: HarperCollins, 1997), 918.

16. See David M. Shribman, "A Renewed Public Interest, Trust in Government," *Boston Globe,* October 16, 2001, A13.

17. Joseph A. Califano Jr., *The Triumph and Tragedy of Lyndon Johnson* (New York: Simon and Schuster, 1991), 340.

18. Memorandum to the President from Walter Jenkins, November 23, 1963, Lyndon B. Johnson Library, Austin, Texas.

19. Goldman, *Tragedy of Lyndon Johnson,* 22.

20. Luci Johnson, interview with the author, Austin, Texas.

21. Jenkins, *History of the United States,* 264.

22. Text of Johnson's remarks to the governors, Lyndon B. Johnson Library, Austin, Texas.

23. Carl Kaysen memorandum to Theodore Sorenson, November 25, 1963, Lyndon B. Johnson Library, Austin, Texas.

24. Michael R. Beschloss, ed., *Taking Charge: The Johnson White House Tapes, 1963–1964* (New York: Simon and Schuster, 1997), 20.

25. Ibid., 20–21.

26. Ibid., 21.

27. Memorandum to the President from George E. Reedy, November 23, 1963, Lyndon B. Johnson Library, Austin, Texas.

28. Notes from Cabinet Meeting, November 23, 1963, author unattributed, Lyndon B. Johnson Library, Austin, Texas.

29. Letter of Lyndon B. Johnson to Marie Tippitt, November 23, 1963, Lyndon B. Johnson Library, Austin, Texas.

Part III

The Great Society in Action

The Politics of the Great Society

Frances Fox Piven and Richard A. Cloward

The features of domestic policy that distinguish the Great Society era are widely agreed on. First, new federal programs were initiated, presumably to deal with such social problems as juvenile delinquency (Juvenile Delinquency and Youth Offenses Act of 1961), mental illness (Community Mental Health Centers Act of 1963), poverty (Economic Opportunity Act of 1964), and blighted neighborhoods (Demonstration Cities and Metropolitan Development Act of 1966).[1] Second, these new programs were targeted to the big cities, and especially to the inner-city populations that were increasingly black and poor. Third, as the number of programs increased, the state and local fiscal contributions customarily required by federal grant-in-aid programs diminished. Fourth, the new programs tended to bypass the state governments, and even to bypass municipal governments, in favor of a range of new organizational participants, including neighborhood groups and nonprofit agencies. Finally, the federal programs permitted—and even seemed to encourage rhetorically—these new entities to wage campaigns to change the practices of established municipal agencies.[2]

Such a massive shift in federal social policy, the rapidity and even urgency with which it was implemented, and the upheaval it caused in federal-local relations, on the one hand, and in local politics, on the other, seems to beg for a large political explanation. But relative to the scale of policy change, the familiar explanations are puny. As usual, one of the favorites fastens on the aspirations of presidents, particularly in this case the aspirations of Lyndon Baines Johnson, who was given to proclaiming his vision of "an end to poverty and racial injustice"[3] or, elsewhere, "I wanted power to give things to people—all sorts of things to all sorts of people, especially the poor and the blacks."[4] Another favored explanation points to "urban problems"—whether crime, mental illness, poverty, or substandard housing—and the inability of state and local governments to deal with these problems. "From the perspective of the Washington policy-maker" says Robert Reischauer, "these governments suffered from three major weaknesses. The first . . . was fiscal starvation . . . the second . . . technical and administrative capacity." And the third was simply a lack of will.[5]

None of this is adequate. Of course Johnson spoke the words attributed to him, there were also urban problems; and deficiencies existed in the fiscal, administrative, and political capacity of state and local governments. These explanations, however, only push the question back a step. Why did Johnson, after a career in the Congress that revealed no such commitments, suddenly become preoccupied with poverty and racial discrimination? Similarly, while there was much to complain of in urban governance, few of these problems were new, and in any case, existing federal programs provided the vehicles if not the funds to help the cities. Why did the problems of the cities suddenly loom so large as to demand action through entirely new programs?

Critics of the Great Society who see the policy initiatives as a big mistake have even less satisfactory explanations as they tend to search for the sources of policy error and not for the political conditions that might explain so large a shift in policy and its specific features, whether in error or not. Margaret Weir, for example, thinks the emphasis of the programs ought to have been on what she calls the structural reform of labor markets, and she points to features of the internal politics of the national administration to explain why this did not happen.[6] Daniel Patrick Moynihan, aghast at the foolhardiness of the Great Society approach and the conflicts it fueled in the big cities, blames muddy and contradictory goals, which he attributes to the cloudy thinking of the academics who advised the policymakers.[7]

But if the policies were mistaken, could it reasonably be because foolish academics were influential or, in the view of Bernard Gifford, because unnamed federal "strategists" relied on "bankrupt" therapeutic and cultural interventions?[8] Why were these particular academics influential, and why were strategists so taken by ideas about therapeutic intervention, if indeed they were? More reasonably, we need an explanation of the "why" behind these specific mistakes: why did they occur on such a large scale, and why were they repeated and even enlarged from one program initiative to another? A satisfactory account needs to go beyond the good or mischief that can be wrought by a handful of not very powerful people. We think that a compelling explanation of the Great Society taken as a whole must deal with politics, for the simple reason that the actors who initiated the programs, repeated them, and enlarged on them were the leading politicians of the nation.

Our political explanation of these events was originally developed in the early 1970s, at the close of the Great Society.[9] We want to review it here because we think that it has stood up well and that subsequent policy developments in the Nixon and Reagan administrations both confirm and add depth to our account, as do reversals in Democratic policy in the 1990s. We contend that the federal policy initiatives, as well as their distinctive administrative features, were efforts to cope with major political disturbances in the Democratic base, and particularly in the base of the presidential wing of the party. The mass movement of American blacks from the plantations to the cities of the South had helped to set off the civil rights movement, which in turn jeopardized white southern support for the party.[10] In short order, the migration of blacks to the ghettos of the big cities of the North and the conflicts that ensued were jeopardizing the northern urban base of the party as well.

We do not mean by this brief statement to imply that the economic and demographic shifts which led to political trouble in the cities were forces external to politics and policy. To the contrary, a full explanation must also take account of the federal politics and policies complicit in agricultural modernization and black rural displacement, as well as the politics and policies that facilitated the subsequent outward movement of urban whites to the suburbs. In other words, there was also a politics of agricultural subsidies, of water and sewer grants, of urban renewal, of highway programs, and of other policies that contributed to the spatial reconfiguration of race and the political troubles that followed.[11] But here we focus on the more limited question of the politics of the Great Society.

The new federal programs directed to the inner city, whatever their legislative titles and rhetorical statements of purpose, were an effort to cope with the political problems set off by demographic upheaval and to do so by incorporating the black newcomers into urban politics. No wonder that, despite the large and diverse programmatic goals announced in the titles of the legislation, the activities funded by the programs recalled those of the old political machine. Local agencies were created, often in storefronts. Staff offered residents help in finding jobs and securing services, and neighborhood leaders were hired as "community workers" to dispense the new federal patronage, much as the old ward heelers had done. Whether the funds were appropriated for delinquency prevention, mental health, antipoverty efforts, or model cities, on the streets of the ghettos, the programs looked very much alike.

This task loomed as large as it did owing to the impact of the black migration on the Democratic voter base. The majority electoral coalition established during the New Deal consisted of the overwhelming Democratic majorities produced by the white South and the big cities. Defections in the South had begun in the presidential contest of 1948, a reflection of economic modernization and the intense conflicts generated by the rising civil rights movement. With southern support leeching, the urban strongholds of the party became more important.

In 1940, 77 percent of the nation's black population lived in the South, where they were, of course, disenfranchised. By the 1960s, the proportion in the South had dropped to half, as rural blacks migrated to the cities of the North, where they became at least nominal participants in electoral politics. One in five residents of the fifty largest cities was now black, and many of the largest cities were well on their way toward black majorities. Moreover, by 1960, 90 percent of these northern blacks were concentrated in ten of the most populous states (California, New York, Pennsylvania, Ohio, New Jersey, Michigan, Massachusetts, Illinois, Indiana, and Missouri) that could produce the electoral college votes to determine the outcome of presidential elections.

There were signs of trouble for the Democrats in the northern cities as well as in the South. The swelling ghettos were encroaching on white neighborhoods, schools, and parks, setting off fierce conflicts between the newcomers and older residents. One need only recall, for example, the bitter and long-lasting battles over school desegregation. Confronted by apparently irreconcilable group demands, mayors generally favored their older, white constituents. Federal funds for public housing had gone unused because the projects had come to be associated with the black poor and thus aroused adamant opposition. Meanwhile, urban renewal funds were used, but to displace blacks in favor of better-off whites and white businesses.[12] Nor were big-city politicians working to mobilize black electoral participation, either in local or national contests.

The 1960 election cast these problems in sharp relief. Kennedy owed his victory to the heavy Democratic vote in key northern cities, especially the black vote. But his good showing in the ghettos was not something that could be taken for granted, a reflection of black loyalty to well-oiled local Democratic parties. To the contrary, while urban blacks had been Democrats for almost a quarter century, there were clear signs of slippage. In 1952, blacks had voted 79 percent for Stevenson; in 1956, the black Democratic vote dropped to 61 percent. Kennedy won back some of these votes (69 percent in 1960) by taking a strong stand on civil rights. But to act on that platform would cause only further defections in the South. Other ways to strengthen the allegiance of urban blacks were needed.

This was no small challenge, given the intransigence of municipal governments and their white constituents. To be sure, the Great Society programs tried to use new moneys to coax municipal agencies into providing services for blacks. But it also took a unique initiative by launching new programs to establish a direct relationship between the federal government and ghetto neighborhoods, bypassing both state and local governments. That state governments were ignored is easy to explain. A number of northern states were clearly not vehicles for the federal strategy since they were controlled by Republicans. And in the South, the reigning Bourbons could hardly be expected to cooperate in new programs for blacks. But either Democratic city governments in the North were also bypassed by many of the programs or city agencies were subjected to a level of federal scrutiny and direction that was unprecedented. These arrangements were strong evidence of the concern felt by the national administration over the failures of urban political organizations to integrate the rising number of blacks, newcomers not only to the cities but to electoral politics as well.

In fact, this was not the first time, nor was it to be the last, that electoral shifts prompted federal initiatives to restructure intergovernmental relations. The New Deal administration had sidestepped recalcitrant state governments to direct grants-in-aid directly to the party's urban strongholds. And when the Nixon and Reagan administrations reversed the pattern of the Great Society, channeling program authority and funds back to the states and away from the older big cities, they were also acting on their distinctive electoral calculus.

In the 1960s, however, a Democratic national administration had come to view both state and city governments as impediments, obstacles to be cajoled or circumvented if the new programs were to reach blacks. Hence the virtually unprecedented initiative of funding a host of other intermediaries, including new agencies created in the ghettos for the specific purpose of receiving the funds. Fully 75 percent of the antipoverty programs, for example, were administered by private agencies, according to the Advisory Commission on Intergovernmental Relations. And to expedite the new programs, the traditional grant-in-aid practice of requiring states and localities to match federal contributions was reduced, to as low as 10 percent in the case of poverty programs, and eliminated altogether in the case of programs funded under the Manpower Development and Training Act.[13] Something similar had occurred during the New Deal, when the new Roosevelt administration had pushed funds for emergency relief out to the states whether or not state governments had provided the matching funds ostensibly required by the Federal Emergency Relief Act.

This is not to say that the Great Society political strategy was mapped out in advance. To the contrary, the strategy emerged step-by-step, shaped by the resistance the federal initiatives faced from big city governments, on the one hand, and by escalating black discontent, on the other. Indeed, the earliest federal programs—launched under the banner of John F. Kennedy's New Frontier—tried to work in collaboration with regular municipal agencies, through schemes defined as "demonstrations," innovations, or efforts at "institutional change."[14] Institutional change was to be accomplished by the carrot and the stick: new funds were granted with strict guidelines and relatively close oversight. Thus, invoking the goal of "institutional change," the Washington officials who administered the juvenile delinquency program (under Robert Kennedy's direction) required as a condition of funding that local governments submit "comprehensive plans" for their own reform. Not surprisingly, once the funds were granted, this strategy turned out not to be very compelling in forcing municipal agencies to shift the distribution of services to black neighborhoods.

But the federal initiatives nevertheless persisted, and enlarged, from the early venture under the rubric of delinquency, to the culminating model cities program. Moreover, as racial conflict in the cities escalated—over school desegregation and police brutality, for example—and when riots flared after 1964, the federal administrators became more aggressive. "Violent protest in the streets," says Robert Wood, "pushed the administration from experimental, innovative activities to full-scale production."[15] Heightened political polarization also increasingly forced the local Great Society projects to take sides with the neighborhoods they served, a stance that often led them to become vehicles for protests against municipal agencies, a development that federal oversight agencies tolerated if they did not endorse it.

We were participants in the events we describe, and our interpretation is informed in part by our experience. The Mobilization for Youth project on the Lower East Side of New York City was launched in 1962 as the first of a series of inner-city projects funded initially by the Kennedy administration juvenile delinquency program. In short order, it became the model and the flagship of the poverty program community action projects. The transition from gang delinquency to poverty was, as it happens, not difficult, for the approach promulgated by the President's Committee on Juvenile Delinquency and Youth Crime was very much influenced by "opportunity theory," a perspective that located the causes of delinquency in blocked opportunities for upward mobility in poor communities.[16] Richard Cloward, one of authors of "opportunity theory," was also one of the local initiators of the Mobilization plan and later a director of the project. Frances Fox Piven was funded by the National Institute of Mental Health, one of the federal agencies involved, to conduct research on the project itself as a political and administrative collaboration between local, city, and federal agencies. Piven's research included interviews with key officials in virtually all the local, municipal, and federal agencies involved, as well as reviewing project archives and attending all project meetings.[17] We were therefore close observers of events as they unfolded in the field and watched as the project was buffeted between intransigent municipal agencies, on the one hand, and heightening neighborhood discontent, on the other.

As might be expected from the focus on opportunity, the Mobilization project emphasized new initiatives in the areas of education and employment. Local school personnel, for example, were to be coaxed into greater responsiveness to poor children through participation in a home visiting program, while the children themselves were to receive tutoring services. Similarly, local youth were to be inducted into the "world of work" through job training and placement programs. But local school personnel were uninterested in and unresponsive to these attempts at their own reform, and relative to the cost of the work programs, the rates of actual job placement that resulted were far from impressive.

Instead, at Mobilization as at other federally funded projects, much of what was gained by the black poor came through income maintenance programs, particularly the Aid to Families with Dependent Children (AFDC) program. No one involved, from the federal politicians who shepherded the key legislative initiatives through the Congress to the local project managers and staff, actually intended this. Poor blacks, it was widely agreed, needed better schools, jobs, health care, housing, and protection from police coercion. But municipal agencies stubbornly resisted efforts to achieve these goals, as did better-organized groups with stakes in these preexisting programs and with the rules and regulations of well-developed bureaucracies to protect those stakes. These groups also had close ties to the urban political apparatus. In the end, it proved far easier to help people make claims for welfare benefits than to change big-city school bureaucracies. And besides, when desperately poor people turned to the new federal projects for help, it was money they needed, and quickly. Welfare was the place to get it.[18]

Thus, while the Mobilization for Youth effort was concentrated on education and employment, it also established "neighborhood service centers" in storefronts on the Lower East Side. The project planners did not think the centers especially novel or important, merely an effort to offer more traditional psychological counseling services to the poor. But center staff found itself deluged by people who needed cash to avoid an eviction, to buy school clothing for their children, or to pay the grocer. Nearly two-thirds of the people who made their way to the first of these storefronts during the initial six months gave "insufficient income" as their main problem.[19] Most of these people were eligible for welfare but not receiving it. Others were receiving benefits but less than that to which they were entitled. In time, Mobilization found itself retooling its center staff, shifting the emphasis from psychiatric casework to training in the rules, practices, and inner workings of the welfare department.

The Mobilization staff had inadvertently, just by making itself available to the local poor, tapped into the immense reservoir of need that had been building up on the Lower East Side and in other urban slums. When southern black sharecroppers migrated to the cities during and after World War II, urban economies could not fully absorb them, and black unemployment rose. Labor department officials later began to use a new term, "subemployment," to describe the resulting spread of irregular work at substandard wages. In 1966, the subemployment rate was 25 percent for blacks, three times the white rate. In central cities, the nonwhite rate was 35 percent. As a result, a huge pool of impoverished people built up, and legally, many of them were eligible for welfare.

Many, however, were not receiving welfare, in part because of the force of norms that led the poor themselves to define the dole as shameful but also because welfare department rules and practices led to the rejection of many of those who did apply. Thus, despite the scale of the migration of the southern poor to the cities, the rolls rose by a mere 110,000 cases between 1950 and 1960. Rising black anger, along with the resources and rhetorical encouragement that the federal programs provided, changed that. Nationally, annual application rates for welfare rose, from 588,000 in 1960 to 1.1 million in 1968. And as protests in the cities escalated, approval rates shot up as well, from a 55 percent national rate in 1960 to more than 70 percent by 1968. By 1973, the welfare rolls had risen fourfold from the level in 1960.

This increase did not happen because the welfare department, in New York City or elsewhere, simply caved in to requests for aid. After all, the nationwide system was everywhere designed to make assistance difficult to obtain. A tangle of bizarre and contradictory rules specified the conditions that might make people ineligible; line workers were cautioned that the withholding of assistance might be more beneficial to the client than the giving of assistance, and supervisors scrutinized only decisions to grant benefits, ignoring decisions to deny and thus systematically discouraging line workers from liberality.

To cope with persistent welfare restrictiveness, the Mobilization for Youth project soon hired lawyers to sue the welfare department over such practices as issuing bus tickets back to the South instead of accepting applications for assistance. Then, as individual complaints piled up, Mobilization shifted its community organizing staff from work with tenants on housing problems, which had not been particularly effective, to work on welfare grievances. By 1965, as urban protests escalated, along with federal promises to wage a "war on poverty," welfare rights protests were spreading throughout New York City. Soon, flanked by movement activists and poverty program workers, poor women across the country were demanding welfare assistance.

The legal assault that Mobilization had pioneered also spread across the country, particularly after 1964, when legal services for the poor became part of the poverty program. As a consequence, restrictive welfare laws were challenged in suit after suit: federal courts struck down state residence laws, man-in-the-house rules, "substitute father" rules, and employable mother rules.[20] In *Goldberg v. Kelly*, the Supreme Court even required that recipients be allowed to challenge welfare decisions through quasi-judicial administrative proceedings called "fair hearings."[21] The Department of Health, Education, and Welfare (later renamed Health and Human Services) also kicked in, issuing new federal regulations that restrained the discretion of local welfare departments, including a regulation requiring that oral requests for aid be considered formal applications. In short, the federal Great Society programs, together with the urban protests that helped shape them, brought something like the rule of law to welfare administration.

In the continuing debate over the Great Society and its consequences, the rise in the welfare rolls is certainly not slighted. Our account helps explain just how the programs came to contribute to mounting claims for welfare. To be sure, there was an irony in this development. Neither Johnson nor his political advisers preferred to solve the problem of political integration posed by urban blacks with welfare benefits. As Henry Aaron has pointed out, no reference was made to welfare in early statements about the "war on poverty."[22] Rather, Johnson said, he wanted to give the poor "opportunity," not relief. But the political resistance to federal efforts to enlarge opportunities for blacks shaped the Great Society strategy on the ground. In the short run, blacks got welfare. And largely because they got welfare, food stamps, and Medicaid, poverty rates fell, and fell sharply, from 15.6 percent in 1965 to 11.4 percent in 1978. The minority poverty rate fell from 42 percent in 1965 to 31 percent in 1978.[23] Poverty in female-headed families dropped from 70 percent in 1966 to 48.6 percent in 1978. In addition, the new nutritional and health programs for the poor resulted in marked declines in black infant mortality, from 40.3 per thousand births in 1965 to 20.9 in 1970.[24] John Schwarz et al., writing in the *New Republic*, summed it up:

> Programs such as food stamps virtually eliminated serious malnutrition among low-income children and adults in America. Medicaid and Medicare greatly increased the access of low-income Americans to health care. In turn, the enlargement of both the nutritional and medical programs led to a decline in the infant mortality rates among minority Americans of 40 percent between 1965 and 1975, a drop that was eight times larger than the decline that had taken place in the ten years prior to 1965. The expansion of government housing programs helped to reduce the proportion of Americans living in overcrowded housing from 12 percent in 1960 to 5 percent in 1980. Those living in substandard housing declined from 20 percent to 8 percent.[25]

Thus the federal effort had dramatic effects on the well-being of the poorest of the newcomers to the cities.

The gains in black political incorporation were just as remarkable, providing additional support for our argument that the Great Society programs can best be understood as a strategy to cement the loyalty of restive blacks to the national Democratic Party. Not least important, the new local resources provided by the federal programs—resources largely independent of existing state and local parties—provided a base for the emergence of new black political leadership, and the rhetoric and practice of citizen participation spurred the political ambitions of the newcomers. "Over the years," says Robert Wood, the "practice of citizen participation produced a new generation of savvy ward politicians and imparted valuable political skills to future council-persons, mayors, and legislators."[26] A generation of black city mayors, state legislators, and congressional representatives began their careers in these programs. Not surprisingly, in the wake of the Great Society, African Americans, whose fealty to the Democratic Party had wavered in the 1950s, became the most loyal Democratic constituency of any population group, supporting the Democrats by majorities that hovered around 90 percent.

Moreover, in the slightly longer term, the growing role of blacks in urban politics also led to gains in education and employment, especially public employment. Linda Williams reports that in 1960, 13.3 percent of the employed African American labor force was working in the public sector. By 1970, 20 percent was on public payrolls. Among black college graduates, 72 percent of females and 57 percent of males were employed by government.[27] Head Start and compensatory education funding to local school districts under Title I of the Elementary and Secondary Education Act resulted in significant education gains.[28] Employment and education were the main areas in which the Mobilization effort had foundered in the early 1960s. But as blacks became a more important political constituency, they did score gains in the municipal public sector and then in county and state government as well. Years ago, Moynihan and Nathan Glazer wondered whether blacks would follow the path of other minorities, particularly the Irish.[29] While the path for blacks was certainly rocky and rutted, in the end it was not entirely different.

Democratic leaders initiated the Great Society programs in an attempt to deal with the political reverberations of massive racial change in the United States. But the programs and their political accomplishments notwithstanding, the conflicts generated by racial upheaval did overtake the party, and by 1968 white backlash contributed to the ascendance of the Republicans to the presidency. The shifts that ensued in the design of programs for the cities provide further support for our interpretation of the programs of the 1960s.

Republican administrations after 1968 were certainly not trying to win the black vote. Not only was that vote now firmly Democratic, but the Republican leadership had also fastened onto a strategy that would persist for decades of playing the "race card" to encourage the shift of white voters to Republican ranks, among both white southerners and the white working class in the cities of the North. Almost immediately upon gaining the presidency, Richard Nixon proceeded to a radical reorganization and slashing of the antipoverty program, including its legal services arm.[30] A larger effort was also begun to reduce the federal role in the cities, at first by shifting from the categorical aid programs, which had governed the local use of federal funds comparatively closely, to block grants. "The Republican preference for block grants," writes Michael Brown, "goes back to the 1960s and their efforts to derail the Great Society."[31] As early as 1965–66, when the Great Society programs were still taking shape, Republicans in Congress were introducing bills to replace categorical grants-in-aid with revenue-sharing measures.[32] The new political calculus was obvious and the logical complement to the Great Society calculus. Revenue sharing and other block-granting measures gave state and local governments a larger measure of control of both the distribution of federal funds and the purposes for which they could be used, permitting the dispersal of federal aid to more Republican–inclined constituencies to support programs preferred by these constituencies.

If the Great Society led to an enlarged, albeit mainly indirect, federal role in liberalizing welfare policy as a means of providing something to blacks, Republican policies worked to reduce the federal role in welfare policy and to restrict the dispersal of benefits. This, too, began early, as Republicans in Congress took the lead in pushing through a series of measures making cash assistance conditional on participation in work programs. When Ronald Reagan gained the presidency, not only were substantial cuts made in benefits but Reagan also floated a proposal to abolish the federal role and turn responsibility for the funding and administration of welfare over to the states. Just as the federal interventions in the cities of the 1960s reflected a Democratic political strategy, so, too, did the emphasis in the 1970s and 1980s on block grants and devolution reflect a Republican political strategy.

One aspect of that strategy was a decades-long rhetorical assault on welfare policy. The core arguments in that campaign are by now familiar. A liberal welfare regime, it was said again and again, had actually caused the poverty it was supposed to reduce. The argument first emerged in the Nixon presidential campaign of 1968. The availability of the dole encouraged both idleness and out-of-wedlock childbearing. The argument gained a certain weight and heft from the books and speeches of such intellectuals as Charles Murray and George Gilder, who in turn were supported by the right-wing think tanks that burgeoned in the 1970s. Throughout the 1980s, Republican politicians such as Ronald Reagan fanned public anger against poor blacks with anecdotes about "welfare queens" who drove fancy cars to cash in their food stamps for vodka. And in 1994, a triumphant Republican Party won the Congress after a campaign that featured a call for radical change in welfare policy under the banner of "personal responsibility."

Meanwhile, the Democratic calculus had changed as well. The constellation of pressures on the party of the 1960s, compounded by the electoral instability generated by demographic shifts and black insurgency, had subsided. Black voters were now loyal Democrats, and blacks had moved up in the party apparatus as well. Meanwhile, however, the effort to integrate blacks had helped to produce a racial backlash that battered the party for more than two decades, with the consequence that it suffered enormous defections from the white South and the white working class of the cities. With the Republicans consistently appealing to white racial antagonism in order to exacerbate these cleavages in the Democratic coalition, blacks had become, in Paul Frymer's words, a "captive constituency."[33] Indeed, looking back over two centuries of party politics in the United States, Frymer concludes that "the success of broad-based parties rests on the marginalization of black interests."[34] Republicans had seized on a strategy of marginalization as a way of weakening Democratic support. By the 1990s, Democrats struggling to recoup, and particularly those associated with the Democratic Leadership Council, were employing a similar strategy.

Moreover, once the disruptive forces of the 1960s had subsided and a measure of political stability had been restored, the age-old preoccupations that have shaped income maintenance policies for the poor since the development of markets in labor reemerged. A too-generous relief policy weakens the bottom of the labor market, for the simple reason that the dole provides an alternative to the worst work at the lowest wages. Welfare is also said to erode other forms of social discipline, not least sexual and family discipline.

In 1996, a Democratic president responded to these changing political conditions and signed the Republican-fashioned Personal Responsibility and Work Opportunity Reconciliation Act of 1996, wiping away the history of uneven and incremental federal liberalization of welfare, including most of the legal rights won in the 1960s. The Aid to Families with Dependent Children program was abolished and replaced with Temporary Assistance to Needy Families, a block grant that largely turned the administration of welfare over to the states. The block granting of Medicaid and food stamps loom as future possibilities.

In sum, once the extraordinary political conditions that had spurred the Great Society programs receded, the political influence temporarily exercised by the minority poor in American politics evaporated. And when it did, the old model of a harsh and stigmatizing poor relief that had always dominated our social policies for the poor was restored.

Notes

1. Robert Reischauer discusses the "spectacular explosion in the number, size and relative importance of federal grants. The number of programs increased

from 132 in 1960 to 379 by 1967," and grant outlays grew from $8.6 billion in 1963 to $20.3 billion in 1969. However, Reischauer is casting a broad net, including virtually all the federal domestic grants of the period ("Fiscal Federalism in the 1980s: Dismantling or Rationalizing the Great Society," in *The Great Society and Its Legacy: Twenty Years of U.S. Social Policy*, ed. Marshall Kaplan and Peggy L. Cuciti [Durham: Duke University Press, 1986],181). We choose here to focus on the policies directed to the cities, which are, after all, the policies that came to be known as the Great Society.

2. David Rosenbloom points to a pattern of "juridical federalism" paralleling these shifts in grant-in-aid programs, which we will not, however, discuss. See "The Great Society and the Growth of 'Juridical Federalism': Protecting Civil Rights and Welfare," in Kaplan and Cuciti, *Great Society*, 208–15.

3. Speech delivered at the University of Michigan, May 22, 1964, cited in Kaplan and Cuciti, *Great Society*, 2.

4. Quoted in Doris Kearns, *Lyndon Johnson and the American Dream* (New York: Harper and Row, 1976), 149.

5. See Reischauer, "Fiscal Federalism," 180.

6. Weir wants to explain why federal policy focused on changing workers' characteristics instead of trying to change the demand for labor. Her explanation focuses on "how the organization of expertise in the federal executive interacted with the strategic perspective of the president" (64). We note in passing that except during economic crises, politicians are not likely to risk the massive business opposition that the public employment programs and tight labor markets that Weir prefers would generate. See Margaret Weir, *Politics and Jobs: The Boundaries of Employment Policy in the United States* (Princeton, N.J.: Princeton University Press, 1992).

7. See Daniel Patrick Moynihan, *Maximum Feasible Misunderstanding: Community Action in the War on Poverty* (New York: Free Press, 1969).

8. See Bernard Gifford, "War on Poverty: Assumptions, History and Results," in Kaplan and Cuciti, *Great Society*, 69.

9. See Frances Fox Piven, "The Great Society as Political Strategy" (271–83) and "The New Urban Programs" (284–313), both in *The Politics of Turmoil*, ed. Richard A. Cloward and Frances Fox Piven (New York: Pantheon Books, 1974).

10. For a more complete development of this argument, see Frances Fox Piven and Richard A. Cloward, *Poor People's Movements: How They Succeed, Why They Fail* (New York: Pantheon Books, 1977), chap. 5.

11. For this sort of larger explanation, see Frances Fox Piven, "Federal Policy and Urban Fiscal Strain," *Yale Law and Policy Review* 2, no. 2 (1984): 291–320, and Frances Fox Piven, "Structural Constraints and Party Development," in *Labor Parties in Postindustrial Societies*, ed. Frances Fox Piven, 235–64 (New York: Oxford University Press, 1991).

12. On the failure of state and city governments to integrate blacks, see Michael Brown, "Ghettos, Fiscal Federalism, and Welfare Reform," in *Race and the Politics of Welfare Reform*, ed. Joe Soss, Sanford F. Schram, and Richard C. Fording (Ann Arbor: University of Michigan Press, 2003).

13. See ibid.

14. Peter Marris and Martin Rein think that it was mainly municipal officials who obstructed the federal reforms. See Marris and Rein, *Dilemmas of Social Reform: Poverty and Community Action in the United States* (New York: Atherton Press, 1967).

15. See Robert Wood, "The Great Society in 1984: Relic or Reality," in Kaplan and Cuciti, *Great Society*, 20.

16. See Richard A. Cloward and Lloyd Ohlin, *Delinquency and Opportunity* (New York: Free Press, 1960).

17. For example, Piven's interviewees included David Hackett, head of the President's Committee on Juvenile Delinquency and Youth Crime, as well as other key staff from the President's Committee, the National Institute of Mental Health (NIMH), and the Office of Economic Opportunity; Congressman Jim Fogarty, chair of the House subcommittee to which NIMH reported; the superintendent of schools in the local school district; the deputy mayor for city administration; the executive directors of most of the settlement houses involved in the project; and board and staff members of Mobilization for Youth itself.

18. And the federal government helped. According to Michael Brown, in 1965 the ceiling on federal public assistance payments to the states originally imposed during the New Deal was "effectively eliminated." Subsequently, the federal match rose to an average of 60 percent of total welfare payments. See "Ghettos, Fiscal Federalism, and Welfare Reform," 59.

19. See Frances Fox Piven and Richard A. Cloward, *Regulating the Poor: The Functions of Public Welfare* (New York: Pantheon Books, 1993), 291–92.

20. In effect, "substitute father" rules made families ineligible when the mother was known to have a relationship with a man.

21. *Goldberg v. Kelly*, 397 U.S. 254 (1970).

22. See Henry J. Aaron, "Six Welfare Questions Still Searching for Answers," in Kaplan and Cuciti, *Great Society*, 105.

23. See Paul Ylvisaker, "Poverty in the United States," in Kaplan and Cuciti, *Great Society*, 54–55.

24. See Linda Williams, *The Constraint of Race: Legacies of White Skin Privilege and the Politics of American Social Policy* (Albany: State University of New York Press, 2001), 179.

25. John E. Schwarz et al., "The War We Won: The Great Society's Fight against Poverty," *New Republic*, June 18, 1984.

26. Wood goes on to say that it also produced scandals and mismanagement, but these have characterized ward politics in the past. See Robert Wood, "The Great Society in 1984: Relic or Reality?" in Kaplan and Cuciti, *Great Society*, 22.

27. Williams, *Constraint of Race*, 182.

28. Sar A. Levitan and Clifford M. Johnson reported in 1986 that 40 percent of the difference in reading achievement between black and white nine-year-olds had been eliminated since 1965. See "Did the Great Society and Subsequent Initiatives Work?" in Kaplan and Cuciti, *Great Society*, 78.

29. See Nathan Glazer and Daniel Patrick Moynihan, *Beyond the Melting Pot:*

The Negroes, Puerto Ricans, Jews, Italians, and Irish of New York City (Cambridge: MIT Press and Harvard University Press, 1963).

30. For a thorough discussion of the changes introduced to the Community Action Program during the Nixon administration, see Andrew Fleischmann, "The Community Action Program and Black Political Power" (senior thesis, Woodrow Wilson School of Public and International Affairs, Princeton University, April 11, 1986).

31. Brown, "Ghettos, Fiscal Federalism, and Welfare Reform," 17.

32. Ibid., 22.

33. See Paul Frymer, *Uneasy Alliances* (Princeton: Princeton University Press, 1999). See also Christopher Malone, "Between Freedom and Bondage: Racial Voting Restrictions in the Antebellum North" (Ph.D. diss., Graduate Center of the City University of New York, 2001), esp. chaps. 2 and 7.

34. Frymer, *Uneasy Alliances*, 7.

The New Politics of Participatory Democracy Viewed through a Feminist Lens

Rosalyn Baxandall

In this essay I examine the contribution of second-wave feminism to new forms of democracy and equality. To establish a foundation for my line of reasoning, I explore why a democratic mobilization to challenge female inequality was necessary and long overdue. Finally, I present a historic overview of the accomplishments and shortcomings of consciousness-raising, because the feminist practice was a key contribution to the idea and practice of participatory democracy.

The women's liberation movement of the 1960s and 1970s was the largest social movement in the history of the United States. Its impact has been felt in every home, school, and business, in every form of entertainment and sport, in all aspects of personal and public life in the nation. Like a river overflowing its banks and seeking a new course, it permanently altered the landscape. For a movement of such breadth, the extent of misinformation, false mythology, and amnesia, even among scholars, is surprising. There are few scholarly studies of the American women's movement. Part of the problem may be the movement's very success: its achievements—the work women do, the treatment women expect, the way women express themselves—have become the very air we breathe, so taken for granted as to be invisible, and consequently we do not ask how they came about.

There are also deeper reasons for the lack of reliable studies of late-twentieth-century feminism, for despite the huge changes in our society brought about by the women's movement, its fundamental ideas are still controversial. Indeed, they underlie the hottest debates of our times, such as abortion rights, contraception for teenagers, welfare, women in the armed forces, gay marriage and adoption, and affirmative action.

The rapid spread of feminism, unlike other social movements or even first-wave feminism, occurred almost overnight and never shared a single focus comparable with that of suffrage. The immediate "tidal wave," with little ebb, lasted until the mid-1970s.[1] In fact, by the end of the 1960s and early 1970s, the women's movement had taken center stage, dwarfing the New Left, a term used to describe the loosely linked groups of mainly white college-aged men and women engaged in challenging the basic values and institutions of American society in the 1960s.

Feminism was long overdue; the sudden surge of activity came from thirty years of pent-up frustration. Women had been largely excluded from the New Deal, owing to benign neglect and sexism, not deliberately like African Americans, who were denied the vote in the Democratic South until the civil rights movement forced change. The National Recovery Act codes and the Social Security Act did not cover the majority of female jobs: domestics, clericals, and agricultural workers. Pay differentials from five cents to twenty-five cents were mandated in a quarter of the codes. The Social Security Act provided grants for mothers with dependent children, but many of its provisions discriminated against female wage earners, especially married ones. Only 8,000 young women, in contrast to 2.5 million men, gained employment in the Civilian Conservation Corps.[2] Women temporarily gained some rights and respect during the war, but afterward they were encouraged to return to the home, and a new form of domestic containment prevailed in kitchens and bedrooms as well as in Pentagon boardrooms.[3]

Women would not become a priority in Kennedy's New Frontier legislation, even though they had been key to his winning the election. The women who participated in the Peace Corps and the poverty programs did gain confidence, organizing experience, and exposure to different sectors of their society and the world. Inadvertently, some of Kennedy's and Johnson's programs, especially in the Peace Corp and antipoverty programs, opened up spaces for women and heightened these women's awareness of gender inequality and female poverty.[4] But these were changes felt in the long term. Women remained on the sidelines in the early 1960s. The fourteen top assistants to the Peace Corp director were all male; women held only 2.4 percent of all executive positions in the Kennedy administration, the same percentage they had held under the two previous presidents.[5] One exception to the pattern of exclusion was Kennedy's Presidential Commission on the Status of Women (PCSW) appointed to thank women for helping make him president. He hoped that this gesture, for the commission had no power, would deflect women and keep them out of his hair. But the commission initiated a continuing process that produced demands and expectations. Its 1963 report called for equal pay for *comparable* work (it understood that *equal* pay for *equal* work would not be adequate because women so rarely did the same work as men), child care services, paid maternity leave, and many other measures that had not yet been achieved.

The PCSW found that the inequality had actually intensified, which heightened their discontent. One study in an all-white sample showed that women in the postwar period were twice as likely as their mothers to enter college but much less likely to complete degrees. Ninety percent of black women, who were much fewer in number, completed their degrees.[6] A survey of five thousand women who graduated from college between 1946 and 1949 found that half these women were unable to find the work they had wanted and been prepared for. By 1956, one-quarter of all white urban college women married while still in college.[7] In 1960, the full-time year-round wages for women workers averaged only 60.6 percent of those of men, down from 63.6 percent in 1957. Black women fared the worst of all, earning only 42 percent of male wages.[8] Women with college degrees, a growing proportion of women workers, were still earning less than men with only high school educations. Married working women paid an emotional as well as economic price, as popular pundits and scholarly publications claimed that joining the paid workforce was unnatural and harmful to their families.

Before 1963, employers could with impunity pay a woman less for performing exactly the same work done by a man. This blatant injustice made equal pay legislation a priority for such women as Eleanor Roosevelt and Ester Peterson, an early Kennedy supporter, experienced lobbyist, labor organizer, and director of the Women's Bureau. Peterson petitioned Kennedy to set up the PCSW and spearheaded the drive for congressional action. She was the assistant secretary of labor and in that capacity directed the collection of data, coordinated the lobbying activities of unions and women's groups, and effected the compromises necessary to pass the Equal Pay Act of 1963.

The Equal Pay Act required employers to pay men and women the same when they performed equal work. The problem was that the labor force was sex segregated, and the vast majority of women worked in jobs different from those of men. Predominantly female occupations paid less; three-quarters of women were secretaries, domestics, saleswomen, elementary school teachers, bookkeepers, nurses, and waitresses. Nonetheless, the Equal Pay Act enabled hundreds of thousands of women to file discrimination charges and win wage increases and back pay. It also drew attention to gender discrimination and set a precedent for government intervention on behalf of equity for women. The Equal Pay Act of 1963, the first political legislation benefiting women directly since 1920, was exceptional for its time.

The next federal initiative on behalf of employed women covered not just wages but all aspects of employment. Title VII of the Civil Rights Act owed its passage to the demands of the black freedom struggle, women professionals, women activists, and conservative legislators who opposed black equality. Title VII had originally been proposed to combat racial discrimination; sex was added to race as a joke by segregationist Howard Smith of Virginia to make correcting discrimination in employment seem ridiculous and prevent the bill from passing. Nearly all the men who spoke for the sexual provision voted against the bill, proving that the inclusion of sex was intended to kill the bill. Martha Griffins, a Democratic representative from Michigan, who intended to introduce the amendment adding sex to the bill, was so appalled that she argued that the vile sexist tone of the debate and raucous laughter should prove to anyone that women were second-class citizens.[9]

Title VII was finally passed in 1964 and signed into law by Lyndon Johnson at a ceremony with no women present and no mention of equal rights for women. Johnson was more acutely aware of the exigencies of political patronage, but he, too, did not make woman a priority, although he passed legislation providing federal aid to education, Medicare, preschool for underprivileged children, employment and training programs, and environmental and consumer programs, all of which benefited women.[10]

Once Title VII had been enacted, the department charged with handling discrimination, the Equal Employment Opportunity Commission (EEOC), treated sex discrimination with disdain and derision. The only woman on the EEOC, Aileen Hernandez, recalled later that the subject of sex discrimination elicited either "boredom" or "virulent hostility."[11] Franklin Roosevelt Jr., EEOC chairman, assured the public at a press conference on the new guidelines that there would be no massive assault on sex-segregated jobs.[12] Women would need to organize and demonstrate, as African Americans had, to win their legal rights.

Determined not to let its momentum stall or its message reach only small elite circles, the PCSW built a network among many existing women's organizations, made special efforts to include black women, and convinced Kennedy to establish two continuing federal committees. Significantly, by 1967, it had stimulated the creation of women's commissions in every state. The state commissions were linked through a Federal Interdepartmental Committee and the Citizens Advisory Council, which became clearinghouses for information. Investigations by the state commissions unearthed ample evidence of women's inequality, persuading many previously dubious women that sexual discrimination required legislation and organization to change. The reports created a climate of awareness and expectation that something should be done. The commission's report, *The American Woman*, which followed publication of Betty Friedan's *Feminine Mystique* (1963) by six months, also struck a chord and had wide reverberations. By October 1965, the government had distributed eighty-three thousand copies. It had been translated into several languages, and Charles Scribner's Son published a commercial version edited by Margaret Mead.[13] Most noteworthy, a network, formed through these commissions, eventually led to the creation of the National Organization for Women (NOW), one of the two streams of the women's movement.

Long frustrated with the government's inaction, the professional and labor union women, who had begun campaigning for women's equality since the New Deal, decided in 1966 to form an organization of their own. Modeled on the National Association for the Advancement of Colored People (NAACP), NOW focused particularly on equal rights for women, in the law and in employment. Perhaps the women figured the time was propitious, as the government had taken positive action on racial discrimination and opened the door a crack with Title VII on gender discrimination.

The creation of NOW is often attributed to Betty Friedan's bestseller, *The Feminine Mystique,* which captured the experience of white, suburban, college-educated women. But NOW included significant working-class and minority leadership. In addition to former leftist Friedan, NOW's founders included black lawyer and minister Pauli Murray, as well as labor union women such as Dorothy Haener of the United Automobile Workers (UAW) and Addie Wyatt of the Amalgamated Meatcutters. African American Aileen Hernandez was NOW's second president. The organization's first headquarters was provided by the UAW. Nevertheless, NOW, like other parts of the women's movement, was initially composed primarily of white middle-class women. After a long-delayed internal affirmative action program, black and Latina women made up one-third of the national staff and leadership by the mid-1990s.

Primarily an organization representing adult professional women and a few male feminists, NOW did not at first attempt to build a mass movement open to all women. Thirty women had attended its founding conference, three hundred its second conference, but NOW from the start effectively created and used the impression that it could mobilize a massive power base—an impression that became reality. When the women's liberation movement, the more radical stream of the women's movement, appeared in the late 1960s, NOW, drawing energy from it, changed to become a mass organization. At the peak of the campaign for the equal rights amendment (ERA) in the mid-1970s, it had approximately 250,000 members in 600 chapters in all 50 states and the District of Columbia.

Reflecting its close ties to the US Women's Bureau (Catherine East of the Women's Bureau and Mary Eastwood of the Justice Department were among NOW's twenty-eight founders), NOW concentrated heavily on employment issues. The organization litigated pioneering class-action lawsuits against sex discrimination in employment and campaigned to elect women to local and national political offices. Its members used their professional and political skills to exert pressure upward to elected or appointed officials.

The initial impetus behind NOW was anger that the EEOC was not enforcing the sex discrimination provisions of the Civil Rights Act of 1965. NOW achieved some immediate results in 1967, when President Johnson issued Executive Order 11375 prohibiting sex discrimination by federal contractors. In the same year, NOW forced the EEOC to rule that sex-segregated want ads were discriminatory (although newspapers ignored this ruling with impunity for years).[14] NOW's legal committee, composed of four high-powered Washington lawyers, three of them federal employees, brought suits against protective legislation that, in the name of protecting women's fragility, kept them out of better jobs. (In arguing one case, the five-foot, one-hundred-pound lawyer picked up the equipment, which the company had claimed was too heavy for women, and carried it around with one hand as she argued to the jury.)

Despite these legal gains, women's lives during the Great Society continued to be limited within both the workplace and the family. Married women could not borrow money in their own name; professional and graduate schools imposed quotas of 5 to 10 percent, or even less, on the number of women they would accept. Union contracts most often had separate seniority lists. Some states excluded women from jury duty, and radio announcers considered female voices to be too abrasive for the air. No women ran large corporations or universities, sat on the Supreme Court, worked as firefighters or police officers, climbed telephone poles, or carried mail. Women could not wear pants to work or school except in snowstorms, and then underneath their skirts. The public believed that a woman who was raped had "asked for it," there was no term for sexual harassment, and on and on. It required grassroots activism and mass mobilization of the women's liberation movement to effect change within the culture, to bring about a "new deal" and make women increasingly equal partners in the egalitarian initiatives of the Great Society. President Johnson and other politicians listened and responded.

I am not going to dwell on the history of NOW, as it has been told many times. The women's liberation movement, the other stream in the revival of feminism, is more complex and difficult to research and unravel and has only begun to be examined.[15] This stream of feminism is often called the "radical wing," whereas NOW was dubbed the "liberal wing" by the press and its members. Sometimes the two streams came together, especially in smaller towns, but mostly they were distinct.[16] Generally, the women's liberation movement was composed of small, informal groups, often without headquarters, a listed telephone number, or elected leaders. It had a more agitprop confrontational style. The National Organization of Women worked within the government; it had a hierarchical structure with dues and paid officials. It was more organized, centralized, and reformist. The group that made up the women's liberation movement was larger by far in total membership and had originated in the late 1960s, developed spontaneously, and coexisted through loose, informal networks. The women were younger and less professional and insisted on women's-only autonomous groups. They were also skeptical that conventional politics could obtain structural changes and redistribute power and wealth. The women's liberation movement challenged the private as well as the public, the psychological as well as the economic, the cultural as well as the legal sources of male dominance.

Where NOW arose from New Deal Democrats and the Old Left, women's liberation arose from civil rights and the New Left, which was rooted in suspicion of formal procedures, elected offices, and leadership. Like the New Left, critique of the United States by those in women's liberation was systemic and all pervasive. They questioned whether the United States was truly a democracy, noting how few people vote and how wealthy interest groups exerted a disproportionate influence on the whole system—who could afford to run for office, what they supported once in office. The women's liberation movement, again like the New Left, questioned the virtual exclusion of people of color and white women from the political process and the way the political process was so obscure to ordinary people that they tuned out and became passive objects rather than subjects of government. Women's liberation believed that participatory, direct democracy, as practiced in the Student Nonviolent Coordinating Committee (SNCC) and Students for a Democratic Society (SDS), two key New Left groups, would restore political subjectivity to citizens. Those in the movement insisted that they contribute actively and directly to decision making, as opposed to merely voting for representatives.

New Leftists were united around a critique of commercialization, conformity, and poverty in a land of plenty. Their goal was to challenge received wisdoms and hierarchical authorities. Activists were often in several groups at the same time or at different times. By the late 1960s, there was a strong sense of unity among radical campaigns for social justice, expressed in the way participants referred collectively to "the movement" in the singular.[17] Reflecting the context of relative prosperity, the mood of New Left activists was optimistic, at times even utopian. This sense of possibility and hope was furthered by the enormous changes that occurred in the 1960s and early 1970s. Southern legal segregation was dismantled; changes were made on college campuses both in curriculum and dorm rules. There were huge antiwar demonstrations that drew media coverage to New Left activism. Jobs and scholarships seemed plentiful, and movement youth lived simply and cheaply, taking part-time jobs and devoting the lion's share of time to activism—meetings, demonstrations, organizing, striking, and building alternative institutions.

Quintessentially a movement of young people, it was correspondingly impatient. In dress, in sexual behavior, in its favorite intoxicants, and above all in its beloved music, it distinguished itself sharply from grown-ups. Most antiwar student and white civil rights activists were from the middle class. But a significant number were poor and came from the working class. For the latter, the movement, and especially SNCC, often provided a means of upward mobility.

By the mid-1960s, some New Left women had begun to examine power relations in areas that the movement's male leaders had not considered relevant to radical politics. The preliminary digging by these women hit a thick vein of grievances about men's power over women inside the movement itself.[18] Women in civil rights and the New Left were, on the whole, less victimized, more respected, and less romanticized than they were in the mainstream culture or the counterculture, but despite their passionate and disciplined work for social change, they typically remained far less visible and less powerful than the men who dominated the meetings and the press conferences.[19]

Women came into greater prominence wherever grassroots organizing was undertaken, as in voter registration in the South and the SDS community projects in northern and midwestern cities.[20] Throughout the civil rights and the student movements, women proved themselves typically the better organizers: of course, some men excelled and some women did not, but on average, women's greater willingness to listen and ability to connect often enabled them to reach across class and even racial lines to empower the previously diffident and also to persevere despite failure and lack of encouragement. Still, they experienced galling frustrations and humiliations. Everywhere and in every organization, women were responsible for keeping records, producing leaflets, telephoning, cleaning offices, cooking, organizing social events, and catering to the egos of male leaders, whereas the men wrote manifestos, talked to the press, negotiated with officials, and made public speeches.[21] This division of labor did not arise from misogyny or acrimony. It was "natural," or so it seemed to most women as well as men—until for some women it began to seem no longer natural at all.

Most accounts of second-wave feminism see the women's movement as a discrete movement rather than as part of the New Left.[22] Feminists often broke from New Left organizations, like the SDS, but they continued the New Left agenda and mode of organizing. Most of the early participants in the women's liberation movement owed the development of their political consciousness and their organizing experience to the 1960s social movements and to community organizing projects such as the Economic and Research Action Project (ERAP). Even though most New Left accounts ignore or minimize women's participation, women were the backbone of the SDS and civil rights initiatives.[23] The women's movement shared many of the New Left's strengths and weaknesses.

From the civil rights movement women gained a commitment to grassroots organizing, an activity in which they particularly excelled. Histories of the New Left have suggested that feminism caused women to withdraw from the antiwar movement,[24] but this was not the case. Instead, most feminists not only continued to participate and even lead antiwar activities but also helped educate many thousands of women in the women's movement about U.S. foreign policy. Moreover, radical women drew on the lessons from the civil rights and antiwar movements to develop a feminist critique of militarism and imperialism that showed their connection to domestic policies and increased inequality at home.

In contrast to NOW's focus on equality in public life, the radical branch of the women's movement placed private life at the center of their theory and practice. Much of the creativity and longevity of feminism is grounded on the claim that the personal is political. This insight, first pronounced in 1968 by Kathy Sarachild of New York Radical Women, empowered both individuals and groups to challenge inequities the culture defined as normal. Such issues as abortion and sexual preference, formerly considered personal, were now placed on the political agenda as legitimate issues. NOW's goal was to gain equal access for women to the public sphere on equal terms with men. While the women's liberation movement, or radicals, supported that goal, it aimed for a broader vision. Radicals insisted that subordination in the public realm could not be separated from subordination in the private realm. Both had to be addressed simultaneously. The radicals also argued that women could not be equal in a society stratified by race and class.

Consciousness-raising (CR) was the major new organizational form, theory of knowledge (CR claimed that knowledge could derive only from lived experience), and research tool of this stream of women's liberation. (CR helped gather a wealth of information about women's lives.) It was especially well adapted for understanding what had been previously personal and unspoken. It was inspired by the Chinese Revolution, derived from reading *Fanshen* by William Hinton, in which women "spoke bitterness to recall pain" in women-only groups. The ideas of Myles Horton from the influential civil rights and labor Highlander school were also influential, as were those of Ella Baker of SNCC. Their philosophy was that "the oppressed themselves collectively, already have much of the knowledge needed to produce change: if they only knew how to analyze what their experiences were, what they know[,] and generalize them . . . they would begin to draw on their own resources."[25] A theme in Ella Baker's early training session was "give light and the people will find a way."[26] The challenge was to build on people's accumulated experience, rather than imposing outside wisdom. The people should "tell it like it is." In the participatory democracy method, members assumed direct and personal responsibility for decisions, which were reached by consensus rather than compromise.

Consciousness-raising was usually practiced in small groups because it depended on encouraging every member to participate fully, reflecting the strong emphasis on equality and democracy in the early women's movement. Feminist CR fused analysis, insight, and action. Consciousness-raising groups had to exclude men because they depended on a feeling of safety and trust. The groups also required that everyone participate equally because each person's experience was considered necessary. Feminists learned painfully through practice that their democratic, participatory ideals were not fully realizable or simple. Feminist CR theory implied that all women's participation was equal. However, some women were more articulate, some shy; some talked too much, others too little.

Nonetheless, CR groups were brilliant organizing tools. They abolished the distinction between organizer and organized, especially when the movement first started. One of the reasons that women's liberation spread so quickly was that anyone, anywhere could take it upon herself to set up a group. When a group grew too large, as they often did, another emerged. "Let a hundred flowers bloom," as the Chinese had said about their revolution. The smallness and autonomy of the CR group was an important principle, inherited in part from the SNCC and SDS critiques of bureaucracy and centralization. The proliferation of small groups proved especially attractive to young, impatient women who could not be bothered with the expensive, political process of running for office and lobbying, or the circuitous politics involved in getting legislation passed.

But radical decentralization of groups was a problem. Many women wanted to join groups but could not find one and grew discouraged. Many women came once and left. As the movement spread and expanded, women joined who were not part of the New Left or the civil rights movement and did not even agree with the radical beliefs of groups such as Redstockings, which had a set of written principals.[27] With the spread of feminism, politically less active women joined, the radical goals of feminism changed, and CR became more of a therapeutic tool. Support groups—from Wall Street executives to religious retreats and commercial enterprises—later appropriated the CR form for therapeutic purposes. NOW began to use CR as well. Most of the appropriations neglected the core of CR. The common denominator in early women's feminist CR was that women share experiences in order to analyze collectively how male dominance worked and how it could be changed.

Different women's groups used different CR forms, some more supportive, some more challenging to participants, such as Redstockings, a feminist group in New York City, with branches in Gainesville, Florida, and San Francisco, California. CR often created emotional and political cohesiveness. Sometimes, especially if women came from different class and racial backgrounds, the process tended to alienate and silence those in the minority. African American and working-class women have written accounts of how they felt silenced by the privileged women's universal assumptions.[28] Consciousness-raising tended to produce generalizations and even theories about women's oppression that were actually particular to middle-class, white, college-educated women. These included antagonism toward the family, which was a traditional refuge from racism for people of color, and idealization of paid work as "liberatory," which ignored the poverty and discrimination that drove so many women of color into low-paying, boring, even dangerous jobs.

Consciousness-raising operated on the supposition that women were the experts on their own experience, as opposed to professionals such as doctors, psychologists, and religious leaders who were usually male and inclined to assume they knew what was best for women. It was posited on an assumption that feminist theory could arise only from the daily lives of women. The uncritical acceptance of CR, however, overemphasized the individual and did not always recognize that experience in itself can produce a variety of interpretations, some subjective and some plain wrong. CR helped to foster hostility to theorizing, which in turn was seen as overly abstract and used by men to put women down. This led to a "do-your-own-thing" attitude that provoked opposing theories as women formed groups to study Marx and later postmodernism to supplement consciousness-raising. These were to broaden into study groups on women's history, anthropology, economics, and many other areas of knowledge, which moved far away from the original CR concept.

However innovative in drawing women into the movement, CR in the longer run contained political as well as intellectual weaknesses. The transition from CR to activism was by no means smooth or inevitable. Making decisions required strategy and tactics and a step back from subjectivity. Some women were unable to grasp the underlying societal forms of domination and saw only the oppressors closest to them: parents, boyfriends, or other women. Groups often became bogged down in emotional battles, and some women left feeling ganged up on, hurt, and excluded.[29]

Women's liberation groups typically had no formal criteria for membership, and anyone who dropped in instantly became a member. There were neither dues nor formal records, and people volunteered for committees by putting their names on sign-up sheets. The search for direct democracy led the movement to revere the principle of "every woman a leader," which had both positive and negative implications. On the one hand, the movement empowered thousands of women who never dreamed they could write a leaflet, speak publicly, talk to the press, chair a meeting, challenge a doctor, assert unpopular points of view, or make risky suggestions. On the other hand, owing perhaps to the heady thrill of rapid transformation and pent-up anger, radical women also turned their anger against women in groups who became too prominent. The suspicion of leaders could be extreme: all ideas were considered to have come from the group, and many leaflets and pamphlets were published without individual names or were signed X or "Sarachild" and often without dates—another reason why researching this stream of the women's movement is arduous. Many women were in rebellion against what they perceived to be oppressive male leadership and would transfer this distaste for leadership to female leadership as well.

Consciousness-raising worked well in small groups with people of similar backgrounds and belief systems. But in larger organizations, the lack of formal procedures could make it harder for some members to have any voice and more difficult to resolve conflicts. Large meetings, often chaotic, became intolerably long and ended with the group unable to reach decisions. Instead of officers, women's liberation had rotating chairs, and thus no one became experienced at chairing large meetings where there was heated conflict. Chairs were often passive and indecisive, and discussion did not remain on the point. As a result, strong-minded women and charismatic individuals resolved the point by will or staying power. Mothers and working women often had to leave the meeting, giving more power to those privileged with time.

Groups, however, do not speak with one voice, and the movement did create individual leaders as all groups do—women with greater confidence, articulateness, experience, and assertiveness. Yet their prominence was frequently unacknowledged. "Heavies," as leaders were called, often provoked resentment from others in the group and on occasion found themselves the targets of snide remarks and open criticism, commonly referred to as "trashing." Many strong leaders simply left, depriving the movement of ideas and direction. Because there were no elected or mutually agreed-on leaders, women who were especially charismatic or attractive or who had media connections would become informally more visible and influential than others. At times, women who were hardly affiliated with the movement were sought out as spokeswomen by the media. Media "stars" often said things that were not true and then their words became myth, harder to dispel than truth.[30]

These problems gave rise to what Jo Freeman in 1970 called "the tyranny of structurelessness."[31] Freeman observed that participatory democracy, with its lack of officers and structure, could actually impede democratic process. She pointed out that leadership, if it is informal rather than formal, became a star system, without accountability to membership, and that participatory democracy often crippled groups and prevented political action. Another problem the women's liberation movement encountered with ultrademocracy was that highly organized sectarian groups, mainly Marxist-Leninist and Trotskyite, stacked meetings and then took over groups.

The leadership problem involved the movement's denial of internal inequalities—utopian hopes became wishful thinking.[32] Feminists so wanted equality that they imagined it was there. Many women, especially working women, were thwarted in their work and private lives by these utopian visions. They left school or jobs to devote themselves to the movement full-time and then could not get back on a career track, or they left husbands hoping the movement would provide emotional sustenance and then found themselves alone and impoverished. Still, the majority of the participants, in their memoirs and at reunions and academic conferences state that the women's liberation movement enhanced their professional and personal lives.[33]

The radical wing of the movement was not an organization, which was its strength and its weakness. As Linda Gordon states, "The vast majority of the newly minted feminists across the country probably did not belong to any organization. Participation in the movement was as much private and domestic as public, it was a new way of challenging a boss, a new way of understanding daily interactions. You were in women's liberation if you thought you were. Indeed, the movement had its greatest impact precisely because it was not primarily an organization—its radical decentralization allowed for maximum creativity and freedom to explore new theoretical hunches and novel activist brainstorms."[34]

The National Organization for Women continues as an organization, but in the 1980s the women's liberation movement dwindled to a smaller presence and then, like most social movements, almost disappeared. But social movements are typically short-lived. Yet feminists, both from NOW and women's liberation, have had an impressive list of judicial and legislative victories, including the legalization of abortion in 1973, federal guidelines against coercive sterilization, and rape shield laws that encourage women to prosecute their attackers. Laws would not have changed without the grassroots pressure from speak-outs, theatrical events at laundromats and on the streets, and mass marches on state and federal capitals. Women in NOW facilitated the change by lobbying and working inside the political process. NOW became more acceptable to the Democratic Party in comparison with the more radical and daring groups such as Redstockings or Women's International Terrorist Conspiracy from Hell (WITCH), another "zap action" group in several states. The existence of a diverse movement pushes leaders of more-respectable women's organizations to more-radical feminist positions. The Great Society programs, legal accomplishments, and liberal rhetoric, which aided the poor and minorities, also helped to create a responsive environment for women's equal rights legislation.

The women's liberation movement established institutions including magazines, journals, and books, among which was *Our Bodies, Ourselves*, written by the Boston Women's Health Collective and translated into twenty languages, with sales of five million copies. Women's liberation also inspired thousands of women's studies programs and major subfields in academic and professional disciplines. Owing to feminist pressure, changes in education have been substantial: curricula and textbooks have been rewritten to promote equal opportunity for girls. In the universities and professional schools, more women are admitted and funded, and a new and rich feminist scholarship has, in some disciplines, overcome opposition and won recognition. The women's movement provided information, data, and testimony to feminists in Congress who were sponsoring relevant bills. The movement was particularly valuable to elected officials, half of whose constituents were women.

Title IX, passed in 1972 to mandate equal access to college programs, has worked a virtual revolution in high school and college sports. In health care, many physicians and hospitals have made major improvements in the treatment of women. About 50 percent of medical students are women. Women successfully fought their exclusion from medical research, and diseases affecting women, such as breast cancer, now receive better funding. In supporting families, feminists organized day care centers, demanded day care funding from government and private employers, developed standards and curricula for early childhood education, and fought for the rights of mothers and for a decent welfare system.

Feminists also struggled for better employment conditions for women. They won greater access to traditionally male occupations, from construction and law enforcement to professions in the military and business. The women's liberation movement insisted that only female reporters could cover their activities. The large majority of these reporters became sympathetic feminists and fought and sued their magazines and newspapers so that women's issues would be covered more fully and sympathetically and more women would be hired. Despite these efforts, most media remain male dominated; indeed, the table of contents of ten leading magazines shows the ratio to be eleven men to three women.[35]

Women also entered and changed the unions and have been successful at organizing previously nonunion workers such as secretaries, waitresses, hospital workers, and flight attendants. As the great majority of American women increasingly need to work for wages throughout their lives, the feminist movement tried to educate men to share in housework and child raising. Although women still do the bulk of the housework and childrearing, it is common today to see men at the playgrounds, in the supermarkets, and at PTA meetings. Feminists turned violence against women, previously a well-kept secret, into a public political issue; made rape, incest, battering, and sexual harassment understood as crimes; and obtained public funding for shelters for battered women. Many institutions, such as women's studies programs, rape crisis centers, and hotlines remain as a legacy of women's liberation. Women can now own credit cards in their own names. But the greatest achievements are intangible: the way women speak, walk, dress, and plan their future and in the nature of their love affairs and friendships. Neither NOW nor the women's liberation movement's organizing drives changed the legal barriers for women in government or the corporate world; men are still 85 percent of the elected officials and 95 percent of the corporate executives. Job discrimination is subtler, but it still exists.[36] Nonetheless, it is difficult to identify an area unchanged by the women's liberation movement. Women now comprise almost half the paid labor force and hold positions in every field, from Supreme Court justices to rabbis and generals.

Ultimately, the women's liberation movement was a struggle for the expansion of democracy and equality. The highest form of democracy is to be found in the movement for democracy. Perhaps in a large, diverse country there is no stable political system that can continually involve all citizens in active participation. Therefore, we need to rely on the regular outbursts of human social creativity and the political activists who help to organize this energy toward social change.

Notes

1. This phrase is used by Sara Evans, *Tidal Wave: How Women Changed America at the Century's End* (New York: Free Press, 2003).

2. Susan Ware, *American Women in the 1930s: Holding Their Own* (Boston: Twayne, 1982), 41.

3. Wini Breines, *Young, White, and Miserable: Growing Up Female in the Fifties* (Boston: Beacon, 1992); Elaine Tyler May, *Homeward Bound: American Families in the Cold War Era* (New York: Basic Books, 1990).

4. I worked for Mobilization for Youth, an early antipoverty program. Most of the women did the grassroots organizing, and the men, the supervising.

5. Cynthia Harrison, *On Account of Sex: The Politics of Women's Issues, 1945–1968* (Berkeley: University of California Press, 1988), 76.

6. May, *Homeward Bound*, 68.

7. Ibid., 68–69.

8. U.S. Department of Labor, Women's Bureau, *Background Facts on Women Workers in the United States*, January 1962.

9. Jo Freeman, *The Politics of Women's Liberation: A Case Study of an Emerging Social Movement and Its Relation to the Policy Process* (New York: Longman, 1975), 53–54; Myra Ferree and Beth Hess, *Controversy and Coalition: The New Feminist Movement across Three Decades of Change* (New York: Twayne, 1994), 63; Susan Hartmann, *From the Margins to the Mainstream: American Women and Politics since 1960* (Philadelphia: Temple University Press, 1989), 55.

10. Robert Dallek, *Flawed Giant: Lyndon Johnson and His Times, 1961–1973* (New York: Oxford University Press, 1998), 195–231.

11. Harrison, *On Account of Sex*, 187, who quotes Frances Kolb, "The National Organization for Women: A History of the First Ten Years," unpublished manuscript, 109.

12. Harrison, *On Account of Sex*, 190, who quotes the *Washington Post*, November 23, 1965.

13. Harrison, *On Account of Sex*, 193.

14. The *New York Times* ignored these orders until 1968, when a small group of women, including myself, from NOW and the New York Radical Women picketed for days. "12 Women Picket *Times* Charging Segregation in Ads," *New York Times*, July 24, 1968.

15. The best books are Rosalyn Baxandall and Linda Gordon, *Dear Sisters: Dispatches from the Women's Liberation Movement* (New York: Basic Books, 2000); Susan Brownmiller, *In Our Time: Memoir of a Revolution* (New York: Dial Press, 1999); and Evans, *Tidal Wave*.

16. Judith Ezekiel, *Feminism in the Heartland* (Columbus: Ohio State University Press, 2002), 195–251.

17. According to Tony Platt, "Sisterhood Is Powerful," *Los Angeles Times*, July 14, 2002. A *Life* magazine survey in 1970 revealed that 11 percent of American students defined themselves as radical leftists.

18. Ruth Rosen, *The World Split Open: How the Modern Women's Movement Changed America* (New York: Viking, 2000).

19. Wini Breines, *The Great Refusal: Community and Organization in the New Left* (New Brunswick, N.J.: Rutgers University Press, 1989).

20. Sara Evans, *Personal Politics: The Roots of Women's Liberation in the Civil Rights Movement and the New Left* (New York: Knopf, 1979); Charles M. Payne, *I've Got the Light of Freedom: The Organizing Tradition and the Mississippi Freedom Struggle* (Berkeley: University of California Press, 1995), 93, 89.

21. Evans, *Personal Politics*; Payne, *Light of Freedom*.

22. Todd Gitlin, *The Sixties: Years of Hope, Days of Rage* (New York: Doubleday, 1987); Maurice Isserman, and Michael Kazin, *America Divided: The Civil*

Wars of the 1960s (New York: Oxford University Press, 2000); and James Miller *Democracy in the Streets: From Port Huron to the Siege of Chicago* (New York: Simon and Schuster, 1987).

23. Jennifer Frost, *An Interracial Movement of the Poor* (New York: New York University Press, 2001).

24. Todd Gitlin, *The Twilight of the Common Dream: Why America Is Wracked by Cultural Wars* (New York: Holt, 1995), 100, and Michael Tomasky, *Left for Dead: The Life, Death and Possible Resurrection of Progressive Politics in America* (New York: Free Press, 1996), 86.

25. Payne, *Light of Freedom*, 70–71.

26. Ibid., 89.

27. Materials about Redstockings are available from the Redstockings Archive, P.O. Box 2625, Gainesville, Florida 32602.

28. bell hooks, *Ain't I a Woman: Black Women and Feminism* (Boston: South End Press, 1981); Barbara Smith, "Feisty Characters and Other People's Causes: Memories of White Racism and U.S. Feminism," in *The Feminist Memoir Project: Voices from Women's Liberation*, ed. Rachel Blau DuPlessis and Ann Snitow (New York: Three Rivers Press, 1998), 476–81.

29. Phyllis Chesler, *Woman's Inhumanity to Woman* (New York: Nation Books, 2001), 455–56.

30. For example, Robin Morgan, the child television star of *I Remember Mama*, had only attended a few meetings, yet she told the press who identified her at the first Miss America contest in 1969 that we burned bras on the boardwalk. This was untrue—fires were not allowed, but the statement is repeated ad nauseam.

31. Jo Freeman, "The Tyranny of Structurelessness," in Baxandall and Gordon, *Dear Sisters*, 73–75.

32. Carol Hanisch, "Struggles over Leadership in the Women's Liberation Movement," in *Leadership and Social Movements*, ed. Colin Barker, Alan Johnson, and Michael Lavalete (Manchester: Manchester University Press, 2001), 77–95.

33. The Veteran Feminists of America (VFA) has held reunions in various cities and states every year (VFA, 220 Doucet Rd., Lafayette, Louisiana 70503). See also DuPlessis and Snitow, *Feminist Memoir Project*; Estelle Freedman, *The History of Feminism and the Future of Women* (New York: Ballantine Books, 2002); Rosen, *World Split Open*.

34. Linda Gordon, "Social Movements, Leadership, and Democracy: Towards Utopian Mistakes," *Journal of Women's History* 14, no. 2 (2002): 112.

35. Jennifer Baumgartner and Amy Richards, *Manifesta, Young Women, Feminism and the Future* (New York: Farrar Strauss, 2000), 100–101.

36. Deborah Rhode, *Speaking of Sex: The Denial of Gender Inequality* (Cambridge: Harvard University Press, 1997), 4–5, 146.

Freedom from Ignorance?

The Great Society and the Evolution of the Elementary and Secondary Education Act of 1965

Patrick McGuinn and Frederick Hess

The Elementary and Secondary Education Act (ESEA) of 1965 was a central component of President Lyndon Johnson's War on Poverty and one of the key legislative achievements of the Great Society. This act marked the first major incursion of the federal government into K–12 education policy, an area that historically had been the domain of states and localities, and initiated a new era of federal involvement in school reform. At the heart of the ESEA was a powerful equity rationale for federal government activism to promote greater economic and social opportunity. The moral clarity behind the ESEA and the Great Society's War on Poverty, however, was not matched by a clear sense of the means by which the government could alleviate educational disadvantages or poverty, which would cause many problems in the design and implementation of the program.

Initially, the ESEA was intended to provide additional resources to disadvantaged students with little federal involvement as to how the resources were utilized by state and local education authorities. Over time, however, federal legislative enactments, bureaucratic regulations, and court mandates in education became increasingly numerous and prescriptive, and federal influence over schools grew significantly. As a result, the political debate shifted from whether the federal government had an obligation to promote educational opportunity, to the effectiveness of these efforts. By the 1980s, growing skepticism about the orientation and efficacy of federal education programs led to a backlash against the ESEA and fueled a reform movement that promoted administrative flexibility, parental choice, and outcome standards. During the 1990s, first Bill Clinton (a New Democrat) and then George W. Bush (a Compassionate Conservative) made education the centerpiece of their efforts to reposition their parties on social-welfare policy and to craft new, more-appealing public philosophies. These developments culminated in the No Child Left Behind Act of 2002, which fundamentally reconfigured the ESEA but also increased the size and scope of the federal role in education in a number of important ways.

The expansion and reform of the ESEA has dominated the politics of education at the national level for the past forty years, and an analysis of the act's evolution can tell us a great deal about the origins and evolution of the Great Society more generally. How did a popular program originally intended to promote opportunity eventually become viewed as a controversial entitlement? How did the federal role in education become more extensive and prescriptive over time despite strong opposition from many quarters? How did the initial federal focus on expanding resources and opportunity for disadvantaged students get transformed into a federal mandate demanding outcome assessment and improvement for all students? How does education come to play a central role in efforts by the Democratic and Republican parties to adapt to post–Great Society politics? In this essay we will seek to answer these questions by examining the evolution of ESEA and the federal role in education over the past four decades. The analysis will also shed light on the nature of the Great Society—particularly on the important ways in which it differed from the New Deal—and the struggle between Democrats and Republicans to define the appropriate uses of federal power in pursuit of expanded opportunity for citizens.

The Political Context of the ESEA

America has a long-standing tradition of local control of schools. The U.S. Constitution is silent on education, and the issue was historically deemed the province of state and local governments.[1] Before the 1950s, federal involvement in education was almost nonexistent; conceptions of equal educational opportunity were less central to political disputes, and broad inequities were not considered problematic. As late as 1930, less than a fifth of adults over twenty-five had completed high school, and education was not perceived by citizens as central to economic success.[2] Progressives had also fought doggedly to convince the public that schooling decisions ought to be entrusted to "nonpolitical" educational professionals. When education did emerge as a political issue, it was typically due to religious and ethnic tensions, rather than more abstract concerns about school quality.[3]

As a result, the issue of elementary and secondary education was largely absent from the national political agenda until the second half of the twentieth century. As Hugh Davis Graham has noted, "Prior to the 1960s, one of the most distinctive attributes of America's political culture had been the tenacity with which the United States, unlike other nations, had resisted a national education policy."[4] Even the ambitious legislative agenda of the New Deal contained remarkably little on elementary and secondary education—only impact aid for school districts adversely affected by the presence of nontaxed governmental institutions.[5] Education gained new prominence in America after World War II, however, as high school completion became the norm and as the GI Bill spurred a dramatic increase in college enrollment.[6] For the first time, education became part of the lexicon of the working-class American and a key to economic and social mobility.[7]

Education gained additional salience in the aftermath of the Supreme Court's 1954 *Brown v. Board of Education* ruling on school segregation and the Soviet Union's 1957 launch of Sputnik, the first orbiting satellite. The Supreme Court's powerful statement in *Brown* on the importance of equal educational opportunity, as well as the civil rights struggles of the following decade, gave rise to a public conception of education as the birthright of a free citizenry.[8] Educational opportunity was increasingly considered vital to ensuring all Americans the chance to better their circumstances. Sputnik, meanwhile, emphasized the importance of education to national security and the cold war competition with the USSR. These developments provided the impetus for passage of the National Defense Education Act (NDEA) of 1958, which provided categorical aid to states to improve math, science, and foreign-language instruction in American schools. The NDEA was an important political precedent and psychological breakthrough for advocates of federal aid to education. Even the opponents of federal aid to education recognized the NDEA's significance, with Barry Goldwater writing during consideration of the bill that it reminded him "of an old Arabian proverb: 'If the camel once gets his nose in the tent, his body will soon follow.' If adopted, the legislation will mark the inception of aid, supervision, and ultimately control of education in this country by federal authorities."[9] Yet as of 1960, even with the NDEA, national support for education remained quite small in absolute dollars (less than $1 billion) and as a percentage of total education spending (around 2 percent). It was also fragmented into several categorical grants with little direct federal oversight. Existing federal aid was generally devoted to narrow ends: statistics collection, specialized research and demonstration grants, vocational education assistance, the school lunch program, and impact aid.

The civil rights movement would create a much greater public awareness of the economic and educational inequalities facing African Americans and other racial minorities in the United States and generate support for a more substantial federal role in schools. A large body of social science research released in the early 1960s documented the terrible educational conditions facing poor children and the dire consequences that these conditions had on their later life prospects. Work by Michael Harrington (*The Other America*), James Conant (*Slums and Suburbs*), and others highlighted the resource and achievement gap between students in poor schools, on the one hand, and students in middle- and upper-class schools, on the other. Poor children, it was also recognized at the time, were concentrated in the inner cities and often from racial minority groups. The consequence, as one observer noted, was that "beginning in the 1950's and continuing through the 1960's and 1970's, Americans generally were made keenly aware of the existence of a number of social injustices. Thus, there developed a climate of public opinion favorable to social reform efforts."[10]

Despite increasing public awareness of the unequal opportunities in American schools, however, the political opposition to an expanded federal role in education remained strong. As Graham has written in his classic work on the period, "to propose federal 'intrusion' into the sanctity of the state-local-private preserve of education was to stride boldly into a uniquely dangerous political mine field that pitted Democrat against Republican, liberal against conservative, Catholic against Protestant and Jew, federal power against states rights, white against black, and rich constituency against poor in mercurial cross-cutting alliances."[11] This opposition had succeeded in defeating a number of proposals by Democrats for increased federal education spending in the 1940s and 1950s, as well as several by President Kennedy's administration in the early 1960s.[12]

The Passage and Content of the ESEA

Kennedy's successor, his vice president and the former Senate majority leader Lyndon Johnson, would capitalize on the growing public awareness of school inequalities, the political goodwill for Kennedy's agenda following his assassination, and the large Democratic majority in Congress following the 1964 election to push again for an education bill.[13] LBJ declared a "war on poverty" and thrust the quest for civil rights to the center of his domestic agenda. He identified his education bill as a crucial component of the broader antidiscrimination efforts begun with the Civil Rights Act of 1964 and of his antipoverty program, which had rejected an income-transfer strategy in favor of an emphasis on job training and education. Johnson believed that "very often, a lack of jobs and money is not the cause of poverty, but the symptom. The cause may lie deeper—in our failure to give our fellow citizens a fair chance to develop their own capacities in a lack of education and training."[14] If education was the key to economic and social mobility, however, too many schools lacked the resources to provide the necessary skills to students from disadvantaged backgrounds. As one observer noted, "The architects of the Great Society have found the school systems, for the most part, ill-prepared and ill-equipped to meet the educational challenges to be encountered in building the Great Society. Furthermore, they learned that most localities today are hard pressed to finance the schools on which success depends."[15]

When LBJ introduced his education plan in 1965, the former schoolteacher argued that "nothing matters more to the future of our country; not our military preparedness, for armed might is worthless if we lack brainpower to build a world of peace; not our productive economy, for we cannot sustain growth without trained manpower; not our democratic system of government, for freedom is fragile if citizens are ignorant."[16] Johnson also saw federal leadership in education as a logical—and essential—extension of the New Deal. During a "state of education" address in February 1968, Johnson remarked that "on January 6, 1941, President Franklin D. Roosevelt set forth to Congress and the people four essential freedoms for which America stands. . . . Today, wealthier, more powerful, and more able than ever before in our history, our nation can declare another essential freedom—the fifth freedom is freedom from ignorance."[17]

From the outset, however, Johnson and his advisers were cognizant of the political obstacles—intense opposition to government support for integration, Catholic schools, and centralized administration—that had defeated previous attempts to expand the federal role in education. What had become known as the "three Rs"—race, religion, and the Reds—remained a substantial barrier. The passage of the Civil Rights Act in 1964, however—and particularly Title VI, which outlawed the allocation of federal funds to segregated programs—would prevent federal education bills from becoming entangled with racial issues as they had in 1956 and 1960.[18] Johnson's commissioner of education Francis Keppel warned in a 1964 memo that the other two "Rs" remained. Any plan to provide substantial new federal aid to schools, he observed, would still meet with intense opposition from states' rights and antigovernment conservatives, as well as create conflict between two important Democratic constituencies: Catholics and the National Education Association (NEA).[19] Catholics opposed any bill that would direct federal money to public but not private schools, while the NEA opposed any diversion of federal education aid to private schools.

Keppel devised an ingenious compromise solution that provided the basis for the Elementary and Secondary Education Act. His plan was to target federal aid to poor *children* regardless of the type of school they attended (whether public or private). This plan had the advantage of spreading money around to a majority of congressional districts, to public and private school children, and to state education agencies for implementation purposes, thereby undercutting most of the potential political opposition to the program. Determined to prevent the bill from getting bogged down by endless public debates in congressional committees, the legislation was drafted in secret by a presidential task force and then passed through Congress quickly, with no amendments and with so little deliberation that it became known as the "Great Railroad Act of 1965."[20] By all accounts, President Johnson's legislative savvy and active lobbying on the bill's behalf were crucial to its passage. As Harold Howe (who succeeded Keppel as commissioner of education in 1965) remarked: "Johnson asserted a very personal influence . . . the 89th Congress voted all the new education legislation through, literally *pushed* by him."[21] The bill was supported by large majorities in both chambers, passing by a vote of 263–153 in the House and 73–18 in the Senate.[22] Johnson signed the measure into law in front of his former elementary school in Texas and declared, "I believe deeply no law I have signed or will ever sign means more to the future of America."[23]

The ESEA was intended to be primarily a redistributive bill, to supplement school spending in the nation's poorest communities and to lend federal muscle to efforts to innovate and improve educational services. The centerpiece of this effort and of the legislation itself was the Title I program, which stated that "the Congress hereby declares it to be the policy of the United States to provide financial assistance . . . to expand and improve . . . educational programs by various means . . . which contribute particularly to meeting the special educational needs of educationally deprived children."[24] Title I was designed to assist communities with a high concentration of low-income families (defined as families earning less than two thousand dollars annually) by raising per-pupil expenditures. The nature of the legislative process, however, meant that the redistributive edge of the ESEA got rubbed off as money was spread around in exchange for political support. In the end, the funding formula was designed to maximize the number of school districts (and thus the number of congressional districts) that would be eligible, and the restrictions on how the money could be spent were loosened considerably. Ninety-four percent of the school districts in America ultimately received ESEA funds, and the act allowed Title I funds to be used for a variety of purposes including hiring additional staff, purchasing classroom equipment, and classroom instruction.[25] The result was that the ESEA would, despite Johnson's initial desire, remain a hybrid program, both distributive and redistributive in its design and impact.[26] The political incentives for local school authorities and state policymakers—and at times national politicians—to disperse education funding broadly would lead to a long-standing struggle over its focus on disadvantaged students.

Congress authorized an initial appropriation of $1.3 billion for the ESEA, which contained five separate titles, although the vast majority of the funds ($1.06 billion) was directed toward Title I. Title II of the ESEA created a five-year program to fund the purchase of library resources, instructional material, and textbooks by state educational agencies (which were then to lend them to local public and private school students). Title III created a five-year program of matching grants to local educational agencies to finance supplemental education centers and services. (It was also allocated $100 million for the first year.) Title IV gave the U.S. commissioner of education the authority to enter into contracts with universities and state educational agencies to conduct educational research, surveys, and demonstrations. This title received $100 million in funding for the five-year period. Finally, Title V provided $25 million over five years to strengthen state departments of education.

The ESEA was the result of widespread agreement among educational policymakers and researchers that the federal government should intervene in what was seen as an educational crisis among poor children. Yet there remained much disagreement over the causes of poverty and educational inequality and what the government should do to address them. There was no consensus among researchers and policymakers about the most important factors influencing educational achievement or what kind of educational reforms were likely to work for disadvantaged students. In addition, a great ideological rift existed between conservatives and liberals about whether the issue of disadvantaged students should be approached from a deficit perspective, a structural perspective, or something else entirely. Conservatives argued that disadvantaged students suffered from a "culture of poverty" and that they could succeed only if they were taught middle-class values.[27] Liberals countered that the primary problem facing poor students was that they attended poor schools. In this view, the structure of the American social, political, and economic systems resulted in inequalities that the schools largely served to replicate. In addition to these debates over educational strategy, policymakers disagreed about which level of government (federal, state, or local) was best suited to achieve school reform.

The mix of programs established under the ESEA reflected the substantial disagreement over the precise cause of educational inequalities among poor children and over the best strategies for eradicating them. As educational historian Diane Ravitch has noted, "the vigorous advocacy of differing theories obscured the fact that educators did not know how best to educate poor children or even whether it was possible to eliminate the achievement gap between poor and middle-income children."[28] As a result, ESEA funds were allocated to support a wide variety of programs in local school systems including teaching innovations, cultural and social enrichment programs, library improvements, parental involvement activities, nutrition programs, and social and medical services. How best to fight poverty and its effects in schools was thus unclear, and no consensus existed even among child development and educational experts on how government aid might be used most effectively to that end. This uncertainty would prove to be a major obstacle in the implementation of the ESEA.

The design as well as the substance of the act were to have important consequences for American education policy. One of the most significant features of the ESEA was what it did *not* do: it did not provide general federal aid to public schools in the United States. Instead, the ESEA provided "categorical" aid that was targeted to a specific student population—disadvantaged students. As Paul Peterson and Barry Rabe would later note, "Passage of the ESEA . . . provided for greatly increased support for public education, but it hardly took the form that traditional education interest groups had long advocated. Instead of a program of general aid, the legislation concentrated resources on educationally disadvantaged children living in low-income areas."[29] And, as we will discuss in more detail, the creation of federal categorical programs required that federal educational institutions shift from what had been largely an information gathering and disseminating role to a more supervisory role in the administration of the new federal funds and programs. Given the political opposition to federal "control" in education, however, it had been impossible to include rigorous compliance provisions in the ESEA or even the kind of administrative requirements that were normally attached to categorical grants.

Many supporters of expanding federal aid for education and of expanding opportunity for those who were poor were concerned that the ESEA's failings—poor targeting, conflicting educational philosophies, and ambiguous implementation authority—greatly limited the potential impact of the legislation. As one liberal Democratic congressman commented at the time, "In 1965, the issue was not good education policy versus bad. The question Congress had to settle in 1965 was whether there was ever going to be federal aid to the elementary and secondary schools of this nation. . . . The 1965 bill, in all candor, does not make much sense educationally, but it makes a hell of a lot of sense legally, politically, and constitutionally. This was a battle of principle, not substance, and that is the main reason I voted for it. If I could have written a bill that would have included provisions to meet the national interest in the education field it would not have been 89–10 [ESEA]."[30] It was thus clear from the start—even to its supporters—that implementation of the ESEA would present many challenges.

Nonetheless, many observers at the time recognized the symbolic significance of the ESEA for national education policy—an important threshold had been crossed and an important federal role in education policy cemented. President Johnson remarked at the time that in one year Congress "did more for the wonderful cause of education in America than all the previous 176 regular sessions of Congress did, put together."[31] And as both the supporters and opponents of federal aid to education acknowledged, the federal role in education was likely to expand after passage of the act despite continuing opposition on some fronts. Congressman John Williams (R-Del.), for example, remarked after passage of the ESEA, "Make no mistake about it, this bill . . . is merely the beginning. It contains within it the seeds of the first federal education system which will be nurtured by its supporters in the years to come long after the current excuse of aiding the poverty stricken is forgotten. . . . The needy are being used as a wedge to open the floodgates, and you may be absolutely certain that the flood of federal control is ready to sweep the land."[32] Indeed, in his classic study of the Johnson years, James Sundquist comments that with ESEA "the national 'concern' for education had become a national 'responsibility.' . . . The question would be, henceforth, not *whether* the national government should give aid but *how much* it should give, for what purposes—and with how much federal control."[33]

The combination of the NDEA and the ESEA dramatically increased federal funding for education both in absolute terms and as a proportion of total education spending. Between 1958 and 1968, for example, federal spending on education multiplied more than ten times, from $375 million to $4.2 billion, and the federal share expanded from less than 3 percent to about 10 percent of all school funding. The beneficiaries of federal aid to education—particularly teachers' unions, parent groups, and state and local education agencies—quickly became a powerful political force in Washington and fought hard to protect existing programs and to create new ones. As Graham notes, "By the end of the Johnson administration, the very proliferation of Great Society programs . . . reinforced the growing triangular networks with a vested interest in maximizing their benefits by pressing willing congressional authorizing committees to exceed by large margins the president's budget requests, especially in education."[34] Although the political survival of the ESEA seemed assured by the end of the 1960s, concern was growing in many quarters about the implementation of federal education programs and their effectiveness in promoting equal education opportunity.

Implementation and Expansion of the ESEA

Policymaking and implementation in education are inherently difficult given the vagaries, conflicting goals, and ambiguities that characterize schooling. It quickly became clear that the implementation challenges surrounding the ESEA were especially difficult and that the compromises required to gain congressional approval of the act in many ways compromised the legislation's original goal of improving educational opportunities for poor children. First, as noted, the legislation itself incorporated multiple goals and methods, some of which were incompatible with one another. Second, the original act gave federal administrators few tools to force compliance with federal directives and goals in the use of ESEA funds. Third, even if such tools had been available, the agency charged with implementing the ESEA, the United States Office of Education (USOE), was for several years after its passage disinclined or unable to make use of the compliance tools it had. Fourth, lingering opposition to federal control of education ensured that attempts to administer the ESEA rigorously would generate a strong political backlash. And fifth, the politics and implementation of the ESEA were greatly complicated by the addition of new purposes and programs to the act in the years following 1965.

Though the goal of the ESEA—to improve educational opportunity for the poor—was clear, the legislation was vague as to how this goal was to be achieved. The ESEA distributed funds to school districts according to the number of poor children enrolled but did not specify which services districts should provide to "educationally deprived" children.[35] The consequence of the ESEA's initial flexibility was that federal funds were used in a wide variety of ways for a wide variety of purposes, and local districts often diverted funds away from redistributive programs.[36] As Graham observed, "The upshot of all this is that when Title I was implemented, it produced not *a* Title I program, but something more like 30,000 separate and different Title I programs."[37]

The original ESEA legislation gave the USOE little power to coerce states to comply with federal regulations or goals or to punish states and school districts that failed to do so. The large amount of discretion accorded to states and school districts in spending the new federal money ensured that compliance with federal goals would be spotty at best. In his examination of the implementation of the ESEA, Joel Berke notes that "federal aid is channeled into an existing state political system and pattern of policy, and a blend distilled of federal priorities and the frequently different state priorities emerges. . . . Federal money is a stream that must pass through a state capitol; at the state level, the federal government is rarely able—through its guidelines and regulations—radically to divert the stream or reverse the current."[38]

The wide latitude given to school districts and the lack of compliance mechanisms in the ESEA were serious barriers to effective implementation of the act. The USOE, however, was also ill-suited to a compliance role. It had long been a small, passive organization that focused on collecting and disseminating statistical data on education and did little else. As Jerome Murphy has noted, the passage of the ESEA did not change the prevailing organizational culture at the USOE, which was characterized by a reciprocal client relationship with state and local education agencies and was strongly opposed to an enforcement role. He quotes an official at the USOE as stating, "Title I is a service-oriented program with predetermined amounts for the states. This sets the framework where the states are entitled to the money. Other than making sure states got their money and making sure it was spent, there was no role for the Office of Education. I don't know anyone around here who wants to monitor. The Office of Education is not investigation-oriented, never has been, and never will be."[39] The result, as John and Anne Hughes note, was that "if USOE had limitations on its policymaking authority and capability—and these have been legion—its ability to enforce its policies has been even more limited. The state agencies and the local districts, by and large, were used to going their own ways, which often meant disregarding federal requirements."[40] Initially, the USOE relied on the assurances of state education officials that they were in compliance with federal guidelines.

Many of the problems at the USOE were visible soon after the passage of the act. Indeed, President Johnson and his advisers became very concerned about the ability of the office to administer federal education programs effectively. As Graham discusses, "The crux of the matter was that too much money was being spent too fast in too many places and under too many categorical programs. . . . [The ESEA faced] already severe problems of implementation [that were exacerbated by] the chaos of a radically reorganized USOE."[41] These concerns, as well as the budgetary constraints imposed by inflation and the Vietnam War, led Johnson to try to reform and restrain the growth of the Great Society's education programs that he had done so much to create. Despite many reservations about its effectiveness, however, the new legislation had quickly developed formidable political constituencies and strong allies in Congress. A growing rift was also developing between LBJ and liberal Democrats in Congress over the Vietnam War and the funding and direction of the Great Society. Steve Fraser and Gary Gerstle have noted that "tensions within the Democratic Party over the issues of poverty and race had already become apparent during the halcyon days of 1960s prosperity. They became much more serious as the costs of defending the 'free world' and, in particular, fighting the Vietnam War began to force cutbacks in domestic social spending."[42] This situation, along with the president's declining public approval ratings, led many congressional Democrats to ignore their president and push to expand the size and scope of the ESEA.

By the 1970s, the additional resources available to the U.S. Office of Education and the agency's gradual adjustment to its new administrative role led it to begin taking its enforcement responsibilities seriously and to reorganize its enforcement efforts to make them more effective.[43] One of the fundamental premises behind the idea of compensatory education, and behind the ESEA more generally, was that state and local education authorities had failed to ensure equal educational opportunities for their students and that they could not be trusted to do so in the future without federal intervention. The distrust of local education authorities—and mounting evidence that states and localities were diverting federal funds to purposes for which they were not intended—ultimately led federal bureaucrats to increase the regulation and supervision of federal aid. As Ravitch has observed, "In this atmosphere of discord and distrust, those with grievances turned naturally to the courts and the federal government to enforce their rights against local school boards. . . . [P]rograms, regulations, and court orders began to reflect the strong suspicion that those in control of American institutions were not to be trusted with any discretion where minorities, women, or other aggrieved groups were concerned."[44] Democrats and their allies in the federal education bureaucracy continued to argue that the best way to help poor students was to direct additional federal money to their schools and to regulate how it was used.

Continuing opposition to federal micromanagement in education and the lack of consensus on how to measure the effectiveness of school reform efforts, however, led federal administrators (using the substantial discretion given to them in the legislation) to focus on school district spending patterns and administrative compliance. The result was that an enormous amount of bureaucratic red tape was created during the 1970s without any kind of concomitant focus on student or school results—everything was judged by procedure and process. In the 1980s, John Chubb noted that "in federal programs that are not explicitly regulatory, as well as those that are, policy has come to be carried out by increasingly detailed, prescriptive, legalistic, and authoritative means."[45] Between 1964 and 1976, for example, the number of pages of federal legislation affecting education increased from 80 to 360, while the number of federal regulations increased from 92 in 1965 to nearly 1,000 in 1977.[46]

One of the most significant consequences of the ESEA was thus the centralization of education policymaking from the local level to the state and federal levels. From 1965 to 1975, federal funds for elementary and secondary education more than doubled.[47] In addition, between 1960 and 1985, the percentage of total education spending provided by the national government grew from 8 percent to 16 percent. Over the same period, the share of local spending dipped from 51 percent to 31 percent, whereas the state share increased from 41 percent to 55 percent.[48] Eligibility for federal education funds was often conditioned on the provision of state matching funds, the creation of central implementation offices, and the collection of a variety of statistical information which necessitated that state education agencies expand their size and activities and become more institutionalized. This was a clear objective of the ESEA, as the original legislation contained funding for the agencies to build up their administrative capacity so that they would be better equipped to handle their new, federally imposed responsibilities. Owing in no small part to the centralization and professionalization of state education agencies mandated by New Deal and Great Society programs, the number of independent school districts in the United States dropped from approximately 150,000 in 1900 to 15,000 in 1993.[49] Administrative centralization at the state level also ultimately made education more susceptible to federal regulation by reducing the number of decision-making foci. In practice, centralization also meant that local decision makers had less and less flexibility in how they ran their schools. As Ravitch states, "During the decade after 1965, political pressures converged on schools . . . in ways that undermined their authority to direct their own affairs. . . . Congress, the courts, federal agencies, and state legislatures devised burdensome and costly new mandates. In elementary and secondary schools, almost no area of administrative discretion was left uncontested."[50]

As opponents of federal control of education had feared, the passage of the ESEA had given a crucial beachhead to those who sought to increase further the federal role in education policy. The act had been based on the idea that the federal government had the obligation to assist "disadvantaged" students and that such assistance would be efficacious. Once this rationale had been enshrined in federal law and court precedent, a number of education-related interest groups worked hard to protect it and to expand the number and type of students considered "disadvantaged" and thus eligible to receive federal Title I aid. These groups included the National Advisory Council for the Education of Disadvantaged Children, the National Welfare Rights Organization, the Legal Standards and Education Project of the National Association for the Advancement of Colored People (NAACP), the Lawyers Committee for Civil Rights under Law, and the National Association of Administrators of State and Federally-Assisted Education Programs.

With the support of these and other organizations, a number of groups representing other disadvantaged segments of the population were able (often with the assistance of the courts) to secure additional federal spending and protections. Amendments to the ESEA in 1968 provided funding and new federal programs for disadvantaged students in rural areas, for dropout prevention programs, and for the support of bilingual programs. Congress strengthened the act in 1974 and reauthorized it in 1978 by wide bipartisan margins. (The $50 billion five-year reauthorization of 1978, for example, passed 86–7 in the Senate and 350–20 in the House.) The education proposals of the Nixon and Carter administrations largely continued in the path established by LBJ by adding over one hundred new categorical programs in education. Migrant children, children for whom English was a second language, delinquent and neglected children, and children with mental and physical disabilities would all eventually be added to Title I. Writing in the 1990s, Michelle Fine notes that "the language of 'risk' is upon us, piercing daily consciousness, educational practices, and bureaucratic policymaking. We have all been quick to name, identify, and ossify those who presumably suffer at the mercy of 'risk factors.'"[51]

The creation and growth of the special education program within ESEA demonstrates how the scope of the act was expanded and some of the consequences of this expansion. A 1966 amendment to the ESEA created a new title (Title VI) to provide grants to programs for "handicapped" children. This new program—like the ESEA itself—continued to expand over time as the definition of "handicapped" was broadened to cover more and more students. In 1970, Title VI was broken off from the ESEA and expanded to form a separate Education of the Handicapped Act. This later became the Education for All Handicapped Children Act (1975) and, most recently, the Individuals with Disabilities Education Act (IDEA). Despite a decline in the total public school population between 1968 and 1986, the number of children in special education programs in the United States during that period increased from 2.3 million to 4.3 million. The cost of providing special education services in the 1990s was estimated at between $25 and $30 billion per year, with the federal government contributing only $4 billion of that total. (The remaining amount constituted an enormous unfunded federal mandate that localities and states had to finance on their own.) Special education programs have become the fastest-growing part of the state and local education budget and the second-largest federal education program.[52]

Some of the expansion of special education programs occurred as a result of direct congressional action, but state and federal courts came to play an increasingly active and expansionist role in education policy during the 1970s. R. Shep Melnick's research has shown how generally expansive interpretations of vague federal statutes by the courts contributed to the dramatic growth of federal regulation and spending in the case of special education. He attributes the sizable growth in special education programs, for example, to the vague language contained in the 1975 Education for All Handicapped Children Act (EAHCA) and the subsequent broad determinations of eligibility by federal courts and administrators. The EAHCA mandated that all school systems provide a "free appropriate public education" to all "handicapped" children; that schools develop an "individualized educational program" for each "handicapped" child; and that schools provide "related services" to "handicapped" children. The act did not, however, specify how the crucial terms—"handicapped," "appropriate," "individualized," or "related services"—should be defined.[53]

Melnick notes that "legislators talked blithely about providing equal educational opportunity and allowing individuals to maximize their potential, without giving serious thought to what this might mean in practice."[54] Because the legislation also granted parents the right to appeal school decisions to the courts, it ensured that judges would ultimately provide those definitions. And judges tended to interpret the EAHCA broadly in terms of protecting the individual rights of children with disabilities. "The courts . . . insist[ed] on a literal interpretation of some phrases (such as the requirement that states educate all handicapped children) and [gave] a liberal interpretation to others (such as 'related services')."[55] These interpretations fueled an increase in federal, and particularly state and local, spending on special education—the federal share alone increased from $14 million in 1965 to $4.3 billion in 1999. The growth of spending on programs for those with disabilities mirrored the growth of education spending for disadvantaged students more generally. Grants for disadvantaged students increased from zero in 1965 to $6.7 billion in 1999; school improvement programs went from $72 million to $1.5 billion; Indian education went from zero to $65 million; and bilingual education went from zero to $385 million (all in inflation-adjusted dollars).[56]

While the design and priorities of some federal programs were questioned, the central idea that the federal government had an obligation to expand the opportunities for those who were disadvantaged through new programs and resources was widely accepted during the 1970s by politicians and the public alike.[57] By 1980, federal spending and influence on schooling had expanded dramatically, and the Elementary and Secondary Education Act had facilitated the centralization, bureaucratization, and judicialization of education policymaking. The case of special education policy (and its many problems) represented an extension of ESEA logic—that the federal government needed to protect the most vulnerable from inequities in state and local school systems. The result was a growing federal involvement in education but also increasingly inflexible and copious regulations and more intrusive court involvement.

President Carter's creation of the cabinet-level Department of Education in 1979 was symbolic of the growth of the national presence in educational policy. By 1980, the department administered approximately five hundred different federal education programs.

The focus of the federal effort in education at this point was on supplying additional resources to promote equity and ensuring an equitable process of determining how these resources were allocated. There was little effort, however, to measure the educational progress of students covered by federal programs or to evaluate the programs' effects on student performance.[58] This fueled the growing perception in the 1970s that federal education policy—like many other federal policies from the Great Society—had become more about providing entitlements and protecting rights than about enhancing opportunity or demanding responsibility. This situation led to growing discontent among Republicans, states' rights advocates, and even some Democrats about the nature and effectiveness of federal education aid and set the stage for a backlash against the ESEA.

The Backlash against the ESEA

Given the difficulties in the design and implementation of the ESEA, it was not surprising that researchers and policymakers began to question the effectiveness of federal education aid. During the late 1960s and 1970s a number of prominent studies were published which argued that ESEA funds and programs had largely failed to improve educational opportunity for disadvantaged students.[59] Joel Berke and Michael Kirst, for example, analyzed data from over five hundred school districts and concluded that the ESEA aid had done little to redress the large inequality in per-pupil expenditures between rich and poor districts.[60] By dispersing ESEA funds widely across school districts, not only was federal assistance poorly targeted to its intended beneficiaries, but the additional resources that came to any particular school were limited.

In addition, because the ESEA was premised on the provision of additional resources rather than the promotion of school reform, federal education aid generally went to support existing state and local programs. This approach came under fire over time as the additional resources failed to generate improvement in student achievement. In a September 1970 speech whose themes would be widely repeated in the following years, Republican president Richard Nixon argued that increased spending on education would not improve educational opportunity unless more fundamental changes in schools were required. Congress had been, he noted, "extraordinarily generous in its support of education . . . [and] much of this activity was based on the familiar premise that if only the resources available for education were increased, the amount youngsters learn would increase." It was time, he argued, to recognize that existing education "programs and strategies . . . are . . . based on faulty assumptions and inadequate knowledge."[61]

By this point the Great Society had come under fire from both conservative and liberal politicians. As Gareth Davies has noted, "The former was increasingly certain that the poor did not deserve the War on Poverty's largesse, and the latter was equally adamant that they were entitled to far more."[62] As a result of the questionable benefits of the ESEA, public support for it and many of the other social welfare programs born during the Great Society began to wane in the 1970s and particularly in the 1980s. There was a growing perception that many programs that had begun as an effort to promote opportunity and self-reliance had morphed into entitlements which encouraged dependency—that opportunity liberalism had transformed into what Davies calls "entitlement liberalism."[63] "Although the very visible War on Poverty program appeared to be aimed at assisting the poor to find a competitive place in the system," Marshall Kaplan and Peggy Cuciti note, "the entitlement programs that evolved seemed premised on a commitment to assist a poverty population that could not, should not, or would not compete."[64]

As the ESEA continued to expand in size and to cover more and more disadvantaged groups despite its apparent failure to deliver on its promise to enhance educational opportunity, support for a fundamental reconsideration of the federal role in education gained momentum. In the 1980 presidential election, Ronald Reagan took advantage of growing public opposition to federal "interference" in schools and the expansion of the welfare state more generally to defeat Democratic incumbent Jimmy Carter.[65] Reagan energized the Republican Party behind a conservative agenda centered on cutting taxes and rolling back the size and scope of the federal government. Once in office, he argued that "it's time to bury the myth that bigger government brings more opportunity and compassion."[66] As part of his New Federalism program, Reagan gained passage in 1981 of the Education Consolidation and Improvement Act

(ECIA), which dramatically reformed many ESEA provisions. The changes reduced the amount of federal funding for education by almost 20 percent, simplified eligibility requirements, and increased flexibility for states in the use of federal education funds.[67]

States' rights advocates celebrated what they thought was the beginning of a new era (or perhaps more accurately a return to an old era) in which the federal government would leave education policymaking to the states. As Graham observed at the time, however, "the Reaganite hostility to a strong federal role in education (beyond defense related R & D) is not shared by a congressional majority that clings with surprising tenacity to the consensus forged during the Kennedy-Johnson years, which survived and even prospered under the Nixon and Ford administrations, and which was strongly reinforced under Carter."[68] By 1980, the ESEA and the federal role in education had been institutionalized and were vigorously defended by teachers' unions, state education agencies, and parent groups. The result, as Ravitch has noted, was that "the new politics of the schools rotated about a state-federal axis rather than a local-state axis."[69]

Republican efforts in the 1980s to roll back federal influence in education also ran into fresh evidence that American schools were in very poor shape. A widely publicized 1983 report on the state of American education, *A Nation at Risk,* painted a dire portrait of the country's public schools and highlighted how far American students lagged behind their foreign counterparts on academic achievement tests. It emphasized that the poor performance of American students was a matter of national security, both in our cold war struggle with the Soviet Union and in our competition in the global economy. The widespread sense that the country was facing an education crisis enhanced public support for increased federal leadership, despite the Republican argument that the best way to improve our schools was to get the federal government out of education policy.[70]

Acknowledging the increased salience of education among voters, Republican George H. W. Bush promised during the 1988 campaign to be an "education president" and convened an unprecedented meeting of the nation's governors in Charlottesville, Virginia, in the fall of 1989 to discuss education reform.[71] Despite much disagreement concerning the proper extent of the federal role, the governors agreed to support the creation of a set of national education goals and to assess the progress of states in meeting them.[72] In April 1991, President Bush introduced his

America 2000 education reform plan, which called for the development of more-detailed standards in the core academic subjects and asked governors to adopt voluntary national testing for fourth, eighth, and twelfth graders.[73] At this point, however, both Republicans and Democrats opposed federal standards and tests, though for very different reasons. Republicans feared that they would inevitably lead to federal control of education, whereas Democrats feared that they would lead to the imposition of tough school accountability measures and a de-emphasis on the importance of increasing federal funding for education. As a result of this bipartisan opposition, Bush's America 2000 bill ultimately died in Congress.

New Democrats, Compassionate Conservatives, and the Battle to Redefine the ESEA

The growing importance of education in the electorate and a shifting political environment in the 1990s produced new political pressures and dynamics for both Republicans and Democrats.[74] The end of the cold war elevated the profile of domestic policy, and in 1992, New Democrats successfully shed the party's tax-and-spend image by employing a rhetoric that emphasized expanding opportunity and shared responsibility. They argued that a skill- and knowledge-based economy required the workers' party to shift from a redistributive model toward one that fostered societal investment in workers.[75] Democratic efforts to reposition themselves and blunt Republican attacks on federal social-welfare policies were evident in the party's 1992 platform, which proclaimed, "Rather than throwing money at obsolete programs, we will eliminate unnecessary layers of management, [and] cut administrative costs." On education, the platform argued, "Governments must end the inequalities that create educational ghettos among school districts and provide equal educational opportunity for all," but also that schools must be held accountable to "high standards of educational achievement."[76]

Education reform became a centerpiece of Bill Clinton's New Democrat philosophy and his 1992 and 1996 presidential campaigns.[77] Republicans, meanwhile, struggled to answer the challenge posed by the New Democrats without abandoning the party's historic free-market and small-government principles. President Clinton capitalized on Republican disagreement on education to seize the initiative on the standards idea. He repackaged the core of Bush's America 2000 plan into the renamed Goals 2000, pushed it through a Democratic Congress, and signed it into law on March 31, 1994.[78] The passage of Goals 2000 and its companion, the 1994 Improving America's Schools Act, marked a significant shift in federal education policy, since for the first time the national government would be involved in influencing the pedagogy and curricular content in mainstream American schools.[79]

The broad scope of Goals 2000 rekindled fears of federal micromanagement in education, and the ESEA remained controversial throughout the remainder of the 1990s.[80] Republicans battled the attempts by Clinton and congressional Democrats to secure large increases in federal education spending and create an assortment of new federal education programs.[81] Extending Reagan's argument that government was the problem rather than the solution, Republicans hoped to reduce federal involvement in education by cutting federal spending, by converting it into block grants or vouchers, or by eliminating the Department of Education entirely. These efforts were largely unsuccessful and, while popular with the party's conservative base, proved unpopular with the general public and particularly with moderate swing voters.[82]

Clinton and the Democrats were largely successful during the 1990s in focusing national attention on the problems in America's schools, in arguing that school improvement should be a federal priority, and in positioning the Democratic Party as the party of education standards and reform. Federal spending on elementary and secondary education increased dramatically during the decade,[83] and national policy moved beyond the original premise of the ESEA—equalizing resources for disadvantaged students—toward a new focus on student performance and accountability for all schools. By the end of the decade there was a growing recognition among many Republicans that the party's opposition to federal activism in education had been costly in national elections and that it needed to develop a more appealing domestic philosophy and policy agenda to compete with Clinton's popular centrist Third Way.

The Republican nominee in 2000, George W. Bush, proclaimed that he was a "compassionate conservative," and education became the central issue of his campaign and a symbol of his break with antigovernment conservatives.[84] Education ranked as one of voters' highest priorities in the election, and Bush developed and disseminated a detailed education reform plan that endorsed a significant expansion of the federal role in schools.[85] He and the Democratic nominee, Al Gore, both called for more federal funding for education, for using tests to allow the federal government to hold all schools accountable for student achievement, and for increased federal support for charter schools.[86] This convergence between the Democratic and Republican parties on education would have been unthinkable only five years earlier and set the stage for a historic compromise on the pending ESEA reauthorization.

The No Child Left Behind Act became law on January 8, 2002, and the centerpiece of the legislation was the requirement that as a condition of accepting federal funds, states test all of their children in grades 3–8 in reading and math every year.[87] States were also required to make the results of their tests publicly available with breakdowns by school, race, and level of poverty and to undertake a series of corrective actions to fix failing schools.[88] The law also dramatically increased federal spending on education and provided for greater flexibility in the use of federal funds by allowing states to transfer funds among different federal programs.[89] Both supporters and opponents of No Child Left Behind agree that it dramatically increased and reshaped the federal role in education, with Richard Elmore calling it "the single largest expansion of federal power over the nation's education system in history."[90]

The Elementary and Secondary Education Act was one of the signal legislative achievements of the Great Society. Its legacy has been enormous and has grown over time as the act has come to shape an increasingly ambitious national effort to reform the country's K–12 schools. The ESEA established a statutory federal commitment to equal educational opportunity and created a number of new national education programs and institutions to promote school improvement. Educational opportunity was elevated to the status of a right, with emphasis placed on the "inputs" (process) rather than on the "outputs" (achievement) of schooling. Thus the ESEA contributed significantly to the dramatic expansion of federal spending, legislation, and regulation in education that has occurred over the past thirty-five years.[91]

The Great Society is often portrayed as a linear extension of the New Deal, but it differed from the New Deal in important ways. As Hugh Heclo and Ira Katznelson have demonstrated, the New Deal sought to alleviate the consequences of poverty, whereas the Great Society sought to eliminate the underlying *causes* of poverty and thereby make redistribution unnecessary.[92] This crucial difference between the two reform movements is perhaps most clearly demonstrated in the realm of education policy, which played little role in the New Deal but was central to the Great Society. The Elementary and Secondary Education Act—along with other Great Society legislation such as the Civil Rights and Voting Rights Acts—moved away from redistribution, which lay at the heart of the New Deal, and attempted to place equality and opportunity at the center of the nation's social welfare policies.

Indeed, it was when federal education policy became perceived as more concerned with securing procedural rights and providing benefits for certain special interest groups than improving student achievement that it lost its original bipartisan political support. During the 1970s and 1980s, Republicans led an effective assault on the ESEA and other Great Society programs by arguing that they had been transformed into entitlements that promoted dependency rather than opportunity and were inconsistent with America's tradition of individualism. Led by Bill Clinton and the Democratic Leadership Council, Democrats responded in the 1990s by acknowledging the failings and limits of the welfare state and by reemphasizing opportunity over entitlement. In response to the success of these Democratic maneuvers, Republicans shifted from attacking the goals of the Great Society to reforming the means by which these goals should be achieved. It was in this vein that George W. Bush pushed Republicans in 2000 to end their efforts to eliminate the federal role in education and to focus instead on reshaping national education policy to emphasize student performance, school accountability, and parental choice.

These broad political developments have helped launch a new era of education policy in which the alliances, policies, and assumptions of the past forty years are undergoing a fundamental shift. The 2002 No Child Left Behind Act, though it technically "reforms" the Elementary and Secondary Education Act, in reality re-creates it. The original ESEA was narrowly targeted (to disadvantaged students) and focused on inputs (providing additional resources to schools). The new ESEA embraces a much broader scope (improving education for all students) and is focused on outputs (measuring the academic achievement of students). It is too early to know whether the latest incarnation of the ESEA will ensure "freedom from ignorance," as LBJ hoped, or what its long-term effect will be on educational opportunity or school governance in the United States. What is clear is that Johnson's primary objective—to enlist the federal government permanently in the effort to promote educational opportunity—has been achieved. Elementary and secondary education policy is now widely considered—by the American public and key elements of both major political parties—to be an important *national* responsibility, a remarkable contrast with the decentralized and even individualistic views of schooling that were dominant before the Great Society and the Elementary and Secondary Education Act.

Notes

1. The origin of federal involvement in education can be traced to the Land Ordinance Act of 1785 and the Northwest Ordinance of 1787, which required that new states guarantee public education for citizens in their constitutions. The federal government became more directly involved in education—and set a precedent for later grant-in-aid programs—with the passage of the Morrill Act in 1862, which supported the creation of a network of land-grant colleges. It was not until 1867, however, that the tiny four-person U.S. Office of Education was established, and it was another five decades before the federal government first provided an annual appropriation for K–12 schooling (with the Smith-Hughes Act of 1917).

2. U.S. Department of Commerce, Bureau of the Census, *Education of the American Population,* U.S. Census of Population, Table 8, Washington, D.C.: 1999.

3. See, for instance, Paul Peterson, *The Politics of School Reform: 1870–1940* (Chicago: University of Chicago Press, 1985), 5–22; Michael Katz, *Reconstructing American Education* (Boston: Harvard University Press, 1987), 16–20; or Diane Ravitch, *Left Back: A Century of Failed School Reforms* (New York: Simon and Schuster, 2000), 241–47.

4. Hugh Davis Graham, *The Uncertain Triumph: Federal Education Policy in the Kennedy and Johnson Years* (Chapel Hill: University of North Carolina Press, 1984), xvii.

5. For more on the educational policies of the New Deal, see Ronald Story, "The New Deal and Higher Education," in *The New Deal and the Triumph of Liberalism,* ed. Sidney M. Milkis and Jerome M. Mileur (Amherst: University of Massachusetts Press, 2002).

6. Whereas in 1940, just 38.1 percent of those aged twenty-five to twenty-nine years old had graduated high school and just 5.9 percent had completed four years of college, by 1970, 75.4 percent had finished high school and 16.4 percent four years of college (U.S. Department of Commerce, *Education,* Table 8).

7. See Diane Ravitch, *The Troubled Crusade: American Education, 1945–1980* (New York: Basic Books, 1983), 10–16.

8. For an extensive account of the context and consequences of the *Brown* decision, see James T. Patterson, *Brown v. Board of Education: A Civil Rights Milestone and Its Troubled Legacy* (Oxford: Oxford University Press, 2001).

9. As quoted in James L. Sundquist, *Politics and Policy: The Eisenhower, Kennedy, and Johnson Years* (Washington, D.C.: Brookings Institution, 1968), 178.

10. James Guthrie, "The Future of Federal Education Policy," *Teachers College Record* 84, no. 3 (1983): 674.

11. Graham, *Uncertain Triumph*, xv.

12. Kennedy's efforts to enact a federal aid to education bill were also complicated by his Catholicism (which heightened fears about federal aid to private and parochial schools) and his narrow victory in the 1960 presidential election (which left him without a strong popular mandate).

13. Johnson won the 1964 presidential election by what was then the largest margin in American history—16 million votes. Johnson's popularity was also widely credited with helping the Democratic Party significantly increase its control of Congress by expanding its majority to 36 in the Senate and 155 in the House. Johnson used his strong popular mandate, as well as the gratitude of many Democratic senators and representatives for the strength of his coattails, to lobby effectively for support of his education agenda.

14. Quoted in Julie Roy Jeffrey, *Education for Children of the Poor: A Study of the Origins and Implementation of the Elementary and Secondary Education Act of 1965* (Columbus: Ohio State University Press, 1978), 3.

15. Tinsley Spraggins, "New Educational Goals and Directions: A Perspective of Title I, ESEA," *Journal of Negro Education* 37, no. 1 (1968): 46.

16. Quoted in Phillip Meranto, *The Politics of Federal Aid to Education in 1965* (Syracuse: Syracuse University Press, 1967), 104.

17. Quoted in Harold Howe, "LBJ as the Education President," in *The Presidency and Education*, ed. Kenneth Thompson (Lanham, Md.: University Press of America, 1990), 102.

18. Meranto, *Politics of Federal Aid to Education*, 132.

19. Joel Spring, *Conflict of Interests: The Politics of American Education* (Boston: McGraw Hill, 1999), 96–97.

20. Paul Peterson and Barry Rabe, "The Role of Interest Groups in the Formation of Educational Policy," *Teachers College Record* 84, no. 3 (1983): 717.

21. Howe, "LBJ as the Education President," 101–2.

22. For a thorough discussion of the political context surrounding the passage of the ESEA, see Meranto, *Politics of Federal Aid to Education in 1965;* Eugene Eidenberg and Roy Morey, *An Act of Congress: The Legislative Process and the Making of Education Policy* (New York: W. W. Norton, 1969); and Graham, *Uncertain Triumph*.

23. "Remarks in Johnson City, Texas, upon Signing the Elementary and Secondary Education Bill, April 11, 1965," in *Public Papers of the Presidents of the United States: Lyndon B. Johnson*, 1965, 2 vols. (Washington, D.C.: Government Printing Office, 1966), 1:412–14, entry 181.

24. Quoted in Joel Spring, *The Sorting Machine: National Educational Policy since 1945* (New York: David McKay, 1976), 225.

25. Eidenberg and Morey, *Act of Congress*, 247.

26. For a detailed explanation of the typology of public policies and what is meant by distribution and redistribution, see Theodore Lowi, "American Business, Public Policy Case Studies, and Political Theory," *World Politics* 16 (July 1964): 677–715.

27. As Diane Ravitch has noted, "From the middle 1950's to the end of the 1960's, a vast literature was produced which sought to account for the low achievement of poor and minority children in urban schools. Books, articles, symposia, seminars, and conferences proliferated around the theme of how to educate the 'culturally deprived,' the 'culturally disadvantaged,' the 'underprivileged,' and the 'lower-class child'" (*Troubled Crusade*, 150).

28. Ibid., 158.

29. Peterson and Rabe, "Role of Interest Groups," 717.

30. Eidenberg and Morey, *Act of Congress*, 93.

31. Quoted in Sundquist, *Politics and Policy*, 16.

32. Quoted in ibid., 215.

33. Ibid., 16.

34. Graham, *Uncertain Triumph*, 193.

35. Jack Jennings, "Title I: Its Legislative History and Its Promise," *Phi Delta Kappan* (March 2000): 4.

36. See Paul Peterson et al., *When Federalism Works* (Washington, D.C.: Brookings Institution Press, 1994), 136–40, for a more detailed discussion of the local tendency to shift federal funds from redistributive programs to other purposes.

37. Graham, *Uncertain Triumph*, 204.

38. Joel Berke, *Answers to Inequity: An Analysis of the New School Finance* (Berkeley: McCutchan Publishing Corporation, 1974), 143.

39. Jerome Murphy, "Title I of ESEA: The Politics of Implementing Federal Education Reform," *Harvard Educational Review* 41 (February 1971): 42.

40. John Hughes and Anne Hughes, *Equal Education: A New National Strategy* (Bloomington: Indiana University Press, 1972), 50.

41. Graham, *Uncertain Triumph*, 22.

42. Steve Fraser and Gary Gerstle, ed., introduction to *The Rise and Fall of the New Deal Order* (Princeton: Princeton University Press, 1989), xix.

43. Hughes and Hughes, *Equal Education*, 57.

44. Ravitch, *Troubled Crusade*, 271.

45. John E. Chubb, "Excessive Regulation: The Case of Federal Aid to Education, *Political Science Quarterly* 100, no. 2 (1985): 287.

46. Ravitch, *Troubled Crusade*, 312.

47. National Center for Education Statistics, *The Condition of Education 2000* (Washington, D.C.: National Center for Education Statistics, 2000), 395.

48. Deil S. Wright, *Understanding Intergovernmental Relations* (Pacific Grove, Calif.: Brooks Publishing, 1988), 195.

49. Michael Newman, *America's Teachers* (New York: Longman, 1994), 166.
50. Ravitch, *Troubled Crusade,* 267.
51. Michelle Fine, "Who's 'At Risk'?" *Journal of Urban and Cultural Studies* (November 1990): 55, 64.
52. R. Shep Melnick, "Separation of Powers and the Strategy of Rights: The Expansion of Special Education," in *The New Politics of Public Policy,* ed. Marc C. Landy and Martin Levin (Baltimore: Johns Hopkins University Press, 1995), 24.
53. Ibid., 157.
54. Ibid., 37.
55. Ibid., 27.
56. National Center for Education Statistics, *Condition of Education 2000,* 409.
57. Marshall Kaplan and Peggy Cuciti, eds., *The Great Society and Its Legacy: Twenty Years of U.S. Social Policy* (Durham: Duke University Press, 1986), 1, 13.
58. Senator Robert Kennedy fought to have testing and accountability measures included in the original ESEA legislation but was rebuffed. Forty years later, however, George W. Bush would remind Ted Kennedy of his brother's efforts in order to enlist his support for No Child Left Behind.
59. See, for example, Bailey and Mosher (1968); Joel Berke and Michael Kirst, *Federal Aid to Education* (Lexington, Mass.: Heath, 1972); Berke, *Answers to Inequity* (1974); McLaughlin (1975); Thomas (1975); and Jeffrey (1976).
60. Berke and Kirst, *Federal Aid to Education,* 45. They found that while Title I (which was explicitly focused on disadvantaged students) had a somewhat redistributive effect, this was erased by the effects of the act's other titles and vocational aid that went disproportionately to wealthier districts.
61. Quoted in Jeffrey, *Education for Children,* 143.
62. Gareth Davies, *From Opportunity to Entitlement: The Transformation and Decline of Great Society Liberalism* (Lawrence: University Press of Kansas, 1996), 78.
63. Ibid., 1–9.
64. Kaplan and Cuciti, *Great Society,* 217. Typical of the growing backlash against the Great Society was Charles Murray's widely publicized book *Losing Ground: American Social Policy, 1950–1980* (New York: Basic Books, 1984), in which the author argued that the poor were worse off after the Great Society than they had been before it.
65. The 1980 Republican platform called for "deregulation by the federal government of public education and . . . the elimination of the federal Department of Education." The platform fretted that "parents are losing control of their children's schooling" and that Democratic education policy had produced "huge new bureaucracies to misspend our taxes" (*Historic Documents of 1980* [Washington, D.C: Congressional Quarterly, 1981], 583–84).
66. Quoted in Sar Levitan and Clifford Johnson, "Did the Great Society and Subsequent Initiatives Work?" in Kaplan and Cuciti, *The Great Society and Its Legacy,* 73.
67. One scholar estimated that the number of regulatory mandates imposed

on states through federal education programs was reduced by 85 percent during the Reagan administration. See Parris N. Glendening and Mavis Mann Reeves, *Pragmatic Federalism: An Intergovernmental View of American Government* (Pacific Palisades, Calif.: Palisades Publishers, 1984), 243. Also, as D. T. Stallings has noted, "The new administration planned to move the Department of Education away from awarding categorical grants and toward the awarding of block grants, with the goal of eventually eliminating federal grants entirely, which would cause the federal role to revert to what it had been in 1838—nothing more than collecting statistics." See D. T. Stallings, "A Brief History of the U.S. Department of Education, 1979–2002," *Phi Delta Kappan* 83, no. 9 (2002): 678.

68. Graham, *Uncertain Triumph*, 22.

69. Ravitch, *Troubled Crusade*, 320.

70. A 1987 Gallup poll, for example, found that 84 percent of Americans thought that the federal government should require state and local educational authorities to meet minimum national standards. See Michael Heise, "Goals 2000: Educate America Act; The Federalization and Legalization of Educational Policy," *Fordham Law Review* 63 (November 1994): 11.

71. Several southern governors who had been active in pushing standards at the state level—Bill Clinton (D-Ark.), Richard Riley (D-S.C.), and Lamar Alexander (R-Tenn.)—played a prominent role at the conference and would later become important players in federal school reform efforts.

72. The six goals were: (1) all children in America will start school ready to learn; (2) the high school graduation rate will increase to at least 90 percent; (3) students in grades 4, 8, and 12 will be competent in English, mathematics, science, foreign languages, civics and government, economics, arts, history, and geography; (4) every school will be free of drugs, violence, firearms, and alcohol and will offer a disciplined learning environment; (5) U.S. students will be the first in the world in mathematics and science achievement; (6) every adult will be literate and will possess the knowledge and skills necessary to compete in a global economy.

73. Bush's plan also proposed the creation of a quasi-private–public New American Schools Development Corporation to design model schools and called for a number of school choice demonstration projects.

74. For a more detailed discussion of the rise of education as an issue in national politics and the evolution of the parties' positions on education, see Frederick Hess and Patrick McGuinn, "Seeking the Mantle of 'Opportunity': Presidential Politics and the Educational Metaphor, 1964–2000," *Educational Policy* 16 (January–March 2002): 72–95.

75. In 1990, the Democratic Leadership Council issued the "New Orleans Declaration: A Democratic Agenda for the 1990s," which specifically called for replacing the "politics of entitlement with a new politics of reciprocal responsibility." See www.ndol.org/print,cfm?contentid=878.

76. See www.presidency.ucsb.edu/platforms.

77. Public opinion polls in 1992 revealed that education had become one of

voters' top priorities and that voters thought Clinton better able than Bush to improve public schools by a staggering 47 percent to 24 percent margin.

78. As with America 2000, the heart of the Goals 2000 program was a set of national education goals. These goals were the six goals set out in America 2000 along, with two others: that teachers have access to professional development, and that every school develop parental partnerships to promote the social, emotional, and academic growth of children.

79. States were required under the Goals 2000 plan to develop targets for the attainment of factual information and intellectual abilities that students should master at specified grade levels. The legislation also embraced a much more ambitious scope for federal education policy; henceforth the federal focus would be the educational performance of all children, not just those who were disadvantaged.

80. These fears were not assuaged by strong and specific language in the legislation that reasserted the primacy of local and state control in education. Though the states were theoretically free to devise their own standards, they were initially required to submit applications to the U.S. Department of Education for approval before receiving Goals 2000 funds. Several states, including Virginia and California, initially refused to accept Goals 2000 funds and mandates.

81. Republicans gained control of Congress in 1994, and the House voted to eliminate funding for Goals 2000 twice (in 1995 and 1996) before compromises with the Senate restored funds for the program. The 1996 national Republican Party platform stated: "We will abolish the Department of Education, end Federal meddling in our schools, and promote family choice at all levels of learning. We therefore call for prompt repeal of the Goals 2000 program."

82. The advocacy of these positions by the party's nominee in the 1996 presidential election, Bob Dole, contributed to a huge disadvantage on education during the campaign, with voters favoring Clinton on the issue by a margin of more than 2 to 1. Louis Harris poll conducted November 1–3, 1996, www.web.lexis-nexis.com/universe/form/academic/s_roper.html, accession number 0267644, question 3.

83. Federal on-budget funds for elementary and secondary education increased 69 percent in constant dollars between fiscal year 1990 and fiscal year 2001. National Center for Education Statistics, *Federal Support for Education: 1980–2001*, NCES 2002-129 (Washington, D.C.: U.S. Department of Education, Office of Educational Research and Improvement, 2002), 3.

84. As governor, Bush had been one of the first Republicans to recognize that the party's traditional position on education was problematic electorally, noting in 1996 that it had played a key role in Dole's defeat and that "Republicans must say that we are for education." Jena Heath, "Bush Education Plan Draws from All Sides," *Austin-American Statesman*, October 22, 1999, A1.

85. Bush discussed school reform more than any other issue during the campaign, and his rhetoric and proposals helped close the education gap between the parties and contributed to his victory over Gore. See Melissa Marschall and Robert McKee, "From Campaign Promises to Presidential Policy: Education Re-

form in the 2000 Election," *Educational Policy* 16 (January–March 2002): 101.

86. Bush's stance strengthened the Republican hand on education and a broad array of policy debates, but it proved to be an unhappy bargain for traditional Republicans and for the radical critics of federal interventionism. The expanded federal role marked a historic departure from Republican doctrine and created the likelihood of future conflicts between the proponents of the opportunity society and the traditional defenders of state and local prerogatives.

87. Thirty-five states did not have such testing at the time of passage. Crucially, however, after much debate, the final bill did not require states to adopt nationally designed tests, allowing them instead to design their own as well as to set their own levels for student proficiency.

88. In addition, students in schools that continued to fail would be given federal money for tutoring and the option to transfer to another public school or to a charter school.

89. It authorized a 20 percent increase in funds for Title I and also established new rules requiring that the additional moneys be directed to the poorest classrooms. The law tripled the money for reading programs (from $300 million to $900 million) and required states to put a "highly qualified teacher" (one who has a college degree, is fully certified, and has passed state competency tests) in every classroom by 2005. For the full text of the No Child Left Behind Act, see www.ed.gov/nclb at the Department of Education. For a detailed analysis of the provisions of the act, see "Major Changes to ESEA in the No Child Left Behind Act," by the Learning First Alliance, at www.learningfirst.org.

90. Richard Elmore, "Unwarranted Intrusion," *Education Next* 2, no. 1 (Spring 2002): 31–35.

91. Defined in terms of the proportion of total education spending in the United States, federal education spending has remained more or less constant at 10 percent from the 1960s to today. The number and total expenditures of federal government education programs, however, has grown dramatically during this period, a trend that appears likely to continue in the future. Total Department of Education outlays increased 57 percent in constant dollars between 1980 and 2000, and in fiscal year 1999 alone the federal government spent $82.8 billion on education. See the *Digest of Education Statistics, 1999* (Washington, D.C.: U.S. Department of Education, National Center for Education Statistics, 2000).

92. See Hugh Heclo, "The Political Foundations of Anti-Poverty Policy," in *Fighting Poverty*, ed. Sheldon Danziger and Daniel Weinberg (Cambridge: Harvard University Press, 1986), and Ira Katznelson, "Was the Great Society a Lost Opportunity?" in Fraser and Gerstle, *Rise and Fall of the New Deal Order*, 200.

Medicare

The Great Society's Enduring National Health Insurance Program

Edward Berkowitz

A high official in the Johnson administration described Medicare as a "real jewel in the crown of the federal government."[1] President Lyndon Johnson, who readily agreed, put Medicare in the company of the Social Security Act of 1935 and the Elementary and Secondary Education Act of 1965 as the most "comprehensive and constructive and beneficial" public acts in the period between the New Deal and the end of his term in 1969.[2] With great pride, he signed the Social Security Amendments of 1965 into law on July 30, 1965, in an impressive ceremony at the Truman Library in Independence, Missouri. This comprehensive piece of legislation included significant provisions related to Social Security and public assistance. Most important, however, it initiated a social insurance program that paid many of the hospital and doctor bills of the nation's elderly, and it started Medicaid, which was federal assistance to the states to help pay for the medical care of welfare recipients and other indigent individuals.

It was President Johnson's pride that prompted him to sign the Medicare bill in the presence of President Harry Truman. Like a dutiful son, Johnson wanted to share his triumph with one of the fathers of national health legislation. Truman had chosen to highlight health insurance in his postwar domestic program and had delivered an unprecedented message on the subject to Congress in November 1945. Fighting for political survival in a nation that knew little about him, Truman hoped that advocating national health insurance would show his desire to embrace and expand President Roosevelt's New Deal agenda. Roosevelt, after all, had never found the right moment to endorse national health insurance. Truman could, in effect, do it for him. The results were less than salutary. Truman won a few points with liberals for his advocacy of health insurance but failed to get Congress to approve the measure. Even the labor unions, whom Truman courted through such actions as vetoing the Taft-Hartley bill, despaired of the federal government's prospects in passing health insurance and deserted the cause by seeking alternatives within their collective bargaining agreements. As he traveled to Independence, Johnson could lay claim to finishing what Truman had started (and, of course, succeeding where Truman, and Kennedy, for that matter, had failed). At last Congress had agreed to national health insurance.[3]

Not all the president's advisers thought it was a good idea to highlight Truman at the signing ceremony. Wilbur Cohen, the assistant secretary of health, education, and welfare who had done much of the staff work on Medicare, worried that Truman's presence would send the wrong signal. People might compare Johnson's law with President Truman's proposals and get the impression that the administration advocated the same things as had Truman. Medicare covered only the nation's elderly, and Medicaid covered the nation's poor. Truman had wanted a program that reached everyone, regardless of age or financial condition.[4] Johnson brushed such objections aside, and the ceremony went off without any untoward political incidents.

It was a moment of triumph for Johnson that marked the apex of his mastery of Congress. Although other victories would follow the passage of Medicare, urban riots, including one in the Watts section of Los Angeles that began only a few weeks later, and foreign wars would tarnish the president's popularity and strain the government's administrative capacity.[5]

Easy in retrospect, with a popular president confronting a compliant Congress, the passage of Medicare required consummate political skill. Throughout the original debate over Medicare, conservatives and representatives of the medical profession harbored two fears. One was that Medicare was only a way station on the road to national health insurance; the other was that the passage of Medicare would provide an opening through which the federal government would regulate the practice of medicine. Medicare proponents went out of their way to assert that neither fear was justified. They repeatedly stressed that Medicare, once passed, would not become the basis for a national health insurance program that covered people of all ages. "The problem of the aged is a unique problem and . . . I can think of no practical way to meet this problem than through the Social Security approach. The younger members of the population do not have the same problem," said Robert Ball, the Social Security commissioner during the Johnson administration. Would Medicare lead to the government's control of medicine? "Emphatically not," replied Ball.[6]

In retrospect, Ball admitted that he had been less than candid. Medicare's design, he noted, was based "entirely on a strategy of acceptability—what sort of program would be difficult for opponents to attack and what kind of program would be most likely to pick up supporters." "Although the record contains some explicit denials to the contrary, we confidently expected it to be a first step toward national health insurance," he said.[7] Despite conservative fears and liberal hopes, the United States never took that step. Medicare was a terminus rather than a point of embarkation. Medicare remains on the books, still a popular program but one that is a memorial to the world as it existed in 1965. It is neither a late addition to the New Deal nor a viable model for national health insurance.

Medicare as a Great Society Program

If the New Deal was about security and disengagement from the labor force through such devices as retirement pensions, unemployment compensation, and pensions for the worthy poor, the Great Society, by way of contrast, was about opportunity and labor force participation. The Great Depression conditioned the programs of the New Deal, and the big postwar economic boom made the programs of the Great Society possible. The New Deal supported hard-pressed Americans at a time of economic catastrophe; the Great Society invested in people at the margins of the labor force at a time of economic opportunity. The New Deal outlook was pessimistic. Many thought the nation had reached a permanent turning point and would remain stuck in a depression mode. The Great Society outlook was optimistic. Continued economic growth would draw African Americans into the economic mainstream and fund advances in medical care that would improve the quality of life and, not coincidentally, the economic productivity of all Americans.[8]

As a piece of legislation and as social policy, Medicare bore many similarities to other Great Society programs. The characteristic programs of the Great Society took the form of federal grants-in-aid to states and localities. The number of federal grant programs increased from 132 in 1960 to 379 by 1967. Outlays for these grants grew from $8.6 billion in 1963 to $20.3 billion in 1969. Whereas federal grants before the Great Society had gone for such basic governmental functions as highways and public assistance, they were now spent for a bewildering number of purposes, from family planning to school breakfasts, from mass transit aid to alcohol and drug abuse.[9]

Medicare was a form of social insurance and not, properly speaking, a federal grant-in-aid program. But one might think of it as a grant-in-aid from the federal government to the nation's hospitals and doctors. In the implementation of Medicare, none of the principal players in the Johnson administration saw their job as challenging hospitals or the medical profession to do a better job; rather, they wished to encourage these institutions to serve a new target group, the elderly. To bring about that result, they offered hospitals and doctors relatively easy money on lenient terms. Robert Ball, who took the lead role in the implementation effort, put it succinctly when he said that "by and large our posture at the beginning was one of paying full costs but not intervening very much in the way hospitals, or at least the better ones, conducted their business."[10] As Ball noted, Medicare simply "accepted the going system of the delivery of care and the program structure was molded on previous private insurance arrangements. Reimbursement of institutions followed the principle of cost reimbursement that had been worked out with the American Hospital Association and the majority of Blue Cross plans. Physician reimbursement followed the direction of private commercial insurance, making payments based, by and large, on what physicians charged their other patients."[11]

It was not a bad deal that the government offered to the medical profession, and all the profession had to do was drop its previous opposition to Medicare and reap the benefits. Elderly individuals who had previously been charity patients in hospitals or who paid the doctors less than regular patients now became as desirable as any other patient. In speeches to groups such as the American Hospital Association, Robert Ball assured them that it was the government's intention to "meet actual costs" of providing services, however widely those costs might vary from one hospital to another and however much they increased over time. As hospitals acquired new equipment, adopted new techniques, and made other improvements, Ball emphasized that the "additional operating costs will be reimbursed," thus providing "the proper financial underpinning to improvements in care."[12] "In most fields, you get only what you pay for," he wrote in an internal agency article describing the implementation effort, and he promised that the federal government would not skimp on its payments for the medical care of the elderly.[13]

Senator Paul Douglas (D-Ill.) captured the tone of Medicare implementation when he said that it was necessary to get the cooperation of hospitals, and "the wheels won't turn unless the axle has a little grease." In this spirit, the government made concessions to the hospitals that even went beyond paying the actual costs of the services rendered. Hospitals, for example, received an extra 2 percent of their allowable costs to cover expenses that could not otherwise be specified. The result was similar to the cushy cost-plus financing common to defense contracts, without the hospitals having to do the hard work of getting the contract in the first place. Instead of concentrating on the marginal costs of serving Medicare patients, the government allowed hospitals to capture a portion of their fixed costs.[14] The result was not much different from other grants-in-aid of the Great Society era. If anything, hospitals and doctors had an easier time securing these grants than did local government agencies competing for public health funds.

Medicare and Civil Rights

Medicare also resembled other Great Society legislation in its connection to initiatives in civil rights. Like civil rights legislation, it guaranteed a previously excluded group—in this case, elderly Americans—access to a system that could improve their quality of life. In a more direct sense, it served as a force for the racial integration of hospitals, in particular the hospitals located in the Deep South. The direct connection between Medicare and civil rights reflected the preoccupations of the era. By way of contrast, civil rights figured only incidentally in the major legislation of the New Deal, although New Deal programs had racial consequences.

The Social Security Act of 1935, for example, excluded farmers and self-employed workers such as domestics and sharecroppers from coverage under the old-age insurance program. As a result, a majority of blacks did not gain Social Security coverage. At the same time, race was not central to the politics of Social Security in the New Deal era, as half of all whites were also not covered. Most farmers were white, not black, and in any case, few farmers clamored for coverage. At a time when a quarter of the labor force could not find a job, the problems of black Americans failed to make an impression on most policymakers.[15]

All that had changed by the time Medicare cleared Congress. Until the advent of Medicare, most health legislation, such as the 1946 Hill-Burton hospital construction program, had been racially permissive in the sense that it did not require local authorities to maintain integrated facilities in order to receive federal funds. Local customs, including those of the Jim Crow South, predominated over national racial standards.[16] If Medicare had passed when it received its first serious congressional hearing in 1957, it too might have been racially permissive and hence racially restrictive. Southern politicians who occupied influential positions on the key congressional committees, such as Harry Byrd (D-Va.) on the Senate Finance Committee or Wilbur Mills (D-Ark.) on the House Committee on Ways and Means, might have insisted on states' rights in hospital accommodations as a price for the passage of the bill. In 1962, when the measure was defeated on the floor of the Senate, and in 1964, when the Ways and Means Committee blocked passage, the fear of racial integration might have helped to doom the bill. In 1965, the year the measure did pass, circumstances were different. Civil rights was, in a sense, a done deal. Title VI of the Civil Rights Act of 1964 required that activities receiving support from the federal government be integrated.[17] Any hospital that expected to receive federal money from the Medicare program, therefore, would have to be integrated.

For the Johnson administration, civil rights compliance presented a problem of many dimensions. The first aspect of the problem was overtly political. Although Congress might have passed the Civil Rights Act of 1964 and the Voting Rights Act of 1965, the Congress with which the administration bargained on vitally important social welfare legislation contained more than its share of southerners with seniority on the Ways and Means and Finance Committees. Herman Talmadge (D-Ga.), for example, occupied an important place on the Senate Finance Committee, yet he remained an ardent opponent of civil rights initiatives. The second aspect of the problem reflected the trade-off between the success of Medicare and other social policy goals of the Johnson administration. Hospitals remained highly segregated institutions in the sections of the country in which Jim Crow social arrangements lingered, because hospital activities involved intimate body functions in which racial taboos were strongest.[18] Yet if all the hospitals in a particular area were not authorized to provide Medicare services, that would mean significant gaps in Medicare coverage. Above all else, Johnson administration officials in the Social Security Administration and elsewhere wanted Medicare to succeed, and civil rights posed a significant obstacle to that goal.

Staff members in the Social Security Administration (SSA) tried to resolve these tensions by steering a cautious course, attempting to get the hospitals in the South to change their practices without, at the same time, alienating southern congressmen. Wherever possible, officials tried to use the federal government as, in effect, an excuse for integration, enabling local authorities to argue that they had no choice.

The Public Health Service received primary responsibility for the civil rights aspects of Medicare implementation. In March 1966, the Public Health Service, which had a long tradition of cooperation with local health officials, mailed a questionnaire to the participating hospitals concerning civil rights. In May 1966, Health, Education, and Welfare secretary John Gardner told Lyndon Johnson that about sixty-nine hundred hospitals had assured the federal government that they were in compliance with Title VI. The government cleared fifty-five hundred of these hospitals, which left fourteen hundred that required further investigation. Gardner estimated that 15 percent of the hospital beds in the country were in areas in which there might be a compliance problem. On the eve of Medicare's start-up on July 1, 1966, Robert Ball had information that in Louisiana, Mississippi, Alabama, and South Carolina less than three-quarters of the general hospital beds had been cleared for Title VI.[19] Indeed, in Mississippi only 34 percent of the hospital beds were in compliance when Medicare started.[20]

Of course, the law contained escape hatches that made it possible to start the program without complete compliance. As early as April 1966, administration officials realized that it was reasonable to assume that some southern hospitals would not take steps to comply with Title VI by July 1. In life-threatening situations, however, the law allowed beneficiaries to receive services from a hospital, even if it was not integrated. Emergency medical services could also be provided by hospitals that failed to meet the Medicare standards. These escape hatches mattered because no one wanted a shortage of participating hospitals at the start of Medicare.[21] As late as the end of 1968, Robert Ball admitted that even then there were a "handful of hospitals, largely in the Delta area of Mississippi and Alabama," that had held out and refused to integrate.[22]

The bulk of the work getting hospitals to comply with Title VI fell on a special detail of Public Health Service and Social Security Administration personnel assembled in April 1966, given a quick orientation at the Center for Disease Control, and then sent into the field to inspect, negotiate, and cajole. The members of the special detail discovered that segregation was intertwined with the health care system. One Social Security employee told the story of a visit to a hospital in Louisiana. When the members of the visiting group got to the laboratory, they were dismayed to see that the blood was labeled "black" or "white." Continuing their tour, they arrived in the nursery and were encouraged to notice black babies alongside white babies. Something about the scene in the nursery nagged at them, however. That night they made an unscheduled visit to one of the employees who worked in the nursery. She told them that someone had come into the nursery with the warning that "feds" were visiting. Hospital employees hastily put the black and white babies together.[23]

Some of this resistance to integration was more symbolic than real. Arthur Hess, Robert Ball's chief deputy, described a visit to a southern hospital in which the administrator and the board members were "ranting and raving but as we were leaving, one board member came up to me and quietly said, 'keep the heat on.'"[24] Some southerners, in other words, used Medicare as a excuse for integrating their hospitals on the pretext that if they failed to do so, they would lose a substantial source of money. They realized that it was expensive and inefficient to maintain separate facilities for whites and blacks.

Still, many things, such as assigning rooms without regard to race or color or inviting black doctors to serve on the staffs of white hospitals, took years to achieve, even though administration officials regarded Medicare as a civil rights triumph. On the sixth day after the formal start of the Medicare hospital insurance program, for example, Robert Ball noted civil rights compliance "by hospitals throughout the country and particularly the hundred and hundred and hundreds of hospitals who have changed their fundamental practices throughout the South," calling it one "of the most encouraging aspects of administration in the whole medicare program."[25]

Medicare as a Form of Social Security

Although Medicare became a core program of the Great Society, rather than of the New Deal, it also formed part of a social policy tradition that began with the passage of the Social Security Act in 1935. Medicare was more than a de novo health insurance program, created by planners in the Kennedy and Johnson administrations. It was also an amendment to the Social Security Act and an extension of the Social Security program. With the creation of Medicare, Social Security expanded from making cash payments to retired individuals and their dependents and survivors into the realm of reimbursing hospitals and doctors for services rendered. Despite this expansion, both the traditional Social Security program and Medicare were aimed at the same population: most Medicare beneficiaries were also Social Security beneficiaries. Like Old-Age, Survivors, and Disability Insurance, Medicare would go to the nation's retirees and their families. Furthermore, people paid for hospital insurance (if not the Part B insurance that paid doctors' bills) through payroll taxes collected during their working lifetimes, just as they paid for Social Security.

On the surface, the creation of Medicare looked as though it were a political improvisation on the part of its primary legislative author, Wilbur Mills. In fact, the insurance provisions of the Medicare legislation took much the same form and raised many of the same questions as did the provisions to cover the elderly in the original Social Security Act. Mills had been less than cooperative on Medicare during the Kennedy administration and before Johnson's landslide victory in 1964. Then, as it became clear that the administration had the votes to pass Medicare, he began to soften. On December 2, 1964, Mills sent a signal that he was willing to accept Medicare. "I can support a payroll tax for financing health benefits just as I have supported a payroll tax for cash benefits," he told the Little Rock Lions Club.[26] Hearings began in earnest in 1965, as Mills carefully worked his way through a set of comprehensive amendments to the Social Security Act that would contain Medicare. When he completed his first review of the bill, he improvised a variation on the administration's Medicare proposal. Mills chose to combine three different approaches in one bill. He accepted the administration's approach to hospital insurance, but added a voluntary program to cover doctors' bills and included an expanded public assistance program to pay the doctor and hospital bills of the medically indigent or those on welfare.[27]

It was the voluntary program to cover doctors' bills that was the stunner. Robert Ball of the Social Security Administration, who had sat in on all the hearings and executive sessions and had spent a career observing the behavior of Mills, believed that Mills did not think of this idea ahead of time but rather came up with it on the spot: "The combination of the fact that the AMA was pushing improvements in assistance, that the Republicans had pushed a voluntary plan with government subsidy for the doctors' bills and that the Administration was pushing hospital bills: I think everything kind of came together and he said, 'why not do them all?'" Robert Ball admitted that everyone in the room was "flabbergasted." Still, after consultation with Wilbur Cohen and the administration's political allies in the labor movement and elsewhere, Ball set his staff to work on designing the specifications for what became known as Medicare Part B. From Ball's perspective, Medicare Part B contained many objectionable features, such as voluntary coverage and financing that combined general revenues and contributions from the elderly themselves (through expenses that they would pay out-of-pocket when they visited the doctor and through deductions that would come from their Social Security checks). While it was not something Ball would have proposed, it nonetheless met the immediate political needs of the Johnson administration. It was acceptable. As Ball noted, it provided a way "to get the program we had been fighting for for such a long time."[28]

In its voluntary and state-federal nature, the Mills proposal, which became the Medicare law, resembled the original Social Security proposals of 1935. Medicare Part A, which paid hospital benefits, borrowed the form, if not the content, of Old-Age Insurance; participation was compulsory, and financing came from payroll taxes. Medicaid, which relied on federal grants to the states, expanded the traditional welfare system. It functioned like Old-Age Assistance (means-tested, partially federally funded but state-administered, payments to the elderly) in that it provided health insurance for those outside the social insurance system. Medicare Part B, a separate program to pay the doctors' bills of Medicare beneficiaries, was both voluntary and financed in part by the elderly themselves and thus bore a resemblance to a program of voluntary old-age annuities that was part of the original Social Security proposal but never passed by Congress. Whether policymakers realized it at the time, Medicare did fit a historical pattern.[29]

Medicare Legislation and State-Federal Tensions in Social Security

Medicaid raised the question of state participation in federal social welfare programs, an issue that had preoccupied Social Security policymakers ever since 1935. The four people who played the most important roles in the creation of the Social Security Act—President Franklin Roosevelt, Labor Secretary Frances Perkins, Committee of Economic Security staff director and University of Wisconsin professor Edwin Witte, and Assistant Secretary of Labor Arthur Altmeyer—all got their starts in state government. They were reluctant to disturb the tradition of local primacy over social policy. In a June 8, 1934, statement on economic security, President Roosevelt emphasized "a maximum of cooperation between states and the federal government."[30] The report of the Committee on Economic Security, chaired by Frances Perkins and written by Witte and Altmeyer, preceded congressional introduction of the legislation and contemplated the return of "primary responsibility for the care of people who cannot work to the State and local governments."[31] The report also suggested considerable variation in the design of unemployment compensation programs so that the states could act, in Justice Louis Brandeis's phrase, as the "laboratories of reform." The planners hoped to learn "through demonstration what is best."[32]

Even after the passage of the Social Security Act, welfare and unemployment compensation were administered by the states rather than the federal government. At first, even federal bureaucrats were reluctant to recommend extensions of federal power, although, as their tenure in Washington lengthened, they lost many of their inhibitions and began to advocate that the federal government expand its social responsibilities at the expense of the states.

One could see this transformation in the field of health. The Social Security Board's original, relatively timid health insurance proposals called for a temporary disability insurance program that would replace wages lost because of illness. It would be linked to unemployment compensation programs and hence run by the states. Health insurance, as proposed in 1938 by Senator Robert Wagner (D-N.Y.), had at least tacit approval of the administration as well as active support from the Social Security bureaucrats, taking the form of federal grants to the states to establish local health insurance programs. Only permanent disability insurance or retirement pensions for people forced to drop out of the labor force because of a physical or mental disability would be a federal program, linked to old-age insurance. None of these proposals gained political traction, and they had largely been abandoned by the start of the Second World War.[33]

In time, federal officials came to regard the states as unreliable and inefficient partners who by handling the same social problems in such disparate ways created chaos rather than coherence. The laboratories of reform often produced inferior products, and a race to the bottom—a desire to keep social welfare taxes and expenditures below those of competing states—only reinforced that tendency. It was tempting and, in the mobilization for war, apparently plausible to take the daring step of bypassing the states. They were already too embedded in the welfare system to be swept aside, but federal bureaucrats nonetheless entertained notions of making unemployment federal and of creating national health insurance and disability programs. They hoped in this manner to establish what Arthur Altmeyer, the former Wisconsin state official who became the chief Social Security administrator in 1936, described in 1943 as a "unified comprehensive system of contributory social insurance with no gaps, no overlaps, and no discrepancies."[34]

Political realities trumped bureaucratic aspirations. Neither the states nor their representatives in Congress were particularly willing to cede power to the federal government. The latter did triumph in the field of old-age insurance, but not in the fields of unemployment compensation or temporary disability. Still, the federal government managed to build on its victory in old-age security to gain its objectives in the fields of (permanent) disability and health, as the passage of disability insurance in 1956 and Medicare in 1965 indicated. Reaching these objectives in fields related to health, however, required considerable compromise with the political forces that protected the interests of state governments.[35]

The process began with a major expansion of the Social Security old-age insurance program in 1950 that brought coverage to the self-employed and other previously excluded individuals and raised benefit levels for all recipients. In a 1952 article Wilbur Cohen, then a staff member of the Social Security Administration, described 1951 as a milestone year, noting that in February for the first time in the nation's history, more people received old-age insurance than old-age assistance. In August, also for the first time, the total amount of insurance payments exceeded the amount of old-age assistance payments.[36]

Even with this apparent federal victory over welfare, states remained very much a part of America's social welfare system. Instead of legislating a federal social insurance program for permanent disability in 1950, Congress chose to create a new category of federal grants for state public assistance programs for those who were permanently and totally disabled. Hence the same Social Security legislation that so greatly expanded Social Security in 1950 also expanded the state welfare programs.[37] It appeared to be an axiom of social welfare politics that once a social welfare function that received federal funding was lodged in the states, it tended to remain there. As interest groups developed vested interests in the state programs, they resisted efforts to federalize them.[38]

Even in the field of health care, which had not been effectively colonized by state governments, the states wielded a great deal of power. The American Medical Association (AMA), which represented the interests of the nonacademic and non-research-oriented segments of the medical profession (nearly all the profession), operated through a grassroots structure that covered the entire country. It was in an advantageous position from which to lobby Congress on the evils of national health insurance. The organization was so effective that it even influenced the outcome of a relatively modest measure in 1952 that would have allowed the federal government to preserve the retirement benefits of people who dropped out of the labor force because of a disability. If the measure had passed, it would have meant that a person who was disabled, unable to maintain his or her Social Security payments because he or she could no longer work, would nonetheless be able to receive retirement benefits at the normal retirement age. When the American Medical Association received word of this bill, it dispatched telegrams to every member of the House saying that the "disability freeze" provisions amounted to socialized medicine and did not belong in a Social Security bill. It argued that if the federal government got into the business of deciding whether someone was disabled, it would be a step on the slippery slope toward government control of medicine. The telegram got the attention of Congress, and by the time the measure reached the Senate, the AMA had lined up enough votes to remove the disability freeze from the legislation.

In a desperate effort to reach a compromise, one of the Senate conferees on the bill proposed that state officials, who were presumably closer to the grass roots and more attuned to predilections of the AMA, be allowed to make disability declarations. Although this provision never went into effect, it established a precedent that Congress used to amend the Social Security program in 1954 and 1956. As a consequence, Social Security Disability Insurance, an important extension of Social Security and a key precedent for health insurance, contained a feature, which persists to this day, of having the federal government contract with state governments to certify someone as disabled. Even Social Security, the primary example of a federal program, operated through state intermediaries in the field of disability.[39]

Once the notion of an intermediary was established, it created a model that was applied to Medicare in the course of the hard political bargaining that preceded its 1965 passage. In both the hospital and doctors' part of the program, the federal government utilized local intermediaries. This notion appealed to Wilbur Mills and to other influential conservatives on the Ways and Means Committee, such as Burr Harrison (D-Va.). On May 15, 1964, Wilbur Mills called Wilbur Cohen and told him that he wanted to sell the head of the national Blue Cross Association on the idea of having the local Blue Cross organizations administer the hospital insurance parts of Medicare. He argued that, if the law were written that way, no private insurance company could then be the administering agent; instead, the nonprofit Blue Cross plans across the nation would assume that role.[40] Mills made many suggestions as he jockeyed for position in the Medicare debate and did not follow through on all of them. Still, the notion of an intermediary was one that he preserved throughout the process of drafting the legislation.[41]

Nor was the idea original with Mills. As early as 1962, Representative Harrison, whose vote the Medicare advocates repeatedly tried to get, hinted he might be receptive to an arrangement that would allow hospitals to designate private, voluntary Blue Cross plans as their agents so that the money went from the federal government to Blue Cross rather than directly to the hospital. Important Republicans, such as Senator Jacob Javits of New York and Representative John Byrnes of Wisconsin, also thought in terms of using intermediaries in Medicare, and they believed that private for-profit insurance companies, not just the nonprofit Blue Cross Plans, could have a role.[42]

In the law that President Johnson signed in the summer of 1965, a hospital did not have to deal with the federal government in billing a Medicare patient. Instead, it could work through an intermediary, most often the local Blue Cross organization. Similarly, a doctor could use the services of an intermediary, most often an insurance carrier, to charge a patient for a medical procedure. The patient might receive a bill in an envelope that said Medicare on the return address, but more likely than not the envelope also included the name of an insurance company. A person in Nebraska would almost certainly deal with a different insurance company than would someone in New Jersey.

Medicare, therefore, was a product of the Great Society but one that had been tempered by the tradition of social insurance as established in the New Deal and by the particular history of health insurance in the period between FDR and LBJ. If health insurance had been included in the Social Security Act of 1935 or immediately after, it would have featured federal grants to the states and less of a role for the private intermediaries for the simple reason that these intermediaries had not yet made their mark on the health care market.

Part B and the Question of Private Responsibility

Part B, the provision of Medicare that paid doctors' bills through a combination of general revenues and payments by the elderly themselves, might be seen as another anomalous feature of Medicare. In fact, it marked the continuation of a long discussion in the Social Security field over the proper divisions of public and private responsibility. Throughout the debate that led to passage of the original Social Security Act, people questioned just how coercive a federal program of income security should be. Should all employers and employees be forced to pay social security taxes, or was it sufficient to require that employers provide pensions for their employees? Social insurance, as it was understood at the time of the New Deal, contained the precedent of self-insurance. Most states did not require employers to buy insurance against the risk of industrial accidents from a state insurance fund. Instead, the states permitted the employers to make their own arrangements, so long as they agreed to pay injured workers the monetary and medical benefits specified in the state workers' compensation laws.

At the time of the Social Security Act, a somewhat similar proposal arose in the field of old-age insurance. An amendment proposed by Senator Bennett Champ Clark (D-Mo.), would have given employees a choice between entering the federal Old-Age Insurance plan or continuing with the employer's private plan, provided that the employer's plan was "not less favorable" than the federal plan. In other words, this amendment would have given employees in industries with established pension plans the chance to opt out of the Social Security system. At least one hundred large companies supported this amendment in the summer of 1935.[43] The Clark Amendment, with a tangible and very powerful constituency behind it, came close to passage.

New Deal planners regarded the amendment as anathema. If younger and more affluent workers dropped out of the Social Security system, the cost to the system would become much greater because of the subsidies to older and less affluent workers contained within Social Security. In a political sense, an already vulnerable system that was not scheduled to start collecting taxes until 1937 and paying benefits until 1942 would become that much more vulnerable. Instead of working to expand the system, comparatively advantaged workers and their employers would concentrate on the expansion of private pensions and neglect Social Security. As it turned out, however, the administration mustered its political strength and defeated the Clark Amendment in conference after it had been passed by the Senate.[44]

The result was that public and private pensions expanded together, and the compatibility of the two eventually became one of Social Security's celebrated virtues. In health care, something different happened: the private sector moved ahead of the public sector in the period between 1935 and 1965. Particularly in the postwar era, employer-based health insurance, aided by favorable tax treatment of the premiums paid by employers, emerged as a standard feature of the American welfare state.[45] The perceived success of this fringe benefit caused government planners to cede health insurance for the working population to private insurance companies and community-based nonprofit health plans such as Blue Cross and Blue Shield. In a further concession to the well-regarded health care system and to the political sensitivities of the American Medical Association, the Medicare proposal, as it emerged after 1957, covered only hospital care, not doctors' bills. The private sector, it seemed, had carved out a sizable niche for itself in American health care finance.

Republicans, even liberal Republicans such as Jacob Javits, hoped to increase the responsibilities of private health insurers through Medicare. In the period between 1961 and 1964, when Medicare was hotly contested in Congress, Javits got the labor movement and the White House to agree on a proposal in the spirit of the Clark Amendment. If a retired person already had a health care plan, then Javits suggested that the federal government should allow the person to remain in the plan and should reimburse the plan for the services it provided. Most Republicans, including Congressman Byrnes, rejected the Javits plan but favored one that was voluntary in nature and included doctor as well as hospital benefits. Mills used the Byrnes proposal as the basis for Part B of Medicare.[46]

Governmental Capability and Recruiting for Part B

The voluntary nature of Part B posed ideological problems for the Johnson administration which were solved through a massive effort that illustrated the federal government's administrative capabilities in the era of the Great Society. Social insurance depended on its compulsory nature, which in turn permitted a broad pooling of risk and eliminated problems common to private insurance. Just as with the Clark Amendment, government officials argued that Part B could lead to the problem known in insurance jargon as "adverse selection." The lingering fear about health insurance and the standard argument against private coverage were that only sick people would elect coverage, driving up costs until it became impossible to offer it at a price people could afford to pay. Covering everyone—the sick and the well—took care of that problem. Part B, however, allowed people the luxury of choice. Someone who did not want to pay for it could decide not to take it. If too many people decided against it, then the possibility existed that the whole program would sink under its growing costs. Even beyond this problem, the voluntary nature of Part B meant it would necessarily involve a tremendous outreach effort to persuade people to sign up for it. The enrollment period started almost immediately, beginning on September 1, 1965, and was scheduled to last only a short time, ending in March 1966 (although Congress did later extend it).[47]

For Robert Ball and his colleagues in the SSA, Part B represented the latest in a series of odd congressional creations related to health care that the organization simply had to accept and make work. For the most part, the SSA had benefited tremendously from its working partnership with

Congress. It was the source of all the benefit increases and program liberalizations, and Congress permitted the SSA an almost collaborative role in the legislative process. On controversial matters, however, Congress had much less discretion, and in recompense for the largesse and in aid of the continuing working relationship, the SSA had to take what Congress gave it. The general strategy was to persuade Congress to start small but create a program that could be expanded in an incremental manner into something much larger—slices of salami that, piled on top of one another, soon made a satisfying sandwich, to use Wilbur Cohen's famous image. Sometimes, however, Congress gave the SSA something fundamentally different from what it wanted and forced SSA to work with it. Examples included a disability insurance administered by the states and, in this instance, a voluntary health insurance program to cover doctors' bills. The Social Security Administration might have tried to sabotage such a program by implementing it in a way that showed it was unworkable, but this was never the style of Social Security bureaucrats. Instead, they did something more subtle. They ran Medicare Part B as if it were not a voluntary program but a regular, compulsory, social insurance program that took a slightly different form.[48]

The Social Security Administration mounted a promotional campaign to sell Part B to the 19 million elderly people who were eligible. Newspapers, radio, and television all contained reminders of the need to sign up. Post office trucks carried Medicare messages, and the post office set out piles of applications in each of its thirty-four thousand offices. The return address for forms was simply "Social Security Office," without a specific address. Those already on the Social Security rolls received special punchcard application forms, and by the middle of November 1965, 8 of the 15 million on the rolls had responded. During one memorable week, a million forms flooded into the SSA mailroom. Eighty-eight percent of those who responded indicated that they wanted to sign on for Part B, which, because it would be subsidized from general revenues, presented its beneficiaries with an extremely attractive deal. In this sense, Congress, with administration's consent, had stacked the deck by making Medicare Part B cheaper than similar coverage could be offered by an insurance company.

Nor was the government content to stop there. As new people applied for Social Security benefits, they learned about Medicare Part B. Welfare recipients and civil service pensioners received special pleas to sign up for Part B. The Social Security Administration secured the addresses of still more people through the Internal Revenue Service (IRS) because of a new feature that required tax filers to put their Social Security number on the return. Hence, someone over sixty-five who had a social security number, had not filed an application for social security benefits, but had filed an income tax return in the past two or three years, could be identified by comparing the SSA computer tapes and the IRS computer tapes.[49] The campaign also included special mailings to nursing homes, urging the administrators to tell their patients about Part B and a special project with the Office of Economic Opportunity, which ran the War on Poverty, to hire people to meet with hard-to-reach groups like those in the inner cities and those shut in at home.[50] The rural counterpart of this project was a joint effort with the Department of Agriculture's Rural Community Development Service to reach people in the countryside who might otherwise be ignored. Church groups, trade unions, and councils on the aged also played key roles.[51]

By May 1966, after Congress extended the deadline to sign up by two months, 90 percent of Americans aged sixty-five or over had signed up for Part B.[52] The SSA had turned out the voters and won the election in a landslide. The potential disadvantages of a voluntary program had been largely overcome because of the high participation rate. Soon after the July 1, 1966, start-up for Medicare, Robert Ball spoke with pride of his agency's efforts. "I truly believe," the Social Security commissioner told his employees, "that the preparation for the administration of the medicare program is absolutely unique in the history of public administration in terms of its being a great cooperative effort involving such a large number of governmental and private organizations working together in a very cooperative spirit."[53]

Rewarding the Private Sector: Picking Part B Carriers

An important part of the preparation to which Ball referred involved picking the private health insurance carriers that would act as intermediaries in the Part B program—an act requiring consummate political skill. Congress, working closely as always with the executive agencies, expected these carriers to be efficient and effective, yet it also hoped that the selection of carriers would produce a "configuration that would be broadly representative of the various types of health organizations qualified to perform the necessary functions." This would, in theory, provide a natural experiment to see which type of organization could best perform the necessary function—a quasi-public organization such as Blue Shield, a private insurance carrier, or perhaps a prepaid group health plan. It was another example of local entities serving as laboratories of reform.[54]

The Social Security Administration, working with the congressionally mandated Health Insurance Benefits Advisory Council, issued qualification criteria in November 1965. In general, the criteria favored large, established health insurance organizations that could demonstrate "unquestionable capability to administer effectively and efficiently . . . for a beneficiary group of significant size." As if to underscore this fact, the SSA required that the intermediary should have experience in making "prompt and proper payment under the concept of 'reasonable charges.'" That necessitated the carrier to know about "customary and prevailing charges for physicians services," as well as having "a wide range of ongoing professional relationships in the field of medical and health care" in the area for which it would administer the Part B supplementary medical insurance program.[55]

In all, 136 organizations submitted proposals to the SSA to be Part B carriers. This figure included nearly all the large commercial insurance companies, most of which were given some territory to administer. The fourteen largest health insurance companies were each chosen to play at least some role in the program. In general, the SSA awarded contracts to Blue Shield in the areas with "strong" Blue Shield plans and to commercial insurance companies in their home bases or where they had a large market share.[56]

Politics played a big role in the final selections. In the state of Alabama, for example, Senator John Sparkman, a congressional stalwart who had run for vice president on the 1952 Democratic ticket, recommended to federal officials that the Life Insurance Company of Alabama be selected. The Alabama Medical Association, the organization representing the doctors in private practice who would have to work with the carrier selected, had no objections to this choice but also recommended the Equitable Life Assurance Society of America. The association preferred commercial insurance over a Blue Shield plan. When the SSA investigated, however, it found the Equitable to be preferable to the Alabama Life Insurance Company, but Robert Ball felt that Senator Lister Hill,

Sparkman's colleague who wielded large influence over the federal health care policy, favored an Alabama organization over an outside company such as the Equitable. Complicating the situation, the SSA believed that the "factual situation" dictated the choice of Blue Cross–Blue Shield of Alabama over both the commercial carriers. As a result of these conflicting forces, the SSA postponed a decision on Alabama.[57]

In the state of Arkansas, the choice was clearer. Congressman Mills wrote a letter in December 1965 indicating that the Arkansas Blue Shield would be an "ideal organization" to serve as the Part B carrier for that state. The SSA had little choice but to go along with its primary patron. Ball told Wilbur Cohen that the Arkansas Blue Shield was "not a particularly strong plan but it is adequate and has the support of both the medical society and Mr. Mills." Since all the interest groups were neatly aligned in that relatively small state, the SSA put aside any scruples it might have had about efficiency and effectiveness and went with Mills's choice.

Across the nation, selection of a Part B carrier was a matter of political negotiation. Hence, federal officials consulted members of the congressional delegations with interests in the selection of a Part B carrier in particular states. Before selecting the Aetna Company for Alaska, for example, Ball and Cohen checked with Senator Ernest Gruening (D-Alaska), and before picking Equitable for Idaho they spoke with Senator Frank Church (D-Idaho).[58] Ball and the SSA accommodated not only the predilections of individual members of Congress but also the often-related concerns of the large commercial insurance companies, such as Prudential in New Jersey or the Mutual of Omaha in Nebraska.

Although the Johnson administration tried hard to diversify the selection of Part B carriers and to include group health plans that operated on a prepaid basis and emphasized preventive care, federal officials always stopped short of confrontation and knew when to yield to political realities. The state of New York was large enough and diverse enough that the SSA felt comfortable dividing it into three areas and awarding part to Blue Shield, part to the Metropolitan Life Insurance Company, and part (Brooklyn) to Group Health Insurance.[59] Started as a health cooperative, this nonprofit company had a strong consumer orientation and enjoyed significant support from labor.[60] For the state of Virginia, however, Ball thought it best to yield to politics. "On the basis of Congressman Jennings' reaction," he told Wilbur Cohen, "we might as well give Virginia to an insurance company and we really need more work for Travelers than we have previously given it on the basis of its general position in the industry."[61]

In the end, the Social Security Administration had a large map of the United States printed on a piece of durable white paper with all the state boundaries carefully drawn. Robert Ball wrote the name of the carrier on the state for which it had been selected. The result was a map dominated by Blue Shield organizations but with room for large private carriers such as Aetna in Iowa, Connecticut General in Connecticut, and Equitable in New Mexico. In this way, the federal government began its program of public health insurance by awarding large contracts to private insurance companies and to organizations that represented the interests of private physicians. To get the program off to a strong start, political accommodation held sway.

The Johnson administration's ability to expand the bureaucracy to take on new and complex tasks facilitated the implementation of Medicare. Even before the formal passage of Medicare, Robert Ball submitted a supplemental budget request that would increase the size of the SSA staff from 38,500 to 44,000 people.[62] A few months after Medicare's passage, Ball upped his requests for extra personnel to some 8,000 new employees who would work both at headquarters and in eighty new social security offices across the country. By the spring of 1966, he talked about opening one hundred new offices and hiring 9,000 new staff members. That did not include the 3,000 temporary employees necessary to get Part B applications processed, who were onboard by May.[63] These people and offices aided an effort that involved processing 8 million new applications for benefits, enrolling 17.2 million in Part B, distributing 19 million health insurance cards, and printing 100 million booklets that explained the program.[64]

Medicare as an End Point in Health Policy

For the most part, the news was good in Medicare's early years, but not even a partisan such as Ball could sustain the mood of euphoria. Although he put his initial energy into making the program work, Ball refused to accept the program as it was given to him by Congress. At first he wanted to expand it to cover more people. Within a few years, however, he lobbied to change it. No longer wishing merely to accommodate the health care industry, Ball and many of his liberal allies began to think in terms of regulating it.

Initially Ball and his colleagues had defended Medicare. In an expansive interview with the trade journal *Hospitals* that appeared at the beginning of 1967, Ball said he "couldn't be anything but pleased that by the middle of November [1966] some two million persons had received inpatient hospital services and that by and large the hospitals had received their reimbursements." Even in this contented recitation of Medicare's achievements and potential, however, some problems appeared. One was the actuarial integrity of the program in the face of rising hospital costs. A second was the limits of the coverage. Ball mentioned, in particular, expanding the program to cover people receiving disability benefits and to pay for prescription drugs.[65]

Only two and a half years later, *U.S. News and World Report* titled a similar interview with Ball, "Is Medicare Worth the Price?" To be sure, he still lauded the program. He believed it meant that, for the first time, many of the nation's elderly had gained access to the nation's best hospitals and that minorities had access to the same care as anyone else. Because Medicare certified hospitals for participation on certain quality standards, it meant, as Ball noted, better hospitals for everyone, not just the elderly. Ball admitted, however, that the cost of the program had become a real concern that he could no longer glibly dismiss. The program was simply spending more money, more quickly, than the actuaries had anticipated. Hospital costs had gone up, as had the rate at which the elderly used hospitals. Similarly, physicians' fees had taken what Ball described as "quite a spurt" in the program's first three years. As a result, the SSA had been forced to increase the monthly premium it charged beneficiaries for Part B coverage from three to four dollars a month, not a large dollar amount but nonetheless a 25 percent increase that was a portent of potential problems.

There were also real abuses of the system, with doctors seeing large numbers of patients in congregate settings such as nursing homes and barely taking the time to stop and say hello. Such "gang visits" violated the spirit of the program, as did seeing patients more than was necessary in order to wring the most money from Medicare. Indeed, over five hundred different doctors collected more than fifty thousand dollars from the program. "I find it disturbing to have this many with such large payments," Ball said.[66]

This cautious yet open criticism of the program reflected a changing political situation. By 1969, with the start of the Nixon administration, influential critics of Medicare were easier to find than they had been in 1965. In Congress, the Senate Finance Committee staff, which objected to Wilbur Mills's predominance over Medicare policy, issued a report in 1970 that took a harsh tone. It commented on how the Medicare program had consistently cost more than the actuaries had predicted because of "soaring costs resulting from price increases and greater than anticipated utilization of covered services." It discussed how Medicare paid more to physicians than did other Blue Shield contracts and described the performance of the private carriers as "erratic, inefficient, costly and inconsistent with congressional intent." The muckraking report uncovered inefficiency and inept administration at all levels of the program.[67]

Such a report might have bothered Lyndon Johnson, but not Richard Nixon. The new president tended to see both Social Security and Medicare as strategic traps in which the Democrats tried to maneuver the Republicans into untenable and unpopular positions. "I am becoming increasingly concerned with the sharply rising costs of both the Medicaid and Medicare program," Nixon told his appointee as secretary of health, education, and welfare in the first days of his administration. According to analysis performed for Nixon by economist Arthur Burns, rising costs created pressures to change the program, possibly by adding general revenues to the hospital part of the program. Nixon and Burns feared that bringing in general revenues would make it "increasingly difficult to resist proposals for progressively liberalizing the program."[68]

Liberals might have welcomed the expansion of the program, but they also saw the need for more-fundamental change. "The more we got into the administration of the program," Robert Ball later said, "the more we saw the need for change." In particular, he saw the notion of reimbursing hospitals for their expenses after the fact, rather than setting up-front limits, as flawed.[69] The Social Security Administration, in other words, had been too accommodating, too willing to accept the existing system.

Seven years after Medicare's passage, Ball believed that the situation with regard to Medicare had changed dramatically from the heady days of its passage and implementation. The public now favored changes in the basic system of health care financing and looked to Medicare "to help provide the leverage to bring about change."[70] According to Ball, the program no longer was being criticized for interfering too much in the health care system but rather for interfering too little. The program, therefore, had to take on responsibility for seeing that the health care system was managed better so as to control costs and improve the quality of care. "What the change adds up to," Ball concluded, "is that as a community we are now willing to say that Medicare is a *health care program* with responsibility for preventing the risk and pain of unnecessary and poor quality care and with the responsibility to see over time that good care is provided." No longer was Medicare a simple social insurance program directed "solely at an economic risk" of the elderly being unable to afford health care.[71]

According to this analysis, more parts of the health care system, rather than less, needed to be brought under the government's control so as to increase the system's efficiency. It would take more than an incremental expansion of Medicare to bring about national health insurance. Indeed, reforms were needed to move the federal government away from accommodation and toward regulation.

The fight for national health insurance would not go the same way as the fight to expand retirement benefits through Social Security.[72] Reading the history of Old-Age Insurance into Medicare, one might have taken an expansive view in 1965. One could have predicted that coverage would expand to encompass different age groups in incremental strides toward national health insurance, much as coverage had been extended to more and more occupational groups under Social Security. One could foresee the triumph of Medicare over Medicaid just as Old-Age Insurance had triumphed over Old-Age Assistance and social insurance always triumphed over welfare. One might also have anticipated that the benefits would become more adequate, perhaps encompassing long-term care as well as hospital stays, in a manner similar to the way in which disability insurance had been added to Old-Age Insurance. In the case of Medicare, however, those developments failed to materialize.

Things started out in an encouraging manner. Philip Lee, a prominent health care official in the Johnson and later the Clinton administrations, commented that he and many others believed that a proposal circulating at the end of the Johnson presidency to provide infants with prenatal and postnatal care would become the vehicle to move national health insurance forward. "We thought by 1975 there would be national health insurance," he said.[73] Health care for infants failed to materialize, except for Medicaid, but that was limited to the nation's poor and administered differently in different states. Incremental expansion of Medicare also took place so that by 1972, for example, it covered disability insurance recipients.

Still, the same legislation that contained this expansion also contained rudimentary steps toward health care planning so as to avoid unnecessary capital expansion, as well as support for experiments on how best to implement the idea of prospective reimbursements rather than paying hospitals their "reasonable costs." Thus, legislation that expanded the program also contained measures to constrain its future growth. Within a few years, the goal of containing health care costs replaced that of passing national health insurance on the policy agenda. Despite repeated attempts by Ball and others, notably President Bill Clinton, to link the two goals, the cause of national health insurance foundered. On the road to national health insurance, America stopped at Medicare, which never developed into the comprehensive program that its proponents desired.[74] In Medicare, then, the creators of the Great Society got a little more than they had bargained for, a system that they ultimately wanted to change but could never disavow. In the end, President Truman's presence at the Medicare signing ceremony made no great difference.

Notes

1. Kermit Gordon quoted in Irving Bernstein, *Guns or Butter: The Presidency of Lyndon Johnson* (New York: Oxford University Press, 1996), 181. Other good accounts of Medicare's passage include Richard Harris, *A Sacred Trust* (New York: New American Library, 1966); Theodore Marmor, *The Politics of Medicare* (London: Routledge, Kegan, and Paul, 1970); and Sheri I. David, *With Dignity* (Westport: Greenwood Press, 1985).

2. "Off-the-Record Review," September 26, 1968, diary backup, container 111, Lyndon Baines Johnson Library, Austin, Texas.

3. Daniel M. Fox, *Health Policies, Health Politics: The British and American Experience, 1911–1965* (Princeton: Princeton University Press, 1988); Daniel S. Hirshfield, *The Lost Reform: The Campaign for Compulsory Health Insurance in the United States from 1932 to 1943* (Cambridge: Harvard University Press, 1970); Monte Poen, *Harry S. Truman and the Medical Lobby* (Columbia: University of Missouri Press, 1979); Jennifer Klein, *For All These Rights: Business, Labor, and the Shaping of America's Public-Private Welfare State* (Princeton: Princeton University Press, 2003).

4. Edward D. Berkowitz, *Mr. Social Security: The Life of Wilbur J. Cohen* (Lawrence: University Press of Kansas, 1995), 236.

5. Robert Dallek, *Flawed Giant: Lyndon Johnson and His Times, 1961–1973* (New York: Oxford University Press, 1998).

6. "The Government's Case on Medical Help for the Aged," *National Observer*, March 25, 1963, Robert Ball Papers, Wisconsin State Historical Society, Madison, Wisconsin; Robert M. Ball, "Medical Care: Its Social and Organizational Aspects—the American Social Security Program," *New England Journal of Medicine* 270 (January 1964): 232–36.

7. Robert M. Ball, "Medicare Recollections," speech delivered July 20, 1995, Ball Papers.

8. Edward Berkowitz, "Losing Ground? The Great Society in Historical Perspective," in *The Columbia Guide to America in the 1960s*, ed. David Farber and Beth Bailey, 98–108 (New York: Columbia University Press, 2001).

9. Robert D. Reischauer, "Fiscal Federalism in the 1980s: Dismantling or Rationalizing the Great Society," in *The Great Society and Its Legacy: Twenty Years of U.S. Social Policies*, ed. Marshall Kaplan and Peggy Cuciti (Durham: Duke University Press, 1988), 181.

10. Ball, "Medicare Recollections."

11. Robert M. Ball, "The Assignment of the Social Security Commissioner" (1972), typescript of report to the Secretary of Health, Education, and Welfare, p. 48, Ball Papers.

12. Robert M. Ball, "Hospitals and Health Insurance for the Aged," speech given at the 67th Annual Meeting of the American Hospital Association, August 30, 1965, Ball Papers.

13. Robert M. Ball, "Health Insurance for People Aged 65 and Over: First Steps in Administration," *Social Security Bulletin* 29 (February 1966): 6.

14. Herman Miles Somers and Anne Ramsay Somers, *Medicare and the Hospitals: Issues and Prospects* (Washington: Brookings Institution, 1967), 188, 163, 180.

15. The debate over coverage exclusions has floundered over the question of intent. Did administrative necessity, indifference to the program, the racist views of southern congressmen, or some other factor cause Congress to limit coverage to industrial and commercial workers on regular payrolls? The most convincing piece on this topic is Gareth Davies and Martha Derthick, "Race and Social Policy: The Social Security Act of 1935," *Political Science Quarterly* 112 (November 1997): 217–35. The best empirical work is Robert C. Lieberman, *Shifting the Color Line: Race and the American Welfare State* (Cambridge: Harvard University Press, 1998).

16. Jill Quadagno, "Promoting Civil Rights through the Welfare State: How Medicare Integrated Southern Hospitals," *Social Problems* 47 (2000): 68–89.

17. The best introduction to this monumental legislation and its effects is Hugh Davis Graham, *The Civil Rights Era: Origins and Development of National Policy, 1960–1972* (New York: Oxford University Press, 1990).

18. For a perceptive history of the hospital, see Charles E. Rosenberg, *The Care of Strangers: The Rise of America's Hospital System* (New York: Basic Books, 1987).

19. John Gardner to Lyndon Johnson, May 23, 1966, Ball Papers; Robert Ball, "Speaking Points," June 30, 1966, Ball Papers.

20. Ball, "Talk Delivered on July 7, 1966, to the Employees of the Social Security Administration," Ball Papers.

21. Alvin M. David to Robert M. Ball, April 18, 1966, Ball Papers.

22. Robert M. Ball, interviewed by David G. McComb, November 5, 1968, pp. 40–41, Oral History Collection, Lyndon Baines Johnson Library.

23. "Recollections (Discussions) by Social Security Administration Officials Knowledge and/or Involvement in Certain Stages of Early Implementation of the Medicare Program (Calendar Year 1966)," group oral interview with Arthur Hess, conducted on September 25, 1992, Atlanta Georgia, transcript, p. 11, Library of the National Academy of Social Insurance, Washington, D.C.

24. Ibid., 12.

25. Robert Ball, talk delivered on July 7, 1966, to the Employees of the Social Security Administration in Baltimore, Maryland, at the Start of the Medicare Program, Ball Papers.

26. "Remarks of Congressman Wilbur D. Mills before the Downtown Little Rock Lions Club," December 2, 1964, box 151, Wilbur Cohen Papers, Wisconsin State Historical Society, Madison, Wisconsin.

27. See Marmor, *Politics of Medicare*, 64–65; Wilbur Cohen to the President, March 2, 1965, box 83, Cohen Papers; Fred Arner, "Wilbur Mills' Three-Layered Cake-It's [sic] 25th Birthday," unpublished manuscript; Harris, *Sacred Trust*, 187.

28. Robert Ball, interview with Peter A. Corning, April 5, 1967, p. 16, Columbia Oral History Collection, Columbia University, New York.

29. See Edward D. Berkowitz, "History and Social Security Reform," in *Social Security and Medicare: Individual vs. Collective Risk and Responsibility*, ed. Sheila Burke, Eric Kingson, and Uwe Reinhardt (Washington, D.C.: Brookings Institution, 2000), 42–43.

30. President Roosevelt's statement and other basic documents related to the Social Security Act are contained in *50th Anniversary Edition: The Report of the Committee on Economic Security of 1935* (Washington, D.C.: National Conference on Social Welfare, 1985).

31. *Report of the Committee on Economic Security* (Washington, D.C.: Government Printing Office, 1935), 7.

32. Ibid., 5.

33. See Hirshfield, *Lost Reform*.

34. Arthur Altmeyer to E. Worth Higgins, January 19, 1943, Record Group 47, Records of the Social Security Administration, Central Files 1935–1947, 056–057, box 60, National Archives, Washington, D.C.

35. See Edward Berkowitz, *America's Welfare State: From Roosevelt to Reagan* (Baltimore: Johns Hopkins University Press, 1991).

36. Wilbur J. Cohen, "Income Maintenance for the Aged," *Annals of the American Academy of Political and Social Science*, January 1952, 154.

37. See Edward Berkowitz, *Disabled Policy: America's Programs for the*

Handicapped (New York: Cambridge University Press, 1987), and Deborah Stone, *The Disabled State* (Philadelphia: Temple University Press, 1984).

38. See Christopher Howard, "Workers' Compensation, Federalism, and the Heavy Hand of History," *Studies in American Political Development*, 2002.

39. Berkowitz, *Disabled Policy*, 41–78.

40. Cohen to the Secretary, May 15, 1964, box 81, Cohen Papers.

41. See Julian Zelizer, *Taxing America: Wilbur D. Mills, Congress, and the States* (New York: Cambridge University Press, 1999).

42. Berkowitz, *Mr. Social Security*, 172–73.

43. "Companies Known to Favor Clark Amendment to Social Security Act," in Dr. Rainhard B. Robbins, "Confidential Material Collected on Social Security Act and Clark Amendment," July 11, 1935, in Murray Latimer Papers, Special Collections, George Washington University Library, Washington, D.C.

44. It was nonetheless a close call, as contemporary evidence reveals. Edwin Witte, exhausted by his service as the staff director of the Committee on Economic Security, spent the summer of 1935 traveling through Europe. In his wanderings, he heard little about the progress of the Social Security bill through Congress. Finally, after the August 14 passage of the bill, he received a wire from America. "I feared," Witte noted, "that it would be necessary to take the Clark Amendment in some form; but it is certainly much better that it has been eliminated, even if (as I am told here) there is some sort of an understanding that the Clark Amendment is to be introduced as a separate bill." See Edwin Witte to Murray Latimer, August 11, 1935, Latimer Papers.

45. Sanford M. Jacoby, *Modern Manors: Welfare Capitalism since the New Deal* (Princeton: Princeton University Press, 1997).

46. Berkowitz, *Mr. Social Security*.

47. For more on the problems posed by voluntary health insurance, see Rashi Fein, *Medical Care, Medical Costs: The Search for Health Insurance Policy* (Cambridge: Harvard University Press, 1986); Mark V. Paul, ed., *National Health Insurance* (Washington, D.C.: American Enterprise Institute, 1981); Victor R. Fuchs, *Who Shall Live? Health, Economics and Social Choice* (New York: Basic Books, 1974); and Kenneth Arrow, "Uncertainty and the Welfare Economics of Medical Care," *American Economics Review* 53 (September 1963): 946.

48. Edward Berkowitz, *Mr. Social Security*, 232–38; Derthick, *Policymaking for Social Security*, 325–34; Berkowitz, *Disabled Policy*, 79–104.

49. Robert M. Ball, "A Progress Report on Medicare," talk delivered at the American Management Association, March 21, 1966, Ball Papers.

50. Robert Ball, "A Report on the Implementation of the Social Security Amendments of 1965," talk delivered November 15, 1965, to regional assistant commissioners and regional commissioners of the SSA in Baltimore, Maryland, Ball Papers.

51. Robert M. Ball, "Health Insurance for People 65 or Over," speech delivered at the American Pension Conference, January 26, 1966, Ball Papers.

52. White House Press Release, May 24, 1966, containing "Progress Report to the President on the Launching of Medicare," Ball Papers; Robert Ball, "A

Report on the Implementation of the Medicare Provisions of the 1965 Amendments to the Social Security Act as of May 23, 1966," Ball Papers.

53. Robert Ball, "Talk Delivered on July 7, 1966, to the Employees of the Social Security Administration in Baltimore, Maryland, at the Start of the Medicare Program," Ball Papers.

54. For background on the distinctions between these sorts of plans, see Paul Starr, *The Social Transformation of American Medicine* (New York: Basic Books, 1982), 290–334, and Lawrence D. Brown, *Politics and Health Care Organization: HMOs as Federal Policy* (Washington, D.C.: Brookings Institution, 1983), 3–74.

55. Robert M. Ball to the Secretary, January 27, 1966, Ball Papers.

56. Ibid.

57. Robert M. Ball to the Undersecretary, January 21, 1966, transmitting "Inquiries and Endorsements Regarding Carriers," January 23, 1966, Ball Papers.

58. Ball to Cohen, February 7, 1966, and other fragmentary materials in Part B carrier materials, Ball Papers.

59. Ball to the Undersecretary, January 21, 1966, Ball Papers.

60. "Group Health Insurance, Inc. of N.Y.," undated write-up in Part B Carrier Materials, Ball Papers.

61. Ball to Wilbur J. Cohen, February 7, 1966, Ball Papers.

62. Ball to the Undersecretary, August 12, 1965, Ball Papers.

63. Ball, "Report on the Implementation of the Social Security Amendments"; "A Report on the Implementation of the Medicare Provisions of the 1965 Amendments to the Social Security Act as of May 23, 1966," from Robert M. Ball, commissioner of Social Security, in John Gardner to Lyndon Johnson, May 23, 1966, Ball Papers.

64. Robert Ball, "Chart Talk on Implementing Medicare," Spring 1966, Ball Papers.

65. "An Interview with Robert Ball," *Hospitals* (January 1, 1967): 46–52, Ball Papers.

66. "Is Medicare Worth the Price?" interview with Robert Ball, Social Security commissioner, *U.S. News and World Report*, July 21, 1969, clipping in Ball Papers.

67. *Medicare and Medicaid: Problems, Issues, and Alternatives*, Report of the Staff to the Committee on Finance, United States Senate, February 9, 1970, pp. 3, 9, 20.

68. Richard Nixon to Robert Finch, January 30, 1969, and enclosures, Ball Papers.

69. Robert M. Ball, "Medicare Recollections," July 20, 1995, Ball Papers.

70. "Address by Robert M. Ball," presented before the Washington Journalism Center, Washington, D.C., January 29, 1973, Ball Papers.

71. Ball, "Assignment of the Social Security Commissioner," 49.

72. See Fein, *Medical Care, Medical Costs*, and Derthick, *Policymaking for Social Security*, 336.

73. Philip Lee, interview with Edward Berkowitz, November 27, 1995,

Washington, D.C., Health Care Financing Administration Oral History Collection.

74. For books on the "demise" of national health insurance, see Jacob S. Hacker, *The Road to Nowhere: The Genesis of President Clinton's Plan for Health Security* (Princeton: Princeton University Press, 1997), and Theda Skocpol, *Boomerang: Health Care Reform and the Turn Against Government* (New York: W. W. Norton, 1996).

Justices and Justice

Reflections on the Warren Court's Legacy

Henry J. Abraham

In his trenchant review of a book on the Warren Court by Lucas A. Powe Jr., a professor of law and government at the University of Texas,[1] A. E. Dick Howard quickly identified the gravamen of the Warren Court's legacy:

> Like some Nordic giant, the Warren Court has been both mythologized and demonized. To civil libertarians and civil rights activists, it is the bastion against such evils as injustice and racism. To conservatives it was an arrow aimed at the heart of the Constitution. Alabama's [Democratic U.S. representative] George Andrews spoke for many such critics when, chiding the Court for its 1962 decision banning prayer in the public schools, he declared, "They put Negroes in the school and now they've driven God out."[2]

Any attempt to analyze and evaluate the performance of the Supreme Court of the United States in our constitutional firmament must address two basic considerations that inform its role: one, of course, is the lifetime membership of justices; the other is the particular membership's perception of the appropriate parameters of its power and authority.

Invoking the ubiquitous dichotomy that governs the latter, namely, "judicial activism" and "judicial restraint," about which so much has been written, the Warren Court was unquestionably an activist tribunal—a judgment that both the proponents and the detractors of its jurisprudence share. It would be clearly apposite to regard it, as does Powe, as "a functioning part of the Kennedy-Johnson liberalism of the mid and late 1960s,"[3] when Justice William Brennan, who had joined the Court in 1956, was assuredly its most successful "Marshaller," in predictable concord with the chief justice, Justices Hugo Black and William Douglas, and at least one of the trio of post-1958 appointments: Justices Arthur Goldberg, Abe Fortas, and Thurgood Marshall.

The meaning of "judicial activism" and "judicial restraint" may be defined by six criteria. *Activist* justices engage in at least several of the following exercises:

1. Going out of their way to find an issue not properly before the Court
2. Construing a statute (or constitutional provision) demonstrably counter to its intent or, more significant, its language
3. Reaching the *constitutional* issue unnecessarily or prematurely
4. Accepting cases for review that have a priori been properly settled below
5. Providing relief in a fashion too generous or too broad to be justifiable under the litigation at issue
6. Patently supplanting the legislative process[4]

In contrast, *restraintist* justices reportedly make decisions generally based on different guidelines:

1. Limiting the circumstances the Court takes into consideration in rendering its rulings
2. Determining the narrowest possible legal grounds for each decision, preferring to rely on statutory rather than constitutional bases
3. Relying on precedent, on stare decisis, overruling it only in extremis
4. Applying either the *letter* of the law rather than a judge-determined *spirit* thereof or the "original intent" of the Founding Fathers rather than embracing the concept of a "living Constitution"
5. Deferring to the "representative" legislative and/or executive branches of the government (unless those two elected bodies have violated the Constitution, legal precedent, or some fundamental legal principle) out of respect for democratic principles, especially the separation of powers
6. Eschewing personal preferences on political and social matters.[5]

Although the formulation of such basic definitions and criteria is obviously not an exact science, a look at the Warren Court's personnel and its jurisprudence will confirm the judgment that it was indeed an activist Court, one that engaged in a plethora of judicial legislating. Such a judgment does not, however, ignore the approbation that greeted its frequently seminal decisions on the part of what was arguably a majority of the body politic, most emphatically and enthusiastically headed by the word of academe.

On September 8, 1953, only eight months after Dwight D. Eisenhower had assumed office, Chief Justice Vinson died unexpectedly, evoking one of Justice Felix Frankfurter's nastiest cracks on record: "This is the first indication I have ever had that there is a God."[6] Eisenhower was thus provided with his initial opportunity to act on a Supreme Court vacancy, and his appointment of Governor Earl Warren of California would revolutionize American constitutional law. It represented a political payment for Warren's swinging of all but eight of the seventy-member California delegation to Eisenhower rather than to Senator Robert A. Taft of Ohio at the 1952 Republican Party convention. Alas, at the end of his presidency, Ike would pronounce his selection of Warren and, later, that of Brennan as his two "biggest political mistakes."[7]

There is no question that Earl Warren provided the leadership for a liberal activist approach to public law and individual rights that went far beyond the Eisenhower brand of progressive Republicanism. The chief justice, usually with Justices Black, Douglas, and Brennan by his side, wrought a constitutional revolution in the application of the Bill of Rights to the states in his generous interpretation of specific constitutional provisions of criminal justice safeguards for the individual ("Yes, but was it fair?" was a standard question he would put to prosecutors); in the broad application and interpretation of both the letter and the spirit of the Civil War Amendments; in rendering any executive or legislative classification by race and nationality or alienage "suspect"; in the liberalization of the right to foreign travel and to vote; in an elevated commitment to freedom of expression; and in many other sectors of the freedom of the individual.

Earl Warren, of course, did not do this alone; the seeds were already there, growing since the 1937 "switch in time that saved nine." But it was he who provided the judicio-political leadership on the Court, encouraged by the aforementioned trio of liberal associate justices. It was he whose assertive view of the judicial role and vision of constitutional fulfillment made possible the judicial revolution that he was determined to achieve, even if that meant letting a personal sense of right and wrong *determine* the outcome of cases, supporting the result with any convenient—and not necessarily logically articulated or inevitably convincing—result. It was Warren whose knowledge of the humanistic capabilities of men and women and applied administrative savoir faire succeeded in "massing" the Court for the big decisions, with results second only to those achieved so dramatically in different constitutional realms by the great John Marshall, a century and a half earlier. And it was he whose dedication to the ideals of equal justice under law gave hope to those who were economically and socially downtrodden; he whose insistence that for democratic society to succeed, its people must have ready access to their government, including the judiciary.

Earl Warren—who involved his clerks heavily in the production of his opinions—was not a great lawyer in the mold of a Roger Taney or a Charles Evans Hughes; not a great legal scholar in the tradition of a Louis Brandeis or a Felix Frankfurter; not a supreme stylist like a Benjamin Cardozo or a Robert Jackson; not a judicial philosopher like an Oliver Wendell Holmes or a Hugo Black; not a resourceful, efficient administrator like a William Howard Taft or a Warren Burger. But he was the chief justice par excellence—second in greatness as an institutional leader only to John Marshall in the eyes of most impartial students of the Court, as well as many of the Warren Court's legion of abiding critics. Like Marshall, he understood and utilized the tools of pervasive and persuasive power leadership available to him; a genuine statesman, an assertive executive in judicial compass, an experienced politician, he knew how to bring people together, how to set a tone, and how to fashion a mood. He was a wise man and a warm, kind human being. He was his Court, *the* judicial activist Court; he viewed law as an instrument to obtain "the right" result. Indubitably, he was the personification of the result-oriented jurist, who rejected constitutional, legal, and historical barriers to the results he regarded as "right"—he was a legislating jurist.

It is a pity that some of the momentous Constitution-revolutionizing opinions Earl Warren wrote were not delivered with more clarity and explicitness, with more careful legal reasoning, more historical proof—a pity because the public he loved and served so conscientiously would have been better able to understand themselves and him. Yet in G. Edward White's frank avowal, the ethical values he found underlying the Constitution were seminal. Warren believed that vindication of the basic moral imperatives of the Constitution as he perceived them was more significant than doctrinal consistency.[8] Still, his aggressive, determined statesmanlike leadership created more milestones in constitutional adjudication and interpretation than did any other chief justiceship save Marshall's.

Among the many prevailing decisions Warren himself wrote, five stand out. The first is *Brown v. Board of Education of Topeka I* (1954), his supreme achievement. His unanimous Court declared compulsory segregation by race in the public schools to be an unconstitutional violation of the Fourteenth Amendment's guarantees of equal protection of the laws.[9] Of this decision, which wrought a veritable sociopolitical revolution in our land—and against which President Eisenhower had lobbied directly with Warren—John P. Frank, a close Court observer and once a clerk to Justice Black, wrote: "Of his individual contributions, history will have enough to say, but it will never need to say more than he wrote in the *Brown* school-segregation opinion."[10]

Second, in *Watkins v. United States* (1957) the Court held 6–1 that "the vice of vagueness" so prevalent in the conduct of congressional investigating committees (particularly the House Committee on Un-American Activities) was an unconstitutional derogation of the due process of law clause of the Fifth Amendment.[11] The chief justice's rambling, passionate opinion constituted virtually a lecture to Congress on fundamental constitutional law.

The third noteworthy case is *Reynolds v. Sims* (1964), where the Court ruled 6–3, in what was arguably a novel and rather dubious interpretation and application of the Fourteenth Amendment, that both houses of a state legislature must be apportioned on a "one person, one vote" basis, with the chief justice holding that "legislators represent people not trees or acres. Legislators are elected by voters, not farms or cities or economic interest."[12] Warren regarded his Court's work in redistricting and reapportionment of even greater fundamental importance than that of desegregation.

Fourth, in *Miranda v. Arizona* (1966), the Court held 5–4 that the confession of a person in custody cannot be used against that individual unless the accused has been provided with a series of six specific and protective rules against self-incrimination.[13] The highly prescriptive nature of Warren's *Miranda* opinion brought down the wrath of many objective constitutional scholars as well as that of law enforcement officials and laypeople.

Finally, *Powell v. McCormack* (1969) was Chief Justice Warren's valedictory opinion before turning over the center seat to U.S. Court of Appeals judge Warren Earl Burger, who had disagreed in the lower court with the outgoing chief in this very case. Here, Warren ruled for his 8–1 Court that the U.S. House of Representatives had improperly excluded the errant Adam Clayton Powell as a member of that body in 1967 because—whatever else Powell might have done, and there was plenty— he did meet the requirements of the Constitution as to age, citizenship, and residence.[14] It was characteristic and fitting that this holding, Warren's last opinion before his retirement at the conclusion of the Court's 1968–69 term, was another lecture to Congress on constitutional law, specifically on the separation of powers and checks and balances; that it was for an almost unanimous Court; and that it dealt with an issue most earlier courts would have declined to hear on the grounds that the issue represented a "political question" into which "thicket" judicial bodies should not venture lest they drown in a "mathematical quagmire"—the argument Justices Felix Frankfurter and John Marshall Harlan II had so warmly, albeit unsuccessfully, pressed on colleagues and country in *Baker v. Carr*, the 1962 "parent" of the 1964 decision in *Reynolds v. Sims*.[15]

Among other key decisions rendered by the Court under Earl Warren's sixteen years at its helm were, for example, such far-reaching and contentious rulings as those of *Engel v. Vitale* (1962), written by Justice Black for a 6–1 Court, declaring unconstitutional—on grounds of a violation of the constitutionally mandated separation of church and state— the daily recitation of state-prepared and prescribed prayers in public schools;[16] *New York Times v. Sullivan* (1964), penned by Justice Brennan for a unanimous court, which vastly extended freedom of the press by holding that a public official could not collect on a defamatory falsehood relating to official conduct unless it could be proved that it "was made with actual malice";[17] the Black-authored 9–0 *Gideon v. Wainwright* (1963) landmark that nationalized the Sixth Amendment's guarantee to counsel in *all* criminal cases;[18] and the highly controversial 1965 Connecticut birth control case of *Griswold v. Connecticut*,[19] in which Justice Douglas's 7–2 majority opinion found a sweeping constitutional zone of privacy, not owing to any *specific* constitutional language but as a result of what he termed "penumbras," "emanations," and "radiations" from five different provisions of the Bill of Rights. Here, the normally solid Warren majority lost its usual faithful ally, Hugo Black, who, together with fellow dissenter Potter Stewart, could "find in the Constitution no language which either specifically or impliedly grants to all individuals a *constitutional* right of privacy."[20] Three of these nine cases were decided unanimously: (*Brown, New York Times,* and *Gideon*); in three, only one justice dissented: (*Watkins,* Clark; *Powell,* Stewart; and *Engel,* Stewart); one, *Reynolds,* saw three dissenters (Frankfurter, Harlan, and Clark); and one, *Griswold,* had two (Black and Stewart). Only one of the nine milestones resulted in a 5–4 vote, the famous (or infamous) *Miranda* case, in which Harlan, Stewart, White, and Clark dissented. Yet that case has withstood all attempts to overturn it, most recently in 2000, when Chief Justice William Rehnquist, hardly an Earl Warren jurisprudential clone, wrote the 7–2 opinion, upholding it.[21]

Only three members of the Warren Court spanned the entire course of the sixteen years of its existence (1953–69); the Chief Justice and Associate Justices Black and Douglas. Warren stepped down in 1969. He had initially announced his retirement one year earlier but withdrew it when the Senate refused to confirm Abe Fortas for the position. Black and Douglas would stay until health dictated their retirements in 1971 and 1975, respectively. These three constituted the center of power and success of the Warren revolution, joined in 1956 by Brennan, who, in the opinion of many Court watchers, ought to share the Warren Court's title. The four encountered little difficulty in finding the necessary fifth vote from one of the other justices, especially during the Warren Court's last seven years (1962–69), when the quartet could count firmly on Justices Goldberg, Fortas, and Marshall. Often in dissent during the chief's 1953–69 tenure were Justices Reed, Clark, Burton, Whittaker, Stewart, and White. For sundry reasons, they were uncomfortable with what they viewed as the Court's forays into judicial activism. Still, it was only during a three-year period at the height of the cold war era that they found themselves more often than not in the controlling majority, one created and lead by Justices Felix Frankfurter and John Marshall Harlan II. It was a short prevailing alliance that was terminated by Frankfurter's retirement in 1962 and his succession by Arthur Goldberg, who quickly joined the Warren quartet's jurisprudential commitment, one followed by Abe

Fortas during his brief tenure from 1965 to 1969, after President Lyndon Johnson had coaxed Goldberg off the Court in favor of his old friend.

As indicated, the two major opponents of the Warren majority's judicial activism were Justices Frankfurter and Harlan II, arguably the two most acute jurisprudential intellectuals then on the Court. Yet Frankfurter was one of the chief architects of *Brown v. Board of Education*, both *Brown I* and *II*.[22] The fundamental civil libertarian, who was a heroic, if ultimately unsuccessful, leader in the struggle to save the lives of Nicola Sacco and Bartolomeo Vanzetti, a longtime Harvard University professor of law, and faithful ally of President Franklin Roosevelt, was described in 1936 by *Fortune* magazine as "the single most influential individual in the United States."[23] The committed champion of the poor, the oppressed, the underdog, the persecuted, this native of Vienna, Austria, was FDR's third appointment early in 1939. A passionate believer in the democratic process with an abiding regard for the British concept of legislative supremacy, he would dedicate his twenty-three years on the high court to the proposition that the people should govern, that it was emphatically up to their elected representatives in the legislature, not to the appointed judiciary, to make laws. Thus, Frankfurter became increasingly known as the articulate and persuasive advocate of judicial abnegation in favor of legislative action. "When in doubt, don't," became the Frankfurter on-bench maxim for judicial involvement. So dedicated was he to the principle of judicial restraint that Yale University's Fred Rodell referred to him sarcastically as "the Supreme Court's Emily Post."[24] Professor Walton Hamilton characterized him as "weaving crochet patches of legal realism on the fingers of the case."[25] Frankfurter's jurisprudential philosophy, of course, enabled him to back FDR's New Deal program totally—enacted as it was by the people's duly chosen representatives in Congress.

In economic-proprietarian legislation, Frankfurter could be found in agreement with the other Roosevelt-appointed justices. But when it came to the interpretation of the Bill of Rights, especially its Black- and Douglas-sponsored "incorporation" of the document, that is, its application to the states, and its "nationalization," he would often part company with Black, Douglas, Warren, and Brennan, for Felix Frankfurter brought the same principled sense of judicial restraint to legislation concerning human and cultural rights as he did to legislation concerning economic-proprietarian issues. He could be a powerful spokesman on behalf of *procedural* due process of law, and he accorded the Fourth Amendment's safeguards against "unreasonable searches and seizures" a place second to none in the Bill of Rights—more so than did his jurisprudential adversary Hugo Black. Yet this champion of human freedom stood like Canute against his *personal* convictions when it came to his role as a jurist. Frankfurter's scrupulous adherence to his perceived duty as judge qua judge, despite his personal beliefs and commitments, is best illustrated by his most famous dissenting opinion, delivered in a seminal civil liberties case. It was handed down in 1943, ten years before Earl Warren became chief justice, when Robert H. Jackson led a 6–3 Court in overruling an earlier Frankfurter opinion and declaring a West Virginia statute that compelled all public school children to salute the flag as a daily exercise to be unconstitutional as a violation of the free exercise of religion clause.[26] Frankfurter wrote:

> One who belongs to the most vilified and persecuted minority in history is not likely to be insensible to the freedoms guaranteed by our Constitution. Were my purely personal attitude relevant I should whole-heartedly associate myself with the general libertarian view in the Court's opinion, representing as they do the thought and action of a lifetime. But as judges we are neither Jew, nor Gentile, neither Catholic nor agnostic. We owe equal attachment to the Constitution and are equally bound by our judicial obligations whether we derive our citizenship from the earliest or the latest immigrants to these shores. As a member of this Court I am not justified in writing my private notions of policy into the Constitution, no matter how deeply I may cherish them or how mischievous I may deem their disregard.[27]

Committed to the proposition that "there is not under our Constitution a judicial remedy for every political mischief," as he put it in his famed 1962 dissent in *Baker v. Carr*,[28] a statement enshrined in many an obituary when he died three years later, he believed that "in a democratic society like ours, relief must come through an aroused popular conscience that sears the conscience of people's representatives," not by judicial fiat.[29]

Frankfurter's credo did not prevail in the Warren Court, but it was carried forward by his jurisprudential disciple and soulmate, John Marshall Harlan II, who was often referred to as "the Justices' Justice." In stark contrast to the judicial posture of his grandfather, John Marshall Harlan I (1877–1911), the grandson spent his sixteen years on the Court arguing for a limited judicial role in political and social issues and for a strict separation of state and federal responsibilities, a jurisprudence not exactly popular with the Warren Court's majority. With almost half of his full opinions in dissent (296 of 613), he never tired of exhorting his colleagues as well as his fellow citizens that the only viable role for the Court ought to be a limited one, that it should at all costs stay out of the Frankfurter-decried "political thicket," that it should eschew the dismantling of federalism. And as he put it so memorably in dissenting from the contentious 6–3 *Reynolds v. Sims* Warren opinion extending the "one person, one vote" rule to *both* houses of state legislators:

> The Constitution is not a panacea for every blot upon the public welfare, nor should this Court, ordained as a judicial body, be thought of as a general haven for reform movements. This Constitution is an instrument of government, fundamental to which is the premise that in a diffusion of governmental authority lies the greatest promise that this Nation will realize for all its citizens. This Court, limited in function in accordance with that premise, does not serve its high purpose when it exceeds its authority, even to satisfy justified impatience with the slow workings of the political process.[30]

The essential legacy of the Warren Court is that it saw the judicial function and its parameters of power and authority differently. Led by a decisive quartet of strong-minded individuals with little or no judicial experience, except for Brennan, but rather with executive (Warren and Douglas) or legislative (Black) backgrounds, it was determined to do what it could to redress the plethora of pat but genuine grievances and patent injustices in the body politic that Congress was evidently both unwilling and unable to accomplish until the Court paved the way in the tumultuous 1950s and 1960s. In doing so it overturned 45 precedents in its 16 years of existence, versus a total of 88 in the 164 years of its predecessors, but this did not appear to trouble the majority of justices, who clearly took the view that if it took judicial legislating to trigger the nascent civil rights and liberties revolution, so be it! "Equal Justice Under Law," the hallowed inscription on the front portals of the Court's magnificent edifice, gave way to "Justice at Any Cost," a result evidently embraced ultimately by the populace and its representatives in Congress, albeit not without considerable toil, trouble, and controversy. There is little doubt, if any at all, that Earl Warren's Court faced and embraced political issues that would very likely not have been resolved, at least not at the time, through the legislative process. More than any other Supreme

Court in our history, with the arguable exception of John Marshall's, the Warren Court practiced judicial activism in extremis. The extent to which that achievement was justified depends, in final contemplation, on one's perception of the nature of the judicial process and the parameters of its authority and power in our fundamental constitutional constellation.

Notes

1. Lucas A. Powe Jr., *The Warren Court and American Politics* (Cambridge, Mass.: Harvard University Press, Belknap Press, 2000).

2. A. E. Dick Howard, review of *The Warren Court and American Politics*, by Lucas A. Powe Jr., "Book World," *Washington Post*, May 7, 2000, 6.

3. Powe, *Warren Court*, 494 n. 1.

4. Henry J. Abraham, "Reflections on Judicial Activism and Judicial Restraint," National Endowment for the Humanities Lecture, Knox College, Galesburg, Ill., June 25, 1985.

5. Michael Ross Fowler, *With Justice for All? The Nature of the American Legal System* (New York: Prentice Hall, 1998), and Henry J. Abraham, *The Judicial Process: An Introductory Analysis of the Courts of the United States, Britain, and France,* 7th ed. (New York: Oxford University Press, 1998), chap. 9, n. 2.

6. As recounted by Joseph L. Rauh Jr., "The Chief," *New Republic*, August 9, 1982, 31. Frankfurter was utterly disdainful of Vinson's intellectual and leadership prowess, and he did not like him personally. The sentiment was mutual. For some of the following material I have relied heavily on my *Justices, Presidents, and Senators: A History of the U.S. Supreme Court Appointments from Washington to Clinton,* new and rev. ed. (New York: Rowman and Littlefield, 1999), chap. 20, "The Warren Court."

7. Impromptu press conference aboard Air Force One, December 1959 and/or January 1960. The statement was repeatedly reiterated by the media.

8. G. Edward White, *Earl Warren: A Public Life* (New York: Oxford University Press, 1982), chap. 16, "Ethics and Activism."

9. 347 U.S. 483. *Bolling v. Sharpe,* 347 U.S. 497 (1954), applied the *Brown* ruling to the District of Columbia on the same day, but on due process of law grounds.

10. John P. Frank, *Marble Palace: The Supreme Court in American Life* (New York: Alfred A. Knopf, 1958), 86.

11. 354 U.S. 178. The sole dissenter was Justice Tom Clark.

12. 377 U.S. 533, at 562. *Reynolds* was the first-born child of Brennan's historic opinion in *Baker v. Carr,* 369 U.S. 186 (1962).

13. 384 U.S. 436.

14. 395 U.S. 486.

15. 369 U.S. 186; 377 U.S. 533.

16. 370 U.S. 421.
17. 376 U.S. 254; quotation at 279.
18. 372 U.S. 335.
19. 381 U.S. 479.
20. Ibid., dissenting opinion, at 507, 509, 511.
21. *Dickerson v. United States,* 68 LW 4566.
22. 347 U.S. 483 (1954) and 349 U.S. 294 (1955), respectively.
23. As quoted by Edward V. Heck, "The Liberals' Spokesman," *Judicature* 78, no. 1 (1954): 55.
24. Fred Rodell, *Nine Men: A Political History of the Supreme Court of the United States from 1790–1855* (New York: Alfred A. Knopf, 1955), 271.
25. As quoted by Rodell, ibid., 271.
26. *West Virginia State Board of Education v. Barnette,* 319 U.S. 624 (1943). The earlier Frankfurter opinion was *Minersville School District v. Gobitis,* 310 U.S. 586 (1940).
27. *West Virginia State Board of Education,* 319 U.S. at 646.
28. 369 U.S. 186, at 270.
29. Ibid., at 270.
30. 377 U.S. 533, at 624–25.

Part IV

Legacies

The Great Society's Civil Rights Legacy

Continuity 1, Discontinuity 3

Hugh Davis Graham

Looking back today at the directions American society has taken since World War II, most scholars see the 1960s as a cultural and political watershed and emphasize the discontinuities that flowed from it.[1] The subtitle of this essay on civil rights policy reflects this view and reads like a baseball score, with discontinuity winning, 3 to 1. The three great discontinuities in civil rights policy that flowed from the watershed of the 1960s are linked closely to the legislation of 1964 and 1965, the breakthrough period of Lyndon Johnson's Great Society program. But the policy changes range through the "long 1960s" and include initiatives by presidents Kennedy (the affirmative action executive order of 1961, the Equal Pay Act and the civil rights bill of 1963) and Nixon (the revived Philadelphia Plan of 1969, the voting rights renewal of 1970, the equal employment amendments of 1972, and Title IX of the education amendments of the same year).

The three major discontinuities were, in order of occurrence: (1) the triumph of liberal nondiscrimination, including the destruction of the biracial caste system in the South; (2) the emergence of race-conscious affirmative action; and (3) the return of mass immigration. The policies that shaped these forces gained momentum from interventions by the Warren Court but were grounded mainly in statutes and administrative directives forged by the elected branches of government. Their impact was accelerated in many instances by judicial decisions that upheld the statutes and agency regulations. But policymaking by the elected branches of the federal government is the main concern of this essay. Together, the three new forces transformed American civil rights policy in ways that were scarcely imaginable in 1960. Indeed, two of them, affirmative action and mass immigration, brought changes that were neither intended nor foreseen by the sponsors of the statutes and executive orders on which they were based.

Arrayed against this tidal wave of discontinuity is the lonely continuity in civil rights policymaking noted in the subtitle. What is this continuity? It is the long process, largely hidden, unforeseen, and unacknowledged, of selecting official minorities.[2] Students of the 1960s, who recognize the decade's debates over nondiscrimination, affirmative action, and immigration reform, may be puzzled by a reference to official minority designation in the 1960s, not recalling this topic in the era's civil rights debates. They would be correct. Controversy over minority preferences flared momentarily during 1964 in the debates over the civil rights bill but was quieted by the pervasive national consensus behind the liberal principle of equal individual rights. The issue of minority preferences returned the following decade, in the national debate over the Bakke case of 1978 involving medical school admissions, and again in the Reagan administration's battles over hiring quotas in the 1980s. Yet a close reading of the evidence, much of it fugitive, reveals that government decisions about which groups are officially recognized as protected minorities and which are not, decisions carrying enormous significance for determining winners and losers in the competition for government benefits, were rooted in civil rights policymaking during the 1940s and 1950s. Whereas passage of civil rights, voting rights, and immigration reforms in 1964–65 and the shift by federal agencies and courts to race-conscious affirmative action policies during 1969–71 marked sharp departures from the past, the evolution of official minority doctrine in the United States reaches from World War II to the end of the century in a seamless process that, though shrouded in obscurity, shows common characteristics, many of them with unintended and problematic consequences.

The Triumph of Liberal Nondiscrimination

Of the three great policy discontinuities, only the first qualifies as a major change that produced the consequences its sponsors intended. This was, however, the most important change of them all: the destruction of the Jim Crow system in the southern and border states, accompanied by a widening national commitment to gender equality as well. It marked the apparent triumph in the 1960s of liberalism's core doctrine, so long compromised by half measures and hypocrisy, of equal individual rights. It was couched in classic liberalism's negative-action language of prohibitions against unequal treatment among citizens who inherently possessed equal rights claims. The major legislative benchmarks of these changes during the baker's dozen years of the "long sixties" are well known: equal pay for men and women in 1963, equal rights in public accommodations and employment in 1964, voting rights and nondiscriminatory immigration in 1965, open housing in 1968, and gender equality in education in 1972.[3]

The breakthrough laws of 1964 and 1965, unlike their predecessors, were radical in intent, and they were effective because they were radical. The radicalism of these measures lay not in their command against harmful discrimination on the basis of race, color, or creed. Such nondiscrimination policy had characterized liberal reform proposals and measures since the Reconstruction era. Rather, the civil rights and voting rights laws of 1964–65 were radical because they permanently expanded federal authority with effective enforcement power over vast areas of behavior previously free of national coercion, including private as well as public employment; customer choice in stores, hotels, restaurants, and places of amusement; and voting procedures. These laws broke the back of Jim Crow and in the process produced more-rapid gap closing in racial incomes, especially in the South, home to half of all black Americans, than did subsequent affirmative action policies in the 1970s and beyond.[4]

Race relations in the American South, for centuries a wellspring of both degradation for blacks and psychosocial corruption for whites, improved dramatically after the 1960s. Yet outside the South, black-white relations hardened in the wake of inner-city riots that largely spared the South, where blacks had won immediate gains from the civil rights and voting rights laws. Ironically, Martin Luther King, the martyred patron saint of the black civil rights movement who was widely vilified by white southerners, was numerically the Great Liberator of far more southern whites than blacks. The movement that King spiritually led broke the shackles of Jim Crow from 11 million African Americans and at the same time destroyed an institutionalized system of racial superiority that warped the socialization of 43 million southern whites. Americans born since the 1960s, exposed to media reports of persistent African American grievances (racial isolation in housing and schools, disproportionate imprisonment, racial profiling by police, low median family income), have only their history, rather than their memory, to tell them how much worse it used to be.[5]

Affirmative Action and Mass Immigration as Unintended Consequences

The other two discontinuities, and the single continuity as well, chiefly represent unintended consequences of policy change. From the viewpoint of policymaking intent, the score could be rephrased as Intended Consequences 1, Unintended Consequences 3. A recent book by Steve Gillon, *That's Not What We Meant to Do*, explores why, and to what degree, the rapid policy changes of the 1960s are so rife with unintended consequences.[6] Few would be so dramatic as affirmative action policy, which in the name of more effective enforcement appeared to violate the very provisions of the Civil Rights Act (Titles VI and VII) on which affirmative action was based. By affirmative action I mean, as most people do in common usage, "hard" affirmative action, the policy of compensatory minority preferences that emerged from Nixon's revived Philadelphia Plan during 1969–71.[7] Hard affirmative action is thus distinguished from the federal government's original, "soft" form of affirmative action, begun by President Kennedy and Vice President Johnson in 1961 through executive order and based on nondiscrimination augmented by various forms of outreach, such as targeted recruiting, training, internships, and the like. As sociologist John Skrentny observes in *The Ironies of Affirmative Action*, hard affirmative action was not sought by the civil rights coalition, was rejected by the legislative leadership of the Great Society, and was prohibited in the Civil Rights Act itself.[8] Its rapid emergence and subsequent consolidation, first in federal agencies and courts and ultimately in the legislative trenches of American policymaking and in corporate boardrooms and university administrations as well, mark it as one of the most successful examples of policy entrepreneurship and interest-group politics in twentieth-century America.

The third discontinuity is the return of mass immigration to America. In passing the Immigration and Naturalization Act of 1965, the Johnson administration and the bipartisan legislative leadership explained that the law would dismantle the national origins quota system constructed in the 1920s. This change was consistent with the administration's drive to eliminate bias from government policy, and it was an important symbolic act in cold war competition. Government leaders pledged, however, that the reform would not significantly change the size and origins of American immigration. Immigration would rise little above customary levels of around three hundred thousand a year, the bill's sponsors said, with most immigrants still coming from Europe. The only significant change would be a shift in European immigration toward countries of origin in eastern and southern Europe, those most penalized by the national origins quotas.[9] Instead, between 1965 and the end of the century, a vast tide of 30 million immigrants arrived, more than three-quarters of them from Latin America and Asia.

Thus the second and third discontinuities, affirmative action and mass immigration, involved unintended consequences and have remained controversial. By all evidence available to researchers, policymakers in the Kennedy and Johnson administrations were sincere in their claims that their reforms would not and should not produce the results that they ultimately did produce: hard affirmative action and mass immigration from Latin America and Asia. What Americans have argued about since the 1960s is not whether the changes brought by affirmative action and mass immigration were intended but whether they were wise. The two issues shared parallel but otherwise not closely related origins in the 1960s. Both issues then stirred controversy during the 1970s and 1980s but seemed little connected to each other. In the 1990s, however, Americans began to notice that the two issues were converging.[10]

The Strange Convergence of Affirmative Action and Immigration Policy

It is from the unanticipated intersection of these two giant-sized unintended consequences, affirmative action and mass immigration from Latin America and Asia, that the continuity factor in this essay, official minority designation, arises. A blockbuster consequence of the convergence of affirmative action and mass immigration has thus gone largely unobserved, as if the emperor wears no clothes. The consequence is that since 1965, approximately 23 million immigrants, from the moment of their arrival in the United States, have qualified for the benefits of affirmative action. This has been true as a matter of law and policy, even though it extends rights and benefits to immigrants while denying them to millions of low-income, native-born Americans and even though millions of the immigrants either remained unaware that they were eligible for affirmative action benefits or were not inclined to ask for them.

The chief rationale of hard affirmative action was to compensate for past discrimination, particularly on behalf of African Americans with their unique history of slavery and segregation. For this reason, the extension of affirmative action benefits to newly arrived immigrants seems strange. Since at least the 1960s, Asians especially have shown among both native-born and immigrant populations levels of attainment in income and education that are higher than that of both other minorities and white families as well. In 1995, for example, Asian families in the United States had a median family income of $48,200 (in 1997 dollars) compared with $42,700 for all white families (including Hispanics) and $25,800 for all black families.[11] Asian family income, most of it reflecting immigrant achievements, was almost twice the level of median black family income. Yet under federal policy, all Asian Americans, like all African Americans, were presumably eligible for affirmative action programs.

Why did American policy extend affirmative action to such a successful group? When controversy over both immigration and affirmative action began to intensify in the early 1990s, especially in economically distressed California, the civil rights coalition was embarrassed by the issue and generally dodged it. Civil rights leaders feared its divisive potential, and they lacked a plausible explanation to account for it. If we are asked, today, by citizens surprised to learn that four out of five immigrants qualify for affirmative action programs, "When did our government make this policy?"—we are stumped for an answer. And we are stumped for good reason, because the government never decided to make such a policy. Instead, the policy emerged in a piecemeal and belated fashion, as a fait accompli, an inadvertent policy consequence of unclear provenance.

In my recent work I have tried to patch together an understanding of how this came to pass.[12] The story is still fragmented, but it is fascinating and instructive. At its center lies the story of when and how the federal government designated a list of official American minorities. Books about the civil rights revolution, published by the thousands, either never asked how America's official minorities were selected or threw little light on the answers. Scrutiny of the public hearings and debates surrounding the nation's revolution in civil rights policy since the 1940s shows almost no discussion of why other minority groups in America were included as official minorities (e.g., Chinese, Argentineans, Pakistanis, Cubans, Spaniards, Portuguese) or why others were excluded (e.g., Jews, Italians, Jehovah's Witnesses, Mormons, Palestinians, Iranians).[13] The answer to the why, when, and how questions have to be teased out of reports and archival documents left by obscure government bureaucrats, men (rarely women) largely unknown to the public and not answerable to voters for their decisions. It is striking that none of the career civil servants and appointed officials who shaped the outcomes showed any awareness that they were sorting out future winners and losers by racial and ethnic ancestry.

A major barrier to designating official minorities in post–World War II America was the liberal political tradition itself, which emphasized equal individual rights, not group rights, and protected them through the negative action of antidiscrimination. Thus the language of the country's modern nondiscrimination law, including Roosevelt's wartime Fair Employment Practices Committee (FEPC), the president's subsequent contract compliance program, the state antidiscrimination commissions pioneered by New York, and the civil rights statutes of the 1960s, banned discrimination on account of race, color, creed (meaning chiefly religion), and national origin but avoided mentioning specific groups.[14]

Two Paths to Minority Group Classification

How, then, did particular groups get singled out under the nondiscrimination law? The record shows two paths leading to specific group identification. One was primarily political, the other administrative. The political path, more visible but less determinative in this process than the administrative path, involved the national investigations and reports of advisory bodies. The most important of these were Truman's Committee on Civil Rights, appointed in 1946, and the U.S. Commission on Civil Rights, established by statute in 1957. Truman's committee, like all civil rights inquiries and reports in the postwar era, emphasized discrimination against black Americans. But the committee's 1947 report, *To Secure These Rights*, also described discrimination against other groups. The report noted the wartime evacuation and internment of Japanese Americans, citizenship limitations on Chinese and Japanese, voting restrictions on American Indians, and school segregation and jury duty restrictions on Mexican Americans. The Truman Committee briefly mentioned incidents of past bias against whites—especially against Jews and against Italians during World War II. But *To Secure These Rights* marked a shift away from the concerns over religious discrimination that had characterized New York's pioneering campaign, for example, against Jewish quotas at Ivy League colleges and bias against Catholic immigrants, and toward an emphasis on color. "Groups whose color makes them more easily identified," the report observed, "are set apart from the 'dominant majority' much more than are the Caucasian minorities."[15] The hearings and reports of the Civil Rights Commission continued this shift. The commission concentrated through 1965 on African Americans and segregation in the South, then shifted to emphasize nationwide discrimination against blacks *and* Latinos.

The ad hoc Truman committee and the continuing Civil Rights Commission provided public education about civil rights abuses and the need for reform. But as advisory bodies, they had no regulatory or enforcement authority. More important to the story about designating official minorities were the decisions of obscure government officials providing staff support in the fledgling civil rights compliance bureaucracy. Needing information about employment patterns to support the work of the president's contract compliance committees, they designed forms for government contractors to fill out showing how their employees were distributed by race, ethnicity, and sex.[16]

Since the concept of group rights was alien to the civil rights bureaucracy until the end of the 1960s, the career civil servants designing survey forms for the contract compliance committees had no notion that their amateurish efforts would have such far-reaching consequences. In his account, Skrentny calls attention to the decisions of David Mann, director of surveys for Eisenhower's contract compliance committee and later for Kennedy's committee as well.[17] In 1956, Eisenhower's committee asked government contractors to count their "Negro," "other minority," and "total" employees. For contractors with large numbers of "other minority" employees, the survey questionnaire added that "the contractor may be able to furnish employment statistics for such groups," including "Spanish-Americans, Orientals, Indians, Jews, Puerto Ricans, etc." Contractors were not provided definitions to guide their count of such groups. Since employment records presumably did not list the employees' religious affiliation, it was unclear how a contractor's visual inspection might identify Jewish workers, how they should define Spanish Americans, or how employers might distinguish between Spanish Americans and Puerto Ricans. As Skrentny observed, employers presumably were given wide latitude by the form's permissive invitation—contractors may be able to furnish further information—and by the enigmatic "etc."

This was a clumsy beginning. The only minority group that contractors were required to identify in the 1956 form was "Negroes." But once minority groups started getting named on the government's civil rights compliance forms, the ethnic organizations kicked into play. The League of United Latin American Citizens (LULAC), the GI Forum, and the Mexican-American Political Action Committee argued that Hispanics had suffered discrimination and deserved equal billing with blacks on the government's new form. The Latino organizations recruited support from Mexican American members of Congress—Henry Gonzales (Texas), Joseph Montoya (New Mexico), and Edward Roybal (California), all Democrats. By 1962, when President Kennedy's contract compliance committee revised the early survey questionnaire into Standard Form 40, "Spanish-Americans" were included with "Negroes" as obligatory reporting categories. A similar campaign by the Japanese American Citizens League, supported by two legislators from Hawaii, Republican Hiram L. Fong in the Senate and Democrat Daniel K. Inouye in the House, persuaded Mann to add "Orientals" as a required category on the standard form. Mann at the same time added American Indians to the standard form, even though Indian organizations had not lobbied to be included and were reluctant to be designated as a protected group. Mann added them to the form anyway, citing his personal conviction that they suffered discrimination and lived in a woeful economic state.[18]

Jews, on the other hand, were dropped from the form. Some black groups had objected to their inclusion, as had some employers. Jewish organizations were sensitive to the anti-Semitic uses of group labels and statistics, and the leading Jewish agencies—the Anti-Defamation League, the American Jewish Committee, and the American Jewish Congress—tacitly agreed to their deletion from the form. Thus by 1962, religion or creed as a category of discrimination associated with specific religious groups had largely disappeared from the government's data bank of enforcement information. Because the First Amendment barred government officials from asking citizens about their religious beliefs and affiliations, the new equal employment opportunity (EEO) forms the government was designing in effect blocked reporting on religious discrimination in employment.

The election of a Catholic president in 1960 and the fading of the Jewish quotas in college and professional school admissions pointed to a rapid decline of religion-based discrimination in postwar America. But the exclusion of religion from the EEO forms helped break the connection with an American past filled with group-based religious discrimination and oppression. When group-based affirmative action later emerged, it would not include Jews, Catholics, Jehovah's Witnesses, Mormons, and other religious groups with a history of discrimination. By excluding religious discrimination as a category, the EEO forms in effect blocked protected minority status not only for groups historically suffering religious discrimination in America but also for new groups, such as Arab Americans, whose presumptive whiteness, it turned out, excluded them from the color-coded selection of official minorities.

The Unplanned Designation of Official Minorities

By 1965, when the newly established Equal Employment Opportunity Commission (EEOC) used the contract compliance committee's Standard Form 40 as the basis for designing its own form, the EEO-1 form, the government had already produced a de facto list of official minorities that employers were required to count and report. Workers were assigned to five ethnic categories on the EEO-1 form: Negro, Spanish American, Oriental, American Indian, and white. Because the Civil Rights Act that created the EEOC also prohibited discrimination on account of race and national origin, none of the five groups could legally be discriminated against in 1965, including whites. But whites, alone among the five listed groups, were not considered a minority.

Thus when the ghetto riots of 1965–68 prompted federal agency officials and judges to speed black job recruitment by devising race-conscious affirmative action programs such as the Philadelphia Plan, the government already had at hand a list of four official minorities. Although individual ethnic organizations lobbied federal officials to pay more attention to their group, there is no record of civil rights leaders addressing the issue of which groups to include on the EEO-1 form, no hearings or record of discussion by the president's contract compliance committees or by the EEOC, and no record of minority rights or women's organizations during 1965–68 asking for race-conscious or gender-specific remedies. Instead, the initiative in both the earlier minority-counting projects and, later, in developing race-conscious affirmative action programs came from appointed federal officials and served their immediate political needs.[19]

There is no need to repeat here the story of the development of affirmative action in the late 1960s and early 1970s. Keyed to the statistical inference of underutilization analysis and pioneered by the EEOC, it required the designation of official minorities. The Labor Department, although it developed the Philadelphia Plan with riots and jobless black workers in mind, drew on the EEO-1 form's list of official minorities—"Negro, Oriental, American Indian, and Spanish Surnamed Americans"—to establish its own form of underutilization analysis.[20]

During these years of commissions to deal with urban riots and violence, a third federal agency, the Small Business Administration (SBA), used the new concept of official minorities to reshape its programs. In 1968 the SBA, responding to appeals from the Kerner commission for special outreach programs to build economic opportunity in the inner cities, established the 8(a) program. It provided grants, subsidized loans, and preferred access to government contracts for "economically or culturally disadvantaged individuals." Aimed principally at the black ghettos, the 8(a) program did not define what it meant by economic or, especially, cultural disadvantage. When African American and Hispanic organizations criticized the 8(a) program as cumbersome and ineffective, the SBA reached out to the new and expanding civil rights constituencies to bolster its support in Congress. In 1973 the SBA published new regulations for the 8(a) program in the *Federal Register*. Henceforth, the status of cultural disadvantage would be *presumed* for all program applicants identifying themselves as black, Hispanic, Asian American, or American Indian.[21]

Characteristics of the Official Minority Selection Process

Thus by 1973, when the leading federal agencies in civil rights enforcement had consolidated their shift from nondiscrimination to an underutilization model of affirmative action, they already had at hand a list of four minority groups on whose behalf the new model would be applied.

What were the most significant attributes and consequences of this selection process, which evolved unevenly in fits and starts over three decades? First, it was a closed process of bureaucratic policymaking, one largely devoid not only of public testimony but even of public awareness that policy was being made. Second, the in-house nature of the government's deliberations narrowed the goals of policy from meeting broad public needs to meeting the more immediate political needs of the agency. Closed deliberations facilitated sheltered bargaining between agency officials, constituent groups, and members of Congress, bargaining that followed the client model of regulatory politics, in which costs are widely distributed among taxpayers and consumers and benefits are concentrated on well-organized interest groups.[22] Before 1965, the government's clumsy, trial-and-error search for useful categories on their fair employment survey forms carried no hint of group entitlement. When nondiscrimination and equal individual rights were the agreed anchors of policy, getting one's ethnic group added to a questionnaire promised little in benefits beyond elevated visibility and prestige. If someone suggested adding Jews or Arab Americans to the survey form, officials could add them—with a shrug and a "Why not?"—without anticipating any particular effect on nondiscrimination policy, which protected all Americans equally against harmful bias. But the shift to hard affirmative action and adverse impact claims during the Nixon years radically changed the stakes of policy.

It is not surprising that the agencies shaping the new definition of official minorities in America—the EEOC, the contract compliance bureaucracies in Labor and other mission agencies, the Office of Civil Rights, the SBA's 8(a) program bureaucracy—became largely captured bureaucracies whose policies rewarded the protected classes that the official minority designations recognized. Hard affirmative action was a brilliant creative stroke for these agencies. It radically enlarged their policy repertoire. It armed previously weak agencies—the EEOC, the Labor Department, the Office of Education—with powerful regulatory authority. It enabled them to speed redistributive justice. At the same time, it allowed them to appease volatile, radicalizing constituencies, quieting criticism by directing a robust new stream of benefits to reward racial and ethnic clientele groups. Best of all, by requiring private firms and other government agencies, including all state and local governments and education institutions, to cover the cost of the new benefits (jobs, promotions, government contracts) to minority constituencies, it freed the civil rights bureaucracy from the necessity of persuading Congress to provide appropriations to pay for them.

Third, the agencies provided no rationale to justify their racial and ethnic categories. Dealing with inherited notions of race that had been abandoned in science and social science, government officials in the 1950s and 1960s drew up questionnaires that reflected assumptions they took for granted. No explanations were provided. What was a race? Who should make that determination, how, and why? Should religious minorities be included? Was anti-Semitism a form of national origin discrimination? Should Europeans from Portugal be regarded as Spanish Americans? Were persons of Middle Eastern or North African ancestry "white"? How should the government categorize persons of racially or ethnically mixed ancestry, and why? Not having to answer questions like these in public, or even in closed conference rooms, made it easier for government officials to adjust their lists pragmatically, winnowing the official minorities down by 1965 to a core of four.

Color-Coding America: Assumptions and Consequences

By that year, the new EEO-1 form, by isolating four minority groups that corresponded to the color-coding of American popular culture—black, yellow, red, and brown—reified a cluster of assumptions about American society that agency officials, shielded from public debate by their closed process, simply took for granted. One implicit assumption was that membership in a minority group carried an automatic presumption of disadvantage in American society. Other attributes of minority individuals that might reflect socioeconomic success, such as income, wealth, and educational achievement, were disregarded. Minority status, in effect, trumped socioeconomic class. A second implicit assumption was that all minority groups were equal in their disadvantage. Although the paradigmatic disadvantaged minority group was indisputably, in 1950s parlance, the Negro American, there was no implication that civil rights remedies could differ for blacks, Hispanics, Asians, or American Indians. Third, the government listing of enumerated minority groups, which erased the lines separating official minorities from each other, drew a line separating official minorities from all other Americans. By 1965, when the EEO-1 form asked employers to use visual identification rather than employee records or queries to assign workers to EEO categories, the white ethnics and religious groups had all been excluded.

Finally, the government officials making these decisions from the beginning privileged the rights claims of African Americans. Black claims came first; all other minority groups played a distant tagalong. This taken-for-granted assumption was almost universally shared by reformers. When speaking of "the" civil rights movement, it was understood that one meant the black civil rights movement. Presidents Kennedy and Johnson, when pressing the civil rights bills of the mid-1960s, rallied Americans exclusively to the justice claims of African Americans. Historically, the assumption of African American primacy seemed self-evident. Politically, it provided the moral power behind the breakthrough legislation of 1964–65. Subsequently, it also provided the rationale for adopting race-conscious remedies under affirmative action, speeding government-subsidized jobs to protesting urban blacks. But it coexisted uneasily with the presumption that all minority groups were equally disadvantaged and were entitled to the same remedies in civil rights enforcement.

By the end of the 1960s, African Americans fit a color-coded model for America most easily. The Black Power movement tended psychologically to unify and darken the racially mixed African American population, aided ironically by the one-drop rule, a racist proviso devised by antebellum slave regimes and used to police segregation laws in the South until the 1960s. The growth of race-conscious affirmative action remedies by federal courts and agencies in the early 1970s spurred competition by other racial and ethnic groups to win protected-class status. As groups got wise, they wanted to get themselves classified as minorities.[23]

Lobbying for specific recognition by minority racial and ethnic groups led the Budget Bureau in 1969 to ban the residual term "nonwhite" from government classification statistics.[24] Spanish Americans, the majority of whom regarded themselves as white, presented special difficulties for classification schemes. Varying widely by national origin (Mexican, Puerto Rican, Cuban, Guatemalan, Venezuelan, Spanish), they were aggregated in the census of 1950, 1960, and 1970 as Spanish-surnamed Americans. To administer the surname classification system, the Census Bureau gathered a list of more than eight thousand names to identify members of this group. But this approach included as Hispanic many who were not—non-Hispanic spouses, Filipinos, American Indians. More problematic, it invited double-counting of African Americans—a race—and Hispanics, who could be of any ethnic group. Hispanic lobbying groups, chiefly La Raza and LULAC, persuaded Congress in 1976, an election year, to pass a statute governing statistical classifications for Hispanics. The law defined Hispanics as persons "tracing their origin or descent from Mexico, Puerto Rico, Cuba, Central and South America, and other Spanish-speaking countries."[25] This clarification, however, did not remedy the problem of double-counting. Moreover, it excluded, at least by implication, persons with origins in non-Spanish-speaking countries (e.g., Brazil, Guiana, Suriname, Trinidad, Belize, or Portugal). Presumably, the Office of Management and Budget (OMB) explained, such persons would be classified by their race, although it was unclear how this might be done or who would do it.

Asian classification presented another set of problems. A geographic as well as a racial classification, it encompassed a vast but ill-defined area of extraordinary cultural and linguistic variety that contained the world's most densely populated nations (China, Japan, India), as well as its most thinly populated areas (Pacific Islands). In the early 1970s, Japanese American and Chinese American organizations began objecting to the term "Oriental," still used by federal agencies. Polynesian Hawaiians and Micronesian Guamanians complained that they were not "Oriental."[26] Americans from the Indian subcontinent, moreover, were classified as Hindu in the 1920, 1930, and 1940 censuses, then were reclassified as "white" or "Caucasian" in the censuses of 1950, 1960, and 1970. But this classification, by the 1970s, left Americans with subcontinent origins out of affirmative action programs. In response, Indian American organizations successfully lobbied the EEOC in the mid-1970s to reclassify Americans with subcontinent origins from white to Asian, a step the EEOC took in 1976 in the EEO-6 form for higher education reporting.[27]

In 1977, the OMB, culminating a process of federal interagency negotiation that had continued through the 1970s, issued Directive no. 15. It established a statistical classification system for all federal agencies that sorted all Americans into one of five groups:[28]

> 1. American Native or Alaskan Native. A person having origins in any of the original peoples of North America and who maintains cultural identification through tribal affiliations or community recognition.

2. Asian or Pacific Islander. A person having origins in any of the original peoples of the Far East, Southeast Asia, the Indian subcontinent, or the Pacific Islands.
3. Black. A person having origins in any of the black racial groups of Africa.
4. Hispanic. A person of Mexican, Puerto Rican, Cuban, Central or South American, or other Spanish culture or origin, regardless of race.
5. White. A person having origins in any of the original peoples of Europe, North Africa, or the Middle East.

To prevent double-counting, Directive no. 15 established a combined classification scheme, requiring that persons be assigned by both racial group (any one of four) and ethnicity (Hispanic or non-Hispanic). The scheme's five categories codified the five-color taxonomy found in the EEO-1 form in 1965, categories that in turn corresponded to American popular culture's cartoonlike depiction of Americans as being either black, white, yellow, red, or brown.

The Assault on the "Ethno-Racial Pentagon"

David Hollinger called this schema "the ethno-racial pentagon."[29] It was based primarily on geographic, not social, cultural, or in any sense scientific criteria. It met the immediate needs of federal agencies for an internally consistent system of demographic classification. Importantly, it also met the political needs of agencies and Congress, under pressure from racial and ethnic lobbies to maximize the size of their constituent groups and certify their presumptive eligibility for affirmative action programs. But the ethno-racial pentagon was riven with internal contradictions. Its racial and ethnic dualism, representing a compromise by skilled federal officials caught between historic traditions of racial pseudoscience and an explosion of multicultural demographics and politics, was basically impossible to reconcile.

In the 1980s, as large-scale immigration strengthened multicultural political currents, the ethno-racial pentagon came under attack. Its "white" classification, a residual category that included peoples of North Africa and the Near and Middle East but oddly excluded Spain, denied government benefits from affirmative action programs to even the most impoverished Americans so categorized, while its Hispanic and Asian classifications extended affirmative action benefits to millions of immigrants. In an age of surging religious fundamentalism and impassioned orthodoxy, it provided no place for religious groups to register their identity. In an age of growing intermarriage and mixed-race parentage, it required Americans, in self-identifying their affiliations, to favor one parent and culture over another. Its rigidities could not accommodate the rapidly proliferating combinations of modern America—Arab Americans, native Hawaiians, Spanish-speaking Filipinos, Hasidic Jews, and, above all, the mixed-race Tiger Woods of twenty-first-century demography. Ironically, the enriched demographic data produced by the new home-language question in the 1970 census and new ancestry questions in the 1980 census—data designed in part to help categorize Americans more accurately—further undermined the contradictions and vulnerabilities of the ethno-racial pentagon.[30]

Growing demands for an "Other" race option in the 1990 census led the OMB in 1988 to consider providing this option. But counterattacks by rights-based racial and ethnic organizations, such as the National Association for the Advancement of Colored People, the Mexican American Legal Defense Education Fund, and La Raza, defeated the effort. The surging mixed-race population in immigrant-rich America, however, increased pressure against the government's ethno-racial pentagon. Following hearings by the House census committee in 1993, the OMB in 1994 reopened the question. Multiracial organizations, using new Internet-based lobbying techniques, hammered federal agencies and Congress for refusing to recognize their unique and proud identities. In 1997 the OMB, responding to this pressure, approved an option for Americans to select more than one racial identity in the 2000 census.[31] The politics of affirmative action were colliding with new patterns of identity politics generated by mass immigration in an increasingly multicultural America.

Affirmative Action for Immigrants?

Today there is wide agreement that the destruction of southern segregation, the development of affirmative action, and the growth of mass immigration are changes rooted in the 1960s, shaped by the reforms of the Great Society and marking sharp discontinuity with the policies of the past. The literature on all three developments is massive, and two of them, affirmative action and mass immigration, remain controversial. Working together, the latter two issues produced rising disputes in the 1980s and 1990s over affirmative action for immigrants. In the 1980s the EEOC, disturbed by "diversity"-based industrial hiring trends that favored Hispanics and Asians over blacks, brought lawsuits against employers in an attempt, largely unsuccessful, to require stricter proportional representation in employment. By the 1990s, Asian and Hispanic businesses had displaced blacks as the chief beneficiaries in the nation's largest single affirmative action budget, the SBA 8(a) minority contract set-aside program. Whereas black-owned firms in 1981 had received 66.9 percent of 8(a) contract dollars compared with 14.7 percent for Hispanic and 7.2 percent for Asian firms, by 1996 the equivalent nationwide percentages were blacks, 34 percent; Hispanics, 26 percent; and Asians, 28 percent. In California, the 8(a) contract dollar percentages for these groups were Asians, 40 percent; Hispanics, 33 percent; and blacks, 23 percent. A 1995 General Accounting Office report showed that of the top twenty-five firms in the 8(a) program in contract dollar awards, only three were black owned.[32] As immigrant communities increasingly took advantage of their official minority status in affirmative action programs, African American resentment grew, and whites, except for some set-aside programs for women-owned businesses, remained excluded entirely.[33] By the year 2000, demographic shifts were increasingly challenging policies rooted in the taken-for-granted assumptions of the 1960s. By the year 2000, whites had become a minority in California, the nation's largest state; racial intermarriage was increasing rapidly, and Tiger Woods appeared to be the model of America's demographic future.

Against this background, the OMB in March 2000—an election year—directed the Census Bureau to classify as a minority all individuals who claimed both white and minority ancestry on the 2000 census forms. The directive read, in part: "Mixed-race people who mark both White and a non-White race will be counted as the latter for purposes of civil rights monitoring and enforcement."[34] Under heavy lobbying by both black and Latino groups, the Clinton administration in effect reaffirmed the one-drop rule, to maximize the census count for official minorities. The controversy surrounding this issue may indicate another watershed in American civil rights policy, marked by widening public controversy over minority identification and rights claims. If so, it could bring to a close an era of underlying continuity in civil rights policy, when government officials in closed deliberations applied taken-for-granted assumptions from the 1940s through the 1970s to produce a list of official minorities in a process that had completed its work before its radical implications had become apparent.

This angle of analysis on policymaking in the Great Society has been little explored. Insights derived from reconstructing processes hidden in the bureaucracy of the American regulatory state, and scrutinizing their consequences, should reshape our understandings about the Great Society and its policy consequences. Most of the important changes in civil rights policy made in the 1960s were shaped in relatively open debate, as befits a democracy. These include desegregating the schools, public institutions, private businesses, and voting booths in the South; enforcing racial and gender equality in education and employment; abandoning the national origins quota system in immigration; and committing the government to nondiscrimination in residential housing. The major policy shifts involving race-conscious affirmative action and protected-class status for official minorities, however, were negotiated primarily behind closed doors in the expanding domain of the civil rights bureaucracy. Opening those doors casts the era of civil rights policymaking in a new light.

Notes

1. The literature on the modern civil rights era is massive. For a comprehensive recent review, see Charles W. Eagles, "Toward New Histories of the Civil Rights Era," *Journal of Southern History* 66 (November 2000): 815–48.

2. Other candidates for policy discontinuity emerge from "whiteness studies," a subfield that emphasizes white hegemony throughout Western and American history. In this vein, particular case studies of policy continuity in the post-*Brown* civil rights era might include segregation in housing and public schools. The school desegregation story, however, includes the unprecedented discontinuity of court-ordered busing in the 1970s, which by mid-decade had produced more racially mixed public schooling in the South than in the rest of the nation. Fair-housing measures also faced a continuity of strong resistance. Yet they include two significant changes: the 1968 ban on housing discrimination and a 1988 fair-housing law that provided the enforcement authority and machinery lacking in 1968. For another view of housing policy, see Douglas S. Massey and Nancy A. Denton, *American Apartheid* (Cambridge, Mass.: Harvard University

Press, 1993). For a challenge to this view, see Hugh Davis Graham, "The Surprising Career of Federal Fair Housing Law," *Journal of Policy History* 12 (Spring 2000): 1–18.

3. Hugh Davis Graham, *The Civil Rights Era: Origins and Development of National Policy, 1960–1972* (New York: Oxford University Press, 1990).

4. John J. Donahue and James J. Heckman, "Continuous versus Episodic Change: The Impact of Affirmative Action Policy on the Economic Status of Blacks," *Journal of Economic Literature* 29 (1991): 1603–44; Dave M. O'Neill and June O'Neill, "Affirmative Action in the Labor Market," *Annals of the American Academy of Political and Social Science* 523 (September 1992): 88–103; Frank Levy, *The New Dollars and Dreams: American Incomes and Economic Change* (New York: Russell Sage, 1998), 97–98.

5. In "Since 1965: The South and Civil Rights," in *The South as an American Problem*, ed. Larry J. Griffin and Don H. Doyle, 145–63 (Athens: University of Georgia Press, 1995), I argue that black-white relations following the 1960s were better in the South than in the North.

6. Steven M. Gillon, *"That's Not What We Meant to Do": Reform and Its Unintended Consequences in Twentieth-Century America* (New York: Norton, 2000).

7. On the emergence of race-conscious affirmative action during the Nixon presidency, see Joan Hoff, *Nixon Reconsidered* (New York: Basic Books, 1994), chap. 3; Hugh Davis Graham, "Richard Nixon and Civil Rights: Explaining an Enigma," *Presidential Studies Quarterly* 26 (Winter 1996): 93–106; and Dean Kotlowski, *Nixon's Civil Rights: Politics, Policy, and Principle* (Cambridge, Mass.: Harvard University Press, 2001).

8. John David Skrentny, *The Ironies of Affirmative Action* (Chicago: University of Chicago Press, 1996).

9. Stephen Thomas Wagner, "The Lingering Death of the National Origins Quota System: A Political History of United States Immigration Policy, 1952–1965" (Ph.D. diss., Harvard University, 1986); Betty K. Koed, "The Politics of Reform: Policymakers and the Immigration Act of 1965" (Ph.D. diss., University of California, Santa Barbara, 1999).

10. Hugh Davis Graham, "Unintended Consequences: The Convergence of Affirmative Action and Immigration Policy," *American Behavioral Scientist* 41 (April 1998): 898–912.

11. Levy, *New Dollars and Dreams*, 209.

12. Hugh Davis Graham, *Collision Course: The Strange Convergence of Affirmative Action and Immigration Policy in America* (New York: Oxford University Press, 2002).

13. A prominent exception was women, technically not a minority group. Since the ratification of the woman suffrage amendment, the twentieth-century feminist movement had been deeply split between the sex-blind model of equal rights for men and women, as symbolized by the equal rights amendment (ERA), and the social feminist model, which emphasized inherent differences be-

tween the sexes and promoted special protective legislation for working women. Equal rights feminists, ineffective through the 1950s, regained national leadership behind the ERA during the 1960s and 1970s. Following the presidential election of Ronald Reagan and the defeat of the ERA, the embittered feminist leadership shifted back toward the difference model and pressed for affirmative action preferences for women, such as women business enterprise (WBE) set-aside contracts in government procurement. See, for example, Rosalind Rosenberg, *Divided Lives* (New York: Hill and Wang, 1992).

14. Paul Burstein, *Discrimination, Jobs, and Politics: The Struggle for Equal Employment Opportunity in the United States since the New Deal* (Chicago: University of Chicago Press, 1985); Merl E. Reed, *Seedtime for the Modern Civil Rights Movement: The President's Committee on Fair Employment Practice, 1941–1946* (Baton Rouge: Louisiana State University Press, 1991).

15. The President's Committee on Civil Rights, *To Secure These Rights* (Washington, D.C.: Government Printing Office, 1947), x.

16. For a detailed description of the development of official minorities, see John David Skrentny, *The Minority Rights Revolution* (Chicago: University of Chicago Press, 2002), chap. 4. The author acknowledges with gratitude Skrentny's generosity in sharing the fruits of his research.

17. Ibid. Skrentny rests his account in part on an unpublished manuscript by Harold Orlans, "The Origin of Protected Groups," prepared by Orlans as part of a Commission on Civil Rights study of affirmative action in higher education in 1986 that was not completed, and shared by Skrentny with me.

18. Orlans, "Origin of Protected Groups," 3–6.

19. Alfred W. Blumrosen, *Modern Law: The Law Transmission System and Equal Employment Opportunity* (Madison: University of Wisconsin Press, 1993), 65–67; Graham, *Civil Rights Era*, 193–201.

20. Hugh Davis Graham, *Civil Rights and the Presidency* (New York: Oxford University Press, 1992), chap. 9; Skrentny, *Minority Rights Revolution*, chap. 4.

21. The SBA's 1973 regulation named five rather than four groups as presumptively culturally disadvantaged: "blacks, American Indians, Spanish-Americans, Asian-Americans, and Puerto Ricans." The curious distinction between Spanish Americans and Puerto Ricans testifies to the imprecision and general sloppiness of the closed bureaucratic processes that produced official minority designations to govern affirmative action policy during its formative years.

22. James Q. Wilson, *Bureaucracy: What Government Agencies Do and Why They Do It* (New York: Basic Books, 1989), 79–83. On clientele capture in civil rights regulation, see Hugh Davis Graham, "Since 1964: The Paradox of American Civil Rights Regulation," in *Taking Stock: American Government in the Twentieth Century*, ed. Morton Keller and R. Shep Melnick, 187–218 (Washington, D.C.: Woodrow Wilson Center Press; New York: Cambridge University Press, 1999).

23. Orlans, "Origin of Protected Groups," 6–7, quoting Bernard Michael, former director of the Federal Inter-Agency Committee on Education.

24. Exhibit K, circular A-46, Bureau of the Budget, August 8, 1969.
25. Public Law 94-311, "Economic and Social Statistics for Americans of Hispanic Origin," June 16, 1976.
26. U.S. Commission on Civil Rights, *To Know or Not to Know: Collection and Use of Racial and Ethnic Data in Federal Assistance Programs* (Washington, D.C., February 1973), 30–31.
27. Nathan Glazer, *Ethnic Dilemmas, 1964–1982* (Cambridge, Mass.: Harvard University Press, 1983), 149–50.
28. Office of Management and Budget, "Directive No. 15: Race and Ethnic Standards for Federal Statistics and Administrative Reporting," *Federal Register* 43 (May 4, 1978): 19269. The OMB formally dates the adoption of Directive 15 as occurring on May 12, 1977, though publication in the *Federal Register* occurred a year later.
29. David A. Hollinger, *Postethnic America* (New York: Basic Books, 1995), 23–50.
30. Charles Hirschman, Richard Alba, and Reynolds Farley, "The Meaning and Measurement of Race in the U.S. Census: Glimpses Into the Future, *Demography* 37 (August 2000): 381–93.
31. Office of Management and Budget, "Revisions to the Standards for the Classification of Federal Data on Race and Ethnicity," *Federal Register* 62 (October 1997): 58782–90. In the 1997 revisions of Directive no. 15, the OMB, under pressure especially from native Hawaiian groups resisting alleged encroachments by Hawaiians of Asian ancestry, split the Asian and Pacific Islander category into two groups, Asian and Hawaiian and Other Pacific Islander.
32. General Accounting Office, *The Small Business Administration: 8(a) Program Is Vulnerable to Program and Contract Abuse* (Washington, D.C.: General Accounting Office, Office of Special Investigations, September 1995).
33. See, for example, the General Accounting Office, *Small Business: Problems Continue with SBA's Minority Business Development Program* (Washington, D.C.: General Accounting Office, GAO/RCED-93-145, Sept. 17, 1993); Graham, *Collision Course*, chap. 5. In fiscal 1994, for example, of the 5,628 firms participating in the 8(a) program, only one-half of 1 percent of the owners (nine women, nine people who were disabled, and eight white men) were not in the presumptively eligible groups.
34. Office of Management and Budget, "Guidance on Aggregation and Allocation of Data on Race for Use in Civil Rights Monitoring and Enforcement," OMB Bulletin no. 00-02, March 9, 1999; Steven A. Holmes, "New Policy on Census Says Those Listed as White and Minority Will Be Counted as Minority," *New York Times*, March 11, 2000, A9.

From Tax and Spend to Mandate and Sue

Liberalism after the Great Society

R. Shep Melnick

The image of the Great Society retains a strong hold on the imagination of liberals and conservatives alike. To conservatives, the LBJ years were the moment of the Great Wrong Turn: unlimited expectations replaced limited government; maximum feasible participation quickly morphed into maximum feasible misunderstanding; real progress against poverty halted just as the official War on Poverty began; the long-awaited triumph of color blindness was jettisoned in favor of a new form of counting by race; and before long, McGovernism had replaced the Truman Doctrine as the cornerstone of the Democratic Party's foreign policy. For most liberals, in contrast, the Great Society was a long-overdue effort to eliminate poverty and subdue racism, tragically cut short by racial backlash at home, imperialism abroad, a duplicitous Texan in the White House, and the success of Richard Nixon's "southern strategy" in 1968. While the right vows to roll back the Great Society, the left dreams of renewing the hope, the ambition, and the political ferment of the 1960s.

Even a cursory look at the policy legacies of the Great Society, on the one hand, and of 1969–76, on the other, should make us think twice before accepting these common images of the Johnson and Nixon years (see Tables 1 and 2). No one can doubt the significance of the policy initiatives of the Johnson administration: the Civil Rights Act of 1964 and the Voting Rights Act of 1965; Medicare and Medicaid; federal aid to

Table 1. Policy Legacy of the Great Society, 1964–1968

Medicare
Medicaid

Civil Rights Act of 1964
Voting Rights Act of 1965
Fair Housing Act of 1968
Immigration reform

Elementary and Secondary Education Act
Head Start
National Endowment for the Arts
National Endowment for the Humanities

Job training programs
Model Cities
Legal Services

National Highway Traffic Safety Act
Truth-in-Lending Act

---

education; and a variety of education and training programs targeted to the poor. But the policy legacy of the Nixon and Ford years is equally impressive: a huge expansion of means-tested programs; recognition of the legal rights of women (including abortion rights), the disabled, linguistic minorities, and the elderly; extensive and expensive health, safety, consumer, and environmental regulation; and affirmative action in school assignments, college admissions, employment, and electoral districting.

Ironically, by the turn of the millennium, most American conservatives had come to terms with the programs established in the 1960s but remained fervently opposed to many of the initiatives of the 1970s. In decrying affirmative action, they call for a return to the color-blind interpretation of the Constitution and Civil Rights Act enunciated by the Johnson administration and its primary spokesman in the Senate, soon-to-be vice president Hubert Humphrey.[1] Similarly, contemporary Republicans support federal aid to education but oppose the proliferation of categorical programs and unfunded mandates that characterized education policy in the 1970s. The welfare reform enacted by the Republican Congress in 1996, too, was designed to reverse policies established in the 1970s not the 1960s. As James Patterson has explained:

Table 2. Initiatives of the Nixon and Ford Years, 1969–1976

Means-tested programs:
- Major expansion of food stamps
- Supplemental Security Income
- Nationalization of Aid to Families with Dependent Children (AFDC) eligibility requirements (through courts)
- Supplemental feeding program for women, infants, and children (WIC) and school lunch, school breakfast, and other nutrition programs
- Earned Income Tax Credit

Major expansion of Social Security, including addition of cost-of-living adjustment

Affirmative action:
- Employment, race, and gender (Title VII)
- College admissions (Title VI)
- School assignment (including busing)
- Electoral districting (Voting Rights Act)

Rights of those with disabilities:
- Section 504 of the Rehabilitation Act of 1973
- Education for All Handicapped Children Act
- Court rulings on rights of those who are mentally ill and institutionalized

Other expansion of civil rights:
- Title IX of Education Amendments of 1972 (gender discrimination)
- Courts recognize gender as "semisuspect" classification
- Abortion rights (*Roe v. Wade*)
- Age Discrimination Act of 1975
- Bilingual education mandates

- Equal Employment Opportunity Act of 1972 (expansion of the Equal Employment Opportunity Commission's enforcement capacity)
- Constitutional amendment giving eighteen-year-olds the right to vote

Environmental regulation:
- National Environmental Policy Act of 1969
- Creation of Environmental Protection Agency (by executive order)
- Clean Air Act of 1970
- Clean Water Act of 1972
- Pesticide amendments of 1972
- Coastal Zone Management Act of 1972
- Endangered Species Act of 1973
- Safe Drinking Water Act of 1974
- Toxic Substances Control Act of 1976
- Resource Conservation and Recovery Act of 1976
- National Forest Management Act of 1976

Other major regulatory statutes:
- Employment Retirement Income Security Act of 1974 (ERISA)
- Federal Election Campaign Acts of 1971 and 1974
- Occupational Health and Safety Act of 1972 (creating OSHA)
- Consumer Product Safety Act of 1972 (creating CPSC)
- Mine Safety and Health Act of 1970 (regulation plus black lung entitlement)
- Magnuson-Moss Warranty Improvement Act of 1974
- Commodity Trading Act of 1974

Neither [Office of Economic Opportunity (OEO) director] Shriver nor Johnson intended their efforts to increase government spending on public assistance. Both hated the very idea of long-term welfare dependency and of costly government outlays for public aid. "Welfare," indeed, remained a dirty word in the lexicon of liberals as well as conservatives in the United States. Instead, Johnson hoped that a "war" on poverty would provide the "opportunity" necessary to help people help themselves. Welfare, thereby rendered unnecessary, would wither away. The goal, Shriver said repeatedly, was to offer a "hand up, not a hand out," to open "doors" to opportunity, not to establish federally financed "floors" under income.[2]

It was under Richard Nixon—the first president to endorse a guaranteed income—that entitlements replaced education and job training as the centerpiece of antipoverty programs.

The second half of the 1960s may have been a wild time, but the programs that emerged now seem rather tame. Conversely, the allegedly conservative 1970s produced many of the policies that liberals are now most determined to defend. When one looks at policy development rather than at presidential rhetoric and election returns, the 1970s cannot be considered a period of conservatism or reaction. Our proclivity to divide American political history according to presidential terms of office in this instance creates a mistaken image of the two decades.

This essay does not seek to denigrate the significance of the Great Society but rather to explore the ways in which the events of the 1960s contributed to the emergence of a "new American political system" and a "new politics of public policy" that produced the initiatives of the 1970.[3] The argument is twofold. On the one hand, the 1960s unleashed new forces and new expectations that could not be quelled by the election of Richard Nixon—or Ronald Reagan or Speaker Newt Gingrich for that matter. These are laid out in the first part of the essay.

On the other hand, the initiatives of the 1970s were the product of political strategies and political visions far different from those of the Great Society. The Great Society relied on forceful and highly visible presidential leadership; the initiatives of the 1970s, on more subtle congressional, administrative, and judicial innovation. The accomplishments of the Great Society were embodied in a few landmark laws; the initiatives of the 1970s in a multiplicity of legislative amendments, bureaucratic rules, and court decisions. The Great Society relied heavily on federal tax revenues; the initiatives of the 1970s tended to rely on litigation to shift costs to private parties and subnational governments. The

Great Society expressed boundless faith in government and substantial trust in administrative expertise; the initiatives of the 1970s were based on deep suspicion of government in general and the executive branch in particular.

Moreover, the Great Society was the product of extraordinary and memorable events: the death of one president and the rapid rise and fall of another; the moral triumph of the civil rights movement; a record-breaking presidential landslide and lopsided Democratic majorities in Congress; unprecedented affluence combined with widespread urban unrest. No one understood better than Lyndon Johnson how fleeting an opportunity this concatenation of events had produced, which is why he pushed his programs through the Eighty-ninth Congress with such memorable speed, zeal, and success. The innovations of the subsequent decade, in contrast, were the product of much more mundane events and far less colorful leaders. Their stories tend to be less dramatic, more technical, harder to follow, and, consequently, often ignored, which is another way of saying that in the 1970s, expansion of the responsibilities of the federal government became routine. That, perhaps, was the most profound legacy of the Great Society.

The New Political Landscape

The 1960s brought five important changes that contributed to the policy initiatives of the 1970s. Some of these—most notably the expansion of the public agenda and the transformation of federalism—lasted longer than others. But all left an indelible mark on the politics of the 1970s.

First and foremost is what James Q. Wilson has called the "lowering of the legitimacy barrier." Before 1964 the federal government played a minor role in civil rights, education, health care, crime prevention, delivery of social services, and promotion of the arts. Whether the national government had the constitutional authority to prohibit discrimination by private actors or to outlaw state literacy tests were highly controversial matters.

Public expectations and constitutional understandings shifted rapidly during the decade. As Wilson explains, "Until rather recently, the chief issue in any congressional argument over new policy was whether it was legitimate for the federal government to do something at all. . . . Once the 'legitimacy barrier' has fallen, political conflict takes a very different form. New programs need not await the advent of a crisis or an extraordinary majority, because no program is any longer 'new'—it is seen, rather, as an extension, a modification, or an enlargement of something the government is already doing. . . . Since there is virtually nothing the government has not tried to do, there is little it cannot be asked to do."[4] This shift is evident not only in the remarkable legislative achievements of the Great Society but also in the grandiose aspirations announced by a president not known for flights of fancy. Lyndon Johnson declared that the federal government was "totally committed" to ending "poverty and racial injustice," thus ensuring "abundance and liberty for all." And this was "just the beginning": "The Great Society is a place where every child can . . . enrich his mind and enlarge his talents. It is a place where leisure is a welcome chance to build and reflect, not a feared cause of boredom and restlessness. It is a place where the city of man serves not just the needs of the body and demands of commerce, but the desire for beauty and the hunger for community."[5] Three decades earlier, when Lyndon Johnson was entering politics, the country was engaged in a bitter debate over whether the interstate commerce clause authorized the federal government to outlaw child labor and establish a minimum wage. Now a president was declaring that the national government should combat boredom, build "community," and help citizens in their search for beauty—shortly before he won reelection by an unprecedented majority. The Great Society, as Patterson has shown, capped a "revolution in expectations" about the "capacity of the United States to create a better world abroad and a happier society at home."[6]

Second, expansion of the responsibilities of the federal government went hand in hand with a redefinition of relations between the national government and the states. The 1960s, Martha Derthick has written, "should be remembered as a time in which the mores of federalism underwent a massive change. The national government moved freshly and boldly into the critically important domains of civil rights, schools, police, and legislative districting. It very much enlarged its place in the domain of welfare. It sought to impart equality to African Americans and political efficacy to the poor. With goals so ambitious across so broad a front, it groped for more effective instruments of influence vis-à-vis state and local governments. And it found them."[7] Significant increases in the number and size of grants-in-aid made the states more dependent on federal financial support. The federal courts not only sought to reform state and local political systems through redistricting but also issued numerous detailed decrees to subnational governments on such matters as school and police practices, criminal procedures, welfare rules, and labor relations. Some of these decrees were based on new readings of the Fourteenth and Fifteenth Amendments, others on novel interpretations of old statutes, and still others on new legislation whose passage reflected the declining political power of state and local governments. New terms had to be invented to describe the new realities of federalism: "unfunded mandates," "cross-cutting requirements," "partial preemption," "implied private rights of action," "commandeering" the state administrative apparatus. Most of these policy instruments originated in efforts to uproot racial discrimination in the South. But they quickly spread to other policy areas, reflecting both the rapid diffusion of legal innovation and what Alice Rivlin has described as "the escalating perception that states were performing badly even in areas that almost everyone regarded as properly assigned to them."[8]

Third, the Great Society helped to create new centers of policy advocacy both inside government and out. Civil rights agencies such as the Equal Employment Opportunity Commission, the Office of Federal Contract Compliance Programs, the Office of Civil Rights in the Department of Health, Education, and Welfare (HEW), the Civil Rights Division of the Justice Department, and the Civil Rights Commission developed close ties with advocacy groups and supported an array of efforts to expand, strengthen, and ultimately redefine nondiscrimination requirements. Legal Services, originally created by OEO director Sargent Shriver as part of the War on Poverty, established sophisticated "backup centers" to put together ambitious reform agendas for welfare, education, health care, housing, and mental illness. The controversial community action and Model Cities programs recruited new advocates for the poor and minorities in cities throughout the country. The Ford Foundation helped out by sponsoring antipoverty efforts such as Mobilization for Youth and later provided seed money to litigation-oriented public interest groups such as the National Resources Defense Council and the Mexican American Legal Defense and Education Fund. Meanwhile, new legislation and judicial doctrines made it easier for such organizations to bring their cases to court and to receive generous attorneys' fees when they won (and even, on occasion, when they lost). The result was a dense and eclectic network of reformers with impressive policy expertise, a bottomless agenda of proposals and demands, and ready access to government officials, congressional aides, and journalists.[9]

Fourth, the combination of the civil rights revolution of the 1960s and the success of northern and western Democrats in the elections of 1958 and 1964 eventually ended southern Democrats' control in Congress. The conservative coalition lost its grip on the House Rules Committee in 1962. Two years later a coalition of determined Senate Democrats and Republicans were willing to violate venerable folkways, circumventing the Judiciary Committee and invoking cloture in order to pass the Civil Rights Act. The number of southern Democrats slowly shrank, and an increasing number of those who remained relied on black votes. By 1970 the liberal Democratic Study Group commanded a solid majority in the Democratic caucus and quickly used its power to redistribute power in the House. A similar shift had occurred more quietly and informally in the Senate a few years earlier. In presidential elections, the civil rights revolution cost Democrats the Solid South, making it hard for them to win the White House. But for a quarter of a century it also helped northern and western Democrats control key party and committee positions in Congress and to pass significant legislation—usually without the support of Republican presidents.

Finally, the Supreme Court appointments of the Kennedy and Johnson administrations created what Lucas Powe has aptly called "history's Warren Court."[10] From 1963 to 1969 these new justices—Byron White, Arthur Goldberg, Thurgood Marshall, and Abe Fortas—joined with Justices Warren, Black, Douglas, and Brennan to produce most of the landmark decisions for which the Warren Court is famous: *Gideon v. Wainwright* (right to counsel); *Abingdon School District v. Schempp* (prayer in school); *Reynolds v. Sims* (one person, one vote); *Heart of Atlanta Motel v. United States* (congressional power to outlaw segregation); *Griswold v. Connecticut* (privacy rights); *Harper v. Virginia Board of Education* (elimination of the poll tax); *Miranda v. Arizona, In Re Gault,* and *Terry v. Adams* (rights of the accused); *Green v. New Kent County* (school integration); *New York Times v. Sullivan* (freedom of the press); *Tinker v. Des Moines School District* and *Brandenburg v. Ohio* (freedom of speech); and *Goldberg v. Kelly* (welfare rights), to name but a few.

To be sure, Johnson's blunder in nominating his friend and informal adviser Abe Fortas—who neither wanted the job nor was willing to curtail financial and political activities incompatible with his new position—

eventually led to the appointment of Warren Burger as chief justice and to a somewhat more cautious Supreme Court. At the same time, though, Johnson's lower-court appointments had a profound influence on legal developments. In effect he packed the D.C. Circuit, the second most important court in the country, with judges who soon brought about the "reformation" of administrative law. Among his district court appointments were W. Arthur Garrity, Miles Lord, Jack Weinstein, and William Wayne Justice. These judges continued to shape public policy long after Lyndon Johnson retired to his ranch. Nudged along by two Democratic presidents, the federal judiciary entered an extended period of activism celebrated by liberals and decried by conservatives.

From Tax and Spend to Mandate and Sue

Given these substantial changes in American politics, it is not surprising that the 1970s were a period of significant policy innovation. During his first term, Richard Nixon was more inclined to take credit for new domestic programs than to oppose them. In his truncated second term, Nixon tried to contain the forces of change but failed. By 1974, Congress was clearly in control of domestic policymaking, creating new programs and revising old ones at a rapid clip. At the same time, the allegedly counterrevolutionary Burger Court was endorsing busing to achieve school desegregation in the North as well as the South, announcing *Roe v. Wade*, laying the legal foundation for affirmative action for private employers, reducing the states' authority to establish welfare rules, and using the equal protection clause to attack gender discrimination.

If the Nixon and Ford years were not ones of conservatism, reaction, or stasis, neither were they characterized by New Deal or Great Society liberalism. Liberal reformers first adjusted their political strategies and eventually revised the meaning of liberalism. To understand this shift, it is useful to start with an obvious and concrete difference between the 1960s and 1970s: in the latter decade, reformers' power base lay in congressional subcommittees, the lower federal courts, and the permanent staff of a few administrative agencies rather than in the White House. This simple fact had a number of important consequences.

First, policy change came not in a few big, highly publicized bangs but in a long series of incremental expansions that were often presented as mere extensions and clarifications of previous programs. Congressional subcommittees focused their efforts on programs within their jurisdiction. Rarely did they attempt to construct comprehensive reform packages that would inevitably invade the turf of other committees. Federal judges relied more on "creative" statutory interpretation and less on overt invocation of novel constitutional arguments.[11] Administrators used old laws to justify new policies. In the 1950s this form of policy innovation would have been far more difficult. But, as noted, the federal government had created so many beachheads in the 1960s that it was hard to find policy areas that were off-limits to such incremental expansion.

The new incrementalism involved not just the proliferation of programs and their steady expansion over time but also a subtle process by which each branch of government could build on the work of the others. New federal mandates on bilingual education, for example, were announced in HEW regulations that expanded on the Supreme Court's decision in *Lau v. Nichols*,[12] which in turn had adopted an expansive interpretation of a previous HEW memorandum interpreting Title VI of the Civil Rights Act and 1968 amendments to the Elementary and Secondary Education Act.[13] Similarly, a complex Environmental Protection Agency (EPA) program to prevent "significant deterioration" of air quality in rural areas began when a federal district court judge, relying on a few fragments of legislative history, ordered the agency to initiate such a policy. The EPA responded by constructing an elaborate regulatory program, which Congress then expanded still further.[14] In school desegregation, HEW and the federal courts similarly ratcheted up federal mandates, each citing the other as an authority on the subject.[15] An HEW attorney who witnessed a similar expansion of federal rules on welfare eligibility described the process as "a sort of four-sided game of leapfrog." As he put it, "If for any reason the federal administrators were inhibited in the development of new rules—perhaps because of the disapproving views of members of an appropriation committee—the courts could assume the lead in developing new legal requirements." Federal administrators could then embed the judicially developed policy in their rule book, "perhaps even embellishing it a bit." Reform "could thus proceed in an ever-ascending spiral with no single participant in the process having the capacity to block progressive development."[16]

Consider the consequences of such steady, incremental growth for means-tested income maintenance programs. As everyone who studies welfare knows, comprehensive welfare reform proposals repeatedly went down to defeat in the 1970s. But in the first half of the decade, food stamps grew from a tiny discretionary program into an entitlement costing nearly as much as Aid to Families with Dependent Children (AFDC); the federal government took over state programs for the disabled and elderly poor and added a new provision for families with disabled children; the courts essentially nationalized eligibility standards for AFDC; and the federal government created the Earned Income Tax Credit, the special supplemental feeding program for women, infants, and children (WIC), entitlements for those suffering from black lung disease and kidney failure, several new housing programs, the school breakfast program, and the Low Income Home Energy Assistance Program. In 1968, federal spending on means-tested program amounted to a little over $53 billion (in 1998 dollars); state and local governments spent an additional $22 billion, for a total of $75 billion. A decade later these figures (again in 1998 dollars) were $160 billion from the federal government and $50 billion from state and local governments, for a total of $210—almost *triple* the real spending of a decade before.[17] Those who paint the 1970s as an era of backlash and conservatism often point out—correctly—that real spending on AFDC declined after 1972. But it is also true that AFDC spending had doubled during Nixon's first term. Moreover, by the mid-1970s, AFDC was just one of many programs providing cash and in-kind benefits to the poor. This incremental expansion of means-tested programs may lack the high drama of the failure of the Family Assistance Plan (which is one reason it has failed to capture the attention of intellectuals), but its cumulative impact on antipoverty efforts has been immense.

The major environmental statutes of the 1970s—particularly the Clean Air Act, the Clean Water Act, and the National Environmental Policy Act—have attracted more scholarly and public attention. The popularity of environmental protection at times produced a bidding war between Democrats in Congress and Republicans in the White House. Here, too, the problem of environmental degradation was handled in a multiplicity of statutes and programs. The dominance of Congress meant that similar risks were treated differently in statutes written by different committees. Moreover, each act was regularly rewritten—almost always made more stringent—as Congress incorporated innovations of the courts and administrators.[18]

One of the most important policy changes of the 1970s, the shift from a color-blind interpretation of civil rights to affirmative action, is particularly hard to trace because the authors of this new set of policies insisted so vociferously that no change was occurring at all. As John Skrentny has shown, advocates of affirmative action in the Equal Employment Opportunity Commission, in the courts, and in civil rights organizations employed a "discourse of tradition" that denied not only "that there was anything new in affirmative action" but also "that any [racial] preferences were taking place."[19] It is worth noting that while presidents and members of Congress usually have incentives to exaggerate their contributions and innovations, judges and administrators often have the opposite incentives: they wish to disguise the novelty of their actions.

A second consequence of the new institutional patterns of the 1970s was that divided government gave a distinctive tone to the political debate of the Nixon-Ford years and a distinctive structure to the laws passed by Congress. Nothing united fractious Democrats in Congress as much as hostility to the White House. As Michael Foley put it, "Nixon's election provided a real tonic to congressional Democrats, for it reduced their internal tensions and integrated the party—and thereby the institution—against a Republican administration. The Senate liberals, in particular, were able to immerse themselves in the occupational therapy of unembarrassed opposition to the White House."[20] In this new political environment a variety of social ills—malnutrition, racial discrimination and segregation, pollution, lack of educational and employment opportunities for those with disabilities—were redefined as consequences of insufficient vigor or callous disregard by the executive branch. Thus food stamp advocates laid the problem of hunger at the feet of the Department of Agriculture and the Nixon administration, leading Nixon aide Daniel Patrick Moynihan to complain that "the more government did to meet the nutritional needs of the poor, the more impassioned grew the insistence that it was not doing enough. . . . The style of the hunger movement was attack, and it attacked whoever was in office, almost regardless of what the officeholder did."[21] The job of liberal program advocates was to confront and expose executive misdeeds, executive indifference to social problems, and executive failure to enforce congressional enactments aggressively. This confrontation and exposure could be achieved in committee hearings, in court suits, through investigative journalism, or, as was often the case, by all three simultaneously.

If bureaucratic fecklessness, Office of Management and Budget foot-dragging, and presidential recalcitrance were key parts of the problem, than elaborate procedures, multiple deadlines, detailed statutory commands, "technology-forcing" requirements, and legislative "hammers" were all essential parts of the solution. Long, complex statutes replaced the broad grants of discretion characteristic of New Deal and Great Society programs. Demanding, even utopian, statutory requirements (such as the 1972 Clean Water Act's goals of making all waters "fishable and swimmable" by 1983 and eliminating all discharges into navigable waters by 1985) had two advantages: first, members of Congress could take credit for ambitious programs, and second, they could blame the executive branch for the inevitable failure to reach these goals.[22]

The new congressional enactments were usually combined with aggressive congressional oversight and judicial review. Many of the new statutes authorized federal courts to hear "action-forcing" suits, without requiring any showing that the litigants had suffered a concrete, particularized injury. Private citizens and public interest groups were encouraged to act as "private attorneys general" to make sure that the law was enforced to the fullest possible extent. Even when such "citizen suit" provisions were absent, federal judges granted standing and recognized causes of action to ensure "that the legislative purposes heralded in the halls of Congress are not lost in the vast halls of the federal bureaucracy."[23] Congress also authorized federal courts to jettison in many circumstances the traditional "American rule" on attorneys' fees—which required all parties to pay their own litigation costs—and to award attorneys' fees to "prevailing" parties. As a result, policy disputes between congressional committees and the White House were often resolved in court suits between agencies and public interest groups. Sometimes these suits remained adversarial; sometimes they became collusive.

Third, program advocates had strong incentives to keep the costs of their programs off-budget. Within Congress their power lay in policy and constituency committees—Education and Labor, Environment and Public Works, Energy and Commerce, Agriculture, Interior, and Judiciary—not the appropriations committees, the revenue committees, or the new budget committees. Just as important were the endemic budget deficits of 1970s and 1980s. Presidents and conservatives in Congress had more leverage when an issue could be framed in terms of balancing the budget and when funding could be cut in appropriation or reconciliation bills. Creating a new tax to fund a new program—as FDR did for

Social Security and LBJ did for Medicare—was seldom within the realm of political feasibility. As the cost of existing programs grew, gobbling up all available revenue, the political incentives to keep the cost of new initiatives off-budget became ever stronger.

One frequently used funding alternative was to impose costs on the private sector. The environmental regulation that originated in the 1970s, for example, cost over $150 billion per year by 1995, almost all paid by consumers in the form of higher prices for goods and services.[24] Another common technique was to impose program costs on subnational governments. State and local school systems, for example, have paid over 90 percent of the cost of complying with the Education for All Handicapped Children Act of 1975. By the end of the decade mayors and governors were describing these "unfunded mandates" as "millstones" that "threaten both the initiative and the financial health of local governments throughout the country."[25] Timothy Conlan reports that "fully half of the thirty-six most intrusive intergovernmental regulations identified in 1982 by the U.S. Advisory Commission on Intergovernmental Relations (ACIR) were created in this period [1969–74]."[26]

Congress also imposed onerous new mandates on federal agencies without providing commensurate additional appropriations. Legislation specified the number of eligibility reviews to be carried out annually by the Social Security Administration; the number of pollution standards, emission limits, and reports to be produced by EPA each year; and the number of days within which agencies must respond to Freedom of Information Act requests. Congress directed the Department of Transportation not only to build highways and fund mass transit (its traditional missions) but also to "relieve congestion, improve air quality, preserve historic sites, encourage the use of auto seatbelts and motorcycle helmets, control erosion and storm water runoff, monitor traffic and collect data on speeding, reduce drunk driving, require environmental impact statements, control outdoor advertising, develop standards for high-occupancy vehicles, require metropolitan area and statewide planning, use recycled rubber in making asphalt, set aside ten percent of construction monies for small businesses owned by disadvantaged individuals"— and more.[27] Piling on new tasks presumably would force administrators to work harder, be more aggressive in regulating private parties and subnational governments, and perhaps eventually squeeze more money from the discretionary budget.

A subtle consequence of these indirect forms of funding new programs is the need to establish the moral culpability of those on whom the cost is imposed. Why should the federal government shift cost for complying with federal rules to the private sector and subnational governments? Because these organizations were shirking their moral responsibilities. If environmental protection or education of those with disabilities were merely problems to be solved, then federal funding would be appropriate. But once they are seen as moral failings on the part of corporations and subnational governments, then it seems only right that the costs be imposed on the guilty.

Finally, since the late 1960s there has been a distinct tendency to frame government programs in terms of individual rights.[28] One reason for this was the power of the Civil Rights Act model. If employers could not discriminate on the basis of race, gender, or national origin (Title VII), then why should they be allowed to discriminate on the basis of age, disability, or sexual orientation? If subnational governments that received federal funds could not discriminate on the basis of race (Title VI), why should they be allowed to discriminate on the basis of gender or disability? With state and local governments increasingly dependent on federal money, what Hugh Davis Graham has called the "cloning of Title VI" became a simple and effective strategy for entrepreneurial members of Congress.[29] Both section 504 of the Rehabilitation Act of 1973 (which prohibits discrimination against the handicapped in any program receiving federal funding) and Title IX of the Education Amendments of 1972 (which prohibits gender discrimination in education programs receiving federal assistance) passed with virtually no debate.[30]

Just as important, the language of rights enabled Congress to build on the initiatives of the federal courts. Sponsors of the Education for All Handicapped Children Act, for example, argued that the legislation was designed to protect constitutional rights already recognized by the courts. The Civil Rights of Institutionalized Persons Act of 1980 encouraged the courts to expand their efforts to reform state institutions for the mentally ill and the developmentally disabled. Conversely, defining issues in terms of rights increased the likelihood that the courts would play a major role in interpreting and enforcing the statute enacted by Congress, which in the 1970s usually strengthened the hand of program advocates. Rights, of course, have undeniable political appeal in the United States. Consumers' bill of rights, patients' bill of rights, airplane passengers' bill of rights, taxpayers' bill of rights—such labeling is often an effective method both to increase the visibility of legislative proposals and to disarm the opposition.

For many years conservatives have loved to deride liberals as "tax-and-spend Democrats." Most Democrats have gone to great lengths to show their constituents that this label does not apply to them. Yet this description of Democrats would not have offended Franklin Roosevelt or Lyndon Johnson. (When Harry Hopkins coined the phrase, it was "tax and tax, spend and spend, elect and elect.") In the most popular programs of the New Deal and Great Society, taxing and spending were explicitly tied together through earmarked taxes and sacrosanct trust funds. In a wide variety of grant-in-aid programs, the federal government used its unmatched capacity to generate tax revenue to promote various state activities, professionalize state agencies, and subtly redistribute resources. Indeed, the Constitution's explicit taxation clause gave special legitimacy to this form of federal activity. Taxing and spending meant using collective resources to solve collective problems—ranging from national defense and law enforcement to unemployment, education, and preservation of natural resources.

Those who supported initiatives of 1970s were hardly averse to spending federal tax dollars. But for reasons laid out above, after the heady days of the Eighty-ninth Congress it was difficult to push large, visible new spending programs through the obstacle course on Capitol Hill. In the 1970s—and subsequent decades as well—the dominant strategy of reformers was not tax and spend but rather mandate and sue. Federal laws, regulations, and court rulings placed new demands on the private sector, subnational governments, and federal agencies. Congress seldom provided financial resources commensurate with these new responsibilities. In each case the mandate came first, followed by a mad scramble to come up with the money.[31]

Since these mandates were bound to generate substantial resistance, they were almost always tied to a powerful enforcement mechanism: the right to sue. This included the federal government's authority to sue private actors and subnational governments (and to impose hefty penalties), the authority of private citizens and public interest groups to sue all levels of government, and the right of private citizens to bring enforcement suits against other private actors who had allegedly violated the law. Congressional committees and federal administrators produced the mandates; federal courts not only entertained the suits but often expanded the mandates in the process. As the stick replaced the carrot, formal rules and legal contestation replaced the bargaining and relatively stable norms of the budgetary process.

Greater Expectations, Declining Trust

So far, this essay has presented the strategies of reformers as tactical adaptations to the distribution of power among and within American national institutions after 1969. But these strategies also reflected powerful trends in American political culture and public opinion. In a famous 1967 study, Lloyd Free and Hadley Cantril noted that the American public is "ideologically" conservative but "operationally" liberal.[32] Although Americans are distrustful of government in general, they support virtually all the particular activities that government undertakes—and want more of almost everything. After 1967 this contradiction grew more intense: public expectations grew, while trust in government declined precipitously. The public expected the federal government to fight racial and gender discrimination, improve education, expand the economic opportunities of the disadvantaged, protect the environment, reduce crime, wage one "war" on drugs and another on cancer, promote energy self-sufficiency (which suddenly became the "moral equivalent of war"), guarantee health care for all, create a growing and full-employment economy, and provide a "safety net" for those unable to find work. When asked what they want from government, citizens typically offer a Gomperesque reply: "more."[33] After the Great Society, it became nearly impossible to argue that any of these tasks was outside the constitutional realm of the federal government.

Yet, as innumerable public opinion polls have demonstrated, confidence in government fell precipitously after 1965. In the mid-1960s, three-quarters of Americans thought the federal government could be trusted to do the right thing most of the time. By the mid-1970s, only about a third of Americans shared that view. Conversely, in the mid-1960s only 30 percent of the public believed the "government is run by a few big interests looking out for themselves." Ten years later over two-thirds agreed with this statement. Despite a few ups and downs, public trust in government has continued to be low ever since.[34]

Surprisingly, between 1965 and 1975, trust in government fell furthest and fastest among those who described themselves as liberals and Democrats.[35] According to Norman Nie, Sidney Verba, and John

Petrocik, by 1972 "liberals were more opposed to big government than were conservatives."³⁶ There were, of course, many reasons for this. Liberals came to identify "big government" with Richard Nixon, the war in Vietnam, the military-industrial complex, captured regulatory agencies, and ineffective, insensitive, unresponsive bureaucracy. Civil rights workers, who had spent years challenging the discriminatory practices of public school systems, state and local governments, and some federal agencies, were not inclined to give public officials the benefit of the doubt. The New Left celebrated participatory democracy and decentralization. For many on the left, the era of centralized, bureaucratic government had come and gone.

This put liberals in the awkward position of arguing that more responsibility and authority should be given to a national government that they—and the American public generally—did not trust. In the 1960s, as Hugh Heclo has explained, "institutional authority was challenged throughout American society at the same time as demands and expectations on government were multiplied. For a great many activists, the federal government was part of the 'establishment' that had to be attacked. And yet it was also the resource that lay most readily at hand to pursue the social reformations [they] urged." Fortunately for these liberal activists, "the paradox of policy expectations and institutional suspicion seemed to yield an answer. Federal policy powers could be vigorously increased so long as they were sufficiently distrusted and controlled by activists. . . . [T]he energetic use of national policy for transforming American society had to be accompanied by an equally vigorous suspicion of that power and whoever might exercise it." In marked contrast to the reform tradition stretching from the Progressives to the New Deal and the Great Society, "to be a reformer was to be pro-activist, but also in a certain sense to be antigovernment. . . . Government responsibilities were to be vastly expanded, while government autonomy had to be restricted at every turn. Distrust required opening up policy-making to public view and assuring access for formerly marginalized groups. Confidence in administrative discretion, expertise, and professional independence had to be replaced by continuous public scrutiny, hard-nosed advocacy, strict timetables, and stringent standards for prosecuting the policy cause in question."³⁷

No one followed this strategy more consistently than the leading policy entrepreneur of the 1970s, Ralph Nader. Nader attacked the auto industry for producing unsafe cars and the federal government for failing to do anything about it. Once Congress created the National Highway Traffic Safety Administration, Nader repeatedly faulted it for insufficient regulatory zeal. This attack continued even when his protégé, Joan Claybrook, was running the agency. As his influence increased, Nader's policy and political goals grew ever more quixotic; nothing seemed to alarm him as much as the prospect of being allied with those in power.[38]

Building public programs by exposing government's failures was the formula that not only resolved liberal activists' ambivalence about government authority but also allowed them to make full use of their allies in the media, on congressional subcommittees, and on the federal bench. After all, journalists, oversight committees, and judges do not run government programs. Their responsibility is to show that something is wrong and to demand (usually indignantly) that the situation be corrected. Casting blame is their job, and if blame could be cast at a Republican administration, so much the better.[39]

The language of individual rights was particularly well suited to the purposes of these ambivalent activists. For the rights most vigorously promoted in the 1970s were at one and the same time *claims for government assistance* and *protections against bureaucratic discretion*. The right to a free and appropriate education, the right to a nutritionally adequate diet, the right to equal access to public transportation, the right to breathe clean air, the right to adequate health care, the right to a workplace free from racial discrimination or sexual harassment—all this required substantial governmental effort. But the fact that these were rights rather than mere programs meant that government officials would be subject to elaborate procedures, multiple rules, and constant oversight. This understanding of rights produced not the limited government we associate with Locke and *Lochner* but the peculiar combination of governmental activism and political fragmentation that Robert Kagan has called "adversarial legalism."[40]

Throughout American history, reformers have searched for methods to keep government agencies responsive to the popular will. Party patronage, rotation in office, presidential leadership, congressional oversight, community action—all have been presented as ways to keep the programs the public wants from degenerating into the powerful, autonomous bureaucracies it fears. For the reformers of the 1970s, the most important instrument for assuring democratic control of bureaucracy was the so-called citizen suit. Citizen suits not only allowed public interest groups to push for more aggressive government action but also enabled private parties to take direct actions against malfeasants in the public and private spheres. Joseph Sax, one of the most important teachers of leaders of the environmental movement, touted such litigation as "a means of access for ordinary citizens to the process of governmental decision-making" and "a repudiation of our traditional reliance upon professional bureaucrats."[41] Reformers could fight city hall and big business by making innovative legal arguments rather than building political organizations with active members.

In odd and unexpected ways, conservatives could sometimes find common ground with this rights-based approach to public policy. Consider the Philadelphia Plan, the first explicit affirmative action program for employment. In response to the urban unrest of the mid-1960s, Lyndon Johnson urged the building-trade unions to negotiate "a national pact with contractors that represented a classic Johnsonian consensus: builders would rebuild the cities, labor would train minority workers in exchange for robust employment, and the federal government would pay for it all."[42] When Richard Nixon took office shortly thereafter, he was significantly less enthusiastic about a massive urban renewal program. Secretary of Labor George Schultz convinced Nixon that the employment "targets" of the Philadelphia Plan provided a way to increase black employment, promote "black capitalism," and reduce public assistance without increasing federal spending or establishing an inefficient public jobs bureaucracy. At the same time, Nixon could stick it to the unions by forcing them to open their rolls to African Americans.[43] Similarly, Nixon saw his Family Assistance Plan as a way to reduce the size and power of the welfare bureaucracy—especially its meddling social workers.[44] Years later the first Bush administration vigorously advocated expansion of the rights of the disabled as a way to move those with a disability from welfare to work. This, too, promised to reduce federal spending, welfare dependency, and bureaucratic paternalism.[45] Regulation and rights rather than bureaucracy and spending—this was the formula that proved so successful after the heyday of the Great Society.

In retrospect it is clear that mandate-and-sue liberalism is not without its own drawbacks. Costly, contentious litigiousness; lack of coordination among programs; lack of transparency and public accountability; neglect of grassroots political organizations— these are among the charges now launched at such programs. Serious problems they may well be, but they are certainly not the product of Great Society liberalism. If conservatives want to understand why their efforts to roll back the welfare and regulatory state have largely failed, they need to see how the programs they attack are themselves the product of a revolt against "big government." And if liberals want to understand present discontents with "big government," they need to acknowledge the extent and the peculiar path of their own success.

Notes

1. See sections 703(a), 703(d), and especially 703(j) of the Civil Rights Act, and Hugh Davis Graham, *The Civil Rights Era: Origins and Development of National Policy, 1960-1972* (New York: Oxford University Press, 1990), 139–52.

2. James T. Patterson, *Grand Expectations: The United States, 1945–1974* (New York: Oxford University Press, 1996), 535.

3. Anthony King, ed., *The New American Political System*, 2nd version (Washington, D.C.: AEI Press, 1990); Marc C. Landy and Martin A. Levin, eds., *The New Politics of Public Policy* (Baltimore: Johns Hopkins University Press, 1995); Sidney Milkis and Richard Harris, eds., *Remaking American Politics* (Boulder, Colo.: Westview Press, 1989).

4. James Q. Wilson, "American Politics: Then and Now," *Commentary*, February 1979, 41.

5. Commencement speech at the University of Michigan, May 22, 1964, www.cnn.com/SPECIALS/cold.war/episodes/13/documents/lbj.

6. Patterson, *Grand Expectations*, vii–viii.

7. Martha Derthick, *Keeping the Compound Republic: Essays on American Federalism* (Washington, D.C.: Brookings Institution, 2001), 147.

8. Alice Rivlin, *Reviving the American Dream: The Economy, the States, and the Federal Government* (Washington, D.C.: Brookings Institution, 1992), 86–87.

9. For a description of the long-term consequences of these changes, see Jeffrey Berry, *The New Liberalism: The Rising Power of Citizen Groups* (Washington, D.C.: Brookings Institution, 1999), and Charles R. Epps, *The Rights Revolution: Lawyers, Activists and Supreme Courts in Comparative Perspective* (Chicago: Chicago University Press, 1999).

10. Lucas A. Powe Jr., *The Warren Court and American Politics* (Cambridge: Harvard University Press, 2000), 209–16; the term "history's Warren Court" is used on p. 207.

11. R. Shep Melnick, *Between the Lines: Interpreting Welfare Rights* (Washington, D.C.: Brookings Institution, 1994), 35–40, 83–92, 207–21, and 249–53.

12. 414 U.S. 563 (1974).

13. Abigail Thernstrom, "E Pluribus Plura—Congress and Bilingual Education," *Public Interest*, no. 60 (Summer 1980); Gareth Davies, "The Great

Society after Johnson: The Case of Bilingual Education," *Journal of American History* 88 (March 2002): 1405–29; Gary Orfield, *Must We Bus? Segregated Schools and National Policy* (Washington, D.C.: Brookings Institution, 1978), 206–11; and Lawrence Fuchs, *American Kaleidoscope: Race, Ethnicity, and the Civil Culture* (Hanover, N.H.: University Press of New England, 1990), chap. 24.

14. R. Shep Melnick, *Regulation and the Courts: The Case of the Clean Air Act* (Washington, D.C.: Brookings Institution, 1983), chap. 4.

15. Stephen Halpern, *On the Limits of the Law: The Ironic Legacy of Title VI of the 1964 Civil Rights Act* (Baltimore: Johns Hopkins University Press, 1995), esp. 58–80.

16. St. John Barrett, "The New Role of the Courts in Developing Welfare Law," *Duke Law Journal* (1970): 23.

17. Committee on Ways and Means, U.S. House of Representatives, *2000 Green Book* (Washington, D.C.: Government Printing Office, 2000), 1398–1400. This increase was not primarily the result of increases in Medicaid. Of the $135 billion increase over the decade, $38 billion (28 percent) came from Medicaid spending. See also Timothy Conlan, *From New Federalism to Devolution: Twenty-Five Years of Intergovernmental Relations* (Washington, D.C.: Brookings Institution, 1998), 82–85.

18. R. Shep Melnick, "Risky Business: Government and the Environment after Earth Day," in *Taking Stock: American Government in the Twentieth Century*, ed. Morton Keller and R. Shep Melnick (Washington, D.C.: Woodrow Wilson Center Press; New York: Cambridge University Press, 1999), 156–84.

19. John Skrentny, *Ironies of Affirmative Action*, 146.

20. Michael Foley, *The New Senate: Liberal Influence on a Conservative Institution, 1959–72* (New Haven: Yale University Press, 1980), 77.

21. Daniel Patrick Moynihan, *The Politics of a Guaranteed Income* (New York: Vintage, 1973), 117, 120.

22. For an example of this dynamic, see R. Shep Melnick, "Pollution Deadlines and the Coalition for Failure," *Public Interest*, no. 75 (Spring 1984).

23. *Calvert Cliffs Coordinating Committee v. AEC*, 449 F.2d 1109 (D.C. Cir. 1971) at 111.

24. Daniel Fiorina, *Making Environmental Policy* (Berkeley: University of California Press, 1995), 121–22, citing figures produced by the Environmental Protection Agency.

25. Edward Koch, "The Mandate Millstone," *Public Interest*, no. 61 (Fall 1980): 42. Koch noted that unfunded mandates were the result of "an ever widening gulf separating the programmatic demands of an activist Congress from its concurrent fiscal conservatism" (43).

26. Conlan, *From New Federalism to Devolution*, 87.

27. James Q. Wilson, "Can the Bureaucracy Be Deregulated? Lessons from Government Agencies," in *Deregulating the Public Service*, ed. John DiIulio (Washington, D.C.: Brookings Institution, 1994), 43.

28. See, generally, R. Shep Melnick, "Courts, Congress, and Programmatic Rights," in *Remaking American Politics,* ed. Sidney M. Milkis and Harris (Boul-

der, Colo.: Westview, 1989), 188–212, and Landy and Levin, *New Politics of Public Policy*.

29. Hugh Davis Graham, "After 1964: The Paradox of American Civil Rights Policy," in Keller and Melnick, *Taking Stock*, 187–218.

30. Robert Katzmann, *Institutional Disability: The Saga of Transportation Policy for the Disabled* (Washington, D.C.: Brookings Institution, 1986).

31. For a review of some of the consequences of the multiplicity of mandates placed on federal agencies and the resulting "disproportionality between agencies' statutory responsibilities and agencies' resources," see Richard Pierce, "Judicial Review of Agency Actions in a Period of Diminishing Agency Resources," *Administrative Law Review* 49 (1997): 61.

32. Lloyd Free and Hadley Cantril, *The Political Beliefs of Americans* (New Brunswick, N.J.: Rutgers University Press, 1967).

33. Albert H. Cantril and Susan Davis Cantril, *Reading Mixed Signals: Ambivalence in American Public Opinion about Government* (Washington, D.C.: Woodrow Wilson Center Press; Baltimore: Johns Hopkins University Press, 1999), chap. 2; William G. Mayer, *The Changing American Mind: How and Why American Public Opinion Changed between 1960 and 1988* (Ann Arbor: University of Michigan Press, 1993), 451–62, 486–90; Fay Lomax Cook and Edith J. Barrett, *Support for the Welfare State: The Views of Congress and the Public* (New York: Columbia University Press, 1992); R. Kent Weaver, *Ending Welfare as We Know It* (Washington, D.C.: Brookings Institution, 2000), chap. 7; Robert Cameron Mitchell, "Public Opinion and the Green Lobby: Posed for the 1990s?" in *Environmental Policy in the 1990s*, ed. Norman Vig and Michael Kraft, 81–99 (Washington, D.C.: CQ Press, 1990). Only two programs consistently provoke public opposition: foreign aid and "welfare." As Cook and Barrett as well as Weaver show, though, the public consistently supports spending on programs that provide "assistance to the poor," especially poor children. The public opposes foreign aid largely because it vastly exaggerates its cost.

34. Gary Orren, "Fall from Grace: The Public's Loss of Faith in Government," in *Why People Don't Trust Government*, ed. Joseph Nye, Philip Zelikow, and David King, 77–107 (Cambridge: Harvard University Press, 1997); Seymour Martin Lipset and William Schneider, *The Confidence Gap* (Baltimore: Johns Hopkins University Press, 1987).

35. Lipset and Schneider, *Confidence Gap*, 333.

36. Norman Nie, Sidney Verba, and John Petrocik, *The New American Vote* (Cambridge: Harvard University Press, 1976), 127.

37. Hugh Heclo, "The Sixties' False Dawn: Awakenings, Movements, and Postmodern Policy-making," *Journal of Policy History* 8 (1996): 50–52.

38. On Nader, see Jerry L. Mashaw and David L. Harfst, *The Struggle for Auto Safety* (Cambridge: Harvard University Press, 1990), 107–8, 118, 194–201; Justin Martin, *Nader: Crusader, Spoiler, Icon* (Cambridge, Mass.: Perseus, 2002); and R. Shep Melnick, "The Lonely Scold," *Claremont Review of Books*, Fall 2003, 57–58. Michael W. McCann provides a rich description of this "new liberal philosophy," its "code of conflict," and the resulting "judicialization of

politics" in *Taking Reform Seriously: Perspectives on Public Interest Liberalism* (Ithaca: Cornell University Press, 1986), chap. 2. According to Heclo, "Policy disputes are likely to begin with presumptions, not of good-faith bargaining in a search for agreement, but of confrontation with adversaries who are hostile to one's cause. . . . [A] great deal of postmodern policy-making is not really concerned with 'making policy' in the sense of finding a settled course of public action that people can live with. It is aimed at crusading for a cause by confronting power with power" (56).

39. For a graphic example, see Martha Derthick, *Agency under Stress* (Washington, D.C.: Brookings Institution, 1990), esp. chaps. 7 and 8. Samuel Huntington has described the 1970s as "the great age of exposure," noting that "exposure could not occur until the authority of the executive branch—that is, the plausible targets of exposure—had been weakened, and it could not occur until the power of the press and Congress—that is, the necessary agents of exposure—had been enhanced." See *American Politics: The Promise of Disharmony* (Cambridge: Harvard University Press, 1981), 190.

40. This essay's description of the initiatives of the 1970s has much in common with Kagan's description of the rise of adversarial legalism. Indeed, this essay could be read as an effort to expand on his discussion of the "roots of adversarial legalism." According to Kagan, adversarial legalism "can be viewed as arising from a fundamental tension between two powerful elements: first, a political culture (or set of popular political attitudes) that expects and demands comprehensive government protections from serious harm, injustice, and environmental danger—and hence a powerful, activist government—and, second, a set of governmental structures that reflect mistrust of concentrated power and hence that limit and fragment political and governmental authority. Adversarial legalism helps resolve the tension." See *Adversarial Legalism: The American Way of Law* (Cambridge: Harvard University Press, 2001), 15. In this essay I try to explain how both of these seemingly conflicting elements were strengthened in the 1960s and 1970s.

41. Quoted in McCann, *Taking Reform Seriously*, 115. In a dissenting opinion, Justice Stephen Breyer has described such private enforcement suits as a method for "promoting the sharing among citizens of governmental decision-making authority" and an effective way to ensure "local control over local decisions"—even when they are brought against state and local governments. See *College Savings Bank v. Florida Prepaid Postsecondary Education Expense Board*, 527 U.S. 666 (1999).

42. Graham, *Civil Rights Era*, 294.

43. Ibid., chap. 13, and Skrentny, *Ironies of Affirmative Action*, 193–209.

44. Moynihan, *Politics of a Guaranteed Income*, 302–27.

45. Thomas Burke, "On the Rights Track," in *Comparative Disadvantage? Social Regulation and the Global Economy*, ed. Pietro Nivola, 242–318 (Washington, D.C.: Brookings Institution, 1997).

The Great Society and the Demise of New Deal Liberalism

Jerome M. Mileur

The domestic New Deal ended in the final years of the 1930s, victim in part of Franklin Roosevelt's Court-packing plan, his executive-reorganization proposals, and his purge campaign—and also by the two-term precedent that made him a lame duck who would be gone by 1941. Predictions of FDR's political departure, however, proved premature as he went on to win a third and a fourth term as president. But in the 1940s, Roosevelt's presidency was centered on the war abroad, not reform at home, and in the aftermath of that war the new liberalism for which he stood was recast to address the realities of a cold war against the threat of international communism.

Liberalism had survived the war. In the United Nations, it made good on Woodrow Wilson's promise of an international organization designed to adjudicate disputes and act internationally to preserve world peace. At home, it produced the GI Bill of Rights, which transformed both American higher education and the lives of hundreds of thousands of returning veterans, and also a full-employment bill, which, though not everything for which its sponsors had hoped, nonetheless pledged the nation to provide jobs for its citizens. Socially, the spirit of the new liberalism—the promise of equal opportunity for all Americans—found expression in the determination of African Americans and women to share fully in the liberty in whose defense the nation had gone to war.

The late 1940s and 1950s, however, were years of frustration for New

Dealers and their progeny. Harry Truman, who came to the presidency upon Roosevelt's death, designed the policies and institutions, military and diplomatic, through which the nation would combat the threat of international communism and, in the Marshall Plan, put a humanitarian stamp on the nation's efforts abroad. As president, Truman took the first formal steps, however halting, toward a federal program to secure the civil rights of the nation's black minority. He also advanced an ambitious agenda of domestic reform in education, housing, and health care, but this for the most part fell victim to the preoccupation with international politics and to the determined opposition in Congress of a bipartisan "conservative coalition" of southern Democrats and midwestern Republicans that had formed in the final years of the thirties to resist the extension of FDR's domestic New Deal.

By the 1960s, history—World War II and its aftermath—had produced changes in liberalism as a public philosophy, while population movements had shifted the electoral ground on which the New Deal political coalition had been built. John F. Kennedy's narrow victory in 1960 was, in many ways, the "last hurrah" for the party of Roosevelt. By the time Lyndon Johnson succeeded to the presidency, liberalism and the Democratic Party majority were at risk. A master of vote counting as leader of the Senate, LBJ had to know the precarious state of things for both liberalism and the party, but from the outset of his presidency, he put national interests above party, especially in the area of civil rights. Kennedy had profiled cases of courage in American politics; Johnson produced a new chapter for the book.

The Quiet Revolution

Politics in the 1960s was noisy, from the traditional hoopla and rhetoric of conventional politics to boisterous public marches and demonstrations, peaceful and otherwise. Highly visible social movements, loud in their declamations, dominated public politics in the years of Camelot and Vietnam. But the politics of the decade had been reshaped in fundamental ways in the years following World War II by a less visible social movement. It was the quiet movement of the American from east to west, north to south, and city to suburb—not to protest but to live—that changed the nation's political landscape and set the political stage for the sixties. On the one hand, this greatest of social movements struck a blow at the political foundations on which the liberalism of Roosevelt and the New Deal rested, and on the other, it created a new geography of American politics that proved less hospitable to liberalism and more receptive to conservatism than was true of America before World War II.

The Democratic Party as remade by Franklin Roosevelt in the New Deal was grounded politically in the big cities of the North—the states above the Mason-Dixon Line from the East Coast west to those bordering the Mississippi River. It was the Democratic organizations in New York, Chicago, Philadelphia, Detroit, and other northern cities that were the electoral muscle in the party coalition. These largely ethnic machines, heavily Irish and Catholic, were reinforced in the 1930s by the "newer races" as Boston's colorful James Michael Curley called them (Italians, Poles, Jews), whose previously mixed party loyalties now went overwhelmingly to the Democrats.[1] Blue-collar workers, especially those who were members of the new industrial unions in the Congress of Industrial Organizations but also skilled workers from the craft unions of the American Federation of Labor, rallied behind the New Deal, attracted by its support for unions and workers: the Wagner Act that strengthened workers in their relations with management, the Federal Home Loan Act that made the American Dream of home ownership a reality for many, the Fair Labor Standards Act that set wage and hour standards for workers, and the Social Security Act that promised security in old age. In addition, women were actively recruited into the party of Roosevelt, where their presence in government was expanded and more visible, as were African Americans, who abandoned the party of Lincoln for that of FDR. All of these new groups were drawn primarily from the urban North.[2]

In 1932, the political geography of American politics—the distribution of Electoral College votes among the states—made the urban North a powerful base on which to build a liberal party in the mold of Roosevelt, one that combined the newer elements of the Democratic Party with a portion of the old and rallied both behind the new liberalism of the New Deal. The South, for centuries the base of the Democratic Party, would be less important, but Democratic majorities were so massive in the old confederacy that the party could lose one-third or more of its vote across the region without losing majorities in most states. Should the losses be greater in the South, the vote in the North was still sufficient to win the presidency. As Table 1 shows, a candidate in

Table 1. Number and Percentage of Electoral College Votes for Selected Presidential Elections by Regions, 1932–2000

	1932–40		1952–60		1964–68		1972–80		1992–00	
	N	%	N	%	N	%	N	%	N	%
North										
Northeast	88	16.6	85	16.0	80	14.9	78	14.5	68	12.6
Mideast	71	13.4	68	12.8	69	12.8	66	12.3	59	11.0
Midwest	137	25.8	131	24.7	129	24.0	126	23.4	112	20.8
South										
Midsouth	55	10.4	55	10.4	51	9.5	50	9.3	52	9.7
Deep South	57	10.7	59	11.1	61	11.3	63	11.8	71	13.2
West										
Plains	58	10.9	54	10.2	53	9.8	53	9.8	57	10.6
Mountain	30	5.7	32	6.0	33	6.1	35	6.5	40	7.4
Coastal	35	6.6	47	8.9	62	11.5	67	12.5	79	14.7

Source: Congressional Quarterly, *Guide to U.S. Elections*

Northeast: New England and New York
Mideast: New Jersey, Pennsylvania, Delaware, Maryland, West Virginia, and Washington, D.C.
Midwest: Ohio, Indiana, Illinois, Missouri, Michigan, Wisconsin, and Minnesota
Midsouth: Virginia, Kentucky, North Carolina, Tennessee, and Arkansas
Deep South: South Carolina, Georgia, Alabama, Mississippi, Louisiana, and Florida
Plains: North Dakota, South Dakota, Nebraska, Kansas, Oklahoma, and Texas
Mountain: Idaho, Montana, Wyoming, Colorado, Utah, Nevada, Arizona, and New Mexico
Coastal: California, Oregon, Washington, and, after 1960, Alaska and Hawaii

1932 who carried only the states of the North—the Northeast, mid-Atlantic, and Midwest—would win the White House with a 55 percent majority in the Electoral College without gaining another vote from any other part of the nation. This was the political geography that elected Roosevelt, returned him to the presidency in a landslide in 1936, gave him a third term in 1940, and a fourth in 1944. It was the same geography that enabled Harry Truman to manufacture a dramatic come-from-behind victory in 1948 and that carried John F. Kennedy to the White House in 1960 with a narrow margin of victory.

After World War II, however, the political geography of the nation began to change slowly but dramatically as a result of the massive movements of population away from the North to the South (especially Florida), to the Southwest (principally Texas), and to the West (mainly California). In addition, many of those who stayed in the old North were moving as well, away from urban centers to the suburbs. The new liberal political coalition of FDR would be challenged philosophically and politically by these movements. By the 1980s, when a new conservatism took firm hold on the American polity, the old North had barely 47 percent of the Electoral College vote, which fell to less than 45 percent by the 1990s. In 1960, the old geography still worked to the electoral benefit of the New Deal coalition, though the margin for error in political calculations was greatly reduced. The party's choice of Los Angeles for its convention attested to the growing political importance of the Golden State, while Kennedy's choice of Lyndon Johnson as his running mate acknowledged the importance of the "new" South, especially Texas, to the success of the party ticket. In the New Deal, the role of the South in national Democratic Party politics had been diminished for reasons both ideological and electoral, but as the population declined in the urban North in the late 1940s and 1950s, the South regained some of its lost importance to the national party.

The narrowness of John Kennedy's win in 1960 reflected the impact of this changing geography on presidential politics. By 1964, population shifts would eliminate altogether any political advantage the Democrats had in the old geography. JFK surely realized that his reelection would be fought on a terrain in which the electoral votes of the urban North would be reduced to near parity with the remaining states and that this in turn meant that the South would be even more important to Democratic Party success. This realization seems most evident in his administration's cautious exercise of executive authority in dealing with the civil rights demands of African Americans, as the two Kennedy brothers, Robert as attorney general and John as president, tried to manage black protest of social and political conditions in the South in order to maintain the loyalty of the party's southern white leadership without losing the moral ground on the issue and, with it, the support of the black civil rights leadership.[3] It was party divisions in Texas that took JFK to Dallas on November 22, 1963.

Lyndon Johnson's landslide victory in 1964 concealed the political implications of changes in the Electoral College that were the consequence of population movements between the states, though Johnson and other party leaders must have recognized the new electoral math that resulted from the new political geography of the nation. When LBJ acknowledged that the Civil Rights Act of 1964 likely meant the loss of the South, he surely understood that it could mean the loss of a great deal more. But the new math held little urgency for any in the party, for in 1965 and 1966 they were launched upon the construction of a Great Society, and by 1967, members of both parties were focused on those Americans in the streets of the nation's cities protesting racial discrimination or on their counterparts on the nation's campuses protesting the war in Southeast Asia.

Nor was great attention given in the early sixties to the other silent social movement following World War II, that from city to suburb, which would also weaken the political muscle of the New Deal coalition.[4] The presidential election of 1960 was the last in which the major cities of the North wielded a clout approximating that on which Roosevelt had rebuilt the Democratic Party in the 1930s. The population of these cities relative to that of their states changed little between the federal census of 1930 and that of 1950, but in the fifties and thereafter there was a great exodus from the older cities into the countryside around them. Postwar prosperity and a new and rapidly expanding federal interstate highway system fed this movement. City after city, as Table 2 shows, saw its political power reduced by one-third to one-half from what it had been in the 1940s. The suburbs had become the new home of the "American dream": a single-family house set neatly on a quarter-acre lot owned by its occupant free from the congestion, squalor, noise, and problems of the big city.[5]

Not only did the growth of the suburbs erode the political power of the big cities, but the suburbs themselves became home to a new style of politics—more independent and activist, more issue oriented and cause centered, less connected to the familiar institutional politics of political parties and interest groups. This new politics of suburbia, which found

Table 2. Percentage of Total State Population in Selected Major Northern Cities for Presidential Election Years 1932–2000

	1932–40 %	1944–48 %	1952–60 %	1964–68 %	1972–80 %	1984–88 %	1992–00 %
Boston	18	17	17	13	11	9	9
New York	55	55	52	46	43	40	40
Philadelphia	20	19	19	17	16	14	14
Cleveland	13	12	11	9	7	5	4
Detroit	32	30	29	21	17	12	11
Chicago	44	43	41	35	30	26	24

Source: U.S. Decennial Censuses of the Population, 1930–90 (Washington, D.C.: Government Printing Office).

expression in the smaller-scale "club politics" and a new "managerial culture," embraced a good-government ethos that viewed with suspicion, if not contempt, the old ethnic, working-class, machine politics of the cities.[6] Indeed, these urban machines, a foundation of the New Deal party system long in decline, now began to disappear altogether, none more dramatically than New York City's famed Tammany Hall, which fell in the early 1960s before the onslaught of reformist forces led by Eleanor Roosevelt and former New York governor Herbert Lehman. Only the Chicago Democratic organization of Richard Daley survived more or less intact through the 1960s, though it was bloodied at the national party's 1968 convention in the Windy City and its delegation to the 1972 convention was thrown out for violating the party's new delegate selection rules.

Like changes in the Electoral College, the political effects of the new power and different political style of the suburbs were not immediately apparent in the early sixties. Democratic success in the presidential contests of 1960 and 1964 helped to conceal them from public view, as they had the population shift between states. John Kennedy's campaign was fought on the old political geography of the 1950s, not the new one that came with the 1960 census. Moreover, his youthful energy, his "star" power on the new medium of television, and his issue- and candidate-centered campaign appealed to the highly individualistic suburban voter in the North. Lyndon Johnson's landslide triumph in 1964, driven by the Republican Party's nomination of Barry Goldwater, was won on the new political geography, but the magnitude of LBJ's win effectively papered over the political pitfalls for his party in this new terrain, and especially for his party's liberals.

Thus as the Democrats entered the decade of the 1960s, the electoral grounds beneath them had shifted greatly, albeit quietly, and if not immediately to the advantage of the Republican Party, these changes were systematically to the disadvantage of the old liberal party coalition forged by Franklin Roosevelt. The Great Society legislation of the sixties, for all its success in redressing long-festering social injustices, none greater than race, also gave the Republicans and their new conservative elites the opportunity to launch a counterattack against the Democrats and liberalism that came to its climax in the presidency of Ronald Reagan in 1981, an administration that redirected the mainstream of American politics away from the channels of liberal reform toward a new philosophical conservatism that grew strategically and tactically from the era of the Great Society.

New Deal Liberalism in the Postwar World

It was not only the political geography of the New Deal that began to shift after World War II. The political liberalism that was the philosophical foundation from which the social and economic programs of the New Deal sprang also began to change. By the 1960s, liberalism was not what it had been a quarter century earlier. The term "liberal" had not held much political significance for most Americans before the 1930s. It was, as Ronald D. Rotunda observes, "literally *born* in the early New Deal," yet by the end of the thirties "it had become a vital symbol used to identify New Deal programs."[7] The term "liberalism" was useful to Roosevelt in several ways. It differentiated the New Deal as a program of reform from the New Freedom of Woodrow Wilson and, perhaps more important, from "progressivism" and the electoral failures of the Progressive Party as recent as 1924.[8] It helped also to deflect conservative criticism of the New Deal as an alien ideology ("socialism" or "communism") that posed a threat to individual freedom. While the term "liberalism" had been used infrequently in American politics, its origins traced to Thomas Jefferson and thus linked FDR's program to the author of the Declaration of Independence (a founder of the Democratic Party) and gave the appearance of following Herbert Croly's advice that reformers use Hamiltonian means to Jeffersonian ends. Finally, it gave FDR a new label for a "new" Democratic Party that stood for his nationalist program of positive government and rejected the states' rights and laissez-faire conservatism of the party's past. It was a symbol around which he could build a new party coalition by appealing to blocs of voters for whom the "old" Democratic Party held little charm.[9]

The new liberalism had emerged in British political thought at the end of the nineteenth century. Harold Laski credited T. H. Green with being the architect of a new positive and collectivist theory of liberalism, as opposed to the older negative liberalism, and he credited it for the major gains Britain had made in social legislation in the first decades of the twentieth century.[10] But it was L. T. Hobhouse who provided perhaps the best statement of the new liberalism. Locating the origins of liberalism in the Renaissance, where it arose as a criticism of tyranny that demanded liberty for the individual, Hobhouse argued that mere criticism was no longer sufficient, because social and economic changes had rendered inadequate this essentially "negative" idea of liberty as the freedom of the individual *from* society. Following the lead of John Stuart Mill, as well as Green, he urged that a "positive" theory of liberty was required to secure the freedom of the individual *within* society. This required equality, for without it, Hobhouse argued, liberty was "a name of noble sound and squalid result."[11] Neither capitalism nor socialism provided an automatic formula for securing both individual liberty within society and social progress. Hobhouse looked instead to a broader understanding of democracy as being social as well as political and to the enlightened self-interest of individuals, who would use their collective power through government to achieve and maintain a rational balance of opportunity through an ongoing political debate about which activities were properly individual and which social. The management of this debate, Hobhouse insisted, required not only democracy but also bold leaders in the public realm.

British liberalism found its way into American politics in the decades before the New Deal. In its economic focus, its social-welfare orientation, and its statist impulses, this new liberalism grew out of a social democratic tradition that was embedded in Progressivism. There were traces in the Progressive Party platforms of 1912 and 1924, with their calls for an expanded role for government in economic regulation and for a graduated inheritance as well as income tax, and also in the New Freedom of Woodrow Wilson. Many Progressives, such as John Dewey and Jane Addams, believed that the era of extreme individualism was passing and that a new more socialized and collectivist world was emerging.[12] Beneath the surface of national politics in the 1920s, a debate was churning among old Progressives, social democrats, and Social Gospelists about the need for greater mutuality in social and economic organization and a more positive role for government in achieving it, from which came a more collectivist liberalism—Dewey called it "renascent liberalism"—that would give important intellectual direction to the New Deal.[13]

For Dewey, this new liberalism was intimately bound up with individualism, pluralism, and the *methods* of science and democracy. Where nineteenth-century liberalism had sought to liberate individuals from constraints of the physical world and thereby provide the opportunity to fulfill their material desires, the new liberalism envisioned a society in which individuals could realize their full potential as human beings. While material security was a prerequisite, the new liberalism called for a new social organization that would "make possible effective liberty and opportunity for personal growth in mind and spirit in all individuals."[14] Dewey believed that all social institutions, including government, existed to solve problems through the practical application of intelligence and the scientific method. To this end, individuals worked with others in social groups to deal with competing claims around particular problems and in doing so would move toward realization of their human potential. Through "scientific method and technological application," the conflicting claims could be settled "in the interest of the widest possible contribution to the interests of all" through the "method of democracy."[15]

More social democrat than New Dealer, Dewey believed that American political institutions, while democratic in form, tended to favor a "privileged plutocracy" and that the "ultimate place of economic organization in human life is to assure the secure basis for an ordered expression of individual capacity and for the satisfaction of the needs of man in non-economic directions."[16] Dewey also insisted that the "general creed of liberalism" had to be formulated into "a concrete program of action," but he was not clear as to the particulars of this program, saying that it would be achieved through experimentation, not argument.[17]

The New Deal was grounded, conceptually, in this new liberalism. Not only did Franklin Roosevelt embrace the liberal label for tactical reasons, he welcomed it as justification for the greatly expanded role to be played by the federal government in the affairs of the nation. His cousin Theodore had shown the potential of the presidency in the hands of an energetic chief executive, but many of Theodore Roosevelt's most dramatic initiatives and achievements—the Panama Canal, the creation of national parks and wildlife preserves, his intervention to end a national coal strike, and even his antitrust prosecutions—had changed neither the institutional capacity of the office significantly nor the place of the national government in the federal system, though TR had shown the potential of the presidency as a bully pulpit from which to speak directly to the American people. In turn, Wilson had shown the potential of the office for policy leadership, moving the national government into new areas of responsibility. With FDR, both the presidency and the federal government grew dramatically. In step with the new liberalism, he built the institutional capacity of the executive branch in general and the

Office of the President in particular beyond anything known before, including even mobilization for World War I. For the second Roosevelt, the new liberalism called for a state-centered nationalism: it was, to be sure, big government, but it was big government with the goal of being on the side of those who needed it.

The New Deal was a whirlwind of action that seemed sometimes contradictory in its effects, but its speech drew consistently on the new liberalism. Indeed, Roosevelt put Dewey's call for experimentation into lay terms, promising that he would try this, try that, and try something else until he found what worked. When conservatives charged that big government was threatening the freedom of individuals, the reply was that, by putting a solid material floor under individuals, the government was not threatening liberty but making it possible for more individuals to realize the fruits of freedom for themselves. Moreover, Roosevelt was intent on bending business to the interests of a common good and on empowering farmers and workers as partners in the design and management of a new and more collectivist economy in which mutualism, not individualism, would govern. In the depths of depression, the programs of the New Deal aimed at economic security—recovery, jobs, and individual protections—and at redrawing the economic balance of power between business, workers, and government. This economic liberalism remade the party battle in America by dividing the sides along class lines—the have-nots against the haves—and transformed the Democrats, the party of Roosevelt, into the new political majority in the nation.

But there was a flaw in FDR's new liberalism that was detected early by Rexford Tugwell, who, in describing the New Deal as a "time of confusion," attributed that confusion to "trying to attain collective organization under individualistic labels."[18] While the new liberalism gave FDR justification for expanding the role of government, he continued to speak more in terms of individual rights than in collectivist principles that obligated individuals to act in concert with the larger community for purposes not immediately their own. Dewey believed that individual self-interest would be enlightened through education and science and lead individuals to appreciate that a "great community" was in the interests of all. Beyond this appeal to reason, the new liberalism contained no compelling theory of collective action that made clear either why or when the interests of the whole should trump those of the individual. Aside from a theory of public order, an essential feature of all theories of governance, there was no moral justification for the use of government coercion in the interests of the common good.[19] Liberty and equality might be the American heritage, but liberalism, even the new liberalism, gave liberty a privileged status, placed equality in a subordinate position, and provided no sure guidance as to when equality should outweigh liberty in the equation of policymaking by liberal governments. Indeed, equality was to be the *means* to the end of greater liberty. The claim for equality was made in the name of *opportunity*, not condition, for the latter smacked of socialism (or, worse, communism) and was thus politically suspect. In the end, the justification for collective action lay in the power of political democracy, where majorities ruled, and in the 1930s, Roosevelt had the votes.

FDR came face-to-face with this flaw early in his first term. The collectivist ideal was evident in both the National Industrial Recovery Act (NIRA) and the Agricultural Adjustment Act, which were the cornerstones of FDR's recovery program and his attempt to build the "cooperative commonwealth" that he had proposed in his Commonwealth Club Address during the 1932 campaign. His aim was to build what William Leuchtenburg in this volume calls an "all-class alliance" in which capital, labor, and agriculture would work together in conjunction with government in the interests of the common good. This was a struggle from the outset in the drafting of the NIRA. The bill sent to Congress was the product of many compromises, but as George McJimsey notes, these compromises were less a matter of give-and-take and "more in the nature of a truce in which each party was inclined to hold the others to strict observance while they maneuvered to improve their own positions."[20]

Roosevelt nonetheless remained optimistic and in signing the bill noted the part he had "in the great cooperation of 1917 and 1918," adding that he was confident that "we can count on our industry once more to join in our general purpose."[21] Such was not to be, as industrialists resisted administration efforts to bring their workers into anything resembling a partnership with them. The NIRA, with its collectivist ideal, was also denounced as "socialism" by a broad range of conservatives, Democrats as well as Republicans. In 1934, when the U.S. Chamber of Commerce convention voted to reject the New Deal, FDR lamented their lack of concern for any interest larger than their own, saying of their convention, "I don't believe there was a single speech which took the human side, the old-age side, the unemployment side."[22] When the NIRA was declared unconstitutional, Roosevelt railed against the Court for a "horse-and-buggy" decision, but he saved his harshest words for industrialists, whom he denounced as "economic royalists" bent on imposing a "new industrial dictatorship" on America. He not only abandoned the all-class strategy but he retaliated, declaring class warfare and winning passage of the wealth tax bill that placed federal levies on inheritances, estates, gifts, corporate incomes, and dividends and also increased income tax rates on the wealthy.

Frustrated in his efforts to build a cooperative commonwealth, Roosevelt turned in a different political direction. As McJimsey observes, he moved away "from 'nation' solutions toward 'group' solutions and to a definition of citizenship that included identification with a social group."[23] Roosevelt had called for an economic bill of rights in his 1932 campaign, and he now set about constructing it, extending new rights to various groups of Americans. The rights of which he spoke were for the most part materialistic: a right to employment, to a decent home, to adequate food and clothing, to protection from unemployment and sickness, to security in old age, and to a good education. In the so-called second New Deal, Roosevelt set about constructing this new realm of rights. The Wagner Act gave workers the right to organize and bargain collectively with management through unions of their own choosing, while the Social Security Act created "entitlements" for the young, the infirm, the unemployed, the elderly, and families. These were *positive* rights—claims that individuals in the various groups had on the government—akin to the "positive liberty" embraced by the new liberalism, consistent as well with the idea of equal opportunity.[24] Increasingly, for Roosevelt, as Eric Foner notes, "civil liberties replaced liberty of contract as the foundation of freedom."[25] In 1939, Attorney General Frank Murphy created a new civil liberties unit in the Justice Department, and in 1941 the Roosevelt administration made the 150th anniversary of the Bill of Rights cause for national celebration.

While conceptually (and constitutionally) different from the *negative* rights in the Bill of Rights, these *positive* rights seemed nonetheless authentically American within the traditional realm of rights that defined freedom for Americans. But this strategy was an individualistic solution to the new liberalism's need for a theory of social action, not the collectivist solution that Tugwell and the more radical New Dealers desired, and it was a solution that would eventually lead liberalism onto some very difficult political terrain. Before that, however, in the early 1940s, Roosevelt's liberalism of positive rights became the central justification for American involvement in World War II. Framed as a battle between freedom and slavery, FDR defined his war aims in terms of securing the Four Freedoms: the freedoms of speech and worship and from want and fear. These were, he told Americans in 1942, "the rights of men of every creed and every race" and were "the crucial difference between ourselves and the enemies we face today," comparing them at times with the Ten Commandments, the Magna Carta, and the Emancipation Proclamation.[26]

The Four Freedoms gained widespread visibility and popularity with Americans, especially as portrayed by the American artist Norman Rockwell. But the message in Rockwell's illustrations, as Foner observes, "with the notable exception of the *Freedom of Speech*, which depicts civic democracy in action, seemed to be that the freedoms Americans were fighting to preserve were private entitlements enjoyed individually or within the family."[27] Under Rockwell's brush, the Four Freedoms, especially the Freedom from Want, suggested that prosperity and abundance were the goals of the war, and whether related or not there was a shift in liberal views of the relationship of government to the private economy. As Alan Brinkley details, the older debates over government ownership of business and of reforming capitalism yielded to consumerism—to concerns about full employment, social well-being, and material comfort—in which government's role was to encourage and manage prosperity largely through fiscal policy.[28]

The allied victory in Europe and Asia thwarted the fascist threat to freedom, only to be followed almost immediately by the rise of a new one: communism. As hot war turned to cold, a new national security state was constructed in Washington to combat the spread of international communism, and with it "anticommunism," long on the periphery of American politics, emerged as a major issue in national politics.[29] For conservatives, anticommunism became the weapon of choice with which to flail liberals for their left-wing sympathies and flirtations, and liberalism for its kinship with socialism. The Left itself had been divided by the approach of war, as liberals tended toward preparedness and socialists toward pacifism, while communists flip-flopped as relations between the Soviet Union and Nazi Germany changed. The cold war and the rise of anticommunism as a political issue exacerbated these divisions, splitting the Left into two organizations: the Progressive Citizens of America (PCA), which included some old New Dealers and socialists, as well as communists, and Americans for Democratic Action (ADA), which included most New Deal liberals and some socialists but was anticommunist, *excluding* communists from membership in an attempt to neutralize the criticisms of the Right.

The new liberalism of Roosevelt thus found itself simultaneously divided within and under attack from without by a reinvigorated conservatism that helped return the Republicans to control of Congress in the 1946 midterm elections for the first time in a quarter century. More and more, the reforms of Roosevelt that produced an enlarged national state and a more powerful executive were decried by conservatives as being no different in their managerial ethos and wish for a planned society from the authoritarian fascist and communist regimes of Europe and thus posed the same threat to freedom at home as had and did those from abroad.[30] While the PCA was reluctant to abandon the dreams of the 1930s, the ADA began to call for a more moderate liberalism—a middle way between the radicalism of the 1930s and the conservatism of the postwar years.[31] The historian Arthur Schlesinger Jr., a founder of the ADA, argued that the political center should be "the home of the new postwar liberalism." Contending that liberalism had no need to invoke Marx at every turn, Schlesinger called instead for a return to the historic idea of liberalism: "a belief in the integrity of the individual, in the limited state, in due process of law, in empiricism and gradualism." He stressed as well the importance of decentralization, checks and balances, and a *plural* conception of the democratic process.[32] The result, as Hugh Heclo writes in this volume, was that the "upbeat liberalism of the earlier Progressive era" was abandoned "in favor of a tough-minded liberal realism."

John Kenneth Galbraith, an economist and fellow ADA member, joined Schlesinger in this reformulation of liberalism. Galbraith argued against both socialism and economic planning in favor of a mixed economy in which business, labor, and government exercised "countervailing powers" over one another, thereby achieving freedom through the interplay of diverse interests and serving the public interest by limiting the capacities of these interests.[33] Similarly, the theologian Reinhold Niebuhr, also a member of ADA, called for a new realism that recognized that man was "fallen" in the biblical sense and not fundamentally good—that men had an overwhelming desire for power which led them to misuse freedom and abuse justice—and he joined in urging a more chastened and moderate liberalism.[34] Of these postwar, cold war liberals, the historian Mary Sperling McAuliffe writes: "The new liberals identified not with the left, as had been the case in the 1930's, but with the center; they identified not with the people but with an elite. Unlike the liberals of the thirties, who had criticized the social order, the new liberals stressed the beneficence of American political and economic institutions."[35]

Cold war liberalism rejected the optimistic notion that progress was inevitable—or was embedded in some grand movement of history—and thus abandoned idealism for a politics of moderation and consensus. Postwar historians and political scientists stressed *stability* rather than conflict in the nation's history and politics, *continuity* rather than change, and they sought an orderly democracy defined more by *procedures* than outcomes that was marked by the "end of ideology" in liberal politics.[36] Democratic politics was a competition among a plurality of interests played by "rules of the game" in a marketplace of ideas.[37] While the cold war liberalism remained committed to the domestic social programs of the New Deal, the assumptions and justifications underlying these programs shifted. Increasingly, *due process* displaced social justice as the principal goal of democracy, as groups sought to share fully in the new positive rights that were the legacy of Roosevelt and the new liberalism of the 1930s.[38] But it was the contest with communism—a "long twilight struggle," as John Kennedy described it—that was the defining issue for cold war liberalism. The forces of freedom had to resist the expansion of this new "totalitarianism" around the globe. A bipartisan foreign policy to contain the spread of communism not only presented a united front but also became the political model for the consensus politics that liberals now thought typified the political democracies of the free world.

Cold war liberalism embraced the domestic reforms of the New Deal, but its calls for completing its social-welfare agenda often seemed more a matter of memory than priority. The collectivist theories of John Dewey and the thirties Left, which had in many ways guided and in all ways justified the more radical society-centered approaches of early New Deal liberalism, had fallen victim to the centrist politics of the cold war at home. As a public philosophy, liberalism now incorporated FDR's rights-centered agenda. Indeed, the last of the great New Deal domestic programs, the Serviceman's Readjustment Act of 1944, better known as the GI Bill of Rights, was an extension of the notion of positive rights, as well as nation's long tradition of caring for its military veterans. The GI Bill transformed public higher education, contributing mightily to its enormous growth after the war as millions of veterans flooded into universities to pursue the better life for which they had fought.[39] It quietly transformed American society as well, contributing importantly to the postwar social movements of the population both to the suburbs and to the growing military, scientific, and industrial complex across the South and the West. In addition, the wartime contributions of African Americans and women led to their demand that they share equally in the freedom of opportunity for which they too had fought and worked. Together, these groups remade American society and politics after 1950.

Liberalism from the Cold War to Camelot

Twenty years of liberal control of the national government ended in 1952 with the victory of Republican Dwight Eisenhower, the supreme allied commander of World War II, over the Democrat Adlai Stevenson. The fifties were years filled with political anxieties. In the first half of the decade, the fall of China, the invasion of South Korea by forces from the North, the execution of Julius and Ethel Rosenberg for spying, and the perjury conviction of Alger Hiss fed fears of a communist threat at home as well as abroad. The Truman administration was assailed constantly for being "soft on communism." Government loyalty investigations, both federal and state, put those suspected of communist sympathies on public display, and framed all collectivist theories of an expanded government as "socialist" or, worse, "communist." These became political attack words used to attack one liberal program after another from national health insurance, which was decried by the American Medical Association as *socialized* medicine, to public housing proposals rejected by real estate interests as *socialized* housing.[40]

The Congress was relentless in its pursuit of national security. Targeting labor unions and immigrants in particular, it passed laws expanding the list of subversive activities, strengthening espionage and sedition laws, and created the Subversive Activities Control Board to police them. Senator Joseph McCarthy of Wisconsin, charging that the Truman administration was "crawling with communists," launched passionate and often reckless investigations that gave his name—"McCarthyism"—to the era.[41] While many liberals, especially those in public office, were initially reticent to speak out against the extraordinary reach and abuses of government investigations, civil libertarians and others denounced them as grave threats to the older constitutional rights of speech, thought, assembly, and due process—negative liberties all—and to the liberal tradition in America. The hunt for subversives led to adjustments in the ideology of labor. The cold war, as Nelson Lichtenstein observes elsewhere in this volume, made the whole discourse of industrial democracy suspect, and unions instead celebrated "free collective bargaining" in contrast with the "slave" labor unions under communism. By mid-decade, with Eisenhower in the White House and McCarthy censured by the Senate, the wildfires of anticommunism had been more or less contained, although the issue continued to burn in the hearts of conservatives and would remain at the center of national politics for another three decades.

In the second half of the decade, the preeminence of anticommunism in domestic politics was challenged by civil rights. The appointment of Earl Warren as chief justice of the Supreme Court ushered in an era of court activism that led to a dramatic and politically controversial expansion of individual rights, positive as well as negative. Nowhere was this more the case than in the Court's 1954 decision *Brown v. Board of Education*, which declared the doctrine of "separate but equal" invalid and ordered the racial desegregation of public schools. The Court thereby placed the volatile issue of rights for black Americans in the national political spotlight. With the decision, black demands for desegregation and an end to Jim Crow grew both more insistent and more public, while white resistance in the South grew more determined. In 1955, the Montgomery bus boycott, through the new medium of television, brought the "southern way of life" and Martin Luther King Jr. into the homes of millions around the nation. With its strategy of nonviolent mass protest, the civil rights movement dramatized the denial of equal rights to blacks with scenes of repression and violence that, initially, won widespread sympathy and support in the North. As violence spread across the Deep South, civil rights became an urgent national issue. The Eisenhower administration tried to give moral leadership on the issue while continuing to treat education as a state responsibility, hoping thereby to avoid both direct involvement and criticism for inaction. But the Court had put the federal government into the struggle in a new way, and when Arkansas governor Orval Faubus blocked the integration of Little Rock's public high school, Eisenhower was forced to intervene, federalizing the National Guard to enforce the high court's ruling.

For the most part, the rights claimed by blacks were the traditional negative ones promised by the Constitution, not the new positive ones associated with liberalism since the thirties. Over the next two decades, the Warren Court would read the Constitution in ways that extended the realm of both positive and negative rights in areas of association, criminal justice, privacy, and more, as well as civil rights. These decisions often invoked notions of social justice, but these appeals to a common good—the equal protection of the laws—were used consistently to achieve individualist and not collectivist ends, the outcome about which Tugwell had fretted in the 1930s.

Now clearly a national issue for which the federal government had a moral as well as constitutional responsibility, civil rights cut across the coalitions of both major parties, but more so the Democrats who were still the party of the white South, a region whose electoral vote was growing in relative importance to the party as northern states and their big cities lost population after World War II. But in the fifties, both parties were arenas of intramural struggles. In the GOP, conservatives had battled for their party's presidential nominations without success throughout the 1940s and 1950s. In the forties, they had watched eastern moderates carry the party to defeat three times and were frustrated again in 1952 when Dwight Eisenhower took the nomination from the conservative favorite, Senator Robert Taft of Ohio. Eisenhower went on to win the White House for the Republicans, but conservatives were disappointed that he made little effort to dismantle the New Deal. Unlike other moderate Republicans, however, Eisenhower had run well across the South. In 1952, he carried the border states of Virginia and Tennessee, as well as Florida; in 1956, he won them again and added Kentucky, Louisiana, and Texas. Party conservatives argued that the South offered the best long-term hope for the party, but only if the GOP abandoned its "me-too" politics and offered a clear and consistent conservative philosophy.

Rather than the South, the Democrats, especially northern urban liberals, were concerned about the North, where Eisenhower had cut seriously into their electoral base.[42] In 1952, many low-income voters and those with a grade-school education, bedrock groups for the Democrats in the thirties and forties, switched in significant numbers to Eisenhower, who also had made inroads among union members, blacks, and Catholics and won a majority among young voters. Stevenson carried the vast majority of the largest cities, but of those over three hundred thousand in population, Ike won seventeen, whereas Thomas Dewey had won only four in 1948.[43] In 1956, these trends continued in the central cities of the fifteen largest metropolitan areas and among black voters.[44] These GOP inroads into their New Deal urban constituency caused a growing anxiety among liberal Democrats, who after 1952 found themselves out of power for the first time in two decades.

For many of the northern liberals, the situation grew only more frustrating after 1954, when the Democrats regained control of Congress but with southern leadership in both houses—Texans Sam Rayburn as Speaker in the House and Lyndon Johnson as majority leader in the Senate—who claimed to speak for the *national* party. Moreover, on becoming majority leader, Johnson announced that his policy would be one of "accommodation" and "cooperation" with the Eisenhower administration. After the 1956 election, when more southern states failed to back the party's presidential ticket, liberals blamed Johnson's policy, which had tolerated southern Democrats joining with the GOP to defeat federal aid to education, civil rights, and other legislation of importance to the North.[45] More and more, liberals argued that the real lesson of 1948 was that the party could win the White House without Dixie, but not without a program of social and economic reform that appealed to the North. Johnson's announcement, after the 1956 election, that he intended to continue his policy of moderation sparked a small revolt by party liberals in the Senate (led by Minnesota senator Hubert Humphrey), who presented their own program, but their effort failed.[46]

Other northern liberals in the party sought to use the Democratic National Committee as the voice of the party's presidential wing. In collaboration with Chairman Paul Butler, they won authorization for the Democratic Advisory Council that would promote the party's "progressive, forward-looking platform."[47] The council attracted prominent national party leaders as members, including Truman; Stevenson; Eleanor Roosevelt, who agreed to serve as a consultant; Dean Acheson, secretary of state under Truman; and Senator Estes Kefauver, the party's 1956 vice presidential nominee. It also drew leading presidential hopefuls for 1960, such as Humphrey and Averell Harriman of New York, as well as leading academic liberals such as John Kenneth Galbraith and Arthur M. Schlesinger Jr.[48] But Johnson, Rayburn, and several southern governors declined to join the council, which they saw correctly as a challenge to their leadership of the party. Indeed, at its first meeting, the council made clear that it was not willing to rest the party's chances for the presidency in 1960 solely on the record of the Democrats in Congress.[49]

The council began to issue statements on a range of topics dealing with both foreign and domestic policy, all designed to appeal to the party's New Deal/Fair Deal liberal base in the North.[50] Its focus on civil rights stirred southern animosity, as did its recommendations calling for an expansion of the role of the federal government in education, housing, and management of the economy. Its criticisms of the Eisenhower administration, especially the handling of Little Rock and Sputnik, were taken by Johnson and Rayburn as tacit criticisms of their leadership in Congress, but these pronouncements also won the attention of the press, which began to treat the council as the national policy voice of the Democrats.[51] In 1958, when the Democrats made major gains in Congress, Butler was quick to claim credit for the council, asserting that the results were a ringing endorsement of its work. Congressional leaders disagreed, arguing instead that the vote was an endorsement of their moderate policy of cooperation with the Eisenhower administration. The intraparty struggles between north and south were made more dramatic by several unsuccessful attempts to replace Butler as national party chair, all of which had their origins in Congress and its southern leadership.[52]

As the 1960 presidential year arrived, both the Democratic and Republican Parties had internal divisions, each with a more liberal or moderate presidential wing and a more conservative congressional wing.[53] With an heir apparent in Vice President Richard Nixon, whose conservative credentials as an anticommunist were impeccable, the division in the Republican ranks seemed less a threat to the party's chances in November than was the case with the Democrats. Conservatives within the party did try to persuade Nixon to take a more conservative stand on civil rights, a position that would appeal more to the party's new southern bloc. Led now by Arizona senator Barry Goldwater, who had emerged as "Mr. Conservative" in the years following the 1953 death of Robert Taft, the new GOP conservatives were a generation removed from the ideological battles of the 1930s, when many in the party believed that only FDR stood between them and a return to being the nation's majority party.[54]

Intraparty strife continued to torment the Democrats into the presidential year. The party was faced with a large field of candidates for the nomination, and unlike in other presidential years, all were national figures, none really a "favorite son." All the candidates, except Johnson, appeared before the Democratic Advisory Council, which hoped to settle on a liberal candidate to back in the race, but in the end its support was divided between Humphrey, Stuart Symington of Missouri, and the party's twice-defeated nominee, Stevenson. Kennedy drew limited support, and Johnson almost none.[55] In March, Chairman Butler provoked yet another controversy, but this time he antagonized the liberals by predicting a Kennedy nomination and speaking somewhat disparagingly of both the Humphrey and Johnson candidacies.[56] Humphrey called for Butler's resignation, adding to the turmoil within the party, which reached a climax just before the convention when former president Truman declared that it had been "rigged" for Kennedy and resigned as a delegate in what was interpreted as an attempt to block a Kennedy nomination. The convention itself seemed anticlimactic as JFK moved with relative ease to a first-ballot victory but then upset northern liberals by choosing Johnson to be his running mate.

For all their differences, the Democrats entered the fall election more or less united with a regionally and seemingly ideologically balanced ticket that was running on a very liberal platform shaped by the party's advisory council.[57] While the platform made some accommodations to southern members of Congress, it made no concessions whatsoever to the Dixiecrat views on either race or the role of the national government. It rested securely on the new liberalism as adjusted by the cold war and civil rights. The platform was programmatic in content, pragmatic rather than philosophical, calling for completion of the New Deal/Fair Deal agenda in education, health, housing, and civil rights, among other areas of traditional liberal concern. The "new frontier," of which Kennedy spoke in his acceptance speech at the Democratic convention, was decidedly more generational and internationalist in definition than ideological.

In his campaign, Kennedy's youthful energy, his "vigah," his promise to "get America moving again" reignited the hopes of many in his party that the long-postponed agenda of liberalism—the unfinished business of Roosevelt's New Deal and of Truman's Fair Deal—would at last be realized. His inaugural address summoned Americans to service for their country ("Ask not what you country can do for you—ask what you can do for your country"). But when Kennedy spoke of a "new generation" of Americans ("born in this century, tempered by war, disciplined by a hard and bitter peace, proud of our ancient heritage"), he was speaking not of New Dealers or Fair Dealers but of cold war liberals. There were echoes of the rhetoric of FDR's new liberalism ("if a free society cannot help the many who are poor, it cannot save the few who are rich"), but his was a rallying call to a "long twilight struggle" against the "common enemies of man" framed in the bluntest of ways: "Let every nation know, whether it wishes us well or ill, that we shall pay any price, bear any burden, meet any hardship, support any friend, oppose any foe to assure the survival and success of liberty." The nation would soon learn that Kennedy fully embraced the bipartisan policy of containment set forth by Truman and pursued by Eisenhower and that he was prepared to take the nation to the brink of nuclear war to prevent the spread of communism in the Western Hemisphere. The Cuban missile crisis not only measured the man; it was the man.

Like postwar liberals generally, Kennedy accepted the domestic reform program of the thirties and forties, for which liberals had fought since Roosevelt set it forth in his economic bill of rights. JFK's rhetorical support heartened old and new liberals alike, but his narrow victory, together with the power of southern Democrats in Congress and his cautious political nature, produced a reluctance to press forward aggressively with a domestic reform agenda. The conservative coalition in Congress discouraged the filing of an education bill. The power of southern Democrats made the "stroke of a pen" to end integration in public housing slow to find paper. A tax cut to stimulate a sluggish economy faced opposition from conservatives in both parties, who were concerned about its impact on federal budget deficits. All the while, Kennedy's popularity grew, but his reluctance to "spend" any of this capital also led to a growing frustration among liberals with his administration.

Kennedy's economic policies, predicated on his belief that government and business were "necessary allies," added to the disappointment of many left-wing liberals, who more often saw the two as natural enemies. These left-liberals deplored Kennedy's approach as "corporate liberalism," which they saw as a continuation of the economic policies of all the reformist administrations of the twentieth century. They believed that "liberalism," not the political Right, was the principal impediment to a truly democratic society.[58] "Whatever its merits for understanding the past," Allen Matusow writes, "the concept of corporate liberalism cut to the heart of the post-1945 American political economy. Intellectual liberals," he continues, "unashamedly asserted the benevolence of large corporations and defended the existing distribution of wealth and power in America. Political liberals assumed corporate hegemony and pursued policies to strengthen it." Matusow concludes that John Kennedy was the "quintessential corporate liberal."[59] Uninterested in antitrust actions and with no particular sympathy for unions, Kennedy aimed at being a public manager in a privately managed economy, not a reformer. Corporate America did not reciprocate this view, and there were confrontations as in the case of the steel industry, but for the most part the New Frontier's approach to business was cautious but friendly.[60]

Kennedy did place himself squarely in the liberal New Deal tradition with his embrace of the idea of positive rights. In early 1962, for example, he announced a consumer bill of rights that echoed FDR's economic bill of rights. In a special message to Congress, as Lizabeth Cohen notes, JFK declared that consumers have "the right to safety, to be informed, to choose, and to be heard," and he called for "specific executive and legislative actions to protect these rights."[61] Like his liberal predecessors, Kennedy looked to the federal government to secure these rights, asserting: "To promote the fuller realization of these consumer rights, it is necessary that existing Government programs be strengthened, the Government organization be improved, and in certain areas, that new legislation be enacted."[62] In 1963, Kennedy also prompted memories of the New Deal battles against joblessness and economic insecurity when he moved to develop a federal program to combat these ancient enemies. From the writings of Michael Harrington and John Kenneth Galbraith, as well as his primary campaign in West Virginia, Kennedy had "discovered" poverty as a political issue.[63] But his tenure in office was cut short before formal proposals could be made, and it would be his successor who would declare "war" on poverty.[64]

But it was the movement for civil rights for black Americans that tormented and ultimately defined his presidency. As the civil rights movement grew more public and aggressive in the South, the Kennedys—John and his brother Robert—grew increasingly concerned about its effects on JFK's reelection chances, and as attorney general, the younger Kennedy tried repeatedly to deflect any negative political fallout from black protests. This became impossible in May 1963, when the explosion of two bombs in Birmingham, Alabama, led blacks to rampage through the streets, attacking police and firefighters, battering cars and burning stores in the first of what was to be a succession of urban riots. Kennedy sent troops to Alabama and decided also to send a civil rights bill to Congress dealing with public accommodations and equal employment opportunity. For the most part, the president's advisers opposed this decision, believing that the legislation could not be passed but would nevertheless destroy Kennedy politically in the South and possibly provoke white backlash in the North. But JFK, as Matusow writes, "brushed aside all objections and bid for command of the civil rights movement."[65]

Six months later, Kennedy was dead, and Johnson made passage of the civil rights bill a priority as a testament to the martyred president. The bill passed in the House of Representatives with relative ease but faced a determined southern Democrat filibuster in the Senate. Passage in the upper chamber thus turned on Johnson's ability to win support for cloture, which was achieved when 27 of the 35 Senate Republicans followed their leader Everett Dirksen in voting to end debate and enactment followed. With remarkable quickness, the Civil Rights Act of 1964 brought down the Jim Crow system of discrimination in public accommodations, largely because southern businessmen were weary of the social "costs" of segregation. The law also facilitated the growth of a "new" South, socially and economically, but at the same time led white voters to renounce their ancient Democratic loyalties in favor of the new conservatism of the Republican Right.[66]

All the Way with LBJ

The first signs of a southern secession from the Democratic Party to the Republicans came in the 1964 presidential election, when five southern states gave their electoral votes to the GOP nominee, Barry Goldwater.[67] By almost every immediate measure, the Goldwater candidacy was a disaster for the Republican Party. Not only did the GOP lose the presidency in a landslide of historic proportions, but it also lost almost forty seats in the House, two in the Senate, and more than five hundred in state legislatures. In Congress, the Democrats had their largest majorities since 1936, with the vast majority of new Democrats being liberals. The "conservative coalition" of southern Democrats and midwestern Republicans lost its veto power, and conservatives were about to see all the liberal programs they had resisted for three decades enacted into law. Lyndon Johnson was poised to construct his Great Society, and by the end of 1965, it was an imposing edifice.[68]

Unlike FDR and the New Deal, which concentrated on economic recovery and personal security, Johnson saw the Great Society as focused more on providing equal opportunities that would enable the poor and oppressed to move into the mainstream of American life. He led off with bills for federal aid to education and national health care, issues that had been before Congress since the Truman administration and were thought by many to be intractable. But LBJ believed that if he could succeed with these, the rest of his program would follow. He proved correct: they passed, and a flood of reform legislation followed that reminded many of FDR's "hundred days." Johnson declared war on poverty, aimed at assisting and, in a new twist, "empowering" the urban poor and minorities by requiring their maximum feasible participation in the design and execution of programs. In over sixty separate messages, he declared war on disease, crime, and ugliness. He attacked juvenile delinquency, unemployment, and the physical deterioration of the cities. He won assistance for older Americans and those who were disabled and also for the arts and humanities. He won enactment of a second major civil rights bill, the Voting Rights Act of 1965, aimed at ending Jim Crow in the voting booth as the previous year's act had ended it in public accommodations.[69] It launched the third great reform era of the twentieth century that, as Shep Melnick writes elsewhere in this volume, extended into the first half of the 1970s.

Johnson had entered politics in the 1930s as a champion of the New Deal devoted to Roosevelt, and he wanted to complete the New Deal. Indeed, he wanted to surpass the record of his mentor and model. But unlike Franklin Roosevelt, and more like Franklin's cousin Theodore, Johnson was pushing a reform program in good economic times in which the need for federal intervention to deal with society's continuing problems was not felt as widely or as acutely as in the depression years of the 1930s. The political coalition that was the force behind his efforts was also unlike that which produced FDR. It was, however, a testament to the political success of the New Deal, for it was an alliance of union members, blacks, women, urban ethnics, public intellectuals, and reform-minded professionals which had come together in the thirties and now controlled the Democratic Party. Missing from the core of the Johnson coalition were the big-city machines of the North, almost all of which were extinct by the mid-1960s, and the white South, whose leaders had been marginalized within the presidential wing of the Democratic Party and whose rank and file was gravitating toward the new Republican conservatism.

Johnson's party, however, lacked the socioeconomic coherence of the New Deal party. It was a party of "haves," as well as "have-nots," and thus differed from the party of Roosevelt in several ways. The focus of the Johnson party on opportunity moved it toward social concerns and away from the economic ones that dominated the depression years—toward quality-of-life issues, not just material and quantitative ones. It was a split-level party, with an upper-middle, white-collar, professional class on top, whose values dominated, and a lower and poorer class on the bottom—the two joined more by social than by economic interests. The two found common ground on the newer issues of the sixties, more so than on the old New Deal agenda. As Nelson Lichtenstein writes in this volume, they shifted the "discourse of liberalism" out of the "New Deal–labor orbit" and into one in which "the racial divide colored all politics."

The new forces within the Democratic party also brought a "new politics"—in part the upper-middle-class "club" politics of the suburbs, concerned with "issues," and in part a lower-class social "movement" politics concerned primarily with the "cause" of civil rights, for which the working-class labor movement in the thirties was the model. Movement politics, however, changed in the sixties as upper-middle class activists (antiwar, consumer, feminist, environmental) adopted the strategy to press their respective causes. For the new upper-middle-class groups, the Democratic Party became less important as an agency of joint endeavor and common purpose through accommodation of differences and more important as an instrument of power through which to pursue their particular goals.[70] The party as an institution suffered from this, and suffered as well, as Sidney Milkis argues, from Johnson's style of leadership, which personalized national politics in the president with success or failure turning on the political skills and abilities of the occupant of the Oval Office. Permitting the party to atrophy would exact a heavy price from Johnson—and the Democrats—in 1968.

The Johnson Democratic Party also marched to a somewhat different idea of liberalism than had its predecessors. While in the spirit of the New Deal, Johnson's program differed conceptually from that of Roosevelt. Consistent with liberalism's historic purpose, both sought to expand opportunity so that individuals might realize their full potential as human beings, but whereas FDR had been preoccupied with material security, LBJ was focused more on social empowerment. The class division within his party produced two strategies of empowerment, one old and one new. The older strategy was now that of positive rights, which had been incorporated into liberalism by Roosevelt in the thirties where it remained central through the forties, fifties, and into the sixties. The Great Society expanded on these rights in new and often controversial ways, none more so than the idea of affirmative action for specific groups in the population. Initially, the target group was African Americans, but later women were added and, eventually, as Hugh David Graham's essay details, so were various nationality groups who came following immigration reform in the sixties.

The new strategy was one of social empowerment, best exemplified by the community action programs of the Office of Economic Opportunity that required the maximum feasible participation of the poor in the administration of programs at the local level. The aim of empowerment was to teach responsibility by giving it and to develop more effective leadership in these communities that could, in turn, take greater advantage of those opportunities that were generally available. In effect, this created new units of government at the local level in which the populations of the target communities had responsibility for programs under federal guidelines that operated largely beyond the reach of state and local governments. Politically, this produced tensions within Johnson's party, as Democratic governors and mayors objected to being bypassed by a Democratic White House in programs that affected their states and communities.[71]

The new politics of the new liberals in the Democratic Party, especially the "amateurs" from clubs and the activists from the upper-status movements, rallied to the call for greater participation and openness in politics. This ethic, which became the standard by which a "democratic" politics would be judged, was framed against the image of an old politics of bosses and backroom deals. Consistent with the empowerment strategies of the Great Society, they held that the individual, with unique capacities honed to the highest through active participation, was the fundamental fact in social and political life and would in turn produce the good society.[72] In this, they stood in sharp contrast to the collectivist ethic of John Dewey, whose much earlier call for a "great community" seemed to anticipate Johnson's for a "great society." Dewey had argued that *society* was the fundamental fact and that the character of the individual was constructed in fundamental ways by the nature of society. It was a view that FDR had seemed to embrace in his ideal of a cooperative commonwealth, only to abandon in frustration in the face of business resistance in favor of regulation and a new realm of positive rights.[73] The calls for greater participation and openness would find their fullest expression in the Democratic Party reforms of its presidential selection process that followed the party's 1968 convention.[74]

Johnson's Great Society promised and delivered a more just and humane America. It also delivered political opportunities to the new conservatives in the GOP. There could no longer be any doubt that "big government" had arrived and that liberals were responsible for it. Conservatives renewed their familiar refrain that big government was a threat to individual freedom at home, but the more surprising and effective intellectual attack on New Deal liberalism came from the New Left.[75] Unlike the Old Left, this New Left was more concerned with social issues than economic ones—with *quality* of life issues more than quantitative ones. For this New Left, politics related to the everyday lives of people, which led to a call for "participatory democracy" and more decentralized policymaking so that all might participate fully in decisions that affected their lives. The idea of participatory democracy, Kevin Mattson writes, "grew out of a 'radical republican' tradition of politics, one that related to the writings of Thomas Jefferson [as] updated in the modern intellectual explorations of John Dewey."[76] Where the New Deal, like Progressivism, had sought Hamiltonian means to Jeffersonian ends, the New Left called for a return to Jeffersonian means. Animated by opposition to Vietnam, the New Left faulted the bureaucratic, top-down power of the liberal state controlled by a power centered in a military-industrial complex. For these critics of liberalism, politics was centered in the everyday lives of citizens, and in the name of realizing a more authentic democracy, they sought to push decision making downward into the grass roots. The New Left critics also embraced an individualism that required an immediate involvement with others. The New Left critique began to shift the national political debate away from economics and toward more cultural issues. In their view of big government and their concern with social and cultural issues, the New Left would occupy common political ground with the new conservatism, though they in no respects made common cause.

But it was the issue of race that provided the great new opportunity for conservatives. The Voting Rights Act of 1965, following the Civil Rights Act of 1964, was a double blow to the "southern way of life"— blows delivered by the northern wing of their party. The 1965 act mandated that federal registrars be sent into areas where a pattern of discrimination against blacks could be documented, the vast majority of which were in the South. But the South was not alone. Indeed, the issue of civil rights was nationalized politically in 1965 when civil rights activists moved to challenge de facto school segregation in Chicago and other major cities of the North that were the foundation stones of the New Deal Democratic Party. The North had rallied to support the cause of civil rights, supporting the federal legislation of 1964 and 1965 that was aimed mainly at the Jim Crow South, but this support faded, sometimes into hostility, when civil rights activists moved into their communities. Open housing, busing, and affirmative action were all perceived as threats by those who inhabited the white ethnic neighborhoods of the inner cities. Largely working-class and built institutionally around the family, the church, and the neighborhood school, these communities often reacted with special outrage when desegregation struck at one of the pillars of their community: the public school.[77]

Democratic prospects in urban America grew more ominous in August 1965 when the Watts section of Los Angeles erupted in widespread rioting, which was followed by rioting in black ghettos in big cities across the North. With college and university campuses alive with antiwar protests, and civil rights marches continuing in both the North and the South, the nation seemed rife with disorder sparked by those who were widely seen as the beneficiaries of Great Society programs. The growing prominence of a new "counterculture" of hippies and yippies, long hair, drugs, free love, communes, and rock and roll added to public concern that the nation's traditional values of family, home, church, and neighborhood were being undermined. Conservatives would capitalize politically on the social disarray, blaming liberals and liberalism for a failure to maintain law and order and for a more general breakdown in the nation's moral order.

Beset by antiwar protesters with their seemingly incessant shout, "Hey, hey, LBJ, how many boys did you kill today?," Lyndon Johnson began to see shrinking public support for his domestic programs, especially those involving race. In September 1966, a Gallup poll reported that 52 percent of those surveyed thought the Johnson administration was "pushing racial integration too fast," as compared with only 28 percent who had held that view a year earlier in April 1965. Similarly, a Harris poll found public support for the Great Society waning. In September 1966 it reported that approval for the War on Poverty had dropped to 41 percent from 60 percent less than a year before in October 1965. The conservative Republican message also appeared to connect with voters. In August 1968, a Gallup poll found that 46 percent of the public thought "big government" was the "biggest threat to the country in the future," almost twice as many as named big labor and roughly four times as many as named big business. In 1968, when Harris asked if "liberals have been running the country too long," almost two-thirds of *working-class whites*, 64 percent, said "yes." Moreover, "when public opinion turned against the Johnson administration," James Reichley notes, "there was little political structure at the national level to shore it up," for LBJ had let the Democratic National Committee atrophy in the years after 1964.[78]

The Republicans made significant gains in the 1966 midterm elections, adding forty-seven seats in the House and three in the Senate. The vote was in part a return to normal two-party politics after the Goldwater aberration two years earlier, but it was also a measure of the growing public doubts about the Great Society at home and disenchantment with the war in Vietnam abroad. For the most part, Senate Republicans had followed Everett Dirksen in supporting escalation of the nation's military involvement in Southeast Asia, though the Goldwater conservatives would have preferred a more aggressive prosecution of the war, whereas party moderates such as John Sherman Cooper of Kentucky were seeking ways to disengage. The GOP moderates were reinforced by the midterm balloting with the addition of Edward Brooke of Massachusetts, Mark Hatfield of Oregon, and Charles Percy of Illinois, whose elections had turned in substantial part on their support for an end to the conflict. Minority Leader Dirksen, who was in declining health, was now faced with a more polarized party, as Republican doves joined with their Democratic counterparts to press for an end to the fighting, while the more conservative Republicans were adamant in their belief that communism had to be defeated in Vietnam.

The war came to dominate American politics in 1967 and 1968. President Johnson chose to pursue a policy of guns *and* butter, hoping to avoid the loss of Southeast Asia to the communists and, simultaneously, to preserve his Great Society programs. Spending on both produced inflation, which had long been a threat to the solidarity of the liberal Democratic coalition.[79] Conservative Republicans, Dirksen among them, supported increased military spending, in part to check expansion of domestic programs and increased spending on them. Historically the champions of balanced budgets, conservatives in the GOP now seemed ready to accept growing federal deficits if that would frustrate the growth of the central government at home. It was a strategy that would find its fullest and most successful application in the early 1980s during the presidency of the ultimate hero of the new conservatives, Ronald Reagan.[80]

The 1968 presidential election was to prove a watershed in the party battles of postwar America. It led to Republican control of the White House for twenty of the next twenty-four years, to divided government during these years, and to the new conservatism, born of the Goldwater candidacy four years earlier, displacing liberalism as the nation's dominant public philosophy. The Democrats entered the fall contest as a crippled party: an incumbent president on the sidelines, a leading candidate for the nomination assassinated, and a nominating convention marked by disorder inside and a violent police reaction against protesters outside.[81] Johnson's vice president, Hubert Humphrey, emerged with the nomination of a deeply divided party, whose national organization was understaffed and heavily in debt. The contest for the Republican nomination, while less violent than the Democrats, was a desultory exercise in which neither the new conservatives nor the party moderates could find a candidate behind whom to mobilize, enabling Richard Nixon to win the GOP nomination with surprising ease. Neither the moderates nor the conservatives had great enthusiasm for Nixon, whose views lay between the extremes of left and right in the party. To moderates, he was not an ideological right-winger; to conservatives, he was not a northeastern "liberal." In November, Nixon won a close contest whose outcome, until the final days, had seemed a foregone conclusion.

But the more significant candidacy in 1968 was that of Alabama governor George Wallace, running as the nominee of the American Independent Party. While the Wallace candidacy rested on civil rights and the politics of race, he knew, as Dan Carter has noted, that many Americans, north and south, who did not think of themselves as racists, nonetheless hated the disorder caused by civil rights and antiwar protesters and saw the counterculture as a serious threat to traditional American values. Wallace capitalized on this. Like conservative Republicans, old and new, he was both strongly anticommunist and hostile to both the liberal welfare state and the taxation required to sustain it. But where Republicans had carried their message to upper-class audiences, Wallace took his to the other end of the spectrum. "The genius of George Wallace," Carter writes, "lay in his ability to link traditional conservatism to an earthy language that voiced powerful cultural beliefs and sympathies with a much broader appeal to millions of Americans: the sanctity of the traditional family, the centrality of overt religious beliefs, the importance of hard work and self-restraint, the celebration of the autonomy of the local community." Carter adds: "George Wallace . . . was the alchemist of the new social conservatism as he compounded racial fear, anticommunism, cultural nostalgia, and traditional right-wing economics into a movement that laid the foundation for the conservative counterrevolution that reshaped American politics in the 1970s and 1980s."[82]

Kennedy and Johnson knew that their support for black civil rights would hurt them and their party in the white South, and both feared that it could provoke a white backlash in the North as well. Goldwater adherents shared this view and believed that, together with a strong anticommunist appeal, they could cut into the Democratic vote in the predominantly Catholic neighborhoods of the Northeast and upper Midwest. The first signs that Wallace might capitalize in all these ways were evident in the 1964 Democratic party primaries, when he won impressive shares of the vote in several northern states—taking over 40 percent in Maryland, one-third in Wisconsin, and almost 30 percent in Indiana. In 1968, as the nominee of the American Independent Party, Wallace won 13.5 percent of the popular vote and carried five southern states (Georgia, Alabama, Mississippi, Louisiana, and Arkansas), while defeating Humphrey but not Nixon in three others (North Carolina, South

Carolina, and Tennessee). He also ran well in the North, especially in the states bordering the Ohio River, as well as in Maryland, Michigan, and Missouri.

As president, Richard Nixon capitalized politically on the more general tactics and message of George Wallace, embracing the so-called southern strategy first advocated by Goldwater in the late fifties. Nixon crafted a more conservative cultural appeal—the "social issue"—that framed the combination of crime, drugs, race, feminism, welfare, and the counterculture as a massive assault on the traditional culture of America, that is, family, work, church, and school, for which liberals and liberalism were to blame. Lyndon Johnson's Great Society drew the fire of the Nixon White House for a liberalism gone astray: the creation of a yet bigger and more bureaucratic government that was more invasive into the lives of ordinary Americans and that taxed the many for programs to benefit the few. But it was the liberalism of the Supreme Court, headed by Earl Warren, that drew the heaviest fire from conservatives for a succession of decisions beginning with school desegregation in the fifties and continuing with state legislative redistricting, school prayer, criminal rights, busing, abortion, and affirmative action through the sixties and into the seventies. The Court was regularly faulted for judicial activism, for *making* law rather than applying the law as Congress had intended. Nixon's promise to restore "law and order" by appointing constitutional conservatives to the federal bench won high approval from social and religious conservatives across the country, especially those in the white South. It touched off a partisan and ideological struggle for control of the federal courts that would continue through the remainder of the twentieth and into the twenty-first century.

The new conservatism of Goldwater continued to grow through the Nixon years. It had found a new leader in 1966 with the election of Ronald Reagan as governor of California. When Reagan ascended to the presidency in 1980, it marked the end of the long—three-quarters of a century—period of liberal reform in America, replacing it with a conservatism that recalled the social Darwinism of the nineteenth century as much as it did the moderate conservatism of the Republican Party through most of the twentieth. The electoral success of the new conservatives was grounded in the politics of race that had produced a secular realignment of the white South from Democrat to Republican, though the issue itself remained embedded in a cluster of cultural concerns, clouded further by an optimistic rhetoric that suggested a new founding. It was "morning in America"—the rebirth of a virtuous America that had been lost in the secularism and hedonism of a misguided liberalism. The new, more populist conservatism cast liberalism as nothing more than an ideology of big government, of tax and spend, and charged liberals with being indifferent, uncaring, and out of touch with ordinary Americans. Big government remained a threat to individual freedom, but now it was the "tyranny" of taxation as much as communism that was the great foe.

Barry Goldwater and George Wallace may have played the pivotal roles in the conservative redirection of American politics that came after the sixties and moved the nation away from the statist liberalism of the New Deal and Great Society, but no figure in the sixties, as the essays in this volume attest, stood taller or was more compelling than Lyndon Baines Johnson. David Shribman describes LBJ as "an old man in a hurry," which he was and for good reason. He surely knew that political changes in the nation—demographic and ideological—meant that time was running out on the New Deal and on his dream of bringing it to completion. Johnson was a man of numbers: his career in the Senate had been built on counting votes; he surely knew how to read the vote count in the Electoral College and the trend lines behind it. Johnson was also a man of the New Deal: his career in Washington had been built on his association with Franklin Roosevelt; he surely knew that cold war liberalism lacked a compelling justification for collective action and that completion of the New Deal depended on him and his leadership. Johnson was finally a man of the South: his electoral success had been achieved by winning the support of voters more conservative than he, especially in the area of civil rights; he clearly knew the political costs to himself and to his party of any effective civil rights legislation. To a remarkable degree, he realized his dream, only to have it overwhelmed by the nightmare of Vietnam that drove him from office.

The sixties exhausted Lyndon Johnson, and they exhausted liberalism as well. The confidence that liberalism had carried from the 1930s into the 1960s had been shaken by a winless war abroad and civil strife at home. The causes were many. The Democratic Party coalition that had championed liberalism since the presidency of Franklin Roosevelt was split between hawks and doves, between a new politics and an old, and between new social priorities and older economic ones. The muscle in the coalition had atrophied as well: the big-city machines were almost gone, as was the South, and the unions that had been a driving force in the thirties had seen their membership shrink from over 30 percent of the workforce in the 1950s to just over half that number by the 1970s, with the biggest losses among the industrial unions. Democratic Party reforms that came after the 1968 convention, driven by demands for greater intraparty democracy and openness, continued the assault on the institutional party begun in the Progressive Era as it empowered the newer elites from the antiwar and other movements of the sixties at the expense of the older party elites.[83] The war in Vietnam had taken its toll, producing in the view of H. W. Brands an "anti-liberal sea change" that "shattered the [cold war] consensus, ravaged popular faith in government, and scorched the earth from which the liberal agenda had sprung."[84] But the Democrats were also victims of their success. The Great Society had, as Johnson hoped, made good on most of the domestic agenda of the New Deal. The long liberal conversation about social and economic problems that had begun in the thirties—about full employment, education, housing, health care—was now displaced by a new conversation about participation, openness, affirmative action, empowerment, and the environment. These newer issues, together with rights, became the language of liberal politics in the seventies, and they cut across the old party coalition in different ways.

In addition, the population movements after World War II had dramatically altered the influence of the urban North and Midwest in national politics. In contests for the presidency, the sizable majority the region held in the Electoral College in the thirties had disappeared altogether: by 1972, it was reduced to parity with the rest of the country. In Congress, seats in the House of Representatives had followed voters from the Rust Belt states to those of the "sun states" and also from city to suburb. Only seniority protected the old liberal interests in Congress, and they were undercut by reforms in the 1970s. In the late 1960s, Richard Scammon and Ben Wattenberg argued that "demography is destiny" in American politics.[85] They were joined by Kevin Phillips, who argued that the new demography, coupled with the new politics of race, would produce a conservative Republican majority in the nation.[86] All were correct. Indeed, the new conservatism was the big winner from the shift of the American population to the west and the south. These areas of growth not only changed the political calculus for the nation but also were the areas in which the new Republican faith took shape and found its leaders.[87]

Most of all, however, liberalism as a public philosophy was beset with an intellectual fatigue. It was under assault from a New Left as well as from a new conservatism, both of which had shifted the focus of political debate from economic to social and cultural issues. To the New Left, liberalism was a spineless doctrine of uncertain purpose, concerned with balancing competing interests through endless bargaining and compromise in a politics of stasis, not with achieving social justice or real democracy.[88] To the new conservatism, liberalism was a morally bankrupt doctrine, a godless secularism, overly intrusive into the marketplace, out of touch with ordinary Americans, and committed to nothing so much as big government and the taxes required to sustain it. The New Left offered theories of participatory democracy, demands for openness, and strategies of empowerment but only the thinnest justification for collective action and the vaguest vision of the good society. The new conservatism, on the other hand, embraced a rhetoric that suggested a new founding—"morning in America"—that would return the nation to its traditional values of family, church, and the flag, which would in turn restore the virtue lost in the secularism of a misguided liberalism.

Since the 1960s, liberals have sought a way, intellectually and politically, to design a new and compelling liberalism around which electoral majorities can be organized. The essays in this volume illustrate the dilemmas left by sixties liberalism. They echo Tugwell's lament in the thirties that the New Deal was trying to accomplish collectivist ends through individualist means—a problem made more challenging by the great expansion of rights in the sixties. The "rights talk" that became liberalism after the sixties has undermined both a more deliberative politics and the institutional structures necessary to sustain it.[89] Nelson Lichtenstein notes in this volume that rights consciousness had little organizational payoff for unions because, "under a regime of rights, it becomes very difficult to privilege a trade union as an institution that stands apart from its membership." The same may be said of their effect on political parties. Similarly, Shep Melnick writes that where a liberalism centered on "taxing and spending meant using collective resources to solve collective problems," the new liberalism of rights meant that "reformers could fight city hall and big business [with] legal arguments rather than building political organizations with active members." To which Hugh Davis

Graham adds that as "minority status . . . trumped socioeconomic class" in the nation's politics, it "drew a line separating official minorities from all other Americans," thereby pitting poor against poor and erasing the economic division that underlay the liberal New Deal electoral coalition.

Lyndon Johnson may have known that his presidency would be the "last hurrah" for the New Deal and for the liberalism that guided it. He most surely wanted that "hurrah" to echo through American history such that he would share greatness with FDR—indeed, that he would be, as William Leuchtenburg recalls, the "greatest of them all, the whole bunch of them." This was not to be. But as Carey McWilliams reminds us, Johnson also wanted a society in which material abundance produced a "richer life of mind and spirit" for all. In this, he knew a good measure of success.

Notes

1. See Gerald H. Gamm, *The Making of New Deal Democrats* (Chicago: University of Chicago Press, 1986).

2. The African American population in the South was overwhelmingly rural in residence, and in the age of Jim Crow, few of them were permitted to vote. The recruitment of blacks into the Democratic Party was led by African American newspapers in the urban North, initially in 1932 by the *Pittsburgh Courier* but in 1936 by newspapers in New York, Chicago, and other major cities. In the latter year, members of the so-called black cabinet, African Americans holding administrative positions in the New Deal, led in the formation of an African American organization to campaign actively for the reelection of Roosevelt, with their energies focused heavily on the urban North. See Nancy J. Weiss, *Farewell to the Party of Lincoln: Black Politics in the Age of FDR* (Princeton: Princeton University Press, 1983).

3. See Allen J. Matusow, *The Unraveling of America: A History of Liberalism in the 1960s* (New York: Harper and Row, 1984), chap. 3.

4. This is not to suggest that there was no attention to these matters. In the late 1950s, Robert Wood was exploring the effects of suburbanization on American politics. See Wood, *Suburbia: Its People and Their Politics* (Boston: Houghton Mifflin, 1958). See also Edward C. Banfield and James Q. Wilson, *City Politics* (Cambridge: Harvard University Press, 1963), and Edward C. Banfield, *The Unheavenly City* (Boston: Little, Brown, 1974).

5. By 1960, suburbanites living in single-family homes outnumbered both urban and rural dwellers. A house of one's own had become, Eric Foner writes, "the physical embodiment of the hopes for a better life" (*The Story of American Freedom* [New York: W. W. Norton, 1998], 264).

6. See Wood, *Suburbia,* and also James Q. Wilson, *The Amateur Democrat*

(Chicago: University of Chicago Press, 1966), and Edgar Litt, *The Political Cultures of Massachusetts* (Boston: MIT Press, 1965).

7. Ronald D. Rotunda, "The 'Liberal' Label: Roosevelt's Capture of a Symbol," in *Public Policy*, ed. John D. Montgomery and Albert O. Hirschman (Cambridge: Harvard University Press, 1968), 380.

8. Liberalism had been used by the editors of the *New Republic* around World War I to denote a reform version of progressivism. See Richard Wightman Fox and James T. Kloppenberg, eds., *A Companion to American Thought* (Malden: Blackwell, 1998), 398.

9. See Rotunda, "'Liberal Label,'" 390–93.

10. See Melvin Richter, *The Politics of Conscience: T. H. Green and His Age* (Cambridge: Harvard University Press, 1964), 267.

11. L. T. Hobhouse, *Liberalism* (New York: Oxford University Press, 1964), 48. See also Stefan Collini, *Liberalism and Sociology: L. T. Hobhouse and Political Argument in England, 1880–1914* (New York: Cambridge University Press, 1979), chap. 4. For a more general treatment of British liberalism, see Michael Freeden, *The New Liberalism: An Ideology of Social Reform* (Oxford: Clarendon Press, 1978).

12. See Michael McGerr, *A Fierce Discontent: The Rise and Fall of the Progressive Movement in America, 1879–1920* (New York: Free Press, 2003), chap. 2.

13. On Dewey's "reformulation" of liberalism, see David Fott, *John Dewey: America's Philosopher of Democracy* (New York: Rowan and Littlefield, 1998), chap. 3. There is a striking parallel between Dewey's arguments and those of Hobhouse.

14. John Dewey, *Liberalism and Social Action* (New York: Capricorn Books, 1963), 57. Dewey regularly contrasted the old and new liberalisms. In *Individualism: Old and New* (New York: Capricorn Books, 1962), he writes: "The earlier economic individualism had a definite creed and function. It sought to release from legal restrictions man's wants and his efforts to satisfy those wants" (76); "Just as the new individualism cannot be achieved by extending the benefits of the older economic individualism to more persons, so it cannot be obtained by a further development of generosity, good will and altruism" (88); "Our problems grow out of social conditions: they concern human relations rather than man's direct relationship with physical nature" (92).

15. Dewey, *Individualism*, 77, 79.

16. Ibid., 88. In *Individualism*, 17, 18, Dewey remarks that the American heritage lies in "the ideal of equality of opportunity and freedom for all," efforts in behalf of which "once constituted our essential Americanism," but that it now guides our politics "only spasmodically" and does not control "their aims or their methods." He finds this "spiritual heritage of equal opportunity and free association" in competition with a second tradition, "one of money and machines that begets a pecuniary culture."

17. Ibid., 91. Dewey's favorable reference to the "creed" of liberalism contrasts with his negative view of "dogma," which he associated with theories of historical inevitability. "Intelligence," he argued, "does not pretend to *know* save

as a result of experimentation, the opposite of preconceived dogma" (ibid., 77). On Dewey's liberalism in thought and practice, see Alan Ryan, *John Dewey and the High Tide of American Liberalism* (New York: W. W. Norton, 1995), chap. 8. Dewey was not a supporter of Franklin Roosevelt; he voted for Norman Thomas in 1932 and 1936.

18. Quoted in Rotunda, "'Liberal Label,'" 380. Conceptually, Dewey recognized the disjunction between the aggregate and the individual. Rather than the individual as the basic fact, he argued that "society in its unified and structural character is the fact of the case," adding that "the mass as an aggregate of isolated units is the fiction." Quoted in Louis Menand, *The Metaphysical Club* (New York: Farrar, Straus and Giroux, 2001), 304–5.

19. Protestant Christianity had provided a justification: that we are our brother's keepers. The Social Gospel movement promoted this as part of its view of the social Jesus, but the growing secularism of liberalism that led ultimately to its constitutional view of an absolute separation between church and state undermined this moral foundation for the liberal state. See Walter Rauschenbusch, *Christianity and the Social Crisis* (New York: Macmillan, 1911), and *Christianizing the Social Order* (New York: Macmillan, 1914). See also Paul M. Minus, *Walter Rauschenbusch: American Reformer* (New York: Macmillan, 1988). It was experience, not moral appeals based on reason, that triumphed after the 1960s. Kevin Phillips makes the point: "The Democratic Party fell victim to the ideological impetus of a liberalism which had carried it beyond programs taxing the few for the benefit of the many (the New Deal) to programs taxing the many on behalf of the few (the Great Society)." See Phillips, *The Emerging Republican Majority* (New Rochelle: Arlington House, 1969), 37.

20. George McJimsey, *The Presidency of Franklin Roosevelt* (Lawrence: University Press of Kansas, 2000), 48.

21. Quoted in William Leuchtenburg, *Franklin D. Roosevelt and the New Deal* (New York: Harper and Row, 1963), 58.

22. Quoted in ibid., 147.

23. McJimsey, *Presidency*, 85.

24. The financial burden of these "economic" rights was borne disproportionately by business and industry and not by the general population of taxpayers. The income tax burden on middle- and working-class Americans was much smaller in the 1930s than it was to become after World War II and especially after the 1960s.

25. Foner, *Story of American Freedom*, 216.

26. Quoted in ibid., 227. Foner adds that not everyone agreed with everything about the Four Freedoms. Conservatives in Congress saw the Freedom from Want as a projection of the New Deal domestic program on the world and reacted by ending a number of what they saw as the more left-wing programs of the New Deal: the Civilian Conservation Corps, the National Youth Administration, the Works Progress Administration, and the National Resources Planning Board. Others, especially business groups, noted the failure to include the freedom of private enterprise, which they argued was fundamental to all the oth-

ers. Even in a time of national mobilization for war, FDR seems not to have forgotten his battles with business interests in the early New Deal; nor, for that matter, had they. Ibid., 227–30.

27. Ibid., 227.

28. See Alan Brinkley, *The End of Reform: New Deal Liberalism in Recession and War* (New York: Alfred A. Knopf, 1995).

29. On anticommunism in American politics, see John Kenneth White, *Still Seeing Red: How the Cold War Shapes the New American Politics* (Boulder, Colo.: Westview, 1998).

30. See James M. Burnham, *The Managerial Revolution* (New York: John Day, 1941), and Friedrich Hayek, *The Road to Serfdom* (Chicago: University of Chicago Press, 1944).

31. See Lionel Trilling, *The Middle of the Journey* (New York: Viking Press, 1947).

32. See Arthur M. Schlesinger Jr., *The Vital Center: The Politics of Freedom* (Boston: Houghton Mifflin, 1949).

33. See John Kenneth Galbraith, *American Capitalism: The Theory of Countervailing Power* (Boston: Houghton Mifflin, 1952).

34. Of Niebuhr's works, see especially *Moral Man and Immoral Society: A Study in Ethics and Politics* (New York: Charles Scribner's Sons, 1932), and *The Irony of American History* (New York: Scribner's, 1952). See also Richard Wightman Fox, *Reinhold Niebuhr: A Biography* (New York: Pantheon, 1985), esp. chap. 10.

35. Mary Sperling McAuliffe, *Crisis on the Left: Cold War Politics and American Liberals, 1947–1954* (Amherst: University of Massachusetts Press, 1978), 63.

36. See Louis Hartz, *The Liberal Tradition in America* (New York: Harcourt, Brace and World, 1955); Daniel Boorstin, *The Genius of American Politics* (Chicago: University of Chicago Press, 1953); Henry B. Mayo, *An Introduction to Democratic Theory* (New York: Oxford University Press, 1960); and Daniel Bell, *The End of Ideology: On the Exhaustion of Political Ideas in the Fifties* (Glencoe, Ill.: Free Press, 1960).

37. See David B. Truman, *The Governmental Process* (New York: Alfred A. Knopf, 1950).

38. Theodore J. Lowi's critique of liberal pluralism and of the role of interest groups in American life ended with a reformist call for a "juridical democracy." See Lowi, *The End of Liberalism: Ideology, Policy, and the Crisis of Public Authority* (New York: Norton, 1969).

39. See Michael J. Bennett, *When Dreams Came True: The GI Bill and the Making of Modern America* (Washington, D.C.: Brassey's, 2000).

40. See Foner, *American Freedom*, 257.

41. See Alonzo L. Hamby, *Man of the People: The Life of Harry S. Truman* (New York: Oxford University Press, 1995), esp. chap. 31. See also Robert J. Donovan, *Tumultuous Years: The Presidency of Harry S. Truman, 1949–1953* (New York: W. W. Norton, 1982), esp. chaps. 16, 17, and 28.

42. The possibility that Eisenhower could transform the two-party battle was made real by the 1954 book of pollster Louis Harris, whose title asked the question, "Is there a Republican majority?" See Harris, *Is There a Republican Majority? Political Trends, 1952–1956* (New York: Harper and Brothers, 1954).

43. See Hugh Bone, *American Politics and the Party System* (New York: McGraw-Hill, 1955), 267.

44. See Robert C. Wood, "The Impotent Suburban Vote," *The Nation*, March 26, 1960, 273, and Henry Lee Mason, "The Negro Voter," *The Nation*, September 17, 1960, 156–57.

45. See Eugene H. Roseboom, *A History of Presidential Elections* (New York: Macmillan, 1957), 527–29.

46. The other senators were Paul Douglas of Illinois, Wayne Morse and Richard Neuberger of Oregon, James Murray of Montana, and Patrick McNamara of Michigan. See Sidney Hyman, "Can a Democrat Win in '60?" *The Reporter*, March 5, 1959, 12.

47. See *New York Times*, November 28, 1956, 1, and Hugh A. Bone, *Party Committees and National Politics* (Seattle: University of Washington Press, 1958), 210ff.

48. Two presidential hopefuls—Senators John F. Kennedy of Massachusetts and Stuart Symington of Missouri—declined membership at the outset, but in 1959 both did join, though neither played a significant or prominent role in its work.

49. See *New York Times*, January 5, 1957, 1.

50. For a summer of council policy positions, see *Congressional Quarterly Weekly Report*, December 11, 1959, 1550–52. See also Philip A. Klinkner, *The Losing Parties: Out-Party National Committees, 1956–1993* (New Haven: Yale University Press, 1994), chap. 2.

51. The council's criticism of the handling of school integration in Little Rock by Arkansas governor Orval Faubus provoked a particularly angry response from southern Democrats, including a call for a third party issued by former Truman cabinet member and former South Carolina governor James Byrnes.

52. On divisions between northern and southern Democrats and attempts to remove Butler as national party chair, see "How Big Is the North-South Democratic Split?," *Congressional Quarterly Weekly Report*, November 1, 1957, 1217–18; "Notable Change Seen in Butler Leadership," ibid., December 5, 1958, 1497–99; "Basic Democratic Divisions Examined," ibid., December 12, 1958, 1515–16, 1520; "Extent of North-South Democratic Split Analyzed," ibid., December 2, 1960, 1929–30, 1932; and Sidney Hyman, "War and Peace among the Democrats," *The Progressive*, September 1959, 30–32. Also involved was the issue of a "loyalty oath," adopted by the 1952 Democratic convention, before Butler became chair, and clearly aimed at the South, that required delegates to pledge support to the national ticket. See Abraham Holtzman, "Party Responsibility and Loyalty: New Rules in the Democratic Party," *Journal of Politics* 22 (August 1960): 485–501. Ironically, Butler had been elected chair by a coalition

of southern and western votes and was opposed by northern and urban interests in the party. He worked hard to rally the south behind the party nominee in 1956, and it was only after this failed that he became an advocate for a strong civil rights position for the party and joined with northern liberals in the formation of the Democratic Advisory Council.

53. See James MacGregor Burns, *The Deadlock of Democracy* (Englewood Cliffs, N.J.: Prentice Hall, 1963).

54. On the rise of Barry Goldwater and the new conservatism, see Robert Novak, *The Agony of the G.O.P., 1964* (New York: Macmillan, 1965). Support for Goldwater was evident at the 1960 Republican convention, as supporters placed his name in nomination, then cheered Goldwater enthusiastically when he spoke to the gathering before the first ballot to withdraw his name. See Robert J. Donovan, *The Future of the Republican Party* (New York: Signet Books, 1964), chap. 3.

55. Liberals had long had doubts about Kennedy as a liberal. Their doubts derived from his family's connections with Senator Joseph McCarthy, from Kennedy's failure to join the ADA, and from a *Saturday Evening Post* article in which he was quoted as saying, "I'm not a liberal at all. . . . I'm not comfortable with those people." See James MacGregor Burns, *John Kennedy: A Political Profile* (New York: Harcourt, Brace and World, 1959), 132–36; quotation is from pages 134–35.

56. See *New York Times*, March 18, 1960, 24.

57. Paul Tillett notes that the council "influenced the resolutions committee despite the absence from the council of the congressional leaders in the party" ("The National Conventions," in *The Presidential Election and Transition, 1960–1961*, ed. Paul T. David [Washington, D.C.: Brookings Institution, 1961], 33–34). Kennedy would draw on the council for appointments to subcabinet and ambassadorial positions, including Stevenson, Harriman, Galbraith, and G. Mennen Williams of Michigan, while many others were named to a variety of posts in the administration.

58. See Gabriel Kolko, *The Triumph of Conservatism* (New York: Free Press, 1963).

59. Matusow, *Unraveling of America*, 33.

60. Kennedy was widely hailed for a speech at Yale University in which he embraced the Keynesian theory of the fiscal and monetary roles for government in its "management" of the economy.

61. Lizabeth Cohen, *A Consumer's Republic* (New York: Alfred A. Knopf, 2003), 345.

62. Quoted in ibid., 352.

63. See Michael Harrington, *The Other America: Poverty in the United States* (New York: Macmillan, 1962), and John Kenneth Galbraith, *The Affluent Society* (Boston: Houghton Mifflin, 1958).

64. See Robert Dallek, *An Unfinished Life: John F. Kennedy, 1917–1963* (Boston: Little, Brown, 2003), 640.

65. Matusow, *Unraveling of America*, 88.

66. See Robert D. Loevy, ed., *The Civil Rights Act of 1964* (Albany: State University of New York Press, 1997).

67. See Bernard Cosman, *Five States for Goldwater* (Montgomery: University of Alabama Press, 1966).

68. *Congressional Quarterly Weekly Report*, November 19, 1965, 2, reported that of sixty-seven pieces of major legislation filed by the White House in 1965, sixty-three were enacted. The four that were not were amendments to the Fair Labor Standards Act, repeal of Section 14-B of the Taft-Hartley Act, home rule for the District of Columbia, and improvements in unemployment insurance.

69. In the end, *Congressional Quarterly* counted 469 proposals that Johnson made to Congress in 1965, of which 321 (64.8 percent) passed. See *Congressional Quarterly Weekly Reports*, ibid., table, 2341.

70. See James Q. Wilson, *Amateur Democrat: Club Politics in Three Cities* (Chicago: University of Chicago Press, 1962).

71. See Daniel P. Moynihan, *Maximum Feasible Misunderstanding* (New York: Free Press, 1969), and John C. Donovan, *The Politics of Poverty* (New York: Pegasus, 1967).

72. See Carole Pateman, *Participation and Democratic Theory* (New York: Cambridge University Press, 1970).

73. Elsewhere in this volume, Hugh Heclo argues that this understanding of individualism in a participatory democracy led to a new conception of liberal citizenship.

74. On the Democratic Party reforms, see William J. Crotty, *Decision for the Democrats: Reforming the Party Structure* (Baltimore: Johns Hopkins University Press, 1978); Bryon E. Shafer, *Quiet Revolution* (New York: Russell Sage, 1983); and Nelson W. Polsby, *Consequences of Party Reform* (New York: Oxford University Press, 1983).

75. See Fred Siegel, "The New Left, the New Right, and the New Deal," in *The Liberal Persuasion*, ed. John Patrick Diggins, 151–63 (Princeton: Princeton University Press, 1997).

76. Kevin Mattson, *Intellectuals in Action: The Origins of the New Left and Radical Liberalism, 1945–1970* (University Park: Pennsylvania State University Press, 2002), 13. There is irony in the fact that John Dewey, whose advocacy of collectivist approaches influenced the New Deal liberalism, should also be a primary source for those on the New Left who mounted an individualist critique of it.

77. See Ronald P. Formissano, *Boston against Busing: Race, Class, and Ethnicity in the 1960s and 1970s* (Chapel Hill: University of North Carolina Press, 1991).

78. Poll results and quote are from James A. Reichley, *The Life of the Parties* (New York: Free Press, 1992), 336–37.

79. See Samuel Lubell, *The Future of American Politics* (New York: Harper, 1952).

80. See David Stockman, *The Triumph of Politics: How the Reagan Revolution Failed* (New York: Harper and Row, 1986).

81. See David Farber, *Chicago '68* (Chicago: University of Chicago Press, 1988).

82. Dan T. Carter, *The Politics of Rage: George Wallace, the Origins of the New Conservatism, and the Transformation of American Politics* (New York: Simon and Schuster, 1995), 12.

83. On the "circulation of elites" in the two major parties in the 1960s and 1070s, see Byron E. Shafer, *The Two Majorities and the Puzzle of Modern American Politics* (Lawrence: University Press of Kansas, 2003), esp. chap. 6.

84. H. W. Brands, *The Strange Death of American Liberalism* (New Haven: Yale University Press, 2001), 125. Brands is not alone in this view. G. Calvin Mackenzie, for example, writes that "it was the war in Vietnam that drew the real boundary between the old politics and the new, the point at which trust in government ended and skepticism began." As for its impact on the Democrats, Mackenzie adds: "The end of the war did not end the spirit of skepticism or the political activism that the war had generated. . . . [I]n the late 1960s the cutting edge of this new political activism, honed in the antiwar and civil rights movements, took on a new enemy: the Democratic Party establishment." See Mackenzie, *The Irony of Reform: Roots of American Political Disenchantment* (Boulder, Colo.: Westview, 1996), 74. See also Louis Galambos, who suggests that Vietnam may have been "the most debilitating episode in the nation's entire history," in *America at Middle Age: A New History of the United States in the Twentieth Century* (New York: New Press, 1983), 120.

85. Richard M. Scammon and Ben J. Wattenberg, *The Real Majority* (New York: Coward-McCann, 1970).

86. Phillips, *Emerging Republican Majority*.

87. See Lisa McGirr, *Suburban Warriors: The Origins of the New American Right* (Princeton: Princeton University Press, 2001); Mary C. Brennan, *Turning Right in the Sixties: The Conservative Capture of the GOP* (Chapel Hill: University of North Carolina Press, 1995); and Matthew Dallek, *The Right Moment: Ronald Reagan's First Victory and the Decisive Turning Point in American Politics* (New York: Free Press, 2000).

88. See Arnold Kaufman, *The Radical Liberal: New Man in American Politics* (New York: Artherton, 1968); Theodore J. Lowi, *The End of Liberalism: Ideology, Policy, and the Crisis of Public Authority* (New York: W. W. Norton, 1969); and William Connolly, ed., *The Bias of Pluralism* (New York: Atherton, 1969).

89. On the nature of American rights and the problems posed, see Mary Ann Glendon, *Rights Talk: The Impoverishment of Political Discourse* (New York: Free Press, 1991).

Contributors

Henry J. Abraham is James Hart Professor Emeritus in the Department of Politics at the University of Virginia. He is the author of numerous works on the American court system, among them *Freedom and the Court: Civil Rights and Liberties in the United States*; *The Judiciary: The Supreme Court in the Governmental Process*; and *Justices, Presidents, and Senators: A History of U.S. Supreme Court Appointments from Washington to Clinton*.

Brian Balogh is associate professor in the Department of History and co-director of the Miller Center's American Political Development Program at the University of Virginia. He is the author of *Chain Reaction: Expert Debate and Public Participation in American Commercial Nuclear Power, 1945–1975*; editor of *Integrating the Sixties: The Origins, Structures, and Legitimacy of Public Policy in a Turbulent Decade*; and the author of numerous essays on recent developments in American political history.

Rosalyn Baxandall is Distinguished Teaching Professor and chair of the American Studies Department at the State University of New York at Old Westbury. An activist, one of the founders of the women's liberation movement, as well as a scholar, Baxandall is the author of *Words on Fire: The Life and Writing of Elizabeth Gurley Flynn*; coauthor of *Picture*

Windows: How the Suburbs Happened; and coeditor of *America's Working Women: An Anthology of Women's Work, 1620 to the Present* and *Dear Sisters: Dispatches from the Women's Liberation Movement.*

Edward Berkowitz is professor of history and of public policy and public administration and director of the Program in History and Public Policy at the George Washington University. His most recent books are *Mr. Social Security: The Life of Wilbur J. Cohen; To Improve Human Health: A History of the Institute of Medicine; The Medical Follow-Up Agency: The First Fifty Years, 1946–1996* (coauthor); and *Robert Ball and the Politics of Social Security.*

Eileen Boris is Hull Professor of Women's Studies in the Women's Studies Program at the University of California, Santa Barbara. She is the author of *Home to Work: Motherhood and the Politics of Industrial Homework in the United States* and *Art and Labor: Ruskin, Morris, and the Craftsman Ideal in America;* coeditor of *Voices of Women's Historians: The Personal, the Political, the Professional* and *Major Problems in the History of American Workers.*

Hugh Davis Graham was professor emeritus in the Department of History at Vanderbilt University. He was the author of several books on civil rights and immigration, including *The Civil Rights Era: Origins and Development of National Policy, 1960–1972* and *Collision Course: The Strange Convergence of Affirmative Action and Immigration Policy in America.* He was the coeditor of *The Carter Presidency: Policy Choices in the Post–New Deal Era* and *The Reagan Presidency: Pragmatic Conservatism and Its Legacies.*

Hugh Heclo is Clarence J. Robinson Professor of Public Affairs at George Mason University. He is the author of several books, including *A Government of Strangers: Executive Politics in Washington* and *Modern Social Politics in Britain and Sweden;* coauthor of *Comparative Public Policy: The Politics of Social Choice in Europe and America;* and coeditor of *The Illusion of Presidential Government.* He has written numerous essays on social policy and the presidencies of Ronald Reagan and George H. W. Bush.

Frederick Hess is director of Education Policy Studies at the American Enterprise Institute. His publications include *Common Sense School Reform; Revolution at the Margins: The Impact of Competition on Urban School Systems;* and *Spinning Wheels: The Politics of Urban School Reform.*

William E. Leuchtenburg is William Rand Kenan, Jr., Professor Emeritus at the University of North Carolina, Chapel Hill. He is the author of many books on American politics in the twentieth century, among them *The Perils of Prosperity, 1914–1932; Franklin D. Roosevelt and the New Deal, 1932–1940; In the Shadow of FDR: From Harry Truman to Ronald Reagan;* and *The Supreme Court Reborn: The Constitutional Revolution in the Age of Roosevelt.*

Nelson Lichtenstein is professor of history at the University of California, Santa Barbara, where he directs the Center for the Study of Work, Labor, and Democracy. He is the author, most recently, of *Walter Reuther: The Most Dangerous Man in Detroit* and *State of the Union: A Century of American Labor;* editor of *Imaging Capitalism: Political Economy and Social Thought in 20th-Century America;* and coeditor of *Major Problems in the History of American Workers.*

Patrick McGuinn is assistant professor of political science at Drew University. His work on education policy has been published in *The Public Interest, Teachers College Record,* and *Education Policy,* and he is author of a forthcoming book, *Educating Politics: The Transformation of Federal Education Policy, 1965–2002.*

Wilson Carey McWilliams was professor of political science at Rutgers, The State University of New Jersey, and the author of *The Idea of Fraternity in America; Beyond the Politics of Disappointment?: American Elections, 1980–1998;* and numerous essays on American politics, philosophy, and literature as well as coeditor of *The Federalists, the Antifederalists, and the American Political Tradition.*

R. Shep Melnick is Thomas P. O'Neill, Jr., Professor of American Politics in the Political Science Department at Boston College and co-chair of the Harvard Program on Constitutional Government. He is author of two books, *Between the Lines: Interpreting Welfare Rights* and *Regulation* *and the Courts: The Case of the Clean Air Act,* and coeditor of *Taking Stock: American Government in the Twentieth Century.*

Jerome M. Mileur is professor emeritus in the Department of Political Science at the University of Massachusetts Amherst. He is the author of numerous essays on American national politics in the twentieth century; editor of *The Liberal Tradition in Crisis: American Politics in the Sixties;* and coeditor of *Challenges to Party Government; America's Choice: The Election of 1996; Progressivism and the New Democracy;* and *The New Deal and the Triumph of Liberalism.*

Sidney M. Milkis is White Burkett Miller Professor and chair of the Department of Politics and co-director of the Miller Center's American Political Development Program at the University of Virginia. He is the author of *The President and the Parties: The Transformation of the American Party System Since the New Deal* and *Political Parties and Constitutional Government: Remaking American Democracy;* coauthor of *Presidential Greatness; The Politics of Regulatory Change: A Tale of Two Agencies; The American Presidency: Origins and Development, 1776–2002;* and *American Government: Balancing Democracy and Rights;* and coeditor of *Remaking American Politics; Progressivism and the New Democracy;* and *The New Deal and the Triumph of Liberalism.*

Frances Fox Piven and **Richard A. Cloward** are the coauthors of a series of books on American politics, poverty, and social movements, including *Poor People's Movements: Why They Succeed, How They Fail; Regulating the Poor: The Functions of Public Welfare; The New Class War: Reagan's Attack on the Welfare State and Its Consequences;* and *Why Americans Still Don't Vote: And Why Politicians Want It That Way.* Piven is Distinguished Professor of Political Science and Sociology at the Graduate Center of the City University of New York. Her latest book, *The War at Home,* is on the domestic causes and consequences of the war in Iraq. Until his death, Cloward was professor of social work at Columbia University.

David M. Shribman is executive editor of *The Pittsburgh Post-Gazette.* Formerly the Washington Bureau Chief for *The Boston Globe,* Shribman writes a nationally syndicated column dealing with national politics. He won the Pulitzer Prize in 1995.

Index

Aaron, Henry, 262
Abingdon School District v. Schempp, 394
abortion, 279
Abraham, David, 106–7
Acheson, Dean, 430
activism: ambivalent, 161, 405; grassroots, women's movement and, 159–60, 278–79, 287n14; judicial, 351–52; LBJ on, 13
Addams, Jane, 419
Adult Education Program, 120
adverse impact claims, 376
Advisory Commission on Intergovernmental Relations, 258, 400
Aetna Company, 340, 341
affirmative action: civil rights bureaucracy and, 383; civil rights policy transformed by, 365–66, 381–82; expansion of, 438; hard vs. soft, 368; identity politics and, 381; immigration policy and, 369–71, 380–83; insider politics and, 173; legal foundation for, Burger Court and, 395; 1970s as beginning of, xv, 58; Nixon and, 406; within NOW, 275; official minority status and, 376, 378, 385n21; policy incrementalism and, 397–98; political impact of, 440; positive rights and, 438; rationale for, 370; therapeutic ethos and, 163; as unintended consequence, 368–69; women and, 384–85n13

AFL-CIO, 84, 86, 101–2, 106
African-Americans: affirmative action and, 370, 406; cold war liberalism and, 411, 427; Democratic Party and, 413, 448n2; democratic pluralism and, 171, 174–75; disenfranchisement of, 271; educational inequalities of, 292; Great Society politics and, 255–59, 263–64; Great Society programs targeted at, 253, 322–23; impact of welfare on, 262–63; in Job Corps, 122–23; LBJ/FDR relationship and, 197–98, 210n28; liberal nondiscrimination and, 367–68; Mobilization for Youth and, 260–62; New Deal and, 152–53, 271; northward migration of, 255–59; official minority status and, 371–72, 378–80, 382, 385n21; political incorporation of, 263–64, 266, 268n26; and public vs. private, 160; unemployment, 261
African-American women, 117–18, 272, 274, 281
Age Discrimination in Employment Act (1968), 104
Agricultural Adjustment Act, 205, 422

agricultural labor, "employable mother" rules and, 142n67
agricultural modernization, 255
Agriculture Department, U.S., 338, 398
Aid to Dependent Children (ADC), 117; employment/welfare policy interconnections in, 129–31; name change of, 131; redefined goals of, 130
Aid to Families with Dependent Children (AFDC): eligibility requirements for, 136; employment/welfare policy interconnections in, 116–17, 129, 131; federal spending for, 397; Mobilization for Youth and, 260; policy incrementalism and, 397; replaced with TANF, 137, 266; -Unemployed Father (AFDC-UF), 131, 142n72; -Unemployed Parent (AFDC-UP), 142n72
Alabama, Medicare in, 326–27, 339–40
Alabama Medical Association, 339
Alaska, 340
Alaskan Natives, 379
Albert, Carl B., 247
Alexander, Lamar, 317n71
alienation, 27, 74–75
Allred, James, 189, 192
Altemeyer, Arthur, 131, 330, 331
Amalgamated Meatcutters, 275
Ambrose, Stephen, 236–37
American Capitalism (Galbraith), 99–100
American Farm Bureau Federation (AFBF), 180n63
American Federation of Labor (AFL), 92, 413
American Federation of State, County, and Municipal Employees, 100
American Hospital Association, 323–24
American Independent Party, 443–44
American Jewish Committee, 373
American Jewish Congress, 373
American Medical Association, 329, 332–33, 335, 427
American Public Welfare Association, 130–31
Americans for Democratic Action (ADA), 57, 425, 453n55
Americans with Disabilities Act (1990), 104

American Woman, The (PCSW report), 274
America 2000, 308–9, 317nn72–73
Andrews, George, 351
anticommunism, 218; cold war liberalism and, 426; conservative strategy and, 223, 294; containment strategy, 433; impact on liberalism, 411–12, 424–25, 427–28; LBJ and 223, 228n27, 294. *See also* cold war
antipoverty programs: of Nixon/Ford, 388–90. *See also* War on Poverty
antiwar movement, 416; civil rights movement and, 4, 21–22; feminism and, 279; New Left and, 278; new politics and, xiv, 34–35; participatory democracy and, xiii; political impact of, 440–41, 443
Appalachia, Job Corps and, 123
Appalachian Regional Development Act, 239
appeasement, 218, 220
Arab Americans, 374
Arkansas Blue Shield, 340
Army Corps of Engineers, 169
Aronowitz, Stanley, 101
Asia, mass migration from, 369–70
Asian Americans, 370, 379, 380, 381, 382, 385n21
Atlanta (Ga.), LBJ's civil rights promotion in, 17
Atlanta Constitution, 18–19

Baker, Ella, 280
Baker v. Carr, 356, 359
Bakke case, 366
Ball, George, 217, 220
Ball, Robert: Medicare, 340; on Medicare abuses, 342; on Medicare and national health insurance, 322; Medicare civil rights compliance and, 326–28; Medicare Part B and, 329, 336, 339–41; on Medicare participation, 338; Medicare reform and, 341–44; on Medicare reimbursements, 323–24
Balogh, Brian, 6
Barkley, Alben, 190
Barrett, Edith J., 409n33
Beer, Samuel, 29, 35, 47n96, 57, 75

Bell, Daniel, 89, 91, 93, 99, 100, 101
Berke, Joel, 300, 306
Berkowitz, Edward, 149
Berman, Shelley, 77
Berry, Jeffrey, 35
bilingual education, 303, 305, 396
Bill of Rights, 353, 356–57, 358–59, 423
Birmingham (Ala.), civil rights demonstrations in, 16, 101, 435
birth control, 356–57
Black, Hugo: Frankfurter vs., 358–59; as judicial activist, 353; as rights liberal, 106, 352; Supreme Court decisions authored by, 356–57; Warren Court and, 357, 360, 394
black capitalism, 406
Black Power movement, 248; color-coding and, 378; Great Society opposed by, 22–23; liberal results orientation and, 150; Markman report on, 27; political culture and, 160
block grants, 264–65, 266, 310, 317n67
Blue Cross, 323, 333–34
Blue Cross–Blue Shield, 335
Blue Cross–Blue Shield of Alabama, 339–40
Blue Shield, 339, 340–41, 343
Booker, Simeon, 42n49
Boris, Eileen, 149, 152, 154, 159, 169
Bornet, Vaughn Davis, 237
Boston Women's Health Collective, 285
Bradlee, Benjamin C., 239
Brandeis, Louis, 87–88, 330
Brandenburg v. Ohio, 394
Brands, H. W., 446, 455n84
Brecher, Jeremy, 101
Brennan, William, 352, 353, 356, 357, 358, 360; Warren Court and, 394
Breyer, Stephen, 410n41
Brinkley, Alan, 236, 424
Brinkley, Douglas, 236–37
Broder, David, 6
Brooke, Edward, 441
Brown, Edmund G., 20
Brown, Michael, 121, 125, 264, 268n18
Brownlow Committee, 47n94
Brown v. Board of Education, 291, 355, 357, 358, 428
Bruce, Lenny, 66

budget balancing, 399
Budget Bureau, 378
Bundy, McGeorge, 246–47
Burckhardt, Jacob, 72–73
bureaucracy: civil rights policy and, 376–77, 383, 385n21; ESEA and, 289, 301–2, 305–6; of labor unions, 85–86, 92, 98–99; mandate-and-sue strategy and, 405–7; modernization and, 74; New Left critique of, 280, 439–40
Burger, Warren, 395
Burkhead, Jesse, 48n105
Burnham, James, 89
Burns, Arthur, 343
Burns, James MacGregor, 214
Burton, Harold, 357
Busby, Horace, 8–9, 16, 42–43n52, 194, 247
Bush, George H. W., 308–9, 317n73, 317–18n77, 406
Bush, George W./Bush administration, 163; ESEA reform of, 290, 310–11, 312, 316n58, 319n86; as governor, 318n84; influence of Great Society on, xv, 177n12; presidential campaign of (2000), 318–19n85; Republican educational policies and, 318n84
business interests: antiunionism of, 84, 88, 105–6; FDR and, 421; JFK and, 433–34; New Deal programs financed by, 450n24; pluralism in, 180n63; public employment programs and, 267n6
busing, for desegregation, 167, 383–84n2, 395, 440
Butler, Paul, 430–31, 452–53n52
Byrd, Harry, 241, 325
Byrnes, James, 452n51
Byrnes, John, 333–34, 336

Caddell, Patrick, xvi
Caesar, Irving, 192–93
Califano, Joseph A., Jr., 241
California, 382, 415; Reagan elected governor of, 20, 444
Cantril, Hadley, 403
capitalism: black, 406; devaluation of, as system of power, 89, 90–91
Carlin, George, 66

Carmichael, Stokely, 22–23, 27
Caro, Robert, 39n18, 194, 212n46, 238
Carpenter, Liz, 202
Carter, Dan, 443
Carter, David, 22
Carter, Jimmy, 36; electoral defeat of (1980), 307; ESEA expansion under, 303–4, 306, 308; "malaise" speech of (1979), xvi, 34
Catholicism, 294, 314n12, 374
Catledge, Turner, 151–52, 203–4
Celebrezze, Anthony J., 132
Census Bureau, 378–79, 382
Center for Disease Control, 327
Chamber of Commerce, U.S., 422
Chapman, Oscar, 197
Charlestown (S. C.), antiunionism in, 103–4
Chesterton, G. K., 76
Chiang Kai-shek, 231n71
Chicago, machine politics in, 417
childcare, 132–33, 272, 285–86
child labor restrictions, 117
China, 221, 229n52, 427
Chinese Americans, 371, 379
Chinese Revolution, 280
Chubb, John, 302
Church, Frank, 340
church/state separation, 356
cities, inner. *See* urban ghettos
Citizens Advisory Council, 274
citizen suits, 168, 405–6, 410n41
civic education, 226
civil disobedience, 158
Civilian Conservation Corps (CCC), 122, 205, 271, 450–51n26
Civil Rights Act (1964), 107; as acknowledgment of racist history, 154; affirmative action as violation of, 368; civil rights policy discontinuities and, 365; conservatives and color-blind interpretation of, 388; democratic pluralism and, 173; ESEA and, 293, 294; expansion of, 134, 159, 165, 401–2; LBJ and, 19, 245, 415; liberal nondiscrimination and, 367; 1964 election and, 23, 24; political impact of, 415, 440; as radical, 367; significance of, 387–88; Title VI, 294, 325–27, 368, 396, 401;
Title VII, 101–5, 159, 166, 273–74, 287n14, 368, 401; Title IX, 285, 365
Civil Rights Act (1965), 275
civil rights agencies, 167–68, 393. *See also specific agency*
Civil Rights Bill (1957), 196–97, 237, 241
Civil Rights Bill (1963), 365, 435
Civil Rights Commission, 371–72, 393
civil rights movement: black disenfranchisement and, 271; Democratic Party and, 16, 394; educational inequalities and, 292; impact of Sixties civics on, 69; impact on pluralism, 157–59, 174; JFK and, 434–35; labor unions and, 84, 95, 101–2, 103; LBJ and, 4–5, 16–28, 32, 42n49, 43n53, 44n75, 205, 242–43; liberal reform ideology and, 4–5; March on Washington (1963), 4, 16, 102; militancy in, 21, 22–23; new politics and, xiv, 15, 32, 33, 34–35, 437; Northern support for, 428; political impact of, 443–45; white backlash against, 21; women in, 278–79; women's movement and, 277
Civil Rights of Institutionalized Persons Act (1980), 401
civil rights policy: cold war and, 156; continuity in, 366, 383–84n2; contract compliance committees and, 372–73; discontinuities in, 365–66, 381–83, 383–84n2; Eisenhower administration and, 428–29; Great Society and, 239, 383; LBJ and, 237; LBJ/FDR relationship and, 196–97; liberal nondiscrimination and, 365–68; mandate-and-sue strategy and, 166; Medicare and, 324–28; New Deal and, 324–25; 1960s vs. 1970s as major period of, 58; official minority status and, 382–83; as radical, 159; unintended consequences of, 368–71. *See also* affirmative action; Civil Rights Act (1964); ethnic/racial minorities, official status of; Voting Rights Act (1965); *specific agency, legislation*
Clark, Bennett Champ, 335
Clark, Joseph S., 139n16
Clark, Tom Campbell, 357
Clark Amendment, 335–36, 348n44

class action suits, 158, 172
class conflict: industrial pluralism and, 88–93, 101; NIRA and, 423
Claybrook, Joan, 405
Clean Air Act, 167, 397
Clean Water Act, 167, 397, 399
Clemens, Elizabeth, 180n63
Clifford, Clark, 205
Clinton, William Jefferson/Clinton administration: ESEA reform under, 290, 309–10; as governor, 317n71; legacy of, 240; national health insurance and, 345; official minority status and, 382–83; and opportunity vs. entitlement, 312; policy mindedness and, 60–61; presidential campaign of (1992), 317–18n77; presidential campaign of (1996), 318n82; state-level educational standards promoted by, 317n71; welfare reform and, 137
Cloward, Richard, xviii; on Community Action Program, 5, 49n116, 155; on Equal Opportunity Act, 152; impact on antipoverty program, 47n96; in Mobilization for Youth program, 259; on therapeutic ethos, 163–64
Cohen, Lizabeth, 434
Cohen, Wilbur, 333, 340–41; Altemeyer on, 131; LBJ and, 7, 9; Medicare Part B and, 329, 337; Truman's presence at Medicare signing and, 321
cold war: impact on Great Society, 155–57; impact on liberalism, 156–57, 411–12, 424–26; industrial pluralism and, 88, 428; LBJ and, 218; liberal reform ideology and, x–xi
cold war liberalism: defined, 426; Great Society influenced by, 170–71; JFK and, xi, 1, 432–35; LBJ and, 156–57; Left and, 223; moral basis for collective action lacking in, 445; political reformulation for, 424–26; rights-based agenda of, 426–27
cold war pluralism, 170–71, 172, 180n63, 426
collective bargaining: decline of, 83–84, 96, 107–8; impact of cold war on, 428; industrial pluralism and, 87–88, 91–93, 169; labor bureaucracies and, 85–86,

88; as positive right, 423; radical disillusionment with, 98, 99, 101. *See also* labor unions
collectivism, New Deal liberalism and, 418–24
Commanger, Henry Steele, 236
Commentary, 98–99
Committee of Racial Equality (CORE), 22–23, 24
Committee on Civil Rights, 172
Committee on Economic Security, 348n44
Committee on Equal Employment, 197–98
Commons, John R., 87
Commonwealth Club, FDR's address at (1932), 177n25, 422
Communications Workers Convention (1964), 11, 41n36
communism, 418, 427
Community Action Program, 148; advocacy groups and, 168; disruptive potential of, 12; empowerment strategies of, 438; equal opportunity and, 149; modern presidency and, 28–32, 34, 155; objectives of, 120; participatory democracy and, xiii, 5, 12, 29–30, 172; political risks of, 31–32, 46–47n92; public interest advocacy and, 393; significance of, 49n116; in War on Poverty, 11–13, 28–32, 48n105
Community Mental Health Centers Act (1963), 253
Community Work and Training, 131–32
Conant, James, 292
Congress, U.S.: anticommunist investigations of, 427–28; cold war pluralism and, 170; Democratic control of, Seventies policy and, 394, 395, 398–99; divided government and, 394, 398–99; EPA and, 165–66; ESEA and, 307; exposure strategy and, 410n39; hearings, 167; LBJ as president and, 204, 205, 294–95, 391; LBJ in, 189–92, 193–94; mandate-and-sue strategy and, 402–3, 405; Medicare and, 325–26, 338–41; micromanagement by, 167; 1964 election and, 435–36; NIRA and, 422; off-budget costs and, 400–401; official

Congress, U.S. (*cont.*)
  minority status and, 379, 380; policy incrementalism and, 395–98; Republican control of (1994), 265, 318n81; rights consciousness and, 401–2; Social Security state-federal tensions and, 332–33; SSA and, 336–37; Warren Court and, 355–56, 394; Ways and Means Committee, 325, 333
Congress of Industrial Organizations (CIO), 103, 413
Conkin, Paul, 20, 34
Conlan, Timothy, 400
Connally, John, 191
Connally, Tom, 187–88, 192, 209n22
Connecticut General, 341
Connolly, Nellie, 247
Connor, Bull, 103
consciousness-raising, 164–65, 279–83
conservation, LBJ/FDR relationship and, 196
conservatism: "compassionate," 290, 310–11; deficit spending as strategy of, 442; educational reform and, 290, 310–11; ESEA and, 294, 296; Four Freedoms and, 450–51n26; Great Society and rise of, xiv, 6, 146, 439–45; Great Society as target of, xiii–xiv, 387; ideological, American public as, 403; impact of Great Society on, xv–xvi, 175–76, 177n12, 388–91; impact of post-WWII demographic shifts on, 446–47; labor unions and, 84, 86, 96; LBJ criticized by, 231n71; LBJ's civil rights promotion and, 40–41n33; liberal reform ideology opposed by, ix–x; mandate-and-sue strategy and, 406–7; Medicare and, 321–22; new, 442, 444–45, 446–47; pluralism and, 175–76; policy mindedness and, 62, 163; rights-based policy of, 406; social, 443–44; think tanks, 265; Vietnam War and, 223
Constitution, U.S.: Amendment I, 373–74; Amendment IV, 359; Amendment V, 355; Amendment VI, 356; Amendment XIV, 355, 393; Amendment XV, 393; Bill of Rights, 353, 356–57, 358–59; Civil War Amendments, 353; conservatives and color-blind interpretation of, 388; as design for limited government, 59; education and, 290; negative rights in, 429; taxation powers in, 402; Warren Court interpretations of, 354–57
consumer bill of rights, 434
consumerism, 424
consumer movement: civil rights movement as model for, 4, 158; government distrusted by, 160–61; impact of Sixties civics on, 69; legitimacy barrier and, 162; new politics and, xiv, 33; public interest advocacy and, xiii
contract compliance committees, 372–73
contracted services, 168
contract set-aside programs, 375, 376–77, 382
Contract with America (1994), 58, 62
Cook, Fay Lomax, 409n33
Cook County (Ill.) Democratic Party, 45n84
Cooper, John Sherman, 441
Corcoran, Thomas G., 57, 189–90, 191, 196
corporations, 89–90, 100, 117
Council of Economic Advisors, 120
counsel, right to, 356–57, 394
counter-counterculture, 69
counterculture, 62, 69, 248, 440–41, 443
courts: desegregation and, 150; ESEA and, 289; federal-state relations and, 392–93; as guardian of rights revolution, 36–37; industrial pluralism supported by, 93; labor union devaluation and, 106–8; LBJ district-court appointments, 395; mandate-and-sue strategy and, 402–3, 405; policy expansion and, 392–93; Roosevelt's packing of, 151–52; Sixties civics and, 53. *See also* Supreme Court; Warren Court
Cox, Archibald, 93
credibility gap, 236
criminal cases, Warren Court and, 355–56
Croly, Herbert, 75, 418
Cronkite, Walter, 14, 191
Cuciti, Peggy, 307
culture of poverty, 116, 119, 296
Curley, James Michael, 413
"cycles of reform," 151–53

Dahl, Robert, 89, 92, 94, 98
Daley, Richard, 26, 45n84, 222, 417
Dallek, Robert, 199, 200–201, 226n11
Davies, Gareth, 11, 12, 118, 307
Davis, Mike, 101
Death of a President (Manchester), 244
Defense Department, U.S., 168
deficit spending, 156, 399, 442
delegitimization, 75–77
Democracy in America (de Tocqueville), 110n18
Democratic Advisory Council, 430–31, 432, 452nn48, 51
Democratic Leadership Council, 266, 312, 317n75
Democratic National Committee, 430
Democratic National Convention: 1928, 186; 1952, 452–53n52; 1964, 23–25, 44n75, 45nn79, 81; 1968, 222, 235; 1972, 207
Democratic Party: African-Americans and, 413, 448n2; ambivalence about government role, 403–4; civil rights movement and, 16, 394, 429; class division within, 437–38; community action programs and, 29; divided government and, 35, 394, 398–99; divisions within (1970s), xiv, 445–46; educational reform and, 290, 292–93, 309–10; ESEA and, 301–2; Great Society politics and, 255–59, 263–64, 265–66; impact of Great Society on, xv–xvi; impact of post-WWII demographic shifts on, 412–18, 429, 446–47; impact of Sixties civics on, 65; impact of Vietnam War on, 445–46, 455n84; labor unions and, 86, 106; LBJ and, 188–89, 207, 234, 244, 301, 435–37; McGovernism and, 387; MFDP controversy in, 23–25, 44n75; New Deal liberalism and, 421; New Deal realignment and, 32–33, 152; New Democrats, 58, 309–10; new politics and, 437–39; 1960 election as "last hurrah" of, 412; 1964 election and, 435–36; North-South split in, 20–21, 429–31, 452–53n52; NOW and, 284; policy reversals in (1990s), 255; post-1968 reforms in, xiii, xiv–xv, 34–35; presidential politics vs., 14;
racial/gender divisions tolerated by, 118; as tax-and-spenders, 402; Vietnam War and, 301. *See also specific president*
Democratic Study Group, 394
Demonstration Cities and Metropolitan Development Act (1966), 253
Dereliction of Duty (McMaster), 238
Derthick, Martha, 166, 392
desegregation: *Brown v. Board of Education*, 291, 355, 357, 358, 428; congressional power and, 394; Democratic Party and, 256; ESEA and, 294; LBJ and, 244; liberal nondiscrimination and, 366–67; mandate-and-sue strategy and, 166, 167, 394, 396; New Left and, 277; as policy discontinuity, 381–82, 383–84n2; racial conflict over, 259; results orientation and, 150
Dewey, John, xii, 9–10, 419–20, 421, 426; on economic individualism, 449n14; on equal opportunity, 449n16; Great Society empowerment strategies vs., 439; on individualism vs. collectivism, 450n18; on liberalism, 449–50n17; New Left and, 454n76
Dewey, Thomas, 430
Dickerson, Nancy and Wyatt, 247
Diem, Ngo Dinh, 206, 219
Dien Bien Phu, fall of, 218
Directive no. 15, 379–80
Dirksen, Everett, 19, 247, 435, 441–42
disability insurance, 328, 330–31, 332–33, 337
disenfranchisement, 271
disinterestedness, 66–67, 70, 157, 175
Dissent (journal), 98
district courts, LBJ appointments to, 395
distrust. *See* government, distrust of
Dobie, Frank, 39n18
Dole, Bob, 318nn82, 84
domestic violence, 286
Dominican Republic, 248
Douglas, Helen Gahagan, 194, 230–31n68
Douglas, Paul, 324
Douglas, William O., 93, 352, 353, 356–57, 358, 360; Warren Court and, 394
dropout prevention programs, 303
Drucker, Peter, 89–90, 93, 109–10n14

Dublin, Robert, 88
Dudziak, Mary, 156
due process, 426
Duggan, Ervin, 20–21
Dunlop, John, 90, 110n16
Dutton, Fred, 13, 41n43

Earned Income Tax Credit (EITC), 137, 397
East, Catherine, 275
Eastland, James, 135
Eastwood, Mary, 275
Economic and Research Action Project (ERAP), 279
economic bill of rights, 10, 423
Economic Opportunity Act (1964), 119–20, 253; community action as core of, 13; Job Corps, 121–28; as New Deal extension, 10; Title II, 120; Title V, 132
Economy Act, 205
education: African-Americans and, 263–64, 268n28; bilingual, 303, 305, 396; centralization of policy in, 302–3, 305–6; federal role in, 289–90, 298, 308–9, 311–13, 313n1, 387–88; federal spending on, 292, 298, 304–5, 306–7, 310, 318n83, 319n91; federal standards/tests, 309, 312, 316n58, 317n70; gender equality in, 367; gender inequality in, 272; GI Bill and, 411; Great Society and equal access to, 149–50; Great Society legislation and, xiv, 8, 239; impact of cold war on, 156; interest groups, 303; mandate-and-sue strategy and, 166; Mobilization for Youth and, 259–60; Native American, 305; policy expansion and, 169, 177n12, 179n44; political context of, 290–93; post-WWII importance of, 291, 313n6; public support for, 308–9, 310–11, 317–18n77, 318n82; reform of, 309–11; rights consciousness and, 162; special education, 166, 304–5; state/local control of, 290–91; War on Poverty and, 116; women's movement and, 285. *See also* Elementary and Secondary Education Act
Education Amendments (1972), 401

Education Consolidation and Improvement Act (ECIA; 1981), 307–8
Education Department, U.S., 306, 310, 317n67, 318n80
Education for All Handicapped Children Act (EAHCA; 1975), 304–5, 400, 401
Education of the Handicapped Act (1970), 304
Ehrenreich, Barbara, 133
8(a) contract set-aside program, 375, 376–77, 382, 385n21
Eisenhower, Dwight/Eisenhower administration: as anticommunist, 433; civil rights policy of, 428–29; as constitutional conservative, 13–14; contract compliance committee of, 372–73; foreign policy of, 247; insider politics of, 156–57; on labor unions, 92; LBJ and, 156–57, 218, 247; presidential election of (1952), 427, 429–30, 452n42; Southern electoral support for, 16; Vietnam War and, 221; Warren Court and, 353
elections, presidential: **1936,** 188, 200, 203–4, 414; **1940,** 414; **1944,** 414; 1948, 414; **1952,** 257, 427, 429–30; **1956,** 257; **1960,** 197, 257, 314n12, 412, 414, 416, 417, 431–32; **1964,** 2, 43–44n65, 199–200, 201–2, 213n54, 314n13, 415, 417, 435–36; **1968,** 20–21, 32, 235, 264, 442–44; **1980,** 6, 307, 417; **1988,** 308; **1992,** 309, 317–18n77; **1996,** 309, 318nn82, 84; **2000,** 214, 226, 234, 310–11, 318–19n85
Electoral College, impact of post-WWII demographic shifts on, 413–18
Elementary and Secondary Education Act (ESEA): amendments (1966), 304; amendments (1968), 303, 396; backlash against, 290, 306–9, 316n65; consequences of, 302–3, 305–6; equity rationale behind, 149–50; expansion of, 290, 301–6; federal role in education and, 289–90; implementation of, 297, 298, 299–301; institutionalization of, 308; LBJ and, 148, 204, 320; No Child Left Behind Act as re-creation of, 312, 319n89; objectives of, 289, 295–96,

299; passage of, 169, 293–95; political context of, 290–93, 294, 313n6; reauthorization of, 304, 311; redistribution in, 316n60; reform of, 290, 309–11, 316n58; school desegregation and, 166; significance of, 311–13; special education programs, 304–5; Title I, 264, 295, 299–300, 303–4, 316n60, 319n89; Title II, 295; Title III, 295–96; Title IV, 296; Title V, 296; Title VI, 304; weaknesses of, 296–98, 299, 306
Ellison, Ralph, 237
Elmore, Richard, 179n44, 311
"employable mother" rules, 118, 130, 142n67, 262
Employee Retirement Income Security Act (1974), 104
employment: African-Americans and, 263–64; consciousness-raising and, 281; low-wage, 117–18, 137; Mobilization for Youth and, 259–60; motherhood and, 129–37; religious-based discrimination in, 373–74; War on Poverty and, 116
Employment Service, U.S., 126
empowerment, 438–39
Engel v. Vitale, 356–57
entitlement: ESEA and, 306, 312; Nixon and, 390; opportunity vs., 11, 312; policy incrementalism and, 397; as positive right, 423; Social Security as, 149; welfare as, 118, 390
environmental legislation, 150–51; divided government and, 399; policy incrementalism and, 397; unfunded, 166–67
environmental movement: citizen suits and, 168; civil rights movement as model for, 4, 158; impact of Sixties civics on, 69; new politics and, xiv, 33; public interest advocacy and, xiii
Environmental Protection Agency (EPA): grassroots distrust of, 161; mandate-and-sue strategy and, 165–66; policy incrementalism and, 396; unfunded mandates of, 166–67
Equal Employment Opportunity Act (1964), 152–53; amendments (1972), 365

Equal Employment Opportunity Commission (EEOC), 104–5; affirmative action and, 382, 398; EEO-1 form, 173, 374–75, 377–78, 380; EEO-6 form, 379; grassroots distrust of, 161; NOW and, 275–76; official minority status and, 375, 376–77, 379; policy incrementalism and, 398; public interest advocacy and, 167–68, 393; sexism and, 273–74, 275–76
equal opportunity: Dewey on, 449n16; entitlement vs., 312; as goal of War on Poverty, 11, 118; Great Society and equalization of, 148–50, 312; New Deal and, 411, 422; New Democrats and, 309; Social Security and, 149
Equal Pay Act (1963), 273, 365, 367
equal pay legislation, 272–73
equal rights amendment (ERA), 275, 384–85n13
equal rights doctrine, 367
Equitable Life Insurance Society of America, 339–40, 341
ethnic politics, 181n78
ethnic/racial minorities, official status of: affirmative action/immigration convergence and, 369, 370–71; civil rights bureaucracy and, 383, 385n21; consequences of, 378–80; controversy over, 380–81, 382–83; cultural assumptions about, 377–78; group identification methods, 371–74; identity politics and, 381, 382–83; liberal nondiscrimination as barrier to, 371; pluralism and, 172, 173; as policy continuity, 366; political impact of, 447–48; religious minorities and, 373–74, 381; selection process for, 375–77; unplanned designation of, 374–75
ethno-racial pentagon, 380–81
Executive Reorganization Act (1939), 1–2
exposure strategy, 404–5

Fair Employment Practices Committee, 101, 371
fair-housing laws, 383–84n2
Fair Labor Standards Act (1938), 117, 413
Falk, Bernard, 162

family: dual-income, 135; feminism and, 281, 285; welfare as entitlement and, 136
Family and Medical Leave Act (1993), 104
Family Assistance Plan, 406
"family values," 137
Fanshen (Hinton), 280
Farley, Jim, 188–89
Farmer, James, 24
Faubus, Orval, 429
Federal Bureau of Investigation (FBI), 68
Federal Deposit Insurance Corp. (FDIC), 205
Federal Emergency Relief Act, 205, 258
Federal Highway Act (1956), 59–60
Federal Home Loan Act (1932), 413
Federal Interdepartmental Committee, 274
federalism: creative, 148; juridical, 267n2; 1960s change in, 392–93
Federalist Papers, The, 232nn93–94
Federal Power Commission, 195
Federal Register, 375
Fehner, Marie, 247
Feminine Mystique, The (Friedan), 274–75
feminism: antiwar movement and, 279; civil rights movement as model for, 4, 158; consciousness-raising and, 281–82; equal rights vs. social feminism, 384–85n13; impact on pluralism, 159–60, 174; LBJ and, 248; New Left and, 279; NOW vs. women's movement, 276–77; rapid spread of, 271; social impact of, 284–86; unreliable scholarship on, 270–71; welfare rights vs., 133–35; workfare programs and, 121; work rights and, 105. *See also* women's liberation movement
Fine, Michelle, 304
Fobes, Catherine, 125, 128
Fogarty, Jim, 268n17
Foley, Michael, 398
Foner, Eric, 424, 448n5, 450–51n26
Fong, Hiram L., 172
food stamps, 262–63, 266, 397, 398
Forbath, William E., 129
Ford, Gerald, 308, 388, 389, 398
Ford Foundation, 90, 148, 168, 393

foreign aid, public view of, 409n33
foreign policy, 8, 214–15, 226n3, 387. *See also* Vietnam War
Fortas, Abe, 196, 352, 357–58, 394–95
Fortune magazine, 91, 358
Forty-five Seconds from Broadway (Simon), 249
Foster Grandparents Program, 124–25
Four Freedoms, 424, 450–51n26
Frady, Marshall, 200
Frank, John P., 355
Frankfurter, Felix, 80n20, 353, 356, 357–60, 361n6
Franklin Delano Roosevelt Memorial Park, 207
Fraser, Steve, 301
Free, Lloyd, 403
Freedom of Information Act (1967), 400
Freeman, Orville, 242
Freylinghuysen, Peter, 125–26
Friedan, Betty, 274–75
Frymer, Paul, 266
Fulbright, J. William, 219

Gainesville (Ga.): LBJ's civil rights promotion in, 19; LBJ's Great Society speech at (1964), 10–11, 199–200
Galambos, Louis, 170
Galbraith, John Kenneth: as cold war liberal, 425; Democratic Advisory Council and, 431; industrial pluralism and, 89, 99–100; influence of, 4–5, 89; JFK and, 434; on Johnson/Roosevelt relationship, 186; on LBJ and Vietnam War, 235; on LBJ as politician, 234; as LBJ speechwriter, 8, 245–46
Gardner, John, 326
Garner, John Nance, 186, 197
Gault, In Re, 394
General Accounting Office, 382
General Motors, 110n14
Gerstle, Gary, 301
GI Bill of Rights, 291, 411, 426–27
Gide, André, 81n41
Gideon v. Wainwright, 356–57, 394
Gifford, Bernard, 254–55
GI Forum, 373
Gilder, George, 265
Gillon, Steve, 368

Gingrich, Newt, 244, 390
Glazer, Nathan, 29, 264
Goals 2000, 309–10, 318nn78–81
Goldberg, Arthur, 92–93, 246, 247, 352, 357–58, 394
Goldberg v. Kelly, 136, 167, 262, 394
Goldman, Eric, 199, 235–36
Goldwater, Barry: Civil Rights Act (1964) opposed by, 23, 24; conservative label embraced by, 62; electoral defeat of (1964), 2, 23, 24, 43–44n65, 199–200, 417; GOP conservatives led by, 431–32; GOP Southern strategy and, 444; LBJ/FDR relationship and, 199; on NDEA, 291–92; as new conservative, 442, 444–45; partisan realignment and, 435; political impact of, 445; at Republican National Convention (1960), 453n54; Vietnam War and, 223
Gonzales, Henry, 172, 373
Goodwin, Richard: on civil rights movement as model, 4; LBJ and, 7; LBJ/FDR relationship and, 199, 200, 211n39; as LBJ speechwriter, 8, 9, 39n19, 211n39; on liberal realism, 67
Gordon, Linda, 160, 284
Gore, Al, 234, 310–11
government: "big," 57–58; divided, 35, 394, 395, 398–99, 442. *See also* public policy
government, public ambivalence about: Franfurter on, 80n20; as Great Society legacy, xvi–xvii; intensification of, during Seventies, xvi–xvii, 34; liberalism and, 160–62, 403–7; Sixties civics and, 53–56, policy mindedness and, 70–77
government, public distrust of: adversarial legalism and, 410n40; doubt vs., 63–64; of motive, 64–65; pervasiveness of, 69–70; pluralism and, 175; policy expectations vs., 70–77, 80n20, 160–62; in popular culture, 65–67; social embedding of, 160; Sixties civics and, 64–70; Vietnam War and, 217
Graham, Bill (White House intern), 45n84
Graham, Billy (evangelist), 77–78
Graham, Hugh Davis, xviii; on affirmative action, xv, 438; on civil rights legislation (1964-65) as radical, 159, 165; on ESEA, 299, 300–301; on federal role in education, 291, 292; on federal-state relations, 401; on Great Society and triangular networks, 298–99; and minority status, 154, 172, 173; on minority status, 447–48; on policy expansion, 169; on Reagan administration and education, 308
grant-in-aid programs: block grants favored over, 264; ESEA and, 297; federal spending on, 266–67n1; federal-state relations and, 253, 257–58, 392–93; historical precedents for, 313n1; juridical federalism and, 267n2; Medicare as, 323–24; tax-and-spend formula and, 402
grassroots, 440
grassroots activism, 159–60, 278
Great Depression, 322
Great Society: academic influences on, 254–55; backlash against, 307; as "big government," 57–58; civic education as requirement of, 226; civil rights policy and, 383; conservative view of, xiii–xiv, 387; controversy over term, 39n19; conventional political explanations for, 253–54; as cyclical reform, 151–53; defined, xii, 7–8; distinctive features of, 253; employment/welfare policy interconnections in, 115–17, 139n16; empowerment strategies of, 438–39; equal opportunity and, 148–50; experts and, 147–48, 155–56; first use of term, 38n6; foreign policy vs., 214–15; historical influences on, 151–57; impact of cold war on, 155–57; impact of Vietnam War on, 21–22, 146, 153, 216–17, 230–31n68, 442; impact on Vietnam War, 222–26; imperium and, 216, 226n16; institutionalization of, 36–37; as "last hurrah" of liberalism, xiii–xiv; LBJ/FDR relationship and, 204; LBJ's promotion of, 6–13; legacy of, xvi–xvii, 33–34, 55, 388; legislation comprising, 239; legitimacy barriers lowered by, 179n46; liberal decline and, xiv, 146, 435–48; liberal reform ideology and, ix–xi; liberal view of, 387; as linear

Great Society (*cont.*)
trend, 153–55; Lippmann's use of, 80n18; major achievements of, 148; Medicare and, 322–24, 334; mistaken policies of, 254–55; modern presidency and, 6, 14, 26, 33–34, 154–55; New Deal as antecedent of, 199; New Deal vs., 311–12, 322–23; new politics and, 13–16; opportunity as goal of, 11; participatory democracy and, xii–xiii; pluralism and, 145; political influence of, xv–xvi, 6, 146, 439–45; politics of, 255–59, 262–64, 436–37; post-LBJ continuation of, xv, 58; post-WWII economic boom and, 322; public support for, 307, 441; qualitative goals of, xii, 8–9, 10, 150–51; Republican dismantling of, 264–66; results orientation of, 150–51; revisionist historical views of, 236–37; as revolution in expectations, 392; Seventies continuation of, xv, 58, 387–91; significance of, xvii–xviii, 49n116; tax-and-spend formula of, 399–400, 402; therapeutic ethos and, 254–55; women's issues during, 276, 286n4; women's movement and, 284; as work in progress, 146–51. *See also specific legislation*
Green, Edith, 48n105, 125
Green, T. H., 418–19
Green v. New Kent County, 167, 394
Gregg, Judd, 163
grievance arbitration, 111n26
Griffins, Martha, 273
Griffiths, Martha, 134
Griswold v. Connecticut, 356–57, 394
Group Health Insurance, 340
Gruening, Ernest, 340
guaranteed income, 390

Hackett, David, 268n17
Haener, Dorothy, 275
Hall, Burton, 112–13n51
Hamilton, Charles, 27
Hamilton, Walton, 358
Harbison, Frederick, 90
Harlan, John Marshall, I, 359
Harlan, John Marshall, II, 356, 357, 358, 359–60

Harlem Community Action Agency (HARYOU-ACT), 29
Harper's Weekly, 99
Harper v. Virginia Board of Education, 167, 394
Harriman, Averill, 431
Harrington, Michael, xi, 4–5, 96, 97, 292, 434
Harris, Herbert, 99
Harris, Louis, 122, 124, 127, 452n42
Harrison, Burr, 333
Harvard Water Program, 168–69
Hatcher, Andy, 42n49
Hatfield, Mark, 441
Hayden, Tom, 96, 97
Head Start, 122, 124, 264
health care: Great Society legislation and, xiv, 8, 149; Medicare as policy end point, 322, 341–45; public vs. private responsibility, 335
Health, Education, and Welfare Department, U.S. (HEW), 104, 120, 127, 239, 262; mandate-and-sue strategy and, 396; Office of Civil Rights, 376–77, 393
health insurance: employer-based, 335; national, 321–22, 344–45, 427; Social Security as precedent for, 331, 333
Health Insurance Benefits Advisory Council, 339
health insurance companies, private, 333–34, 337, 338–41
Heart of Atlanta Motel v. United States, 394
Heclo, Hugh: on individualism and participatory democracy, 454n73; on interest group pluralism, 170; on liberal realism, xiii, 157, 425; on New Deal vs. Great Society, 311; on pluralism, demise of, 145, 175; on policy mindedness, 147; on political culture in 1960s, 160, 404; on therapeutic ethos, 164
Heineman Task Force on Government Organization, 29, 47n99
Herberg, Will, 89, 110n22
Hernandez, Aileen, 274, 275
Hess, Arthur, 327
Hess, Frederick, 147, 150, 166
Highway and Traffic Safety Act, 239
Hill, Lister, 339–40

Hill-Burton hospital construction program, 325
Hinton, William, 280
hiring quotas, 366
Hispanics, 373, 378–79, 380, 381, 382, 385n21
Hiss, Alger, 427
Hobhouse, L. T., 418–19
Hoffa, Jimmy, 96
Hollinger, David, 380
Home Owner's Loan Corporation, 205
Hoover, J. Edgar, 247
Hopkins, Harry, 199, 402
Horton, Myles, 280
hospital insurance, 328
hospitals, Medicare and, 323–28, 335
Hospitals (trade journal), 342
Hospital Workers Local 1199, 100, 103–4
House of Representatives: Civil Rights Bill (1963) passed in, 435; impact of post-WWII demographic shifts on, 446; 1964 election and, 435–36; Rules Committee, 394; Un-American Activities Committee, 355; Ways and Means Committee, 325, 333
housing: civil rights policy and, 383–84n2; Great Society legislation and, xiv, 8; open-housing bill, 23, 28, 367; political impact of, 440; public, 427
Housing and Urban Development Act (1965), 239
housing discrimination, 383–84n2
Howard, A. E. Dick, 351
Howard University, 22, 116
Howe, Harold, 294
Hoyer, Steny H., 129
Hughes, John and Anne, 300
Hulsey, Byron, 171
Humphrey, Hubert, 33; Democratic Advisory Council and, 430–31; Job Corps and, 122; on Johnson/Roosevelt relationship, 195–96; LBJ's first days in office and, 247; on left-liberal critics of LBJ, 223; MFDP controversy and, 23–24, 25; 1968 election and, 442; presidential election (1960) and, 430–31, 432; Vietnam War and, 224; War on Poverty and, 10
Huntington, Samuel, 410n39

identity politics, 181n78, 381, 382–83
ideology, political activism and, 68–69
illiteracy programs, 120
immigrant women, 117–18
immigration, mass, 368–69; anticommunist investigations and, 427; civil rights policy transformed by, 365–66, 381–82
Immigration and Naturalization Act (1965), 239, 368–69
immigration policy: affirmative action and, 369–71, 380–83; ethno-racial pentagon and, 380–81; LBJ administration and, 148; liberal nondiscrimination and, 367; unintended consequences of, 368–69
imperium: Great Society and, 216, 226n16; in liberal societies, 224–25; social/"people's," 232n87
Improving America's Schools Act (1994), 310
income taxes, 450n24
Indian Americans, 379
individualism: collectivism vs., 450n18; economic, 449n14; New Deal liberalism and, 418–24; New Left and, 440; in participatory democracy, 454n73
Individuals with Disabilites Education Act (IDEA), 304
Industrial Commission, U.S., 87
Industrialism and Industrial Man (Kerr, Dunlop, et al.), 90
industrialization, pluralistic theory and, 90–91
industrial pluralism: collective bargaining as, 87–88, 91–93; demise of, 98–101, 105; ideological rooting of, 88–93; impact of cold war on, 88, 428; labor unions and, 91–93, 105, 107, 108, 169–70
inequality, 148–49
inflation, 442
inner cities. *See* urban ghettos
Inouye, Daniel K., 172
In Re Gault, 394
insider politics, 156–57, 170–71, 172–73, 174
Intermodal Surface Transportation Efficiency Act (1991), 59–60
Internal Revenue Service (IRS), 338

International Brotherhood of Teamsters, 84, 86, 96
internationalism, 215, 218, 226n4, 228
interstate highway system, 59–60, 156, 416
Ironies of Affirmative Action, The (Skrentny), 368
iron triangles, 170, 172

Jackson, Robert H., 359
Jacobs, Paul, 98–99
Japanese American Citizens League, 172, 373
Japanese Americans, 371, 379
Javits, Jacob, 333–34, 335–36
Jefferson, Thomas, 418, 439
Jehovah's Witnesses, 374
Jenkins, Philip, 237–38
Jenkins, Walter, 242
Jet magazine, 42n49
Jewish Anti-Defamation League, 373
Jews, 372, 373–74
Job Corps: creation of, 119–20; employment/welfare policy interconnections in, 124–28; gender differentiation in, 125–28, 152; impact on home/family, 116, 125; lack of childcare and, 128; negative publicity of, 123–24; objectives of, 121–22; origins of, 122; racial makeup of, 122–23
Johnson, Clifford M., 268n28
Johnson, James, 20
Johnson, Lady Bird, 201–2, 207, 247
Johnson, Luci, 243
Johnson, Lyndon Baines/Johnson administration: abdication of, 32–33; advisers of, Vietnam War and, 217–20, 228nn27, 30; as anticommunist, 218; aspirations of, and Great Society, 254, 392; civil rights movement and, 4–5, 16–28, 32, 42n49, 43n53, 44n75, 242–43; civil rights policy of, 378; cold war pluralism and, 171; community action programs and, 28–32, 46–47n92; complexity of, 39n18, 234–35; congressional campaign of (1937), 187–89; congressional campaign of (1944), 210n24; as congressman, 189–92, 193–94, 254; conservative critics of, 225, 231n71; conservative vs. liberal views of, 387;
contemporary view of, 235–36; crudeness of, 205, 206; current reputation of, 214, 226n2, 226n3; as Democratic campaign manager, 191–92; district-court appointments of, 395; downfall of, 205–7; electoral mandate of, 314n13; ESEA and, 293–95, 298, 300–301; father-figures of, 185; FDR imitations of, 186; FDR's death and, 194; first days in office, 243–44, 245–48; foreign policy credentials of, 218; ghetto visits and, 26–28, 31, 45n84, 46nn87 90; Great Society promoted by, 6–13, 38n6; Howard University speech of, 22; as internationalist, 215, 218, 228n20; JFK compared to, 240–43, 245; as JFK's running mate, 415; on Job Corps, 123–24; Kennedy (Robert) and, 41n43, 45n79; last days in office, 235; left-liberal critics of, 223, 225, 231n77; liberation rhetoric of, 161; on mastery, 153; Medicare and, 320–22; MFDP controversy and, 44n75, 45n81; Michigan speech of (1964), xii, 7–9, 39n19, 147–48, 161; modern presidency and, 437–38; as nationalist, 215–17, 221–22; New Deal and, 151–52; as New Deal liberal, 1–6; new politics and, 32, 437–39; Nixon years compared to, 387–90; personality of, 200–201, 205, 206–7, 220–22, 226n11, 229–30n57; on political activism, 13; political legacy of, 33–37, 239–40; as politician, 13–16, 19, 40–41n33, 41n36, 45n84, 156–57, 171, 187, 234, 235, 241, 294–95, 314n13, 321–22, 391, 435–37; in popular opinion, 239; as president, 201–7, 235; presidential campaign of (1964), 199–200, 213n54; presidential election of (1964), 415, 417; as presidentialist, xi, 3, 155; public support for, 441; public support for Vietnam War and, 224–26, 230–31n68, 231n83, 232nn93–94; revisionist historical views of, 233–38; RFK and, 230n57; rights revolution and, 36–37; as romantic, 241–42; senate campaign of (1941), 192–93, 209n22; senate campaign of (1948), 210n28; as sena-

tor, 194–97, 430; significance of, 248–49, 445–48; State of the Union address (1964), 212n48, 243; State of the Union address (1966), 8, 161; strengths of, 242–43, 248–49; Supreme Court appointments of, 357–58, 394–95; as teacher, 226n11; as Texas NYA director, 3–4, 9, 30–31; two-tiered politics of, 224–25; Vietnam War and, 146, 153, 220–22, 229n44; War on Poverty and, 48n105, 116; weaknesses of, 243, 248; women's issues and, 273, 275–76. *See also* Great Society; Johnson/Roosevelt relationship

Johnson/Roosevelt relationship: beginnings of, 186–89; competition in, 200–207, 212n48; FDR as presidential role model, xi, 1, 14, 37–38n3, 198–99, 200–207; LBJ's congressional career and, 189–92; LBJ's congressional race (1944) and, 210n24; LBJ's exaggerations of, 185–86, 208n5; LBJ's senate career and, 194–97; LBJ's senate race (1941) and, 192–93, 209n22; LBJ's senate race (1948) and, 210n28; LBJ's vice-presidential career and, 197–98; personal, 190–91; resentment in, 201; revisionist historical views of, 236; Vietnam War and, 205–6, 207, 216

Johnson Treatment, 239
Joint Chiefs of Staff, 217–18
journalism: impact of Sixties civics on, 65; mandate-and-sue strategy and, 405
judicial activism, judicial restraint vs., 351–52
Justice Department, U.S., 167–68, 275, 423; Civil Rights Division, 393
Juvenile Delinquency and Youth Offenses Act (1961), 253
juvenile delinquency programs, 120, 253, 258–59

Kagan, Robert, 161, 405, 410n40
Kaplan, Marshall, 307
Kappell, Fred, 247
Karl, Barry, xvii
Katz, Michael, 120
Katzenbach, Nicholas, 25–26
Katznelson, Ira, 311

Kaysen, Carl, 246
Kearns, Doris, 226n11
Kefauver, Estes, 430
Kennedy, Jacqueline, 244
Kennedy, John F./Kennedy administration: assassination of, 198, 235, 243–44, 293, 415; black support for, 257; civil rights policy of, 16, 61, 205, 365, 368, 378, 415, 434–35; as cold war liberal, xi, 1, 426, 432–35; contract compliance committee of, 372, 373; as corporate liberal, 433–34; Democratic Advisory Council and, 452n48; educational reform and, 314n12; juvenile delinquency programs, 120, 259; LBJ as running mate of, 415; LBJ compared to, 240–43, 245; liberal credentials of, 453n55; Medicare and, 328; New Frontier, 258, 271, 432, 434; in popular opinion, 233, 238–39, 244; positive rights and, 434; presidential election of (1960), 412, 417, 432; Supreme Court appointments of, 394; Vietnam War and, 217, 221; women's issues and, 271–73, 274

Kennedy, Robert F.: assassination of, xv, 235; civil rights protests and, 415; ESEA and, 316n58; juvenile delinquency program administered by, 258; LBJ and, 41n43, 45n79, 230n57, 246; McClellan Committee and, 96; OEO and, 199

Kennedy, Ted, 177n12, 316n58
Keppel, Francis, 294
Kerr, Clark: industrial pluralism and, 89, 90–91; influence of, 89; on labor unions, 85, 92; as neo-Weberian, 100; radical disillusionment and, 93, 94
Key, V. O., 86–87
Keystone Job Corps Center for Women, 127
Khrushchev, Nikita, 221
King, Martin Luther, Jr., 173, 428; as antiwar activist, 21–22; assassination of, xv, 235; FBI operations against, distrust and, 68; LBJ and, 21–22, 23, 244; MFDP controversy and, 44n75; Southern race relations and, 367–68. *See also* civil rights movement

King v. Smith, 136
Kirst, Michael, 306
Kopaid, Sylvia, 113n51
Korean War, 218, 223, 427
Kornhauser, Arthur, 86
Ky, Nguyen Cao, 206, 220

Labor Department, U.S., 119, 120, 376–77
labor standards, 117
labor unions: anticommunist investigations of, 427; civil rights movement and, 84, 95, 101–2, 103; corruption in, 84, 95–96; court decisions regarding, 106–8; declining political influence of, 83–84, 105; devaluation of, 84–87, 105; fragmentation of, 86; impact of cold war on, 427–28; industrial pluralism and, 91–93; institutionalization of, 85–86, 92, 98–99, 112–13n51; LBJ's criticism of, 223; McClellan Committee hearings and, 105–6; Medicare and, 336; national health insurance and, 321; New Deal and, 413; New Deal political realignment and, 152; Philadelphia Plan and, 406; pluralism in, 180n63; public perception of, 96; racial/gender divisions maintained by, 118; radical disillusionment with, 93–98, 112n47; rights consciousness and, 83, 103–8, 447; solidarity principle undermined, 106–7; striking rights, 106–7; women in, 285; women's movement and, 274–75, 285
land-grant colleges, 313n1
Landon, Alf, 188
Land Ordinance Act (1785), 313n1
Landrum, Philip, 130
Landrum-Griffin Law (1959), 106
Landy, Marc, 226n2, 226n3
La Raza, 379, 381
Laski, Harold, 418
Latham, Earl, 91
Latin America, mass immigration from, 369
Latinas, 117–18
Lau v. Nichols, 396
"law and order," 444
Laws (Plato), 215

Lawyers Committee for Civil Rights under Law, 303
League of United Latin American Citizens (LULAC), 172, 373, 379
League of Women Voters (LVW), 180n63
Lee, Philip, 344
legalism, adversarial, 405, 410n40
Legal Services, 118, 262, 264, 393
legitimacy, 58–59, 75–77, 162–63, 179n46, 391–92
Lehman, Herbert, 417
Leiserson, William, 87
Lemann, Nicholas, 135, 201
Leuchtenberg, William: on LBJ and "all-class alliance," 422; on LBJ and Great Society, 146, 151; on LBJ's political aspirations, xi, 2, 448
Levitan, Sar A., 268n28
Lewis, John, 24
liberalism: ambivalence about government role, 160–62, 403–4; conservative view of, 447; corporate, 433–34; Dewey on, 449–50n17; equal individual rights doctrine of, 367; ESEA and, 296; exposure strategy of, 404–5; FDR's use of term, 418, 420; federal expansion supported by, 177n12; Great Society and decline of, xiv, 146, 435–48; grievance arbitration and, 111n26; impact of cold war on, 156–57, 411–12, 424–26; impact of Great Society on, xv–xvi; impact of post-WWII demographic shifts on, 412–13; impact of social movements on, 157–60; imperium and, 224–25; individualism vs. collectivism in, 418–24, 428–29; intellectual fatigue of, 447; labor union devaluation and, 85, 95, 98; LBJ and, 2–3, 223, 225, 438; mandate-and-sue strategy and, 402–3, 405–7; New Deal, 418–24; New Left view of, 447; operational, American public as, 403; policy incrementalism and, 395–98; policy mindedness and, 61–62; positive vs. negative rights and, 423–24; programmatic, 67–68, 150; qualitative, 40n31; racial/gender divisions tolerated by, 117–18, 125, 154, 159, 271; radical disillusionment and, 93–94; redefining,

40n31; results orientation of, 150–51; rights-based, 161–62, 177n25; secularization of, 450n19; Vietnam War and, 223. *See also* cold war liberalism
liberal nondiscrimination, 365–68, 371, 375–76
liberal realism, 66–68, 71–72
liberal reform ideology: civil rights movement and, 4–5; conservative reaction to, ix–x; evolution of, x–xi; modern presidency and, 35; qualitative goals of, xiii
liberation rhetoric, 281
Lichtenstein, Nelson: on cold war and industrial democracy, 428; on labor and pluralism, 169; on labor and rights consciousness, 447; on liberalism and labor, xiii, 146; on new politics, 437; on pluralism, demise of, 145, 175; on suprapartisan politics, 181n68
Life Insurance Company of Alabama, 339–40
Life magazine, 57, 80n24, 244, 287n17
Lippmann, Walter, 221; disinterestedness and, 157; on distrust, 66; "Great Society" in works of, 80n18; and legitimacy, 75; on policy expectations, 56–57; Vietnam War and, 220, 222
Lipset, Seymour Martin, 89, 92, 93, 94
Literary Digest, 188
Little Rock (Ark.), school desegregation in, 429, 431
lobbying, 180n63
local educational agencies, 298
local governments: block grants and, 264–65; education and, 290–91; ESEA and, 299, 301–2; federal grant-in-aid programs and, 323; federal off-budget costs and, 401; Great Society politics and, 253, 256–59, 268n14; weaknesses of, 254
Lodge, Henry Cabot, 230n57
Long, Russell, 135–36
Lott, Trent, 244
Louchheim, Katie, 201
Louisiana: "employable mother" rules in, 130; Medicare and civil rights compliance in, 326–27
Lowi, Theodore, 98, 171, 451n38
Low Income Home Energy Assistance Program, 397

Lubell, Samuel, 86
Luce, Henry, 57
Lynd, Alice and Staughton, 101

Maass, Arthur, 168–69
MacArthur, Douglas, 218
McAuliffe, Mary Sperling, 426
McCann, Michael W., 409–10n38
McCarthy, Joseph, 427, 453n55
McCarthyism, 427–28
McClellan, John, 95–96
McClellan Committee hearings (1957, 1958), 84, 95–96, 105–6
McCone, John, 246–47
McCormack, John, 247
McGovern, George, 214, 226n3, 234, 235
McGovern-Fraser Commission, 34
McGovernism, 387
McGuinn, Patrick, 147, 150, 166
Machiavelli, Niccolò, 226n3
McJimsey, George, 422, 423
Mackenzie, G. Calvin, 455n84
McKissick, Floyd, 22–23
McMaster, H. R., 238
McNamara, Robert S., 121, 217, 224, 246
McNeese brothers, 125
McPherson, Harry, 6–7, 20, 21, 25–26, 36–37
McWilliams, Wilson Carey, 33, 146, 151, 153, 448
Maddox, Lester, 20
Madison, James, 232nn93–94
Magnuson, Warren, 247
Maguire, Richard, 246
Mahoney, George P., 20
Malcolm X, 173
Manchester, William, 244
mandate-and-sue strategy, 165–66, 390–91; as adversarial legalism, 410n40; exposure strategy, 404–5, 410n39; as judicialization of politics, 409–10n38; policy incrementalism and, 395–98; public ambivalence about government and, 403–7; rights consciousness and, 405–7; as Seventies strategy, 402–3; weaknesses of, 406–7
"man in the house" rules, 118, 136, 262

Mann, David, 372–73
Manpower Development and Training Act (1962), 258
"manpower" programs, 116–17, 138, 139n16
Mansfield, Harvey, 226n3
Mansfield, Mike, 205, 224
March on Washington (1963), 4, 16, 102
Marcuse, Herbert, 226n4
Markman, Sherwin, 27–28, 46n87
Marris, Peter, 268n14
Marshall, John, 354
Marshall, Thurgood, 352, 357, 394
Martin, Louis, 43n53, 197–98
Marwick, Arthur, 78–79n1
Marx, Karl, 216, 228n20
Marxism, 216
Marxists, The (Mills), 112n47
mastery, quest for, 153
maternalism, 137–38
maternity leave, 272
Mattson, Kevin, 439
Matusow, Allen, 434, 435
maximum work hour restrictions, 117
Mead, Margaret, 274
Meany, George, 247
media: civil rights movement and, 158; exposure strategy and, 410n39; impact of Sixties civics on, 65; LBJ and, 223, 248; male domination of, 285; mandate-and-sue strategy and, 405; Medicare promotional campaign and, 337; women's movement and, 283, 288n30
Medicaid: block granting of, 266; creation of, 320; criticism of, 343; financing of, 329; impact on poverty, 262–63; LBJ administration and, 148; limitations of, 344–45; Medicare vs., 321; objectives of, 320; significance of, 387–88
medical profession: fears about Medicare, 321–22; Medicare reimbursements to, 323–24, 329–30, 335, 337, 342–43
Medicare: civil rights legislation and, 324–28; criticism of, 342–44; as end point in health policy, 322, 341–45; expansion of, 344–45; as grant-in-aid program, 323–24; as Great Society program, 239, 322–24, 334; as health care program, 344; impact on poverty, 262–63; implementation of, 323–24, 341; LBJ administration and, 148; LBJ and, 235, 320; Medicaid vs., 321; Part A, 329; passage of, 320–22, 334; payroll tax for, 328–29, 399–400; regulation of, 341–42; significance of, 387–88; as Social Security, 328–30; Social Security state-federal tensions and, 330–34. *See also* Medicare Part B
Medicare Part B: adverse selection and, 336; cost of, 337; features of, 329; financing of, 329–30; private carriers selected for, 338–41; public vs. private responsibility, 334–36; SSA and enrollment in, 336–38
Melnick, R. Shep: on big policy, 58, 163, 167–68; on liberal distrust of government, 160, 161; on mandate-and-sue policy, 63; on New Right and policy mindedness, 147; on 1970s Great Society reforms, xv, 436; on public ambivalence about government, 34; on rights-based liberalism, 447; on special education programs, 304–5
mental illness programs, 253
Metropolitan Life Insurance Co., 340
Mexican American Legal Defense and Education Fund, 168, 174, 381, 393
Mexican-American Political Action Committee, 172, 373
Mexican Americans, 372
Michel, Sonya, 132
Michels, Robert, 94–95
Michigan, University of, LBJ's Great Society speech at (1964), xii, 7–9, 39n19, 147–48, 161
Milazzo, Paul, 168–69
Mileur, Jerome, 6, 146, 151
Milkis, Sidney: on civil rights movement, 158; on LBJ and Community Action Program, 155; on LBJ and liberation rhetoric, 161; on LBJ and modern presidency, xii, 146, 437–38; and LBJ as great president, 226nn2–3; on rights-based liberalism, 162
Mill, John Stuart, 419
Millis, Harry, 87
Mills, C. Wright, 85, 94–95, 99, 100, 112n47

Mills, Wilbur, 325, 328–29, 333, 336, 340, 343
Mine Safety Act (1969), 104
minimum wage, 102, 117, 137
minorities, official. *See* ethnic/racial minorities, official status of
Miranda v. Arizona, 355–56, 357, 394
Miroff, Bruce, 15, 16
Mississippi, Medicare and, 326–27
Mississippi Freedom Democratic Party (MFDP), 23–25, 44n75, 45n81
Mittelstadt, Jennifer, 130
mixed races, 381, 382–83
Mobilization for Youth, 168, 259–62, 264, 286n4, 393
Model Cities Program, 14, 168, 259, 393
Montoya, Joseph, 373
Morgan, Robin, 288n30
Mormons, 374
Morone, James, 30
Morrill Act (1862), 313n1
Morse, Wayne, 132
Moyers, Bill, 7, 12–13, 21, 39n19, 199
Moynihan, Daniel Patrick, 29, 30, 116, 254, 264, 398
Moynihan Report (1965), 121
multiculturalism, 65, 380–81
multi-objective planning, 168–69
Murphy, Frank, 423
Murphy, Jerome, 300
Murray, Charles, 136, 265
Murray, Pauli, 275
Mutual of Omaha, 340
Myers, Charles A., 90

Nader, Ralph, 158, 160–61, 404–5
National Advisory Council for the Education of Disadvantaged Children, 303
National Association for the Advancement of Colored People (NAACP): LBJ and, 24; Legal Defense Fund, 168; Legal Standards and Education Project, 303; NOW modeled on, 274; OEO and, 123; official minority status and, 381; rights consciousness and, 103, 106
National Association of Administrators of State and Federally-Assisted Education Programs, 303
National Association of Manufacturers, 96
National Committee of Citizens for Johnson, 197
National Defense Education Act (NDEA; 1958), 156, 291–92, 298
National Education Association (NEA), 294
National Electrical Manufacturers Association, 162
National Endowment for the Arts, 148
National Endowment for the Humanities, 148
National Environmental Policy Act (1969), 397
National Highway Traffic Safety Administration, 405
National Industrial Recovery Act (NIRA; 1933), 205, 271, 422–23
National Institute of Mental Health, 259, 268n17
nationalism, 215–17, 221–22, 421
National Manpower Council, 119
National Organization of Women (NOW), 274–77; activism of, 159, 287n14; civil rights movement as model for, 159, 274; Legal Defense Fund, 168; social impact of, 284; women's movement contrasted with, 276–77, 279
national origins quota system, 369
National Resources Defense Council, 393
National Resources Planning Board (NRPB), 9–10, 30–31, 450–51n26
National Security Action Memorandum, 247
National Security Council, 156
National Urban League, 24
National Welfare Rights Organization, 136–37, 162, 303
National Youth Administration, 3–4, 9, 12, 30–31, 450–51n26
Nation at Risk, A (1983 report), 308
Native Americans, 305, 371–72, 379, 385n21
Natural Resources Defense League, 168
Nebraska, 340
Negro American Labor Council, 24
Neighborhood Youth Corps, 119–20, 125
neoconservatism, 62, 175
Nevins, Alan, 236

New Deal: civil rights as incidental in, 324–25; cold war liberalism and, 426–27; collective bargaining and, 87; Democratic Party and, 32–33; disinterestedness as foundation of, 157; economic bill of rights, 10; Great Society as expansion of, xiv, 8–9, 10–11, 199; Great Society vs., 311–12, 322–23; impact of WWII on, 411; interest group bargaining in, 169; "labor question" and, 84; LBJ and, 1–6, 151–52, 196, 241–42; legacies of, 117–18, 152; legitimacy of, 179n46; liberalism of, 418–24; liberal reform ideology and, ix–xi, 35; localized activism lacking in, xii; Medicare and, 334; modern presidency as legacy of, 5–6, 15, 155; New Left attack on, 439–40; northern urban foundation of, 413–14; NOW and, 277; NYA and, 30–31; opposition to, 422–23, 450–51n26; political coalition for, 152–53; progressive influences on, 9–10; qualitative goals of, 10; redistribution in, 312; sexism in, 271; tax-and-spend formula of, 165, 399–400, 402; Truman presidency and, 411–12; as work in progress, 241–42
New Democrats, 58, 309–10
New Federalism, 307–8
Newfield, Jack, 33
New Freedom, 419
New Frontier, 258, 271, 432, 434
New Industrial State, The (Galbraith), 100
New Jersey, 340
New Leader, 91–92
New Left: civil rights movement as model for, 158; Dewey and, 454n76; feminism and, 279; impact on Great Society, 8–9; impact on pluralism, 158, 174; individualism of, 440; labor unions and, 100–101; liberalism and, 447; New Deal and, 439–40; new politics and, 33, 34–35; Old Left vs., xiii; participatory democracy and, xii–xiii, 165, 439; pluralism rejected by, 94–95, 100–101; policy mindedness and, 62; therapeutic ethos and, 164–65; women in, 278–79; women's movement and, 271, 277–79, 280

New Left Review, 101
New Men of Power (Mills), 94
New Mexico, 341
New Republic, 195, 263, 449n8
New Right: democratic pluralism and, 175; policy mindedness of, 147
New York City: decline of machine politics in, 417; Mobilization for Youth program in, 259–62
New York Radical Women, 279, 287n14
New York State: Medicare carriers in, 340; workfare programs in, 133
New York Times, 99, 151–52, 193, 202, 203–4, 287n14
New York Times v. Sullivan, 356–57, 394
Nicolau, George, 29
Nie, Norman, 403–4
Niebuhr, Reinhold, 67, 68, 80n23, 89, 91–92, 425–26
Nixon, Richard M./Nixon administration: affirmative action and, 406; civil rights policy of, 365, 376; divided government and, 35, 395, 398; domestic spending increases under, 58, 397; ESEA backlash under, 306–7; ESEA expansion under, 303–4, 308; Great Society politics and, 255, 258, 264; LBJ and election of, 233, 239; and liberalism, decline of, xv; liberal policy opposed by, 165; Medicare criticized by, 343; policy legacy of, Great Society compared to, 387–90; in popular opinion, 233; presidential election (1960) and, 431; presidential election of (1968), xv, 35, 442–44; rights-driven programs of, 162; Southern strategy of, 16, 444; Vietnam policy of, 220, 231n71
No Child Left Behind Act (2002), 177n12, 179n44, 311, 312, 319n89
nonviolent resistance, 158
North, the: civil rights support in, 428; New Deal political grounding in, 413–14; partisanship changes in, 256, 429–30; post-WWII migration from, political impact of, 414–16
Northwest Ordinance (1787), 313n1

Occupational Safety and Health Act (1970), 104

Ochs, John, 246
Office of Civil Rights, 376–77, 393
Office of Economic Opportunity (OEO), 268n17; authorization of, 118; contracted services in, 168; criticism of, 46–47n92, 47n99; executive control of, 47n94; grassroots distrust of, 161; impact on civil rights movement, 32; LBJ/FDR relationship and, 199; Medicare promotional campaign and, 338; policy expansion and, 168; War on Poverty run by, 116, 120, 148. *See also* Community Action Program
Office of Education, U.S. (USOE), 150, 166, 299–301, 313n1, 376–77
Office of Federal Contract Compliance Programs, 393
Office of Management and Budget (OMB), 379–80, 381, 382, 398–99
Office of Manpower Administration, 119
Ohlin, Lloyd, 47n96
old-age assistance, 329, 332, 344
old-age insurance: coverage exclusions in, 325, 346n15; expansion of, 331–32; Medicare as, 328, 330, 344; old-age assistance vs., 149; public vs. private responsibility, 335; Social Security Act (1935) and, 117
Old Left, xiii, 277
Olds, Leland, 195
one-drop rule, 378, 382
"one person, one vote" principle, 167, 355, 394
On the Line (Swados), 96–97
open-housing bill, 28, 367
opportunity. *See* equal opportunity
opportunity theory, 259
Orfield, Gary, 166
Orloff, Ann Shola, 137–38
Orwin, Clifford, 225
Other America, The (Harrington), 5, 97, 292
Our Bodies, Ourselves (Boston Women's Health Collective), 285

Panama Canal incident, 222, 248
parental choice, 312
parent groups, 298
Parmet, Herbert, 32–33
participatory democracy: Community Action Program and, 5, 29–30, 172; failure of, 158; individualism in, 454n73; New Left and, xii–xiii, 165, 439; Sixties civics and, 53; therapeutic ethos and, 165; women's movement and, 277
partisan politics: Great Society politics and, 255–59; impact of post-WWII demographic shifts on, 412–18, 429, 446–47; impact of Sixties civics on, 65, 78; LBJ's view of, 223; Southern realignment of, 16, 256, 265–66, 443–45. *See also* Democratic Party; elections, presidential; Republican Party
Passamaquoddy Project, 208n5
patriotism: civic education and, 226; LBJ's Vietnam policy and, 221–22, 231n70
Patterson, James, 148, 237, 388–90, 392
payroll taxes, 328–29, 399–400
Peace Corps, 271–72
Pearson, Drew, 205
Percy, Charles, 441–42
Pericles, 224–25, 226
Perkins, Frances, 330
Personal Responsibility and Work Opportunity Act (1996), 137, 265
Peterson, Ester, 272–73
Peterson, Paul, 297
Petrocik, John, 403–4
Philadelphia Plan, 162, 173, 365, 374–75, 406
Phillips, Kevin, 446
Piven, Frances Fox: on Community Action Program, 5, 49n116, 155; on Equal Opportunity Act, 152; Mobilization for Youth research of, 259, 268n17; on therapeutic ethos, 163–64
Plato, 215
Pledge of Allegiance, 359
pluralism: cold war, 170–71, 172, 180n63, 426; conservative ascendancy as, 6; democratic, 171–76, 180n63; expansion of, 169–76; Great Society and survival of, 145; Great Society as death of, 145, 175; historical phases of, 180n63; identity politics and demise of, 181n78; industrialization and, 90–91;

pluralism (*cont.*)
  interest group, 175; labor unions and, 169–70; leftwing criticism of, 172; liberalism and, 419–20; mainstream deconstruction of, 98; suprapartisan politics and, 181n68. *See also* industrial pluralism
police brutality, 259
policy mindedness, 56–63; cold war pluralism and, 170; as democratic tendency, 72–75; distrust and, xvi, 70–77, 160–62; Great Society and, xv–xvi, 147; liberal realism and, 67–68; modernization and, 73–75; political influence of, 147. *See also* public policy
Political Man (Lipset), 92
poll taxes, elimination of, 167, 394
pollution control, 166–67
popular culture: color-coding of, 377, 380; impact of Sixties civics on, 65–67, 77
populism, 180n63
Port Huron statement, xii, 9, 97, 161
poverty: causes of, 296; culture of, 116, 119, 296; deserving vs. undeserving, 307; educational inequality and, 292, 296–97, 315n27; education/employment programs and, 260–62; "environmental" concept of, 119; impact of welfare on, 262–63; inequality and, 148–49; liberal "quality of life" concerns and, 4–5, 26–27; New Deal vs. Great Society approaches to, 311–12. *See also* War on Poverty
Powe, Lucas A., Jr., 351–52, 394
Powell, Adam Clayton, 356
Powell v. McCormack, 356–57
Power Elite, The (Mills), 99
pregnancy, 128
Pregnancy Discrimination Act (1978), 104
presidency, modern, 146; civil rights movement and, 16–28; community action programs and, 28–32, 34; democracy vs., xii; FDR and, 5–6, 420–21; Great Society and decline of, 6, 14, 26, 33–34, 154–55; LBJ and, 437–38; as linear trend, 154–55; as New Deal legacy, 5–6, 15; new politics and, 13–16, 32, 33–34; public interest advocacy

and, xiii; reconstructive politics and, 37–38n3; social movements vs., 41n43
presidentialism, xi, 3, 155
President's Commission on Juvenile Delinquency and Youth Crime, 259, 268n17
President's Commission on the Status of Women (PCSW), 272–73, 274
press freedoms, 356, 394
Price, Don K., 47n99
Prisoners of the American Dream (Davis), 101
privacy, right of, 357, 394
private sector: mandate-and-sue strategy and, 402–3; Medicare and, 333–34, 337, 338–41; Seventies off-budget costs and, 400–401
Progressive Citizens of America (PCA), 424–25
Progressivism: collective bargaining and, 87; disinterestedness and, 66–67, 157; "labor question" and, 84; liberal reform ideology and, ix–xi, 35; modern presidency as legacy of, 155; social democratic tradition and, 419
proministrative state, 155–56, 172
Promise of an American Life, The (Croly), 75
Protestant, Catholic, Jew (Herberg), 110n22
Protestantism, 450n19
protests: Great Society politics and, 259; influence of civil rights movement on, 158; LBJ and, 248; welfare and, 261–62; women and, 274
Prudential, 340
Public Health Service, 326, 327
public interest advocacy, xiii, 35, 61, 158; affirmative action and, 368; civil rights agencies and, 393; cold war pluralism and, 170; democratic pluralism and, 175; educational, 303; litigation-oriented, 393–94; pluralism and, 180n63; public policy and, 167–68
public policy, 73; centralization of, 302–3, 305–6; as confrontation, 410n38; divided government and, 398–99; expansion of, 165–69, 177n12, 179nn44, 46; exposure strategy and, 404–5; favored

explanations for Great Society shifts in, 253–54; Great Society politics and, 255–59; incremental changes in, 395–98; judicialization of, 409–10n38; legitimacy of, 162–63, 391–92; mandate-and-sue strategy and, 165–66; off-budget funding of, 399–401; pluralism and, 169–76; revisionist historical views of, 237–38; therapeutic ethos and, 163–65; unfunded, 166–67, 400. *See also* civil rights policy; policy mindedness
public vs. private: Medicare and, 334–36; policy expansion and, 169; social movements and, 159–60; therapeutic ethos and, 163–65; women's movement and, 159–60, 164–65, 279
Pueblo incident, 248
Puerto Ricans, 385n21

Quadagno, Jill, 120, 125, 128

Rabe, Barry, 297
race riots: affirmative action and, 374–75; black-white relations and, 367; Community Action Program and, 31; ghetto visits and, 31, 46n90; Great Society politics and, 259; LBJ and, 22, 23, 248, 321; liberal results orientation and, 150; New Deal political coalition and, 152–53; political impact of, 440–41
Rachlin, Carl, 134
racial justice, 69
racial minorities. *See* ethnic/racial minorities, official status of
racial politics, 264–66
racism, 172–74; Great Society and, 153–54; inequality and, 148–49
radical intellectuals, labor union devaluation and, 85, 93–98, 112n47
radio, 65
Randolph, A. Philip, 24, 102
rape crisis centers/hotlines, 286
Raskin, A. H., 99
Rauh, Joseph, 24
Ravitch, Diane, 296, 301–2, 308, 315n27
Rayburn, Sam, 191, 197, 202–3, 430
RCA, 123, 168
reading programs, 319n89
Reagan, Ronald/Reagan administration, 78, 390; California gubernatorial election of (1966), 20, 444; deficit spending and, 442; ERA defeat and, 385n13; ESEA backlash under, 307–8, 316–17n67; Great Society politics and, 255, 258, 265; hiring quota controversy and, 366; influence of Great Society on, xv, 240; policy mindedness and, 62; post-WWII demographic shifts and, 417–18; presidential election of (1980), 6, 307, 417; welfare rollbacks of, 265
Reagan "revolution," xvii, 58
Rebel without a Cause (film; 1955), 76
recession, 95
reconstructive politics, 37–38n3
Redmon, Hayes, 13, 21–22
Redstockings, 281, 284
Reed, Stanley Forman, 357
Reedy, George, 6, 9, 39n19, 196
Reese, Ellen, 142n67
regulatory politics, 376
Rehabilitation Act (1973), 104, 401
Rehnquist, William, 357
Reichley, James, 441
Reilly, Richard, 317n71
Rein, Martin, 268n14
Reischauer, Robert, 254, 266–67n1
religion, 359, 373–74, 381
Republic (Plato), 215
Republican National Convention: 1952, 353; 1960, 453n54; 1964, 23
Republican Party: conservative resurgence in, 431–32; Contract with America (1994), 58, 62; divided government and, 35; divisions within (1930s), xiv; educational reform and, 290, 310–11, 312, 318n81, 318n84, 319n86; ESEA backlash and, 307–9, 316n65; Goals 2000 and, 318n81; Great Society politics and, 258, 264–66; impact of post-WWII demographic shifts on, 412–18, 429, 446–47; influence of Great Society on, xv–xvi; labor unions and, 86, 106; marginalization strategy of, 266; Medicare and, 335–36; 1964 election and, 435–36; 1968 election and, 442; policy mindedness in, 62–63; Southern strategy of, 429. *See also specific president*
Reuther, Walter, 23–24, 25, 98

revenue sharing, 264–65
Reynolds v. Sims, 167, 355, 356, 357, 360, 394
Richmond Times Dispatch, 18
Riesman, David, xi
rights consciousness, 36–37; ambivalent activism and, 405; conservative exploitation of, 406; ESEA and, 306; foundation of, 177n25; labor unions and, 83, 103–8, 447; mandate-and-sue strategy and, 405–7; pervasiveness of, 104; pluralism killed by, 145; Seventies policy and, 401–2; social movements and, 158
right to earn, 129, 133–34
"right to resign" doctrine, 106–7
riots. *See* race riots
Rivlin, Alice, 393
Roberts, Juanita, 39n18
Rockwell, Norman, 424
Rodell, Fred, 358
Roe v. Wade, 395
Romney, George, 247
Roosevelt, Eleanor, 187; Democratic Advisory Council and, 430; equal pay legislation and, 272; Johnson (Lady Bird) compared to, 201–2; LBJ and, 185–86, 196–97, 210n24; Tammany Hall attacked by, 417
Roosevelt, Elliott, 189
Roosevelt, Franklin Delano/Roosevelt administration: all-class strategy of, 422–23; civil rights and, 205; Commonwealth Club address of (1932), 177n25, 422; court-packing by, 151–52, 187–88, 203–4, 206, 411; death of, 194; economic bill of rights of, 10; foreign policy of, 411; on Four Freedoms, 424; inaugural speech (1933), 186; liberalism as defined by, 418, 420; modern presidency as legacy of, 5–6, 420–21; national health insurance and, 321; northern urban political support for, 413–14; party "purge" campaign of, 16–17; race issues and, 16, 42–43n52; reform and war strategy of, 206, 207; on right to earn, 129; Social Security state-federal tensions and, 330; State of the Union address (1933), 212n48;

State of the Union address (1944), 10. *See also* Johnson/Roosevelt relationship
Roosevelt, Franklin Delano, Jr., 197, 199–200, 274
Roosevelt, Jimmy, 185
Roosevelt, Theodore, 420, 436
Rosenberg, Julius and Ethel, 427
Rosenberg, Norman L. and Emily S., 238
Rosenbloom, David, 267n2
Ross, Arthur, 88
Rotunda, Ronald D., 418
Rowan, Carl T., 41n36
Rowe, James, 46–47n92, 190, 192, 195, 196
Roybal, Edward, 373
Ruckelshaus, William, 166–67
Rural Community Development Service, 338
Rural Electrification Commission, 191
Rusk, Dean, 217, 228n27, 231n77, 246
Russell, Richard, 214; LBJ and, 18, 44n65, 218, 220, 241; on Rusk, 228n27; Vietnam War and, 218, 220

Sahl, Mort, 66, 77
St. Lawrence Seaway, 156
Salinger, Pierre, 247
San Antonio Express, 196
Sanders, Beulah, 134, 135
Sanders, Carl E., 18, 44n65
San Marcos (Texas), community action program in, 13
Sarachild, Kathy, 279
Sax, Joseph, 406
scabbing, 106
Scammon, Richard, 446
Schattschneider, E. E., 98, 171
Schlesinger, Arthur, Jr., 40n31, 67, 80n23, 157, 425; Democratic Advisory Council and, 431
schools: accountability measures in, 309, 312; busing, for desegregation, 167, 383–84n2, 395; centralization of, 302–3; desegregation of, 256, 259, 355, 396, 428; improvement programs, 305; Mobilization for Youth and, 259–60; Pledge of Allegiance in, 359; prayer in, 356, 394; state/local control of, 290–91

Schultz, George, 406
Schwarz, John, 263
Securities Exchange Act (1934), 205
self-incrimination, 355–56
Selma (Ala.), civil rights marches in, 19, 36
Sen, Amartya, 73
Senate, U.S.: Civil Rights Bill (1963) filibustered in, 435; divided government and, 394; Finance Committee, 325–26, 343; Judiciary Committee, 394; LBJ as president and, 294–95; LBJ in, 194–97; 1964 election and, 435–36; Select Committee on Poverty, 125–26
September 11 (2001) terrorist attacks, xviii, 55–56, 226, 240
Seventies, the: as "age of exposure," 410n39; divided government during, 398–99; Great Society reforms during, xv, 58, 387–91; influence of Sixties on, 390–95; institutional patterns during, 395–403; mandate-and-sue strategy during, 402–3; off-budget costs during, 399–401; policy incrementalism during, 395–98; public interest advocacy during, xiii; rights-based policy during, 401–2
sex education, 53–54, 128
sexism: Burger Court and, 395; EEOC and, 273–74, 275–76; Kennedy administration and, 271–73; liberal tolerance of, 117–18, 125, 154, 159, 271; maternalism and, 137–38; state role in, 153; Title VII and, 273–74, 287n14
sexual harassment, 286
sexual orientation, 279
Shakespeare, William, 234
Sheehy, Peter, 164
Shi, David Emory, 238
Shklar, Judith, 129
Shribman, David, 146, 151, 445
"Shrinking the Group" (Sheehy), 164
Shriver, Sargent: community action programs and, 12–13, 47n92; on Job Corps, 123, 125; LBJ/FDR relationship and, 199; Legal Services and, 393; as OEO director, 47n94, 390; on War on Poverty, 5, 116, 124
Shulman, Harry, 88
Simon, Neil, 249

Sixties, the: civil rights policy discontinuities during, 365; community vs. centralized control, 31; defined, 78–79n1; equal rights legislation during, 367; historical controversy over, 238; impact of post-WWII demographic shifts on, 412–18; labor union decline during, 83–84; LBJ and, 245; new politics during, xiv–xv, 13–16, 412; popular culture during, 65–67; quality of life concerns during, xi, 10; 9/11 attacks as end of, 55–56; Seventies policy and, 390–95; social movements during, 4–5
Sixties civics: delegitimization and, 75–77; distrust, 64–70, 160; impact of, 53, 65, 77–78; paradoxes of, 53–56; policy mindedness, 56–63, 147, 170; policy mindedness/distrust united in, 70–77; uncivility of, 76–77
Skerry, Peter, 174
Skowronek, Stephen, 37–38n3
Skrentny, John, 368, 372–73, 398
Slichter, Sumner, 98
Sloan, Alfred, 110n14
Slums and Suburbs (Conant), 292
Small Business Administration (SBA), 375, 376–77, 382, 385n21
small business loans, 127
Smathers, George, 247
Smith, Al, 186
Smith, Howard, 273
social conservatism, 443–44
social Darwinism, 444
social democracy, 145, 180n63, 419–20
social feminism, 384–85n13
Social Gospel movement, 450n19
social insurance, 334, 336
socialism, 97, 164, 418, 422, 425, 427
social movements: impact of Sixties civics on, 68–69; impact on pluralism, 157–60. *See also* antiwar movement; civil rights movement; consumer movement; women's liberation movement
Social Security: disability freeze in, 332–33; Disability Insurance, 333; as entitlement, 149; expansion of, 344; LBJ on, 204; Medicare as, 328–30; public vs. private responsibility, 335; racial/gender divisions maintained by, 117;

Social Security (*cont.*)
  state-federal tensions in, 330–34; taxes and funding of, 399–400
Social Security Act (1935): 1939 amendments, 130; 1956 amendments, 130; 1962 amendments, 131–32; 1965 amendments, 320; 1967 amendments, 132; Clark Amendment, 335–36, 348n44; coverage exclusions in, 325, 346n15; influence of, 152; major participants in, 330; Medicare and, 328; as New Deal legacy, 117; racial/gender divisions maintained in, 117, 271; working-class support for, 413
Social Security Administration (SSA): Congress and, 336–37; Medicare civil rights compliance and, 326, 327; Medicare enrollment and, 336–38; Medicare Part B carriers and, 339–41
Social Security Board, 330
Socrates, 226
Sorenson, Theodore, 16
South, the, 20; African-American population in, 448n2; antiunionism in, 86, 103–4, 106; desegregation in, 150, 265, 277, 365, 367–68, 381–82; disenfranchisement in, 271; "employable mother" rules in, 142n67; impact of Title VII in, 102; LBJ's civil rights promotion in, 17–19, 40–41n33, 43–44n65; Medicare and hospital integration in, 324–28; New Deal political geography and, 413–14; partisan realignment in, 16, 256, 265–66, 443–45; post-WWII migration to, political impact of, 414–16
South Carolina, Medicare and, 326
Southern Christian Leadership Council, 103
Southwest, post-WWII migration to, political impact of, 414
Soviet Union: internationalism and, 226n4, 228n20; as nuclear threat, 229n52; Sputnik launch, 156, 291
space race, 248
Spanish Americans. *See* Hispanics
Sparkman, John, 339–40
speech, freedom of, 394
sports, Title IX and, 285

Sputnik, 156, 291, 431
Stallings, D. T., 317n67
Standard Form 40, 172–73, 373, 374
state educational agencies, 298, 302–3
state governments: block grants and, 264–65; Burger Court and, 395; education and, 290–91; ESEA and, 299–300, 301–2; federal grant-in-aid programs and, 253, 257–58, 323; federal off-budget costs and, 401; Great Society programs and bypassing of, 253, 257; New Deal programs and bypassing of, 257–58; "one person, one vote" principle in, 355; residency requirements in, 262; weaknesses of, 254; welfare requirements and, 395; workfare programs, 133
states' rights, 58–59, 294, 306, 308
Steelworkers Trilogy, 111n26
Stevenson, Adlai, 57, 214, 218, 257, 430
Stewart, Potter, 357
Stone, Walker, 39n18, 41n33
Strike! (Brecher), 101
strikes, 99, 106–7, 111n26
student aid, 148
student movement: leftist orientation of, 287n17; New Left and, 277–78; participatory democracy and, xiii; and public vs. private, 159
Student Nonviolent Coordinating Committee (SNCC), 173; Great Society opposed by, 22–23; MFDP controversy and, 24; New Left and, 278; women's movement and, 277, 280
Students for a Democratic Society (SDS): industrial pluralism and, 101; Port Huron statement of, xii, 9, 97, 161; women in, 279; women's movement and, 277, 280
subemployment, 261
"substitute father" rules, 262
suburbanization, political impact of, 412, 416–18, 427, 448nn4–5
"suitable home" rules, 118
Sundquist, James, 298
Sununu, John E., 163
suprapartisan politics, 171, 181n68
Supreme Court: class action suits and, 172; FDR's packing of, 151–52, 187–

88, 203–4, 206, 411; mandate-and-sue strategy and, 165–66; public policy established by, 167; role of, 351. *See also* Warren Court

Supreme Court decisions: *Abingdon School District v. Schempp*, 394; *Baker v. Carr*, 356, 359; *Boys Market* decision, 107; *Brandenburg v. Ohio*, 394; *Brown v. Board of Education*, 291, 355, 357, 358, 428; *Engel v. Vitale*, 356–57; *Fibreboard* decision, 107; *First National Maintenance Corp.* decision, 107–8; *Gideon v. Wainwright*, 356–57, 394; *Goldberg v. Kelly*, 136, 167, 262, 394; *Granite State* decision, 106–7; *Green v. New Kent County*, 167, 394; *Griswold v. Connecticut*, 356–57, 394; *Harper v. Virginia Board of Education*, 167, 394; *Heart of Atlanta Motel v. United States*, 394; *King v. Smith*, 136; *Lau v. Nichols*, 396; *Lucas Flower* decision, 107; *Miranda v. Arizona*, 355–56, 357, 394; *New York Times v. Sullivan*, 356–57, 394; *Powell v. McCormack*, 356–57; *In Re Gault*, 394; *Reynolds v. Sims*, 167, 355, 356, 357, 360, 394; *Terry v. Adams*, 394; *Tinker v. Des Moines School District*, 394; *Watkins v. United States*, 355, 357

survivor's insurance, 117, 328
Swados, Harvey, 96–97, 98, 100
Symington, Stuart, 432, 452n48
systems analysis, 168

Taft, Robert A., 62, 353, 429, 431
Taft-Hartley Act (1947), 92, 96, 321
Talmadge, Herman, 18, 325–26
Tammany Hall, 417
taxation: constitutional legitimacy of, 402; Great Society programs dependent on, 390; for New Deal programs, 450n24; payroll, 328–29, 399–400; poll taxes, 167, 394; Seventies political infeasibility of, 399–400
tax cuts, 120
taxpayer revolts, 58, 135
Taylor, Maxwell, 219
teachers, competency tests for, 319n89
teachers' unions, 298

television, 248
Temporary Assistance for Needy Families (TANF), 137, 266
Tennessee Valley Authority, 205, 206
Terry v. Adams, 394
Tet offensive, 217–18, 232n84, 235
Texas, University of, 244
That's Not What We Meant to Do (Gillon), 368
therapeutic ethos, 163–65, 254–55
think tanks, 61, 265
Third Way, 310
Thornberry, Richard, 246
Thucydides, 224–25
Thurow, Lester, 11
Tillett, Paul, 453n57
Tillmon, Johnnie, 129, 154
Tindall, George Brown, 238
Tinker v. Des Moines School District, 394
Tippitt, Mrs. J. D., 246, 247
Tocqueville, Alexis de, 36, 72, 73, 110n18, 217, 226
Tonkin Gulf crisis, 223, 231n70
To Secure These Rights (Truman Committee report), 371–72
trade unions. *See* labor unions
Tragedy of Lyndon Johnson, The (Goldman), 236
training, 116, 122, 127
Transportation Department, U.S., 59–60, 400
Truman, David, 91
Truman, Harry/Truman administration, 246, 247; as anticommunist, 427, 433; civil rights and, 205; insider politics of, 156–57; LBJ and, 156–57; at Medicare signing, 320–21, 345; national health insurance and, 320–21; political frustrations of, 411–12
Truman Committee on Civil Rights, 172, 371–72
Truman Doctrine, 387
Tucker, Ray, 188
Tugwell, Rexford G., 57, 421, 423, 429, 447
Tully, Grace, 196

U.S. News and World Report, 342
underclass, 119, 242

unemployment, 119, 261
unemployment compensation, 330–31
unemployment insurance, 117
Unfinished Nation, The (Brinkley), 236
unions, labor. *See* labor unions
United Auto Workers (UAW), 23–24, 86, 97–98, 275
United Church Women, 126
United Electrical Workers, 100
United Farm Workers, 100
United Nations, 411
United Steel Workers (USW), 92–93
universities: impact of Sixties civics on, 69; New Left and curriculum changes at, 277–78; women's studies programs at, 285, 286
urban ghettos: Great Society politics and black migration to, 255–59; Great Society programs targeted at, 253; LBJ administration visits to, 26–28, 31, 45n84, 46nn87, 90. *See also* race riots
Urban Institute, 129
urban renewal, 406
U-2 incident, 218

Valenti, Jack, 42n49; LBJ Great Society speech and, 7, 8, 9; LBJ's first days in office and, 246; on LBJ's speaking style, 211n39
Van De Mark, Brian, 226n16
Verba, Sidney, 403–4
Veteran Feminists of America (VFA), 288n33
Vietcong, 220, 232n84, 235
Vietnam War: "arrogance of power" and, 216; government distrust and, 68, 160, 217; honor and, 220–21; impact of defeat in, 217, 226; impact of Great Society on, 222–26; impact on Democratic Party, 445–46, 455n84; impact on Great Society, 21–22, 146, 153, 216–17, 230–31n68, 301, 442; imperium and, 224–25; labor support for, 84; LBJ and public support for, 224–26, 230–31n68, 231n83, 232nn93–94; LBJ as liberal and, 8, 33; LBJ/FDR relationship and, 205–6, 207, 216; LBJ's advisers and, 217–20, 228nn27, 30; LBJ's first memorandum on, 247–48; LBJ's motivations for continuing, 220–22; and liberalism, decline of, xv; liberal vs. conservative views of, 236; limited war strategy, 220–24, 229n44; modern presidency and, 33; new politics and, 455n84; patriotism and, 221–22, 231n70; Pleiku attack, 222; in popular opinion, 233; proministrative state and, 156; revisionist historical views of, 240; Tet offensive, 217–18, 232n84, 235; Tonkin Gulf crisis, 223, 231n70. *See also* antiwar movement
Village Voice, 33
Vinson, Frederick Moore, 353, 361n6
Virginia, 340–41
Vital Center, The (Schlesinger), 67
Volunteers in Service to America (VISTA), 120
Voting Rights Act (1965): civil rights policy discontinuities and, 365; expansion of, 159, 165; LBJ and, 19–20, 148, 235; liberal nondiscrimination and, 367; political impact of, 440; in popular opinion, 233; as radical, 367; renewal of, 365; significance of, 149, 387–88
vouchers, 310

Wagner, Robert, 87–88, 331
Wagner Act (1935): industrial pluralism and, 87–88, 169; LBJ on, 204; positive rights in, 423; rights consciousness in, 102, 104; working-class support for, 413
Wallace, George, 20–21, 75, 443–44, 445
Wallace, Lurleen, 20
Wallas, Graham, 75, 80n18
Wall Street Journal, 96
Ward, Geoffrey, 212n46
War on Poverty: Adult Education Program, 120; backlash against, 307; Community Action Program, 11–13, 28–32, 48n105, 120; criticism of, 47n99; employment/welfare policy interconnections in, 116, 118–21, 138, 152; ESEA and, 289; ghetto visits and, 28; Head Start, 122, 124; LBJ's ambivalence about, 28, 48n105; "manpower" programs in, 119–21; NYA and, 199; ob-

jectives of, 5, 10–11, 118; presidential politics and, 14; private administration of, 258; reauthorization of, 48n105; Republican dismantling of, 264; sociological influences on, 47n96, 48n105; Vietnam War and, 231n70; VISTA, 120
War on Terrorism, xviii
Warren, Earl, 353–55, 358, 360, 394, 428
Warren Court, xiv; as activist tribunal, 351–53, 354, 360–61, 394–95, 444; civil rights policy and, 365–66; conservative backlash against, 444; dissenters in, 358–60; legacy of, 351, 360–61; major decisions of, 355–57; members of, 357–58; positive rights and, 428–29; Warren as Chief Justice of, 353–55
Washington Post, 18, 163, 201–2
Watergate scandal, 160
Water Quality Act (1965), 151
Watkins v. United States, 355, 357
Watson, Pa, 190
Wattenberg, Ben, 446
Watts race riots, 22, 321, 440–41
Weaver, R. Kent, 409n33
Weber, Max, 94–95
"web of rules," 110n16
Weeks, Christopher, 121–22, 131
Weir, Margaret, 116, 254, 267n6
Welborn, David, 48n105
welfare: eligibility requirements for, 118, 261–62; as entitlement, 118, 137, 390; Great Society politics and, 268n18; hearings for, 167, 262; impact on poverty, 262–63; Mobilization for Youth and, 260–62; New Deal programs, 117–18; policy incrementalism and, 396–97; protests and, 261–62; public view of, 409n33; racialization of, 138; Republican rollbacks in, 264–66; time limits, 137; work rules, 137. *See also* Aid to Dependent Children; Aid to Families with Dependent Children
welfare fraud, 118
"welfare mothers," 135–36
"welfare queens," 265
welfare reform, 137–38
welfare rights, 136, 167, 262, 394
welfare rights movement, 136–37; community action programs and, 49n116;

equal rights feminism vs., 133–35; new politics and, xiv; protests by, 262
West, post-WWII migration to, political impact of, 414
West Virginia, 359
White, Byron, 357, 394
White, G. Edward, 355
White, Lee C., 44n75
White, Theodore H., 80n24, 244
White, William S., 193, 194, 195
white backlash, 21, 264, 265–66
White Collar (Mills), 94
white flight, 255
Whitehead, Alfred North, 55, 56, 59, 73
whiteness studies, 383–84n2
whites, 380–81, 382
Whittaker, Charles E., 357
Wicker, Tom, 204
widows, as deserving poor, 130
Wiley, George, 134–35
Wilkins, Roy, 24
Williams, Aubrey, 3, 195
Williams, John, 298
Williams, Linda, 263
Wilson, James Q., 58, 59, 162, 391–92
Wilson, Woodrow, 411, 418, 419, 420
Wirtz, Alvin, 215, 228n30
Wirtz, Willard, 120
Witness to America (ed. Ambrose and Brinkley), 236–37
Witte, Edwin, 87, 330, 348n44
women: affirmative action and, 384–85n13; cold war liberalism and, 411, 427; Democratic Party and, 413; democratic pluralism and, 174–75; divorced/unmarried, as undeserving poor, 130; impact of increased employment, 121; Job Corps and, 125–28, 152; New Deal and, 117–18, 271
women business enterprises (WBE), 385n13
Women in Community Service (WICS), 126
Women's Bureau, 272–73, 275
women's councils, 126
Women's International Terrorist Conspiracy from Hell (WITCH), 284
women's liberation movement: civil rights movement and, 277; consciousness-

women's liberation movement (*cont.*) raising in, 164–65, 279–83; decentralization in, 280–81; grassroots activism of, 159–60, 278–79; historical overview of, 271–79; impact of Sixties civics on, 69; internal inequalities in, 283–84; labor unions and, 274–75; leadership in, 275, 282–83; media portrayals of, 283, 288n30; New Left and, 271, 277–79, 280; new politics and, xiv, 33; NOW contrasted with, 276–77, 279; organization of, 276–77, 282–84; participatory democracy and, 277; policy mindedness in, 60; and public vs. private, 159–60, 164–65, 279; rapid spread of, 271; right to earn and, 133; social impact of, 270, 284–86; therapeutic ethos and, 164–65; unreliable scholarship on, 270–71. *See also* feminism; National Organization of Women

women's studies programs, 285, 286

Wood, Robert, 259, 263, 268n26, 448n4

work ethic, 149

Work Experience, 132

"work experience" programs, 127

workfare programs, 121, 130–31

Work in America (HEW report), 104

Work Incentive Program (WIN), 132, 154

working class: Great Society and, 441; New Deal and, 413; in New Left, 278; in NOW leadership, 275

workplace discrimination, 133, 159, 272, 286

work rights, 102–5

Work Rules, 133

Works Progress Administration, 450–51n26

World War II: anti-white bias during, 372; demographic shifts following, political impact of, 412–18, 429, 446–47; FDR reform and war strategy and, 206, 207; GI Bill and education following, 291; impact on liberalism, 411–12; impact on New Deal, 411; LBJ's criticism of labor unions during, 223; positive rights and American involvement in, 424

Wright, Gavin, 102

Wyatt, Addie, 275

Yarborough, Ralph, 247

Yarmolinsky, Adam, 121, 123, 129

Young, Andrew, 103

Young, Whitney, 24